THE OXFORD HANDBOOK OF

CONFLICT MANAGEMENT IN ORGANIZATIONS

THE OXFORD HANDBOOK OF

CONFLICT MANAGEMENT IN ORGANIZATIONS

Edited by
WILLIAM K. ROCHE
PAUL TEAGUE
and
ALEXANDER J. S. COLVIN

OXFORD
UNIVERSITY PRESS

OXFORD
UNIVERSITY PRESS

Great Clarendon Street, Oxford, OX2 6DP,
United Kingdom

Oxford University Press is a department of the University of Oxford.
It furthers the University's objective of excellence in research, scholarship,
and education by publishing worldwide. Oxford is a registered trade mark of
Oxford University Press in the UK and in certain other countries

© Oxford University Press 2014

The moral rights of the authors have been asserted

First Edition published in 2014

Impression: 1

Published in the United States of America by Oxford University Press
198 Madison Avenue, New York, NY 10016, United States of America

British Library Cataloguing in Publication Data
Data available

Library of Congress Control Number: 2014939077

ISBN 978-0-19-965367-6

Printed and bound by
CPI Group (UK) Ltd, Croydon, CR0 4YY

Contents

PART 1: THEORETICAL PERSPECTIVES

PART 2: APPROACHES TO CONFLICT MANAGEMENT

PART 3: EXEMPLARS AND INNOVATORS

PART 4: INTERNATIONAL DEVELOPMENT

LIST OF FIGURES

LIST OF TABLES

LIST OF CONTRIBUTORS

Ariel C. **Avgar** is Assistant Professor at the School of Labor and Employment Relations at the University of Illinois at Urbana-Champaign. His research focuses on two primary areas of interests. First, he studies conflict and its management in organizations. Among a number of research projects in this area, he is currently working on a study of conflict management patterns and practices in Fortune 1000 firms in the United States. He is also conducting research on social networks and conflict in teams of scientists.

Greg J. Bamber is a Professor at Monash University, Melbourne. His research includes HRM outsourcing/shared services, dispute settlement, and workplace change in healthcare. His (joint) publications include *Up in the Air: How Airlines Can Improve Performance by Engaging their Employees* (Cornell) and *International and Comparative Employment Relations* (Sage), which has been published in other languages. Before moving to Australia, he was educated in and worked in Britain. He researches with and advises international organizations, enterprises, and other organizations.

Martin Behrens is Programme Director at the Institute of Social and Economic Research in the Hans Böckler Foundation (WSI) and Lecturer at the Institute for Sociology at the University of Göttingen. His research focus is on comparative industrial relations and on German employers' associations, works councils, and labor unions. Recent publications include *Das Paradox der Arbeitgeberverbände (The Paradox of Employers' Associations)* (Edition Sigma, 2011) and 'Still Married after all these Years? Union Organizing and the Role of Works Councils in German Industrial Relations', *Industrial and Labor Relations Review*, 2009, 62: 275–93.

John Benson is Professor and Head of the School of Management at the University of South Australia. Prior to taking up his present appointment, John was Chair of the MBA Programme in International Business at the University of Tsukuba, Japan after having spent many years as Reader in the Department of Management, University of Melbourne, Australia. His major research interests are Japanese management and unions, the restructuring of Chinese industry. His most recent monographs include *Trade Unions in Asia* (Routledge, 2008) co-edited with Ying Zhu, *The Everyday Impact of Economic Reform in China* (Routledge, 2010) co-authored with Ying Zhu and Michael Webber, and *The Dynamics of Asian Labour Markets* (Routledge, 2011) co-edited with Ying Zhu.

Lisa Blomgren Amsler (formerly Lisa Blomgren Bingham) is the Keller-Runden Professor of Public Service at Indiana University's School of Public and Environmental Affairs, Bloomington. She was Visiting Professor of Law at the University of Nevada Las Vegas from 2010 to 2012. She has co-edited three books and authored over seventy articles, monographs, and book chapters on dispute resolution and collaborative governance. Bingham received several national awards, including the Rubin Theory-to-Practice Award from the International Association for Conflict Management and Harvard Program on Negotiation for research that makes a significant impact on practice in 2006 for her research on the U.S. Postal Service employment mediation program REDRESS©. She is Elected Fellow of the National Academy of Public Administration. Her current research examines dispute systems design and the legal infrastructure for collaboration, dispute resolution, and public participation in governance. She is currently working on a book entitled *Dispute System Design: Preventing, Managing, and Resolving Conflict* with Janet Martinez and Stephanie Smith (Stanford University Press, forthcoming).

William Brown is Emeritus Master of Darwin College and Emeritus Professor of Industrial Relations at Cambridge University. He was previously Director of the Industrial Relations Research Unit at the University of Warwick. He is on the Panel of Arbitrators of the Advisory, Conciliation and Arbitration Service and was a member of its Council. He chairs the dispute procedure of the Fire and Rescue Services. He was a foundation member of the Low Pay Commission, which fixes the National Minimum Wage.

John W. Budd is the Industrial Relations Land Grant Chair at the University of Minnesota's Carlson School of Management. His current research interests include employee voice and frames of reference on work, the employment relationship, and conflict. He is the author of *Employment with a Human Face: Balancing Efficiency, Equity, and Voice* (Cornell), *Labor Relations: Striking a Balance* (McGraw-Hill), *Invisible Hands, Invisible Objectives: Bringing Workplace Law and Public Policy Into Focus* (Stanford), and *The Thought of Work* (Cornell).

Alexander J. S. Colvin is the Martin F. Scheinman Professor of Conflict Resolution at the ILR School, Cornell University, where he is also Associate Director of the Scheinman Institute on Conflict Resolution and Associate Editor of the *Industrial & Labor Relations Review*. His research and teaching focuses on employment dispute resolution, with a particular emphasis on procedures in nonunion workplaces and the impact of the legal environment on organizations. His current research projects include an empirical investigation of the outcomes of employment arbitration and a cross-national study of labor and employment law change in the Anglo-American countries. He is co-author (with Harry C. Katz and Thomas A. Kochan) of the textbook *An Introduction to Collective Bargaining and Industrial Relations*, 4th edition (Irwin-McGraw-Hill).

Brian Cooper is Senior Lecturer in the Department of Management, Monash University, Australia. He lectures in research methods and has extensive experience in quantitative business research methodology. His research interests include the relationship between human resource management and employee outcomes. He has published extensively in the area of employee voice and workplace participation.

Joel Cutcher-Gershenfeld is Professor and former Dean in the School of Labor and Employment Relations at the University of Illinois, United States. He is an award-winning author who has co-authored or co-edited ten books and over eighty-five articles on negotiations, high performance work systems, dispute resolution systems, organizational learning systems, and engineering systems. Joel was the 2009 President of the Labor and Employment Relations Association (LERA). Joel holds a Ph.D. in Industrial Relations from MIT and a B.S. in Industrial and Labor Relations from Cornell University.

Gill Dix is Head of Strategy at the Advisory, Conciliation and Arbitration Service (Acas). Acas is a government-funded independent body responsible for providing conciliation services and improving employment relations in Britain. In Acas, Gill manages the organisation's governance team, and a programme on public policy analysis and strategic planning. She has a background in social and public policy research, working in academia, and the voluntary and public sector bodies prior to joining Acas. Gill was Head of Research and Evaluation at Acas for twelve years and has written on a range of industrial relations subjects including being a co-author on the 1998 and 2004 Workplace Employment Relations Studies, an internationally recognized survey mapping patters of industrial relations in Britain. She has a particular interest in dispute resolution, consultation, and employee engagement.

Adrienne E. Eaton is Professor in and Chair of the Labor Studies and Employment Relations department at the School of Management and Labor Relations at Rutgers University. Her research focuses on labor-management partnerships, union organizing under neutrality, and card check and the impact of unionization on particular occupational groups including managerial workers and graduate student employees. She's the co-author along with Tom Kochan, Paul Adler, and Robert McKersie of the book *Healing Together: The Kaiser Permanente Labor-Management Partnership*, editor with Jeff Keefe of *Employment Dispute Resolution in the Changing Workplace*, and author of numerous articles published in journals like *Industrial and Labor Relations Review, Industrial Relations, Labor Studies Journal,* and *Advances in Industrial and Labor Relations.* She is past Editor of the Labor and Employment Relations Association.

Cynthia Estlund is the Catherine A. Rein Professor at the New York University School of Law. She has written dozens of journal articles on labor and employment law and workplace governance, and is the author of two books, *Regoverning the Workplace: From Self-Regulation to Co-Regulation* (Yale University Press, 2010) and *Working Together: How Workplace Bonds Strengthen a Diverse Democracy* (Oxford University Press, 2003).

Howard Gadlin has been Ombudsman and Director of the Center for Cooperative Resolution at the National Institutes of Health since the beginning of 1999. From 1992 through 1998 he was University Ombudsperson at UCLA. He was also Director of the UCLA Conflict Mediation Program and Co-director of the Center for the Study and

Resolution of Interethnic/Interracial Conflict. While in Los Angeles he served as Consulting Ombudsman to the Los Angeles County Museum of Art. Prior to coming to UCLA, he was Ombudsperson and Professor of Psychology at the University of Massachusetts, Amherst.

John Godard is Professor in the School of Business at the University of Manitoba, and Chief Editor of the *British Journal of Industrial Relations*. His work has generally focused on the associations between national institutional environments, employer practices, and both union and worker outcomes, although he has also published a number of papers on labor law and strike activity. His work has appeared mainly in the *British Journal of Industrial Relations, Industrial and Labor Relations Review*, and *Industrial Relations*.

Gaye Greenwood is Senior Lecturer in the Faculty of Business and Law, Auckland University of Technology. She is a registered mediator with experience in negotiation, communication coaching, and mediation of employment relationship problems in education, health, franchise, and small business sectors. She specializes in research and teaching in negotiation and conflict management.

Brian S. Klaas is Professor of Management and Senior Associate Dean at the Darla Moore School of Business, University of South Carolina. He also serves as the Director of the Riegel & Emory HR Center. He received his Ph.D. from the University of Wisconsin-Madison and has published widely on topics relating to employee voice, organizational conflict and dispute resolution, and HR systems.

Thomas A. Kochan is the George M. Bunker Professor of Work and Employment Relations at MIT's Sloan School of Management, Co-Director of the MIT Institute for Work and Employment Research, and Chair of the MIT Faculty. He received his Ph.D. in Industrial Relations from the University of Wisconsin in 1973. He is past President of the Industrial Relations Research Association and the International Industrial Relations Association.

J. **Ryan Lamare** is Assistant Professor in Labor Studies and Employment Relations. He received his B.S., M.S., and Ph.D. from Cornell University's School of Industrial and Labor Relations and held academic positions at the University of Limerick and the University of Manchester prior to joining Penn State. Dr. Lamare's research interests include: labor and employment arbitration; ADR in the securities industry; the development of ADR systems in organizations; the role of unions in politics; employment relations and HR at multinational companies; and quantitative research methods. He has published extensively on these issues in journals such as *Industrial and Labor Relations Review, Industrial Relations*, and *Journal of World Business*. Dr. Lamare has also worked previously for a non-profit workers' rights organization, and has held visiting academic appointments in Ireland, the United Kingdom, and New Zealand.

Paul L. Latreille is Professor of Management at the University of Sheffield. He holds a visiting position at Westminster Business School's Centre for Employment Research, is Research Fellow of the IZA, Bonn, and Associate of the Economics Network. He is an editorial board member for *Work, Employment and Society* and serves on the Professional Mediators' Association advisory group. His main research interests are in applied labor economics and employment relations, focusing on workplace conflict, mediation, and employment tribunals. He has published extensively for both academic and policy audiences and has led and/or been involved in projects on these issues for various bodies including the ESRC, the Department for Business, Innovation and Skills, the Ministry of Justice and Acas.

David Lewin is the Neil H. Jacoby Professor of Management, Human Resources and Organizational Behavior at the UCLA Anderson School of Management. He has published twenty books and more than 150 articles. Among his books are *The Modern Grievance Procedure in the United States; Human Resource Management: An Economic Approach; Contemporary Issues in Employment Relations;* and *The Oxford Handbook of Participation in Organizations.* He is President of the national Labor and Employment Relations Association (LERA) and Chair of the LERA 2013 Program Committee.

David B. Lipsky is the Anne Evans Estabrook Professor of Dispute Resolution in the School of Industrial and Labor Relations, and Director of the Scheinman Institute on Conflict Resolution at Cornell University. He served as the President of the Labor and Employment Relations Association in 2006. In his research and teaching activities he primarily focuses on negotiation, conflict resolution, and collective bargaining. Lipsky served as Dean of the School of Industrial and Labor Relations at Cornell from 1988 until 1997 and has been a member of the Cornell faculty since 1969. He received his B.S. in 1961 from the ILR School at Cornell and his Ph.D. in economics from M.I.T. in 1967.

Mingwei Liu is Assistant Professor of Labor Studies and Employment Relations at Rutgers University. His research interests fall into two broad areas. The first is Asian industrial relations, with a specific focus on Chinese employment relations, trade unions, human resource management, and skill development. The second is high performance work practices, with a specific focus on the healthcare and heavy machinery industries.

Douglas M. Mahony is Assistant Professor of Management and Axelrod Fellow at the College of Business and Economics, Lehigh University. His primary areas of research focus on group and organizational conflict, and nonunion dispute resolution processes and outcomes. He received his Ph.D. in Industrial Relations and Human Resource Management from Rutgers University.

Ian McAndrew is Associate Professor, Otago Business School, University of Otago, New Zealand. He teaches, researches, and practices in the area of employment relations and the processes of negotiation, mediation, and alternative dispute resolution. He practiced in the labor relations field in the US for fifteen years, was a mediator and adjudicator member of the New Zealand Employment Tribunal from 1993 to 2002 and remains an active mediator and tribunal adjudicator.

John Purcell is Associate Fellow of the Industrial Relations Research Unit at Warwick Business School, University of Warwick. He is Deputy Chairman of the Central Arbitration Committee (CAC) and an Acas arbitrator. His main publications include *Human Resource Management in the Multi-divisional Company* (Oxford University Press, 1994) and *Strategy and Human Resource Management* (written with Peter Boxall) (Palgrave, 3rd edition, 2011) and the *Oxford Handbook of HRM* (Oxford University Press, 2007) edited with Peter Boxall and Patrick Wright. Recent research has been on the effect of people management practices on business performance, the role of front line managers in the delivery of effective people management, contingent workers and temporary work agencies and the impact of the Information and Consultation of Employees Regulations. His book, written with Mark Hall, *Consultation at Work: Regulation and Practice* was published by Oxford University Press in 2012.

Erling Rasmussen is the Professor of Work and Employment at the Auckland University of Technology, New Zealand. He has worked in employment relations in academia, and the public and private sectors since the late 1970s. He has extensive experience of employment relations research, public policy formation and evaluation, including involvement in the development of New Zealand legislation and in externally funded New Zealand and international research projects.

William K. Roche is Professor of Industrial Relations and Human Resources at the School of Business, University College Dublin and Honorary Professor at the School of Management, Queen's University Belfast. He was awarded his D.Phil. from the University of Oxford, where he was Heyworth Memorial Prize Research Fellow of Nuffield College. He has led and contributed to strategic reviews of industrial relations and dispute resolution by a number of Irish public agencies, including the Labour Relations Commission, the National Economic and Social Council, and the National Centre for Partnership and Performance.

Mary Rowe has a PhD in economics and joined MIT in 1973. She has been an MIT Ombudsperson for decades, and also Adjunct Professor of Negotiation and Conflict Management. She helped to start and develop earlier ombuds associations, which subsequently became the International Ombudsman Association. The website <http://web.mit.edu/ombud> includes Rowe's articles on the ombuds profession, ombuds effectiveness and elements of practice, micro-inequities, micro-affirmations, harassment, integrated conflict management systems, and bystander behavior.

Richard Saundry is Associate Professor of Human Resource Studies at Plymouth University and is Visiting Fellow of the Centre for Employment Relations, Innovation and Change (CERIC) at the University of Leeds and also at the Institute for Research into Organisations, Work and Employment (iROWE) at the University of Central Lancashire (UCLAN). His current research interests include conflict management, workplace dispute resolution, trade union organization and renewal, and the nature of work in the audio-visual industries. He has published extensively in peer-reviewed academic journals. He has led a number of projects funded by the Economic and Social Research Council, the Department for Trade and Industry (now BIS), the TUC, and the Advisory, Conciliation and Arbitration Service.

Paul Teague is Professor of Management at the Management School, Queen's University Belfast and is Visiting Professor at the School of Business, University College Dublin. He has written widely on the theme of the employment relations consequences of deeper European integration. The themes of social partnership and employment performance, workplace conflict management and human resources in the recession currently dominate his research activities. He has worked with the Irish Government, EU, ILO, and the Belgium Government to develop policies and programmes in these areas. A book that examines systematically the HR strategies of companies based in Ireland in response to the recession, *Recession at Work*, which was co-authored with Bill Roche, Anne Coughlan, and Majella Fahey, was published by Routledge in 2013.

Julian Teicher is Professor of industrial relations in the Department of Management at Monash University. He has published eleven books and monographs and more than ninety refereed papers and book chapters on workplace relations, human resources, and public management. His research covers issues including employee voice and participation, bargaining and dispute resolution, occupational health and safety, skill formation, privatization, and e-government.

Peter Urwin is Professor of Applied Economics and Director of the Centre for Employment Research at the University of Westminster Business School. Peter has a particular focus on the issues faced by government policymakers in the areas of employment relations, education and skills, equality and diversity. He has carried out research for most of the major UK government departments. His work with Acas and other agencies has appeared in a range of policy publications and academic journals.

Bernadine Van Gramberg is Professor and Deputy Dean of the Faculty of Business and Enterprise at Swinburne University of Technology. Her research interests and publications span the areas of alternative dispute resolution, industrial relations law and policy, and public sector management.

INTRODUCTION

Developments in Conflict Management

WILLIAM K. ROCHE, PAUL TEAGUE, AND
ALEXANDER J. S. COLVIN

CONFLICT management in organizations has undergone considerable change in recent years. Innovative ADR practices have emerged across a number of countries. These have been concerned with handling individual grievances and group conflicts. They have been introduced in non-union and unionized organizations and within and outside the collective bargaining process. There are also signs of a growing interest in proactive measures to prevent the occurrence of conflict in workplaces.

The field of conflict management and in particular ADR has seen a growth not only in the numbers of experts of various kinds working inside organizations, but also in the numbers of consulting houses, independent consultants, and external experts providing services to organizations. Conflict resolution agencies like the Federal Mediation and Conciliation Service in the US and the Advisory Conciliation and Arbitration Service in the UK have also changed the ways in which they provide third-party services to the parties to conflict in the world of work. Professional bodies regulating and providing training for those involved in conflict resolution have emerged or grown in a number of countries. Business and law schools, universities, and independent education providers now also commonly provide specialist modules on conflict management and ADR for professional, graduate, executive, and undergraduate students.

The knowledge base for these developments mainly takes the form of prescriptive textbooks that outline the options available for organizations when designing conflict management arrangements and that provide advice on how to practice standard and new approaches to conflict management. Frequently these make portentous claims about the outcomes of conflict management practices for the stakeholders affected: organizations, employees, and trade unions. These claims are variably supported by research evidence and in some instances not empirically supported at all.

A considerable and high quality academic literature has also developed, including high-caliber research studies conducted by leading figures in the field. Much of this literature is scattered across specialist conflict management and general journals spanning the fields of HRM and industrial relations. Up to now no authoritative international review has been available to inform professional practice or synthesize academic knowledge. In the more readily available literature "how to" books, often of uncertain or untested validity, continue to dominate the scene.

The growing interest in conflict management and ADR is an international, indeed global trend, evident in Europe, the US, Canada, Australia, New Zealand, and parts of Asia, particularly Japan and more recently China. In the countries of Continental Europe, by contrast, developments have been patchy and are also often closely aligned with formal judicial activities in employment grievances and industrial disputes.

Developments in conflict management and ADR are rooted in a number of secular trends which attract analysis in this book. These include the emergence of more extensive employment rights, the decline in trade union density and contraction in the coverage and scope of collective bargaining, the reduced incidence and seriousness of industrial conflict, the rising cost of litigation, and the growing intensity of competition. Also important has been the growing prevalence of new forms of work organization, often associated with human resource innovations that seek to minimize conflict at work and provide more expeditious, less adversarial, and more effective practices for resolving workplace conflict. In workplaces where collective bargaining continues to be conducted, competitive pressures have led to a series of changes in both how collective bargaining has been conducted and in approaches to conflict resolution. Developments in conflict management involve innovations in the handling of grievances among individual employees and also sometimes work groups—providing alternatives to litigation or adjudication by administrative agencies. They have also involved innovations in the conduct of collective bargaining and dispute resolution.

Developments in conflict management are also evident in public service organizations. The widespread restructuring of public service agencies from the 1980s, especially in Anglo-Saxon countries, as well as the growing influence of the new public management (NPM) paradigm have put a premium on organizational and workforce attributes such as flexibility and agility with respect to work and employment practices, providing a further stimulus to new forms of conflict management and conflict resolution—especially in the case of groups like the police who provide essential public services and sometimes operate under restrictions with respect to their freedom to take industrial action.

As the book illustrates, developments in conflict management in organizations are diverse and highly variable both within and across countries and global regions. They are also inextricably intertwined with institutions and legal traditions and with changes in these. This makes it difficult to provide a conceptual overview or integrating framework for the field as a whole.

Table I.1 Conflict Management in Organizations: Alternative Practices and Trends

	Conventional	ADR
Individual Grievances	• Multi-step grievance & disciplinary procedures with provision for arbitration following an impasse in union represented workplaces • Resort to employment tribunals & litigation in courts	• Open-door policies • 'Speak-up' & related systems • Organizational ombudsperson • External and internal mediators • Review panels of managers or peers • Union/non-union employment arbitration • ADR-led conflict management systems • Proactive conflict prevention • Proactive line and supervisory engagement in conflict handling
Collective Disputes	• Multi-step disputes procedures, usually with provision for external conciliation, arbitration, or adjudication following an impasse	• Assisted bargaining/mediation within procedure to avoid impasse • Brainstorming & related techniques • Interest-based bargaining with facilitation • Fact finding • Arbitration, mini-trials, & med+arb • Intensive communications surrounding change management • ADR-led conflict management systems • Proactive conflict prevention • Proactive line and supervisory engagement in conflict handling

Source: Roche, W. K., and Teague, P. 2012 'The Growing Importance of Workplace ADR', *International Journal of Human Resource Management*, 23(3): 449.

Nevertheless we find Table I.1 useful as a means of portraying both the overall "architecture" of the field and of distinguishing developments in conflict management. The table distinguishes between conventional approaches and ADR with respect to both grievance handling and dispute resolution. Conventional or long-established practices, especially in Anglo-American countries, have involved multi-step grievance procedures with provision at the final stage for grievance arbitration, particularly in unionized workplaces, or resort to external agencies or the civil courts. Conventional procedures for handling collective bargaining disputes are also commonly provided for multiple steps, involving successively higher levels of management and progressively more senior or professional union representatives and officials as disputes escalate through the steps of the procedure. Again, arbitration might be involved as the final step (or the penultimate step when industrial conflict is permitted), either in the case of disputes of interests or rights, or where there may be provision in procedures to resort to conciliation, arbitration, or adjudication by external agencies.

If the practices associated with conventional approaches to conflict management are straightforward enough, the concept of ADR poses more problems. The term originated in the US to describe a series of conflict resolution practices intended as alternatives to litigation or the resort to administrative agencies in cases involving individual employment grievances. ADR was also commonly associated with grievance handling in non-union firms. The concept thus understood could encompass conventional practices as well as those described in the table as forms of ADR. However the concept of ADR is more commonly used to describe practices that not only seek to provide alternatives to litigation or administrative investigation but that also depart from conventional approaches in various important ways, for example by emphasizing problem solving over establishing who is right, or by favoring the involvement of employees in the design and monitoring of procedures.

Less commonly encompassed within the term ADR, but often seen also as a new development is the involvement in conflict resolution of line managers and supervisors in a proactive manner. The key features of such an approach are such things as line managers and supervisors being made responsible and in some cases held formally accountable for conflict handling in organizations, as well as the provision of training and support for line managers involved in this activity.

In recent decades the term ADR also began to be used to describe innovations in collective dispute procedures and group conflict management practices, whether within or outside the sphere of collective bargaining. The kinds of innovations that have arisen here are distinct from long-established approaches in unionized firms. Practices such as "assisted negotiations," "fact finding," "interest-based bargaining," and mediation-arbitration (usually shortened to "med+arb") have become associated with ADR on both sides of the Atlantic and in other countries where they emerged.

As innovations in grievance handling and dispute resolution gathered pace, some commentators pointed to the emergence of "conflict management systems," sometimes called "integrated conflict management systems," even regarding this as the new frontier of conflict management in organizations. The concept of conflict management systems has been developed in the main with respect to individual grievance handling practices, where it calls attention to the use of interrelated sets of practices of different kinds. Conflict management systems prioritize the use of ADR practices that are "interest-based" in the sense of seeking to address the underlying concerns of parties affected by grievances rather than to determine which one is acting or not acting in accordance with rights bestowed by company policies, collective agreements, employment law, or even social conventions. Conflict management systems also make provision for "rights-based" practices, for example review panels or arbitration, where these are preferred by the parties to grievances, whether *ab initio* or as "fall-back" arrangements where interest-based practices fail to resolve grievances. In combing these different types of practices, provision is also made for easy movement between interest-based and rights-based processes and even for their simultaneous use. Parties are no longer restricted to the series of linear steps that characterized traditional conflict management procedures but are allowed to skip steps or "loop back" from later to earlier stages of procedure. The literature on conflict management systems has had less to say about how practices for handling collective disputes might be configured along the same or similar lines. It seems clear nevertheless that the same overall approach is commonly understood to extend to the handling of collective conflict.

Of course, not all practices or developments fit easily into this framework and some indeed may be orthogonal to the categories on which it is based. Changes within conventional procedures, adaptations to ADR practices, or developments beyond the range of either set of approaches, need to be allowed for and to be understood on their own terms, especially when the focus is on Continental European countries and on Asian countries less directly affected by Anglo-American developments.

The book aims to cover major developments in conflict management practices and also to review the changing contours of conflict management in major countries across global regions. Part 1 examines the changing context and theoretical conceptualizations of conflict management, reviewing the objectives of conflict management in organizations, trends in industrial conflict, developments in employment rights, and HRM perspectives on conflict management.

Part 2 examines both conventional approaches to conflict management and a range of practices associated with ADR. Grievance procedures under collective bargaining are considered, as is grievance handling in non-union firms. The role of third parties in conflict management is reviewed, as is the role of line managers. Important innovations are also covered in chapters that deal with the role of the organizational ombudsperson, interest-based bargaining, mediation, and the nature and outcomes of conflict management systems.

Part 3 presents a series of case studies of exemplars and innovators in conflict management. These cases cover mediation, interest-based bargaining and labor-management partnerships, and the conduct of med+arb. While the focus of the book is on conflict management within organizations, a case study of a significant initiative in "judicial mediation," as practiced by employment tribunals in the UK, is also presented. This covers a form of employment mediation that occurs under the aegis of courts or administrative agencies and with parallels also in some countries in Continental Europe.

Part 4 of the book reviews trends in conflict management in major countries from different regions of the global economy. These reviews examine the development of conflict management both in the context of distinctive national institutions that shape employment relations and labor markets, and against the background of convergent secular trends that increasingly affect all major economies and all stakeholders in organizations.

PART 1

....

THEORETICAL

PERSPECTIVES

....

INTRODUCTION TO PART 1

WILLIAM K. ROCHE, PAUL TEAGUE,
AND ALEXANDER J. S. COLVIN

CONFLICT management and dispute resolution has been a notoriously under-theorized area. In part this may derive from its close connection to the world of practice and the reality that many of the leading thinkers in this area have been scholar–practitioners, well aware that the neat models of theory often do not translate cleanly into the messy world of practice. Although some distinctive theories have arisen in the study of conflict management in organizations, more generally thinking in this field has been influenced by broader perspectives from the fields of labor and employment relations and of law. The contributions to this section draw on theoretical insights from those fields, but also develop analyzes that more specifically consider the problem of how we think about the implications of conflict and its management and resolution within organizations.

Budd and Colvin begin by providing an overview of four different perspectives on the employment relationship and analyze how these inform the goals and assumptions of conflict management. Conflict management is marginalized as a concern in the neoliberal egoist frame of reference, which relies on market mechanisms to resolve conflicts. By contrast, conflict is a central concern of the critical frame of reference, which emphasizes the inherent nature of conflict between labor and capital and its embeddedness in broader societal inequalities, making organizational efforts at conflict management suspect. This stands in contrast to the unitarist frame of reference, whose emphasis on the possibility and desirability of aligning employer and employee interests makes organizational conflict management both feasible and important as organizations seek to address the types of interpersonal and behavioral problems that can undermine effective organizational functioning. Meanwhile the pluralist frame of reference sees employer–employee conflicts as being more structurally embedded than the unitarist frame, yet more amenable to resolution than the critical frame, due to the assumption of the mixed motive nature of the employment relationship with both conflicting and aligned interests.

Budd and Colvin go on to develop an explicitly pluralist perspective on conflict management. Central to this perspective is the idea that there are legitimate, but also conflicting, interests across all the parties to labor and employment relations that need to be taken into account and balanced in resolving conflict. The three goals of efficiency, equity, and voice provide a framework for analyzing the contrasting interests that need to be balanced in conflict management. From the pluralist perspective, successful procedures and systems for conflict management will be ones that provide a balancing of these goals and ideally jointly maximize achievement of all three.

Godard develops a critical or radical perspective on issues of labor and employment conflict. This begins with the identification of industrial conflict as being endemic in capitalist economies and a product of the nature of the capitalist employment relationship with its basic antagonism between labor and capital. One consequence of this inherent nature of conflict in the employment relationship is the "balloon theory" that even as one manifestation of conflict may be reduced other forms of conflict will expand to compensate. From this perspective, the historical decline in strike activity seen across a number of countries does not represent an improvement in working conditions and diminution of conflict, but more likely its repression and migration to other forms. A critical or radical perspective indicates that the problem of workplace conflict is far more structurally embedded and intractable than is suggested by much of the conflict management literature. Micro-level attempts at conflict management that are limited to the workplace or organizational level will not be able to address the real sources of conflict in the employment relationship. To the degree that workplace conflict is to be better understood, it will require a broader analysis that recognizes the national and international structures of society and the economy within which it occurs.

Estlund provides an alternative perspective on workplace conflict that draws on the growing new governance perspective in the field of law. A starting point to this analysis is to note the broad shift in recent decades away from labor law and collective bargaining as the central institutions for workplace conflict resolution and toward individual employment rights and litigation as the leading mechanisms. Despite their obvious differences, however, there are parallels between collective bargaining and litigation in that they are both catalysts of conflict and mechanisms of conflict resolution. Both are also major sources of fear for employers, affecting the way in which they behave in relation to employees. Organizational conflicts in both forms serve as means for employees to pursue justice, as the threat of costly conflict induces employers to operate the workplace in a more just fashion.

Estlund argues that pressures from statutory employment rights and litigation have the potential to push employers toward a system of regulated self-regulation. This can occur through "reflexive" mechanisms in which organizations respond to and internalize mandates emanating from the public sphere of the legal system. A key mechanism is the rewarding of effective self-regulation by organizations through providing relief from external enforcement regimes. Although there are risks to this approach, Estlund argues for a stronger form of "co-regulation" in which deferral to organizational self-regulation is contingent on a significant measure of employee collective voice in the workplace. Unions provide a natural structure for co-regulation of the workplace; in the absence of unions it will be necessary to set up institutional structures, such as representative elections and access to resources and sources of power, in order to allow non-union employee representatives to fulfill a parallel function.

Mahony and Klaas provide a human resource management perspective on conflict management. They focus on the options and ability for employees to exercise voice under the employer-promulgated procedures that are, at least in the United States, the most widespread mechanism for conflict management. An initial question is what options do organizations provide to employees to exercise voice and what factors drive the adoption and structure of employer-promulgated procedures? Procedures adopted in non-union organizations feature a range of different structures and vary across a series of dimensions, including: informal versus formal processes; internal versus external decision-makers; binding versus non-binding procedures; and rights versus interest based procedures. Factors driving organizations to adopt these procedures include both external pressures from union organizing and litigation, and internal determinants such as complementarity with high performance work systems and other human resource (HR) benefits.

In contrast to other perspectives, Mahony and Klaas show the importance of individual employee level factors in conflict management from the human resource management (HRM) perspective. Organizational level procedures will be dependent on individual employee willingness to exercise voice, which will be affected by factors such as the risks associated with voice, behaviors, and attitudes of organizational leaders, employee loyalty and organizational identification, and the degree to which the organization makes voice a legitimate activity. Managerial reactions to employee voice will be a central component of whether employees use voice and the effectiveness of voice mechanisms for managing and resolving conflict within organizations. Managers can have negative reactions to employee exercise of voice, particularly if the voice mechanism used is more formal and if it is presented in a more challenging manner. For HR policy and practice, research in this area indicates the importance of encouraging leader openness to employee voice for the effective management of conflict in organizations.

These contrasting theoretical perspectives on conflict management illustrate the importance of considering the foundational assumptions about conflict and the employment relationship in general in thinking about issues of conflict management. Too often writing on conflict management proceeds with implicit assumptions about the nature of conflict and the normative value of conflict management procedures. These chapters suggest that conflict and its resolution in organizations is a sphere of activity worthy of deep study, but that conflict in organizations may not be amenable to a simple process of management and reduction, nor is that necessarily desirable.

CHAPTER 1

THE GOALS AND ASSUMPTIONS OF CONFLICT MANAGEMENT IN ORGANIZATIONS

JOHN W. BUDD AND ALEXANDER J. S. COLVIN

INTRODUCTION

CONFLICTS in organizations can take many forms, which gives rise to diverse approaches to conflict management. Often overlooked, however, is that different conflict management strategies are implicitly rooted in distinct models of conflict that embrace certain goals and assumptions. These assumptions lead scholars and practitioners to diagnose the sources of a conflict in certain ways, and when paired with a specific set of desired goals, point to preferred methods of conflict management. This chapter seeks to make these connections explicit by contrasting the assumptions and goals of four alternative perspectives. This is then followed by additional discussion of one of these approaches—the pluralist approach.

The discussion starts with a consideration of the goals of conflict management in organizations because it is these goals that provide the desired ends for organizational and societal participants. Then the different perspectives on the relative importance of these goals are considered, as are the differing assumptions about conflict in organizations that generate different views on how to best achieve these goals.

The Goals of Conflict Management in Organizations

The trilogy of efficiency, equity, and voice is a useful framework for considering the goals of conflict management in organizations (Budd and Colvin, 2008). In general terms, efficiency is the effective, profit-maximizing use of labor and other scarce resources, equity is fairness in the distribution and administration of rewards and policies, and voice is the ability of participants to have meaningful input (Budd, 2004). Applying these concepts to the domain of conflict management allows us to ask what the parties to the employment relationship desire from a system of conflict management (see Table 1.1).

One goal of conflict management is efficiency. The effective management of conflict is important so that conflict minimizes disruptions to the productive efficiency of an organization. Whether overt or quietly festering, clashes between supervisors and

Table 1.1 The Goals of Conflict Management

Goals	Selected Key Elements
Efficiency	
Effective use of scarce resources	Eliminates barriers to performance
	Does not interfere with productive deployment of resources
	Cost effective
	Speedy
	Flexibile
Equity	
Fairness and justice	Unbiased decision-making
	Reliant on evidence
	Consistent
	Effective remedies
	Opportunities for appeal
	Coverage independent of resources
Voice	
Participation in design and operation	Input into design and operation of a dispute resolution system
	Hearings
	Obtaining and presenting evidence
	Representation by advocates and use of experts

subordinates, co-workers, union leaders and managers, or other organizational actors can be disruptive and undermine individual and organizational performance. A conflict management system should be able to resolve these conflicts so that they are removed as barriers to performance. Note further that this efficiency objective is not only an organizational goal; indeed, conflicts that hinder job performance can be detrimental to individual employees while conflicts that waste resources or disrupt the provision of goods and services are harmful to society. Efficiency should therefore be a widespread goal of conflict management.

Another aspect of efficiency as a goal of conflict management is that it is desirable to resolve conflicts in an efficient way. Specifically, an efficient conflict resolution system conserves scarce resources, especially time and money. A system that manages conflict in a slow fashion and takes a long time to generate a resolution is inefficient; a system that produces a quicker resolution rates more highly on the efficiency dimension. Similarly, a costly dispute resolution system, whether due to the involvement of large numbers of participants, the use of high-paid experts, or other reasons, is inefficient. A costly conflict management system is also one that interferes with organizational efficiency, such as through excessive constraints on managerial decision-making or by restricting the organizational flexibility needed to adapt to changing business needs.

A second objective of conflict management is equity, which includes concerns about justice, fairness, and due process. Equitable conflict management systems are those in which outcomes are linked to objective pieces of evidence and which include safeguards that prevent arbitrary or capricious decision-making. As such, equitable conflict management outcomes are those that are consistent with the judgment of a reasonable person who does not have a vested interest in a particular outcome. Fairness also requires that similar circumstances be handled in a similar fashion and yield similar, though not necessarily identical, resolutions. Moreover, an equitable conflict management system treats all participants with respect, sensitivity, and privacy while also generating appropriate and effective remedies when rights are violated. The equity dimension can also include the extent to which a conflict management system has widespread coverage independent of resources or expertise. As with the efficiency dimension, equity is a concern of all participants. Employees might have the strongest desire for conflict management approaches that are not biased against them, that use standards of evidence, and that generate consistent outcomes, but employers are likely to also value conflict management systems that are not biased against *them*. Also, if equity increases employee buy-in and therefore creates enduring resolutions, then an equitable conflict management system can serve an employer's as well as an employee's interests.

The third dimension of a framework for considering the goals of conflict management is voice—that is, the extent to which a conflict management system is participatory. A conflict management system that is unilaterally designed and administered by managers lacks voice. In contrast, a system shaped by the input of employees as well as employers scores higher on the voice dimension. Similarly, participation in the actual conflict management system is an important element of voice. In a grievance hearing, this includes important aspects of due process such as having a hearing, presenting evidence in one's defense, and being assisted by an advocate if desired. As with the equity dimension, voice might be a particular concern for employees, but being able to have input into how procedures are designed as well as the ability to present evidence and use experts are presumably of interest to employers too. And if employee participation in conflict resolution creates more enduring resolutions, then voice can be important to employers as well as employees.

Another common framework for considering conflict management is organizational justice, especially distributive and procedural justice (Greenberg and Colquitt, 2005). Indeed, there are important complementarities between this justice approach and the efficiency, equity, and voice framework. In particular, the measures of distributive and procedural justice that have been developed can be useful for creating measures of aspects of equity and voice. However, there are multiple limitations in using organizational justice as an over-arching framework for understanding the broad goals of conflict management in organizations:

1. Efficiency is not well captured in the distributive and procedural justice framework, yet it is a critical element of conflict management.

2. As constructs, distributive and procedural justice are now well developed and therefore typically associated with specific measures (Colquitt and Shaw, 2005). The way these measures have been defined in this literature is with a focus on capturing individual subjective perceptions of fair treatment. This is a relatively narrow psychologically based vision of organizational justice that is rooted in one particular approach to understanding conflict, the unitarist perspective, and fails to give sufficient attention to issues of power and institutions. Efficiency, equity, and voice are more general concepts. This generality is useful because, as will be developed below, different paradigms have different visions of the specifics of efficiency, equity, and voice. In this way, efficiency, equity, and voice can provide an overall framework that includes diverse perspectives.

3. Distributive and procedural justice are commonly seen as provided by employers and desired by employees. As such, while organizational justice is an important predictor for understanding employee behaviors (Conlon, Meyer, and Nowakowsi, 2005), a different approach is needed to capture the goals of employers and the broader societal goals of a conflict management system. Admittedly, some aspects of procedural justice are part of the dimension of voice, but the construct of voice goes beyond procedural fairness in the conduct of a conflict management system to include broader issues such as input into the design of the system and the rules under which decisions are made.

The dimensions of efficiency, equity, and voice provide an analytical framework for thinking about the key elements of a conflict management system and for analyzing the extent to which a conflict management system fulfills each dimension. For example, an analysis of the processes for resolving individual disputes over unfair dismissals, suspensions, and other unfair labor practices in Korea through the Labour Relations

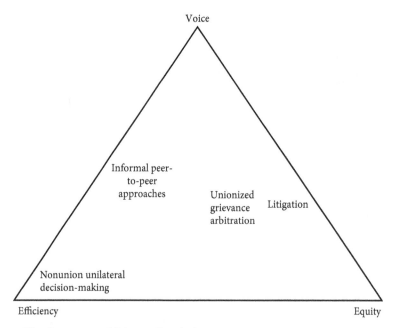

FIGURE 1.1 The Geometry of Dispute Resolution

Commission finds that this system is efficient, includes some elements of voice (especially via hearings), but lacks equity because decision-making is politically influenced and lacks effective remedies (Croucher, Joung, and Miles, 2013). In New Zealand, in contrast, the employment dispute resolution system can be slow, but it provides high levels of equity via low-cost access to impartial mediators and has expanded opportunities for direct participation in the process (Radich and Franks, 2013).

At a high level of generality, this can also provide a useful framework for comparing approaches to conflict management. As an example, Figure 1.1 locates a non-union, uni-lateral conflict management approach where efficiency is high (resolution can be speedy with few managerial constraints) but equity (little consistency) and voice (little partici-pation) are low. An informal approach to resolving co-worker conflicts in which the parties are encouraged to work things out would add more voice, but not much equity. A litigation-based system, in contrast, is quite costly and slow, so it scores low on the efficiency dimension but high on the equity dimension because of the strong procedural safeguards. There is some amount of voice through the right to be heard and to appeal, but this is typically handled by experts rather than the participants themselves. A union-ized grievance procedure also involves due process protections and more participation by the parties, rating higher on the voice dimension, and is somewhat more efficient than a litigation-based system. In this way, the efficiency, equity, and voice approach can provide a very useful framework for comparing these and other conflict management systems.

THE ASSUMPTIONS OF CONFLICT MANAGEMENT IN ORGANIZATIONS

The framework of efficiency, equity, and voice provides a useful schema for thinking about the goals of conflict management in organizations. But how do or should organizations pursue these goals through systems of conflict management? This depends on one's assumptions of where conflict in organizations comes from, which in turn are rooted in one's frame of reference for how the employment relationship works. This section therefore first outlines four frames of reference on the employment relationship (Budd and Bhave, 2010). This is then followed by an explicit comparison of the implications for differing views on conflict and conflict management.

Four Frames of Reference on the Employment Relationship

Dating back at least to Adam Smith and other 18th-century classical economists, mainstream economic thought has seen the employment relationship as a market-mediated transaction between consenting economic agents. Labor is seen as a commodity traded in competitive labor markets no different from other markets. Wages and salaries, benefits, and other terms and conditions of employment, therefore, are set by the invisible hand of the labor market. Economic actors, including employers and employees, are seen as rational and self-interested, but they are protected against the excess demands of others because such demands cannot survive in ideally competitive markets. As advocated by proponents of today's neoliberal market ideology, then, it is best to leave employees and employers to pursue voluntary, mutually beneficial transactions buying and selling units of productive labor based on what the competitive labor market supports. Owing to the twin emphases on markets and self-interest, this is labeled the neoliberal egoist frame of reference.

Karl Marx criticized the classical economists' reduction of work to a generic commodity and, as witness to the deep exploitation of 19th-century labor, challenged the faith in competitive markets as a mechanism for achieving social welfare. In Marxist and related perspectives, then, employers are viewed as the owners and controllers of the means of production so that they have both the incentive and the ability to continually drive for greater profits at the expense of labor (Hyman, 1975). The employment relationship is furthermore seen as much more than a market-focused economic transaction because:

1. Workers are valued as innate human beings entitled to dignity and freedom, not just as commoditized, productive resources; and
2. Laws and other social constructions grant ownership and control rights to certain classes.

Consequently, the critical employment relationship frame of reference that is today most closely associated with radical, heterodox, and feminist scholarship in sociology, economics, and industrial relations emphasizes sharp conflicts of interests and unequal power dynamics between employers and employees that are deeply rooted in multiple layers of societal institutions.

In the early 20th century, progressive employers sought to replace aggressive supervisory methods and other high-conflict practices with more cooperative strategies. This was based on a new management philosophy that employer and employee interests can be aligned in a win-win fashion (Kaufman, 2003). In other words, rather than seeing employers and employees with distinctly opposing interests as a fundamental, structural aspect of capitalism, as in the critical perspective, employer-employee conflicts in this perspective are believed to be the result of poor managerial practices which can be corrected by improved methods of management. The development of this view coincided with the emergence of industrial psychology that de-emphasized coldly rational decision-making in favor of behavioral elements such as fairness, social pressure, and cognitive limitations, and also de-emphasized narrow economic interests in favor of psychological interests. These are roots of a third frame of reference on the employment relationship that today is most closely associated with scholars in industrial/organizational psychology, organizational behavior, and human resource management. This is labeled the unitarist employment relationship because it rests on the assumption that that employees and employers share a unity of many of their interests. Profitability and other organizational goals are seen as resulting from and supported by fulfilling work, fair treatment, and the satisfaction of employees' other intrinsic desires.

Lastly, an alternative approach to redressing the stark inequalities of the early 20th-century employment relationship is rooted in seeing the employment relationship as one that is bargained between employers and employees in the context of imperfectly competitive labor markets that typically give employers a bargaining power advantage. This is the foundation of the pluralist frame of reference that today is found mostly in industrial relations, institutionalist labor economics, labor law, and related fields. This frame of reference lies somewhere in the middle of the other perspectives. Like the neoliberal egoist perspective, it largely sees the employment relationship as an economic one, but, as in the other frames of reference, it rejects the idealism of perfectly competitive labor markets and the view that labor is no more than a commodity. Furthermore, while the critical perspective emphasizes deeply embedded, structural conflicts of interests between employers and employees, and while the unitarist perspective emphasizes shared interests, the pluralist perspective sees employees and employers as having a mixture of common and conflicting interests. Both want profitable organizations and productive workers, but conflicts between, for example, wages and profits, flexibility and security, or speed and safety are also seen as inherent, structural conflicts. But employer as well as employee interests are viewed as legitimate. So the employment relationship is a complex one defined by a plurality of legitimate interests. Unequal bargaining power is viewed as undermining the fulfillment of legitimate employee interests, and, in the extreme, degrading human dignity and undermining democracy, so institutional interventions such as labor unions or

minimum wage laws that bolster workers' bargaining power to create a more equal playing field are seen as important safeguards against unchecked economic incentives and
markets that are valuable for allocating and effectively using scarce resources.

Four Views on Conflict and Conflict Management in Organizations

The four frames of reference on the employment relationship instructively reveal four
differing views on conflict, and thus divergent preferred methods of conflict management in organizations (see Table 1.2). It is important to make these differences explicit to
promote a deeper understanding and enhanced interdisciplinary dialogue.

Given its emphasis on free choice and market-based opportunities, conflict does not
play a central role in the neoliberal egoist frame of reference. Employees, employers, and
other economic agents are believed to freely choose their best opportunity so conflicts
should not arise. If an agent can get a better deal by choosing a different course of action,
s/he should do so. As such, all conflicts are resolved by the opportunities presented by
the competitive marketplace. A potential conflict, for example, between an employee
who wants a higher wage and an employer that does not want to pay this is resolved by
the marketplace—the employee is free to quit if s/he can find a higher wage elsewhere,
and the employer will be unable to attract or retain workers if it pays less than the going
rate. In this way, conflict is resolved through the mechanism of market clearing transactions in which each party engages in any available exchanges that maximize individual
utility under existing resource constraints.

The focal conflict management system in the neoliberal egoist frame of reference
is therefore the invisible hand of the competitive market. Again, this is rooted in the
assumptions of this perspective, especially the embrace of individual self-interest, free
choice, and competitive markets. In this paradigm, moreover, the invisible hand conflict
management system is seen as fulfilling market-based visions of efficiency, equity, and
voice. Efficiency is valued as the most important objective, and is seen as best accomplished through the invisible hand of the competitive market which will optimally allo-
cate scarce resources to their most beneficial uses. The market is thus seen as the most
efficient method of conflict management. A manager, for example, who interferes with
the competitive market by agreeing to a higher-than-market wage to settle a dispute
with an employee distorts competitive outcomes and thereby undermines efficiency.
Moreover, this market-driven approach is also viewed as fulfilling equity because supply and demand determine terms and conditions of employment that reflect economic
value, not coercion or exploitation, and are thus considered fair. This has been labeled
"marginal productivity justice" (McClelland, 1990). Similarly, voice is seen as something
that is fulfilled through the freedom to choose among the options that the market provides. In other words, voice is exercised more by one's feet than one's written or verbal expression. Through the lens of the neoliberal egoist frame of reference, then, the

Table 1.2 Four Frames of Reference on Conflict in Organizations

Frame of Reference	Structure of the Employment Relationship	View of Conflict in Organizations	Preferred Method of Conflict Management	Achievement of Conflict Management Goals
Neoliberal Egoist	Competitive labor markets. Labor as a commodity.	Conflicts are resolved by the market. Exchanges occur when self-interests and market-provided opportunities align.	Perfectly-competitive economic markets.	Markets generate efficient resource allocation. Fairness defined by market acceptability. Voice is the freedom to choose.
Critical	Employment inequalities embedded in systemic, societal inequalities. Labor as economic and psychological beings and democratic citizens.	Employees and powerful employers have inherent, antagonistic conflicts of interest.	Systematic shift in power relations through broad societal change.	Equity and voice are paramount and require significant societal change to achieve due to systemic power imbalances.
Unitarist	Imperfect labor markets. Labor as psychological beings.	Employers and employees primarily have shared interests and conflict is mostly interpersonal or a product of organizational dysfunction.	HR policies to align employer-employee interests. Personal interventions to resolve interpersonal, behavioral conflicts.	Alignment of interests promotes efficiency, equity, and voice through psychological satisfaction and individual productivity.
Pluralist	Imperfect labor markets. Labor as economic and psychological beings and democratic citizens.	Employers and employees with unequal bargaining power have some shared interests and some conflicting interests.	Institutionalized processes that balance bargaining power and respect the rights and interests of all parties.	Balancing efficiency, equity, and voice to meet competing yet legitimate interests.

preferred system of conflict management via the invisible hand fulfills market-based visions of efficiency, equity, and voice.

In contrast, conflict and power are fundamentally important and central issues in the critical frame of reference. For example, Marx (1867/1936: 363) argued that "the directing motive, the end and aim of capitalist production, is to extract the greatest possible amount of surplus-value, and consequently to exploit labor-power to the greatest possible extent." This puts antagonistic employer-employee conflict squarely at the heart of the critical model of the employment relationship, although modern critical scholarship also recognizes that accommodation and consent by employees as well as employers are also important (Hyman, 2006). In this way, the employment relationship is not seen as a voluntary, win-win, or bargained exchange, but as a contested exchange (Bowles and Gintis, 1990). Unlike in the pluralist model that sees employer-employee conflict as largely economic in nature and independent of broader societal institutions, the critical frame of reference emphasizes the social embeddedness of power differentials, and thus conflict, in organizations.

From this type of critical perspective, then, traditional forms of conflict management in organizations are viewed with skepticism. The labor market is not viewed as a neutral forum for resolving conflicts by indicating what is acceptable via supply and demand, but is seen as a socially based instrument of power that perpetuates inequality (Hyman, 1975). Human resources policies and practices to purportedly align employer and employee interests are interpreted as methods for subtly disguising and perpetuating managerial authority (Bolton and Houlihan, 2007). Labor law that promotes collective bargaining in a regulated fashion is seen as a method for channeling worker discontent into forums that provide less of a threat to corporate power and thus perpetuate rather than challenge the status quo (Klare, 1978; Stone, 1981).

Apparent satisfaction of true equity and voice for workers in traditional systems of conflict management, therefore, is argued to be more of an illusion than reality (efficiency is not a priority in the critical frame of reference). As such, if antagonistic employer-employee conflict is structurally embedded within capitalism, then the way to truly resolve this conflict is to change the system. Beyond advocating for deep changes in societal institutions to redress employer-employee conflict, the critical perspective is also useful in highlighting the socially embedded nature of conflict in organizations and in raising important questions about the true nature of conflict management approaches within organizations.

At the opposite end of the spectrum, the assumptions of the unitarist frame of reference essentially assume away the existence of structural employer-employee conflict. Rather, because the employment relationship is viewed as primarily characterized by shared interests between employees and employers, the existence of employer-employee conflict in a specific organization is viewed as a suboptimal state of affairs that can be redressed by improved managerial practices. In other words, with well-informed managers, employer-employee conflict is not significant and there is no need for conflict management systems to resolve this type of conflict in organizations.

In practice, however, managers can be imperfect and employees can misperceive situations so some organizations have non-union dispute resolution systems ranging from open door policies to formal grievance procedures (Colvin, Klaas, and Mahony, 2006). Through the lens of the unitarist frame of reference, in addition to being reactions to outside legal pressures (Colvin, 2003), these systems are best seen as mechanisms that serve employer-employee alignment through employee commitment and the monitoring of deviant cases (Olson-Buchanan and Boswell, 2007). This approach to conflict management is seen as efficient because it typically does not involve expensive hearings, the final decision is generally left to a manager rather than an outsider, and the resulting increased employee commitment as well as improved managerial practices can promote improved individual and organizational performance. Equity and voice are typically seen in terms of individual perceptions of fairness so these goals are seen as fulfilled through the pursuit of distributive and procedural justice in the operation of these non-union dispute resolution procedures.

Within the unitarist frame of reference, conflict among individuals, not between employers and employees as a structural feature of the employment relationship, is much more important, and research analyzes diverse forms of interpersonal, behavioral conflict within organizations (De Dreu and Gelfand, 2008). For example, conflict among co-workers or team members can occur because of relationship conflicts rooted in cultural, political, social, personality, or other differences, and can occur because of task conflicts stemming from differing views about how to accomplish job responsibilities or communication breakdowns (Jehn, Bezrukova, and Thatcher, 2008). Conflict management thus takes the form of interventions to prevent or resolve these conflicts, such as diversity training, team-building exercises, or individual counseling and coaching. Interpersonal conflict in the form of workplace aggression such as harassment, abusive supervision, or bullying are also unfortunate realities of organizational life, but again these conflicts are seen as rooted in situational and individual differences such as negative organizational climate, stress, lack of self-control, or perceptions of injustice (Raver and Barling, 2008). Again, these behavioral conflicts are seen as deviant, not inevitable, even between supervisors and subordinates, and the conflict management response is prevention and resolution through appropriate managerial practices.

Lastly, in the pluralist frame of reference, employer-employee conflicts of interest are viewed as an inherent, structural feature of at least part of the employment relationship. In other words, some interests are assumed to conflict while others can be aligned. As such, conflicts of interest are to be managed rather than seen as deviant as in the unitarist perspective. But in contrast to the critical frame of reference, pluralist thought does not view the employment relationship as always dominated by broader societal divisions and instead it is believed to be possible to manage these conflicts of interests in ways that truly respect the plurality of interests found in the employment relationship. If employers and employees had equal power, presumably they could manage their own conflicts without formal structures or institutions, but the pluralist frame of reference is premised upon an inequality of bargaining power because of imperfect labor markets (Budd, 2004). As such, the absence of institutional intervention is seen as favoring employers, so institutional intervention is needed to create more of a balance and prevent employers from taking advantage of less-powerful employees. Note that in the unitarist frame of reference, this is less of a concern because employers are seen as desiring alignment of interests so they should not opportunistically take advantage of employees. But in the pluralist perspective, employers are seen as having this motivation, at least with respect to issues characterized by conflicts of interests such as wages versus profits, especially in tough economic times: "recessions, depressions, and major industrial downsizings are a mortal threat to advanced, mutual gain [human resource management] systems and can quickly transform employees from high-valued human resource assets to low-valued disposable commodities" (Kaufman, 2008: 278).

Since a plurality of legitimate interests can sometimes be aligned but sometimes conflict in the pluralist frame of reference, conflict management needs to respect the legitimacy of multiple interests and find a balance. The assumptions of the pluralist perspective thereby focus attention on institutionalized methods of resolving conflicts of interests between employers and employees, especially collective bargaining and interest arbitration, as well as on methods of resolving conflicts of rights, especially formal grievance procedures, rights arbitration, and litigation. It is here where balancing efficiency, equity, and voice comes to the fore, not only in terms of the objectives of the employment relationship (Budd, 2004), but also in terms of the goals of conflict management. By seeing workers as citizens of democratic communities rather than as economic or psychological agents as in the neoliberal egoist or unitarist frames of reference, equity and voice are conceptualized in the pluralist perspective in terms of minimum standards and rights consistent with dignity and democracy (Budd, 2011). So rather than distributive and procedural justice, pluralist conflict management procedures seek to satisfy rich conceptualizations of equity and voice that include due process and broad-based participation as equals. But efficiency is also viewed as a legitimate interest, so the goal is to balance efficiency, equity, and voice.

Putting all of this together yields four different frames of reference on conflict and conflict management in organizations (see Table 1.2 above). Making explicit the underlying assumptions of these alternative perspectives is important for a better understanding of conflict and conflict management. Moreover, this explicit analysis reveals the broad classes of conflict management approaches that can be used, and suggests the applicability, pros, and cons of each class—all of which are intimately tied to the underlying goals and assumptions.

As an example, consider non-union dispute resolution procedures such as open door policies, management appeal procedures, and peer review panels. Such procedures are advocated by some as a way for aggrieved employees to voice their complaints and achieve remedies when warranted (Olson-Buchanan and Boswell, 2007), but heavily criticized by others (Stone, 1996). These sharply differing views on non-union dispute resolution are directly related to the divergent goals and assumptions embraced by participants to these debates. In particular, note that the design and desirability of non-union dispute resolution procedures are squarely rooted in the goals and assumptions of the unitarist frame of reference. The presence of these procedures is intended to signal to employees that they will enjoy distributive and procedural justice at this organization, which is believed to create high levels of engagement and thus productivity. This philosophy is very much part of an overall belief that happy workers are productive workers. Moreover, there is not a perceived problem with managers retaining final decision-making authority because of the unitarist philosophy that organizations are best off aligning employer and employee interests in a win-win fashion.

In contrast, the pluralist and critical approaches assume that employers have both the incentive and the power to prioritize organizational over individual employee interests. Moreover, by seeing workers as citizens in democratic communities, the pluralist and critical approaches believe that workers are entitled to due process and meaningful participation, not just managerial-provided distributive and procedural justice. From the critical perspectives, open door policies and other non-union dispute resolution procedures are seen, at best, as hollow schemes that fail to deliver equity and voice and, at worst, as manipulative tools that mollify workers through the appearance, but not the reality, of a meaningful forum for redressing their grievances. Even union grievance procedures are seen as having similar failings from some critical perspectives (Stone, 1981). The pluralist perspective on non-union grievance procedures is more mixed, though also skeptical. From a pluralist perspective, non-union grievance procedures represent an improvement on unfettered management discretion, but fall short of providing the level of voice and equity found in union procedures, and to be truly effective, external institutional pressures are needed to help counter-balance the inherent inequality of bargaining power in the employment relationship (Colvin, 2003). Lastly, others taking a neoliberal egoist perspective might criticize non-union dispute resolution procedures for being unnecessary interferences with the ability of managers to adjust to the realities of the competitive market. Carefully note how these criticisms are better understood once one understands the underlying goals and assumptions, and how these differing views of non-union dispute resolution procedures are linked to different underlying perspectives on these goals and assumptions. The same is true for debates over other forms of conflict management systems in organizations.

BALANCING EFFICIENCY, EQUITY AND VOICE: THE PLURALIST APPROACH TO CONFLICT MANAGEMENT IN ORGANIZATIONS

As the chapters by John Godard and by Doug Mahony and Brian Klaas in Part I of this Handbook discuss the critical and unitarist approaches in more detail, and active conflict management plays little role in the neoliberal egoist approach relying on the market, the remainder of this chapter focuses on the pluralist approach, which also reflects our own perspective as scholars in this area. Throughout these discussions it is important to remember the underlying goals and assumptions that inform the analyzes.

The essence of the pluralist perspective is that it sees the employment relationship as involving both common and conflicting interests amongst the parties that are legitimate and need to be balanced. The metrics of efficiency, equity, and voice provide a useful analytical framework for analyzing the implications of different assumptions and goals for conflict management in organizations. Taking an explicitly pluralist perspective, however, the trilogy of efficiency, equity, and voice is not just an analytical tool, but is also a set of goals that represent key interests that should be balanced when developing systems for managing conflict in organizations.

Why from a pluralist perspective do we emphasize the importance of balancing efficiency, equity, and voice in conflict resolution systems? First note that efficiency, equity, and voice might often conflict with each other. Equity requires objective evidence, unbiased decision-making, and appeals to neutral parties, whereas voice entails participating in hearings. These two dimensions can conflict with each other (such as when third-party control overrides the voices of the participants) and together they can conflict with the efficiency emphasis on quickness and low cost. Against this backdrop of potentially conflicting dimensions, we assert that dispute resolution systems should *balance* efficiency, equity, and voice.

The importance of balancing competing objectives is rooted in the need to balance the competing rights of various stakeholders. In particular, an employer's property rights to use their employees as they see fit must be balanced with employees' rights to equity and voice. This is because work is a fully human activity, not a purely economic transaction, so employees as well as employers have human rights in a democratic society (Budd, 2004). Taking a slightly different tack, due process protections in the civil arena are so important that they are written directly into the Magna Carta and US Constitution; these rights are so critical that they should not be checked at the factory gate or office door and disregarded in the employment relationship.

There is also an analytical rationale for balancing efficiency, equity, and voice: pluralist industrial relations thought predicts that employment systems work better when competing interests are balanced than when imbalances or inequalities exist (Budd, Gomez, and Meltz, 2004). Workplace dispute resolution systems are therefore hypothesized to be more effective and stable when efficiency, equity, and voice are balanced. Compared to unbalanced dispute resolution systems, balanced systems should have greater legitimacy, produce more effective and durable resolutions, and prevent the recurrence of disputes. As a result, practitioners and policymakers should design dispute resolution systems that balance efficiency, equity, and voice. It can be difficult to know when a balance has been achieved. Rather, the idea of balancing efficiency, equity, and voice as a guiding principle is put forth as what philosophers call a regulative ideal—something to strive for even if it is not achieved or if you do not know when it is achieved. With this foundation and frame of reference, specific systems for resolving workplace rights disputes from a pluralist perspective using the triangular framework presented in Figure 1.1 are analyzed. By situating conflict resolution procedures within the triangle of efficiency, equity, and voice, it is possible to identify the degree to which different procedures and systems either do or do not enhance balancing of these goals. From a normative perspective, pluralists emphasize policy innovations that result in movement towards the middle of the triangle and satisfying all three of the goals simultaneously.

Traditional pluralist perspectives have emphasized the strengths of union representation and collective bargaining in achieving balance in meeting the goals of employment relations. In the area of conflict management, the grievance arbitration procedures used in unionized workplaces in the US have a relatively strong provision of voice and especially equity (though the limitation of coverage to unionized workplaces limits equity when considering the entire US employment system). There are concerns with voice to the extent that the process is very formal. The larger weaknesses are in the area of efficiency with significant concerns regarding cost, speed, and flexibility. In comparison, expedited arbitration performs better on the efficiency dimension because of reduced costs and increased speed, but at the expense of a degree of equity and voice. The inclusion of a mediation step before arbitration improves efficiency with only minor trade-offs with equity and voice and thus has the potential to better balance efficiency, equity, and voice. Thus pluralists have favored innovations such as the use of grievance mediation in unionized settings to enhance the functioning of conflict management systems (Brett and Goldberg, 1983). A broader concern for pluralist scholars is the shrinking coverage of union representation and collective bargaining in many countries. This raises the, as yet unresolved, question for pluralists of whether alternative institutions for worker representation such as works councils or newer forms of employee representation can provide equivalent degrees of balancing the interests of efficiency, equity, and voice as union procedures have in the past.

In comparison to union procedures, non-union grievance procedures tend to emphasize efficiency at the expense of equity and voice. The imbalance in favor of efficiency is seen most strongly in open door policies that provide little protection of equity or voice. Management appeal procedures provide a limited enhancement of equity through the formalization of structures for reviewing employee complaints, while continuing to emphasize efficiency through management control of the process and outcomes. Peer review and ombudsperson procedures represent more substantial attempts to achieve greater balance in the geometry of dispute resolution in the non-union workplace. Peer review enhances equity and voice through the mechanism of employee involvement in the grievance decision-making process. Ombudspersons enhance equity and voice through a relatively flexible, informal approach to assisting employees in getting complaints heard and resolved. Both peer review and ombudsperson procedures require more substantial commitment of resources by the company as well as limitations on management discretion, resulting in some sacrifice of efficiency. Although not involving the strongly developed institutional structure of union grievance procedures, these procedures are noteworthy as indicating attempts within non-union workplaces to achieve an improved balance between efficiency, equity and voice in dispute resolution. While from a unitarist perspective, organizations might be expected to adopt these types of non-union procedures in order to resolve interpersonal disputes and improve internal organizational functioning, pluralists tend to be more skeptical of the extent to which these internal employer motivations will produce a true balance given the inherent inequality of bargaining power in the employment relationship. As a result, research from a pluralist perspective has emphasized the importance of external institutional pressures, particularly from the legal system and from the threat of union organizing, as necessary to produce greater balancing of interests in the structure and operation of non-union grievance procedures (Colvin, 2003).

For resolving employment law disputes, both employment law mediation and arbitration represent attempts to rebalance the geometry of dispute resolution relative to litigation. Employment litigation is a system with a strong imbalance in favor of equity, with some strong voice elements, but a lack of efficiency. Employment law arbitration imbues the system with greater levels of efficiency, but leads to questions of whether it sacrifices too much in the areas of equity and voice. The compulsory nature of most employment law arbitration schemes also raises very serious concerns with equity and voice. Relative to arbitration and litigation, mediation provides a greater balancing of efficiency, equity and voice for resolving employment disputes. The main question in regard to mediation is whether it is appropriate, given its emphasis on private, consensual dispute resolution, for employment law cases that involve major questions of public policy. However, for more routine employment law cases, employment mediation provides arguably the better balance in dispute resolution.

Overall, these three examples of union, non-union, and employment law procedures, illustrate how pluralist perspectives tend to favor more strongly than other perspectives the development of alternative dispute resolution procedures and conflict management systems. For pluralists these procedures and systems provide ways to balance more effectively the sometimes competing goals of efficiency, equity, and voice. Pluralists also tend to be optimistic about the potential of institutions and public policy to promote greater balance between these goals within the employment relationship.

CONCLUSIONS

Underlying this chapter is a simple yet powerful and overlooked logic: perspectives on conflict management in organizations are rooted in the intersection of one's objectives and one's view on the source of conflict. Consequently, it is important to start with an explicit understanding of the goals and assumptions of conflict management. To that end, this chapter presents a framework of efficiency, equity, and voice as a useful schema for explicitly considering the key goals of any dispute resolution system. In evaluating or designing specific conflict management systems, these dimensions can be operationalized through a range of specific measures (Budd and Colvin, 2008). This chapter further considers the underlying assumptions to the broad classes of approaches to conflict management and presents a framework of four frames of reference. This framework uncovers the broad classes of conflict management approaches that organizations can use—especially the invisible hand of the competitive market and the visible hand of managerial practices, policies, and interventions—as well as the institutional interventions that others might advocate—ranging from formal grievance procedures and litigation or labor court systems to more systemic institutional changes that change the underlying power relations in the capitalist employment relationship—and allows us to consider under what conditions each method is desirable.

Although frequently hidden from view, the goals and assumptions that underlie each of the chapters in this Handbook as well as the implementation or critique of real-world conflict management systems are important to understand. From this will come a deeper understanding, an improved basis for implementation within organizations, and a more rigorous foundation for considering the need for institutional reform, whether voluntary or mandated by public policy.

REFERENCES

Bolton, S. and Houlihan, M. (eds) 2007. *Searching for the Human in Human Resource Management: Theory, Practice and Workplace Contexts*. Basingstoke, Hampshire: Palgrave Macmillan.

Bowles, S. and Gintis, H. 1990. "Contested Exchange: New Microfoundations for the Political Economy of Capitalism." *Politics and Society*, 18(2): 165–222.

Brett, J. M. and Goldberg, S. B. 1983. "Grievance Mediation in the Coal Industry: A Field Experiment." *Industrial and Labor Relations Review*, 37(1): 49–69.

Budd, J. 2004. *Employment with a Human Face: Balancing Efficiency, Equity, and Voice*. Ithaca, NY: Cornell University Press.

Budd, J. 2011. *The Thought of Work*. Ithaca, NY: Cornell University Press.

Budd, J. and Bhave, D. 2010. "The Employment Relationship." In A. Wilkinson et al. (eds), *Sage Handbook of Human Resource Management*. London: Sage, 51–70.

Budd, J. and Colvin, A. J. S. 2008. "Improved Metrics for Workplace Dispute Resolution Procedures: Efficiency, Equity, and Voice." *Industrial Relations*, 47(3): 460–79.

Budd, J., Gomez, R., and Meltz, N. M. 2004. "Why a Balance is Best: The Pluralist Industrial Relations Paradigm of Balancing Competing Interests." In B. E. Kaufman (ed.) *Theoretical Perspectives on Work and the Employment Relationship*. Champaign, IL: Industrial Relations Research Association: 195–227.

Colquitt, J. and Shaw, J. 2005. "How Should Organizational Justice be Measured?" In J. Greenberg and J. Colquitt (eds), *Handbook of Organizational Justice*. Mahwah, NJ: Erlbaum, 113–52.

Colvin, A. J. S. 2003. "Institutional Pressures, Human Resource Strategies and the Rise of Nonunion Dispute Resolution Procedures." *Industrial and Labor Relations Review*, 56(3): 375–92.

Colvin, A. J. S., Klaas, B., and Mahony, D. 2006. "Research on Alternative Dispute Resolution Procedures." In D. Lewin (ed.) *Contemporary Issues in Employment Relations*. Champaign, IL: Labor and Employment Relations Association, 103–47.

Conlon, D., Meyer C., and Nowakowski, J. 2005. "How Does Organizational Justice Affect Performance, Withdrawal, and Counterproductive Behavior?" In J. Greenberg and J. Colquitt (eds), *Handbook of Organizational Justice*. Mahwah, NJ: Erlbaum, 301–27.

Croucher, R., Joung, K., and Miles, L. 2013. "Evaluating South Korean Legal Channels for Individual Employment Disputes through Budd and Colvin's Framework." *Comparative Labor Law and Policy Journal*, 35(1): 45–65.

De Dreu, C. and Gelfand, M. (eds) 2008. *The Psychology of Conflict and Conflict Management in Organizations*. New York: Erlbaum.

Greenberg, J. and Colquitt, J. (eds) 2005. *Handbook of Organizational Justice*. Mahwah, NJ: Erlbaum.

Hyman, R. 1975. *Industrial Relations: A Marxist Introduction*. London: Macmillan.

Hyman, R. 2006. "Marxist Thought and the Analysis of Work." In M. Korczynski, R. Hodson, and P. Edwards (eds), *Social Theory at Work*. Oxford: Oxford University Press, 26–55.

Jehn, K., Bezrukova, K., and Thatcher, S. 2008. "Conflict, Diversity, and Faultlines in Workgroups." In C. De Dreu and M. Gelfand (eds), *The Psychology of Conflict and Conflict Management in Organizations*. New York: Erlbaum, 179–210.

Kaufman, B. 2003. "The Quest for Cooperation and Unity of Interest in Industry." In B. Kaufman, R. Beaumont, and R. Helfgott (eds), *Industrial Relations to Human Resources and Beyond: The Evolving Process of Employee Relations Management*. Armonk, NY: M.E. Sharpe, 115–46.

Kaufman, B. 2008. *Managing the Human Factor: The Early Years of Human Resource Management in American Industry*. Ithaca, NY: Cornell University Press.

Klare, K. 1978. "Judicial Deradicalization of the Wagner Act and the Origins of Modern Legal Consciousness, 1937–1941." *Minnesota Law Review*, 62(3): 265–339.

Marx, K. 1867. *Capital: A Critique of Political Economy*. Tr. S. Moore and E. Aveling (1936). New York: The Modern Library.

McClelland, P. 1990. *The American Search for Justice*. Cambridge, MA: Basil Blackwell.

Olson-Buchanan, J. and Boswell, W.R. 2007. "Organizational Dispute Resolution Systems." In C. De Drue and M. Gelfand (eds), *The Psychology of Conflict and Conflict Management in Organizations*. New York: Erlbaum, 319–50.

Radich, J. and Franks, P. 2013. *Employment Mediation*, 2nd ed. Wellington: Thomson Reuters.

Raver, J. and Barling, J. 2008. "Workplace Aggression and Conflict: Constructs, Commonalities, and Challenges for Future Inquiry." In C. De Dreu and M. Gelfand (eds), *The Psychology of Conflict and Conflict Management in Organizations*. New York: Erlbaum, 211–44.

Stone, K. V. W. 1981. "The Post-War Paradigm in American Labor Law." *Yale Law Journal*, 90(7): 1509–80.

Stone, K. V. W. 1996. "Mandatory Arbitration of Individual Employment Rights: The Yellow Dog Contract of the 1990s." *Denver University Law Review*, 73: 1017–50.

CHAPTER 2

LABOR-MANAGEMENT CONFLICT

*Where it Comes From, Why it
Varies, and What it Means for
Conflict Management Systems[1]*

JOHN GODARD

*You know as well as we do that right is only in question between equals in
power, for the strong do what they can and the weak suffer what they must.*
(Athenian negotiators speaking to their
Melian counterparts, in 415 BC. Grayling, 2009: 245)

The extent to which labor-management conflict is an endemic problem of capitalist economies has always been a matter of some debate. It has also often been a matter of faith. Different bodies of literature seem to proceed from quite different assumptions, with their contributors failing to question these assumptions or acknowledge that competing assumptions even exist. Too often, they seem not even to be aware of their own assumptions let alone those of others. Where scholars do recognize that competing sets of assumptions may exist, they typically do so in order to categorize the work of various authors or to distinguish between differing "frames of reference." Rarely do they address the implications of differing assumptions for actually understanding the manifestation of labor-management conflict.[2]

This matters, because the "causes" of labor-management conflict are likely to have critical implications for the effectiveness of various methods, systems, or structures for its management. It is made especially serious by the increased tendency of many to see this conflict as pathological and to believe that it can be readily addressed through more voluntaristic and positive sum techniques, without meaningful legal or institutional change. Many such remedies have been advocated in one form or another over the past century. These range from the application of "scientific" principles, to improved communication and counseling, to integrative or mutual gains bargaining, to new techniques of "human resource management," to "alternative dispute resolution" techniques. Yet although these remedies may not have been entirely ineffective, this conflict, or its manifestation in some form, seems to have stayed with us, not just in strikes, but in alternative guises such as turnover, disengagement, and resistance. It has also varied considerably, often independently of the rise and fall of these remedies. These remedies may make a difference in individual cases, and it is even possible that this conflict has declined over time as they have become more sophisticated. Yet they often seem to serve as little more than Band-Aids, failing to address the actual sources of this conflict and decaying over time. This may be especially true for conflict management systems, which seem to exist largely at the behest of employers and to be targeted at the overt manifestation of this conflict rather than its sources or alternative, more covert manifestations. Indeed, these systems are typically poor substitutes for legal rights and protections. Not only do such rights and protections help to ensure the fair and just resolution of labor-management conflicts, they also help to prevent them in the first instance, by creating the conditions for a fair and just employment relation (Edelman et al., 1993: 502–8).

It seems fitting, therefore, that any effort to study conflict management systems begin with the study of conflict itself—where it comes from, why it varies, how it can be resolved or even eliminated and, indeed, whether it should be resolved or eliminated. It also seems important that, on the one hand, the assumptions of various bodies of literature are acknowledged and, on the other hand, that the possibility of systemic sources of conflict within capitalist employment relations is broached. Accordingly, this chapter begins with a brief review of various perspectives on labor-management conflict in the literature, and the assumptions associated with each. It then turns to a discussion and development of an institutional conflict perspective on the employment relation, first identifying systemic sources of conflict within (and attributable to) capitalism and the capitalist employment relation, then identifying institutional sources of variation therein. This analysis is then drawn on to account for variation in conflict since the World War II, with a particular focus on strike activity, where it has gone, and what the implications may be for conflict management systems.

Throughout, the term 'conflict' is used as short-hand for 'labor-management conflict'. It generally does not refer to other forms of conflict or sources thereof (e.g., interpersonal), which are outside of the scope of this chapter. Conflict management systems are defined as they are commonly understood in the literature, as non-adversarial organizational systems designed to resolve, and to an extent prevent, disputes between employees and their employer. In turn, for working purposes, the capitalist employment relation is defined in terms of its central characteristic, as a relationship of subordination in which individuals are hired and employed to serve the ends of their employer.

PERSPECTIVES ON CONFLICT

Identification of distinctive perspectives on conflict (or industrial relations in general) is always something of a "mug's game," because much depends on the choice of (often implicit) criteria for distinguishing perspectives. Even then, these perspectives tend to blur into each other, and attempting to identify their boundaries can be somewhat arbitrary. Often (as is the case here), they are creations of the author and are not as well developed in the actual literature—in part because the assumptions underlying much of the literature can be vague or taken for granted. Nonetheless, doing so is useful for framing the literature and then attempting to go beyond it. In the current case, the primary criterion used to distinguish them is the extent to which conflict is assumed to be ephemeral, bearing little association with the nature of capitalism and readily addressed without institutional intervention, versus whether it is assumed to be endemic to these institutions and difficult to address without substantial institutional intervention and reforms. Six perspectives are identified, beginning at the former end of the continuum and proceeding to the latter. They are labeled as: 1) the neoliberal perspective, 2) the managerial perspective, 3) the evolutionary perspective, 4) the industrial pluralist perspective, 5) the neo-corporatist perspective, and 6) the radical perspective.

The **neoliberal perspective** is seldom found in the literature on conflict, but seems to increasingly underlie both employer and state behavior in liberal market economies. This perspective essentially assumes that conflict, and especially striking, is illegitimate. When employees enter into the employment relation, they agree to subordinate themselves to employer authority. Should they be unhappy with the exercise of this authority, including the terms and conditions established by the employer, they are free to quit. Markets operate so as to ensure that "bad" employers, or those who do not provide terms and conditions commensurate with employees' human capital, have difficulty attracting and retaining labor and hence an incentive to adjust accordingly.

Although adherents to this perspective may acknowledge a role for voice mechanisms, and may allow for limited dispute resolution systems (e.g. over contractual disagreements), they do not recognize the legitimacy of actual conflict in any form other than exit behavior. Strikes are in this respect simply attempts to "hold up" employers (Malcomson, 1997). Alternative forms of conflict (other than quits) are a violation of employee obligations and constitute "moral hazard." Both are to be repressed. One way is through government policies that render various conflicts illegal or virtually so. Another is through laws that provide employers with the authority to maintain discipline, ultimately by being able to dismiss employees with impunity should they be deemed unsatisfactory. Employees then have little choice but to accept employer authority and behave accordingly, in accordance with the opening quotation for this chapter.

The **managerial perspective** has increasingly come to dominate the literature on conflict and has traditionally been dominant in the management literature and in the new institutional economics. Essentially, this perspective views conflict as often legitimate yet unnecessary, and in this sense as not endemic to the employment relation. There are essentially two variants to this perspective, one which is management centered, and one which is state centered.

The management-centered perspective was originally associated with the human relations school (Mayo, 1933; Roethlisberger and Dickson, 1939; Whyte, 1950, 1965). But it has subsequently become implicit in much of the management literature. It assumes

that conflict is for the most part a result of mistaken managerial policies and practices and/or work design. These may result in misunderstandings or violate employee
needs, values or expectations. Thus, for example, it can be addressed through adoption of "new" forms of work design and employment practices, which ensure that
suitable employees are hired and employees are both motivated and empowered to
develop and apply their skills in accordance with employer goals (Lawler, 1992). These
systems may not always, however, forestall possible conflict. Some form of conflict
management system can thus play a critical role, ensuring that any discord that might
arise is addressed before it spreads. A general assumption is that both parties benefit
from a harmonious or "unitary" relationship and that such a relationship is readily
attainable.

The state-centered perspective derives from the early work of Hicks (1932), and has
been developed in neo-institutional economics. It assumes that conflict, and strikes in
particular, essentially reflect mistakes or misjudgments (Siebert and Addison, 1981). In
this view, the parties tend to be rational, self-interested actors, and it is in their interests
to arrive at that agreement that would result if there was a strike, but without undergo-
ing the costs associated with one. The implication is that, to the extent that strikes or
alternative forms of conflict become widespread, it is ultimately because policymakers
have failed to design institutions or adopt policies that allow the parties to make the
calculations necessary for, or to facilitate, a settlement. In this regard, disputes serve an
informational function—especially as to the ability of the employer to grant concessions
(Hayes, 1984; Tracy, 1987) but also as to the depth of employee discontent (Mauro, 1982),
and in this regard may facilitate their own resolution. However, they should not occur
in the first instance, and can be avoided by a combination of the appropriate macroeconomic (especially monetary) policies and dispute resolution systems (e.g. conciliation,
arbitration).

The **evolutionary perspective** essentially derives from traditional sociological theory
and industrial sociology, beginning with the work of Emile Durkheim and continuing
with the work of industrialization (Kerr et al., 1964), "post-industrial" (e.g. Bell, 1973;
Piore and Sabel, 1984) and "postmodern" (e.g. Crook et al., 1992; for a review, see Kelly,
1998: 108–25) theorists. In essence it is the simplest of the six perspectives. It assumes
that industrialization processes give rise to heightened conflict, due to heightened dis-
location and insecurity on the one hand (Mayo, 1933),[3] and often oppressive and dangerous working conditions and employer practices on the other (Blauner, 1963; Woodward,
1965). However, as industrialization proceeds and gradually comes to be displaced by
post-industrial and then "postmodern" institutions and working conditions, these
sources of conflict diminish, lowering the level of discontent and perceived injustice.
Employment less significant to the identities and orientations of workers (Bauman,
2004), which become increasingly focused around racial, ethnic, or affinity groups
(Piore and Safford, 2006). As a result, conflict in all of its forms, but especially at work,
gradually diminishes.

The **industrial pluralist perspective** argues that conflict is endemic to the capitalist employment relation (as defined above), attributable largely to interest differences,

power imbalances, and often fluctuating economic conditions. These sources are, however, partly offset by commonalities of interest and can be resolved amicably provided that the appropriate workplace representation and bargaining systems are established and able to function effectively (Clegg, 1975; Kochan, 1980; Budd, 2004; Katz et al., 2008). This perspective differs from the managerial perspective, because it (traditionally) recognizes the importance of power relations and independent collective representation, which in turn matter because of inherent interest conflicts. In this respect, shifting economic and political conditions (especially business cycles) can alter the relative power, expectations, or resources of the parties, creating conditions that essentially embolden one side and/or generate resistance from the other until such time that expectations adjust and a new settlement is achieved. For example, low unemployment tends to generate heightened expectations from workers, in part because they are less fearful of job loss. This may be reflected in strikes (Ashenfelter and Johnson, 1969; Kaufman, 1982), but also in alternative forms of conflict (Godard, 1997; McGovern et al., 2007). Yet as long as effective bargaining and tribunal (e.g. grievance) systems are in place and there is an approximate balance of power, differences between the parties can generally be resolved (albeit with varying levels of favorability to each) and levels of conflict contained.[4] Otherwise, conflict will manifest itself in a variety of alternative forms, from weaker performance to higher absenteeism and turnover or, in the case of employers, capital flight.

The **neo-corporatist perspective** is most associated with political sociology, and particularly power resource and political exchange theories of the state (Korpi, 1978; Korpi and Shalev, 1980). It argues that the extent to which conflict is endemic depends on the power resources of the labor movement and on national policies and institutions that reflect and institutionalize these resources, thereby achieving a political balance between labor and capital or even a power advantage for labor. Where these policies and institutions enable workers and their representatives to function as "partners" in both the workplace and the broader polity, various sources of conflict are more readily resolved to the lasting satisfaction of both parties through political exchange. Thus, under this perspective, it is not just a matter of whether systems for the resolution of conflict are in place, but rather whether national policies and institutions ensure a relatively equal relationship between labor and capital, and whether there is a sufficient institutional capacity for addressing both macro and micro level sources of conflict and making adjustments should they become necessary.

The **radical perspective** is largely associated with Marxian political economy (Miliband, 1969; Harvey, 1982, 2005) and (to an extent) with early labor process theory (Braverman, 1974), although a number of variants of it have been developed in the field of industrial relations (Hyman, 1972, 1975; Fox, 1974; Edwards, 1990, 2003; Gall, 2003; Blyton and Turnbull, 2004). It generally assumes that conflict is endemic to the capitalist employment relationship and that it will always be problematic, if not in the form of strikes, then in various forms of workplace resistance (Hyman, 1972; Fleming and Spicer, 2007). This conflict reflects a basic antagonism between labor and capital, as the latter seeks to extract a maximum of value from the former, often through coercive methods but also through more sophisticated systems of control designed to achieve "consent" (Burawoy, 1979, 1985). To the extent that these systems are effective, the likelihood for conflict is reduced. However, an implicit assumption of much of this literature seems to be that these systems break down over time, often due to contradictory forces at work within the broader political economy of capitalism.

Of particular interest in this regard is the argument that capitalist economies are inherently subject to long-term cycles of positive growth, followed by major economic crises and downturns (Aglietta, 1979; Gordon et al., 1982; Kotz et al., 1994; Kelly, 1998). Although this argument is not just a radical one, radicals use it to account for variation in conflict in general and strikes in particular. For example, Kelly argues that each turning point between these "upswings" and "downswings" represents a "rupture" in labor-capital relations, normally generating heightened discontent and an upsurge in worker mobilization, followed by a period of employer and state counter-mobilization efforts until such time that a new, more stable regime of accumulation is achieved (Kelly, 1998: 86). Thus, widespread conflict and instability tend to be inevitable, although they vary considerably over long-term economic cycles.

These perspectives all contain particular implications not just for understanding conflict, but also for the likely effectiveness of various forms of conflict management system. However, it seems that only the managerialist perspective is entirely supportive of such systems, because it is based on the assumption that conflict is generally not inherent to the employment relation and hence can be resolved through more voluntaristic means, without resorting to power or altering either the employment relation or its broader institutional environment in any fundamental way. As one moves away from this perspective, towards the radical end of the continuum, these systems become either less legitimate or less able to satisfactorily address the real sources of conflict.[5] The important question then becomes not so much which of these perspectives is right (or most right) per se, but rather whether there are indeed fundamental sources of conflict within capitalist economies. Although some perspectives (especially the radical perspective) assume this, these sources are typically not well identified. Yet it is arguable that any attempt to manage conflict must begin with an awareness of these sources and the arguments associated with them. Below, an "institutional conflict" approach is developed, which as its name suggests focuses on the institutional sources of conflict in capitalist economies. The analysis first identifies sources of conflict attributable to the institutional foundations of capitalism and of the capitalist employment relation. In doing so, it essentially develops a Marxian approach to understanding conflict, especially as developed by Richard Hyman in his book, *Strikes* (1972) and adopted in the author's own work (Godard, 2004, 2011b: 27–71). The analysis then moves beyond this approach to identify potential sources of variation, and arguing that institutional variation across (and potentially within) nations plays a critical role in addressing the sources of conflict and managing it.

The Institutional Sources of Conflict

The starting point for understanding conflict at work has to be with structurally ingrained conflict between capital, as represented by employers, and labor, as represented by their employees. Most simply, it is in the interests of the employers to extract as much work from the employees for as little cost as is possible, other things equal. It is in turn in the interests of the employees to provide a minimal amount of labor for as much compensation as possible, other things equal. Of course "other things equal" represents a very large caveat. Nonetheless, this argument underscores the most basic, underlying source of conflict.

If the parties were in a symmetrical relationship, as in many economic relations, this source of conflict might be relatively easy to address, and could readily lend itself to a simple process of conflict resolution should the parties be unable to come to agreement. Yet the unique characteristic of the employment relationship is such that it engenders a relationship of subordination, under which employees are formally subject to the authority of employers. In what we might think of as "pure" capitalism, employers have by virtue of their property rights no requirement to exercise this authority in any way except to earn a profit, and individuals take on the status of commodities or resources to be deployed and managed in accordance with managerial interests. This not only means that the relationship is asymmetrical, it also means that employees always have a basic reason to distrust the employer's exercise of authority.

This would be less of a problem, at least with regard to conflict, if a formal contract could be written and enforced to establish precisely what employees could be asked to do and not do for a given level of compensation. But this is typically not possible because of the indeterminacy of the employment relationship (Offe, 1976; Edwards, 1986; Kaufman, 2002). Generally, a "psychological" contract is established instead, with each party adhering to particular expectations as to the behavior of the other. But there is generally not any basis for enforcing this contract, and management can violate it with impunity. Because of this, and because this contract is in effect "coerced" on the one hand (workers are in a largely reactive position), and difficult to monitor on the other, there can be little certainty that it will ensure full worker compliance or cooperation, and trust issues remain. As such, it may give rise to only a passive acquiescence, with workers refraining from overt conflict but little more.

Further to this, workers are, in an objective sense, alienated from their labor. This alienation derives not so much from the design of their jobs (below), but rather from the nature of the capitalist employment relation. Workers do not own, nor do they have any legal control over, the means, process, product, or proceeds of their labor. Once they enter into an employment relation, their labor is no longer their own, but rather that of their employer. They become a resource to be used by the employer for the employer's interest, and are required to act in accordance with this interest even though it is not their own. In the objective/legal sense therefore, there is little reason why they should develop any identification with the process by which they labor and, indeed, they can be expected to resist this process, because it on the one hand devalues and objectifies them, yet on the other hand requires them to act in accordance with interests that are not their own, even if it may not always be clear whose interests these are (Smith, 2012).

These sources of conflict are aggravated by a variety of additional, more variable sources. The first are broader inequalities that are endemic to all capitalist economies and attributable to broad power imbalances, especially between those who live primarily off of returns from capital and those who do not, but also to inequalities in opportunity and labor market power. The second is the design of work itself, which is determined by what best serves the interests of the employer rather than of those who actually do the work itself, thereby resulting in a bias towards heightened stress levels and lowered intrinsic value—both of which are aggravated by employer efforts to reduce labor costs and extract a maximum of labor. The third is the lack of security generated by an economy in which labor is discarded just as is any other resource should the employer deem this to be in the interests of capital, and which is aggravated by economic cycles and fluctuations that alter the interests of capital and hence the demand for labor. These sources of conflict derive from the broader political economy of capitalism rather than (necessarily) from within the employment relation, yet the employment relation serves as an outlet for their manifestation.

These conditions are to an extent offset by various sources of cooperation. One is simply the coercion of a market economy, where individuals may find themselves with little choice but to subordinate themselves to employer authority and cooperate accordingly in order to earn a living. As discussed below, this may give rise to a variety of less-visible manifestations of conflict, but it still provides the major basis for cooperation. Another are laws and state policies that directly or indirectly repress or undermine the ability to engage in various forms of conflict without employer or state retribution. A third is dominant norms that underpin economic systems and, essentially, provide moral legitimacy for an established order and various fairness criteria against which this order, and the actual condition of individuals and treatment afforded them within this order, can be judged. These norms may reflect a variety of historical influences, but they generally reflect biases that favor of capital.

None of these negates the sources of conflict, which remain fundamental to the capitalist employment relation; rather they only shape how and the extent to which it comes to be manifest. Indeed, some theorists working from the Marxian tradition (e.g. Sapsford and Turnbull, 1994) have argued for a "balloon theory," whereby if the prevalence of one form of conflict is reduced, then other forms expand to compensate. In other words, the volume of conflict does not change; only its shape does, as happens when one squeezes a balloon. Thus, the level of conflict is constant; it is only the form it takes that varies. In this regard, conflict may be manifest in a variety of forms, many of which may not entail intentional acts of conflict yet do reflect the existence of this conflict. It follows that, in addition to strike and grievance activity, insubordination at work, sabotage, absenteeism, turnover, and other forms of active resistance, it can include instrumentalism, disengagement, depression, interpersonal aggression, substance abuse and a variety of additional behaviors outside of the workplace as well as in it. The sources of conflict identified by radicals are not argued to be the sole or necessarily even the primary cause of these behaviors. They are, however, considered to be one such cause, and can become a major cause should alternative means of addressing conflict be blocked. Indeed, under a radical perspective, a basic failure of most alternative perspectives on conflict, but especially of managerial perspectives, is the inability to understand that these forms of behavior do indeed reflect institutionally ingrained conflicts, the manifestation of which tends to go "underground" if more overt forms of conflict are blocked.

INSTITUTIONAL VARIATION IN CONFLICT

There are two major possible limitations to the above arguments. First, the balloon theory does not take into account the costs relative to the benefits of conflict manifestation. Should the costs of the "weapon" of choice be substantially increased through repressive laws, employees may shift to another weapon, but if this weapon was less effective to begin with, it is unlikely that any increase in its use will fully offset the decrease in the initial weapon of choice. This of course assumes that rational calculation plays a major role in employee decisions, and that employees are able to exercise some control over their discontent. From the perspective adopted here, however, this control involves internal repression and, in fact, the inability to properly express or voice discontent can itself increase the overall level thereof. The result may therefore be a variety of dysfunctional behaviors that reflect this discontent, even if these behaviors may not normally be intended or viewed as manifestations thereof. Indeed, it is possible that repression can actually enhance the level of discontent, if only because employees are now prevented from freely expressing this discontent in what might otherwise be a "healthy" form. Thus, repressing strikes as means of discontent may result in disengagement, with employees lowering their expectations as to what to expect from their work and their level of commitment to their work, with various costs for the employer. This possibility is returned to below, because whether repression reduces, increases, or has no overall effect on the manifestation of conflict is ultimately an unanswered empirical question. In any case, balloon theory is not essential to a Marxian approach.

Second, and more important, the factors identified may indeed be endemic *to* capitalism (and possibly not only capitalism), but many also vary quite considerably *within* capitalism, both over time and across nations. First, international institutions and "architectures" (e.g. the post-war Bretton Woods consensus) can have important implications for both the balance of power between labor and capital and the extent to which the relationship between them is stable. To the extent that these two sides confront each other as "equals" in the international economy, and economic conditions are relatively stable, then a relatively stable accord may be possible—especially if this is accompanied by economic growth and national-level accords, thereby allowing for rising profits while at the same time enabling capital to "buy off" discontent through the provision of rising living standards.

The same is generally the case for national level institutions and conditions. Although these cannot eradicate all of the sources of conflict, they can (as neo-corporatists argue) substantially reduce or ameliorate them. It is in this regard useful to distinguish between distinctive varieties of capitalism. In "corporatist" or "social market" economies, such as Germany, workers tend to have substantial stakeholder rights. These exist not only in the workplace, but also at the employer, the sectoral, and ultimately the national levels. In addition, economic and social institutions are structured so that employers focus on the production of high quality goods and services. It therefore tends to be in their interests to provide workers with secure, high quality employment. The result is a substantial lessening of the sources of conflict identified above and a heightened capacity to resolve those conflicts that occur. In contrast, "liberal market" economies, such as the United States, provide workers with few if any stakeholder rights, and institutions are structured so as to encourage the short term maximization of shareholder value. Thus, the sources of conflict identified are left unaddressed, and there is little institutional capacity for resolving conflict when it occurs. It is thus not surprising that strike activity has historically been much lower in Germany and continues to be – despite some weakening of the German system in recent years (Streeck, 2009).

Specific labor and employment laws and policies may also make a substantial difference. This may be so in at least two respects. First, these laws and policies can create the conditions for resolving or addressing various sources of conflict before they become manifest. Most obvious in this respect are collective bargaining laws and various forms of employment tribunal, both of which essentially serve as institutional means of conflict resolution. In turn laws providing workers with various rights, whether they are rights to a particular minimum vacation allowance, or to health and safety rights, or to protections against job loss, may substantially lessen the scope for conflict. More generally, economic policies can affect both the levels of inflation and levels of employment, both of which can affect the relationship between the parties and the extent to which workers are likely to become discontent with the terms of their employment.

Micro-organizational level factors may also lessen the extent to which conflict is manifest and possibly the implications of some of the sources of conflict identified above. This may be especially true in liberal market economies such as the US, where workers enjoy fewer rights and protections and institutional systems of conflict resolution are weak. In the US, for example, "high road" management models have long been advocated as means of overcoming worker recalcitrance and lessening the likelihood that they will engage in collective action. Since the 1980s, particular attention has been paid to "new" work and HRM practices, under which there is extensive teamwork, autonomy, training, participation systems, and performance management systems. Although both the effectiveness of these practices for employers and their effects on workers has not always been clear (Godard, 2004), they in theory help to empower workers and to generate a "mutual gains" enterprise, in which workers gain more through cooperation than the manifestation of conflict. It would also appear that, although only a small minority of workers has union representation, a sizeable minority has some form of management established representation system or "company union," and that these are accompanied by practices and systems designed on the one hand to ensure employee loyalty (e.g. through selection processes) and on the other hand to promote perceptions of fairness and justice that are similar to those in a union workplace (e.g. seniority rules, internal justice systems, objective job classifications and pay grades). Indeed, although the latter more "bureaucratic" practices have found little favor in the management literature, they have long been associated with internal labor markets in the US, and may be seen as substituting for legal rights and protections that would normally be imposed by the state or negotiated in collective bargaining (Godard and Frege, 2013).

These arguments largely follow from the alternative perspectives discussed earlier. The question arising, however, is just how important they are. This is especially so for more micro-organizational factors. From a Marxian perspective, it may be argued that these factors fail to adequately address the underlying courses of conflict, instead serving as means to control workers, and that they are largely necessitated by these sources. Although they may matter, it is only at the margins, often delaying conflict or shifting it into alternative forms, so that apparent declines in one form of conflict only manifest themselves in other forms over time. For example, new HRM practices may function largely by requiring employees to feign loyalty to employer goals, by monitoring workers and disciplining them for "misbehavior," and by linking pay and advancement opportunities to largely subjective performance evaluations. If so, they may only distort the manifestation of conflict, causing employees to manifest it in alternative forms. Similarly, high-performance work practices accompanied by a so-called mutual gains approach may lessen overt conflict over the short term, but they may also be undermined by widespread skepticism, distrust, and ultimately resistance, especially if the employer is able to violate various promises at such time that they are deemed too costly or restrictive.

Similar arguments may be made with regard to national-level institutions and policies. From a Marxian perspective, capital is normally able to regain the upper hand, and over time, states are driven to adopt policies that weaken worker power, thereby in turn enabling them to renege on past accommodations. Yet institutional variation would appear to have been far more ingrained than some Marxists have assumed. Moreover, to the extent that they are established, strong rights and protections can make a significant difference in the manifestation of conflict. This will become especially evident in the next section.

These arguments are both abstract and superficial, but they provide a useful starting point for really trying to *understand* conflict (and employment relations) within capitalist economies and why it varies. They point to the need for an "institutional" analysis of conflict, because they suggest not only that conflict is attributable to the institutions of capitalism but also that this conflict may vary substantially in accordance with variation in these institutions. Below, this is illustrated with reference to the history of strike activity since World War II. Although strike activity is only the most visible form of conflict, it is perhaps the most potentially destabilizing form and (the balloon theory notwithstanding) is often assumed to reflect deeper discontent that is manifest in alternative forms of conflict as well. It thus provides a point of entry for discussing the modern history of conflict at work in general.

A Brief Modern History of Conflict: Strike Activity (in Particular) Since World War II

Consistent with the discussion so far, strike activity or the threat thereof has historically been a significant problem in most Western economies. However, there was substantial reason to believe that it could become especially serious after the end of the Second World War, and this could undermine economic growth. This concern is often believed to have provided the impetus for post-war accords in most nations, which in terms of this volume, might be thought of as "macro" systems (including institutions) for the management of conflict.

In reality, these accords, or at least their foundations, often pre-dated the Second World War and in some if not many cases reflected a long history of development. For example, Sweden's Saltsjöbaden agreement, creating a partnership between labor and capital, was signed in 1938, and arguably reflected a long history of democratic compromise in that country (Olsen, 1992). Germany also had a long history of democratic rights and corporatist interest associations prior to the onset of Nazism, providing the basis for the stakeholder model that was to develop after the war. In the case of the US, the effort to develop an accord began with the new deal legislation of the 1930s.

What is of interest, here, however, is that these accords appeared to be strengthened in most developed nations after the war and, in some nations, established for the first time. In the US, for example, there was the famous Treaty of Detroit signed between the Big Three automakers and the United Autoworkers Union in 1950, under which the union essentially agreed to maintain discipline on the shop floor in return for guaranteed annual pay increases and improved benefits (Levy and Temin, 2010). In Britain, matters were more complex, as incomes policies adopted in the 1950s only served to undermine industry-level bargaining and encourage often informal and highly contentious productivity bargaining at the workplace level (Howell, 2005). However, there were substantial welfare reforms in the late 1940s, and an increased "institutionalization" of trade unions and collective bargaining within the economy (Hyman, 2001: 96–8). In Canada, there were similar developments.

Perhaps more important, these accords may be seen as part of an emergent "international architecture" of capitalism and the consensus around it. A central part of the consensus around this agreement was the adoption of a Keynesian economic model, in which full employment was to be a key objective of monetary policy, and a belief that collective bargaining was a means of not only "institutionalizing" conflict but also of generating income gains for workers. These gains would in turn help to sustain economic growth. So although national accords varied extensively, there was a core set of policies and principles to which all Western nations generally subscribed. These were reinforced by the Bretton Woods Agreement of 1944, which established an international system of rules and institutions to regulate economic relations between nations.

During the 1950s and early 1960s, this architecture was largely credited for creating industrial stability. Where the former meant growing economic surpluses, the latter meant that workers and their unions had sufficient power (and confidence) to win a share of these surpluses in return for labor peace, which was in turn an important precondition for stable economic growth. Workers came to enjoy steadily improving living standards, job security, and social progress (e.g. health care) in return for accepting the conditions of their employment. This did not mean an end to workplace-level conflict or of related forms of resistance, both of which were virtually inevitable responses to the everyday circumstances in which workers found themselves (Lupton, 1963; Fairris, 1994). But it did mean a lower propensity to strike than otherwise and relatively conservative labor movements.

By the mid-1960s, as market growth began to slow and inter-firm competition began to rise (Arrighi, 2007: 123–30). It became increasingly difficult for unions to hold employers to their side of the bargain without cutting into profit levels or passing on the costs of doing so through price increases. Coupled with a failing monetary regime, massive inflationary increases in US defense spending, and a slowing of productivity growth rates (Glyn, 2006), the result was ultimately stagflation, a declining rate of profit, and a weakening if not breakdown of the accord.

Consistent with managerialist theories of strikes in the new institutionalist economics (Gramm, 1986; Gramm et al., 1988; Crampton and Tracey, 2003), these conditions in turn meant an increase in the complexity of negotiations, as workers (and their negotiators) lacked full information about management's ability to grant concessions, and employers became increasingly insecure about the economic future. Yet more important, they meant that most post-war accords, and the conflict management systems they embodied, could no longer be sustained. Not only did this mean an end to labor peace, it essentially involved a broken promise. As such, it may even have increased the overall stock of discontent (Kelly, 1998: 98). Strike activity mushroomed in many developed Western economies in the late 1960s and early 1970s. Strike statistics can suffer from important flaws (Franzosi, 1989). However, in nine developed nations for which there is reasonably accurate data, the average days lost per thousand workers increased from 168 for the period from 1960 to 1964, to 288 for the period from 1965 to 1969, to 408 for the period from 1970 to 1974.[6]

Britain may in this regard be considered the "paradigm case" for the rise of strike activity. Sluggish productivity growth rates during the 1950s had already meant lower profit levels and a more fragile accord than elsewhere, one that had already begun to break down by the early 1960s. Initially, this breakdown was manifest in short, unofficial walkouts often not reflected in official strike statistics. Thus, even though there was little hard evidence of a problem, there was a widespread perception that "things [we] re not right" (McCarthy, 1970: 234). Yet official strikes increased in frequency, reaching their historic peak in 1970 (Lyddon, 2007: 365). These were initially short in duration, as workers demonstrated growing discontent with working conditions and government imposed constraints on pay increases. However, they became increasingly lengthy in the mid-1970s (strike frequency was in many years no higher than in the early 1960s), as employers grew more resolute in bargaining and workers found themselves having to fight harder just to maintain past gains. Worsening matters were attempts by employers to restore profits and weaken labor through workplace rationalization and technological changes thereby giving rise to strikes over work rules and job security as well as pay.[7]

Yet although the available data suggest a very substantial increase in days lost due to strike activity not just in Britain but in most developed Western economies by the early 1970s, they also suggest that there was considerable cross-national variation (Godard, 2011a). These differences were especially pronounced between the quintessential liberal market economies of the US, the UK, and Canada and their quintessential neo-corporatist counterparts of Germany, Sweden, and the Netherlands. Although the latter all underwent very substantial increases in strike activity in at least one year between 1970 to 1974, they lost an average of only 50 days per thousand workers per annum during this period, compared to an average of roughly 650 days among the countries in the former category. Annual days lost exceeded 200 in only one of these countries, and even then only once (211, in Sweden in 1972); in contrast, annual days lost never dropped below 200 for any country in the former group during this period.

These differences largely reflect the varied institutional capacity of the nations in these two categories. In particular, the generally higher levels of strike activity within liberal market economies would appear to be ultimately explained by their lack of institutional capacity to renegotiate post-war accords. These nations lacked the strong centralized bargaining structures, related peak association structures, and state policy repertoires necessary to effectively address the economic crisis through some form of corporatist bargain. Labor movements were too weak to extract convincing concessions from governments and too decentralized for their leaders to be able to impose discipline on their members (either to engage in concerted action or to refrain from striking), while employers were more exposed to market competition and subject to greater pressure to restore profits due to a much greater reliance on stock market financing. These countries were already also characterized by greater inequality, more authoritarian workplace structures, and weaker social programs, rendering the sources of conflict identified earlier more problematic. Thus, neo-corporatist settlements and related policy initiatives (e.g. wage and price controls), both of which might have strengthened or at least renewed the terms of the post-war accord (as was the case in coordinated/social democratic economies) largely failed.

In Britain in particular, the labor movement lacked both the level of centralization and internal discipline of its continental counterparts (see Hyman, 2001: 98–9). Corporatism was at odds with both British state traditions and the structure of its business system, the former of which relied on voluntarism and hence minimal state involvement, the latter of which was decentralized, largely market driven, and increasingly reliant on stock market financing. These were further aggravated by labor law reforms in 1971 and then 1974 and 1975 that were at odds with the tradition of voluntarism and, largely as result, may only have exacerbated the strike problem.[8] As a result, attempts to achieve a settlement notoriously collapsed in the winter of discontent (1978–9). This helped to creating the opening for Thatcherism, which was able to portray strike activity as illegitimate, unions that engaged in it as irresponsible, and laws that repressed it as justifiable.

In the US, where a tradition of minimal state involvement and a distrust of "big labor" had already meant a gutting of labor laws and an ongoing stagnation if not decline in union coverage (Godard, 2009a), employers were free to adopt an increasingly aggressive stance towards unions. The use of permanent striker replacements became particularly prevalent, especially after the Reagan government resorted to this strategy in the air traffic controllers (PATCO) strike of 1984. In Canada, efforts to move towards a more corporatist system in the 1970s also failed, and there was shift towards neoliberalism in the 1980s, although a state policy tradition emphasizing peace and stability (Godard, 2013) meant that labor laws were strengthened somewhat in the apparent belief that doing so would ameliorate conflicts associated with the certification process and help to win labor moderation.[9]

In contrast, Germany, the Netherlands, and Sweden, each of which had a strong tradition of social partnership and collaboration, were able to find more consensual solutions to the problems of the 1970s (despite some increases in conflict). In all three cases these solutions were accompanied by a new or even strengthened accord (Jacobi et al., 1998: 207–208; Visser, 1998: 288; Kjellberg, 1998: 82), although in Sweden there was a ten-day general strike in 1980. This strike notwithstanding, the experience of these nations is largely consistent with neo-corporatist theories of strike activity (e.g. Korpi and Shalev, 1980).

It would be mistaken to view state policy responses in isolation from broader developments common to the international political economy, especially as these gave rise to a new institutional architecture in the 1980s. Particularly important was the almost universal rejection of Keynesianism in the major Western economies, the deregulation and globalization of financial markets, and the growth in world trade, facilitated by international agreements and tariff reductions beginning in the 1980s. These broader, more general developments played a particularly important role in liberal market economies, again especially in Britain, helping to create an environment that was increasingly hostile to strike action. They also helped to create the essential conditions for low inflation (Glynn, 2006: 6) and increased rates of profit. But, in the process, the balance of power had shifted away from labor and towards capital, leaving labor in no position to affect a return to some variant of the post-war accord. In Britain and the US it is likely that this shift mattered as much to the ability of labor to resist national reforms (e.g. Thatcherism,

Reaganism) as it did to lower strike activity per se, with these reforms in turn reinforcing and institutionalizing the "new realities" of the ensuing decades.

In short, this analysis suggests that industrial conflict is indeed a systemic problem of capitalism, but that the extent to which this is so may be substantially affected by both the international architecture of capitalism at a particular period in time and by institutional capacities of states to ameliorate and manage it. It can also be argued that specfic state polices matter, although these policies and their effectiveness tend to be conditioned by broader institutional traditions and constraints. So, for example, British governments may be seen to have made a number of policy errors in the 1950 and 1960s, yet these errors largely reflecting an institutional system that was inadequate to the task confronting them.

If couched in the terms of this handbook, therefore, it seems to be clear from this analysis that it is institutions in a broad sense that matter to the management of conflict and that the more micro conflict management systems popularized in recent decades may have about the same effect as shooting peas at an elephant: each shot may make its mark, but in the broader scheme of things, it may make little difference. The analysis also suggests that these systems—at least as commonly understood—may be largely redundant in economies with neo-corporatist traditions and institutions, where the sources of conflict are muted and conflict itself can be managed effectively through established institutional mechanisms. It would therefore seem that if we are actually concerned to manage this conflict, it is necessary to worry less about employer level systems and more about international and national ones and, in particular, the more deep seated sources of conflict (and injustice) they address or fail to address. Yet the analysis so far only tells part of the story. Strike activity reduced significantly after the 1970s and has continued to reduce since then. This has been especially so in liberal market economies. Although days lost due to strike activity was to remain much higher in these countries than in their neo-corporatist counterparts, it still declined massively, so that by the early 2000s it was substantially below early 1960s levels (Godard, 2011a: 286). The question, therefore, is one of where the conflict has gone in these economies.

WHITHER CONFLICT?

As discussed more fully elsewhere (Godard, 2011a), there are essentially five plausible explanations for what has happened to conflict in liberal market economies:

- Increasingly repressive state policies, coupled with a more hostile international architecture, have effectively worked as the neoliberal perspective assumes; indeed, the heightened conflict of the 1960s and 1970s might have been avoided had these policies been adopted sooner.
- The conflict that was manifest in the form of strikes in the late 1960s and the 1970s has shifted to alternative forms of conflict, as postulated by the "balloon thesis;"

indeed, increased repression may even have resulted in an increase in the overall manifestation of covert conflict, as industrial pluralists argue, potentially increasing the perceived need for and role of conflict management systems (Gall and Hebdon, 2008).

- The conflict during the late 1960s and the 1970s largely reflected sources of discontent and misunderstandings that have been substantially "conquered" by the shift away from traditional blue collar work, coupled with new employer policies and, perhaps, increased adoption of conflict management systems.
- New employer policies contain a significant repressive element, serving more as mechanisms of monitoring and control, and, coupled with repressive government policies, have forced the expression of conflict "underground," as manifest in widespread depression, drug use, disengagement, and related pathologies (Ackroyd and Thompson, 2000; Morrill et al., 2003).
- Conflict, and the distrust and discontent from which it derives, has shifted from the economic to the political and social realms, resulting in a growing disenchantment with political and social institutions and either the gradual dis-integration of societies or the establishment of new forms of solidarity (Heckscher and McCarthy, 2013) and identity orientations (Piore and Safford, 2006).

These are big questions, and the research that can shed light on them has typically been limited in both quality and quantity. It has yielded little by way of a conclusive finding, beyond suggesting that none of these explanations can be ruled out, and that all can probably contribute to our understanding of where the conflict has gone (Godard, 2011a). Yet a number of them suggest that repression has played an important role. This raises an even bigger question, which is whether the decline in strike activity and, ultimately any corresponding decline in alternative forms of conflict, is necessarily a good thing.

Many forms of conflict may be seen not as pathological, but rather as means of voicing or acting upon discontent, and ultimately as means for achieving stronger rights and protections at work and beyond (welfare state policies). To the extent that the decline in strike activity reflects a genuine improvement in the quality of the employment experience, then it might be considered as a good thing, and conflict is not only unlikely to have migrated elsewhere, but is likely to have declined in all or most of its forms. But to the extent that it reflects heightened repression, the opposite may be considered to be the case, and it is likely that conflict has, indeed, gone underground, with potentially insidious consequences. From the perspective developed in this chapter, conflict will remain an endemic "problem" in the employment relation, especially in liberal market economies, as long as the underlying sources of conflict remain or are not addressed through broader institutional means, and any substantial decline in its overt manifestation will likely reflect repression as much or more than any improvement in the conditions of work. The question that then arises is whether proponents of conflict management systems may be complicit in this repression.

Conclusions: Whither Conflict Management Systems?

This chapter has sought to address the sources and manifestations of conflict within capitalist economies, and in so doing to place the study of conflict management systems in a broader frame than is normally the case. To do so, it has essentially been argued that conflict may be far more intractable as a problem of capitalist economies than is often assumed in the conflict management literature—unless these economies are characterized by some form of neo-corporatism or there is a broader international architecture capable of sustaining labor capital accords, thereby helping to lessen the extent to which these sources pertain and providing institutional environments that allow for their effective resolution. In effect, therefore, this chapter argues for a much broader perspective on conflict management systems than is typically adopted in the literature, one which essentially recognizes the importance of international and national institutional architectures as the true systems for managing conflict.

Throughout, however, the relevance of the analysis for the study of conflict management systems at more micro levels has been developed, especially as these are the levels that the current literature is typically couched. The analysis suggests that, although these systems may have some function in neo-corporatist economies, it is likely that they are largely redundant in these economies owing to broader conflict management systems that characterize and even define them. The question that emerges is, therefore, what function more micro systems may serve in liberal market economies, such as the US, the UK, and Canada, where they seem to have become widespread, at least sufficiently so as to warrant a handbook comprised of chapters written by leading academics and published by a leading university press.

The remaining chapters of this handbook address this question far more fully than can be the case here. Yet the analysis in this chapter suggests that the effectiveness of micro-level systems is likely to be limited, and that any finding to the contrary is likely to be suspect. These systems may appear to serve organizational interests, but they do little to address the real sources of conflict and hence to advance the real quality of the employment relation or the rights and protections of employees. In fact, they may serve more to retard than to advance the sorts of meaningful institutional and policy changes needed to achieve either outcome, serving as very poor, ersatz substitutes for the real thing. Although they may in some cases create the illusion of effectiveness for employees, this is likely because individuals have little alternative but to engage with them, and this engagement in turn enables them to achieve a better outcome than otherwise. But, because these systems do little to address the underlying sources of conflict, they may in the long run prove of limited value even for employers—except possibly as means to avoid unions and to reduce the burden of litigation (Colvin, 2003; Seeber and Lipsky, 2006: 749). Their apparent effectiveness may be greater if accompanied by the appropriate work and human resource policies

(Colvin, 2003; Seeber and Lipsky, 2006: 749), yet although these policies may make a positive difference, they suffer from the same limitations—which is why they are often far less widespread and effective than proponents suggest that they should be (Godard, 2004).

Is this a fair critique? Again, the evidence is unclear; so much depends on the reader's underlying assumptions and biases. But in a book about conflict management systems, it will hopefully encourage readers to bring these biases to the fore and to engage more critically with the material in each chapter. The question the reader may want to ask is not what makes various mechanisms function more (or less) effectively from the point of view of the individuals and actors involved, but rather whether they essentially serve to distort and repress conflict, ultimately to the detriment of society. Specifically, does advocacy for, and the study of, these mechanisms amount to little more than a cul-de-sac, one that draws attention away from the real sources of conflict and the legal and institutional changes needed not just to address them, but also to ensure the greater attainment at work of democracy, justice, fairness, and related civic principles long considered to be at the core of Western civilization?

NOTES

1. Parts of this chapter draw from Godard (2011a.) Comments welcome. The author thanks Alexander Colvin for his comments on an earlier version.
2. An important exception is Roberto Franzosi's (1995) excellent analysis of strikes in Italy, which identifies and then tests a variety of different perspectives. Unfortunately, this is not only a rare exception, it also does not extend to the literature on conflict in general.
3. Although Mayo is (correctly) considered to be the father of the human relations school and to an extent of managerialism, his major book, *Human Problems of an Industrial Civilization*, essentially argued along the lines of the evolutionary perspective. This is a classic case where authors may straddle differing perspectives.
4. Scholars traditionally associating themselves with this perspective have (especially in the US) also advocated "new" forms of work and employment practices during the 1990s (e.g. Kochan and Osterman, 1994), as did their managerialist counterparts. The extent to which this represented a shift towards a managerialist perspective has been a matter of some debate (Godard and Delaney, 2000; Kochan, 2000; Godard and Delaney, 2002), although much turns on the importance attached to the role of independent and effective collective representation under these practices.
5. In reflection of contemporary realities (especially in the US), some scholars who consider themselves to be working in the tradition of industrial pluralism now seem to be supportive of these systems. These systems are at most, however, second best under this perspective because they do not engender autonomous collective representation or legal rights and protections, and they do not address power imbalances.
6. These countries include the US, the UK, Canada, Germany, Sweden, the Netherlands, Belgium, Australia, and New Zealand. The statistics cited here and in the next paragraph are originally from selected tables in van der Velden et al. (2007), as depicted in Godard (2011).

7. As Edwards (1982: 15) points out, disputes over non-wage issues continued to account for roughly six out of ten strikes in the UK throughout the 1970s.
8. The 1975 reforms were, however, followed by a substantial increase in union density, although the extent to which they were responsible for this increase is unclear.
9. It is possible that these reforms did indeed help to account for the decline in strike activity, although it is more likely that this decline reflected high unemployment and job insecurity in other liberal market economies.

REFERENCES

Ackroyd, S., and Thompson, P. 2000. *Organizational Misbehaviour*. London: Sage.

Aglietta, M. 1979. *A Theory of Capitalist Regulation*. London: New Left Books.

Arrighi, G. 2007. *Adam Smith in Beijing*. London: Verso.

Ashenfelter, O., and Johnson, G. 1969. "Bargaining Theory, Strike Activity, and Industrial Strike Theory." *American Economic Review*, 59: 35–49.

Bauman, Z. 2004. *Identity*. Cambridge: Polity Press.

Bell, D. 1973. *The Coming of the Post-Industrial Society*. New York: Basic Books.

Blauner, R. 1963. *Alienation and Freedom*. Chicago: University of Chicago Press.

Blyton, P., and Turnbull, P. (2004). *The Dynamics of Employee Relations*. 3rd edn. Basingstoke: Palgrave Macmillan.

Braverman, H. 1974. *Labor and Monopoly Capital*. New York: Monthly Review Press.

Budd, J. 2004. *Employment with a Human Face*. Ithaca, NY: Cornell Press.

Burawoy, M. 1979. *Manufacturing Consent*. London: Verso.

Burawoy, M. 1985. *The Politics of Production*. London: Verso.

Clegg, H. 1975. "Pluralism in Industrial Relations." *British Journal of Industrial Relations*, 13: 306–21.

Colvin, A. 2003. "Institutional Pressures, Human Resource Strategies, and the Rise of Nonunion Dispute Resolution." *Industrial and Labor Relations Review*, 56(3): 375–93.

Crampton, P. and Tracy, J. 2003. "Unions, Bargaining, and Strikes." In J. T. Addison and C. Schnabel (eds), *International Handbook of Trade Unions*. Cheltenham, UK: Edward Elgar.

Crook, S., Pakulski, J., and Waters, M. 1992. *Postmodernism: Change in Advanced Society*. London: Sage.

Edelman, L., Erlanger, H., and Lunde, J. 1993. "Internal Dispute Resolution and the Transformation of Civil Rights in the Workplace." *Law and Society Review*, 27(3): 497–534.

Edwards, P. 1990. "The Politics of Conflict and Consent: How the Labour Contract Really Works." *Journal of Economic Behavior and Organization*, 13: 41–61.

Edwards, P. 2003. "The Employment Relationship and the Field of Industrial Relations." In P. Edwards (ed.), *Industrial Relations: Theory and Practice*. 2nd edn. London: Blackwell, 1–36.

Edwards, P. K. 1986. *Conflict at Work*. Oxford: Basil Blackwell.

Edwards, P. K. and Scullion, H. 1982. *The Social Organization of Industrial Conflict: Control and Resistance in the Workplace*. Oxford: Blackwell.

Fairris, D. 1994. "Shopfloor Relations in the Postwar Capital-Labor Accord". In D. Kotz, T. McDonough, and M. Reich (eds), *Social Structures of Accumulation*. Cambridge. Cambridge University Press.

Fleming, P. and Spicer, A. 2007. *Contesting the Corporation: Struggle, Power, and Resistance in Organizations*. Cambridge: Cambridge University Press.

Fox, A. 1974. *Beyond Contract: Work, Power, and Trust Relations*. London: Faber.

Franzosi, R. 1989. "Quantitative Strike Research." *Industrial and Labor Relations Review*, 42(3): 348–62.

Franzosi, R. 1995. *The Puzzle of Strikes: Class and State Strategies in Postwar Italy*. Cambridge: Cambridge University Press.

Gall, G. 2003. "Marxism and Industrial Relations." In P. Ackers and A. Wilkinson (eds), *Understanding Work & Employment*. Oxford: Oxford University Press, 316–24.

Gall, G. and Hebdon, R. 2008. "Conflict at Work." In P. Blyton, N. Bacon, J. Fiorito, and E. Heery (eds), *The Sage Handbook of Industrial Relations*. London: Sage Publications, 558–605.

Glyn, A. 2006. *Capitalism Unleashed*. Oxford: Oxford University Press.

Godard, J. 1997. "Managerial Strategies, Labour and Employment Relations, and the State: The Canadian Case in Comparative Perspective." *British Journal of Industrial Relations*, 35(Sept.): 399–426.

Godard, J. 2004. "A Critical Assessment of the High Performance Paradigm." *British Journal of Industrial Relations*, 42(2)(Apr.): 349–78.

Godard, J. 2009. "The Exceptional Decline of the American Labor Movement." *Industrial and Labor Relations Review*, 63(1): 81–107.

Godard, J. 2011a. "What Has Happened to Strikes?" *British Journal of Industrial Relations*, 49(2): 282–305.

Godard, J. 2011b. *Industrial Relations, the Economy, and Society*. 4th edn. Toronto: Captus Press.

Godard, J. 2013. "Labour Law and Union Recognition in Canada: A Historical Institutionalist Perspective." *Queen's Law Journal*, 38(2): 394–417.

Godard, J. and Delaney, J. 2000. "Reflections on the High Performance Paradigm's Implications for IR as a Field." *Industrial and Labor Relations Review*, 53(3): 482–502.

Godard, J. and Delaney, J. 2002. "On the Paradigm Guiding Industrial Relations Theory and Research: Reply to Thomas Kochan." *Industrial and Labor Relations Review* (US), 55(3)(Apr.): 542–44.

Gordon, D., Edwards, R., and Reich, M. 1982. *Segmented Work, Divided Workers: The Historical Transformations of Labor in the United States*. New York: Cambridge University Press.

Gramm, C. 1986. "The Determinants of Strike Incidence and Severity: A Micro Level Study." *Industrial and Labor Relations Review*, 39(3): 361–76.

Gramm, C., Hendricks, W., and Kahn, L. 1988. "Inflation, Uncertainty, and Strikes." *Industrial Relations*, 27: 114–29.

Grayling, A. C. 2009. *Towards the Light: The Story of the Struggles for Liberty and Rights that Made the Modern World*. London: Bloomsbury.

Harvey, D. 1982. *The Limits to Capital*. Oxford: Basil Blackwell.

Harvey, D. 2005. *A Brief History of Neoliberalism*. Oxford: Oxford University Press.

Hayes, B. 1984. "Unions and Strikes With Asymmetric Information." *Journal of Labor Economics*, 2: 57–78.

Heckscher, C., and McCarthy, J. 2014. "Transient Solidarities: Commitment and Collective Action in Post-Industrial Societies." *British Journal of Industrial Relations*, 51(4): forthcoming.

Hicks, J. R. 1932. *The Theory of Wages*. London: Macmillan.

Howell, C. 2005. *Trade Unions and the State*. Princeton: Princeton University Press.

Hyman, R. 1972. *Strikes*. Glasgow: Fontana/Collins.

Hyman, R. 1975. *Industrial Relations. A Marxist Introduction*. London: Macmillan.

Hyman, R. 2001. *Understanding European Trade Unionism: Between Market, Class, and Society*. London: Sage.

Jacobi, O., Keller, B., and Muller-Jemtsch, W. 1998. "Germany: Facing New Challenges." In A. Ferner and R. Hyman (eds) *Changing Industrial Relations in Europe*. Oxford: Blackwell, 190–238.

Katz, H., Kochan, T., and Colvin, A. 2008. *Collective Bargaining and Industrial Relations*. 4th edn. New York: McGraw Hill.

Kaufman, B. 1982. "Determinants of Strikes in the United States 1900–1977." *Industrial and Labor Relations Review*, 35(4): 473–91.

Kaufman, B. 2002. "The Employment Relations System: A Guide to Theorizing." In B. Kaufman (ed.), *Theoretical Perspectives on Work and the Employment Relationship*. Illinois: IRRA.

Kelly, J. 1998. *Rethinking Industrial Relations*. London: LSE/Routledge.

Kerr, C., Dunlop, J. T., Harbison, F. H., and Myers, C. A. 1964. *Industrialism and Industrial Man*. 2nd edn. New York: Oxford University Press.

Kjellberg, A. 1998. "Sweden: Restoring the Model?" In A. Ferner and R. Hyman (eds) *Changing Industrial Relations in Europe*. Oxford: Blackwell, 74–117.

Kochan, T. 1980. *Collective Bargaining and Industrial Relations*. Homewood, IllL: Richard D. Irwin.

Kochan, T. 2000. "On the Paradigm Guiding Industrial Relations Theory and Research. Comment of John Godard and John Delaney: Reflections on the High Performance Paradigm's Implications for IR as a Field." *Industrial and Labor Relations Review*, 53(4): 704–9.

Korpi, W. 1978. *The Working Class in Welfare Capitalism: Unions and Politics in Sweden*. London: Routledge and Kegan Paul.

Korpi, W. and Shalev, M. 1980. "Strikes, Power, and Politics in Western Nations 1900–1976." In M. Zeitlin (ed.), *Political Power and Social Theory*, vol. 1. Greenwich, CN: JAI Press.

Kotz, D.M., McDonough, T., and Recih, M. 1994. *Social Structures of Accumulation: The Political Economy of Growth and Crisis*. Cambridge: Cambridge University Press.

Lawler, E.E. 1992. *The Ultimate Advantage: Creating the High Involvement Organization*. San Francisco: Jossey Bass.

Levy, F. and Temin, P. 2010. "Institutions and Wages in Post-World War II America." In C. Brown, B. Eichengreen, and M. Reich (eds), *Labor in the Era of Globalization*. Cambridge: Cambridge University Press.

Lupton, T. 1963. *On the Shop Floor: Two Studies of Workplace Organization and Conflict*. Oxford: Pergamon.

Lyddon, D. 2007. "From Strike Wave to Strike Drought: The United Kingdom 1968–2005." In S. van der Velden, H. Dribbusch, D. Lyddon, and K. Vandaele (eds), *Strikes Around the World, 1968–2005*. Amsterdam: Aksant Academic Publishing, 339–65.

Malcomson, J. M. 1997. "Contracts, Hold-Up, and Labor Markets." *Journal of Economic Literature*, 35(Dec.): 1916–57.

Mauro, M. 1982. "Strikes as a Result of Imperfect Information." *Industrial and Labor Relations Review*, 35(4): 522–38.

Mayo, E. 1933. *Human Problems of an Industrial Civilization*. New York: MacMillan.

McCarthy, W. E. J. 1971. "The Nature of Britain's Strike Problem." *British Journal of Industrial Relations*, 84(2): 224–36.

McGovern, P., Hill, S., Mills, C., and White, M. (2007). *Market, Class and Employment*, Oxford: Oxford University Press.

Miliband, R. 1969. *The State in Capitalist Society*. New York: Basic Books.

Morrill, C., Zald, M. N., and Rao, H. 2003. "Covert Political Conflict in Organizations." *Annual Review of Sociology*, 29: 391–415.

Offe, K. 1985. "The Political Economy of the Labour Market." In C. Offe (ed.), *Disorganized Capitalism*. Cambridge, MA: MIT Press.

Olsen, G. 1992. *The Struggle for Social Democracy in Sweden*. Aldershot, UK: Avebury/Gower.

Piore, M. and Sabel, C. 1984. *The Second Industrial Divide*. New York: Basic Books.

Piore, M. and Safford, S. 2006. "Changing Regimes of Workplace Governance." *Industrial Relations*, 45(3): 299–325.

Roethlisberger, F. and Dickson, W. 1939. *Management and the Worker*. Cambridge, MA: Harvard University Press.

Sapsford, D. and Turnbull, P. 1994. "Strikes and Industrial Conflict in Britain's Docks: Balloons or Icebergs?" *Oxford Bulletin of Economics and Statistics*, 59(3): 249–65.

Seeber, R., and Lipsk, D. 2006. "The Ascendancy of Employment Arbitrators in US Employment Relations: A New Actor in the American System?" *British Journal of Industrial Relations*, 44(4): 719–56.

Siebert, S. W. and Addison, J. 1981. "Are Strikes Accidental?" *Economic Journal*, 91: 389–404.

Smith, A. 2012. "On Shopworking." *New Left Review*, 78(Nov./Dec.): 99–114.

Streeck, W. 2009. *Reforming Capitalism: Institutional Change in the German Political Economy*. Oxford: Oxford University Press.

Tracy, J. 1987. "An Empirical Test of the Asymmetric Information Model of Strikes." *Journal of Labor Economics*, 5: 149–73.

van der Velden, S., Dribbusch, H., Lyddon, D., and Vandaele, K. (eds), 2007. *Strikes Around the World, 1968–2005*. Amsterdam: Aksant Academic Publishing.

Visser, J. 1998. "The Netherlands: The Return of Responsive Corporatism." In A. Ferner and R. Hyman (eds), *Changing Industrial Relations in Europe*. Oxford: Blackwell, 283–314.

Whyte, W. F. 1950. "Framework for the Analysis of Industrial Relations: Two Views." *Industrial and Labor Relations Review*, 3(2): 393–401.

Whyte, W. F. 1965. "A Field in Search of a Focus." *Industrial and Labor Relations Review*, 18(3): 305–22.

Woodward, J. 1965. *Industrial Organization*. Oxford: Oxford University Press.

....

CHAPTER 3

EMPLOYMENT RIGHTS AND WORKPLACE CONFLICT

A Governance Perspective

....

CYNTHIA ESTLUND

CONFLICT is endemic to organizational life. In extreme cases, conflict among co-workers or between workers and bosses can escalate into murderous rage—as it did outside the Empire State Building in September 2012 (Brown, 2012)—or into revolutionary regime change—as it did in Poland in the 1980s. More often, workplace conflict coalesces into collective labor unrest, and flows into established labor law channels for union organizing and collective bargaining. Most workplace conflict unfolds in less dramatic fashion, however, and is either resolved internally or left to fester and to take a toll on the organization in the form of resentment, turnover, low productivity, deterioration of workers' health and happiness, or, especially in the US, litigation. This chapter focuses on the experience in the US, where the shift away from collective labor relations and toward litigation has been particularly dramatic.

While employment litigation has become a salient feature of workplace relations in the US, it is a relative newcomer to the great historical drama of labor-management conflict and conflict resolution. During the tumultuous era of liberty of contract and the labor injunction that culminated in the early 20th century, courts were seen as inhospitable to workers and their grievances. The National Labor Relations Act of 1935 (NLRA), which remains the basic framework legislation for collective labor relations in the US, was crafted and interpreted to minimize the judicial role in collective labor disputes in favor of arbitrators, administrative bodies, and the parties themselves. Outside the union setting, and until the mid-1960s, workers had few legal rights and were relegated to the tender mercies of managers and markets. When and where markets and managers converged to create strong internal labor markets and long-term employment relations, workers often fared reasonably well. Or at least the core (mostly white and male) workers in primary industries and leading firms fared reasonably well. Racial minorities and women were largely excluded from those relatively comfortable positions.

With help from litigation under the Civil Rights Act of 1964 (CRA), women and minorities began to gain access to those internal labor markets just as their foundations began to crumble under pressure from economic and technological developments. The erosion of internal labor markets undercut the potential gains from antidiscrimination and other wrongful discharge litigation, for the jobs at stake were less likely to last. But the erosion of internal labor markets also made legal rights more important, for it stripped workers of some non-legal protections against the vicissitudes of the external labor market. In the meantime, union density has fallen to just over 11% of the labor force, and to less than 7% in the private sector (Bureau of Labor Statistics, 2013). Without labor unions or strong internal labor markets, most workers are left with little more than their individual "market power" and a collection of legal rights against discrimination, retaliation, or other forms of mistreatment.

The growing body of statutory employee rights is sometimes said to serve as a "union substitute," and to partly explain workers' declining willingness to take the risks involved in forming a union. At least to most workers who have experienced union representation, the formal right to file a complaint or bring a lawsuit after the fact in case of actionable employer misconduct is a far cry from access to union representation and union power in a functioning collective bargaining relationship. Unions enable workers to pursue their own collectively self-determined *interests*, not merely their societally determined legal *rights*. And the litigation process—formalistic, lawyer-driven, strewn with procedural hurdles and technicalities—displays little of the human drama and solidarity of a union organizing drive or a strike. And yet there are some intriguing parallels between collective bargaining and litigation, and their relationship to organizational (and societal) conflict, that are worth exploring, for they may suggest a path forward in our post-collective bargaining era.

This chapter first explores several parallels between litigation and collective bargaining (primarily as it evolved in the US private sector under federal labor law) as modes of workplace dispute resolution. The point of that exploration is to lay the foundation for arguing that employment rights, litigation, and regulation might be following, or at least could follow, a path pioneered by the labor movement in leveraging workplace disputes and the need to resolve them into pressure for more participatory structures of workplace governance. It then turns to the forms of governance—regulated self-regulation and internal dispute resolution—that are beginning to take shape under the shadow of litigation and regulation. Those structures could be creatively and consciously molded into a system of "co-regulation" that would secure for workers some of what collective bargaining was meant to deliver: a form of participation through collective representation in the resolution of workplace disputes—in the first instance "rights disputes," but potentially "interest disputes" as well.

Conflict and Conflict Resolution Through Collective Bargaining and Litigation

At first blush, collective bargaining and litigation represent nearly opposite approaches to the problem of workplace conflict. Collective bargaining emerges out of bottom-up mobilization of workers (within a public statutory framework); litigation stems from top-down legislative enactments (which sometimes follow workers' mobilization). Collective bargaining represents a privatized system of dispute resolution (again, within a public framework); litigation is quintessentially public and judicial dispute resolution (though the rise of mandatory arbitration challenges this distinction). Collective bargaining is designed primarily to resolve interest disputes (though it also helps workers to enforce legal rights and resolve rights disputes); litigation seeks to resolve legal rights claims (under laws that aim to serve workers' interests). There are many important differences between the two approaches to workplace conflict; yet, as the many parenthesized qualifications suggest, they have more in common than first meets the eye.

First, both collective bargaining and employment litigation strike fear into the hearts of employers, and have generated a thriving industry of avoidance—"union avoidance," "litigation avoidance"—and a raft of human resource management (HRM) practices designed to keep them at bay (Colvin, 2012). Interestingly, many of the very same HRM practices—especially internal review and grievance systems—are designed to help avoid both litigation and unionization (Colvin, 2003). Indeed, as some of the economic underpinnings of internal labor markets have eroded, it seems that what is left of internal labor markets, and of organizational norms of fair treatment, is underpinned by employers' twin fears of unionization and litigation. Workers' right to form a union, however frayed, and their potential right to file a lawsuit, however fraught or frustrated, entail a kind of latent power on the part of workers to which we will return.

Second, both collective bargaining and litigation have the somewhat paradoxical quality of serving both as a mechanism of conflict resolution and as a catalyst of conflict. Collective bargaining and its signature system of grievance arbitration is above all a system of dispute resolution (Colvin, 2012). Collective bargaining aspires to resolving interest disputes by generating a collective contract. During the term of the contract most labor-management disputes take the form of contractual rights disputes to be resolved between the parties or by a jointly chosen arbitrator. Yet unions and collective bargaining are obviously associated with conflict—at least in the process of bargaining for an agreement, and at lower levels during the term of the agreement. That is partly because unions derive bargaining power from their ability, at least periodically, to galvanize workers' discontent and to sharpen its focus on the employer. Conflict in the form of strikes both depends on *and builds* solidarity among workers. The decline of unions is thus perhaps as much a product of the decline of strikes as it is a cause (Getman, 2010).

But let us be clear: unions are also associated with conflict because they give workers the power to challenge management's unilateral governance of the workplace and the allocation of revenues. There are, after all, conflicting interests between labor and capital, workers and managers. And there is likely to be more conflict, or at least more open conflict, when both sides in this contest are organized and have some power.

Employment litigation is also simultaneously a mechanism of conflict resolution and a catalyst of conflict. Litigation is a notoriously disputatious mode of dispute resolution, and that is a big part of why it is so feared by employers. There is the adversarial process of litigation itself, of course, but there is also the organizational conflict associated with litigation, which is one of its large though less obvious costs, alongside attorney fees, expenditure of managerial time, reputational harms, and monetary or other remedies. Of course litigation only happens when there is already a dispute of some sort. But the ritualized combat of litigation sharpens the conflict and often appears more fearsome to employers than the conflicts that produce the litigation. And that is partly for the same reasons that fuel employer resistance to collective bargaining: employment litigation allows employees to contest employer power. Without litigation and the rights it asserts, employers (those who do not have to deal with a union) would be largely free to rule the workplace on a take-it-or-leave-it basis, and to eject those who create conflict, or bring it to the surface, by complaining about their treatment.

Third, the groundbreaking laws that launched both the system of collective bargaining and modern employment litigation—the NLRA of 1935 and the CRA of 1964—were themselves conceived in the midst of intense social conflict, and were intended in part to quell that conflict by channeling it into more peaceful and constructive (though still conflictual) channels. Again, that is especially obvious in the case of collective bargaining. The New Deal labor legislation largely solved "the labor question"—many decades of episodically violent labor-management conflict that had fractured communities and undermined the legitimacy of basic public institutions (especially police and courts)—by establishing a peaceful mechanism for resolving disputes at the bargaining table. But bargaining under the NLRA scheme was hardly conflict-free. It was backed up by lawful "economic weapons"—chiefly the strike and various employer countermeasures—to which the parties could resort to press their bargaining demands. The law both legitimized and regulated those economic weapons, especially with the Taft-Hartley amendments of 1947, and the resulting conflicts were both less violent and less political than the street battles and sit-in strikes of the 1930s. But as the latter receded from memory, the organized economic combat associated with collective bargaining appeared far more conflict-ridden than the non-union alternative, in which labor conflict may simmer under the surface, but rarely breaks into the open or poses a challenge to managerial power.

Like the NLRA, the CRA of 1964, which launched the modern era of employment litigation, was enacted in the midst of strife. The civil rights movement and the violent resistance that it met in some parts of the country posed the greatest domestic threat to political and social order since the great labor battles of the 1930s. In that context, the CRA was enacted in part to quell unrest and to end violent public and private resistance to equality rights by recognizing those rights, backing them with the force of federal law, and affording peaceable channels for their vindication (Eskridge, 2002). Much as with the NLRA, this monumental piece of legislation was enacted on the strength of convictions about the justice of the cause and support for its prospective beneficiaries, but also out of a belief that it was necessary (if hardly sufficient) to secure social peace. Adversarial combat in the courts, however troublesome to the employers that now had to reckon with it, was preferable to the existential conflict that was building up on the streets. As with the NLRA, the CRA did not immediately quell social conflict, and may have even fueled it for a while by embracing the justice of the cause that was still being resisted, often violently. Yet there seems little doubt in either case that the strife would have been more serious and longer-lasting had Congress failed to act.

Running through these two tales is a fourth parallel that speaks to the nature of organizational conflict more broadly. In the context of workplace disputes—collective and individual disputes, "interest disputes," and "rights disputes"—conflict is not simply a social evil to be avoided or suppressed, it is also a by-product of, and a means for, the pursuit of justice. When workers actively pursue their rights and interests against employers who are not giving them what they think they deserve, conflict results. If workers lacked either legal rights or collective representatives, workplaces themselves might be fairly peaceful, for employers could simply fire or refuse to hire those who contest their unilateral power—the union activists and rights-conscious minority workers, for example. But unaddressed grievances, when they are shared among groups of workers, have a tendency to pile up and spill into the society at large, creating a more dangerous (and politicized) type of conflict. In both the 1930s and the 1960s, conflict arising from shared grievances helped spur Congress to empower employees and compel employers to deal with them more fairly, and to do so by legitimizing non-violent though still costly forms of conflict between workers and employers.

That brings us to a fifth parallel between labor-management conflict and conflict over employment rights, and a step closer to this chapter's thesis: while conflict is associated with employees' pursuit of just claims and legitimate interests, there is no bleak and inexorable choice between rampant conflict on the one hand and injustice on the other. For the proponents of both collective bargaining rights and statutory employment rights, it was mainly the latent *threat* of costly conflict, not its frequent occurrence, that was supposed to induce the parties (mainly the employer) to construct a more just state of affairs.

That is rather obvious in the case of equal employment rights. The proponents of equal employment legislation could hardly have imagined that it would be desirable, or necessary, or even possible to pursue full-blown litigation against every employer that was engaged in discrimination before the law was passed. Proponents assumed that the articulation of new employee rights, backed by the threat of enforcement, would be enough to induce most employers to reform themselves. And so they did, to varying degrees and in ways to which we will return. "Litigation avoidance" was certainly one factor in the manifold organizational reforms that large and medium-sized firms pursued in the wake of Title VII and the first wave of litigation (Edelman, 1999; Dobbin, 2009). That is mostly how law works, after all: by inducing voluntary compliance. And that is how the *prospect* of discrimination litigation helped to transform day-to-day workplace life even though *actual* litigation is relatively rare and occurs outside of the workplace and usually after the plaintiff has left it.

The parallel scenario under the NLRA is more complex. Some of the law's chief proponents hoped that it would usher in an era of labor-management cooperation. Once employers were faced with the legal duty to recognize employees' chosen union representative, and with the prospect of legally protected strikes in support of employee demands, the rational response would be to sit down and work things out, and to construct a cooperative and mutually beneficial relationship (Barenberg, 1993). That idealized aspiration bears a passing resemblance to what developed over the next few decades in the widely unionized core industries—including heavy manufacturing, transportation, and communications. Strikes occurred periodically, but for the most part employers accepted the union's existence and the need to coexist under a collective agreement. Most workplace disputes were routinely worked out informally between union officials and their company counterparts through a grievance process that could, but rarely did, culminate in arbitration. Labor-management peace and cooperation through collective bargaining, and through the legitimization and regulation of conflict, largely prevailed for a few decades in a sizable unionized sector.[1]

But there was another path by which the NLRA encouraged employers to reform themselves: the path of union avoidance through union substitution. In the non-union sector (including most white-collar jobs within partly unionized companies), companies developed sophisticated HRM practices that were designed in part to deliver to workers some of what they might hope to gain from unionization: internal labor market norms of fair treatment and job security, grievance procedures, managerial control over abusive or arbitrary supervisors, and often higher-than-market-clearing wages (Kochan et al., 1994; Wachter, 2012). In a rather different way than envisioned by the NLRA's proponents, the law's protection of the right to unionize and bargain collectively brought a measure of fairness and decency into many non-union organizations. Fairness and decency perhaps, but not democracy. On the contrary, "high-road" HRM practices are typically coupled with sophisticated anti-union strategies; and the resulting combination of carrots and sticks has proven highly effective in discouraging union organizing and confining the sphere of "industrial democracy" through collective bargaining to a small fraction of the private sector workforce (Bisom-Rapp, 1999; Godard, 2001). (Moreover, the NLRA prohibits employers from establishing alternative non-union forms of employee representation; this problem is discussed below.)

Therein lies one major difference between litigation and collective bargaining as forms of workplace dispute resolution. Litigation is not generally regarded as a good in itself; and so voluntary compliance without actual litigation is a nearly unambiguous good. But collective bargaining and union representation are not only means to the end of higher wages or better working conditions, nor are they merely systems of conflict resolution. They are the law's chosen embodiment of workplace democracy. The success of the non-union HRM model, though due partly to the satisfaction of employee preferences, is a loss on the less tangible dimension of democracy.

The brilliance of the NLRA and the system of collective bargaining that it institutionalized was in simultaneously transforming labor-management conflict from violent to non-violent forms, and leveraging that conflict into a form of democratic self-governance within industry. Collective bargaining and grievance arbitration were elaborate systems for the resolution of labor-management conflict, but they were also vehicles for workers' representation in workplace governance. Of course that system is now a shrunken and embattled vestige of its former self. But the question that is pursued in the remainder of this chapter is whether something comparable could and should arise out of the elaborate web of employee rights and rights of action that has surpassed the collective bargaining system in its impact on the workplace.

THE RISE OF EMPLOYEE RIGHTS AND OF REGULATED SELF-REGULATION[2]

Employment law creates neither a coherent nor an effective instrument of workplace governance. Unlike the NLRA, it was not meant to do that. But it has become a hydra-head of duties and liabilities for employers, and those liabilities have to be managed. The managerial practices that have evolved under the shadow of employment laws (and other laws) have effectively inaugurated a new mode of workplace governance: regulated self-regulation.

As noted above, Title VII and the wave of discrimination litigation that followed generated the growth of internal grievance procedures and equal employment offices within firms, with the aim of preventing or redressing potential discrimination complaints and avoiding lawsuits. Similarly, the enactment of the Occupational Safety and Health Act (OSHA) spurred the growth of internal health and safety departments. Corporate compliance structures were put in place to manage proliferating employment law liabilities (as well as liabilities under environmental, securities, consumer safety, and other regulatory regimes). At their best, corporate compliance efforts aspire not only to avoid liabilities but to internalize the public values and goals behind the law. At their worst, these programs may be mere window dressing—a glossy façade behind which business goes on as usual.

Even as employers publicly embrace corporate compliance and social responsibility, they continue to push back politically and legally against the burdens of regulation and litigation. Employers' tirades against the "litigation crisis" have yielded few legislative rollbacks, but they have produced doctrinal and procedural hurdles to plaintiffs' success, such as mandatory arbitration, which is discussed below (Clermont and Schwab, 2004).[3] Challenges to the efficacy of regulation and litigation of workplace rights and standards have come not only from employers, however, but from scholars and employee advocates as well. Observers from a range of perspectives have argued that:

- the post-war regulatory regime is losing its grip in the face of rapidly changing markets, technology, and firm structures (Breyer, 1982; Dorf and Sabel, 1998);

- uniform legislated labor standards cannot address the range of concerns and contexts that workers face (Weiler, 1990);
- "adversarial legalism" and "regulatory unreasonableness" are undermining the pursuit of public regulatory goals (Bardach and Kagan, 1982); and
- civil litigation is a costly, slow, and often inaccessible mechanism for securing workplace rights and adjudicating disputes (Dunlop Commission, 1995; Outten, 1999; Estreicher, 2001; Sternlight, 2004).

Some of these critiques echo the very arguments that led New Dealers to turn to collective self-governance, and to unionization and collective bargaining as the primary vehicles for addressing workplace disputes and the inequities of the labor market. This time around, however, many critics, courts, and regulators have converged instead on the concept of "self-regulation." Proponents of self-regulation have argued for using public law to encourage employers to regulate their own practices rather than as a direct instrument of control. They point to the growth and increasing sophistication of corporate compliance structures as evidence that self-regulation makes sense.

The concept of self-regulation has begun to shape the external law of the workplace. Most important in the present context: courts responsible for enforcing employee rights have begun to formalize the role of internal compliance procedures—most notably in the sexual harassment context, but also more broadly—and to defer to private dispute resolution schemes (including arbitration), granting employers a partial shield against litigation and liability based on those schemes. These developments bring the main locus of rights enforcement inside the firm or under the firm's control. The internal compliance regimes of large firms must be seen in that light: as efforts not simply to comply with the law but to secure the legal advantages of self-regulation and a partial shield against liability. This chapter focuses on the internal structures, and particularly the dispute resolution structures, that have arisen to deal with the expanding array of "rights claims" under employment laws.

From Managing Conflict Under the Shadow of Employment Law to Regulated Self-Regulation

Employers have invested heavily in dispute resolution procedures as the linchpin of their strategies of litigation avoidance and management. But it is worth distinguishing two different kinds of strategies: systemic strategies seek to avoid lawsuits by internalizing compliance and complaints, and contractual strategies seek to induce or require employees either to waive liability after a dispute has arisen or to waive the right to litigate future disputes in favor of arbitration.

Systemic Litigation Avoidance Strategies

In recent decades, many non-union employers have crafted internal grievance and dispute resolution mechanisms, which vary in their complexity from simple open-door policies to multi-step processes involving peer review, mediation, and arbitration. These systems are thought to enhance employee morale, longevity, and performance; to quell interest in unionization; and to allow management to rationalize discipline and monitor supervisors. That being said, it is clear that the threat of litigation helped to spur the dramatic growth of these systems in medium and large-sized firms (Edelman, 1992, 1999). It has become near gospel among human relations professionals that corporate due process systems help to avoid litigation (as well as unionization) by resolving disputes within the firm and by flagging and potentially correcting actions that may be found or plausibly claimed to be discriminatory.

These corporate due process regimes typically afford "some kind of hearing," usually before a relatively impartial company official, not only for legally actionable claims but for other complaints of unfair treatment (Edelman, 1990). At a minimum these procedures afford a sober second look and a check against the personal tyranny of low-level supervisors; they administer a dose of procedural regularity and soften the sharp edges of employment at will. Yet many observers cast a skeptical eye upon these internal grievance procedures for their failure to fully realize employee rights, as well as for their tendency to assimilate complaints of discrimination to the ordinary run of personnel conflicts (Edelman, 1993, 2001; Krawiec, 2003). Moreover, there is little solid evidence about how well these internal enforcement systems actually work (Krawiec, 2003; Lawton, 2004). Some scholars see promise; others see costly but largely symbolic gestures.[4]

So long as internal grievance procedures played no direct role in the adjudication of formal legal complaints, their shortcomings posed little threat to the enforcement of legal rights. These internal systems might avoid or remedy some discrimination; or they might avert some legal claims by mollifying grievants or persuading them that their case was weak. But if the employee did file a formal complaint, it would still follow the course charted by external law, culminating in public administrative or judicial adjudication (or settlement under the shadow of adjudication), without regard to its fate within the corporate hierarchy.

That changed with the Supreme Court's 1998 decisions in *Burlington Industries* v. *Ellerth*[5] and *Faragher* v. *City of Boca Raton*.[6] The Court reaffirmed employers' liability for supervisors' discrimination and harassment, regardless of whether high-level managers knew or approved of the conduct. But with respect to one type of discrimination—the creation of a discriminatory hostile environment without any tangible adverse employment action—the Court offered the employer an affirmative defense: the employer could escape liability by showing that it "exercised reasonable care to prevent and correct promptly any sexually harassing behavior," and that the employee "unreasonably failed to take advantage of any preventive or corrective opportunities provided by the employer or to avoid harm otherwise," (*Faragher* v. *City of Boca Raton*,[6] at 807, 1998). A year later the Court effectively extended a version of the "self-regulation defense" to tangible adverse actions: The Court held that "good faith efforts to comply with Title VII," in the form of antidiscrimination policies and procedures, would bar punitive damages against the employer for intentional discrimination in promotions (and presumably discharges) (*Kolstad*,[7] at 544, 1999).

With these decisions, the Court transformed employers' internal compliance and grievance procedures into front-line mechanisms for enforcing antidiscrimination law and avoiding liability. No longer is the law merely casting a "shadow" beneath which firms may devise whatever procedures they believe will best avoid liability. Nor is this wholesale self-regulation, in which firms are freed from external scrutiny. Rather, the law is now regulating the process of self-regulation. Courts are charged with distinguishing sham processes from effective ones—with deciding whether employer's policies and practices are "reasonable" and demonstrate good faith. Employers in turn have to look to external legal standards to assess the adequacy of their own internal antidiscrimination policies. If courts do their job well, these doctrines should promote organizational practices that reduce the incidence of discrimination and harassment and offer better recourse to aggrieved employees. But if judicial oversight is cursory, and litigation ends up being barred by a mere pretense of internal process, then employers may be able to insulate themselves from the litigation threat that has driven much internal workplace reform. Deregulation under the guise of self-regulation is a serious risk with a doctrine that rewards employers not just for preventing discrimination but for convincing a court that they tried to prevent it, or would have tried if the plaintiff had come forward earlier.

Contractual Litigation Avoidance Strategies

Employers cannot contract out of discrimination liability for claims that have not yet arisen, for that would amount to contracting out of the mandatory prohibition of discrimination (Estlund, 2007). But employers can and do contract out of liability for existing claims through severance agreements that waive those claims as a condition of severance pay (Issacharoff, 1996). Employers can also contract out of civil *litigation* of future claims—and this is the focus here—by demanding that employees sign mandatory arbitration agreements as a condition of employment. In *Gilmer* v. *Interstate/Johnson Lane Corp.*[8] and *Circuit City Stores, Inc.* v. *Adams*,[9] the Supreme Court upheld the enforceability of employees' agreements to submit future legal claims against the employer to an arbitrator rather than to a court. Since *Gilmer*, many employers have thus taken employment disputes out of the courts and into the more private and party-controlled arbitral forum (Colvin, 2003, 2012).

Both the rise of mandatory arbitration and the proliferation of internal grievance procedures represent organizations' efforts to tame the litigation threat. Both seek to ameliorate the tension between outside legal norms and internal organizational needs, partly by bringing the organization into closer conformity with outside norms, and partly by domesticating those outside norms and the means of their enforcement. And both represent forms of *regulated* self-regulation in the enforcement of employee rights. In the case of mandatory arbitration, employers write arbitration agreements, and they design the process and dictate how arbitrators are chosen; yet they do so subject to the power of courts to reject or redact unfair or legally invalid provisions (*Gilmer*, 1991).[10]

Whether this form of self-regulation is sufficiently well regulated is another question: judicial supervision is episodic, and it often takes a form that may encourage employers to overreach.[11] Employees, for their part, face a serious collective action problem in deciding whether and how to challenge an arbitration agreement at the time it is presented to them. They also risk incurring the employer's disfavor by signaling a willingness to sue in the future. All in all, an individual employee has little to gain and a lot to lose in questioning or attempting to alter an arbitration agreement presented by the employer as a condition of employment. The upshot is that arbitration agreements give employers considerable control over the adjudicatory process. There is some empirical evidence that arbitrators themselves may be subtly biased in favor of employers whom they see in multiple disputes (the so-called "repeat player effect") (Bingham, 1995; Hill, 2003; Colvin, 2011). But there is little doubt that the employer, who foresees repeated resort to the arbitration process in employment disputes, has an incentive to invest in devising an arbitration system that serves its interests to the degree that is possible.

IMPROVING THE REGIME OF REGULATED SELF-REGULATION THROUGH WORKER REPRESENTATION

So there are grounds for concern about the move toward self-regulation in the enforcement of employment rights. But there are also reasons to channel those concerns into improving, and better regulating, self-regulatory structures, rather than into outright reversal of the move toward self-regulation. For the rise of more and less regulated versions of self-regulation is no mere flash-in-the-pan. It follows a trajectory that has become increasingly familiar, and widely analyzed, in the law of corporate criminal law, securities law, and environmental law, among other areas, across much of the developed world.

In workplace regulation, as elsewhere, there has been a shift away from direct top-down mechanisms of legal control and toward "reflexive" mechanisms for encouraging effective self-regulation, and the internalization of public values, by organizations themselves (Lobel, 2004). Many of these mechanisms, including most of those extant in the US law of the workplace, take a conditional or quasi-contractual form. Self-regulation is not mandated but is encouraged and rewarded, most tangibly by the promise of relief from some aspect of the background enforcement regime. Those self-regulatory privileges are conditioned on what the law recognizes as adequate self-regulatory activity. In this chapter that is called "regulated self-regulation."

Proponents of regulated self-regulation see the evolution of more efficient and effective systems for enforcing legal norms, systems that introduce flexibility and responsiveness into the regulatory regime, and reduce the costs and contentiousness associated with litigation, while promoting the internalization of public law norms (Bardach and Kagan, 1982; Ayres and Braithwaite, 1992). Detractors see the same trends as a dressed-up form of deregulation, one that allows firms to deflect public scrutiny by engaging in "cosmetic compliance" and window-dressing (Blackett, 2001; Krawiec, 2003). Much in the debate turns on whether courts and regulators can be counted on to distinguish effective from ineffective systems of self-regulation. If courts and regulators cannot (or will not) reliably distinguish real from cosmetic compliance, then regulated self-regulation may become a thinly disguised form of deregulation.

The Risks and Opportunities of Regulated Self-Regulation in the Workplace

The diffusion of self-regulation within the law of the workplace deserves special attention. The shift toward self-regulation is based in large part on the recognition that those who are best situated to detect, report, and avoid organizational misconduct are the insiders employed by the organization. Systems that activate the monitoring capabilities of those insiders have enormous potential to improve corporate compliance beyond what ordinary law enforcement can do. In the case of labor standards and employee rights, the firm's employees are not only the best potential monitors of misconduct but are the primary beneficiaries of the law. That fact, unique to the law of the workplace, creates both distinct opportunities and distinct risks in the self-regulation of employee rights and labor standards.

The distinct opportunities are quite obvious. The convergence of interest and information—of motive and means—on the part of employees within self-regulating firms would seem to magnify their monitoring role. Whatever altruistic or organizational motive employees have to report unsafe consumer products or financial shenanigans, they have an additional intrinsic and self-interested motive to report dangerous working conditions or denial of overtime pay. To be sure, employees still face collective action problems, at least in the non-union workplace, for most workplace laws secure "public goods" within the workforce or some subset of it. They affect employees as a group, and the collective benefits of compliance, as well as the costs to the employer, are much larger than the benefits to any one employee. So individual employees do not have enough incentive to speak up, even apart from their fear of reprisals. But if that problem can be overcome, activating employees within internal compliance systems has a huge potential pay-off.

But distinct risks arise from those same employees' economic dependence on the employer. Employees, especially those who are terminable at will, may fear reprisals if they report or complain about misconduct (unless they have already quit or been fired). Of course that may also deter employee "whistleblowers" under environmental or consumer safety or securities laws. But those non-labor laws benefit outsiders to the organization who may have enforcement tools of their own. Private enforcement by shareholders, citizens, or consumers faces hurdles, such as lack of inside information, but it is not hampered by the economic dependence of an employment relationship. In the case of employment laws, however, fear of reprisals may inhibit employees in both their internal whistleblowing and their private enforcement efforts. Employees' fear of reprisals may be the Achilles heel of the system, allowing employers to fend off liability or regulatory scrutiny on the basis of compliance systems that do not do the job.

From Self-Regulation to Self-Governance by Way of Co-Regulation

What will it take to create an effective system of regulated self-regulation in the workplace? Among other things, it will take effective forms of employee representation within the self-regulatory process. But it is important to note that the need for stakeholder representation in a system of regulated self-regulation is not unique to the workplace setting. Across an array of regulatory arenas, the work of John Braithwaite and others shows that effective self-regulation requires the participation of the regulated firm, the government, *and* the primary beneficiaries of the relevant legal norms (Braithwraite, 1982, 1985, 2009; Ayres and Braithwaite, 1992).[12] And whether the beneficiaries of the relevant legal norms are consumers, patients, shareholders, air breathers, or workers, they must be represented in some organized form that allows them to influence and monitor self-regulatory processes. Organized participation by regulatory beneficiaries supplements public regulatory oversight and provides a check against covert cheating or paper compliance by regulated organizations, and against "regulatory capture," or unwarranted deference toward those organizations on the part of agencies (or courts) charged with enforcement (Ayres and Braithwaite, 1992).

Effective employee participation in self-regulation requires not only avenues for individual reporting by employees, but also some organized form of collective representation with an existence both inside and outside the workplace. First, such organizations can address the collective action problems associated with the "public good" of compliance with employment laws. Second, such organizations enjoy independence and insulation from reprisals, fear of which inhibits individual employee participation. Third, a collective entity may enable workers to exert some power in decision-making and to counter the opportunistic impulses that may lead firms to cheat on their self-regulatory commitments. Some form of collective employee representation that is independent of the employer may thus be essential to effective self-regulation of labor standards and employee rights.

Unions would seem to fit the bill.[13] They address collective action problems, blunt the fear of reprisals, and put collective clout behind employee concerns; and they do indeed appear to improve compliance with employment laws in the fraction of workplaces in which they now represent workers (Rabin, 1991; Weil, 2002; Morantz, 2013). But unions themselves are unlikely to be the primary vehicle for employee representation going forward, given the drastic decline in unionization and the ever dimmer prospects for a dramatic reversal of that trend. There is more below on the mechanisms by which unions improve compliance with external law, for therein may lie clues to how employees can be effectively represented in the process of self-regulation, and how self-regulation might thereby be improved, in the non-union context.

Whatever the specifics of how employees might be collectively and effectively represented in self-regulatory processes, it is important to recognize that the quasi-contractual structure of regulated self-regulation creates an avenue for encouraging the adoption of those measures. For the law can and does impose conditions on firms' ability to secure the legal advantages of self-regulation. To the extent that firms construct compliance systems with an eye to securing favorable legal and regulatory treatment, they must meet conditions set by law, and those conditions should be designed to ensure the efficacy of self-regulation. For the reasons outlined above, one of those conditions should be the effective collective participation of the employees whose rights and working conditions are at stake. So when policymakers and public agencies set the conditions for admission to a less adversarial enforcement track based on self-regulatory programs, or when courts decide whether to uphold a mandatory arbitration agreement or whether a firm's internal antidiscrimination structures should entitle it to a partial defense against liability, they should ensure that the affected employees have an effective organizational voice in the relevant self-regulatory process. The partial migration of employment law and its enforcement inside firms thus creates not only the need, but also the opportunity, to revive employees' voice inside firms.

The term "co-regulation" is used here as shorthand for a regime of effective employer self-regulation in which employee beneficiaries have a genuine collective voice. "Co-regulation" and its requisites, including employee representation, could be thought of as a kind of official "high road" for employment practices. Any self-regulatory privileges that the law and legal actors deal out in the employment arena—partial defenses to liability, more congenial and cooperative enforcement tracks—should be reserved for firms that follow principles of co-regulation. Unlike much of what now passes for corporate self-regulation, a system of co-regulation provides safeguards against cosmetic compliance and against self-deregulation that critics legitimately fear.[14] Now let us turn to what a co-regulatory approach might entail in the context of workplace dispute resolution systems.

SOME ASPECTS OF CO-REGULATION IN THE RESOLUTION OF WORKPLACE CONFLICT

To begin with, co-regulation is about securing compliance with external law. In the context of workplace dispute resolution, it is about "rights disputes." That is only a subset of workplace disputes, of course, but that is where the law is able to set standards of fairness as conditions for self-regulatory privileges. It is likely, and fortunate, that fair procedures for rights disputes will end up providing fairer recourse for some interest disputes, or ordinary personnel disputes, as well.

The law already sets some standards of fairness in dispute resolution procedures to which the employer seeks legal deference. That is most clear in the law of arbitration, where courts have to decide whether to enforce arbitration agreements (Colvin, 2011). The extent of judicial authority to oversee the fairness of arbitration agreements remains unsettled (Cole, 2011; Horton, 2011; Resnik, 2011). The law of arbitration could be improved from a co-regulatory perspective by adopting something like the "Due Process Protocol," or an updated version of it, as a condition for upholding mandatory arbitration agreements. Fairness standards should similarly govern any internal dispute resolution structures on which an employer seeks to base a partial defense to liability.

But let us hone in on the still largely missing element of employee representation. It is not the only element of co-regulation that is important to the fairness and legitimacy of dispute resolution processes, but it is an under-appreciated and under-explored element. Elsewhere I have explored the nature of the employee representation that might complete a system of workplace co-regulation—why union representation may be the best, but cannot be the only, form of employee representation that passes muster, and what sort of non-union representation schemes, with what safeguards, might fulfill the requisites of co-regulation (Estlund, 2010). Those are hard and complex issues. I will pursue them briefly here in the context of workplace dispute resolution. But first let us take account of existing forms of participation within the already-emerging regime of regulated self-regulation and in non-union workplaces more generally.

Traces of Participation Within Self-Regulation

Collective bargaining and employment litigation serve both as modes of dispute resolution and as catalysts of conflict. Both procedures do both of those things by enabling workers to put some clout—collective economic power or the power of state enforcement—behind claims that employers might otherwise be able to ignore, given the ordinary vectors of labor market pressure. And both collective bargaining and employment litigation lead to the creation of internal dispute resolution mechanisms (including arbitration) that aim to keep disputes from escalating into more costly forms of conflict. But both do more than establish structures of dispute resolution; they establish modes of workplace governance (Colvin, 2012). Collective bargaining and collective dispute resolution structures democratize workplace governance by enabling workers to transform their interests into contractual rights and to enforce those rights through jointly administered procedures. Employment statutes and litigation rights, and the grievance and compliance procedures that they engender, also bring about a shift in the nature of workplace governance toward what I have called regulated self-regulation. But is it, or can it be, a shift toward a more democratic mode of workplace governance?

It is worth observing at the outset that, even without the move to co-regulation, the extant regime of regulated self-regulation has a modestly participatory dimension. For a central element of corporate compliance programs, and of the legal framework for corporate self-regulation, is the encouragement and protection of employee reporting of misconduct, including claimed employment law violations. Firms acting under the shadow of public law (Title VII doctrines, organizational sentencing guidelines under criminal law, for example) have created structures through which individual workers are invited to bring their complaints or reports of non-compliance to organizational actors with some power to resolve those complaints (Moberly, 2008). Public law plays other supporting roles as well, sometimes prescribing internal reporting procedures, and more often prohibiting retaliation against internal employee reporters (Moberly, 2006). Encouraging and protecting employee whistleblowing is very far from "democracy," but it is a modestly democratizing step toward improving legal compliance, or the "rule of law," in workplace governance.

Employers have taken other potentially democratizing steps voluntarily, without legal encouragement or oversight. Many employers have adopted "peer review" procedures for employee discipline. Some corporations are designing systems to resolve both employee–employer grievances and disputes between employees. These systems, if properly implemented, can increase employee commitment to the workplace, reduce tension between external norms and internal organizational needs, and decrease litigation costs (Stone, 2001; Colvin, 2003; Estlund, 2005). Questions remain, however, whether these procedures constitute a form of employee voice and participation, or a mechanism for managerial co-optation of employee resistance.

Many firms have gone further, and created informal structures of collective employee voice in some firm decision-making. For example, employee affinity groups are nearly ubiquitous in large firms as part of their diversity management portfolios (Dobbin, 2009). Affinity groups enable subsets of employees—minority racial and ethnic groups, women, parents, disabled workers, for example—to meet and convey shared concerns to management. The actual impact of these groups on their members' welfare and advancement in firms is not well understood (Dobbin and Kalev, 2013: 268). But it seems plausible that, in hosting such groups, an organization signals a willingness to meet reasonable demands, and risks catalyzing group discontent if it fails to do so.

Most ambitious among employers' participatory initiatives are workforce-wide employee representation structures through which employees participate in workplace governance and often discuss wages and benefits (Freeman and Rogers, 1999; Kaufman and Taras, 2000; Frege and Godard, 2010). Managers have diverse motives for creating these representational structures, but they surely include a desire to resolve disputes and grievances that might otherwise ripen into those more disputatious forms of dispute resolution, litigation and unionization. And it appears that many of these non-union representation schemes are performing fairly well from employees' perspective, perhaps by better enabling workers to communicate their concerns and get satisfactory responses from management (Frege and Godard, 2010).

Rather little is known about how these representational structures work (Kaufman and Taras, 2000). That is partly because most of them probably violate federal labor law. Section 8(a)(2) of the NLRA prohibits employers from interfering with or dominating any labor organization, which is defined in turn to include any structure of employee representation through which employees "deal with" employers, or engage in give-and-take, about terms and conditions of employment. Most of these employer-established non-union representation schemes run afoul of the law.[15] That is an unsettling fact.

There is of course a longstanding debate over whether Section 8(a)(2) makes sense today.[16] The current posture of de jure prohibition and de facto laissez-faire seems untenable. But should the reality be brought in line with the law or vice versa? In particular, how should the law treat structures of informal non-union collective representation from the perspective of promoting the fair resolution of workplace disputes, especially rights disputes?

Until recently, the law basically adopted a posture of laissez-faire toward employers' internal dispute resolution structures: employers could decide for themselves what internal structures would help them to avoid litigation (provided they did not violate the law). But those structures made no difference in how litigation would proceed if it came to pass. Since the advent of mandatory arbitration, and the decisions in *Faragher, Ellerth,* and *Kolstad,* the law is clearly engaged in the enterprise of regulating employers' own dispute resolution structures. Without mandating them, courts are encouraging them, judging their adequacy, and dealing out regulatory advantages to those that pass muster. At best, the regulation of employers' self-regulation can promote the realization of employee rights and the penetration of public values into organizations. But without effective employee representation in the design and implementation of those self-regulatory structures, there is reason to doubt that those internal procedures are trustworthy enough to warrant regulatory deference. The law should not be dealing out regulatory concessions to self-regulators unless employees are effectively represented within the "self" that is being regulated (Estlund, 2010).

In other words, having gone down the path toward regulated self-regulation in the workplace, the law must take additional steps to democratize internal governance structures. Crucially, one need not embrace the intrinsic value of democracy in the workplace to recognize that worker representation in the machinery of self-regulation—and specifically in the machinery of dispute resolution and employee reporting—is an important safeguard of the legitimacy and integrity of those structures. The core idea of co-regulation is thus to better realize the public norms and values embodied in employment rights and labor standards by democratizing workplace governance. Co-regulatory reforms would extend the parallel trajectories of employment rights and litigation and of union organizing and collective bargaining from conflict toward shared governance. Of course even parallel trajectories might be quite distant from one another; as is conceded elsewhere, co-regulation is unlikely to deliver to workers the kind of voice and power that they had in some unionized workplaces in the heyday of collective bargaining (Estlund, 2010: 241–2).

The upshot is that neither prohibition nor permissive laissez-faire is the right approach to non-union representation schemes. Neither, however, is it necessary to mandate or mandatorily regulate such structures (though that is what other advanced industrial economies of the world do through "works councils" or other forms of employee consultation). What is required is the development of legal standards, including standards for employee representation structures, that can safeguard the integrity of internal and arbi-tral dispute resolution structures, and thereby justify the deference that self-regulating employers are claiming in the context of public rights disputes.

How Can Non-Union Employee Representation Work in a Co-Regulatory Regime?

So let us consider briefly what employee representation in internal dispute resolu-tion procedures, including arbitration, might look like. We know what it looks like in the union workplace, and it is clear that collective bargaining and its signature grievance-arbitration processes do contribute to compliance with employee rights and labor standards under external law. But what about in the non-union setting? We might do well to ask: By what mechanisms do unions improve compliance with external law, and can any of those mechanisms be reproduced or approximated in the non-union setting?

The focus here will be chiefly on the role of worker representatives in the fair *imple-mentation* of dispute resolution systems as opposed to their basic design. That is because, as noted above, a co-regulatory approach to workplace dispute resolution should include indices of fairness in the design of dispute resolution schemes. For example, for any mandatory arbitration of "rights disputes," that would include guarantees of arbi-trators' neutrality (at least as robust as those under existing law). But how are any such guarantees to be monitored and implemented in particular workplaces and cases? The difficulty of that question is one of the reasons for requiring employee representation in dispute resolution processes. So let us focus on the nature and functions of employee representation in dispute resolution schemes.

Three ways in which unions address the difficulties that individual employees face in pursuing rights-claims and other grievances have already been suggested: unions help to solve collective action problems; they reduce or blunt employees' fear of reprisals; and they put independent collective power behind employee interests. It is important to note that unions do these three things (especially the last) only because—or to the extent that—unions actually represent workers. That, along with independence and power, is difficult to achieve with non-union representation, and it is discussed below.

Unions help to solve collective action problems in at least four ways. First, they pool information about worker concerns and employer practices (for example, the fact that several workers are being required to work off-the-clock to clean up after their shift, or are finding small discrepancies in their paychecks that may suggest manipula-tion of time records, both practices that have been documented in large retail opera-tions (Greenhouse, 2009)). Second, unions pool workers' interests in pursuing shared concerns that may not be worth pursuing for the individual, but that can be efficiently pursued on behalf of the group (as with off-the-clock work and time-shaving). Third, they can develop technical, legal, and practical expertise that it is not worthwhile or feasible for individual workers to acquire (such as knowledge about the proper classification of workers under the FLSA, and skilled advocacy for workers within grievance-arbitration processes). Many of these advantages of unions stem from a fourth feature: as repeat players in the use of dispute resolution machinery, unions have a greater incentive and ability to shape the decision-making process in employees' interest; and arbitrators, who depend on repeat business, have an incentive to reach decisions that both sides regard as fair.

None of these capabilities is categorically beyond the reach of non-union representative bodies, though some pose challenges. The pooling of information and interests within the particular group of workers is the least challenging criterion; it would seem mainly to require proximity and open lines of communication between workers and their representatives within the workplace. That may be harder in large, or highly dispersed, or fragmented workplace organizations. But these problems recall the question, posed but postponed above, of how to ensure the representativeness of a non-union employee representation body. If "representativeness" is understood to require not only elections but elections within reasonably sized units that map onto workplace networks and interests—for example departments, level (rank-and-file versus supervisory), or work locations—then those representatives should be able to pool workers' knowledge and interests as well.

The third function of unions—their accumulation of technical and legal expertise—depends partly on scale. Unions have their own resources, drawn from thousands of workers from many workplaces in the same industry, and they enjoy economies of scale that are not available to a non-union workplace-based representative. Public regulators might partially fill that gap by serving as a resource and training center for non-union representatives, and by developing and disseminating "best practices" regarding fair internal procedures for reporting and dispute resolution. Unions' status as "repeat players" is important in part for their incentive to invest in developing fair dispute resolution machinery. Public resources and public standards for what counts as a fair dispute resolution process can help address this need. The "repeat player" effect on arbitrators also depends partly on unions' scale and continuity over time. It may be only over multiple workplaces and several years that any one arbitrator can expect to meet the same employee representative repeatedly. That is less likely in the case of workplace-based non-union representatives. But that gap, too, may be partially filled by dedicating modest public regulatory resources to the support of employee representatives.

On the whole, it seems that non-union employee representatives can do some but not all of what unions do to overcome collective action problems in the design and implementation of dispute resolution procedures.

Employees' vulnerability to reprisals is the Achilles heel of any system of self-regulation. Unions guard against reprisals and the disabling fear of reprisals in at least two ways. First, they can pursue some grievances as an institution, thus enabling individuals to make complaints anonymously vis-à-vis the employer. That is something that a non-union representation structure should be able to do, provided that the designated representatives themselves are protected from reprisals.[17] That points to the second mechanism by which unions guard against reprisals: they typically secure strong job security in the form of contractual just cause protection both for ordinary employees and for union representatives.[18] Just cause protection, backed by "industrial due process," confers much greater security against reprisals than does the right to bring a retaliation complaint or lawsuit, where burdens of proof, procedural roadblocks, and delay fall on the complainant.

The remarkable staying power of "employment at will" in the United States might seem to put the desideratum of "just cause" protection beyond reach for non-union workers. But the law could and should provide that one criterion for the adequacy of internal self-regulatory structures is that employee representatives must enjoy not only protection against reprisals but also just-cause protection by contract. The law should ensure that retaliation or the threat of retaliation for legitimate activities of an employee representative or informant should trigger not only expeditious and adequate remedies for the employee but also serious sanctions for the offending employer.

Finally, and behind all of the foregoing mechanisms, unions potentially put collective economic power behind their representation of employee concerns, and they are accountable to workers and independent of the employer. These are the features of unions that are most difficult to approximate, much less replicate, in the non-union setting. Let us begin with the question of power. Ultimately unions' power still rests largely on the ability to strike (or to use other collective "economic weapons"). We will not dwell on the difficult question of how powerful unions' economic weapons are in today's perilous legal and economic landscape. The question is what power, if any, non-union representatives could put behind their demands for compliance with legal rights and labor standards.

One answer is the law itself; that is, the ability to trigger costly, disruptive, and embarrassing litigation against the employer. If power in this context is the ability to bring undesirable consequences to bear on employers that resist workers' demands, and if the demands in question consist of well-founded rights claims, then the law itself, and the existence of private rights of action, give workers power that collective representation enables them to deploy more effectively. (For example, a representative entity might be able to organize aggregate litigation, or even pursue litigation itself on behalf of the workers.) That proposition might seem to ignore the very phenomenon of regulated self-regulation that we are seeking to improve here. That is, if employers can dodge the threat of public enforcement through mandatory arbitration, and can limit the extent of their liabilities through internal grievance procedures, employees' power is accordingly limited. Co-regulation offers a way out of this conundrum. Workers' representatives must have both a meaningful role within self-regulatory processes (including arbitration) and the ability to escape those processes when they are ineffectual or skewed. So arbitration agreements should not be enforceable unless workers have effective representation in the design and operation of the arbitration system. Workers' representatives must be empowered to exercise the outside option of judicial enforcement, and to blow the whistle on ostensibly responsible self-regulators, when they can show that internal processes are not trustworthy.

Representation, Accountability, and Independence

US labor law seeks to ensure unions' representativeness, independence, and accountability in several ways. It confines collective bargaining (through which unions perform nearly all their functions) to unions that enjoy majority support in the relevant group of workers; and it requires election of key union officials, with rules designed to ensure some measure of democratic accountability to workers. (Crucially, US labor law also bars employer interference with and domination of labor organizations, broadly defined; that provision poses some paradoxical hurdles in the present context, as we have seen.) There are other labor law regimes that can ensure unions' accountability, often with less state involvement in trade union affairs. But the point is that unions cannot perform their functions in an industrial relations system—including their function in promoting industrial peace and conflict resolution—unless they are reasonably accountable to workers.

Putting aside for the moment the hurdles posed by Section 8(a)(2), it seems equally clear that, for a non-union representative body to serve its functions within a system of regulated self-regulation, it must have some institutional guarantees of "representativeness." At a minimum, its members must be chosen by workers. That probably requires elections in most instances, and elections within reasonably small units that map onto workplace networks and worker interests, for example departments, pay and authority level (rank-and-file versus supervisory), and work locations. This is not the place for further elaboration of the form that elections would take (though European experience with works councils and other consultation mechanisms would provide useful models; Rogers and Streeck, 1994).

It is worth repeating the point that election of employee representatives would not be mandatory; it would be one condition for entry into a co-regulatory system. It may be that, to many employers, a requirement of elected employee representatives would appear so onerous or risky that it would be a deal-breaker—too high a price for entry onto the co-regulatory "high road." So be it. To gain the regulatory concessions and the reputational boost that ostensibly responsible employers seek, they should have the burden of proving the requisites of effective self-regulation. Employee representation is a critical structural safeguard against the risks of cheating, backsliding, and "cosmetic compliance" that attend any system of self-regulation (Krawiec, 2003).

CONCLUSION

In some ways the trend toward self-regulation in employment law is a re-enactment of the New Deal embrace of self-governance over external public regulation as the primary mode of protecting workers and improving wages and working conditions. We are once again moving toward internal lawmaking and law enforcement within a public law framework, and away from direct public regulation or judicial resolution of workplace disputes. This time around, however, workers have been largely cut out of the internal governance schemes.

It is troubling that the trend toward self-regulation, and toward public reliance on self-regulation, has gained ground at the same time that the existing system of collective representation in workplace governance has lost so much ground. The corporate "self" that is gaining the prerogative to regulate itself is less likely than ever to encompass employees other than as individuals, who face familiar and daunting impediments to effective bargaining or intervention on their own behalf. Fortunately, the emerging system of regulated self-regulation contains the ingredients of a partial solution to the problem: the law sets conditions on self-regulatory privileges and concessions, and those conditions should include some reasonable form of employee representation.

NOTES

1. It is clear in hindsight that this fairly peaceful accommodation in the union sector was partly contingent on regulatory, geographic, and technological hurdles to competition that began to fall, or were deliberately dismantled, in subsequent decades.
2. This section draws heavily from Estlund, 2010.
3. For critical accounts of employer responses to litigation and regulation, see Edelman et al., 1992; McGarity and Shapiro, 1996.
4. Among the more skeptical accounts, see Bisom-Rapp, 2001; Selmi, 2005; Bagenstos, 2006; Krieger and Fiske, 2006. Among the more favorable assessments, see Sturm, 2001; Green, 2003. Some commentators see potential as well as the need for safeguards not yet in place (Carle, 2006; Hart, 2007).
5. *Burlington Industries* v. *Ellerth*, 524 US 742 (1998).
6. *Faragher* v. *City of Boca Raton*, 524 US 775 (1998).
7. *Kolstad* v. *American Dental Association*, 527 US 526 (1999).
8. *Gilmer* v. *Interstate/Johnson Lane Corp.*, 500 US 20 (1991).
9. *Circuit City Stores, Inc.* v. *Adams*, 532 US 105 (2001).
10. Employers are also somewhat constrained by the standards that arbitrators and their professional organizations have set for the fairness of the process. The major arbitration provider organizations have agreed to the "Due Process Protocol" for the conduct of employment arbitrations (Estlund, 2010).
11. A court faced with an invalid clause—say, barring the award of attorneys' fees to prevailing Title VII plaintiffs—might simply strike the clause while enforcing the rest of the agreement. In that case the employer risks nothing by including such a provision and may deter some litigation. Or a court might enforce the agreement to arbitrate and leave the contested issue to arbitration itself (with very limited post-arbitration judicial review). In the meantime, prospective plaintiffs and their attorneys bear the burden of uncertainty and may be deterred from proceeding at all.
12. The application of this principle in the workplace harkens to the concept of tripartism in labor relations and labor regulation, which goes back at least to John Commons (Kaufman, 2003).
13. On the role of unions in enforcing employment rights and labor standards, see generally Rabin, 1991; Craver, 1998; Weil, 2002.

14. The concept of co-regulation proposed here resonates strongly with David Levine's proposal in the late 1990s for "conditional deregulation." (Levine, 1998).
15. The survey questions posed by both Freeman and Rogers and Frege and Godard were designed to identify structures that appeared to violate Section 8(a)(2).
16. See, e.g., Craver, 1992; Hyde, 1993; Summers, 1993; Barenberg, 1994; Estreicher, 1994; Jacoby, 1995; LeRoy, 1999; Weiler, 2001; Hirsch and Hirsch, 2006.
17. The problem of reprisals is a familiar one in the domain of corporate compliance, but current law on the matter is highly unsatisfactory: The law strongly encourages and rewards "effective compliance systems," which must include employee reporting procedures and assurances that those who use them will suffer no reprisals. But the law does not require that non-retaliation promises be legally binding, and employers routinely get by with, and get legal credit for, unenforceable promises (Moberly, 2008).
18. Union officers and stewards also often enjoy "super-seniority" protections against layoff under the collective bargaining agreement (Elkouri and Elkouri, 2003).

References

Ayres, I., and Braithwaite, J. 1992. *Responsive Regulation: Transcending the Deregulation Debate*. New York, NY: Oxford Press.

Bagenstos, S. R. 2006. "The Structural Turn and the Limits of Antidiscrimination Law," *California Law Review*, 94: 1–47.

Bardach, E. and Kagan, R. A. 1982. *Going by the Book: The Problem of Regulatory Unreasonableness*. Philadelphia, PA: Temple University Press.

Barenberg, M. 1993. "The Political Economy of the Wagner Act: Power, Symbol, and Workplace Cooperation." *Harvard Law Review*, 106(7): 1379–496.

Barenberg, M. 1994. "Democracy and Domination in the Law of Workplace Cooperation: From Bureaucratic to Flexible Production." *Columbia Law Review* 94(753): 879–983.

Bingham, L. 1995. "Is There a Bias in Arbitration of Non-Union Employment Disputes? An Analysis of Actual Cases and Outcomes." *International Journal of Conflict Management*, 6: 369–86.

Bisom-Rapp, S. 1999. "Bulletproofing the Workplace: Symbol and Substance in Employment Discrimination Law Practice." *Florida State University Law Review*, 26: 959–1049.

Bisom-Rapp, S. 2001. "An Ounce of Prevention is a Poor Substitute for a Pound of Cure: Confronting the Developing Jurisprudence of Education and Prevention in Employment Discrimination Law." *Berkeley Journal of Employment and Labor Law*, 22: 1–48.

Blackett, A. 2001. "Global Governance, Legal Pluralism and the Decentered State: A Labor Law Critique of Codes of Corporate Conduct." *Indiana Journal of Global Legal Studies*, 8: 401–47.

Braithwaite, J. 1982. "Enforced Self-Regulation: A New Strategy for Corporate Crime Control." *Michigan Law Review*, 80: 1466–507.

Braithwaite, J. 1985. *To Punish or Persuade: Enforcement of Coal Mine Safety*. Albany, NY: State University of New York Press.

Braithwaite, J. 2009. *Regulatory Capitalism: How it Works, Ideas for Making it Better*. Northampton, MA: Edward Elgar Publishing.

Breyer, S. G. 1982. *Regulation and Its Reform*. Cambridge, MA: Harvard University Press.

Brown, R. D. 2012. *Dying on the Job: Murder and Mayhem in the American Workplace*. Lanham, MD: Rowman & Littlefield Publishers.

Bureau of Labor Statistics. 2013. Economic News Release: Union Members Summary. Available at <http://www.bls.gov/news.release/union2.nro.htm> accessed 23 Sept. 2013.

Carle, S. D. 2006. "Acknowledging Informal Power Dynamics in the Workplace: A Proposal for Further Development of the Vicarious Liability Doctrine in Hostile Work Environment Sexual Harassment Cases." *Duke Journal of Gender Law and Policy*, 13: 85–113.

Clermont, K. M. and Schwab, S. J. 2004. "How Employment Discrimination Plaintiffs Fare in Federal Court." *Journal of Empirical Legal Studies*, 1: 429–58.

Cole, S. R. 2011. "On Babies and Bathwater: The Arbitration Fairness Act and the Supreme Court's Recent Arbitration Jurisprudence." *Houston Law Review*, 48: 457–506.

Colvin, A. J. S. 2003. "Institutional Pressures, Human Resource Strategies and the Rise of Nonunion Dispute Resolution Procedures." *Industrial and Labor Relations Review*, 56: 375–92.

Colvin, A. J. S. 2011. "An Empirical Study of Employment Arbitration: Case Outcomes and Processes." *Journal of Empirical Legal Studies*, 8: 1–23.

Colvin, A. J. S. 2012. "American Workplace Dispute Resolution in the Individual Rights Era." *International Journal of Human Resource Management*, 23: 459–75.

Craver, C. B. 1992. "The National Labor Relations Act Must Be Revised to Preserve Industrial Democracy." *Arizona Law Review*, 34(397): 429–31.

Craver, C. B. 1998. "Why Labor Unions Must [and Can] Survive." *University of Pennsylvania Journal of Labor and Employment Law*, 1: 15–47.

Dobbin, F. 2009. *Inventing Equal Opportunity*. Princeton, NJ: Princeton University Press. <http://scholar.harvard.edu/dobbin/publications/inventing-equal-opportunity> accessed 23 Sept. 2013.

Dobbin, F., and Kalev, A. 2013. "The Origins and Effects of Corporate Diversity Programs." In Q. M. Roberson (ed.), *Oxford Handbook of Diversity and Work*, 253–281. New York: Oxford University Press. <http://scholar.harvard.edu/dobbin/publications/origins-and-effects-corporate-diversity-programs> accessed 23 Sept. 2012.

Dorf, M. C. and Sabel, C. F. 1998. "A Constitution of Democratic Experimentalism." *Columbia Law Review*, 98: 267–473.

The Dunlop Commission on the Future of Worker-Management Relations, Final Report 1995: 59–60.

Edelman, L. B. 1990. "Legal Environments and Organizational Governance: The Expansion of Due Process in the American Workplace." *American Journal of Sociology*, 95: 1401–40.

Edelman, L. B., Abraham, S., and Erlanger, H. 1992. "Professional Construction of Law: The Inflated Threat of Wrongful Discharge." *Law and Society Review*, 26: 74–84.

Edelman, L. B., Erlanger, H. S., and Lande, J. 1993. "Internal Dispute Resolution." *Law & Society Review*, 27: 497–534.

Edelman, L. B., Fuller, S. R., and Mara-Drita, I. 2001. "Diversity Rhetoric and the Managerialization of Law." *American Journal of Sociology*, 106: 1589–641.

Edelman, L. B., Uggen, C., and Erlanger, H. S. 1999. "The Endogeneity of Legal Regulation: Grievance Procedures as Rational Myth." *American Journal of Sociology*, 105: 406–54.

Elkouri, F., Elkouri, E., and Rubin, A. 2003. *How Arbitration Works*. 7th edn. Arlington, VA: BNA Books.

Eskridge, W. N., Jr. 2002. "Some Effects of Identity-Based Social Movements on Constitutional Law in the Twentieth Century." *Michigan Law Review*, 100: 2062–407.

Estlund, C. 2005. "Rebuilding the Law of the Workplace in an Era of Self-Regulation." *Columbia Law Review*, 105: 319–98.

Estlund, C. 2007. "Between Rights and Contract: Arbitration Agreements and Non-Compete Covenants as a Hybrid Form of Employment Law." *University of Pennsylvania Law Review*, 155: 379–445.

Estlund, C. 2010. *Regoverning the Workplace: From Self-Regulation to Co-Regulation*. New Haven, CT: Yale University Press.

Estreicher, S. 1994. "Employee Involvement and the 'Company Union' Prohibition: The Case for Partial Repeal of Section 8(a)(2) of the NLRA." *New York University Law Review*, 69(125): 149–55.

Estreicher, S. 2001. "Saturns for Rickshaws: The Stakes in the Debate over Predispute Employment Arbitration Agreements." *Ohio State Journal on Dispute Resolution*, 16: 559–74.

Freeman, R. B. and Rogers, J. 1999. *What Workers Want*. Ithaca, NY: Cornell University Press.

Frege, C. and Godard, J. 2010. "Cross-national Variation in Representation Rights and Governance at Work." In A. Wilkinson, P. Gollan, M. Marchington, and D. Lewin (eds.), *The Oxford Handbook of Participation in Organizations*. Oxford: Oxford University Press.

Getman, J. 2010. *Restoring the Power of Unions: It Takes a Movement*. New Haven, CT: Yale University Press.

Godard, J. 2001. "High Performance and the Transformation of Work? The Implications of Alternative Work Practices for the Experience and Outcomes of Work." *Industrial and Labor Relations Review*, 54: 776–805.

Green, T. K. 2003. "Discrimination in Workplace Dynamics: Toward a Structural Account of Disparate Treatment Theory." *Harvard Civil Rights-Civil Liberties Law Review*, 38: 145–228.

Greenhouse, S. 2009. *The Big Squeeze: Tough Times for the American Worker*. New York, NY: Anchor Books.

Hart, M. 2007. "The Possibility of Avoiding Discrimination: Considering Compliance and Liability." *Connecticut Law Review*, 39: 1623–48.

Hill, E. 2003. "AAA Employment Arbitration: A Fair Forum at a Low Cost." *Dispute Resolution Journal*, 58: 8–21.

Hirsch, J. M. and Hirsch, B. T. 2006. "The Rise and Fall of Private Sector Unionism: What Next for the NLRA?" *Florida State University Law Review*, 34(1133): 1152–72.

Horton, D. 2011. "Arbitration As Delegation." *New York University Law Review*: 86: 437–99.

Hyde, A. 1993. "Employee Caucus: A Key Institution in the Emerging System of Employment Law." *Chicago-Kent Law Review*, 69(149): 187–90.

Issacharoff, S. 1996. "Contracting for Employment: The Limited Return of the Common Law." *Texas Law Review*, 74: 1783–815.

Jacoby, S. M. 1995. "Current Prospects for Employee Representation in the U.S.: Old Wine in New Bottles?." *Journal of Labor Research*, 16(387): 389–91.

Kaufman, B. E. 2003. "John R. Commons and the Wisconsin School on Industrial Relations Strategy and Policy." *Industrial and Labor Relations Review*, 57: 1–30.

Kaufman, B. E. and Taras, D. 2000. *Nonunion Employee Representation: History, Contemporary Practice and Policy*. Armonk, NY: M.E. Sharpe.

Kochan, T. A., Katz, H. C., and McKersie, R. B. 1994. *The Transformation of American Industrial Relations*. Ithaca, NY: ILR Press.

Krawiec, K. D. 2003. "Cosmetic Compliance and the Failure of. Negotiated Governance." *Washington University Law Quarterly*, 81: 487–544.

Krieger, L. H. and Fiske, S. 2006. "Behavioral Realism in Employment Discrimination Law." *California Law Review*, 94: 997–1062.

Lawton, A. 2004. "Operating in an Empirical Vacuum: The Ellerth and Faragher Affirmative Defense." *Columbia Journal of Gender and Law*, 13: 197–278.

LeRoy, M. H. 1999. "Employee Participation in the New Millennium: Redefining a Labor Organization Under Section 8(a)(2) of the NLRA." *Southern California Law Review*, 72: 1651, 1706–9.

Levine, D. I. 1998. *Working in the Twenty-First Century: Policies for Economic Growth Through Training, Opportunity, and Education.* Armonk, NY: M.E. Sharpe.

Lobel, O. 2004. "The Renew Deal: The Fall of Regulation and the Rise of Governance in Contemporary Legal Thought." *Minnesota Law Review*, 89: 342–470.

McGarity, T. O. and Shapiro, S. A. 1996. "OSHA's Critics and Regulatory Reform." *Wake Forest Law Review*, 31: 587–660.

Moberly, R. E. 2006. "Sarbanes-Oxley's Structural Model to Encourage Corporate Whistleblowers." *Brigham Young University Law Review*, 1107–80.

Moberly, R. E. 2008. "Protecting Whistleblowers by Contract." *University of Colorado Law Review*, 70: 975–1042.

Morantz, A. D. 2013. "Coal Mine Safety: Do Unions Make a Difference?" *Industrial & Labor Relations Review*, 66: 88–116.

Outten, W. N. 1999. "Negotiations, ADR, and Severance/Settlement Agreements: An Employee's Lawyer's Perspective." *Practicing Law Institute: Litigation and Administrative Practice Course Handbook Series*, 604: 235.

Rabin, R. J. 1991. "The Role of Unions in the Rights-Based Workplace." *University of San Francisco Law Review*, 25: 169–263.

Resnik, J. 2011. "Fairness in Numbers: A Comment on *AT&T v. Concepcion, Wal-Mart v. Dukes,* and *Turner v. Rogers.*" *Harvard Law Review*, 125: 78–170.

Rogers, J., and Streeck, W. 1994. "Worker Representation Overseas: The Works Council Story." In R. B. Freeman (ed.) *Working under Different Rules.* New York, NY. Russell Sage Foundation.

Selmi, M. 2005. "Sex Discrimination in the Nineties, Seventies Style: Case Studies in the Preservation of Male Workplace Norms." *Employee Rights and Employment Policy Journal*, 9: 46–95.

Sternlight, J. R. 2004. "In Search of the Best Procedure for Enforcing Employment Discrimination Laws: A Comparative Analysis." *Tulane Law Review*, 78: 1401–99.

Stone, K. V. W. 2001. "The New Psychological Contract: Implications of the Changing Workplace for Labor and Employment Law." *UCLA Law Review*, 48: 519–642.

Sturm, S. 2001. "Second Generation Employment Discrimination: A Structural Approach." *Columbia Law Review*, 101: 458–568.

Summers, C. W. 1993. "Employee Voice and Employer Choice: A Structured Exception to Section 8(a)(2)." *Chicago-Kent Law Review*, 69(129): 141–8.

Wachter, M. 2012. "The Striking Success of the National Labor Relations Act." In C. Estlund and M. Wachter (eds), *Research Handbook on The Economics of Labor and Employment Law.* Northampton, MA: Edward Elgar Publishing.

Weil, D. 2002. "Regulating Noncompliance to Labor Standards: New Tools for an Old Problem." *Challenge*, 45: 47–74.

Weiler, P. C. 1990. *Governing the Workplace: The Future of Labor and Employment Law.* Cambridge, MA: Harvard University Press.

Weiler, P. C. 2001. "A Principled Reshaping of Labor Law for the Twenty-First Century." *University of Pennsylvania Journal of Labor & Employment Law*, 3(177): 198–200.

CHAPTER 4

HRM AND CONFLICT MANAGEMENT

DOUGLAS M. MAHONY AND BRIAN S. KLAAS

INTRODUCTION

EMPLOYEES face choices when deciding how to respond to a perceived injustice or wrongdoing in the workplace. While doing nothing (silence) is one option, some may opt to exit the organization, others may engage in revenge seeking, and some may choose to voice their concerns (Hirschman, 1970; Freeman and Medoff, 1984; Pinder and Harlos, 2001; Aquino, Tripp, and Bies, 2006). For employees seeking to remediate the perceived injustice or voice their concerns, their options are often determined by their employer's human resource practices. When redress is sought, the typical first step is to utilize their employer's conflict resolution system. These systems vary across organizations and impact both the employee's ability to exercise voice and ultimately their justice perceptions.

Support for an employer's ability to sanction or discipline an employee stems from their ownership rights and, for managers, from their positional power within the organizational hierarchy (Banderet, 1986). Within non-unionized organizations, the employer retains the right to design the procedures and determine the outcomes, sanctions or remedies associated with employment disputes. A number of employers, however, have voluntarily relinquished their rights to determine such outcomes to third party decision-makers. Employment disputes, if unresolved or if they represent a statutory or public policy violation, may also escalate to (or fall under) the jurisdiction of the public justice system either through specialized labor tribunals or through ordinary-law courts (Wheeler and Rojot, 1992).

As a human resource policy, providing employees with a mechanism (or mechanisms) for the expression of voice is thought to provide several benefits, including reduced willingness to quit, less likelihood of supporting union organizing, and greater levels of employee satisfaction and organizational performance (Lewin and Mitchell, 1992; MacDuffie, 1995; Bae and Lawler, 2000; Cappelli and Neumark, 2001; Wang, Li, Lawler, and Zhang, 2011). While the concept of employee voice encompasses many forms our primary focus is on voice mechanisms for resolving conflicts that arise from the employment relationship. As such, we focus on the employer-promulgated options that an employee has in exercising his or her voice. We are particularly interested in mechanisms of employee voice that are direct such that, it is the employees themselves who utilize the organization's conflict management system to address disputes or complaints arising from the employment relationship. This is in contrast to other broader forms of voice that are often indirect such as employee involvement or problem solving committees, joint partnerships or committees. Although through the latter form employees may seek to raise complaints about employment conditions or treatment, it is done in a collective and representational form. Our focus is on individual centered mechanisms for dispute resolution that are utilized as an alternative to more traditional forums.

This chapter examines the nature of the options with a focus on informal and formal mechanisms. It considers the various determinants of an organization's decision to grant their employees voice in the resolution of workplace conflicts. It then examines the determinants of employee willingness to use voice mechanisms and discuss steps that organizations may take to reduce the barriers voice usage. It further examines managerial reactions to voice usage and discusses ways to enhance managerial receptivity to voice processes. The chapter concludes with a discussion of implications for HR policy and practice.

Human Resource Management Practices and Alternative Conflict Resolution

Generally, organizations have considerable discretion when designing their dispute resolution processes. Two notable exceptions to this discretion involve circumstances when the employer is bound by a collective bargaining agreement or when they operate under laws that establish specific forums or representative structures for evaluating employee claims of mistreatment or wrongful termination. This section begins by briefly describing these exceptions before turning to non-union forms of dispute resolution.

Within unionized settings, formal mechanisms and procedures have arisen over time that serve to channel employee voice over disputes arising from the implementation of the collective bargaining agreement (Lewin and Peterson, 1988). In the North American context, the predominant mechanism for resolving employment disputes for employees arising from collective bargaining agreements remains the grievance process—a multi-step progressive system that has changed little since its introduction and which typically culminates in labor arbitration (Eaton and Keefe, 1999). Within this formalized process, the initial steps often involve informal attempts to resolve the dispute (Lewin, 1987). Through elected representatives, employees are able to exercise voice by calling attention to mistreatment, alleged managerial wrongdoing, or perceived contract violations. As such, labor arbitration functions as an alternative to the courts with respect to adjudicating disputes arising from the application and enforcement of collective bargaining agreements (Stone, 1981). The courts in the US have affirmed the appropriateness of labor arbitration as a mechanism to resolve alleged statutory violations in employment practices (Mahony and Wheeler, 2010).

Many countries outside the US rely on specialized labor tribunals or formal labor courts to resolve employment disputes and thus serve as a mechanism of employee voice (Wheeler, Klaas, and Mahony, 2004). These mechanisms represent neutral and highly formalized structures for addressing employment disputes. In addition to enforcing statutory and contractual rights, these adjudicative bodies typically incorporate the broader concepts of individual justice between the employee and employer (Wheeler and Rojot, 1992).

In workplaces not governed by collectively bargaining contracts or under the jurisdiction of state-sanctioned forums for dispute resolution (e.g. specialized labor courts, works councils), employers retain the right to design and implement mechanisms for resolving disputes arising from the employment relationship (Roche and Teague, 2012). Typically, the nature and design of such systems are influenced by the firm's overall human resource practices and strategies. Consequently, there remains substantial variation in both the structure and nature of these systems. This variation ranges from informal and ad hoc approaches to highly structured and often binding approaches involving third-party decision-makers. These processes further vary in the extent to which the disputant retains some measure of control into the process and whether acceptance of the outcome is voluntary versus mandatory processes that produce binding outcomes.

In light of this variation, scholars have sought ways to categorize these systems in an effort to aid comparisons and evaluations of justice and fairness. For example, Ury, Brett, and Goldberg (1988) and Costantino and Merchant (1996) each delineate three approaches to resolving disputes: power based, rights based, and interest based. Power-based methods (e.g. strikes, lockouts, or work-to-rule tactics) traditionally rely upon collective action to influence an outcome. The remaining two methods, rights based and interest based, are intended to address individual-level concerns rather than collective concerns. Rights-based systems are primarily concerned with the determination of the individual disputant's rights or entitlements under the law or contract. Interest-based systems, in contrast, are concerned with resolving the dispute such that the respective interests of the parties may be mutually satisfied. Bendersky (2003) using the locus of decision-making authority as her central organizing principle further identifies three approaches to managing conflict at work. The first, rights based, relies on the determination by external third parties who form judgments and issues decisions based on prevailing employment laws or contracts of employment. As such, this definition is consistent with that of Ury et al. (1988) and Constantino and Merchant (1996). The second category, identified as "interest-based neutrals," also relies on a third party to the dispute, but the ultimate the resolution is left to the parties to the dispute. Consistent with earlier definitions of interest-based approaches, the third-party neutral is focused on helping the parties to achieve an outcome that is mutually acceptable and that addresses the concerns and desires of the parties to the dispute. Lastly, "negotiated processes" refers to systems where the individual disputant seeks resolution without the use of third-party intervention. Still others talk about dispute resolution processes as systems of dispute resolution. Such systems incorporate multiple approaches that may or may not yield complementarities (Constantino and Merchant, 1996; Rowe, 1997; Bendersky, 2003).

Looking across the myriad categorizations, employer promulgated systems of workplace dispute resolution typically vary along four dimensions:

- Informal versus formal processes. The first dimension is whether the system involves informal or formalized processes. Informal systems, sometimes referred to as negotiated systems of ADR (Bendersky, 2003), encompass systems that put the onus on the individual to raise their dispute with management or with a co-worker in an effort to achieve a satisfactory resolution. Included in this definition are any processes or attempts by an individual to satisfy their concerns, needs, or wants that do not involve invoking the organization's formal dispute resolution process (Olson-Buchanan and Boswell, 2002). In formal systems, employers define the boundaries and scope through which an employee may have input into the resolution. Such systems have clearly articulated and linear steps that the disputant must adhere to. If a satisfactory result is not achieved then the disputant may escalate the dispute to the next step.

- Internal versus external. The second dimension focuses on the extent to which disputes are resolved internally or rely on external, third parties. Internal systems cover a range of procedures that exclusively involve members of the disputant's organization. Other dispute resolution processes call for the use of neutral third parties to either facilitate or determine outcomes in disputes. Informal systems exclusively involve internal decision-makers while formal processes may involve either internal or external parties.

- Binding versus non-binding. Wheeler et al. (2004) differentiated among employer-sponsored dispute resolution mechanisms by the extent to which they intrude upon managerial prerogatives. What they labeled as *soft* dispute resolution systems are those that do not result in a final and binding decision on both the employer and employee but rather provide a forum for achieving a mutually agreed upon solution. *Hard* systems, in contrast, rely on third-party decision-makers (either internal or external to the organization) to produce final and typically binding decisions. Stated differently, does the system result in a decision that is binding upon both parties or is either party able to pursue their claim often through adjudication in the courts? In systems that are non-binding both parties maintain their right to further pursue their claim if they are dissatisfied with the outcome reached in the final step of the then employer's dispute resolution process. In contrast, in processes that result in a binding decision the parties are generally precluded from challenging the outcome of the final step.

- Rights based versus interest based. As discussed above, organizations may choose to either limit or expand the purpose and thus scope of their dispute resolution procedures. Rights-based systems narrow the use of employee voice to those disputes stemming from legal or contractual rights or entitlements. Rights-based systems therefore focus on determining whether a violation occurred, and if so, whether the offender receives their due punishment (Darley, Carlsmith, and Robinson, 2000). In these systems, the punishment is the outcome and thus the future interests or concerns of the employee's peers or the organization are not explicitly considered.

Systems that afford employees the widest latitude to express concerns or issues are deemed interest-based systems. The intent is to find a resolution that mutually satisfies the interests of the parties involved (Bendersky, 2003). Interest-based mechanisms may also serve restorative justice outcomes by incorporating the voices of the victim or stakeholders to the dispute. Focusing on interests helps to foster justice by explicitly incorporating a constructive dialog between the relevant stakeholders (Christie, 1997). In interest-based models, therefore, the focus is on restoring the victim rather than seeking retributive sanctions (Braithwaite, 2002).

Combining these four dimensions we find that informal systems are internal, non-binding, and interest based. Formal systems of voice may or may not include external third parties, may be either interest or rights based, and may produce either a binding or non-binding outcome. However, interest-based systems may only yield non-binding outcomes. Most ADR systems involve a mix of informal and formal voice mechanisms. The next section briefly reviews several common employer promulgated conflict resolution mechanisms through which employees may exercise their voice.

Non-union Alternative Dispute Resolution Procedures

Open door policies are typically the first step in an organization's multistep dispute resolution process (Foulkes, 1980). As such, employees are encouraged, or in some cases required, to discuss an array of problems first with their immediate supervisor or another higher-level manager without the fear of reprisal (McCabe, 2002; Mahony and Klaas, 2008). Open door policies therefore represent informal dispute resolution procedures that involve internal decision-makers only, produce outcomes that are non-binding, and typically focus on an interests-based resolution to the conflict.

Increasingly, employers are adding an ombudsperson to their dispute resolution system. Ombuds are internal neutrals whose primary role is to facilitate the resolution of the dispute by serving as a go-between the disputant and management (Kandel and Frumer, 1994; McDermott and Berkeley, 1996). By facilitating communication between the parties, the ombudsperson seeks an interest-based resolution by helping both sides achieve a mutually acceptable settlement. To the extent that ombuds are not able to impose binding resolutions on either party the employee is able to retain some control over the outcome. This is formal dispute resolution mechanism to the extent that the boundaries and scope of the Ombud's authority is predetermined by the organization. As mechanisms of voice, one criticism of Ombuds stems from their status as an employee. Specifically, employees may question the Ombud's independence from management thus limiting their perceived effectiveness (Cooper, Nolan, and Bales, 2000).

A growing number of organizations have incorporated mediation into their dispute resolution strategy (Feuille, 1999). In multi-step processes, mediation typically serves as the penultimate step prior to adjudication or arbitration. The mediation process relies on rules and agreed upon norms and is thus a formal voice mechanism. While mediation largely utilizes third-party neutrals, many organizations are training and developing internal mediators to facilitate the resolution of employment disputes (Lipsky, Seeber, and Fincher, 2003). Whether internal or external, mediators are not empowered to issue final or binding decisions. Rather, they employ an interest-based approach and aim to provide opportunities for the parties to identify a mutually agreeable solution to an employment problem in a relatively non-adversarial setting (McDermott and Berkeley, 1996). It may further lead to early settlement while serving to redirect emotions (Harkavy, 1999). This is particularly beneficial for disputants who remain employed by the organization (Mahony and Klaas, 2008). As these are non-precedent setting and confidential settings, mediation may afford the parties greater flexibility when discussing possible resolutions and lead to options that are best suited to the idiosyncrasies of each case (Cooper, Nolan, and Bales, 2000).

The use of peer review panels is frequently associated with other high-performance work practices (General Accounting Office, 1995; Colvin, 2003). As a formal dispute resolution approach, peer review emerged in the 1970s and 1980s as part General Electric's overall union avoidance strategy (Grote and Wimberly, 1993). While the structure of peer review varies considerably across organizations, they are each intended to shift many employee relations decisions to an internal committee comprised of an employee's peers (Cooper, Nolan, and Bales, 2000). In a hearing-like setting, these panels are charged with interpreting and applying employer policies within the context of the dispute and thus represent a rights-based process (Ewing, 1989). For the majority of peer review panels, the decisions reached are final and binding. In the US, peer review panels that can only issue either non-binding decisions or recommendations risk being declared a labor organization by the National Labor Relations Board and thus violate the Section 8(a)(2) of the National Labor Relations Act (see *Keeler Brass Automotive Group* (1995);[1] *Sparks Nugget, Inc.* (1980)[2]).

One of the most controversial of the employer promulgated systems of voice currently in use is employment arbitration. This approach utilizes an external third-party neutral to resolve employment disputes in highly formalized court-like procedures bound by rules and standards. Organizations that adopt this process do so as an alternative to litigation and at times as part of their overall union avoidance strategy. This approach has steadily gained in popularity among employers since the early 1990s (Howard, 1995). Presently, it is estimated that approximately one-third of non-union employees are covered by arbitration agreements (Colvin, 2011).

In practice, employment arbitration agreements may be included in individual contracts of employment as a mechanism to resolve all disputes arising under the terms of that contract. With other employers, the arbitration procedures are designed to cover whole classes of employees (Lipsky and Seeber, 2006). Most arbitration procedures restrict the nature of claims to those for which the law already provides a remedy, such as statutory claims of discrimination, and are thus limited to pursuing only rights-based issues. However, a minority of employers have allowed their procedures to apply to any dispute arising out of the employment relationship, thus serving to address both interest- and rights-based issues. Finally, employers may further choose to implement arbitration procedures that are voluntary and thus may serve as a beneficial and viable alternative to litigation (Wheeler, Klaas, and Mahony, 2004). However, the preponderance of procedures require employees to waive their rights to sue their employer as a precondition of employment, and agree to arbitrate employment disputes. These mandatory procedures result in binding outcomes.

As noted above, organizations often invest significant resources in order to ensure access to voice processes and, more broadly, to encourage employees to voice concerns and ideas to organizational decision-makers (Colvin, 2003; Harlos, 2010). And, as suggested, such investments are designed to achieve a number of organizational objectives (Lewin, 1987; Olson-Buchanan and Boswell, 2009). While research has documented how firms are able to benefit from such investments (Olson-Buchanan and Boswell, 2008; Brinsfield, Edwards, and Greenberg, 2009), there are substantial challenges associated with actually realizing these benefits (Burris, 2012). The impact of voice systems and processes depends on how employees evaluate opportunities for voice as well as how managers and others within the organization react to the actual usage of voice. However, responses by employees and managers potentially can be affected by a number of HR policies and practices. Thus, from an HR perspective, it is critical to understand what policies and initiatives are likely to support efforts by the organization to effectively manage the voice processes in organizations. Two questions are likely to be particularly relevant in understanding how to effectively manage voice processes. First, given what we know about what determines employee willingness to exercise different forms of voice, what steps can managers and organizations take to reduce barriers to voice usage? Second, given what we know about managerial reactions to voice, what steps can be taken to facilitate managerial receptivity to voice? We will first review what is known about factors that determine the usage of voice and also factors that determine managerial reactions to voice. We then will discuss the implications of what is known about these factors for HR policy and practice.

EMPLOYER WILLINGNESS TO IMPLEMENT ADR

Scholars from multiple academic disciplines have sought to articulate the motivations and benefits to firms who adopt mechanisms of employee voice. Economists, industrial relations scholars, legal scholars, human resource and organizational scholars have each put forth explanations that are at times complementary and at other times competing. The trend towards integrating or incorporating workplace dispute resolution mechanisms has evolved for myriad reasons ranging from economic, legal, and strategic. This range of internal and external forces influencing the adoption of dispute resolution procedures is briefly discussed here.

From an economist's perspective there are, to some extent, competing theories explaining the reasons for an employer's willingness to invest in the resources necessary to implement ADR procedures. For example, an employer may invest if they believe that doing so would aid their efforts at union avoidance. Under this theory, employers strive to provide avenues for employees to express their concerns or to challenge employment decisions in an attempt to serve as a substitute to the well-established union grievance system. Recent research supports this theory, particularly for organizations that adopt peer review (Colvin, 2003, 2004). Peer review systems were particularly prevalent in organizations that experienced significant union organizing attempts and who were in otherwise highly unionized industries (Colvin, 2003). Of the many forms of alternative dispute procedures peer review appears especially well suited to a union substitution strategy as such procedures provide employee involvement and input into addressing employment disputes. In practice, peer panelists focus on the application of the employer's rules and judge cases on the extent to which the employer's rules were applied and thus do not consider broader fairness or justice issues (Wheeler, Klaas, and Mahony, 2004).

Alternatively, as Kaufman and Levine (2000) note, to the extent that employers operate under the doctrine of employment at will, it may be more efficient from a transaction cost perspective to simply terminate employees rather than investing in the resources necessary to implement and administer conflict resolution system. They further put forth a market imperfections argument which suggests that employers may have little to no direct experience with the costs associated with defending allegations of wrongful termination. This lack of experience translates into less motivation to adopt formal alternative dispute resolution systems (Kaufman and Levine, 2000). The efficacy of this market imperfections argument, however, is diminished given the prevalence of organizations that have instituted a formal dispute resolution procedure (Delaney, Lewin, and Ichniowski, 1989; Feuille and Chachere, 1995; Colvin, 2003). Indeed, a growing body of research cites the restrictions and limits on the at-will status of employees coupled with the perceived risks of litigation associated with wrongful termination claims as an important determinant for the adoption of ADR procedures and binding employment arbitration in particular (Colvin, 2006). Aside from the perceived risks associated with awards in employment disputes, the legal expenses associated with defending employ-ment claims (irrespective of their individual merit) perhaps reflects the largest eco-nomic threat to employers (Estreicher, 2001). To that end, ADR represents a cheaper and faster opportunity for employers to resolve employment disputes (Wheeler et al., 2004). While ADR, particularly mandatory and binding processes, may help employers resolve disputes faster, with less risk, and at lower cost, litigation pressures are not the sole motivator for the adoption of ADR. In particular, they do not fully explain the wide-spread use of informal or formal non-binding forms of conflict resolution.

With respect to internal determinants of ADR, the strategic human resource man-agement literature shows substantial evidence supporting the link between what are deemed components of high-performance work systems (HPWS) and firm level outcomes. While the term "HPWS" covers a range of ideas and approaches to work (Osterman, 1994; Appelbaum et al., 2000), central although not exclusive to most con-ceptualizations is the inclusion of voice mechanisms to enhance employee participation and involvement (Appelbaum and Batt, 1994; Pil and MacDuffie, 1996). In addition to ensuring employees have the skills and motivation to perform well, the opportunity for input or voice is also considered central to achieving the gains associated with HPWS (Boxhall and Purcell, 2003).

Providing employees with voice mechanisms is associated with numerous benefits to the organization including aiding with overcoming information asymmetries (Freeman and Lazear, 1995), reducing some transaction costs (Kaufman and Levine, 2000), and enhancing procedural justice perceptions (Hammer, 2000). Support within the strategic HR literature has been found for the practice of implementing bundles of HR processes. Specifically, performance gains are likely to be enhanced when complementarities exist among the bundled HR practices (MacDuffie, 1995; Huslid, 1995; Ichnioswki et al., 1996). Research has further shown the importance of including voice mechanisms within an organization's overall HR system (Appelbaum and Batt, 1994; Becker and Huselid, 1998; Capelli and Neumark, 2001). Opportunities for voice enhances employee perceptions of fairness and justice—outcomes both associated and consistent with other elements of HPWS (Kochan and Osterman, 1994; Folger and Cropanzano, 1998). Lastly, Roche and Teague (2012) found that conflict management practices, when embedded within broader high-performance practices, were linked with lower turnover and absenteeism, and increased labor productivity.

EMPLOYEE WILLINGNESS TO USE VOICE

The impact of organizational efforts to provide meaningful voice within the workplace depends on employee perceptions regarding voice opportunities, particularly the likely benefits as well as the risks associated with using voice. A broad range of determinants of employee usage of voice have been examined, in a number of different institutional contexts. Many of these determinants relate to individual differences that affect the willingness to make suggestions or identify concerns within the workplace. For example, "Big Five" personality characteristics have been found to be related to the use of informal voice as have individual differences such as proactivity and felt responsibility (LePine and Van Dyne, 1998; LePine and Van Dyne, 2001; Seibert, Kraimer, and Crant, 2001; Botero and Van Dyne, 2009; Thomas, Whitman, and Viswesvaran, 2010; Bjorkelo, Einarsen, and Matthiesen, 2010). While important, such determinants are unlikely to be subject to organizational influence and, as such, will not receive significant attention in this chapter.

Numerous studies have also shown that both formal and informal voice are associated with factors that provide motivations to exercise voice, such as aversive workplace conditions, overall levels of workplace conflict, and abusive supervisor behavior (Katz, Kochan, and Gobeille, 1983; Miceli, and Near, 1984; Miceli and Near, 1985; Miceli and Near, 1988; Labig Jr. and Greer, 1988; Klaas, 1989; Bemmels, Reshef, and Stratton-Devine, 1991; Turnley and Feldman, 1999; Bamberger, Kohn, and Nahum-Shani, 2008). These factors all relate to conflict or workplace difficulties that might potentially be addressed via the use of voice. These factors are indicators of the likely need for voice, not processes that might inhibit or facilitate voice in response to a given workplace environment. As such, these factors are not the primary focus of this chapter, as we are concerned with how organizations might influence the willingness of employees to use voice when they see opportunities to suggest process improvements or highlight workplace concerns.

One set of factors that may be subject to organizational influence relates to behavior and attitudes exhibited by leaders regarding employee use of voice. Findings suggest that where leaders are seen as being open to new ideas, employees are more likely to engage in informal voice by suggesting ways to improve processes and performance in the unit (Burris and Detert, and Chiaburu, 2008; Detert and Trevino, 2010). Further, research has shown that informal voice regarding ways to improve processes and performance is more frequent when leader–member exchange is high and when a manager is perceived as a transformational leader (Van Dyne, Kamdar, and Joireman, 2008; Botero and Van Dyne, 2009; Liu, Zhu, and Yang, 2010).

Attitudes toward the organization also have been found to affect the willingness to use voice, though the relationship appears to vary with the type of voice (Klaas, Olson-Buchanan, and Ward, 2012). Employees who more strongly identify with the organization and who are more loyal to the firm are also more likely to engage in informal voice to improve organizational processes and performance (Liu, Zhu, and Yang, 2010). Such a relationship is very consistent with what might be expected in light of the exit, voice, loyalty, neglect model (Farrell, 1983; Rusbult, Farrell, Rogers, and Mainous, 1988; Mellahi, Budhwar, and Li, 2010). Employees who are more strongly committed to the organization are more willing to accept the risks associated with exercising voice in order to improve organizational processes. The relationship has been observed both for informal voice and voice designed to suggest improvements within the context of suggestion systems and other more formal systems for voice (Lipponen, Bardi, and Haapamaki, 2008).

Similar findings have been observed with regard to job satisfaction. While dissatisfied employees may be more likely to use voice than satisfied employees at a given point in time (Allen and Keaveny, 1985), satisfied employees are more likely to engage in voice (at least informal voice) in response to deteriorating conditions (Busbult, Farrell, Rogers, and Mainous, 1988; Olson-Buchanan, 1997). More satisfied employees may be more motivated to maintain a positive workplace environment and, therefore, more willing to use informal voice in response to the emergence of factors that would damage that environment.

It is important to note, however, that this positive relationship between voice and variables such as organizational identification and loyalty has not been observed for all forms of voice. Evidence suggests that the nature of the impact associated with loyalty and organizational identification is likely to be different when addressing formal voice designed to protest workplace treatment. Loyalty has been found to discourage formal voice that is protesting treatment within the organization (Olson-Buchanan and Boswell, 2002; Luchak, 2003; Tangirala and Ramanujam, 2008). Research suggests that when employees have concerns about treatment within the workplace, at least some formal mechanisms for addressing those concerns are seen quite differently from more informal mechanisms. Raising a problem informally may be viewed as consistent with collaborative problem-solving. Using a formal process often calls for third-party intervention and publically challenges managerial decision-making. With many systems for formal voice, usage is a signal that an employee's relationship with a manager and/or the organization is in need of repair. As such, formal voice for protesting workplace treatment may often be viewed as a last resort (Boroff and Lewin, 1997; Olson-Buchanan and Boswell, 2002). Not surprisingly, then, more-loyal employees tend to prefer informal to formal processes for protesting workplace treatment.

However, it should be noted that structures for formal voice differ substantially. Many such structures are explicitly designed to be used only after informal processes have failed and, moreover, tend to be adversarial in nature (Klaas, Olson-Buchanan, and Ward, 2012). Such structures make it particularly likely that a negative relationship would emerge between loyalty and organizational identification and use of this form of voice. What is less clear is whether this negative relationship exists when the system for formal voice is less adversarial and when norms and systems exist to encourage this form of voice (Kolb, 1987; Amadei and Lehrburger, 1996). For example, systems that rely on an ombudsman for resolving disputes allow for issues and concerns to be addressed in a less confrontational manner, frequently allowing for mediation processes to be employed. As an additional example, within the unionized sector, formal grievance processes are supported by the involvement of the union, with union representatives providing social support to those raising concerns about workplace treatment (Lewin and Peterson, 1988; Klaas, 1989). Such social support has the potential to make voice registering protest seem legitimate and desirable, even among employees who identify with the organization.

Another category of factors that have been found to affect usage of voice relates to the perceived risks associated with exercising voice. This set of factors is particularly relevant in that organizations have at least some influence with regard to the risks that are perceived to be associated with voice. Studies consistently show that the willingness to use informal voice to suggest improvements within the organization is significantly affected by perceptions of psychological safety. Where the climate in the unit and the behavior of the leader signal that it is appropriate and desirable to offer ideas and make suggestions, such informal voice is much more likely (Edmondson, 1999; Detert and Burris, 2007; Burris, 2012).

Evidence has also emerged to suggest that risk is important with regard to voice that is used to address concerns about workplace treatment. For example, in the whistle-blowing literature, researchers have found that this form of voice will be more likely when individuals believe that it will be supported within the organization (Miceli and Near, 1984; Miceli and Near, 1985; Miceli and Near, 1988; Near and Miceli, 1996; Lee, Heilmann, and Near, 2004) and when policies or regulations protect individuals from retaliation for the exercise of this form of voice (Miceli and Near, 1989; Near, Dworkin, and Miceli, 1993; Miceli, Rehg, Near, and Ryan, 1999). This issue of perceived risk can also be seen in the role that anonymity has been found to play in encouraging the use of whistle-blowing (Elliston, 1982; Miceli et al., 1988).

The importance of perceptions regarding the risks associated with using voice can also be seen in research showing that informal voice is more likely among employees who have alternative employment opportunities (Rusbult et al., 1988). Employees who believe they could easily obtain employment elsewhere are, perhaps, less likely to be concerned about negative reactions to any suggestions that they offer. In a similar vein, formal voice protesting treatment in the workplace is more likely among employees who see the firm as being more dependent upon employees. Where the firm is seen as being highly dependent on the workforce, employees are, perhaps, more likely to see the firm as being reluctant to react harshly to the exercise of voice (Bacharach and Bamberger, 2004).

Perceptions of risk can also be affected by questions about whether voice is a legitimate or appropriate activity. Organizations are hierarchical structures and, in many such structures, norms emerge about whether employees should offer ideas and suggestions or raise concerns about workplace treatment. Where norms within the organization stress the legitimacy of voice, the perceived risk associated with using voice is likely to be lower. Evidence for this argument can be found in research showing that informal voice is more frequent among employees who work in groups that value voice (Morrison, Wheeler-Smith, and Kamdar, 2011). Research has also shown that organizational policies and initiatives designed to affect the legitimacy of voice affect the frequency with which voice is actually used. Publicity campaigns designed to highlight the need for employees to improve organizational processes through the use of the suggestion system have been found to affect the usage of this form of voice as has the use of rewards and recognition (Leach et al., 2006; Rapp and Eklund, 2007). Organizational policies that obligate voice also have been found to be important. Such obligations both legitimize voice and create risks for not exercising voice. Specifically, the use of whistle-blowing is more common when organizational policies mandate the reporting of wrongdoing and when organizational roles explicitly require such reporting (Trevino and Victor, 1992; Rothwell and Baldwin, 2007a, 2007b).

Organizations may also be able to affect the usage of voice by virtue of policies and procedures that affect the perceived utility associated with voice. For example, the use of informal voice was found to be higher among employees who perceived themselves as being influential within their work group and having high levels of personal control over the work group (Tangirala and Ramanujam, 2008b; Venkataramani and Tangirala, 2010). Where such influence and control is high, employees are more likely to see themselves as being able to influence how suggestions or concerns are perceived, making it more likely that voice will yield positive results. The impact associated with perceived utility of voice can also be seen in research on voice exercised via suggestion systems. Managerial indifference and delayed responses have both been found to negatively affect use of this form of voice, just as the presence of a learning culture has been found to positively affect voice of this sort (Gorfin, 1969; Leach, Stride, and Wood, 2006).

MANAGERIAL REACTIONS TO EMPLOYEE USE OF VOICE

Whether systems or processes for voice are likely to be effective will depend, in part, on how managers react to actual usage of voice, whether it be formal or informal. Hostile reactions to the use of voice, for example, may well raise concerns among employees about the likely consequences for them personally if they offer suggestions or raise concerns (Burris, 2012). Indeed, one of the more consistent findings within the literature on informal voice is that employee voice behavior is significantly determined by perceptions about whether the leader is open to suggestions and concerns (Detert and Burris, 2007; Walumbwa and Schaubroeck, 2009). Perceptions regarding psychological safety have also been found to significantly affect voice. Where employees see the use of voice as being risky, due to concerns about how others might react, voice is much less likely (Edmondson, 1999; Burris, Detert, and Chiaburu, 2008). And leadership behavior is likely to be a key factor in determining perceptions of psychological safety (Detert and Trevino, 2010). For many employees, the relationship they have with their supervisor is very important and concerns about damaging that relationship may well limit the willingness to exercise voice. Indeed, Milliken, Morrison, and Hewlin (2003) found that roughly a quarter of the employees studied stated that concerns about damaging their relationship with a supervisor limited their use of voice.

Reactions from supervisors are also critical because defensiveness on the part of a manager may affect whether ideas and concerns are actually considered, as opposed to being dismissed without serious consideration. Since voice is often encouraged in order for managers to obtain information about key developments and potential process improvement, managerial reactions are likely to be a critical factor in determining whether this objective is achieved (Milliken, Morrison, and Hewlin, 2003). Where managers take offense or react in a defensive way to suggestions or concerns, their capacity to learn from employee input is likely to be substantially reduced, as is the capacity for the organization to benefit from employee input.

Given the potential implications associated with negative managerial reactions to the usage of voice, questions are raised about whether indeed such negative reactions are observed in a meaningful way and also about factors that may limit the potential for such negative managerial reactions. It should be noted, of course, that reactions to voice may vary across different forms of voice. Voice that is constructive and designed to improve organizational processes and performance may well be seen very differently than voice that takes the form of a formal complaint, particularly when that formal complaint is made to a higher-level manager after being denied by an employee's immediate supervisor. Arguably, informal suggestions are least likely to be seen as self-seeking, confrontational, or a threat to the authority of the manager. However, even with informal voice focused on suggestions for improving unit processes and performance, evidence suggests significant potential for negative managerial reactions. In a laboratory study that manipulated key attributes associated with the message, the context, and the source, it was found that managers rated the performance of employees more negatively when employees used voice to present a problem without also identifying a solution (compared to when voice identified a solution to the concern raised). Similarly, when an employee was not already seen as trustworthy, the usage of voice also resulted in lower performance evaluations. Finally, when voice was not considered timely, the usage of voice resulted in negative evaluations (Whiting, Maynes, Podsakoff, and Podsakoff, 2011). This study is interesting because it suggests that while there may be conditions under which voice can be used without negatively affecting managerial evaluation of employee performance, there are also likely to be many situations where the usage of voice will be viewed negatively by a manager. This study also identified important mediating processes, suggesting that negative evaluations are less likely when the voice is seen as constructive and when the employee engaged in voice is seen as more likeable.

A similar pattern of findings was observed by Burris (2012) who found that informal voice that was presented in a more challenging manner lead to more negative evaluations of the employee, in comparison to voice that was seen as more supportive. Further, the use of challenging (versus supportive) voice led managers to perceive employees as being less loyal and more threatening.

Negative managerial reactions to voice have also been documented with the use of more formal voice. Field research has shown that increased grievance activity by an employee is associated with lower performance evaluations (Klaas and DeNisi, 1989). Such a pattern is consistent with the suggestion that voice, particularly formal grievances made to more senior managers, can be seen as a challenge to the manager, potentially affecting how the manager perceives the employee and their performance. It should be noted, however, that the effects observed could also be due to objective changes in the performance of the employee, perhaps in reaction to incidents that led to the filing of the grievance (Boswell and Olson-Buchanan, 2004). It is also important to note that the field research examining formal grievance activity did not explore the conditions likely to minimize the potential for negative managerial reactions. While the laboratory work examining informal voice has offered insight to how organizations might work to minimize managerial reactions to this form of voice, research is relatively silent on policies or procedural mechanisms that might be used to reduce negative managerial reactions.

Research examining the conditions that discourage hostile reactions to voice has only begun with regard to informal voice aimed at improving unit performance and processes (Burris, 2012). And, as noted above, research examining managerial reactions to formal voice as well as voice protesting workplace treatment is very limited. However, further research is clearly warranted. Consider when voice is being used to protest treatment by a manager or an organization. Such voice requires an employee to challenge a manager, making defensive reactions more likely. The challenging nature of this voice is even more apparent when this type of voice is also formal in nature, because formalization typically requires the employee to appeal a manager's decision to a higher-level manager or third-party decision-maker. Such voice is more likely to be seen as challenging managerial authority and, further, demands a "solution" that has already been rejected by the manager (Klaas, Olson-Buchanan, and Ward, 2012). It should be stressed that further research addressing conditions that might pre-empt negative reactions by managers will be necessary before it is possible to offer precise guidance with regard to HR policies and initiatives.

Researchers examining conditions that affect reactions to informal voice aimed at process improvements found that communication practices used by employees when engaging in voice played an important role (Whiting, Maynes, Podsakoff, and Podsakoff, 2011; Burris, 2012). Similarly, a focus on communication practices might be justified when examining voice used to protest workplace treatment (whether done via formal or informal means). Little is known about whether negative reactions are mitigated by communication that incorporates a neutral presentation style, the documentation of events, and the referencing of accepted standards within the workplace. Further, because of the challenging nature of this type of voice, employee expression of regret for creating difficulties for the manager may well be impactful. Issues relating to timing of voice aimed at workplace treatment also deserve future research attention. In some instances, voice is used to demand immediate rectification and in other instances voice is used to alert the manager to the need for some form of action at some point. With the latter, the manager is allowed some latitude and discretion. In some instances, a decision about a response must be made within the context of a single meeting with all parties involved. In other instances, questions and responses are addressed in an iterative fashion, potentially altering reactions to voice.

Procedural factors deserve attention as well, as voice to protest workplace treatment can be made in a variety of ways. Procedures can encourage or allow for voice to be presented directly by the employee in an unsolicited fashion, to be solicited by the manager as part of a structured process for getting feedback, to be presented through a third party, or to be expressed anonymously (Olson-Buchanan and Boswell, 2009). Procedural factors that affect how voice is presented have the potential to affect tendencies toward defensive reactions to criticism which, in turn, may affect attributions made about the employee. As such, the literature might well benefit from research examining how procedural variation affects managerial reactions to voice used to protest workplace conditions.

Research may also be called for with regard to the role played by employee attributes in determining how voice protesting treatment will be perceived by managers. With informal voice protesting treatment, negative reactions may well be mitigated by the strength of the relationship between the employee and the manager. Where that relationship is strong, attributions regarding why voice is being used are likely to be very different compared to when there is a weak relationship (Bradfield and Aquino, 1999). Where the relationship is strong, managers are more likely to attribute voice to there being problematic issues within the workplace. However, with formal voice, the employee must typically escalate their grievance to a higher level within the organization, after having been denied by their immediate manager. When a strong relationship exists between a manager and an employee, the manager may view an employee "going over his/her head" as a violation of their psychological contract, making a negative reaction even more likely. Managerial attributes also deserve attention in that attributes such as self-control potentially are quite relevant in affecting reactions to voice. Negative reactions are often hypothesized because of defensive reactions to the criticism implied in voice used to protest treatment. However, where managerial self-control is greater, managers will likely resist defensive reactions to criticism, making them more capable of understanding the issues being raised without forming negative attributions about the employee. Validation provided for the use of voice may also be relevant and deserving of attention by researchers. Such validation could come in the form of the outcome associated with voice, such as when an employee's appeal to a higher-level manager is actually granted by the manager. Such validation could also come in the form of cultural norms within the organization that emphasize the right of an employee to raise concerns about treatment, even through formal processes that consume the time and energy of senior managers. Such a validation culture could also come in the form of well-established and clearly accepted formal processes for exercising voice.

The degree to which the manager's authority and reputation are being challenged may also play an important role and, thus, may deserve research attention. For example, when assessing managerial reactions to voice used to protest workplace conditions, consideration might be given to whether the manager in question is responsible for the decision being challenged or whether the manager in question is reviewing concerns about a lower-level manager's decision. Where a manager is not responsible for the decision being challenged, defensive reactions may be less likely to result, reducing tendencies towards negative attributions about the employee (Bradfield and Aquino, 1999). Attention might also be given to the distinction between managerial reactions to voice expressed specifically to the manager versus reactions in a manager observing voice protesting treatment expressed to a superior within the organization.

While research attention has been given to managerial reactions to voice, attention to date has been somewhat limited (Whiting, Maynes, Podsakoff, and Podsakoff, 2011). And given the importance of managerial reactions in determining the impact associated with systems for voice, additional research in this area is clearly needed.

Implications for HR Policy and Practice

Systems and initiatives designed to allow for and encourage voice are intended to accomplish a number of important human resource objectives. However, whether firms are actually able to achieve these objectives depends on a number of factors relating to how voice processes are managed and implemented in organizations (Brinsfield, Edwards, and Greenberg, 2009). This chapter focuses on how the management of voice processes might affect the willingness of employees to actually use voice and managerial reactions to voice when it is used. From an HR perspective, the most critical factors are those potentially under the control and influence of the organization (McCabe, 1997).

First we will discuss factors with the potential to affect managerial reactions to the use of voice. As noted, these reactions are critical both because they affect whether employees will be willing to use voice going forward and because they affect the organization's capacity to extract content and ideas for improvement from employee use of voice (Whiting, Maynes, Podsakoff, and Podsakoff, 2011). And recognizing that there are different types of voice, with managerial reactions operating differently for these different forms (Klaas, Olson-Buchanan, and Ward, 2012), it is important to also consider how organizations should address managerial reactions to voice across alternative forms. However, it is also important to note that managerial reactions to voice have been found to be important across a broad range of types of voice. From an organizational standpoint, then, effective implementation of systems for voice is likely to require efforts to affect how managers evaluate and respond to voice within the workplace.

The arguments above imply that if organizations are to benefit from systems and processes for employee voice, they may also need to invest in efforts to encourage managerial receptivity to voice. Questions about how to encourage such receptivity raise complex issues, however. While voice may be important for organizational effectiveness, there may well be a point where voice becomes excessive and counterproductive. In some instances, voice (both formal and informal) may be designed to annoy and irritate, perhaps in an effort to exact retribution for prior managerial decisions (Skarlicki and Folger, 1997; Tripp and Bies, 2009). In other instances, employees may fail to exercise appropriate prudence and caution in the use of voice, consuming time and disrupting the productive exchange of information (Pyrillis, 2010). Thus, organizations are confronted with the challenge of encouraging managerial receptivity to voice, but not necessarily in an indiscriminate fashion.

The research cited above highlighted the importance of leader openness and of efforts to encourage employees to perceive their environment as being one where it is safe to exercise voice (Burris, Detert, and Chiaburu, 2008). For organizations, then, questions exist about how best to create norms that encourage managerial behavior that suggests an openness to ideas and concerns. Research has not specifically addressed which policies and practices are critical here. However, a range of plausible options exist. For example, where skip-level managers actively seek voice from employees in a unit, the manager for that unit is likely to more actively seek ideas and concerns so as to not be surprised by what is revealed in the skip-level discussions. Additionally, norms regarding leader openness could be encouraged by incorporating openness to ideas and feedback in systems for 360-degree performance review systems. Organizations could also require managers to document ideas and feedback received as well as constructive responses that were taken over time.

Organizations might also encourage managerial receptivity to voice via efforts to help employees exercise voice in a way that will decrease prospects for a defensive or hostile reaction. In the case of informal voice, such efforts are likely to focus on encouraging constructive communication. In orientation and training programs, giving attention to the need for employee input may be highly appropriate. And in doing so, it may also be appropriate to give attention to methods of exercising voice, with a focus on offering alternatives when criticisms are raised, providing suggestions within a time frame and a forum that allows for a productive response, and using language that is supportive rather than confrontational (Burris, 2012).

With regard to formal voice, attention to structure and process may be relevant to discouraging defensive or hostile reactions. For example, where voice can be provided in an anonymous fashion, while managers may still be defensive, the anonymous nature of voice may pre-empt hostile reactions (Miceli, Roach, and Near, 1988; Frese, Teng, and Wijnen, 1999; Fairbank, Spangler, and Williams, 2003). Similarly, with regard to voice that is designed to protest concerns about treatment by a manager, systems that focus on mediation rather than on adjudication by third parties may have the potential to reduce hostile managerial reactions (Amadei and Lehrburger, 1996). Where the dispute resolution focuses on adversarial processes, formal voice may lead to more hostile reactions (compared to when conflict is addressed in a forum that is focused on facilitating problem-solving). Further, where guided by an ombudsman or a mediator, it may be possible for concerns to be raised in a fashion that is less accusatory.

Efforts to affect managerial reactions to voice are an important part of any effort to ensure that systems for voice are actually used in the way intended. However, it is also important to address employee attitudes and perceptions, as they will affect whether voice processes will be used as intended (Naus, Van Iterson, and Roe, 2007). Consider, for example, the role played by organizational loyalty and identification. Many best practices with regard to employee relations are designed to affect organizational identification and loyalty and these characteristics are associated with increased use of informal voice (Olson-Buchanan and Boswell, 2009). However, these same attributes are negatively related to the willingness to use formal voice when confronted with workplace conflict (Olson-Buchanan and Boswell, 2002). Thus, if organizations attempt to increase informal voice via best practices with regard to employee relations, reductions in the use of formal voice might well be expected. Such reductions would, indeed, be expected unless efforts are also made to structure formal voice processes in a way that would be appealing to loyal and committed employees through increasing the collaborative nature of the formal process, reducing the adversarial nature, providing social support to those considering formal voice, or otherwise altering organizational norms about formal voice.

Findings about the importance of the perceived legitimacy of exercising voice highlight additional ways that organizations might be able to encourage voice (Fuller, Marler, and Hester, 2006; Fuller, Barnett, Hester, Relyea, and Frey, 2007). For example, among organizations that utilize formal systems for encouraging voice, there are differences in the degree to which efforts are made to validate voice usage (Olson-Buchanan and Boswell, 2009). Even where voice is informal, opportunities exist to showcase suggestions or concerns that have been raised and the actions taken in response. Showcasing is also possible where voice is formal, including when it is used to protest managerial actions. Regular communication regarding the number of instances where formal voice was used and efforts to highlight instances where the organization took corrective action in response to employee input may well be critical to helping employees to see the legitimacy of employee voice.

Similar attention may also be called for with regard to actions that demonstrate the likely utility of using voice. Timely responses to suggestions or concerns are likely to be important in that it highlights the employee's capacity for impacting organizational outcomes. Further, perceived utility may also be affected by demonstrating that consideration was given to the input provided by employees, even if the organization does not follow the suggestion made by the employee (Lind and Tyler, 1988).

While there remain important unanswered questions with regard to employee and managerial reactions to voice processes and systems, the available evidence highlights policies, initiatives, and processes through which organizations may be able to better achieve some of the objectives associated with organizational voice procedures and initiatives. Quite clearly, there is substantial diversity across firms in why they make use of voice, with some giving far greater attention to minimizing legal risk and union avoidance (Budd and Colvin, 2008). But to the extent that a firm is attempting to make use of voice to benefit from employee input, build employee commitment, and providing meaningful alternatives to more disruptive responses to workplace conflict (Blancero and Dyer, 1996; Bies, Tripp, and Kramer, 1997; Bies and Tripp, 1998; Bradfield and Aquino, 1999), consideration of the practical implications highlighted here may well be warranted.

NOTES

1. *Keeler Bass Automotive Group*, 317 NLRB 1110 (1995).
2. *Sparks Nugget, Inc.* 230 NLRB 275 (1977).

REFERENCES

Allen, R. E., and Keaveny, T. J. 1985. "Factors Differentiating Grievants and Nongrievants." *Human Relations*, 38(6): 519–34.

Amadei, R. N. and Lehrburger, L. S. 1996. "The World of Mediation: A Spectrum of Styles." *Dispute Resolution Journal*, 51(4): 62–86.

Appelbaum, E., Bailey, T., and Berg, P. 2000. *Manufacturing Advantage: Why High Performance Work Systems Pay Off*. Cornell University Press: Ithaca, NY.

Appelbaum, E. and Batt, R. 1994. *The New American Workplace: Transforming Work Systems in the United States*. Ithca, NY. Cornell University/ILRR Press.

Aquino, K., Tripp, T., and Bies, J. 2006. "Getting Even or Moving On? Power, Procedural Justice, and Types of Offense as Predictors of Revenge, Forgiveness, Reconciliation, and Avoidance in Organizations." *Journal of Applied Psychology*, 91(3): 653–68.

Bacharach, S. and Bamberger, P. 2004. "The Power of Labor to Grieve: The Impact of the Workplace, Labor Market, and Power-Dependence on Employee Grievance Filing." *Industrial & Labor Relations Review*, 57(4): 518–29.

Bae, J. and Lawler, J. J. 2000. Organizational and HRM Strategies in Korea: Impact on Firm Performance in an Emerging Economy. *The Academy of Management Journal*, 43(3): 502–17.

Bamberger, P., Kohn, E., and Nahum-Shani, I. 2008. "Aversive Workplace Conditions and Employee Grievance Filing: The Moderating Effects of Gender and Ethnicity." *Industrial Relations*, 47(2): 229–59.

Banderet, M. E. 1986. "Discipline at the Workplace: A Comparative Study of Law and Practice of 13 Countries." *International Labour Review*, 125(4): 383–99.

Becker, B. and Huselid, M. 1998. "High Performance Work Systems and Work Performance: A Synthesis of Research and Managerial Implications." In G. Ferris (ed.), *Research in Personnel and Human Resources Management*, 16: 53–101. Stamford, CN: JAI Press.

Bemmels, B., Reshef, Y., and Stratton-Devine, K. 1991. "The Roles of Supervisors, Employees, and Stewards in Grievance Initiation." *Industrial & Labor Relations Review*, 45(1): 15–30.

Bendersky, C. 2003. "Organizational Dispute Resolution Systems: A Complementarities Model." *Academy of Management Review*, 28(4): 489–503.

Bies, R. J. and Tripp, T. M. 1998. "Revenge in Organizations: The Good, the Bad, and the Ugly." In R.W. Griffin, A. O'Leary-Kelly, and J. Collins (eds), *Dysfunctional Behavior in Organizations: Deviant and Violent Behavior*. Stamford, CT: Elsevier/JAI Press, 49–67.

Bies, R. J., Tripp, T. M., and Kramer, R. M. 1997. "At the Breaking Point: Cognitive and Social Dynamics of Revenge in Organizations." In R. A. Giacalone and J. Greenberg (eds), *Antisocial Behavior in Organizations*. Thousand Oaks, CA: Sage Publications, Inc, 18–36.

Bjorkelo, B., Einarsen, S., and Matthiesen, S. B. 2010. "Predicting Proactive Behavior at Work: Exploring the Role of Personality as an Antecedent of Whistle-blowing Behavior." *Journal of Occupational & Organizational Psychology*, 83(2): 371–94.

Blancero, D. and Dyer, L. 1996. "Due Process for Non-union Employees: The Influence of System Characteristics on Fairness Perceptions." *Human Resource Management*, 35(3): 343–59.

Boroff, K. E. and Lewin, D. 1997. "Loyalty, Voice, and Intent to Exit a Union Firm: A Conceptual and Empirical Analysis." *Industrial & Labor Relations Review*, 51: 50–63.

Boswell, W. R. and Olson-Buchanan, J. B. 2004. "Experiencing Mistreatment at Work: The Role of Grievance Filing, Nature of Mistreatment, and Employee Withdrawal." *Academy of Management Journal*, 47(1): 129–39.

Botero, I. C. and Van Dyne, L. 2009. "Employee Voice Behavior: Interactive Effects of LMX and Power Distance in the United States and Colombia." *Management Communication Quarterly*, 23(1): 84–104.

Boxall, P. and Macky, K. 2009. "Research and Theory on High-performance Work Systems: Progressing the High Involvement Stream." *Human Resource Management Journal*, 19: 3–23

Boxhall, P. and Purcell, J. 2003. *Strategy and Human Resource Management*. NY: Palgrave MacMillan.

Bradfield, M. and Aquino, K. 1999. "The Effects of Blame Attributions and Offender Likableness on Forgiveness and Revenge in the Workplace." *Journal of Management*, 25: 607–31.

Braithwaite, J. 2002. *Restorative Justice and Response Regulation*. Oxford, UK: Oxford University Press.

Brinsfield, C. T., Edwards, M. S., and Greenberg, J. 2009. "Voice and Silence in Organizations: Historical Review and Current Conceptualizations." In J. Greenberg and M.S. Edwards (eds), *Voice and Silence in Organizations*. Bringley, UK: Emerald Group Publishing, 3–33.

Budd, J. W. and Colvin, A. J. S. 2008. "Improved Metrics for Workplace Dispute Resolution Procedures: Efficiency, Equity, and Voice." *Industrial Relations*, 47(3): 460–79.

Burris, E. R. 2012. "The Risks and Rewards of Speaking Up: Managerial Responses to Employee Voice." *Academy of Management Journal*, 55(4): 851–75.

Burris, E. R., Detert, J. R., and Chiaburu, D. S. 2008. "Quitting before Leaving: The Mediating Effects of Psychological Attachment and Detachment on Voice." *Journal of Applied Psychology*, 93: 912–22.

Cappelli, P. and Neumark, D. 2001. "Do 'High-performance' Work Practices Improve Establishment-level Outcomes?" *Industrial & Labor Relations Review*, 54: 737–75.

Christie, N. 1977. "Conflict Property." *British Journal of Criminology*, 17: 1–15.

Clarmont, K. M. and Schwab, S. J. 2004. "How Employment Discrimination Plaintiffs Fare in Federal Court." *Journal of Empirical Legal Studies*, 1(2): 429–58.

Colvin, A. J. S. 2003. "Institutional Pressures, Human Resource Strategies and the Rise of Non-union Dispute Resolution Procedures." *Industrial & Labor Relations Review*, 56(3): 375–92.

Colvin, A. J. S. 2004. "Adoption and Use of Dispute Resolution Procedures in the Non-union Workplace." In D. Lewin and B. E. Kaufman (eds) *Advances in Industrial and Labor Relations*, 13: 69–95.

Colvin, A. J. S. 2006. "Flexibility and Fairness in Liberal Market Economies: The Comparative Impact of the Legal Environment and High Performance Work Systems." *British Journal of Industrial Relations*, 44(1): 73–97.

Colvin, A. J. S. 2011. "An Empirical Study of Employment Arbitration: Case Outcomes and Processes." *Journal of Empirical Legal Studies*, 8(1): 1–23.

Cooper, L. J., Nolan, D. R., and Bales, R. 2000. *ADR in the Workplace*. St. Paul, MN: West Group.

Costantino, C. A. and Merchant, C. S. 1996. *Designing Conflict Management Systems: A Guide to Creating Productive and Healthy Organizations*. San Francisco, CA: Jossey-Bass Publishers.

Darley, J. M., Carlsmith, K. M., and Robinson, P. H. 2000. "Incapacitation and Just Deserts as Motives for Punishment." *Law and Human Behavior*, 24: 659–83.

Darley, J. M. and Pittman, T. S. 2003. "The Psychology of Compensatory and Retributive Justice." *Personality and Social Psychological Review*, 7: 324–36.

Detert, J. R. and Burris, E. R. 2007. "Leadership Behavior and Employee Voice: Is the Door Really Open?" *Academy of Management Journal*, 50: 869–84.

Detert, J. R. and Trevino, L. K. 2010. "Speaking Up to Higher-ups: How Supervisors and Skip-level Leaders Influence Employee Voice." *Organization Science*, 21: 249–70.

Delaney, J. T., Lewin, D., and Ichniowski, C. 1989. *Human Resource Policies and Practices in American Firms*, BLMR #137. Washington, DC: US Department of Labor.

Dyne, L. V., Ang, S., and Botero, I. C. 2003. "Conceptualizing Employee Silence and Employee Voice as Multidimensional Constructs." *Journal of Management Studies*, 40(6): 1359–92.

Eaton, A. E. and Keefe, J. H. 1999. "Introduction and Overview." In A. E. Eaton and J. H. Keefe (eds), *Employment Dispute Resolution and Worker Rights in the Changing Workplace.* University of Illinois, Chicago, IL: Industrial Relations Research Association, 1–26.

Edmondson, A. C. 1999. "Psychological Safety and Learning Behavior in Work Teams." *Administrative Science Quarterly,* 44(2): 350–83.

Eisenberg, T. and Hill, E. 2003. "Employment Arbitration and Litigation." *Dispute Resolution Journal,* 58: 44–55.

Eisenberg, T. and Schlanger, M. 2003. "The Reliability of the Administrative Office of the U.S. Courts Database: An Initial Empirical Analysis." *Notre Dame Law Review,* 78: 1455–96.

Elliston, F. A. 1982. "Anonymity and Whistleblowing." *Journal of Business Ethics,* 1(3): 167–77.

Estreicher, S. 2001. "Saturns for Rickshaws: The Stakes in the Debate over Predispute Employment Arbitration Agreements." *Ohio State Journal on Dispute Resolution,* 16(3): 559–70.

Ewing, D. W. 1989. *Justice on the Job.* Boston, MA: Harvard Business School Press.

Fairbank, J. F., Spangler, W. E., and Williams, S. D. 2003. "Motivating Creativity Through a Computer-mediated Employee Suggestion Management System." *Behaviour & Information Technology,* 22: 305–14.

Farrell, D. 1983. "Exit, Voice, Loyalty, and Neglect as Responses to Job Dissatisfaction: A Multidimensional Scaling Study." *Academy of Management Journal,* 26: 596–607.

Feuille, P. 1999. "Grievance Mediation." In A. E. Eaton and J. H. Keefe (eds), *Employment Dispute Resolution and Worker Rights in the Changing Workplace.* Champaign, IL: IRRA, 187–217.

Feuille, P. and Chachere, D. T. 1995. "Looking Fair or Being Fair: Remedial Voice Procedures in Non-union Workplaces." *Journal of Management,* 21: 187–232.

Foulkes, F. K. 1980. *Personnel Policies in Large Nonunion Companies.* Englewood Cliffs, NJ: Prentice-Hall, Inc.

Freeman, R., and Lazear, E. 1995. "An Economic Analysis of Works Councils." In J. Rogers and W. Streeck (eds), *Works Councils: Consultation, Representation, and Cooperation in Industrial Relations.* Chicago, IL: University of Chicago Press, 27–50.

Frese, M., Teng, E., and Wijnen, C. J. D. 1999. "Helping to Improve Suggestion Systems: Predictors of Making Suggestions in Companies." *Journal of Organizational Behavior,* 20(7): 1139–55.

Fuller, J. B., Barnett, T., Hester, K., Relyea, C., and Frey, L. 2007. "An Exploratory Examination of Voice Behavior from an Impression Management Perspective." *Journal of Managerial Issues,* 19(1): 134–51.

Fuller, J. B., Marler, L. E., and Hester, K. 2006. "Promoting Felt Responsibility for Constructive Change and Proactive Behavior: Exploring Aspects of an Elaborated Model of Work Design." *Journal of Organizational Behavior,* 27: 1089–120.

General Accounting Office 1995. *Employment Discrimination: Most Private-Sector Employers Use Alternative Dispute Resolution.* Washington, DC: GAO.

Grote, R. and Wimberly, J. 1993. "Peer Review." *Training.* Mar.: 51–5.

Hammer, T. H. 2000. "Non-union Representational Forms: An Organizational Behavior Perspective." In B. E. Kaufman and D. G. Taras (eds), *Nonunion Employee Representation: History, Contempormy Practice, and Policy.* Armonk, NY: M.E. Sharpe, 176–95.

Harkavy, J. R. 1999. "Privatizing Workplace Justice: The Advent of Mediation in Resolving Sexual Harassment Disputes." *Wake Forest Law Review,* 34: 135–63.

Harlos, K. 2010. "If You Build a Remedial Voice Mechanism, Will They Come? Determinants of Voicing Interpersonal Mistreatment at Work." *Human Relations,* 63: 311–29.

Hirschman, A. O. 1970, *Exit, Voice and Loyalty Responses to Declines in Firms, Organizations and States*. Cambridge, MA: Harvard University Press.

Howard, W. M. 1995. "Arbitrating Claims of Employment Discrimination." *Dispute Resolution Journal*, 50: 40–50.

Huselid, M. A. 1995. "The Impact of Human Resource Management Practices on Turnover, Productivity, and Corporate Financial Performance." *The Academy of Management Journal*, 38(3): 635–72.

Ichnioswski, C., Kochan, T. A., Levine, D., Olson, C., and Strauss, G. 1996. "What works at work: Overview and Assessment." *Industrial Relations*, 35(5): 299–331.

Katz, H. C., Kochan, T. A., and Gobeille, K. R. 1983. "Industrial Relations Performance, Economic Performance, and QWL Programs: An Interplant Analysis." *Industrial & Labor Relations Review*, 37(1): 3–17.

Kandel, W. L. and Frumer, S. L. 1994. "The Corporate Ombudsman and Employment Law: Maintaining the Confidentiality of Communications." *Employee Relations Law Journal*, 19(4): 587–602.

Kaufman, B. E. and Levine, D. I. 2000. "An Economic Analysis of Employee Representation." In B. E. Kaufman and D. G. Taras (eds), *Nonunion Employee Representation: History, Contemporay Practice, and Policy*. Armonk: M.E. Sharpe, 149–75.

Klaas, B.S. 1989. "Determinants of Grievance Activity and the Grievance System's Impact on Employee Behavior: An Integrative Perspective." *Academy of Management Review*, 14: 445–58.

Klaas, B. and DeNisi, A. S. 1989. "Managerial Reactions to Employee Dissent: The Impact of Grievance Activity on Performance Rating." *Academy of Management Journal*, 32(4): 705–17.

Klaas, B. S., Olson-Buchanan, J. B., and Ward, A. K. 2012. "The Determinants of Alternative Forms of Workplace Voice: An Integrative Perspective." *Journal of Management*, 38: 315–45.

Kolb, D. M. 1987. "Corporate Ombudsman and Organization Conflict Resolution." *Journal of Conflict Resolution*, 31(4): 673–91.

Labig Jr., C. E. and Greer, C. R. 1988. "Grievance Initiation: A Literature Survey and Suggestions for Future Research." *Journal of Labor Research*, 9(1): 1–27.

Leach, D. J., Stride, C. B., and Wood, S. J. 2006. "The Effectiveness of Idea Capture Schemes." *International Journal of Innovation Management*, 10(3): 325–50.

Lee, J. H., Heilmann, S. G., and Near, J. P. 2004. "Blowing the Whistle on Sexual Harassment: Test of a Model of Predictors and Outcomes." *Human Relations*, 57(3): 297–322.

LePine, J. A. and Van Dyne, L. 1998. "Predicting Voice Behavior in Work Groups." *Journal of Applied Psychology*, 83(6): 853–68.

LePine, J. A. and Van Dyne, L. 2001. "Voice and Cooperative Behavior as Contrasting Forms of Contextual Performance: Evidence of Differential Relationships with Big Five Personality Characteristics and Cognitive Ability." *Journal of Applied Psychology*, 86(2): 326–36.

Lewin, D. 1987. "Dispute Resolution in the Non-union Firm: A Theoretical and Empirical Analysis." *The Journal of Conflict Resolution*, 16: 209–39.

Lewin, D. and Mitchell, D. J. B. 1992. "Systems of Employee Voice: Theoretical and Empirical Persepectives." *California Management Review*, 34(3): 95–111.

Lewin, D. and Peterson, R. B. 1988. *The Modern Grievance Procedure in the United States: A Theoretical and Empirical Analysis*. Wesport, CT: Quorum.

Lind, E. A. and Tyler, T. R. 1988. *The Social Psychology of Procedural Justice*. New York, NY: Plenum Press.

Lipponen, J., Bardi, A., and Haapamaki, J. 2008. "The Interaction between Values and Organizational Identification in Predicting Suggestion-making at Work." *Journal of Occupational & Organizational Psychology*, 81(2): 241–8.

Lipsky, D. and Seeber, R. 2006. "Managing Organizational Conflicts" In J. Oetzel and S. Ting-Toomey (eds), *The Sage Handbook of Conflict Communication*. Thousand Oaks, CA: Sage Publications, 359–90.

Lipsky, D., Seeber, R., and Fincher, R. 2003. *Emerging Systems for Managing Workplace Conflict*. San Francisco, CA: Jossey-Bass.

Liu, W., Zhu, R., and Yang, Y. 2010. "I Warn You because I Like You. Voice Behavior, Employee Identification, and Transformational Leadership." *Leadership Quarterly*, 21(1): 189–202.

Luchak, A. A. 2003. "What Kind of Voice do Loyal Employees Use?" *British Journal of Industrial Relations*, 41(1): 115–34.

Mahony, D. and Wheeler, H. 2010. "Adjudication of Workplace Disputes." In K. Dau-Schmidt, S. Harris, and O. Lobel (eds), *Labor and Employment Law and Economics*. Northampton, MA: Edward Elgar Publishing, 361–96.

Mahony, D. M. and Klaas, B. S. 2008. "Comparative Dispute Resolution in the Workplace." *Journal of Labor Research*, 29(3): 251–71.

McCabe, D. M. 1997. "Analysis of Organizational Due Process Procedures and Mechanisms — The Case of the United States." *Journal of Business Ethics*, 16: 349–56.

McCabe, D. M. 2002. "Administering the Employment Relationship: The Ethics of Conflict Resolution." *Journal of Business Ethics*, 36(1) 33–48.

McDermott, E. P. and Berkeley, A. E. 1996. *Alternative Dispute Resolution in the Workplace*. Westport, CT: Quorum Books.

MacDuffie, J. P. 1995. "Human Resource Bundles and Manufacturing Performance." *Industrial and Labor Relations Review*, 48: 197–221.

Mellahi, K., Budhwar, P. S., and Li, B. 2010. "A Study of the Relationship between Exit, Voice, Loyalty, and Neglect and Commitment in India." *Human Relations*, 63(3): 349–69.

Miceli, M. P. and Near, J. P. 1984. "The Relationships among Beliefs, Organizational Position, and Whistle-blowing Status: A Discriminant Analysis." *Academy of Management Journal*, 27: 687–705.

Miceli, M.P. and Near, J.P. 1985. "Characteristics of Organizational Climate and Perceived Wrongdoing Associated with Whistleblowing Decisions." *Personnel Psychology*, 38(3): 525–44.

Miceli, M. P. and Near, J. P. 1988. "Individual and Situational Correlates of Whistleblowing." *Personnel Psychology*, 41(2): 267–81.

Miceli, M. P. and Near, J. P. 1989. "The Incidence of Wrongdoing, Whistle-blowing, and Retaliation: Results of a Naturally Occurring Field Experiment." *Employee Rights & Responsibilities Journal*, 2(2): 91–108.

Miceli, M. P., Rehg, M., Near, J. P., and Ryan, K. C. 1999. "Can Laws Protect Whistleblowers?" *Work & Occupations*, 26(1): 129–51.

Miceli, M. P., Roach, B. L., and Near, J. P. 1988. "The Motivations of Anonymous Whistle-blowers: The Case of Federal Employees." *Public Personnel Management*, 17(3): 281–96.

Milliken, F. J., Morrison, E. W., and Hewlin, P. F. 2003. "An Exploratory Study of Employee Silence: Issues that Employees Don't Communicate Upward and Why." *Journal of Management Studies*, 40(6): 1453–76.

Morrison, E. W. and Milliken, F. J. 2000. "Organizational Silence: A Barrier to Change and Development in a Pluralistic World." *Academy of Management Review*, 25(4): 706–25.

Morrison, E. W., Wheeler-Smith, S. L., and Kamdar, D. 2011. "Speaking Up in Groups: A Cross-level Study of Group Voice Climate and Voice." *Journal of Applied Psychology*, 96(1): 183–91.

Naus, F., Van Iterson, A., and Roe, R. 2007. "Organizational Cynicism: Extending the Exit, Voice, Loyalty, and Neglect Model of Employees' Responses to Adverse Conditions in the Workplace." *Human Relations*, 60(5): 683–718.

Near, J. P., Dworkin, T. M., and Miceli, M. P. 1993. "Explaining the Whistle-blowing Process: Suggestions from Power Theory and Justice Theory." *Organization Science*, 4(3): 393–411.

Near, J. P., and Miceli, M. P. 1996. "Whistle-blowing: Myth and Reality." *Journal of Management*, 22(3): 507–26.

Olson-Buchanan, J. B. 1997. "To Grieve or Not to Grieve: Factors Related to Voicing Discontent in an Organizational Simulation." *International Journal of Conflict Management*, 8(2): 132–47.

Olson-Buchanan, J. B. and Boswell, W. R. 2002. "The Role of Employee Loyalty and Formality in Voicing Discontent." *Journal of Applied Psychology*, 87: 1167–74.

Olson-Buchanan, J. B. and Boswell, W. R. 2008. "An Integrative Model of Experiencing and Responding to Mistreatment at Work." *Academy of Management Review*, 33(1): 76–96.

Olson-Buchanan, J. B. and Boswell, W. R. 2009. *Mistreatment in the Workplace: Prevention and Resolution*. Part of the *Talent Management Essentials* book series, ed. S. Rogelberg. New York: Wiley-Blackwell.

Osterman, P. 1994. "How Common is Workplace Transformation and Who Adopts it?" *Industrial and Labor Relations Review*, 47(2), 173–88.

Pil, F. K. and MacDuffie, J. P. 1996. "The Adoption of High Involvement Work Practices." *Industrial Relations*, 35: 423–55.

Pinder, C. C. and Harlos, K. P. 2001. "Employee Silence: Quiescence and Acquiescence as Responses to Perceived Injustice." *Research in Personnel and Human Resources Management*, 20: 331–69.

Pyrillis, R. 2010. "Companies Grapple with Viral Vents." *Workforce Management*, 89(12): 6–8.

Rapp, C. and Eklund, J. 2007. "Sustainable Development of a Suggestion System: Factors Influencing Improvement Activities in a Confectionary Company." *Human Factors and Ergonomics in Manufacturing*, 17(1): 79–94.

Roche W. and Teague, P. 2012. "Do Conflict Management Systems Matter?" *Human Resource Management*, 51(2): 231–58.

Rothwell, G. R. and Baldwin, J. N. 2007a. "Ethical Climate Theory, Whistle-blowing, and the Code of Silence in Police Agencies in the State of Georgia." *Journal of Business Ethics*, 70(4): 341–61.

Rothwell, G. R. and Baldwin, J. N. 2007b. "Whistle-blowing and the Code of Silence in Police Agencies." *Crime & Delinquency*, 53(4): 605–32.

Rowe, M. 1997. "Dispute Resolution in the Non-union Environment: An Evolution toward Integrated Systems for Conflict Management?" In S. Gleason (ed.), *Workplace Dispute Resolution: Directions for the 21st century*. East Lansing: Michigan State University Press, 79–106.

Rusbult, C. E., Farrell, D., Rogers, G., and Mainous III, A. G. 1988. "Impact of Exchange Variables on Exit, Voice, Loyalty, and Neglect: An Integrative Model of Responses to Declining Job Status Satisfaction." *Academy of Management Journal*, 31(3): 599–627.

Seibert, S. E., Kraimer, M. L., and Crant, J. M. 2001. "What do Proactive People do? A Longitudinal Model Linking Proactive Personality and Career Success." *Personnel Psychology*, 54: 845–74.

Skarlicki, D. P. and Folger, R. 1997. "Retaliation in the Workplace: The Roles of Distributive, Procedural, and Interactional Justice." *Journal of Applied Psychology*, 82(3): 434–43.

Stone, K. v. W. 1981. "The Post-War Paradigm in American Labor Law." *The Yale Law Journal*, 90(7), 1509–80.

Tangirala, S. and Ramanujam, R. 2008b. "Exploring Nonlinearity in Employee Voice: The Effects of Personal Control and Organizational Identification." *Academy of Management Journal*, 51(6): 1189–203.

Thomas, J. P., Whitman, D. S., and Viswesvaran, C. 2010. "Employee Proactivity in Organizations: A Comparative Meta-analysis of Emergent Proactive Constructs." *Journal of Occupational & Organizational Psychology*, 83(2): 275–300.

Trevino, L. K., and Victor, B. 1992. "Peer Reporting of Unethical Behavior: A Social Context Perspective." *Academy of Management Journal*, 35(1): 38–64.

Tripp, T. M and Bies, R. J. 2009. *Getting even: The Even: The Truth about Workplace Revenge and How to Stop It*. San Francisco: Jossey-Bass.

Turnley, W. H. and Feldman, D. C. 1999. "The Impact of Psychological Contract Violations on Exit, Voice, Loyalty, and Neglect." *Human Relations*, 52(7): 895–922.

Ury, W. L., Brett, J. M., and Goldberg, S. B. 1989. *Getting Disputes Resolved: Designing Systems to Cut the Costs of Conflict*. San Francisco, CA: Jossey-Bass Publishers.

Van Dyne, L., Kamdar, D., and Joireman, J. 2008. "In-role Perceptions Buffer the Negative Impact of Low LMX on Helping and Enhance the Positive Impact of High LMX on Voice." *Journal of Applied Psychology*, 93(6): 1195–207.

Venkataramani, V. and Tangirala, S. 2010. "When and Why do Central Employees Speak Up? An Examination of Mediating and Moderating Variables." *Journal of Applied Psychology*, 95(3): 582–91.

Walumbwa, F. O. and Schaubroeck, J. 2009. "Leader Personality Traits and Employee Voice Behavior: Mediating Roles of Ethical Leadership and Work Group Psychological Safety." *Journal of Applied Psychology*, 94: 1275–86.

Wang, S., Yi, X., Lawler, J., and Zhang, M. 2011. "Efficacy of High-performance Work Practices in Chinese Companies." *International Journal of Human Resource Management*, 22: 2419–41.

Wheeler, H. N., Klaas, B. S., and Mahony, D. M. 2004. *Workplace Justice Without Unions*. Kalamazoo, MI: W.E. Upjohn Institute for Employment Research.

Wheeler, H. N. and Rojot, J. 1992. "General Comments." In H. N. Wheeler and J. Rojot (eds), *Workplace Justice: Employment Obligations in International Perspective*. Columbia, SC: University of South Carolina Press, 363–83.

Whiting, S. W., Maynes, T. D., Podsakoff, N. P., and Podsakoff, P. M. 2011. "Effects of Message, Source, and Context on Evaluation of Employee Voice Behavior." *Journal of Applied Psychology*, 97(1): 159–82.

PART 2

....

APPROACHES TO CONFLICT
MANAGEMENT

....

INTRODUCTION TO PART 2

WILLIAM K. ROCHE, PAUL TEAGUE, AND ALEXANDER J. S. COLVIN

AT the core of conflict management in organizations are the various practices and procedures through which organizations seek to resolve and sometimes prevent conflict in the workplace. The contributions to this section examine the major ways in which organizations handle conflict management, whether arising from individual grievances or collective disputes. Both conventional approaches reliant on standard grievance and dispute resolution procedures are considered and also a series of alternative dispute resolution approaches that seek in different ways to depart from conventional practices, sometimes providing an alternative to civil litigation or resorting to administrative agencies established to administer employment laws. Practices have also evolved that combine conventional "rights-based" procedures with innovative "interest-based" options, especially as exemplified by the influential concept of conflict management systems.

Obviously a longer empirical research tradition surrounds the handling of individual grievances and collective disputes through conventional procedures. Indeed, the process of collective bargaining and associated ways of resolving conflict have been a core—arguably for long "the" core—concern of the discipline of Industrial Relations. As collective agreements commonly regulated grievance handling, especially in the US, the grievance handling process has also been the subject of a substantial volume of research. Grievance handling has also received attention in the newly established discipline of human resource management (HRM) from the 1980s, though most commonly as one of a series of practices that might define the presence or level of HRM in organizations, and more unusually as a focus in its own right. An empirical literature has been building on different forms of alternative dispute resolution (ADR) and on conflict management systems, but the literature in these areas has been dominated by "how to do" books and publications—not infrequently making ambitious and even portentous claims as to the outcomes associated with innovations in these areas.

The contributions to Part 2 of the book take a sober look at different approaches to conflict management, informed by empirical research and often by first-hand professional experience of the workings of specific practices, such as the organizational ombudsperson or third-party intervention in collective disputes.

David Lewin focuses on the operation of conventional multi-step grievance procedures in the context of collective bargaining, mainly drawing on experience in the US, where the scope for grievances tends to be tightly circumscribed by collective agreements. Discipline, pay and conditions, and work assignments are the most common issues involved in grievances, and collectively bargaining grievance procedures culminate in arbitration. Grievance mediation, provided by independent professionals or public agencies, is shown to have grown significantly in incidence. The use of mediation to resolve contract renewal disputes in collective bargaining is also growing in the US, and is mandated in some industries. The grievance resolution process is found to be associated with lower performance ratings, high absence from work, and higher quit rates for parties filing grievances. Similar effects are observed for the supervisors of grievants. This may be attributed either to management in practice retaliating against both grievants and their supervisors; or being "shocked" through what is revealed in the grievance process into a recognition of poor performance on the part of both parties that is subsequently tackled more rigorously. Lewin highlights the paradox of research findings that show that *levels* of grievance activity are negatively associated with a series of organizational outcomes, whereas the *presence* of grievance procedures in "bundles" of human resource (HR) practices is seen to enhance organizational performance. This paradox might be attributable to the problem of distinguishing any specific effects of grievance procedures in studies of the effects of general HR bundles.

The effects of ADR-like grievance practices in non-union firms are assessed positively by managers and employees. Lewin is emphatic that both conventional grievance procedures under collective bargaining—whether or not augmented by mediation—and ADR practices in non-union organizations are fundamentally reactive in nature in that they involve responses to incidents of conflict after they have occurred. Even where grievance procedures form part of bundles of HR practices that might overall be portrayed as proactive, the main stimulus to the adoption of grievance procedures and practices appears to be the threat of litigation and perhaps union avoidance. Defensive postures are thus seen to be paramount in developments in conflict resolution.

Willy Brown's chapter on third-party processes in employment disputes complements Lewin's analysis by examining the use of mainly conventional practices in collective disputes. Brown discusses the changed environment of industrial conflict where strike levels and union density have both declined in many countries—the two trends being closely linked but also reflecting an underlying change in competitive conditions that have rendered strike action generally riskier and less effective. Growing exposure to international competition, the deregulation and liberalization of public sector monopolies in many countries, and the growing use of outsourcing in public service organizations means that the leverage unions once gained through industrial action, or by threatening sanctions, has declined significantly. The changed environment has affected third-party intervention. High-risk confrontational bargaining has given way to the greater use of voluntary procedures for conflict resolution, involving third-party agencies and specialists. The diversity that once existed in approaches to dispute resolution within Europe and beyond has given way to convergence around the use of non-judicial means of settling disputes—although judicial and legal traditions of dispute resolution remain strong in some European countries. The advisory functions of third-party agencies have also expanded in a number of countries.

Collective bargaining, whether "distributive" or "integrative", is a complex process that is affected by relationships both between and within the bargaining parties. Third-party interventions in disputes serve to increase information flows between negotiators/disputants and to guide the parties toward settlements that reflect market pressures and other local realities, including notions of fairness. Brown discusses the methods used by third parties in seeking to facilitate settlements. Conciliation is shown to involve an extended repertoire of skills, ranging from facilitating information exchange, framing issues in dispute in a manner that allows for movement, reframing issues to generate options not originally salient to the parties, and serving as a provider of solutions that the parties can accept—even if with reluctance. Other less conventional third-party roles are also discussed, including "med+arb" and "arb-med", where the conciliator acts as arbitrator or drafts an arbitration judgment that is not disclosed to the parties unless they fail to reach agreement through mediation. "Final-offer" arbitration is also sometimes used, where the arbitrator is required under their terms of reference to find definitively in favor of the last claim of the union or the last offer of the employer.

"Interest-based bargaining" (IBB) involves a departure from conventional approaches to collective bargaining and conflict management and has garnered considerable international attention in recent decades. Joel Cutcher-Gershenfeld's chapter examines IBB, drawing mainly on experience in the US, where this approach has been most widely practiced. The nature of IBB is outlined and the approach is contrasted with conventional "positional" bargaining. Analytically, the contrast between the two approaches is clear-cut and covers all phases of the negotiating cycle from preparation to the implementation of agreements. The focus is on joint problem solving by pooling information and generating options for agreement.

Cutcher-Gershenfeld locates the genesis of IBB in the decline in union density in the US private sector which is seen to have polarized bargaining activity into both increasingly conflictual negotiations and IBB. About one in three bargaining relationships in the early 2000s in the US is seen to have involved IBB. IBB is more prevalent in the public sector, where the language associated with it is commonly explicitly deployed in negotiations. Little systematic evidence is available on the incidence of IBB in other countries. As to the outcomes of IBB, Cutcher-Gershenfeld reports that IBB in Canada and the US is more likely to be associated with innovative bargaining outcomes in such areas as joint governance, workplace flexibility, and job security. In Canada, though not in the US, IBB was also more likely to have involved concessions by trade unions.

Alexander Colvin's chapter focuses on conflict management in non-union firms that employ more than 90% of US employees in the private sector. These rely on grievance procedures to manage conflict. The majority of non-union firms possess formal procedures. Grievance procedures have been adopted primarily as a means of union avoidance or "substitution", in response to the threat of employment litigation and out of a concern to institute justice on the job as a component of HR strategies. Colvin highlights the continuing diversity that characterizes grievance procedures in non-union firms, ranging from open door policies, sometimes involving formal investigation of grievances, multi-step processes which typically make provision for appeals, to peer or management review boards. Mediation also has become a growing feature of non-union grievance procedures, and organizational ombudsperson's offices are found in some large organizations. Arbitration was seldom used until the 1990s, when the US Supreme Court judgment in the Gilmer case encouraged employers to adopt arbitration in employment disputes as a means of avoiding litigation. For employees litigation involves a "high risk, high reward system" and for employers a slow-moving, highly uncertain process that carries a risk of large damages. Internationally, non-union grievance procedures are found to be variably prevalent across liberal market economies; their varying use reflects different legal traditions and systems.

Research indicates that both grievance rates and employees' "win rates" are quite similar across non-union and collective-bargaining based grievance procedures. Employees are found to be more likely to take grievances where the final step in procedures involves non-managerial decision-making, either by peer review panels or arbitrators. Procedures that provide for robust or enhanced "procedural fairness" in these ways result in positive workplace outcomes, e.g. a commitment to remain working for the organization. Colvin highlights that research findings from unionized firms revealing that employees who file grievances subsequently attain lower performance ratings apply also under non-union grievance procedures, but not, it appears, findings that they are also more likely to quit or to report negative work and employment attitudes.

The chapter by Latreille and Saundry examines the nature, genesis, and effects of mediation. Much international discussion in the area revolves around the uses of different types of mediation or of different "mediation styles". Latreille and Saundry discuss the core principles underlying mediation, particularly its voluntary and confidential nature. The dominant paradigm views mediation as a form of facilitated problem solving, whereas the "transformational mediation" paradigm emphasizes positive change in the underlying relationship between the parties to conflict. Both approaches are used, but in practice many mediators deploy a range of different approaches when handling the same cases.

The genesis of mediation is found in the search by employers for speedier and lower-cost ways of resolving conflict. Although the evidence available on these outcomes remains too scant to be treated as definitive, it is found to be broadly consistent with these objectives. Mediation is seen as providing employees with less confrontational and less destructive ways of resolving grievances and by allowing individuals to air their grievances before a neutral third party. International evidence reveals high levels of satisfaction on the part of people who have been involved in workplace mediation. The incidence of the use of mediation in firms and public sector agencies has been rising significantly internationally, although the uptake of mediation in small firms is substantially lower than in large establishments. Where data are available—in the UK—the volume of mediation activity within firms with this conflict resolution option appears modest.

Assessing contributors to the effectiveness of mediation poses methodological problems. However, success in resolving conflict is found to be influenced by the timing of interventions (neither too early nor too late in conflicts), the skills of mediators, and the parties' commitment to the process. More general effects on culture change within organizations have also been reported. Latreille and Saundry believe that the mediation literature tends often to neglect the significance of power relations between the parties, and the significance of this issue for the process and its outcomes is examined in the chapter. A number of ways in which mediation may be shaped by power relations is explored, including mediation becoming a transmission mechanism for the superior power of the employer over the employee, or a means of transposing violations of employment rights into localized personal disagreements between people. At the same time the chapter recognizes that rights-based procedures within firms may in practice provide scant protection for employees, whereas mediation may be capable of challenging or muting the power of managers. Unions may also support mediation programs where they have an input into their design and oversight, viewing them as a means of extending their influence in workplaces.

The chapter by Rowe and Gadlin examines the work of the organizational ombudsperson (OO) as a gatekeeper and facilitator of both interest-based and rights-based conflict management and resolution. The genesis and diffusion of OOs is traced to developments from the 1960s involving waves of employment regulation, reflective of a growing concern with diversity, civil rights and justice, and cultural change at work. These developments in turn led to a growing emphasis by employees on autonomy, self-expression, and self-determination in the workplace. A further impetus was provided by the growing influence of ADR more generally. As Row and Gadlin see it, the OO field grew rapidly because it "caught the ADR wave", while also affirming the value of formal rights-based approaches to conflict resolution.

The office of the OO works independently of line management and usually reports to the CEOs or boards of organizations. Their approach is "eclectic" and concerned with informing the parties to conflicts of the different ways in which conflicts can be resolved, while maintaining an ethical focus on fair process. OOs also focus on the systemic implications of underlying patterns and trends in conflict and grievances and thus may play a proactive role in conflict management and organizational improvement. OOs may also act as the integrative coordination mechanism for conflict management systems in organizations, whether these systems are formally designed or operate in a less coordinated way. Some of the skills and competencies of OOs mirror those of mediators (active listening, communicating respect, generating options, etc.), while others appear more distinctive (assessing claims that could involve criminal behavior or safety violations, and working as coaches). Surveys reveal high levels of satisfaction with the work of OOs, although systematic studies of the effectiveness of the role have not been undertaken.

The chapter discusses variations in the mode of operation of OOs, particularly differences in the degree to which they may be mainly affiliated to rights- or interest-based approaches to conflict resolution. International variations are also considered, the key differentiator here being whether OOs modeled their role on the classic public ombudsperson, or alternatively sought to develop a wider range of activities that encompassed interest-based options for resolving conflict. Rowe and Gadlin discuss the challenges and dilemmas involved in the work of OOs. They recognize that independence, freedom from bias, and neutrality may be hard to maintain given that OOs are employed by the organizations in which they operate.

The chapter by John Purcell shifts the focus from formal procedures and practices for conflict resolution to the role of line managers in workplace conflict. As Purcell writes, line managers are at the heart of most conflict, whether causing it, experiencing it, dealing with it, or coping with the consequences. Being allocated too much work by line managers emerges from UK surveys as the single most frequent source of workplace conflict, with managers themselves more at risk of this than non-managerial employees. The Great Recession had led to an increase in work stress and pressure, especially in the public sector. Much of this pressure and stress is attributed to changes in work organization, which are often poorly managed. These work experiences are most pronounced among professional and technical workers in large multi-establishment organizations, and often reflect an underlying work culture in which aggression and humiliation are tolerated as features of management.

Under the sway of modern HRM and expanding employment rights, line managers have become much more centrally involved in the management of employees. But they still often attribute low priority to HR issues, or seek to avoid dealing with these. Support is often not forthcoming from senior managers, and line managers' authority to make decisions on HR issues often appears to be ambiguous. Little training is also commonly provided. Purcell highlights the features of effective line management involvement in managing workplace conflict. Trust in line managers, embedded in organizational routines and practices, is seen to be pivotal and to be connected with employees' perceptions of organizational justice. Trust in practice involves behavioral consistency and integrity, communication, concern with employees' well-being, and sharing of control by promoting job autonomy. Effective line management involvement in conflict resolution also requires making provision for due process in organizational

systems, such as performance management, operating formal grievance procedures, and following codes of practice on conflict management and the use of ADR.

The chapter by Roche and Teague on conflict management systems deals with a currently highly influential concept and associated
body of theory. Although interest in conflict management systems
originated in empirical studies of grievance handling under collective
bargaining, most of the literature in the area is prescriptive and deals
with resolving conflict outside the process of collective bargaining or
in non-union settings. The theory of conflict management systems is
persuasive in proposing that a combination of rights-based and interest-based options within firms, with primacy attributed to the latter,
represents the most effective means of managing conflict and leads
to the most beneficial outcomes for employees and employers and
unions. Conflict management systems theory advocates the provision
of multiple access points to conflict resolution practices, the simultaneous use of rights-based and interest-based practices, and freedom
to move or "loop" backwards and forwards between levels and stages
of conflict resolution rather than having to follow any series of prescribed linear steps. The focus of the prescriptive literature is toward
individual grievance handling, although some contributors also cover
collective forms of interest-based dispute resolution or prevention like
IBB. The conflict management systems literature also recognizes the
role of line and supervisory managers in conflict resolution.

The antecedents of conflict management systems have been identified as including crises in more traditional grievance and dispute resolution procedures, the advent of flatter, more agile and team-based
forms of organization, the explosion in employment litigation, and
other secular trends such as HRM, globalization, and declining union
density and power. There are few systematic studies of the prevalence
of conflict management systems. In the US, where this approach to
conflict management appears most widely prevalent, it has been estimated that about a third of Fortune 1000 companies possess some features of conflict management systems. Outside the US, the prevalence
of conflict management systems, even in large firms, appears very considerably lower.

Integral to conflict management systems theory, as Roche and
Teague see it, is the postulate of systems effects resulting from complementarities between different practices. Because of complementarities, each type of conflict resolution option is rendered more effective
through its coexistence in a system that involves other options. Of
particular importance is that systems should involve combinations of
interest-based and rights-based options. Little empirical research on

the operation of conflict management systems has yet been undertaken and the case accounts of conflict management systems available in the public domain point to mixed experiences and outcomes.
While a major quantitative study, using data derived from three case-
study sites, reported evidence consistent with the complementarities postulated, Roche and Teague report research on Ireland which
failed to establish the presence of complementarities between interest-based and rights-based options for conflict management—albeit
in firms without purpose-designed conflict management systems.
Notwithstanding the prominence and influence of conflict management systems theory as a paradigm for best practice in designing conflict management arrangements, Roche and Teague believe that basic
research still needs to be conducted on the outcomes, operation, and
antecedents of conflict management systems.

Viewed collectively, the contributions to this section of the book
address or pose a number of common themes. First, contributors
identify trends in the external and internal environments of organizations that influence changes in approaches to conflict management
and in particular the growing use of various forms of ADR. More
intense international competition and declining union density and
influence have been associated with unions' willingness to adopt less
confrontational postures in collective bargaining and to embrace
forms of third-party intervention in disputes. The same developments
have been associated with the advent of IBB. Convergence between
national systems of dispute resolution has also been traced to these
developments. Other trends involving an expansion in employment
rights and sometimes a growing propensity to litigate or refer grievances to administrative bodies have been linked with the adoption of
various forms of ADR. Greater line management involvement in conflict resolution is seen to be rooted in similar developments. Within
organizations, commitment to HRM, sometimes in tandem with
union avoidance, has been identified as a contributor to ADR, as has
the advent of less hierarchical and more team-based forms of organization, which may amplify the negative effects of conflict and attach a
premium to the speedy and fair resolution of workplace problems.

Second, a number of contributors address the theme of whether
approaches to conflict management should be viewed in the main as
reactive or proactive. While the establishment of OO offices, the use of
mediation in some instances as a culture change mechanism, and the
development of conflict management systems appear to point to proactive postures, perhaps more commonly as Lewin claims, approaches
to conflict management reveal essentially reactive postures within
organizations. Brown's observation that third-party institutions in a

number of countries have been devoting more resources to their advisory functions also seems to point toward more proactive public policy postures toward conflict resolution.

Finally, it is clear that considerable work needs to be done in establishing the outcomes of ADR practices and systems for stakeholders in the workplace. Whether some of the negative effects of conventional grievance resolution on the parties immediately involved carry through to forms of ADR (as appears to be the case) is an obvious concern; but questions remain to be resolved concerning the more general outcomes of ADR for employers, employees, and unions. More analytical and sophisticated case-study and quantitative research will be required for a more definitive assessment of these innovations than is currently possible.

CHAPTER 5

COLLECTIVE BARGAINING AND GRIEVANCE PROCEDURES

DAVID LEWIN

INTRODUCTION

THE process of collective bargaining during which a company's management and unionized employees negotiate over new terms and conditions of employment occurs every few years, with three-year agreements being most common in the US. These negotiations can be protracted due to deep-seated conflicts and therefore sometimes feature employee strikes and employer lockouts. But such overt manifestations of workplace conflict are far less common today than in prior eras, in part because of the decline of employee unionism (and thus formal collective bargaining) in most developed nations, and in larger part because of the potentially increased costs that result from strikes and lockouts. These costs, manifested in lost sales revenue and employee jobs and income, stem from increasing global economic competition, deregulation and technological change or, in other words, market capitalism in which consumers can more readily switch their purchases to other firms. Stated differently, overt conflict involving interest (i.e. contract) disputes among labor and management has receded markedly in developed nations in recent years, indeed, decades.

By contrast, conflict between management and labor over rights disputes involving existing terms and conditions of collective bargaining agreements continue apace. The forum in which such disputes are pursued, heard, and ultimately resolved is the grievance procedure. Indeed, in most collective bargaining agreements, the bulk of the pages (and thus words) are devoted to the grievance procedure. These include specification of the scope of issues covered by the procedure, eligibility to use the procedure, representation of the parties in grievance processing, and the number and type of procedural steps (Katz and Kochan, 1999; Budd, 2010). While the primary focus of this chapter is on collective bargaining and grievance settlement in the US, characteristics of this "system" may readily generalize to other countries, especially in the Anglo-American world.

By banding together into a union and negotiating a collective bargaining agreement with an employer, employees basically enhance their power and share that power with the employer over numerous aspects of the employment relationship (Kaufman, 2010a). Conceptually, a grievance procedure represents one of the most concrete manifestations of this alteration of power, in particular by tempering the authority of an employer unilaterally to manage employees and impose discipline on them. Further, a grievance procedure enables labor and management to resolve disputes that might otherwise fester, go unresolved, and lead to work slowdowns, strikes, and lockouts that would disrupt the production of goods and services. Generations of industrial relations scholars have celebrated grievance procedures in terms of their contribution to maintaining production and work, preserving industrial peace and, most fundamentally, promoting industrial democracy (Chamberlain and Kuhn, 1965; Budd, 2010). Some empirical evidence and case examples support this favorable perspective on grievance procedures (Katz and Kochan, 1999; Lewin, 1999). But other empirical evidence and case examples paint a more mixed picture of grievance procedures (Bemmels and Foley, 1996; Boroff and Lewin, 1996).

The Grievance Procedure as a Reactive Mechanism

For an employee to invoke the grievance procedure, that is, file a grievance, the employer must have taken some action with which that employee disagrees. Following Hirschman (1970), such disagreement signals deterioration of the employment relationship. By filing a grievance, the aggrieved employee challenges the employer's decision—exercises voice—and thereby seeks to redress the deterioration at hand. In this fundamental sense, the grievance procedure is a reactive or ex-post facto mechanism.

In truth, employment relationship conflicts typically do not result in the filing of written grievances. Rather, such conflicts are informally discussed by the aggrieved employees and their immediate supervisors (or managers) and are usually resolved without ever entering the formal grievance procedure. In this regard, one US study of unionized grievance procedures estimated that approximately 12 grievances are settled informally for every one grievance that is settled through the formal grievance procedure (Lewin and Peterson, 1988). This suggests that employee voice is far more commonly exercised in employment relationships than is indicated by formal grievance filing and settlement activity.

When employees file formal grievances, most of them are settled at the first step of the grievance procedure and the bulk of remaining grievances are settled at the second step. Relatively few grievances make their way to the final step of the grievance procedure, which in US unionized contexts is almost always third-party arbitration. More specifically, about 60% of unionized employee grievances are settled at the first procedural step, about 30% at the second step, about 7% at the third step, and about 3% at the final (arbitration) step (Lewin and Peterson, 1988). This empirical evidence can be interpreted to mean that most grievances are settled as close as possible to their sources of origin, which comports with a long-standing principle of effective employment conflict resolution (Chamberlain and Kuhn, 1965; Katz and Kochan, 1999). Alternatively, this evidence can be interpreted to mean that the costs of grievance processing and settlement rise rapidly as grievances are pursued through higher steps of the procedure. Hence, employee-grievants and management settle for suboptimal, that is, second- or third-best, solutions.

WHAT DO EMPLOYEES GRIEVE ABOUT?

The most prevalent issue over which employees file grievances in the US is discipline, which ranges from relatively minor docking of pay for occasional or persistent lateness in reporting for work to termination for violation of a company policy concerning, for example, theft. In the US and certain other nations, "termination for cause" basically means that an employee has broken the rules and is therefore ineligible for unemployment insurance payments (which are provided to employees laid off for economic reasons). The typical grievance procedure also reflects the principle of progressive discipline wherein discipline imposed for employee violations of company policies and practices becomes more severe for repeat offenses (Jacoby, 1986). This internal discipline and due process system closely resembles that of the external judicial system, which is why it is sometimes referred to as a system of industrial justice (Budd, 2010).

Empirical studies of grievance procedure usage find that grievances are also often filed over issues regarding pay, work assignments, working conditions (such as safety), and supervision. Men are more likely than women to file grievances over these types of issues, as are younger workers compared to older workers. Further, women are relatively more likely than men to file grievances over (lack of) access to training for current and higher-level jobs, whereas older workers are relatively more likely than younger workers to file grievances over (lack of) promotions and performance evaluations (Lewin and Peterson, 1988). Women are somewhat more likely than men to file grievances over gender discrimination, including sexual harassment, but are far more likely than men to file lawsuits alleging gender discrimination at work. Extant evidence also indicates that Asians and Latinos are significantly less likely than Anglos to file grievances over virtually any issue, and that African-American grievance filing rates are roughly similar to those of Anglos (Boswell and Buchanan, 2004).

Grievance Procedure Dynamics

When a unionized employee files a written grievance, a shop steward or union grievance committee member usually assists him/her. Submitting a grievance in writing is a significant act because it puts the employee on record as challenging a management decision. For industrial relations scholars, formal grievance filing constitutes the premier expression of voice in the employment relationship and, more fundamentally, the main evidence of why and how unionization provides workers with a mechanism to exercise such voice (Lewin, 2005).

Once a grievance is filed, management must respond. At the first step of the grievance procedure, the employee's direct supervisor or another supervisor or front-line manager typically meets with the employee to discuss the substance of the grievance. Following this discussion and consistent with grievance procedure provisions of the collective bargaining agreement, the employee-grievant receives a written response from management that contains proposed terms of settlement. If the employee-grievant accepts those terms, the grievance is closed (i.e. ended). As indicated above, about 60% of all grievances filed by unionized employees are settled at the first step of the procedure.

If an employee-grievant rejects management's proposed settlement at the first grievance step, the grievance moves to the next step. At this step, a second-level supervisor, manager, human resource specialist or labor relations specialist typically represents management and a shop steward or union grievance committee official typically represents the employee. When these representatives meet to discuss the substance of the grievance, the employee-grievant and his/her immediate supervisor typically are not present. Following this discussion, the employee-grievant receives a written response from management that contains proposed terms of settlement. If the employee-grievant accepts those terms, the grievance is closed. As indicated above, about 30% of all grievances filed by unionized employees are settled at the second step of the procedure.

If an employee-grievant rejects management's proposed settlement at the second grievance step, the grievance moves to the next step. At this step, a senior management official and a top-level union grievance committee member or union official represent management and the employee-grievant, respectively. These representatives then meet to discuss the content of the grievance, sometimes doing so with the employee grievant or his/her immediate supervisor being present and sometimes not. Following this meeting, the employee-grievant receives a written response from management containing proposed terms of settlement. If the employee-grievant accepts those terms, the grievance is closed. As indicated above, about 7% of all grievances filed by unionized employees are settled at the third step of the procedure.

If the employee-grievant rejects management's proposed settlement at the third grievance step, the grievance moves to the next or final step, which in virtually all instances is third-party arbitration. This step is considerably more formal than the preceding steps. To illustrate, the arbitrator holds a hearing at which management and employee-grievant representatives are present. These representatives as well as witnesses for each party give sworn testimony that is transcribed by a professional transcriptionist. Each party provides the arbitrator with supporting documents and exhibits. In some instances, audio and video recordings of the arbitration hearing are also made. Further, an arbitrator may require the parties to submit post-hearing briefs. As indicated above, about 3% of all grievances filed by unionized employees are settled at the final (arbitration) step of the procedure.

GRIEVANCE ARBITRATION

When unionized employee grievances reach the arbitration stage, management and union representatives jointly select the arbitrator and each party pays half the costs of arbitration. Grievance procedure provisions of collective bargaining agreements typically spell out the method of arbitrator selection. For example, this type of provision may specify that the parties will request a list of several potential arbitrators from the American Arbitration Association (AAA), National Academy of Arbitrators (NAA), Judicial Arbitration and Mediation Services (JAMS) or other organization specializing in employment dispute resolution. Once received, the parties review the list of arbitrators and each side may strike the names of individual arbitrators that it deems unacceptable. If one or more of the listed arbitrators are acceptable to both sides, the parties will rank these arbitrators and request that the top-ranked arbitrator be assigned to the grievance case. If that arbitrator is unavailable, the parties will request the next-highest ranked arbitrator. If none of the arbitrators on the original list are acceptable to one or the other party or are otherwise unable to serve, a second list of potential arbitrators will be requested and the arbitrator selection process proceeds in exactly the same way as with the original list until an arbitrator is selected and assigned to the grievance case.

Following completion of the arbitration hearing and the parties' submission of post-hearing briefs, the arbitrator will render a written decision and transmit it to the parties. In unionized grievance procedures, an arbitrator's decision is final and binding on the parties. This principle is spelled out in the grievance procedure provisions of a collective bargaining agreement—an agreement voluntarily negotiated by management and union representatives on behalf of their respective organizations and constituents. While one or the other of these parties may be sufficiently dissatisfied with an arbitrator's decision to challenge that decision in a court, the US Supreme Court has consistently ruled that where collective bargaining agreements contain grievance procedures culminating in binding arbitration, any grievances that arise thereunder must be settled via arbitration and cannot be appealed to or reviewed by the courts (Chamberlain and Kuhn, 1965). This deferral to arbitration doctrine has clearly strengthened the decision-making power of arbitrators in rights arbitration cases.

Expedited Arbitration

Because arbitration is the final step of unionized grievance procedures and is the most formal component of such procedures, a substantial amount of time—as much as one year—may lapse between the initial filing of a grievance and an arbitrated grievance decision. Stated differently, there is a negative correlation between the speed of grievance settlement and the number of grievance procedure steps used to resolve grievances. For the employee-grievant, this may mean that (industrial) justice delayed is (industrial) justice denied. It also may mean that management experiences a prolonged period of uncertainty about the resolution of the grievance issue at hand. For these reasons some unionized grievance procedures permit the use of expedited arbitration, which basically means skipping certain steps of the procedure, typically the second and/or third steps. When expedited arbitration occurs, the amount of time between initial grievance filing and an arbitration decision is substantially reduced, specifically by 40%–50% (Lewin, 1997).

While the speedier justice and uncertainty reduction rationales for expedited arbitration imply that this type of arbitration will be widely used, the evidence suggests otherwise. By skipping intermediate steps of the grievance procedure, the parties forgo opportunities for grievance settlement at lower steps of the procedure (recall that about 37% of unionized employee grievances are settled at the second and third steps). Such lower-step settlements also avoid the costs associated with arbitration. Further, the binding nature of arbitrator decisions may set precedents for handling certain employment relationship disputes that limit the flexibility that management and union representatives may prefer to retain in dealing with similar future disputes.

Still further, most grievance procedure provisions of collective bargaining agreements limit the type of infractions and the discipline associated with such infractions for which expedited arbitration may be invoked. To illustrate, grievances challenging discipline for drunkenness at work may not be subject to expedited arbitration, whereas grievances challenging discipline for theft at work may be subject to expedited arbitration. In another example, grievances challenging termination may be subject to expedited arbitration whereas grievances challenging suspension from work may not be subject to expedited arbitration. Hence, the benefit of speedier grievance settlement that is associated with the use of expedited arbitration must be balanced against the behavioral and procedural limitations on the use of expedited arbitration.

Grievance (Rights) Mediation

Grievance mediation is substantially different from grievance arbitration. The main difference between these two processes is that an arbitrator has decision-making power whereas a mediator does not. The arbitrator's power stems from the grievance procedure provisions of the collective bargaining agreement in which the parties affirm that the arbitrator is empowered to make decisions in grievance cases that reach the arbitration stage and that the parties will be bound by those decisions. By contrast, the mediator cannot rule on or decide any grievance issues. Instead, the mediator attempts to move the parties closer to reaching agreement on the grievance issue at hand by serving as an intermediary communicator of settlement proposals proffered by both sides, offering his/her own recommendations for grievance settlement, and convincing the parties to accept those recommendations or otherwise reach agreement. Therefore, the mediator basically attempts to influence the parties' behavior and his/her influence and persuasion skills and abilities largely determine the effectiveness of the mediation process (Feuille, 1999).

While grievance mediation is not as prevalent as grievance arbitration, its use has increased considerably. This is because mediation services have become more available, professionalized and well known, mediated grievance disputes settle more quickly and at lower cost than arbitrated grievance disputes, mediation enhances the likelihood that the parties will settle rights disputes on their own rather than risking a potentially negative binding arbitration decision, and grievance mediation has been relatively successful in certain industries such as coal mining, steel manufacturing, airlines and health care (Brett and Goldberg, 1983; Bingham, 2004). Several professional organizations exist to provide such services, of which the longest-standing and best known is the US Federal Mediation and Conciliation Service (FMCS). Others include the aforementioned AAA, NAA, JAMS and the Labor and Employment Section of the American Bar Association (ABA). However, the parties to a grievance are not required to use one of these organizations to identify or select a grievance mediator.

Contract (Interest) Mediation and Other Dispute Resolution Procedures

Mediation is also increasingly used to assist in settling contract disputes among labor and management. An important difference between these disputes and grievance disputes is that with an occasional exception, contract disputes in the US private sector are not settled through arbitration. (The main exception is professional sports, particularly major league baseball in which final-offer arbitration is used to settle contract disputes between players and team owners.) Put differently, rights arbitration is quite common whereas interest arbitration is quite rare in this sector. Therefore, the parties to contract disputes either reach negotiated agreements on their own or avail themselves of mediation services to help reach such agreements. In some disputes, mediation is invoked while the parties continue to negotiate. More often, mediation is requested after an employee strike or an employer lockout or both have occurred.

In some respects, contract mediation resembles grievance mediation, as when a mediator communicates one party's proposed terms of settlement to the other party or when a mediator proposes his/her own terms of settlement to the parties. In other respects, however, contract mediation differs from grievance mediation. To illustrate, a contract dispute involves all employees in a bargaining unit whereas a grievance dispute may involve a few employees but typically only one employee in a bargaining unit. A contract dispute may feature interrupted or suspended negotiations whereas a grievance dispute usually features continuous negotiations. In rights disputes internal mediation may occur in which a human resources or labor relations staff professional serves as the mediator, whereas in contract disputes external mediation will occur if the parties choose the mediation option. For these reasons, a mediator is more likely to communicate one party's proposed settlement to the other party in a grievance dispute and more likely to offer his/her own terms of settlement in a contract dispute. Nonetheless, in both instances, a mediator attempts to persuade the parties to reach a settlement. Hence, unlike an arbitrator's effectiveness, a mediator's effectiveness in bringing about a contract dispute settlement depends largely on his/her ability to influence the parties' perceptions and behavior—just as it does in grievance mediation.

In a few US industries, notably railroads and airlines, contract mediation is mandated rather than being an optional choice of the parties to a contract dispute. This requirement is spelled out in the (1926) Railway Labor Act (RLA), which initially applied only to railroads but was subsequently extended to airlines (Hegji, 2012). Enactment of this law was grounded in the belief that the highly unionized railroad industry (and, later, the airline industry) was so essential to the national economy that special measures had to be taken to prevent strikes and lockouts. Hence, the RLA provides for a standing National Mediation Board whose function is to assist labor and management to reach a settlement in the event of a contract dispute (National Mediation Board, 2010). Mediation services provided by the Board are closely similar to those provided by mediators in other industries.

In the US private sector more broadly, the National Labor Relations Act (NLRA) contains provisions for dealing with national emergency strikes that authorize the US President to appoint a Board of Inquiry, which basically serves as a fact-finding panel, when a particular contract dispute threatens national health or safety. If the Board's findings and recommendations do not motivate the parties to a contract dispute to settle that dispute, the US Congress may adopt those recommendations or variants thereof and then legislate a resolution of the dispute. These national emergency dispute provisions were invoked relatively often during the immediate post-World War II period, about once annually during the subsequent three decades, and hardly at all thereafter (Cullen, 1968; LeRoy and Johnson, 2001). This experience mirrors the decline in private sector unionization and collective bargaining from the mid-1950s to the present.

In the US public sector, mediation is rarely used in rights disputes but frequently used in contract disputes. For certain public services, especially police and fire protection, state and local laws usually prohibit employee strikes (and employer lockouts) and often mandate mediation as a substitute contract dispute settlement procedure. In some instances, these laws specify multiple contract dispute resolution procedures, including mediation, fact-finding and arbitration. Fact-finding basically involves the appointment of a special expert panel charged with analyzing the contract dispute, obtaining comparative pay, benefit and related data pertinent to the dispute, and offering recommendations for settling the dispute. Empirical evidence indicates that such substitute procedures, especially arbitration, are effective in settling public sector contract disputes, meaning that they curb strikes (and lockouts) and result in contract settlements that are not significantly different from (i.e. higher than) settlements resulting from negotiated agreements in which substitute dispute resolution procedures are not invoked (Lewin, Keefe, and Kochan, 2012).

SCOPE OF ISSUES

The scope of issues over which unionized employees may file grievances are defined by and limited to those terms and conditions of employment specified in a collective bargaining agreement. Such terms and conditions typically cover pay (e.g. regular pay, overtime pay, shift pay), fringe benefits (e.g. retirement plan, health-care plan, vacations, sick leave), job classifications, work shifts, supervision, layoffs, discipline and due process, and more. Unionized employees may file grievances involving any of these terms and conditions of employment and over discipline imposed for violating company policies and practices pertaining to these terms and conditions. They may not file grievances over other company policies and practices even if those policies and practices impact certain aspects of employment and employment relationships (Budd, 2010).

In the US in particular, the concept of private property is dominant. Among other things, this means that business owners retain the right to lead and manage their businesses as they see fit subject only to certain regulations and to contractual arrangements they may reach with employees and others, e.g. customers, suppliers, shareholders, and community groups. This same concept applies to executives and managers of businesses—in agency theory terminology, the agents of the business owners or principals—and is sometimes referred to as the doctrine of management's reserved rights (Chamberlain and Kuhn, 1965). This means that even where a company's employees are unionized and a collective bargaining agreement is in place, those employees may not file grievances over any company policy or practice or any term and condition of employment not covered by the collective bargaining agreement. It also means, of course, that grievance arbitration does not apply to these company policies, practices and non-covered terms and conditions of employment.

To illustrate, a unionized company's decision to close a plant, store, or service bureau and lay off its employees is not subject to grievance filing or grievance arbitration unless the collective bargaining agreement specifies that layoffs should be effectuated in reverse order of seniority and the company fails to do so. The same can be said of a unionized company's decision to move certain of its facilities elsewhere, resulting in layoffs of employees in the original locations. Similarly, a unionized manufacturing company's decision to reconfigure the specifications of its products is typically not covered by the collective bargaining agreement, and employees may therefore not file grievances over the changed specifications. In each of these examples, unionized employees may attempt to negotiate with the company in order to have these areas of decision-making covered by the next collective bargaining agreement. Unless and until they do, however, the grievance procedure, including grievance arbitration, cannot be invoked to challenge such decisions irrespective of their impacts on unionized employees.

GRIEVANCE ACTIVITY AND COLLECTIVE BARGAINING POWER

It is well known that the grievance procedure is sometimes used to influence collective bargaining between management and unionized employees (Kuhn, 1961; Katz and Kochan, 1999). In particular and typically at the behest of union officials, unionized employees may file a large number of grievances shortly before the expiration of an existing collective bargaining agreement or when negotiations commence over a new collective bargaining agreement or at a critical juncture in those negotiations. Further in this regard, unionized employees may "load up" on issue-specific grievances, filing them over pay in some instances, work rules in other instances, and supervision in still other instances. By using the grievance procedure this way, unionized employees attempt to influence bargaining power between labor and management (Sayles, 1958).

Because most collective bargaining agreements are multi-year agreements, this type of grievance filing behavior occurs relatively infrequently. Indeed, such behavior provides an incentive to management and union officials to increase the duration of a new collective bargaining agreement. Analytically, flooding the grievance process serves to slow employee work and to shift some of management and union officials' time from work to grievance handling. Such down time results in a loss of productivity, which represents the cost that unionized employees attempt to impose on management in seeking enhanced terms and conditions of employment. Also analytically, however, this cost can be compared to the cost of other unionized employee tactics undertaken to influence collective bargaining, such as working to rule, heightened sickness and absenteeism from work, and wildcat strikes. In turn, management may respond by holding fast to its bargaining position, disciplining employees for work slowdown, absenteeism and absences, and/or locking out employees for violating the terms of the collective bargaining agreement.

POST-DISPUTE RESOLUTION OUTCOMES

The literature on unionized grievance procedures focuses mainly on the antecedents of grievance filing, the dynamics of grievance processing, and the outcomes of grievance settlement, especially the parties' relative win-loss rates. More recently, research attention has turned to post-dispute resolution outcomes or, in question form, "What happens after grievances are settled?" This question derives from an industrial relations-based conceptualization of the grievance procedure as a mechanism for reversing an employee's deteriorated relationship with an employer, and from an organizational behavior-based conceptualization of the grievance procedure as a mechanism for providing restorative justice (Hirschman, 1970; Boroff and Lewin, 1997; Goodstein and Aquino, 2010).

The clearest answer to this question comes from studies that use a quasi-experimental research design to select a sample of a company's unionized employees who file grievances (i.e. grievants) and an accompanying sample of the same company's unionized employees who did not file grievances (i.e. non-grievants). In this design, the sample of grievants is the treatment group and the sample of non-grievants is the control group (other variables, such as job content, are also controlled). These two groups are then compared with respect to job performance, promotions and work attendance before grievances are filed (by the first group), during the grievance-processing period, and after grievances are settled. They are also compared with respect to turnover after grievances are settled. The findings from studies that have used this type of research design (Lewin and Peterson, 1988; Lewin and Peterson, 1999; Lewin, 2008b) are as follows.

Prior to the filing of grievances, grievants and non-grievants do not differ significantly in terms of job performance ratings, promotion rates and work attendance rates. The two groups also do not differ significantly on any of these measures during the grievance filing and settlement period. During the 1–3-year period following the settlement and closure of grievance cases, however, grievants have significantly lower job performance ratings and promotion rates, insignificantly lower work attendance rates, and significantly higher voluntary (and insignificantly higher involuntary) turnover rates than non-grievants. These findings, which have been replicated in a variety of unionized settings as well as in laboratory studies conducted by psychologists (Klaas and Denisi, 1989; Olson-Buchanan, 1996), suggest that employment relationship deterioration is not reversed and restorative justice is not achieved through the unionized grievance procedure. The findings also support the characterization of the unionized grievance procedure as a reactive system of employment dispute resolution. It is reactive because an employee must have experienced an event that eventually causes him/her to file a grievance. If the employee chooses not to do so, then a company's management may be unaware of the issue or problem at hand and the particular grievance issue may fester and go unresolved. Stated differently, the grievance procedure is invoked only after an employment relationship has deteriorated (Hirschman, 1970; Boroff and Lewin, 1997; Lewin, 2005). This ex-post approach to employment conflict resolution contrasts with the ex-ante or proactive approach that is often claimed to be a component of high-involvement work systems (HWIS), which are addressed more fully below.

Additional support for these conclusions comes from a subset of the aforementioned studies in which company-specific samples of supervisors of grievants are compared with company-specific sample of supervisors of non-grievants along the same pre-, during and post-employment dispute resolution measures (Lewin and Peterson, 1988). The findings indicate that prior to employee grievance filing and during the grievance filing and settlement period there are no significant differences between the supervisors of grievants and the supervisors of non-grievants with respect to job performance ratings, promotion rates, and work attendance rates. By contrast, during the 1–3-year period following grievance settlement, supervisors of grievants have significantly lower job performance ratings and promotion rates, insignificantly lower work attendance rates, and significantly higher turnover rates, especially involuntary turnover rates, than supervisors of non-grievants. These findings have also been replicated in a variety of unionized settings and constitute additional evidence of the aforementioned reactive nature of the unionized grievance procedure (Lewin and Peterson, 1999).

They do more than this, however. That employee-grievants and their supervisors have higher involuntary turnover rates (significantly higher in the case of supervisors) than non-grievants and their supervisors during the period following grievance settlement suggests that management retaliates against employees who file grievances—exercise voice—and especially against those who supervise them (Lewin and Boroff, 1996; Boroff and Lewin, 1997). Such retaliation may also be reflected in grievants' and supervisors of grievants' significantly lower post-grievance settlement job performance ratings and promotion rates compared to non-grievants and supervisors of non-grievants, in particular because neither of the treatment groups differed significantly from the control groups on these measures either prior to or during the period of grievance filing and settlement.

This retaliation explanation appears to be at odds with strategic human resource management (SHRM) theory, which posits that a grievance or grievance-like procedure is a component of a set of high-involvement type human resource management practices that enhance organizational performance. Other such practices include employment continuity, selective hiring, team-based work in a relatively decentralized organization, some pay contingent on organizational performance, considerable training and development, low status differentials, and substantial information-sharing with employees (Pfeffer, 1998). Following this reasoning, a company (or other organization) will benefit from having a grievance procedure in place through which employees—unionized and non-union alike—can exercise voice. Therefore, from a SHRM perspective, a grievance procedure together with certain other practices reflects a proactive approach to managing a company's workforce.

Some empirical evidence supports this view. For example, several studies (e.g. Huselid, 1995) report significant positive coefficients on one or another high-involvement human resource management type independent variable (measured as an index) in regression equations in which return on investment (ROI), revenue growth, and market value serve as dependent variables. In these studies, a grievance or other type of employment dispute resolution procedure is typically included as a component measure of high-involvement human resource management practices, which constitutes the main independent variable of interest. The findings from this research are often discussed in terms of the gain in ROI or revenue growth or market value associated with a firm being one standard deviation above the mean of the high-involvement human resource management index.

Other researchers, however, contend that these findings must be regarded skeptically if not rejected because the modeling is incorrect and therefore the regression equations are misspecified (e.g. Kaufman, 2010b). In particular, the causality (or true association) here may run from business performance to human resource management practices rather than the other way around, meaning in plainer language that relatively more successful firms will be more likely than less successful firms to adopt (costly) high-involvement human resource management practices. Further, human resource management-business performance researchers do not take account of or control for the effects of marketing practices, financial management practices, and operating or information technology practices in specifying and testing their ROI, revenue growth, and market value equations.[1]

More fundamentally, this research measures the availability of a grievance or grievance-like procedure but not its use. Other, relatively more industrial relations-oriented research, finds that grievance procedure usage is significantly negatively associated with productivity and product quality and significantly positively associated with labor costs (e.g. Katz, Kochan and Gobeille, 1983). Further, case studies of new employee consultation and team-based work initiatives in the pulp and paper and automobile manufacturing industries, respectively, find that such initiatives substantially reduced employee grievance filing rates while also substantially increasing productivity and product quality (Ichniowski, 1992; Rubinstein and Kochan, 2001). Hence, consistent with HIWS research, the availability of a grievance procedure is apparently associated with positive organizational outcomes whereas the use of a grievance procedure is apparently associated with negative organizational outcomes.

The retaliation explanation of why grievants and their supervisors fare more poorly than non-grievants and their supervisors after grievances are settled is not the only explanation. Another explanation may be termed "revealed performance" and refers to a company's discovery after the fact of grievance filing and settlement that employees who file grievances and their supervisors are poorer performers than employees who do not file grievances and their supervisors (Lewin and Peterson, 1999). The validity of this explanation depends in large part on whether and the extent to which grievance procedure usage shocks management into paying closer attention to the management and measurement of employee performance.

Two quite different examples support this alternative explanation. First, in litigation over employment disputes, especially cases involving claims of age, gender and race discrimination in the context of layoffs, employee performance appraisal data that companies produce in attempting to defend themselves against such claims typically show no statistically significant differences between those laid off and those retained (Cascio and Bernardin, 1981). As a result, especially when defendants lose such cases, companies will take steps to tighten their performance appraisal practices, sometimes including by adopting a forced distribution of employee performance appraisal ratings. In other words, this type of litigation shocks management into paying closer attention to performance management.

Second, it has long been claimed that when employees unionize and negotiate a collective bargaining agreement with management, a company re-examines most if not all of its operating practices and winds up changing some, perhaps many, of them. This can involve changes in workflow, work scheduling, inventory control, record keeping, job design, job assignments, performance evaluation, and especially supervision. As a consequence, productivity and efficiency are enhanced. This is known as "union shock" theory and has been used to explain why unionized and nonunion companie can coexist in the same industry or sector (Chamberlain and Kuhn, 1965; Rees, 1977; Lewin, 2005). Due to collective bargaining, pay and benefits—costs—will be higher in the unionized than in the non-union sector, but productivity will also be higher. In other words, unit labor costs will be roughly the same in the two sectors. Hence, both the litigation shock and the union shock examples support the revealed performance explanation of differential post-grievance settlement outcomes as between grievants and their supervisors and non-grievants and their supervisors.

COMPARING UNION AND NON-UNION GRIEVANCE PROCEDURES

Until relatively recently, grievance procedures prevailed largely, if not exclusively, in unionized companies. Over the last quarter-century or so, and especially during the early 21st century, grievance procedures and variants thereof have spread widely among non-union companies. Recent studies estimate that a majority, perhaps even two-thirds, of publicly traded non-union companies has adopted such procedures (Colvin, Klaas, and Mahoney, 2006; Lewin, 2008a). These procedures are sometimes referred to as alternative dispute resolution (ADR), meaning that they are an alternative to litigation. They are also sometimes referred to as non-union employee representation (NER), meaning that they are an alternative to unionization (Gollan and Lewin, 2013).

From a business strategy perspective, it may make good sense to provide employees with an internal voice mechanism, such as a grievance or grievance-like procedure (Lipsky, Seeber, and Fincher, 2003). After all, many companies claim that "people (meaning employees) are our most important asset" or that they compete for customers largely based on the quality of their human capital or intellectual capital (Pfeffer, 1998). If these claims are at all valid, then adoption of a grievance or grievance-like procedure may be well advised because it gives valuable human assets a voice in the way they are supervised and managed. Recent evidence indicates that both management and employees of non-union companies have similar views of the benefits and costs of grievance procedures. To illustrate, a study of grievance-like (ADR) procedures in four non-union companies found that company executives and employees rated a) identifying/redressing ineffective supervision/management, b) clarifying company HR policies and practices, and c) reducing employee dissatisfaction as among the main benefits of these procedures (Lewin, 2010). This same study found that company executives and employees rated a) loss of productive time, b) reduced supervisor morale, and c) retention of low-performing employees as among the main costs of these procedures. Further, when asked about whether or not the benefits of the grievance (ADR) procedure exceeded its costs, 85% of the 20 interviewed executives and 84% of the 790 surveyed employees responded "yes," and another 5% of the executives and 8% of the employees responded "about equal."

Non-union grievance procedures increasingly feature arbitration as the final step, spurred in part by recent US Supreme Court decisions supporting deferral to arbitration in non-union rights disputes similar to the doctrine enunciated by the court about 50 years ago in unionized rights disputes (Chamberlain and Kuhn, 1965; Lipsky, Seeber, and Fincher, 2003; Colvin, 2013). There are considerable differences, however, between arbitration invoked under a collective bargaining agreement and under an individual employment contract. In the former, company management and the union representing the employee jointly select the arbitrator. In the latter, arbitrator selection practices are more varied. In some instances the company alone selects the arbitrator, while in other instances the company and the employee or an employee representative (such as a peer or outside counsel) jointly select the arbitrator. In the former, company management and the union representing the employee split the costs of arbitration. In the latter, the company alone pays the costs of arbitration. In the former, a shop steward or union grievance committee member or union officer represents an employee. In the latter, an employee may be unrepresented or represented by a peer or occasionally by outside counsel depending upon arbitration provision specifications. In the former, the collective bargaining agreement spells out the scope of issues covered by arbitration. In the latter, the company alone specifies the issues covered by arbitration. For these reasons, non-union employment dispute arbitration has often been characterized as one-sided or employer-dominated (Colvin, Class, and Mahoney, 2006).

Stepping back, it is important to keep in mind that the debate over non-union firms' adoption of grievance and grievance-like procedures is in essence a debate about availability rather than use. Recall that grievance procedure availability is positively associated with organizational performance whereas grievance procedure usage is negatively associated with organizational performance. The evidence supporting these conclusions comes mainly from studies of non-union grievance procedures with respect to availability, and from studies of unionized grievance procedures with respect to use. Furthermore, non-union employees use their grievance procedures about half as often as unionized employees use their grievance procedures, and about half as many non-union employee grievances as unionized employee grievances reach the arbitration stage of the grievance procedure. This implies that there is a smaller negative effect on organizational performance of grievance procedure usage in non-union than in unionized contexts. Nonetheless, in both contexts the grievance procedure is an ex post facto, reactive mechanism for dealing with employment-related disputes.

Conclusions

The unionized grievance procedure has long been regarded as exemplifying the main mechanism through which employees exercise voice in the employment relationship. While this procedure remains in place and continues to operate in unionized settings, far more employees are covered by non-union grievance procedures than by unionized griev-ance procedures. This is because US private sector unionization has declined markedly to about 7% of the total workforce; non-union firms have a variety of incentives for adopt-ing grievance and grievance-like ADR procedures and a substantial majority of them have done so; and grievance-like ADR procedures cover larger proportions of non-union com-pany workforces than are covered by unionized company grievance procedures. As with unionized grievance procedures, non-union ADR procedures increasingly feature arbi-tration as the final employment dispute resolution step. In a non-union setting, however, arbitration is considerably more one-sided—employer sided—than in a unionized setting.

In both settings, there is an important distinction between grievance procedure avail-ability and grievance procedure usage. The extant literature indicates that grievance procedure availability is significantly positively associated with organizational perfor-mance, whereas grievance procedure usage is significantly negatively associated with organizational performance. In addition, evidence from studies of post-employment dispute resolution (i.e. usage) indicate that grievants and their supervisors fare more poorly with respect to job performance, promotions and turnover following griev-ance settlement than non-grievants and their supervisors. This may be due to retali-ation by management against employees who file grievances and the supervisors of those employees or, alternatively, because grievants and their supervisors are poorer job performers than non-grievants and their supervisors. Nonetheless and taken as a whole, this evidence supports the proposition that the grievance procedure is a reactive, after-the-fact mechanism.

If this is so, how can everyday employment disputes be handled more proactively, that is, ex ante? The HR-business performance and Strategic Human Resource Management (SHRM) literatures suggest an answer to this question, which is to include a grievance or grievance-like procedure as a component of a broader set of high-involvement human resource management practices (Kaminski, 1999). Clearly, many firms have done just this, but much less clear is whether they have done so for strategic reasons or, alterna-tively, to avoid employee unionization and/or employment dispute litigation. Available evidence, especially concerning court decisions supporting deferral to arbitration in employment disputes, suggests that the litigation threat is the main explanatory variable in this regard. As such, the rise of non-union grievance procedures can be explained as a defensive initiative and, in this sense, is no (or not much) different from the rise of unionized grievance procedures in an earlier era. Stated differently, the search continues for a more proactive approach to employment dispute resolution, whether in unionized contexts featuring collective bargaining agreements or in non-union contexts featuring individual employment contracts.

NOTE

1. This is an omitted variables issue rather than a misspecification issue but it, too, calls into question the contribution of high-involvement human resource management practices to company financial performance.

REFERENCES

Bemmels, B. and Foley, J. 1996. "Grievance Procedure Research: A Review and Theoretical Recommendations." *Journal of Management*, 22: 359–84.

Bingham, L. B. 2004. "Employment Dispute Resolution: The Case for Mediation." *Conflict Resolution Quarterly*, 22: 145–74.

Boroff, K. E. and Lewin, D. 1997. "Loyalty, Voice, and Intent to Exit a Union Firm: A Conceptual and Empirical Analysis." *Industrial and Labor Relations Review*, 51: 50–63.

Boswell, W. R. and Olson-Buchanan, J. B. 2004. "Experiencing Mistreatment at Work: The Role of Grievance-Filing, Nature of Mistreatment, and Employee Withdrawal." *Academy of Management Journal*, 47: 129–40.

Brett, J. M. and Goldberg, S. B. 1983. "Grievance Mediation in the Coal Industry: A Field Experiment." *Industrial and Labor Relations Review*, 37: 49–69.

Budd, J. W. 2010. *Labor Relations: Striking a Balance*. 3rd edn. New York: McGraw-Hill/Irwin.

Chamberlain, N. W. and Kuhn, J. W. 1965. *Collective Bargaining*. 2nd edn. New York: McGraw-Hill.

Cascio, W. F. and Bernardin, H. J. 1981. "Implications of Performance Appraisal Litigation for Personnel Decisions." *Personnel Psychology*, 34: 211–26.

Colvin, A. J. S. 2003. "Institutional Pressures, Human Resource Strategies, and the Rise of Non-union Dispute Resolution Procedures." *Industrial and Labor Relations Review*, 56: 375–92.

Colvin, A. J. S. 2013. "Participation Versus Procedures in Non-Union Dispute Resolution." *Industrial Relations*, 52, S1: 259–83.

Colvin, A. J. S., Klaas, B., and Mahoney, D. 2006. "Research on Alternative Dispute Resolution Procedures." In D. Lewin (ed.), *Contemporary Issues in Employment Relations Champaign*, IL: Labor and Employment Relations Association, 103–47.

Cullen, D. E. 1968. *National Emergency Strikes*. Ithaca, NY: Cornell University Press.

Feuille, P. 1999. "Grievance Mediation." In A. E. Eaton and J. H. Keefe (eds), *Employment Dispute Resolution and Worker Rights in the Changing Workplace*. Champaign, IL: Industrial Relations Research Association, 187–218.

Gollan, P. J. and Lewin, D. 2013. "Employee Representation in Non-Union Firms: An Overview." *Industrial Relations*, 52, S1: 173–93.

Goodstein, J. and Aquino, K. 2010. "And Restorative Justice For All: Redemption, Forgiveness, and Reintegration in Organizations." *Journal of Organizational Behavior*, 31: 624–28.

Hegji. A. 2012. *Federal Labor Relations Statutes: An Overview*. CRS Report for Congress. Washington, DC: Congressional Research Service (26 Nov.), 1–14.

Hirschman, A. O. 1970. *Exit, Voice and Loyalty*. Cambridge, MA: Harvard University Press.

Huselid, M. 1995. "The Impact of Human Resource Management Practices on Turnover, Productivity, and Corporate Financial Performance." *Academy of Management Journal*, 38: 635–72.

Ichniowski, C. 1992. "Human Resource Practices and Productive Labor-Management Relations." In D. Lewin, O. S. Mitchell, and P. D. Sherer (eds), *Research Frontiers in Industrial Relations and Human Resources*. Madison, WI: Industrial Relations Research Association, 239–72.

Jacoby, S. M. 1986. "Progressive Discipline in American Industry: Its Origins, Development and Consequences." In D. B. Lipsky (ed.), *Advances in Industrial and Labor Relations*, 3: 213–60. Greenwich, CT: JAI Press.

Kaminski, M. 1999. "New Forms of Work Organization and Their Impact on the Grievance Procedure." In A. E. Eaton and J. H. Keefe (eds), *Employment Dispute Resolution and Worker Rights in the Changing Workplace*. Champaign, IL: Industrial Relations Research Association, 219–46.

Katz, H. C. and Kochan, T. A. 1999. *Introduction to Collective Bargaining and Industrial Relations*. 2nd edn. Irwin.

Katz, H. C., Kochan, T. A., and Gobeille, K. 1983. "Industrial Relations Performance, Economic Performance, and QWL Programs: An Interplant Analysis." *Industrial and Labor Relations Review*, 37: 3–17.

Kaufman, B. E. 2010a. "The Theoretical Foundation of Industrial Relations and Its Implications for Labor Economics and Human Resource Management." *Industrial and Labor Relations Review*, 64: 817–51.

Kaufman, B. E. 2010b. "SHRM Theory in the Post-Huselid Era: Why It is Fundamentally Misspecified." *Industrial Relations*, 49: 286–313.

Klaas, B. S. and DeNisi, A. S. 1989. "Managerial Reactions to Employee Dissent: The Impact of Grievance Activity on Performance Ratings." *Academy of Management Journal*, 32: 705–17.

Kuhn, J. W. 1961. *Bargaining in Grievance Settlement: The Power of Industrial Work Groups*. New York: Columbia University Press.

LeRoy, M. H. and Johnson, J. H. 2001. "Death by Legal Injunction: National Emergency Strikes Under the Taft-Hartley Act and the Moribund Right to Strike." *Arizona Law Review*, 43: 63–134.

Lewin, D. 1987. "Dispute Resolution in the Non-union Firm: A Theoretical and Empirical Analysis." *Journal of Conflict Resolution*, 3: 465–502.

Lewin, D. 1997. "Workplace Dispute Resolution." In D. Lewin, D. J. B. Mitchell, and M. Zaidi, M. (eds), *The Human Resource Management Handbook*, Part II. Greenwich, CT: JAI Press, 197–218.

Lewin, D. 1999. "Theoretical and Empirical Research on the Grievance Procedure and Arbitration: A Critical Review." In A. E. Eaton and J. H. Keefe (eds), *Employment Dispute Resolution and Worker Rights in the Changing Workplace*. Champaign, IL: Industrial Relations Research Association, 137–86.

Lewin, D. 2005. "Unionism and Employment Conflict Resolution: Rethinking Collective Voice and its Consequences." *Journal of Labor Research*, 26: 209–39.

Lewin, D. 2008a. "Resolving Conflict." In P. Blyton, N. Bacon, J. Fiorito, and E. Heery (eds), *The Sage Handbook of Industrial Relations*. London, UK: Sage, 447–68.

Lewin. D. 2008b. "Workplace ADR: What's New and What Matters?" In S. E. Befort and P. Halter (eds), *Workplace Justice for a Changing Environment: Proceedings of the Sixtieth Annual Meeting, National Academy of Arbitrators*. Washington, DC: Bureau of National Affairs, 23–9.

Lewin, D. 2010. "Mutual Gains." In A. Wilkinson, P. J. Gollan, M. Marchington, and D. Lewin (eds), *The Oxford Handbook of Participation in Organizations*. Oxford, UK: Oxford University Press, 427–52.

Lewin, D. and Boroff, K. E. 1996. "The Role of Loyalty in Exit and Voice: A Conceptual and Empirical Analysis." In D. Lewin and B. E. Kaufman (eds), *Advances in Industrial and Labor Relations*, 7: 69–96. Greenwich, CT: JAI Press.

Lewin, D. and Peterson, R. B. 1988. *The Modern Grievance Procedure in the United States*. Westport, CT: Quorum.

Lewin, D. and Peterson, R. B. 1999. "Behavioral Outcomes of Grievance Activity." *Industrial Relations*, 38: 554–79.

Lewin, D., Keefe, J. H., and Kochan, T. A. 2012. "The New Great Debate about Unionism and Collective Bargaining in U.S. State and Local Governments." *Industrial and Labor Relations Review*, 65: 749–78.

Lipsky, D. B., Seeber, R. L., and Fincher, R. D. 2003. *Emerging Systems for Managing Workplace Conflict*. San Francisco, CA: Jossey-Bass.

National Mediation Board (NMB). 2010. *Annual Performance and Accountability Report, FY2010*. Washington, DC: NMB.

Olson-Buchanan, J. B. 1996. "Voicing Discontent: What Happens to the Grievance Filer After the Grievance?" *Journal of Applied Psychology*, 81: 1–11.

Pfeffer, J. 1998. *The Human Equation: Building Profits by Putting People First*. Boston, MA: Harvard Business School Press.

Rees, A. 1977. *The Economics of Trade Unions*, rev. edn. Chicago: University of Chicago Press.

Rubinstein, S. A. and Kochan, T. A. 2001. *Learning from Saturn: Possibilities for Corporate Governance and Employee Relations*. Ithaca, NY: Cornell University Press.

Sayles, L. R. 1958. *Behavior of Industrial Work Groups: Prediction and Control*. New York: Wiley.

CHAPTER 6

....

THIRD-PARTY PROCESSES IN EMPLOYMENT DISPUTES

....

WILLIAM BROWN

INTRODUCTION

....

THIRD-PARTY processes cover all forms of neutral intervention in dispute resolution. They provide a flexible range of practices and procedures whereby outsiders can be brought in to break deadlocks and achieve settlements between employers and either organized labor or individual employees. They apply just as much to the persuasive efforts of conciliators and mediators as to the binding awards of arbitrators and industrial tribunals. In practice, these different forms of intervention often merge into each other. If, for example, a conciliator fails to get the disputing parties to resolve their differences, then they may move on to help distill those differences into workable terms of reference for subsequent arbitration. Both formal and informal processes have their part to play.

At the start of the 20th century the growing prosperity of many advanced economies was threatened by increasing industrial unrest. Strike action by relatively small numbers of organized workers could paralyze economic life. The remedies for this problem introduced by different countries were varied. So was their resilience, with most countries changing their legislative framework more than once over the following decades. Countries differed, especially in the extent to which they provided for third-party processes. Some left disputes for the courts to sort out; some created, in effect, special courts; some effectively took disputes out of the reach of the courts altogether; and some offered third-party neutrals as an optional aid. By the 21st century a worldwide decline in strikes since 1980 has reduced the need for third-party intervention. But circumstances have changed in other ways, and the nature of interventions has changed as the world economy has opened up. This chapter describes this changing context and its implications. It describes how institutions have been changing in response. It then discusses the dynamics of intervention in collective employment disputes and the varied third-party approaches that are used to resolve them.

The Changed Environment

For most of the 20th century, industrialized democracies had experienced historically high levels of disputes. In the mid-1960s, for example, the average annual number of days lost through strikes per thousand workers was 870 for the US and 190 for the UK (Clegg, 1972: 316). Towards the end of the century, however, there was a sharp worldwide decline in strike incidence, especially in private sectors. This is evident for both the developed and the developing world (Godard, this volume; Silver, 2003: 126; Serrano et al., 2012: 73). Although directly comparable data are hard to come by, in most OECD countries industrial disputes, especially those in the private sector, have come down to levels that are far lower than at any time on record. In Britain, for example, in the first decade of the 2000s, the average level of strikes diminished to less than one-tenth of the level of thirty years earlier. The private sector, which until the 1980s was highly strike prone, has seen strikes become a rarity. Half of all British strikes so far in the 2000s, accounting for over three-quarters of working days lost, have been in the public sector.

At the same time trade union membership in many countries has been in historical decline. Between 1980 and 2011, the density of trade union membership—expressed as a percentage of the employed workforce—for all the OECD countries fell from 33% to 18%. Although membership held up in Scandinavia, for most countries it has declined substantially despite periods of comparatively strong economic growth. For example, between 1980 and 2011 union density fell as follows: in Australia from 54% to 18%; in Canada from 38% to 29%; in France from 18% to 8%; in Germany from 35% to 19%; in Italy from 50% to 35%; in Japan from 31% to 18%; in the Netherlands from 35% to 18%; in the UK from 50% to 26%; and in the US from 21% to 11%.

Over these thirty years, each country has its own story of changing relationships between trade unions and government, and of consequent legal change. However, some underlying structural changes have been more widespread internationally. Notable is the contraction in size of a highly unionized public sector (in the UK from 36% of all employees to 26% over the period). Also important has been the shrinking of an often highly unionized private manufacturing sector (in the UK from 38% of all employees to 13%). The result for most countries has been a proportionately larger, hard-to-organize private services sector. As a consequence, trade union presence has diminished substantially in the private sectors of many advanced economies. For example, in 2010 the density of unionization of the private sector as a whole had fallen to 14% in the UK, 17% in Japan, and as low as 7% in the US (Brownlie, 2012; Kochan, 2012; JILPT, 2012).

There is no reason to suppose that the worldwide decline in strikes and in union membership since around 1980 is a passing phase. The evidence suggests that both are a direct consequence of an increasingly globalized economy. It has been a period in which the competing world's workforce has doubled as a result of the full entry into the world markets of China, India and the old Soviet bloc. International trade has consistently expanded twice as fast as world product. Foreign direct investment has consistently increased twice as fast as international trade. Ownership of enterprises has become progressively more international, and mobile between countries. The challenge to what are almost invariably nation-based private sector trade unions has been overwhelming. All too often, a well-organized trade union, mounting a credible threat of a strike, has seen the employers, equally credibly, threaten to move the work elsewhere in the world. There is clear evidence from Britain that, since 1980, collective bargaining has diminished most rapidly and farthest in those sectors where competition has intensified the most (Brown et al., 2009: 40). It is reflected in the declining share of national income in many countries that is going to wages (International Labor Organization, 2012: 44). The globalized economy is a savage environment for trade unions.

This has profoundly altered the way in which trade unions can operate. Ever since they began, trade unions have deployed two distinct strategies to get the best for their members. The more conspicuous strategy was that of winning and defending benefits by threats of strike action. It essentially involved confrontation with management, with unions attempting to bargain for a better share of limited resources. The alternative strategy lay in engaging with management in a more cooperative way. By engaging in consultation, unions would give employers the opportunity to carry their workers with them in more productive working, and thereby win more resources for all. Whether and how unions deployed these confrontational and cooperative strategies depended very much upon the employers and the markets that those employers faced.

Trade unions are at their most effective in their confrontational mode when they can negotiate with all the employers competing with each other in a self-contained market for some product or service, or negotiate with a single employer whose product market position is overwhelmingly strong, preferably one of monopoly, or where labor costs are a small component of overall costs, so that controlling them is a low management priority. The globalization of product and capital markets has challenged these strategies. This is not only because in some ways competitive pressures have become more intense, but also because the internationalization of monopolistic enterprises has enabled them to outmaneuver strong unions by relocating or outsourcing production to less-unionized countries. Even for public sector employers, whose monopoly position is unavoidably more robust, there has been a tendency to privatize where possible and, failing that, to outsource aspects of the work to the private sector. Public sector trade union membership has generally remained high relative to private enterprise, but any appetite by unions for confrontational bargaining has been much tempered by a realistic fear of further outsourcing.

It is, then, hardly surprising that both strike levels and trade union membership have fallen across the world. It is not only trade unions but also national governments that are losing influence over labor standards as the world economy becomes ever larger and more open. This is influencing third-party intervention.

Changes in the Institutions of Third-Party Intervention

Governments have traditionally felt obliged to intervene in industrial disputes when unresolved conflicts have caused unacceptable disruption for the wider society. The result has typically been the creation of quasi-judicial processes, insulated from the vagaries of politics. Even within the European Union, let alone more widely, there is great variety in these third-party institutions. Above all, they differ in the extent to which they are dominated by the judiciary as opposed to being dominated by non-legal specialists and representatives of employers and labor. In recent years, however, they have been changing. Despite the very different legal and political backgrounds of European countries, there are some important common patterns to this change (Valdés Dal-Ré, 2003b). One reflection of this is a softening in diversity. The once sharp contrast between countries avoiding direct legal intervention, and those depending on it, is diminishing. For example, once "voluntarist" Britain has seen increased statutory regulation of disputes, while France and Spain have seen a shift to a less judicial approach.

The most important contemporary trend is a preference for voluntary rather than judicial means of settling disputes. There is a growing tendency in most pre-2004 EU countries to try to solve labor disputes without resorting to court proceedings. The immediate benefits lie in lower costs and faster resolution, and also in greater flexibility of outcome. But in the long run what is more important is that voluntary solutions tend to build greater commitment and self-reliance for the disputants. One authoritative analyst has compared unfavorably "the winner-loser outcome that a legal process always produces" with "the capacity of conciliation and mediation formulas to generate or renew agreements and to create a stable negotiating channel and synergies for continuing negotiation" (Valdés Dal-Ré, 2003b: 46). It was with this in mind that in 2000 the European Commission proposed to encourage the spread of voluntary conciliation, mediation and arbitration procedures for dispute resolution.

The more exposed that industrial relations are to competitive markets, then, in general, the more voluntary procedures can be relied upon to resolve disputes. Confrontational bargainers may be able slug it out for weeks in the shelter of a monopoly, with their customers suffering impotently. But once their product market becomes exposed to competition, a prolonged strike may drive their custom elsewhere, never to return, and the incentive to reach a settlement becomes much sharper. Britain and Holland are two examples of countries that have seen greatly increased success in strike avoidance through voluntary means in response to a harsher competitive environment (Goodman, 2000; De Roo, 2003). In Britain the success rate of collective conciliation has risen five-fold since the 1980s. The logic of markets, in terms of potential loss of business and jobs, has a greater influence in the long run than the decisions of judges.

It is not easy, however, to break away from a judicial system of dispute resolution. Generally, the more specialized a country's industrial judicial arrangements are, the less is the incentive for them to develop non-judicial conflict resolution methods. On this spectrum, the Mediterranean countries are at the specialist end, while Britain, Ireland and Holland are at the less judicially constrained end. Much also depends upon whether there is a strong tradition of collective bargaining and what in Europe has come to be called "social dialog". That is, whether there is substantial consultation between employer and trade union bodies. Denmark, Sweden, Holland and Finland have developed such mature bargaining relationships that third-party intervention mainly gives a stamp of added legitimacy to solutions already reached independently by the parties themselves. By contrast, France and Portugal still rely heavily upon the legal system to deal with industrial problems (Valdés Dal-Ré, 2003b). The shift of emphasis from judicial to voluntary means of dispute resolution is evident beyond Europe. It reflects a growing demand for what is commonly called "alternative dispute resolution" (ADR)—that is, at its most basic, the resolution of disputes without recourse to legal procedures—that extends far beyond employment to include, for example, community disputes.

Accompanying this shift to voluntary dispute resolution, another widespread development in the context of employment has been the growth of an advisory function for third-party agencies. This advisory role reflects a more general change in attitude, that is evident for many public services, that prevention is better than treatment. In Britain, for example, this has altered the priorities of fire brigades, police forces, and prison and health services. More effort is being devoted to preventing fires, crimes, reoffending, and ill-health. In industrial third-party agencies, the intention of the advisory role is to shift resources from settling disputes through conciliation, to pre-empting future disputes by encouraging good procedures and employment practices. No agency has thrown itself more wholeheartedly into this pre-emptive advisory work, over and above dispute resolution, than the British third-party intervention agency the Advisory, Conciliation and Arbitration Service (ACAS). Something approaching half of its resources are devoted to running advisory projects, training events, disseminating best practice, and staffing telephone helplines (ACAS, 2011). Unsurprisingly, one of ACAS's slogans is "when we're not working on today's cures, we are working on tomorrow's preventions."

It is a change to be found in many countries. For example, the US Federal Mediation and Conciliation Service (FMCS) has moved from a position in the 1980s when all of the mediators' time was devoted to current dispute resolution, to one where a third of their time is now concerned with conflict prevention, such as through "relationship-building training" programs. The Canadian FMCS offers a wide-ranging "preventative mediation" program. Legislation has moved the New Zealand system towards a more facilitative and advisory approach. The Irish Labour Relations Commission and the Northern Ireland Labour Relations Agency have both developed advisory services to help propagate best practice, not only in dispute resolution but in employment practice more generally.

The emerging picture is clear. The opening up of the world economy and of public services to wider competition is changing the nature of third-party intervention. There is diminishing scope for employers and trade unions to battle out their differences in the sheltered arena of a national market or a monopoly service. To do so is to risk annihilation. Trade unions are being forced to shift their manner of operating away from confrontation towards a much greater reliance on cooperation with employers. This has always been a part of their behavior, but external competitive pressures are forcing it to become dominant. The implications for third-party intervention agencies are far-reaching. There is less call for them to resolve collective disputes by judgements according to some legal code or abstract principles of justice or precedent. The contesting parties increasingly need to be guided to a settlement that reflects the very real and evident demands of the market pressures bearing down upon them. The question to be resolved becomes not what is implied by law, but what will work.

What will work in practice is usually what is locally felt to reflect reality. However much the outcome may be constrained by harsh competitive necessity, it is unavoidably bound up with notions of fairness and of natural, if not legal, justice. Settlements that are perceived to be "unfair" are liable to undermine employee morale and to sour the employment relationship. Consequently, a major part of the task of the third-party process is to help the protagonists, and those whom they represent, to adjust their expectations, and their perceptions of what is "fair", to the shifting realities of the markets in which their business is located. Central to achieving this is giving each side a good hearing and aiding an outcome on the basis of evidence that both sides have seen, heard, provided, and had a chance to challenge. Notions of "fairness" in employment are usually locally formed. They are best locally maintained.

THE BARGAINING PROCESS

An understanding of third-party processes is helped by some analysis of the relationship into which the intervention is being made. The context of the power relationship in collective bargaining is distinctive. Unlike many commercial relationships, employers and employees are heavily dependent on each other. However bitter the dispute of the day, both sides know that, in the near future, they will have to pick up the bits and make amends. Bargainers on both sides are usually acutely anxious to avoid the mutual damage of strike action. They try to take into account changing market conditions in making their claims and offers. A shrewd understanding of each other's market position and organizational strength, and an informed awareness of the credibility of a strike threat, can lead to a shift in the balance of advantage being reflected in the agreed settlement without any strike action being necessary. In John Hicks' seminal theoretical analysis, should the two sides have perfect information about each other's strengths, weaknesses, and preferences, agreement would be reached without the occurrence of strikes (Hicks, 1932).

But when the two sides have different evaluations of their relative market and organizational strength, a strike may be precipitated. The employer may call what they believe to be the union's bluff. Or the union may believe that the employer has not appreciated how the union's strength has increased, perhaps as a result of raised employee aspirations. In either case, the open fighting out of a strike can be a worthwhile investment for whichever side emerges as the winner, with consequences lasting well beyond the current bargaining period.

Whether or not a given negotiation involves a strike, the outcome may carry heavy implications for the survival of the business as well as for the continuing relationship between employer and their employees' union. As a result, the negotiating process tends to have considerable complexity. Effective collective bargaining requires sophistication on the part of those involved and the commitment of time and money. This is deemed worthwhile if it avoids damaging disputes, or if it results in the more efficient management of change. The most serviceable analysis of the complexities of collective bargaining is that by Walton and McKersie (1965). They identified, from a substantial number of observed negotiations in the US, four distinct processes that can be found at work in parallel with each other.

The first process, which fits the popular conception, is what they called "distributive bargaining." This is a "zero-sum" bargain over how the "cake" should be divided up. It is typical of simple annual pay claims. In terms of behavior, it is characterized by a rather formal process, for which opposing parties meet round a table, make statements for the record, often use aggressive language, and edge towards compromise by means of a series of adjournments. Distributive bargaining was a dominant feature of the more confrontational form of collective bargaining that has diminished markedly since the 1980s, as noted above.

The second process is "integrative bargaining." This is a "positive-sum" process that is characterized by both sides taking a problem-solving approach. More recently in the US it has been referred to as "interest-based" or "mutual gains" bargaining (Katz et al., 2008:192). Confrontational language is minimized and informality emphasized. Such bargaining is usually carried out away from the normal place of work, perhaps at a weekend retreat in a country hotel. The objective is to encourage both sides to adopt lateral thinking and flexible attitudes in order to facilitate concessions and improved ways of working. In Britain it became a feature of the "workplace partnership" agreements that flourished, with government and Trades Union Congress encouragement, at the end of the 1990s. Although the word "partnership" quickly fell from favor, an emphasis on integrative bargaining continues to be a feature of the more consultative and cooperative style of collective bargaining that characterizes the British private sector of the 2000s as, indeed, it always has been in the public sector (Oxenbridge and Brown, 2004).

But negotiators do not operate as free agents, and Walton and McKersie identified two further, complementary processes. One process, which they described as "intra-organizational bargaining," is the way in which the negotiators seek to manage the attitudes and preferences of the organizations on whose behalf they negotiate. Informal networking, report-back meetings, and statements to the media are important in this. The other, described as "attitudinal structuring," is a more diffuse process whereby they seek to influence the wider climate of opinion and expectation, not least of the opposing side. It is sometimes called the "framing" of attitudes, and can call for strategies redolent of wartime propaganda.

Before considering how these parallel processes are relevant for third-party intervention, it is necessary to reflect on two further crucial aspects of negotiations. The first concerns the internal politics of each side—their intra-organizational efficiency. The second is the relationship between the individual bargaining agents who confront each other. Both of these contribute towards the necessary conditions for effective negotiation.

An important determinant of the effectiveness of a negotiation arises from the intra-organizational complexity of the two opposing parties. Whether trade unions or employers, they often comprise uneasy coalitions of interests. The greater their heterogeneity, the bigger the task of intra-organizational bargaining whereby divergent interests can be reconciled and agreement reached on a compromise set of priorities and bargaining objectives. Failure can lead to paralysis. Much depends upon the clarity of the coalition's decision-making constitution. Much also depends upon the skill and sensitivity of the individuals who have to administer it.

Taking the employers' side first, this is a particularly important issue for employers' associations involved in multi-employer, sectoral bargaining. Forming a united front against the unions is bound to be difficult for employers who are in direct competition with each other in their product market. It is especially so where the employers concerned differ substantially: in size; in the extent to which their sales are in specialized niches; or in the extent to which they rely upon export markets. Such heterogeneity creates substantial constitutional challenges for the maintenance of unity.

The challenge of maintaining a united front is a different one for trade unions. Unions often have to mobilize a credible threat of collective action. Or, at the very least, they have to mobilize consent to an eventual agreement, often across a diversity of markets, skill levels, and occupational interests. In support of this, the union movement has developed a substantial rhetoric of egalitarianism and solidarity, which is best understood as a functional necessity rather than as purely ideological. Of necessity, unions place great emphasis on constitutional rectitude and democratic procedures. Joint union negotiating committees typically have carefully balanced representative membership and precise standing orders to ensure the clear legitimation of decisions. Usually they are required to ratify provisional bargaining settlements through a final democratic consultation with the rank and file. When constitutional rectitude within the union side breaks down, settlement with the employers can become all but impossible.

Failures of internal decision-making within the opposing bargaining parties arise from ambiguous authorization procedures, from inadequate means of disseminating information and explanation, and from inconclusive mechanisms of internal debate. The more constraints that are placed on the negotiating committee, the more difficult it is to establish a bargaining mandate and achieve its ratification. This, then, is a key condition for effective negotiation: an efficient and clear constitutional arrangement for decision-making within each of the opposing bargaining parties. The greater the intra-organizational constraints under which the individual negotiators are obliged to operate, the less their chance for success will be in the cut-and-thrust of side-deals, trade-offs, face-savers, and compromises that will ease the way to agreement.

A key determinant of the effectiveness of a negotiation is the quality of the bargaining relationship between the opposing negotiators. This is basically concerned with the efficiency with which the individual agents exchange information in their continuing dialog. The bargaining relationship can be defined as the extent to which the negotiators are able to make each other aware of the constraints under which they operate, and of the likely reactions of one organization to actions by the other. The better the bargaining relationship is, the better the information exchange is. And, as a result, the better the relationship, the more accurate (and less costly) will be each side's anticipation of the way in which the opposing side might respond to fresh developments (Brown, 1973: 134).

With a strong bargaining relationship, the negotiators have a greater freedom of action and maneuver than when it is weak. They can informally float possible solutions in a way that is "without prejudice" and thus will not be held against them should their suggestions fail. They can allow the other side to put on a public show of strength or outrage without overreacting. They will be aware that such a show was intended to placate intra-organizational pressures behind the negotiators putting it on, and not to antagonize the negotiators they face. They can provide their opposing negotiators with insights into the underlying priorities of the side they are representing, and of the strength of feeling of their constituents on different bargaining issues. They can help the opposing negotiators to manage their respective organizations by arranging for them to earn personal credit, albeit for small victories. They can dress up outcomes in such a way as to reassure their opposite numbers that the making of concessions will not be accompanied by humiliation (Batstone et al., 1977: 171, 264).

This is not to say that, at times, even negotiators with excellent bargaining relationships may not see advantage in tactical ploys that increase the uncertainty confronting their opponents. Schelling (1960) wrote the classic game-theoretic analysis of the many tricks used by negotiators. They include making themselves unavailable at key phases of negotiations, and unexpectedly making apparently binding commitments. An ability to ride out each other's bargaining tactics without damaging the bargaining relationship is a sign of professionalism. But in the long-run, the power relationship will be managed most efficiently, and with least use of costly sanctions, if the bargaining relationship is strong.

One way of describing a strong bargaining relationship is that it has a high level of trust. It is a reciprocal business relationship between professional negotiators. It may, or may not, involve affective friendship, but it frequently does. Close but professional friendships are a feature of some of the most productive bargaining relationships. There are, of course, inherent dangers if the professional negotiating teams become too close. Any strong bargaining relationship can mutate into a self-serving stitch-up between consenting professionals if they are not exposed to some sort of democratic or managerial accountability. The more isolated the negotiators are from those whom they represent, the greater the danger of this.

One consequence of the decline of collective bargaining, and of the contracting-out of many personnel management functions, is that the negotiating skills touched on here are much less evident than was the case in the 1980s and 1990s. But even with the best intra-organizational constitutions, and the subtlest of bargaining relationships between the negotiators, agreement is sometimes elusive. At this point it may help to bring in an outsider, and the way that role works sheds further light on the bargaining process.

METHODS OF THIRD-PARTY INTERVENTION

Third-party intervention has long provided a safety net for collective bargaining. Most countries have some sort of state-sponsored conciliation and arbitration service. They are state sponsored because a service paid for by the disputants usually has its independence challenged. Some countries have had legal requirements to use such interventions—Canada's compulsory conciliation and Australia's compulsory arbitration endured for most of the 20th century. Most such services have some sort of arrangement to ensure independence from government as well as the involvement of both employers and trade unions. For example, the UK's ACAS is run at arms' length from government by a council constituted on a "social partnership" basis, with equal numbers of representatives from union and employer backgrounds (Brown, 2000; Sisson and Taylor, 2006). In the US, where much third-party intervention is done on a commercial basis, there are a range of safeguards intended to uphold the independence of the third party (Kochan and Zack, 2013).

There is a spectrum of third-party interventions, from conciliation to arbitration. At one extreme, conciliation may amount simply to facilitating information exchange between the disputing parties. At the other, arbitration is a quasi-judicial process in which a formal hearing leads to an "award" that is binding on the disputants. But in practice there is a range of more-or-less active interventions between these extremes, some of which may be referred to, more commonly in the US, as mediation.

One part of the conciliator's role is the relatively passive one of transmitting perceptions and proposals between the disputing parties, who are usually kept in separate rooms. But in practice such a role quickly becomes more active. An important first step is, perhaps surprisingly, to get the parties to agree on what it is that they are in disagreement about. This can take time as they often have different perceptions of what is in dispute and what issues underlie it. Getting agreed understanding of the issue, and getting agreement to put aside tangential controversies over causes and motives, often paves the way to reaching a settlement. Many an arbitration has been averted because the intricate process of agreeing the terms of reference has led to the issue being resolved.

Effective conciliation can call on a variety of skills. The disputing parties have often become so bogged down in particular ways of looking at the issues in contention that the fresh eye of the conciliator may allow them to be repacked in novel and more acceptable ways. An important early part of the conciliator's task is getting each party, independently and alone, to describe and analyze the issues, testing and rephrasing and probing ambiguities in order to clarify the disputing parties' thinking. The conciliator's fresh eye and genuinely naïve questions may help the parties to avoid worn pathways of thought. Lateral thinking is always helpful.

Another phase may be one of getting the parties, again in isolation from each other, to discuss the hypothetical worst possible outcome of a failure to agree, and to reflect aloud about its more unpleasant implications. If done before an adjournment, when they can brood on it, this may improve the acceptability of hitherto unacceptable compromises. Both sides are, metaphorically, made to look over the precipices down which they could drop if agreement is not reached. A successful conciliator is far from passive. He or she may have to make the opposing parties extremely uncomfortable during the course of the process. Eventual agreement typically comes not through rational argument and sweet reason, but through the painful adjustment of expectations to a more realistic appreciation of the options and the costs.

Preventing loss of face by the negotiators is often important in a third-party intervention. This applies at both the personal and the public level. Negotiators who have been stuck in each other's company through long meetings will place considerable store in emerging with their mutual respect and their self-esteem intact. But during the negotiations they may have used some fairly outrageous, possibly moralistic and tendentious arguments. They may have conceded some previously passionately defended "over my dead body" positions. The conciliator will know that they will reach agreement easier if both sides can envisage a dignified exit in each other's eyes. Considerable store is thus placed on devising what is often called a "silken ladder" down which those who have to make major concessions can climb. It may involve the puffing up of a minor favorable concession, subordinate to the main issue at stake, to look like a major one. It may require a robust (but actually unenforceable) agreed statement of intent about the future. If the bargaining relationship is good, the negotiators will work with the conciliator to protect each other's self-esteem.

At the public level, it is important to ensure if possible that neither negotiator should have reason to fear that they might be humiliated either by the media or in the eyes of their respective organizations. An old adage was "mourn in victory; cheer in defeat"— meaning that it was foolish in terms of long-term relations for the perceived winner to emerge triumphant. Settlements are often followed by sound bites in televised interviews about the courage and toughness of the opposition, and statements of the sort: "this is a victory not for either side but for common-sense." It may be necessary to deliberately string out the proceedings and to crash into deadlines in order to give the public impression of a hard-fought bargain.

It usually helps to have a number of variables in play, around which concessions can be traded. It particularly helps if the two sides differ slightly in the priority they place on these, or in their perception of the importance ascribed to them by their respective organizations. At one extreme, a settlement involving multiple components can often be "sold" relatively easily to each organization because different aspects of it can be stressed to the different audiences. But a single-issue dispute is more difficult. A conciliator may be able to create negotiating space by, in effect, breaking down a single-issue bargain into separate items. Each side may then be able to soften the unpopular aspects of the settlement with their respective constituencies by choosing which to emphasize.

The conciliation process often grinds to a standstill, with neither side willing to make any further concessions, however ingenious the conciliator's suggestions may have been. It may be that one or both sides are unwilling to be seen to make the difficult compromises to attain a settlement that they both can privately see is the only one that is feasible. Their constituents may, for example, have publicly forbidden such compromises. The appropriate action may then be for the third party, acting as what in the UK is usually called a mediator, formally to propose it, and for the two sides to take it as an arbitrated award. This process, which is sometimes called "med-arb", leaves both sides free publicly to "blame" the third party for what they have reluctantly gone along with. In a slightly different process, called "arb-med", the third party, with proceedings stalled, writes down an award, and informs the negotiators of this, but does not reveal the details to them, producing and imposing it only if they fail to reach agreement through mediation. This can play effectively on the negotiators' need to be seen by their constituents to be reaching an agreement, and one they know that they can live with (Kochan and Zack, 2013).

Another hybrid is what is sometimes called a "single-text" strategy in which the third party attempts to build up the text of an agreement incrementally, going to and fro between the parties until the successive drafts have reached a point that is acceptable to both. This can be particularly useful if the negotiators feel it necessary to provide written reassurances for their constituents on ancillary anxieties. Even if no conclusion is in sight, the third party can play a constructive role by what is sometimes called "advisory" arbitration, which involves issuing a set of non-binding recommendations for resolving the dispute, in effect thereby indicating the direction of travel when there is a resumption of negotiations (Kochan and Zack, 2013).

In straightforward arbitration, the arbitrator is very evidently there to be blamed for his or her award. In the US this is made more complicated because the same arbitrator is commonly used by the same organization on many occasions over the years. The desire of the arbitrator to appear independent in order to retain the relationship with the organization may create inappropriate pressures to "balance" successive decisions between the two sides. In the British context the arbitrator will normally have no future contact with the organization that was in dispute. The prime objective of the arbitration is to protect the continuing relationship between the opposing parties from the consequences of their clash. It helps to achieve this if the relationship between the organization—both employer and union sides—and the arbitrator per se is wholly expendable.

It should be emphasized that arbitration can only function effectively as an infrequently used support, not as a regular substitute, for negotiated settlements. Its purpose can be seriously undermined if negotiators come to expect that proceedings may end up in arbitration. If that is the case, they may consider it rational to make their final negotiating positions unrealistically to their advantage in the hope that the arbitrator, in striking a balance, will unduly favor them. Far from converging, positions may then become polarized. Compromise becomes more difficult because it discourages realistic intra-organizational bargaining within the two sides.

To counter this, a form of arbitration that is sometimes used is "final offer" arbitration, sometimes also known as "pendulum," or "flip-flop," or "forced choice" arbitration. In this, the arbitrator is given no option but to choose either the final offer of the employer or the final claim of the trade union. They cannot go for any middle ground. Final offer arbitration is favored in some public services and also as part of so-called "no strike" procedures in some commercial organizations. But while the underlying rationale is sensible, its use is limited. One problem is that many negotiations deal in bundles of issues, and a stark choice between the two specific bundles on offer may not be a helpful basis of settlement. More generally, final offer arbitration, by its nature, means that there is an outright winner and a loser, which a normal arbitration, aimed at encouraging compromise and building bargaining relationships, will seek to avoid.

Labor arbitrations have many functions. One is simply to be there as an option during the conciliation process, used as a threat of an unknown arbitrator in order to encourage a negotiated outcome. As already mentioned, another function of the prospect of an arbitration is to get the parties to analyze their dispute more clearly by forcing them to work out and agree terms of reference. This is itself a negotiation, because good terms of reference have to set sufficiently tight limits to constrain the damage that an incompetent arbitrator might inflict.

Another function of arbitration is to provide either side with the chance to kick an embarrassment out of play so it will not sour their wider relationship. One typical example would be where a middle manager has made a mistake, perhaps by neglecting some informal arrangement to which the workforce felt entitled by custom and practice. The senior management may not want to be seen to be climbing down, but they are content to have the manager's hapless decision reversed by an arbitrator. Another common example at a time of diminishing trade union power is when management and the local union negotiators have concluded a deal that is seen to be sensible if not generous, only to have it rejected in a ballot of the union members. The restoration of something like the lost deal by an arbitrator will set relations back on course. Arbitrators are accustomed to, in effect, being used tacitly to protect an otherwise functional collective bargaining arrangement.

The actual procedure of arbitration can also have intrinsic utility. A basic rule is that nothing that the arbitrator reads is not also read, and open to challenge, by the other side. Everything that the arbitrator hears is also heard, and thus can be challenged, by the other side. The arbitrator's questioning, always with both sides present, usually uncovers issues that neither side has articulated, and often allows the competing cases to be set out with a stark clarity that exposes any weaknesses. There is often a therapeutic value, quite irrespective of the final award, in the arbitration hearing process. Each side has to listen while the other sets out its case and has it probed by the arbitrator. Each side has an opportunity to challenge the other side's case, in what is almost always a surprisingly calm and constructive atmosphere.

The arbitrator's written award augments this process. Usually relatively brief, it sets out the background to the dispute, and then summarizes the two sides' arguments as concisely and as strongly as possible. The objective at this stage is to make each side feel not only that their case has been understood, but that they have put forward their respective arguments effectively. Then the arbitrator writes what are sometimes called "general considerations," which is a terse statement of the points that appear to be relevant to deciding the award, usually put in such a way that suggests that neither side is wholly right or wrong. Such points might relate to existing agreements, special circumstances, agreed custom and practice, and reasonable expectations. It is not a legally reasoned argument, intended to create any sort of case law, but a set of pertinent comments. The words of the actual award stick very closely to those of the initial terms of reference in order to minimize the chance that unforeseen precedents might be set. Under most procedures there is no right of appeal because it is not a judicial process. In the UK there have been several thousand ACAS arbitrated awards since ACAS was established in 1976. Despite their not being legally enforceable, they have, without any exception, been adhered to by both sides.

The possibility of arbitration plays an important role in the breaking of deadlocks in employment disputes. But arbitration is best seen as supporting conciliation rather than the other way round. The conciliator's objective is to facilitate independent collective bargaining, and the possibility of arbitration provides the conciliator with a form of sanction. Used sparingly, it may be indispensable, but neither arbitration nor the conciliation it supports provide a substitute for a strong, embedded bargaining procedure.

Conclusion

Since the 1980s, there has been a substantial decline in overt employment disputes worldwide. The underlying cause was the internationalization of competition and of enterprise ownership and the consequential decline in trade union membership and collective bargaining. The character of third-party intervention for conflict resolution has changed as a result. It has become less judicial and more focused on facilitating voluntary settlements. Third-party agencies have devoted more resources to advisory work to pre-empt conflict, improve employment practices, and to the facilitation of cooperative approaches to employment relations.

This chapter has analyzed the various third-party processes appropriate to these new circumstances. It has demonstrated how their utility depends upon an understanding of the conduct of the continuing bargaining relationship necessary for the effective management of the shifting disparities of power between employers and organized labor. Independent conciliators can play a valuable, but fundamentally subordinate, role in support of collective bargaining. Arbitration is most effective if it is, in turn, subordinate to conciliation and the various forms of mediation. The management of collective bargaining is best left as far as possible to the immediate parties to the employment relationship.

REFERENCES

ACAS 2011. *Annual Report and Accounts 2010/2011*. London: ACAS.

Batstone, E., Boraston, I., and Frenkel, S. 1977. *Shop Stewards in Action*. Oxford: Blackwell.

Brown, W. 1973. *Piecework Bargaining*. Oxford: Blackwell.

Brown, W. 2000. "Putting Partnership into Practice." *British Journal of Industrial Relations*. 38(2): 299–316.

Brown, W. A., Bryson, A., Forth, J., and Whitfield, K. 2009. *The Evolution of the Modern Workplace*. Cambridge: CUP.

Brownlie, N. 2012. *Trade Union Membership 2011*. London: BIS.

Clegg, H. A. 1972. *The System of Industrial Relations in Great Britain*. Oxford: Blackwell.

De Roo, A. 2003. "Labor Conciliation, Mediation and Arbitration in the Netherlands." In Valdés Dal-Ré, F. (ed.), 2003a. *Labor Conciliation, Mediation and Arbitration in European Union Countries*. Madrid: Ministerio de Trabajo y Asuntos Sociales.

Goodman, J. 2000. "Building Bridges and Settling Differences: Collective Conciliation and Arbitration under ACAS." In Towers, B. and Brown, W. (eds), 2000. *Employment Relations in Britain: 25 Years of the Advisory, Conciliation and Arbitration Service*. Oxford: Blackwell.

Hicks, J. R. 1932. *The Theory of Wages*. London: Macmillan.

International Labor Organization, 2012. *Global Wage Report 2012–13: Wages and Equitable Growth*. Geneva: ILO.

JILPT 2012. *Japanese Working Life Profile 2012/2012*. Tokyo: Japan Institute for Labor Policy and Training.

Katz, H. C., Kochan, T. A., and Colvin, A. J. S. 2008. *An Introduction to Collective Bargaining and Industrial Relations*. Boston: McGraw-Hill.

Kochan, T. A. 2012. "Collective Bargaining: Crisis and its Consequences for American Society." *Industrial Relations Journal*, 43(4): 302–16.

Kochan, T. A. and Zack, A. M. 2013. "A Potential Roadmap towards Workplace Fairness in China: With some Lessons from US Experience." *International Journal of Comparative Labor Law and Industrial Relations*, forthcoming, 29(2).

Oxenbridge, S. and Brown, W. 2004. "Achieving a New Equilibrium? The Stability of Co-operative Employer-Union Relationships." *Industrial Relations Journal*, 35(5): 388–402.

Schelling, T. C. 1960. *The Strategy of Conflict*. New York: Galaxy, OUP.

Serrano, M., Xhafa, E., and Fichter, M. (eds), 2012. *Trade Unions and the Global Crisi: Labor's Visions, Strategies and Responses*. Geneva: ILO.

Silver, B. J. 2003. *Forces of Labor: Workers' Movements and Globalization since 1870*. Cambridge: CUP.

Sisson, K. and Taylor, J. 2006. "The Advisory, Conciliation and Arbitration Service." In L. Dickens and A. C. Neal (eds), *The Changing Institutional Face of British Employment Relations*. Alphen aan der Rijn: Kluwer Law International.

Valdés Dal-Ré, F. (ed.), 2003a. *Labor Conciliation, Mediation and Arbitration in European Union Countries*. Madrid: Ministerio de Trabajo y Asuntos Sociales.

Valdés Dal-Ré, F. 2003b. "Synthesis Report on Labor Conciliation, Mediation and Arbitration in the European Union Countries." In F. Valdés Dal-Ré (ed.), *Labor Conciliation, Mediation and Arbitration in European Union Countries*. Madrid: Ministerio de Trabajo y Asuntos Sociales

Walton, R. E. and McKersie, R. B. 1965. *A Behavioral Theory of Labor Negotiations*. New York: McGraw-Hill.

CHAPTER 7

....

INTEREST-BASED BARGAINING

....

JOEL CUTCHER-GERSHENFELD

INTRODUCTION

....

IN 1933 Mary Parker Follett delivered a series of invited lectures inaugurating the Department of Business Administration in the London School of Economics. Building on a 1924 address to the US Bureau of Personnel Administration, she introduced the concept of "integration" into the literature on conflict resolution (Graham, 1995), commenting:

> There are three ways of settling differences: by domination, by compromise and by integration. Domination, obviously, is a victory of one side over the other. This is not usually successful in the long run for the side that is defeated will simply wait for its chance to dominate. The second way, that of compromise, we understand well, for that is the way we settle most of our controversies—each side gives up a little to have peace. Both of these ways are unsatisfactory. In dominating, only one [side] gets what it wants; in compromise neither side gets what it wants.... Is there any other way of dealing with difference?
> There is a way beginning now to be recognized at least and sometimes followed, the way of integration.... the extraordinarily interesting thing about this is that the third way means progress. In domination, you stay where you are. In compromise likewise you deal with no new values. By integration something new has emerged, the third way, something beyond the either-or.

The core principles of interest-based bargaining in organizations build on this insight—representing an approach to negotiations and conflict resolution that aims to improve on both domination and compromise.

In the book *Getting to Yes: Negotiating Agreement Without Giving In,* Fisher and Ury (1983) make the central recommendation to focus on interests rather than positions. They define the alternative approaches as follows: "Your position is something you have decided upon. Your interests are what caused you to so decide". Thus, a focus on interests often involves interactive dialogue to appreciate fully the reasons why something might be important to a party. Positions tend to generate win-lose or compromise agreements, while a focus on interests increases the potential for mutual gains solutions— well-crafted solutions that satisfy interests relevant to all parties.

The term "interest-based bargaining" or "IBB" has been most clearly institutionalized in the labor-management context, particularly in the US public sector, where parties will directly refer to conducting an "IBB" negotiation. In many other organizational settings, parties may employ an interest-based approach in the course of conflict management, but may not necessarily use that label for the interactions. The next section of this chapter, which is focused on practice, will present illustrative examples from training and facilitated interventions to anchor the contrast between positional and interest-based negotiations. The focus is on the labor-management context, where the IBB ideas are clearly established. In this section, the author's personal experience and the field observations of others will be the primary source of artifacts and illustrative materials. This section of the chapter is offered as a practicum in the interest-based approach to labor negotiations.

Getting to a deeper understanding of interests is central to various domains of scholarship and action including "industrial relations," "conflict resolution systems," "negotiation theory," "transformational mediation," and "appreciative inquiry." These ideas and others are considered more fully in the theory section of this chapter, with a wide variety of sources cited. Emerging domains of growing importance, involving polarization in the private sector, the "public interest" in the public sector, and "stakeholder alignment" in public-private partnerships represent new frontiers for the interest-based approach that are highlighted in the final section of this chapter.

Practical Skills

The traditional, positional model of negotiations involves setting target and resistance points on each issue in advance of negotiations, overstating opening positions, committing to these positions publically, channeling all communications through a single spokesperson, giving as little as possible for what you get, always trying to keep the other side off balance, mobilizing your constituents, dividing constituents on the other side, never doing what is termed "bargaining against yourself" (that is, making an offer and then making another offer without first getting a counter-offer), and, a reluctantly accepted agreement is a sign of success. This model was captured well by Walton and McKersie (1965) as a purely distributive model, combined with certain forms of negative attitudinal structuring and aggressive internal organizational tactics.

Table 7.1 Positional and Interest-Based Bargaining Compared Across Five Phases in the Negotiations

Phases in Negotiations	Selected Positional Behaviors and Guidelines	Selected Interest-Based Behaviors and Guidelines
Phase I: Preparing	• Set target and resistance points for each issue • Identify weaknesses in what you anticipate will be the counter-arguments from the other side • Prepare your counter-arguments for what you anticipate will the other side's positions	• Identify your own interests and what you anticipate to be the other side's interests for each issue—including each side's constraints • Generate multiple options as part of preparations for each issue • Collect data jointly relevant to each issue
Phase II: Bargaining Over How to Bargain	• Discuss and agree on ground rules for the negotiation	• Discuss and agree on ground rules for the negotiation • Clarify the intent to take an interest-based approach • Charter joint subcommittees as appropriate • Discuss and agree on joint training as appropriate
Phase III: Opening and Exploring	• Overstate opening demands • Make demands public • Channel negotiations through a single spokesperson • Maintain an informal back channel between chief negotiators	• Frame opening statements as questions or as overarching interests • Signal openness to multiple options for resolution • Jointly brainstorm options, taking into account all relevant interests
Phase IV: Focusing and Agreeing	• Do not "bargain against yourself" • Use leverage to compel agreement • Draft agreements to maximize personal advantage	• Seek mutual gains on individual issues and combinations of issues • Draft agreements to minimize risk of misinterpretation
Phase V: Implementing and Sustaining	• Begin preparations for next negotiations (no matter how many years away)	• Establish joint processes for implementation • Use mutually acceptable metrics to track progress relative to each side's interests

The combination of behavioral elements was subsequently termed a "forcing" strategy in Walton, Cutcher-Gershenfeld, and McKersie (1994). Forcing is contrasted with a "fostering" strategy that combines integrative problem solving (rooted in information sharing and brainstorming), along with positive attitudinal structuring and support- ive internal organizational tactics (each side helping the other to address and resolve internal differences). Inexperienced negotiators and observers will frequently equate interest-based bargaining with fostering, but that is an incomplete perspective—all negotiations, positional and interest based, will involve a mixture of forcing and fos- tering.[1] This reflects the underlying mix of common and competing interests that are invariably found among negotiating parties.

In the private sector in the US, the power of unions has been on the decline for a number of decades (Kochan, Katz, and McKersie, 1986) and the approximately 13,000 annual private sector labor negotiations have increasingly moved toward conflictual or cooperative ends of a spectrum, with the interest-based approach reported in approximately one-third of labor-management relationships (characterized by practices such as the use of joint train- ing, joint subcommittees, and joint brainstorming) (Cutcher-Gershenfeld and Kochan, 2004). At a practical level, the contrast between positional and interest-based negotiations can be found at each stage of a five-phase bargaining model that has been used for over fif- teen years by Cutcher-Gershenfeld, McKersie, Kochan, Segal, and Peace in a seminar enti- tled "Negotiating Labor Agreements," first developed under the auspices of the Program on Negotiation at the Harvard Law School.[2] The five phases in the model are listed in Table 7.1, with sample positional and interest-based behaviors and guidelines noted at each phase. Note that Phases I, III, and IV of this model are similar to many bargaining models, and Phases II and V are less common but particularly relevant for interest-based bargaining.

In order to get a better understanding of the practical aspects of interest-based bar- gaining, consider illustrative examples for each of the five phases.

Phase I: Preparing

The first phase of collective bargaining is preparation. Below is a sample copy of a prepa- ration worksheet used in the seminar on "Negotiating Labor Agreements" (Figure 7.1). This is designed to be used by a party for its own internal preparations, though some parties have also used it for joint preparations. Note that this worksheet prompts prep- aration that takes into account history, the interests of multiple parties, multiple rele- vant options, and additional considerations. Of course, more than three or four entries might be made in the various categories. This goes well beyond preparation that is only focused on target and resistance points for specific positions or counter arguments for anticipated demands from the other party.

How parties prepare for bargaining has an enormous influence on what follows. The contrast between positional and interest-based negotiations can thus be seen at the out- set in the degree to which preparation is just focused on positions or whether it involves consideration of the interests of all parties and other factors.

Issue analysis worksheet	
Issue:	
Background data: What data or history is relevant to review on this issue? • • •	
Union's interests: What are the union's core concerns or interests on this issue?	**Management's interest:** What are management's core concerns or interest on this issue?
• • • •	• • • •
Options: What are some options to consider on this issue – especially mutual gains options? • • •	
Additional considerations: Other stakeholders, power dynamics, potential standards, etc. • •	

FIGURE 7.1 Sample Worksheet to Prepare for Interest-Based Bargaining

Phase II: Bargaining Over How to Bargain

While all negotiations involve some degree of what is termed "bargaining over how to bargain," this process is particularly important where potential new, interest-based processes are under consideration (Cutcher-Gershenfeld, 1994). In 2007 the UAW and Ford were facing one of the most challenging negotiations in the history of these two organizations. Ford had lost over $12 billion in 2006 as demand for its vehicles plummeted from over 4 million in 2000 to nearly half that level. Consequently, approximately half of the workforce of over 100,000 individuals would be displaced. In the end, the workforce adjustment was achieved without a single involuntary layoff (through retirement and separation incentive packages, combined with training programs and other supports). Fundamental changes were made to improve the operational effectiveness of the engine, stamping and assembly plants. One key element in the adjustment process was a shift toward a more interest-based approach to collective bargaining. Prior to the shift, one senior negotiator commented on the existing, more positional process as follows: "The definition of insanity is doing the same thing over and over again, but hoping for a different result." (Cutcher-Gershenfeld, 2011). The change in the bargaining process was achieved through two off-site joint conferences entitled "bargaining over how to bargain," involving over 300 of the negotiators who would be populating the twenty-four subcommittees involved in the national negotiation. Figure 7.2

Startup: Confirm working group membership,meeting logistics and establish simplified charter
Scope: Use charter to identify issues to be addressed by the working group what is and is not "in scope"

Potential Standardized Process:

1. **Opening and Shared Version:** Define the issue, including opening statements and resolutions, and develop a shared version of success
2. **Joint Data Collection:** Jointly assemble, prepare and analyze background data
3. **Analyze Underlying Interests:** Analyze the interests of labor management and other stakeholders-what is at stake for each
4. **Generate Options:** Brainstorm options, particularly options that build on the data and the identified interests
5. **Negotiate Agreements:** Where appropriate, negotiate agreements or potential elements of agreements
6. **Main Table Calibration:** Provide periodic updates and final report to the main table
7. **Anticipate Implementation:** Anticipate implementation, including recommended communication/ training plans and sustainment

Calibration: Schedule periodic main table reports

FIGURE 7.2 UAW-Ford Seven-Step Process for 2007 National Negotiations

presents that seven-step process that emerged from these conferences and that was utilized in the negotiations.

Note that the formal negotiations do not start until step 5. In advance of that, the parties chose to engage in constructing a shared vision of success on the issue (including very contentious issues, such as product sourcing), joint data collection, analysis of interest, and generation of options. Being intentional about the bargaining process reflects an appreciation for the fact that the process matters when it comes to negotiation outcomes. Also, this illustrates that an interest-based approach is not necessarily reserved only for "cooperative" issues.

Phase III: Opening and Exploring

The framing of issues (Goffman, 1974; Tversky and Kahneman, 1981) and brainstorming (Osborn, 1963) are social processes that have been documented and studied for decades, though there is more recent research that points to wide variation in brainstorming processes and outcomes (Santanen et. al., 2004). An interest-based approach to bargaining involves the constructive use of framing and brainstorming in ways that contrast with positional negotiations. To illustrate the contrast, consider the quotes in Figure 7.3 from a union opening statement in the case of a Midwestern energy utility where the parties were engaged in interest-based bargaining. The quotes were recorded live at the negotiations and are presented here with headings for two of bargaining issues in the format used in the "Negotiating Labor Agreements" seminar materials:

Job Security:

How can we ensure long-range workforce planning and implementation, increases in productivity and utilization of represented employees? How can we ensure that our local union members are the workforce of priority and choice for this company? What can we do to address issues such as seniority accumulation for bidding and the job posting process? What can we do to incorporate the language from the largest bargaining unit and apply it to members of the other bargaining unit involved in this negotiations? How to firm up commitments made at the close of the 1999 negotiations? How can we ensure apprenticeships within the respective classifications – US DoL recognized apprenticeships? How to provide entry level work with pre-apprentice qualifications and appropriate skill transfer? How can we address contracting and outsourcing issues?

Training:

What can we do to improve the Training Advisory Groups (TAG) structure and functionality? How can we improve the quality and timing of training and education? What training can be implemented jointly?

FIGURE 7.3 Opening Statements from Interest-Based Collective Bargaining Negotiations

Note how these opening statements are primarily questions and the questions are designed to open up dialog in ways that would not happen with positional demands. In the case of the question, "How can we ensure that our local union members are the workforce of priority and choice for this company?" the management team was expecting a demand that there be no subcontracting of bargaining unit work. In response, management was ready to assert its management rights and reject the demand. Instead, when faced with the question, the result was an extended dialog on management's views of its own workforce in comparison to subcontracted workers. This led to brainstorming on multiple options and an agreement on joint workforce planning. Constructive framing and brainstorming will not resolve all bargaining issues, but they reduce the risk of positional impasse and increase the potential for identifying mutual gains solutions.

Phase IV: Focusing and Agreeing

All negotiations make a transition from opening up issues to a process of focusing toward a solution. Some end in impasse, some with an imposed solution, some with a compromise for both parties, and some with an outcome that serves the interests of all parties. In order to achieve that latter, the interest-based approach emphasizes generating as many options as possible. As a result, the process of focusing toward an agreement is more intentional, involving the elimination of non-viable options, the combination of connected options, the invention of variations on options, and other ways of simplifying or enhancing what emerged through the brainstorming of options. What are sometimes termed "supposals" might be raised—not proposals, but exploratory hypotheticals that are offered in the spirit of constructing elements of an agreement.

Ultimately, the most visible measure of an interest-based negotiation process is the degree to which agreements are reached that might not otherwise have been achieved.

In the case of the quote on job security in Figure 7.3, for example, the parties achieved an agreement on workforce planning that both sides said would not have been possible if the union had initially demanded no subcontracting of bargaining unit work. This did not fully shield the parties from subsequent tensions around job security, but it did position them better to address these issues.

As will be discussed further in the concluding section of this chapter, an important frontier for interest-based bargaining involves taking into account the interests of multiple stakeholders. For example, when Kaiser Permanente and the Coalition of Unions representing over 100,000 members of the health-care organization's workforce reach agreements that go beyond wages, hours, and working conditions in order to improve the quality of health-care delivery, it stands out as taking into account the interests of patients and the broader society (Kochan et al., 2009). Imagine trying to tackle one of the most challenging elements of the health-care system, reducing medical errors, via a positional process; this complex issue that is fraught with shame, blame, and potential lawsuits has been addressed by these parties via an interest-based approach.

Phase V: Implementing and Sustaining

Follow-through on negotiated agreements is important in all negotiations. Indeed, a limitation of positional negotiations is the way that resentment from the power dynamics in negotiations can spill over in the form of non-compliance or "paybacks" afterwards. By contrast, an interest-based approach will often reveal interests on the part of all parties around fully realizing the gains from an agreement that features mutual gains. Thus, interest-based bargaining models will give more prominence to the effective joint implementation and sustainment of negotiated agreements than is found in positional models (where there is more focus on enforcement of negotiated agreements by one side or the other).

A relatively simple but effective aide to implementation is presented in Figure 7.4. Entitled "The 5Ws and How" worksheet, this tool is designed to be completed during or immediately following bargaining. The example relates to the implementation of health and safety commitments developed during negotiations that involved an energy utility and its union partners in Portland, Oregon. By specifying the "who, what, when, where, how, and why" of an agreement, the parties gain in a number of ways. First, some gaps in the negotiated language or differences in how the language was intended by each party are often revealed, which are better identified sooner rather than later during the life of the agreement. Second, having a set of milestones and resources specified (the "when" and the "how") provides a timing plan for those with implementation responsibilities and the opportunity for advance dialog on the degree to which this plan is feasible. Third, the document itself is a communications and deployment tool, allowing front-line supervisors and union representatives to literally be on the same page when workers ask about the application of a negotiated agreement to their work area.

Taken together, the examples and artifacts organized around the five phases of the bargaining model have been designed to illustrate the contrast between a more traditional, positional approach to negotiations and the interest-based approach.

Who:	What:	When:
• All employees operating under this initiative • Officers, Managers and supervisors • Safety reps • The continuous improvement safety committee • The safety department • Training and reporting department • The communications department • The joint accord committee	A process that will: • Create a positive, safe work environment • Focus on the presence of safety, not just the absence of accidents • Foster accurate safety data reporting Employees recognized by supervisors and co-workers for engaging in safe behaviors through: • Training in "catching people doing things right" • Providing real-time recognition on the job • Tracking "near misses" and good catches" • Identifying improvement opportunities • Reallocation of safety incentive funds from use on "safety cards" to a "safety fund" for safety and protective gear for bargaining unit employees in high risk jobs Continue investigating, recording and learning from safety incidents	*First quarter* • Wrapping up old program (sunset though 12/31/2010)with payouts • New mechanism for access to funds established • Communication via internet hub site, supervisor meetings, voice blast from CEO, and others • Training for supervisors, managers, officers, and safety reps on roles and responsibilites and 'train the trainer' • Begin front-line work force training by supervisors and safety reps *Second quarter* • Front-line workforce training supervisors and safety complete (April) • Continued meeting by continuous improvement safety committee • Adjusted feedback process with safety data established (with forward looking data analysis increasingly integrated over time) • Identifying ways of tracking and recognizing positive safety behaviors • Identifying ways of setting goals at all management levels *Third quarter* • Ongoing check and adjust • Ongoing reporting on progress at all levels
Why: • Everyone comes to work expecting to be safe, but safety data on lost time incidents has us at the market average – we are capable of doing better • The existing program was not translating into sufficient improvements in safety results • We need a comprehensive process that fosters a safety mentality and a safety culture – this is a step in that direction • We have been recognizing accident avoidance, rather than promoting safe behavior • It is imporatant to ensure that all incidents are reported. There is concern about underreporting, which is a barrier to problem-solving and improvement • There is a pyramid effect where single, smaller incidents add up to larger, catastrophic incidents	**How:** • A process, not a program • Communications via video conference, asynchronous video, e-mail, and phone • This is one step in a larger journey of culture change with respect to safety • Next steps will emerge through the joint partnership process • Developed using the kaizen process and coordination via continuous improvement safety committee • Executive level champion: Gregg Kantor • Comprehensive integration of safety into executive visits and business sessions • Interest-based approach to problems	**Where:** • Training for safety reps, supervisors, managers and officers at training facilities (training trainers) • Front-line workforce training on location (by safety reps and supervisors)–by shift • Ongoing – every location; recognition in the field

FIGURE 7.4 Implementation Planning Worksheet (5Ws and How for Health and Safety)

Importantly, the interest-based approach still involves the need to address difficult and divisive issues around which hard bargaining will occur. There will still be a combination of forcing and fostering in interest-based bargaining. While positional bargaining risks forcing that is unrestrained and fostering that is superficial, the interest-based approach has a greater likelihood of forcing that is more restrained and fostering that is more robust (Walton, Cutcher-Gershenfeld, and McKersie, 1994).

OUTCOMES OF INTEREST-BASED BARGAINING

There have been a number of case studies reporting innovative outcomes as a result of the use of interest-based bargaining—highlighting innovations that can be traced to practices such as brainstorming, the use of joint subcommittees, etc. There have been far fewer studies that look across multiple cases or that follow cases over extended periods of time. The more comprehensive studies that have been conducted do report increased innovation as a result of the use of interest-based processes, but some trade-offs as well. Selected findings on outcomes associated with interest-based bargaining are summarized here.

In one study comparing contract language from nineteen Canadian interest-based collective bargaining negotiations with nineteen traditional negotiations (matched by industry) it was found that the IBB negotiations featured more changes in contract language on joint governance and organizational innovation (Paquet, et al., 2000). At the same time, a greater number of the IBB negotiations also involved union concessions. While it is not possible to distinguish the degree to which any adverse selection may be involved in the choices of the IBB process, it does suggest that the more problem-solving oriented process does increase the likelihood of increased union influence on managerial prerogatives in exchange for increased union willingness to make concessions on other matters.

In a study of a comprehensive application of interest-based negotiations principles in the context of the integration of more than a dozen hospitals in the Minneapolis/St Paul, Minnesota, community, Preuss and Frost (2003) found that the process accounted for important successes in system integration, rationalization, and delivery improvement. At the same time, the use of interest-based processes was not sustained in subsequent years—pointing to important challenges in sustaining innovation.

There have been three national surveys on collective bargaining practice in the US, in 1996, 1999, and 2003, all sponsored by the Federal Mediation and Conciliation Service (FMCS). In all cases, large national random samples of nearly one thousand matched pairs of union and management negotiators were surveyed. Drawing on the first two surveys, Cutcher-Gershenfeld and Kochan (2004) reported on contractual outcomes in key categories associated with labor-management innovation. In each case, the measure was whether the negotiators reported new or modified contract language (but not the specific terms that were in the agreement). A clear connection was found between key "transformational" contractual outcomes (such as increased workplace flexibility and increased job security) and the bargaining process. A more detailed analysis of outcomes, using the 2003 survey data, was presented by Cutcher-Gershenfeld (2005), including the data presented in Figure 7.5. In the cases of work rule flexibility, joint committees, employee involvement, team-based work systems, work-family issues, and workplace safety, the interest-based bargaining process was associated with a greater number of instances with new or revised contract language. This was not the case for new pay systems (such as gain sharing, profit sharing and pay-for-knowledge, or job security). In contrast to the Canadian study, the instances of concessions were much less common where interest-based bargaining was in use. Further, wage and benefit agreements were more common. These results should be treated with caution, however, since there is selection bias in parties using an interest-based approach versus those who do not.

In a comprehensive, multi-year study of Kaiser Permanente and the coalition of unions representing Kaiser Permanente employees, Kochan and co-authors (2009) documented how hundreds of joint committees and task forces were addressing issues such as patient satisfaction, operational efficiencies, absenteeism, and even a complex issue such as reducing medical errors. Similarly, a detailed case study of the UAW-Ford 2007 national negotiations (Cutcher-Gershenfeld, 2011) documented outcomes with respect

	Union and Mgt. do not both report use of IBB in last neg.	Both Union and Mgt. report use of IBB in last neg.
NON-WAGE OR BENEFIT OUTCOMES		
Work Rule Flexibility	22.7%	68.4%
Gain Sharing, Profit Sharing, Pay-for-Knowledge	10.4%	5.3%
Joint Committees	3.1%	10.5%
Job Security	3.6%	0.0%
Employee Involvement	1.4%	21.1%
Teams	0.5%	5.3%
Work/ Family	7.3%	10.5%
Workplace Safety	8.1%	15.8%
WAGE AND BENEFIT OUTCOMES		
Wage Reduction	0.2%	0.0%
Wage Freeze	8.5%	0.0%
Benefit Reduction	8.1%	10.5%
Wage Increase	73.9%	100.0%
Benefit Increase	23.9%	63.2%

FIGURE 7.5 Reported Contractual Changes and the Use of Interest-Based Bargaining

to retiree health care and a new entry-level wage, tied to job creation commitments that would not have happened as they did without interest-based approaches.

UNDERLYING THEORY

There are many frontiers in the scholarly literature that are relevant to the study of interest-based bargaining and IBB as a phenomenon holds great promise as a source of practical data for study in these various areas. The focus here is on a few key domains, including the literatures on industrial relations, conflict resolution systems, decision science and the social psychology of negotiation, mediation (particularly the concept of transformative mediation), appreciative inquiry, and the social constructionist approach to knowledge. In each case, selected opportunities for new research will be highlighted.

As was noted above, interest-based bargaining has figured prominently as characteristic of the cooperative end of the spectrum in an increasing polarization in US labor-management relations (Cutcher-Gershenfeld and Kochan, 2004). While no national data are available comparing public and private sectors, data from a decade ago in the few states where the US Federal Mediation and Conciliation Service (FMCS) serves both public and private sectors, revealed that the parties did have greater awareness and use of interest-based bargaining in the public sector. Specifically, in 2003, approximately 70–80% of union and management negotiators in the selected public sector states where the FMCS provides services reported some experience using the interest-based approach (a range is provided since union and management responses were not identical). By contrast, approximately 15–30% of private sector union and management negotiators reported some experience using the interest-based approach (Kochan, Cutcher-Gershenfeld, and Ferguson, 2004). Given the recent attacks on public sector collective bargaining in the US it will now be important to examine the resiliency of the interest-based approach in states where the public sector laws have changed.

This entire volume on conflict management in organizations provides testimony to the many organizational systems and processes in which an interest-based approach to negotiations may be relevant. At a time when non-union systems for conflict management in organizations (including complaint procedures ending in arbitration) have become more prevent that the traditional unionized grievance procedures (Lipsky, Seeber, and Fincher, 2003), interest-based bargaining represents an interesting bridge since it involves tools and methods that are similar in the unionized and nonunion sectors. In this context, there is a need to more fully understand the cases where parties using the interest-based approach in collective bargaining are extending this approach to grievance handling. For example, Kaiser Permanente and the coalition of unions have rewritten the grievance procedure to emphasize informal "issue resolution" before a formal grievance process is employed (Kochan et al., 2009). The research by Lipsky, Seeber, and Fincher (2003) points to a new social contract around the handling of conflict in organizations and it will be important to see if there is a broad convergence between union and non-union front-line dispute resolution systems.

In the field of decision science, the role of biases in human judgment has long been established (Nisbet and Ross, 1980; Raiffa, 1982; Neale and Bazerman, 1985). Recent scholarship in this area has important implications for interest-based bargaining. Bazerman and Tenbrunsel (2011) document how people can believe that they are making wise decisions that are morally or ethically defensible when there are actually "blind spots" that impair their judgment. The central premise of interest-based bargaining emphasizes constructive, rational problem-solving interactions. On the one hand, the presence of diverse viewpoints (labor and management from different levels in the organization) is an important check against these blind spots. On the other hand, there is a need for additional field research to document the degree to which interest-based negotiations processes are vulnerable to forms of "group think" among the negotiators and other biases precisely because they are more collaborative.

The literature on transformative mediation celebrates the many ways in which mediators can reinterpret polarized positions, building on cues from the parties and constructing new paths toward resolution (Bush and Folger, 1994). While the language of "interests" is not always used in this literature, the heart of this approach involves

probing and dialog to get past surface-level positions and more fully understand underlying hopes, fears, priorities, etc. This approach has been criticized in that mediators
are not resolving the original dispute but their reinterpretation of the dispute, or that
mediators can bring independent expertise and engage in technical problem solving
without the need for reinterpretation (Williams, 1997). Proponents counter, however,
that it is precisely through such a process that mediators can constructively address
power differences and enable all parties to a dispute to feel empowered by a resolution.
This approach will still involve conflict, but in the form of constructive confrontation
(Burgess and Burgess, 1996). One promising area of research in this context involves the
degree to which interest-based negotiators end up serving as quasi mediators of internal differences before, during, and following negotiations. This domain, which Walton
and McKersie (1965) highlighted as intraorganizational negotiations, features a form of
internal interest-based bargaining and mediation that merits further study—to see the
degree to which this too involves the transformation of disputes.

The literature on appreciative inquiry (AI) emphasizes the positive in social situations and utilizes a process of asking provocative questions (Cooperrider and Srivastva,
1987; Cooperrider and Whitney, 2005; Bushe, 2010). The sample opening statement in
Figure 7.3 features questions that are illustrative. Many practitioners of interest-based
bargaining have been drawn to AI, adding this focus on the "positive" to their commitment to get beyond superficial positions. In particular, some federal mediators make
extensive use of the AI approach as they "orchestrate" progress toward agreement, while
others engage in more traditional "deal making." The contrast between "orchestration"
and "deal making" by mediators was introduced by Kolb (1983) before the growth of the
appreciative inquiry and interest-based approaches and it would be timely to revisit the
analysis of how mediators operate with these additional tools and techniques in mind.

More generally, there has been a sea change in the field of psychology around what is
termed "positive psychology" where the focus is on constructive and resilient orientation and personality, rather than the dysfunctional focus that has historically characterized psychology (Fredrickson, 2001). The interest-based approach does call forth a more
positive orientation in comparison to positional negotiations, even with hard issues on
the table. Thus, interest-based bargaining represents a promising context in which we
can see the limits and the potential for maintaining a positive approach in highly contentious situations.

Underlying many of these literatures is a social constructionist approach to theory
and practice. The social constructionist approach holds that social or physical phenom-
ena do not have intrinsic meaning—only the meaning that we assign based on the social
context in which we function. As such, interests are not fixed or predetermined and
interest-based bargaining can involve the reinterpretation or redefinition by parties of
what they see as being in their interest.

While the social constructionist approach can be unsettling, it also brings great transformational potential since new perspectives are generated. Kenneth Gergen (1978)
argues that more traditional, positivist approaches are less likely to be transformational
than the more "generative" approaches that come from social construction, stating: "It

may be useful, then, to consider competing theoretical accounts in terms of their *generative capacity, that is, the capacity to challenge the guiding assumptions of the culture, to raise fundamental questions regarding contemporary social life, to foster reconsideration of that which is 'taken for granted' and thereby to furnish new alternatives for social action"* (p. 1346). Needless to say, these comments echo back to Mary Parker Follett's quote in the prologue—the focus on interests rather than positions enables the discovering of more integrative "third ways" of managing conflict.

FUTURE OPPORTUNITIES AND CHALLENGES

Interest-based bargaining represents the institutionalization of a core dictum in conflict management, which is to focus on interests, not positions (Fisher and Ury, 1983). It has its roots in the concept of integration, introduced by Mary Parker Follett nearly a century ago and documented in the labor-management context by Walton and McKersie in 1965. This chapter has attempted to serve as both a guide to the terrain—mapping the institutional form in the labor-management arena, documenting outcomes, and identifying selected signposts for future directions in theory and practice.

In the collective bargaining context, even though awareness and use of interest-based bargaining is relatively high (with thousands of instances each year), relations in the US are polarized around cooperative and conflictual extremes. At the conflictual end of the spectrum, certain interest-based tactics can still be used by one party to steer adversarial behaviors in a more constructive direction. For example, it is possible to respond to a highly positional demand with questions to better understand why that demand is important to the other party—surfacing interests that make an interest-based solution more likely. In effect, the negotiator is doing the work of both parties to make things more interest based. One future opportunity for theory and practice is to more fully examine the use of interest-based tactics in these highly contentious situations. As noted above, the public sector in the US in particular provides an increasingly polarized domain in which these questions might be pursued.

At the more cooperative end of the spectrum, an important frontier involves taking into account the interests of stakeholders other than labor and management. In the public sector, this includes systematic efforts to take into account the public interest (Cutcher-Gershenfeld and Rubinstein, 2013). To illustrate this point, consider this contract language from Article 24 in the collective bargaining agreement in the San Juan Unified School District:

> The District and the Association agree to take responsibility and be held accountable for the improvement of the quality of teaching and learning which represents an expanded role in public education. It is in the best interest of the San Juan Schools

that the District and the Association cooperatively engage in activities and communication which demonstrate mutual respect for all stakeholders and results in the improvement of student achievement through development of common goals, a cooperative, trusting environment and teamwork. It is the [parties'] belief that actively and constructively involving all relevant stakeholders contributes significantly toward achieving these goals.

Shared responsibility and accountability for results are at the core of a continuous improvement model. Joint responsibility for student success means that educators share in celebrating what works and share in identifying together areas that are not working and are in need of improvement.

Note the strong statements taking into account the interests of students, parents, and the community—all parties that are distinct from labor and management. In citing this language and other data on public sector parties taking into account the public interest, Cutcher-Gershenfeld and Rubinstein (2013) suggest that the future of collective bargaining as an institution may rest, in part, on the degree to which the public sees its interests reflected in the process and outcomes. Thus, a second future opportunity centers on the degree to which interest-based bargaining can incorporate the interests of parties in addition to labor and management.

A final opportunity for interest-based bargaining lies in extensions outside of collective bargaining to systems or societal-level conflict management and governance. This can include systems associated with energy, transportation, health care, education, defense, food, etc. Many of the systems-level institutional arrangements are incomplete for what can be considered the two core functions of institutions—creating value or mitigating harm (Cutcher-Gershenfeld and Lawson, 2010). That is, these systems do not fully engage all stakeholders in "expanding the pie" to the greatest extent possible and inadequately addressed conflicts pose risks of "externalities" and even system failures. Conflict in these systems is rooted in well-known countervailing forces and dynamics, including the "tragedy of the commons" (Hardin, 1968), the "iron law of oligarchy" (Michels, 1915), the "logic of collective action" (Olson, 1965), the "iron cage" of isomorphism (DiMaggio and Powell, 1983), and "structural holes" (Burt, 1998). Alternative institutional models with both public and private elements have been identified as promising (Ostrom, 1990) though hard to scale or sustain. How is interest-based bargaining relevant in this context? In these cases there are n stakeholders each with multiple interests, and the literature on public disputes has demonstrated the applicability of the interest-based model to conflict resolution (Susskind and Cruikshank, 1987). Further, the interest-based model is proving central to research on the alignment of stakeholders in these systems—a necessary foundation for more robust, agile, and sustainable institutional arrangements (Cutcher-Gershenfeld and Lawson, 2010). Thus, the interest-based negotiations lens may be an important foundation for understanding ways to avoid gridlock and govern effectively in settings well beyond the workplace.

Notes

1. For example, when training union and management leaders in the early 1990s in Poland, the terms "integrative" and "distributive" were initially translated as "the good approach" and "the bad approach."

2. This seminar has been delivered over fifty times from 1997 to the present, with average workshop attendance of more than 75 individuals from unions and management in the public and private sectors. Materials from the seminar is used to illustrate key points in this chapter.

References

Bazerman, M. H. and Tenbrunsel, A. E. 2011. *Blind Spots: Why We Fail to Do What's Right and What to Do about It*. Princeton: Princeton University Press.

Burgess H. and Burgess, G. 1996. Constructive Confrontation: A Transformative Approach to Intractable Conflicts. *Mediation Quarterly*, Summer, 13(4): 305–22.

Burt, R. 1992. *Structural Holes: The Social Structure of Competition*. Cambridge, MA: Harvard University Press.

Bush, R. A. B. and Folger, J. P. 1994. *The Promise of Mediation*. San Francisco: Jossey-Bass.

Bushe, G. 2010."Appreciative Inquiry Is Not (Just) About the Positive." *Oxford Leadership Journal* 1(4), Oct.: 1–9.

Cooperrider, D. L. and Srivastva, S. 1987. "Appreciative Inquiry in Organizational Life." In W. A. Pasmore and R. W. Woodman (eds), *Research in Organizational Change and Development*, 1: 129–69. Greenwich, CT: JAI Press.

Cooperrider, D. L. and Whitney, D. 2005. *Appreciative Inquiry: A Positive Revolution in Change*. San Francisco: Berett-Koehler.

Cutcher-Gershenfeld, J. 1994. "Bargaining Over How to Bargain in Labor-management Negotiations." *Negotiation Journal*, Oct.: 323–35.

Cutcher-Gershenfeld, J. 2005. "US Collective Bargaining in a Global, Knowledge-Driven Economy: Assessing the Capacity for Institutional Transformation." Research Seminar, Cornell School of Industrial and Labor Relations (Oct.).

Cutcher-Gershenfeld, J. 2011. "Bargaining When the Future of an Industry is at Stake: Lessons from UAW-Ford Collective Bargaining Negotiations." *Negotiation Journal*, Apr.: 115–45.

Cutcher-Gershenfeld, J. and Kochan, T. 2004. "Taking Stock: Collective Bargaining at the Turn of the Century." *Industrial and Labor Relations Review*, 58(1), Oct.: 3–26.

Cutcher-Gershenfeld, J. and Lawson, C. 2010. "Valuing the Commons: A Fundamental Challenge Across Complex Systems." NSF/SBE 2020 White paper on Future Research in the Social, Behavioral & Economic Sciences. Available at: <http://www.nsf.gov/sbe/sbe_2020/submission_detail.cfm?upld_id=313>.

Cutcher-Gershenfeld, J. and Rubinstein, S. 2013. "Innovation and Transformation in Public Sector Employment Relations: Future Prospects on a Contested Terrain." *The Ohio State Journal on Dispute Resolution*, 28(1): 107–44.

DiMaggio, P. J. and Powell, W. W. 1983. "The Iron Cage Revisited: Institutional Isomorphism and Collective Rationality in Organizational Fields." *American Sociological Review*, 48 (2): 147–60.

Fisher, R. and Ury, W. L. 1983. *Getting to YES: Negotiating Agreement Without Giving In.* New York: Penguin.

Follet, M. P. 1940. *Dynamic Administration: The Collected Papers of Mary Parker Follett.* H. C. Metcalf and L. Urwick (eds). New York: Harper & Brothers, Publishers.

Fredrickson, B.L. 2001. "The Role of Positive Emotions in Positive Psychology: The Broaden-and-Build Theory of Positive Emotions. *American Psychologist,* 56: 218–26.

Gergen, K. J. 1978. "Toward generative theory." *Journal of Personality and Social Psychology,* 36: 1344–60.

Goffman, E. 1974. *Frame Analysis.* Cambridge, MA: Harvard University Press.

Graham, P. (ed.) 1995. *Mary Parker Follett. Prophet of Management: A Celebration of Writings from the 1920s.* Boston, MA: Harvard Business School Press.

Hardin, G. 1968. "The Tragedy of the Commons." *Science,* 162 (3859): 1243–48.

Kochan, T., Katz, H., and McKersie, R. 1986. *The Transformation of American Industrial Relations.* New York: Basic Books.

Kochan, T. A., Cutcher-Gershenfeld, J., and Ferguson, J.-P. 2004. *"Report to the Federal Mediation and Conciliation Service on the Third National Survey."* Washington, DC: FMCS (1–50).

Kochan, T. A., Eaton, A. E., McKersie, R. B., and Adler, P. S. 2009. *Healing Together: The Labor-Management Partnership at Kaiser Permanente.* Ithaca: Cornell University Press.

Kolb, D. 1983. *The Mediators.* Cambridge, MA: MIT Press.

Lipsky, D. B., Seeber, R. L., and Fincher, R. 2003. *Emerging Systems for Managing Workplace Conflict: Lessons from American Corporations for Managers and Dispute Resolution Professionals.* San Francisco: Jossey-Bass.

Michels, R. 1915. *Political Parties: A Sociological Study of the Oligarchical Tendencies of Modern Democracy.* Tr. from the 1911 German source by E. Paul and C. Paul. New York: The Free Press.

Neale, M. and Bazerman, M. 1985. "The Effects of Framing and Negotiator Overconfidence on Bargaining Behaviors and Outcomes." *Academy of Management Journal,* 28(1): 34–49.

Nisbett, R. and Ross, L. 1980. *Human Inference: Strategies and Shortcomings of Social Judgment.* Englewood Cliffs, NJ: Prentice-Hall.

Olson, Jr., M. 1965. *The Logic of Collective Action: Public Goods and the Theory of Groups,* Cambridge, MA: Harvard University Press.

Osborn, A. F. 1963. *Applied Imagination: Principles and Procedures of Creative Problem Solving.* 3rd edn. New York, NY: Charles Scribner's Sons.

Ostrom, E. 1990. *Governing the Commons: The Evolution of Institutions for Collective Action.* Cambridge: Cambridge University Press.

Paquet, R., Gaétan, I., and Bergeron, J.-G. 2000. Does Interest-Based Bargaining (IBB) Really Make a Difference in Collective Bargaining Outcomes? *Negotiation Journal,* 16: 281–96.

Preuss, G. A. and Frost, A. C. 2003. The Rise and Decline of Labor–management Cooperation: Lessons from Health Care in the Twin Cities. *California Management Review,* 45(2): 85–106.

Raiffa, H. 1982. *The Art and Science of Negotiation.* Cambridge, MA: Harvard University Press,.

Santanen, E., Briggs, R. O., and de Vreede, G.-J. 2004. "Causal Relationships in Creative Problem Solving: Comparing Facilitation Interventions for Ideation." *Journal of Management Information Systems.* 20(4): 167–98.

Susskind, L. E. and Cruikshank, J. 1987. *Breaking the Impasse: Consensual Approaches to Resolving Public Disputes.* New York: Basic Books.

Tversky, A. and Kahneman, D. 1981. "The Framing of Decisions and the Psychology of Choice." *Science,* 211(4481): 453–8.

Walton, R. and McKersie, R. 1965. *A Behavioral Theory of Labor Negotiations.* New York: McGraw Hill.

Walton, R., Cutcher-Gershenfeld, J., and McKersie, R. 1994. *Strategic Negotiations: A Theory of Change in Labor-Management Relations.* Boston: Harvard Business School Press.

Williams, M. 1997. "Can't I Get No Satisfaction? Thoughts on *The Promise of Mediation.*" *Mediation Quarterly*, 15(2): 143.

CHAPTER 8

......

GRIEVANCE PROCEDURES IN NON-UNION FIRMS

......

ALEXANDER J. S. COLVIN

INTRODUCTION

......

NON-UNION grievance procedures were often traditionally regarded as a residual category. In examining workplace dispute resolution, the primary historical focus was on the well-established grievance procedures found in unionized workplaces. Even with the increased focus on individual employment rights and declining emphasis on collective bargaining and union representation, the emphasis in dispute resolution has been on the role of the courts and public administrative and adjudicatory agencies. Meanwhile grievance procedures in non-union workplaces, where examined at all, have been relegated to a secondary role as poor copies of their counterparts in unionized workplaces or limited supplements to formal public procedures for enforcing individual employment rights.

Yet these perspectives miss the increasingly central role of non-union grievance procedures in resolving conflicts for employees. For the now 93% percent of American private sector employees who are not represented by unions, non-union grievance procedures represent the only workplace dispute resolution mechanism potentially available to them (Colvin, 2012). Similarly, although litigation in the public courts is notionally available to all employees, in practice relatively few cases will provide the type of substantive claims and potential damages that can produce a plausible claim to be litigated. For most employees and most workplace disputes, non-union grievance procedures will be the only avenue available to attempt to achieve some redress for unfair treatment in the workplace.

Non-union grievance procedures are characterized by a high degree of diversity in their origins, structures, usage, and impact on the workplace (Westin and Felieu, 1988;

Ewing, 1989). Procedures range in type from relatively simple open door policies to elaborate peer review panels with formal jury-like procedures to provide due process. Motivations for their introduction range from efforts to improve management human resource practices to efforts to ward off union organizing drives and protect the organization from lawsuits (Colvin, 2003a). Some non-union grievance procedures are virtually never used by employees whereas others are utilized at levels closer to those found in grievance procedures in unionized workplaces. More effective non-union grievance procedures may serve to correct poor management decision-making and enhance employee commitment and retention, yet employees who utilize non-union grievance procedures can also be subject to retaliation and punishment (Lewin, 1990). The role and impact of non-union grievance procedures in the workplace is a complex and varied one, not subject to simple, generalized characterizations as either a panacea or a canard in the search for workplace justice.

In examining non-union grievance procedures, the initial focus of this chapter will be on the experience with these procedures in the United States. The reason for this emphasis is that American organizations were the first to adopt these procedures and they are clearly the most widespread and best developed in the U.S. This reflects both the relative weakness of American unions and resulting large non-union sector of the U.S. economy and also the strong role of individual employment rights litigation threats which encourage many American companies to adopt procedures. However, after examining the American experience in this area, I will turn to examining that of other countries, in particularly some of the alternative regulatory approaches affecting procedures found in different countries.

A Typology of Procedures

What are we talking about when we refer to non-union grievance procedures? An initial problem is to define the boundaries of this phenomenon. Although conflicts arise in all workplaces, in not all is there some type of procedure to resolve these conflicts. In smaller and more informal organizations, conflicts may be handled directly by managers without recourse to any systematic procedure. Instead a manager may use his or her individual discretion to deal with a complaint from an employee or to respond to a conflict that is observed to be occurring in the workplace. This is certainly a form of conflict management, but does not rise to the level of a grievance procedure. If we are simply dealing with managerial discretion in responding to workplace conflict, then we may find one approach being used one day and an entirely different one another. Indeed the manager may choose to respond to one grievance raised by an employee and ignore or suppress a different grievance raised by another. As a threshold, the existence of a non-union grievance procedure implies that the organization has some type of standard, systematic procedure to respond to employee grievances. There may be flexibility in how conflicts are handled and elements of discretion retained by decision-makers, but the key factor is that there needs to be some type of formal procedure through which an employee's grievance can be raised and resolved.

If we start with this relatively basic definition, survey evidence suggests that a majority of American non-union workplaces have some type of grievance procedure (Berenbeim, 1980; Delaney, Lewin, and Ichniowski, 1989; Edelman, 1990; Feuille and Chachere, 1995; Colvin, 2003a). The simplest of these are open door policies, which typically involve a statement of organizational policy so that employees should feel free to bring concerns or complaints to management who will then attempt to address the problem (Feuille and Delaney, 1992; Wheeler, Klaas, and Mahony, 2004; Colvin, Klaas, and Mahony, 2006). Open door policies may specify who complaints can be brought to, often the employee's supervisor, a more senior manager, or a human resources representative. Open door policies may include statements that there will be no retaliation against employees who bring complaints under the policy.

Although many open door policies involve little more than aspirational statements by the organization with little to back them up, some organizations undertake more elaborate efforts to encourage and monitor usage of the open door policy. Perhaps the most extensive system based around this concept is IBM's open door procedure, which dates back to the more informal open door policy followed by the company's Chairman Tom Watson in the 1950s (Ewing, 1989). IBM's modern open door procedure is a formalized investigation procedure, under which employee complaints trigger the rapid deployment of an executive level manager to investigate the conflict and report the results back to the Chairman's office. Although commitment of this level of resources and effort is unusual, open door policies are a widespread feature of American non-union workplaces and may be an important supplement to other types of non-union grievance procedures.

Most non-union grievance procedures involve some structure for appeal of an adverse decision against the grieving employee (Feuille and Chachere, 1995; Colvin et al., 2006). A common example would be a disciplinary decision by a supervisor, such as a warning for absenteeism or a suspension for workplace misconduct, that the employee thought was unjustified. Under a typical procedure, the employee can file a grievance seeking to have this disciplinary decision reversed. A central feature of grievance procedures then is who the grievance can be appealed to. In many procedures there are multiple levels or steps of appeal to successively higher level decision-makers. The neutrality and independence of these decision-makers is a central feature determining the degree of due process that the grievance procedure provides. We can classify different types of non-union grievance procedures by the decision-makers in the procedure and by their degree of independence from the normal management chain of command.

Many basic non-union grievance procedures simply instruct the employee to pursue complaints up the standard chain of command. The first step might involve discussing the concern with the employee's supervisor. The grievance could be pursued further by raising it with the next highest level of manager with supervisory responsibility. The procedure may terminate with an appeal to the plant or facility manager or it may provide that the employee can appeal the grievance to a more senior level executive at the divisional or corporate level. Grievance procedures of this nature have the advantage from the organizational perspective that they respect the existing structure of managerial authority reflected in the chain of command. Lower level decisions may be reversed by higher management, but this is done in the same way that lower level operational decisions can also be reviewed and reversed by higher level decision-makers in the organization. At the same time, this replication of the existing chain of command structure provides the grieving employees with relatively little independence of review in the appeal. The fear will be that higher level managers will have a natural tendency to support and affirm the decisions of the subordinates who report to them.

To provide more independent review of grievance and reduce the danger of simply reinforcing the existing decision-making process, some non-union grievance procedures provide for review of complaints by managers outside the direct chain of command above the employee. For example, this may involve a procedure step in which rather than an executive from the employee's own division reviewing the grievance, it is instead reviewed by an executive from another division within the company. Having more senior executives review the grievance in later steps of the procedure may also be directed at achieving a similar goal of removing the decision-making in the review process from the immediate managerial hierarchy of the specific plant or facility involved. In addition to providing a degree of independence from the most closely involved managerial actors, shifting decision-making in the grievance procedure to a higher level in the organization may also serve to provide more focus on the interests of the company as a whole in resolving the conflict. Lower level management may be more likely to be concerned about reaffirming their authority in the workplace and prioritizing the production goals of their specific unit in reviewing grievances. By contrast, higher level management, particularly if not directly connected to the management of the unit where the grievance arose, are more likely to emphasize broader organizational priorities such as ensuring consistency in application of organizational policies and protecting the organization from external threats of litigation or union organizing. These organizational priorities may lead such decision-makers to provide a more rigorous review aimed at ensuring the employee was not treated unfairly.

Management appeals boards provide a procedural structure that emphasizes these objectives of providing review by decision-makers who are higher up in the organization and less directly connected to the management of the specific unit involved in the grievance (Feuille and Chachere, 1995). Under management appeals board procedures, a panel of executives, usually three in number, hears and decides the employee's grievance (Colvin et al., 2006). The executives on the panel will commonly include both operations and human resources managers as well as executives both from the grievant's division and from other divisions in the company. Given the relatively elaborate and expensive nature of this step, taking substantial managerial time, it is usually used as a later step in grievance procedures after efforts to resolve the grievance at the workplace level have been unsuccessful. The use of management appeals boards provides grievants with the benefits of multiple decision-makers reviewing the case and the perspectives of managers less directly connected to the situation. Although this provides more independent review than typical non-union grievance procedures, it still involves managers serving as the decision-makers in the procedure. By contrast, to provide greater independence and neutrality in non-union grievance procedures some organizations have adopted procedures that include non-managerial decision-makers.

Peer review procedures are an innovation that employs non-managerial employees from within the organization as decision-makers in the grievance procedure (Colvin, 2003a, 2003b). A peer review panel will commonly consist both of employees who are peers of the grievant and managers, with the peer employees being a majority on the panel (Feuille and Chachere, 1995). A common structure is to have a five-member panel with three peer employees and two managers (Colvin, 2004a). Peer review panel procedures first become well-known through the example of a GE plant that adopted them in the 1970s in response to a series of union organizing drives. By providing the peer review panels, management at the plant hoped to better respond to employee grievances and convince the workers that they could obtain fair treatment and employee involvement in decision-making through a non-union procedure. Research suggests that peer review panel procedures have been adopted in increasing numbers of organizations in recent decades (Colvin, 2003a).

Arbitration in the workplace dispute resolution arena has been strongly associated with the grievance procedures of unionized workplaces. Final and binding decision-making by independent neutral Labor Arbitrators as the last step of grievance procedures is one of the most long-standing and stable elements of American labor relations. By contrast, until recently arbitration was virtually absent from non-union workplaces. The only exceptions were a small number of employers who had introduced arbitration as the final step of their non-union procedures to mimic the union system of labor arbitration and provide a substitute for union representation to guard against organizing drives. The best known example of this is the non-union grievance procedure at Northrop, which since the late 1940s has featured arbitration as its final step (Westin and Felieu, 1988). Despite the positive experiences of Northrop with this system, the vast majority of non-union employers remained unwilling to turn over decision-making authority in their organizations to an independent third-party neutral arbitrator. This aversion to arbitration in the non-union workplace changed dramatically in the 1990s. As will be described in more detail in the section titled "Factors Leading to Procedure Adoption", a shift in the law of arbitration opened up the possibility for employers to use non-union arbitration agreements as a shield against claims being brought against them in the courts. Through the 1990s and 2000s arbitration procedures focused on potential employment law claims spread rapidly, with estimates suggesting around a quarter of non-union employees being covered by them by the early 2000s (Colvin, 2007) and perhaps by a third more at present (Lewin, 2008).

The types of procedures described so far all involve an appeal by the employee to a decision-maker who determines the outcome of the dispute. In these determination type procedures, the employee is presenting a grievance to the decision-maker in hopes of receiving a decision with some type of remedy (Colvin et al., 2006). A separate category of procedures are those that do not involve a determination by a decision-maker, but rather an effort to facilitate a negotiated or consensual resolution of the conflict. The classic example of a facilitation type procedure is mediation. In traditional third-party mediation, an independent neutral mediator attempts to assist the parties to a dispute in reaching a negotiated resolution. Some non-union grievance procedures include mediation as a step, particularly as a prelude to arbitration in procedures that use arbitration as the final step of the procedure (General Accounting Office, 1997; Colvin, 2004a).

Where effective, these mediation procedures hold the potential for producing faster, cheaper, and more mutually satisfactory resolutions to conflicts than the more formal and involved procedures of arbitration. In addition to formal mediation by outside third-party neutrals, some non-union grievance procedures include internal mediation steps where someone within the organization attempts to mediate the dispute. Human resource managers often do this on an ad hoc basis, but some organizations have attempted to systematize this process by providing structured mediation training and making it a defined step within the grievance procedure. Another approach to internal mediation is the use of peer mediation, where regular employees not specialized in the employment relations function serve as mediators for disputes among their fellow employees (Lipsky, Seeber, and Fincher, 2003). This will often involve a program of training given to employees who volunteer to serve as peer mediators within the organization.

Ombudsperson offices provide a more extended organizational commitment to facilitating conflict resolution in the workplace. An ombudsperson is a designated neutral within the organization tasked with responding to employee concerns and complaints (Kolb, 1987; Bingham and Chachere, 1999). The ombudsperson will not try to determine the outcome of a complaint, but rather uses a range of techniques including information gathering, conciliation, and mediation, to attempt to facilitate a satisfactory resolution of the conflict. An ombudsperson serves as an organizational neutral, situated outside of the standard chain of command and emphasizing confidentiality of complaints received to protect against retaliation toward employees using the office. At the same time, the ombudsperson works within the organization, and successful ombudsmen tend to have significant experience with and knowledge of the organization which allows them to more effectively navigate the internal policies, structures, and politics of the workplace in helping to resolve conflicts. Although many ombudsmen effectively balance these roles, they can cause tensions where a conflict develops into a more formal legal claim against the organization and the ombudsperson's role as a neutral may be compromised by demands to testify in legal proceedings (Cooper, Nolan, and Bales, 2000). Ombudsperson offices are used in a number of larger non-union firms, however, the expense of hiring someone into a full-time in-house neutral role makes this type of procedure impractical for small or mid-sized organizations.

Factors Leading to Procedure Adoption

Why do non-union organizations adopt grievance procedures? In the United States, there is no legal requirement that an employer have any type of internal workplace dispute resolution procedure for employees. In non-union workplaces there is no institutionalized actor like the union pushing for the adoption of procedures in organized workplaces. Nor do non-union employers receive the benefits of grievance procedures that accrue to their unionized counterparts of having the procedure substitute for the disruptions of direct industrial action or attempts to enforce collective bargaining agreements through the courts. It might be expected that the non-unionized employer would simply rely on the prerogatives of managerial authority and use its own discretion on how to deal with problems in the workplace. Indeed, the continued adherence to the doctrine of employment at-will in American employment would seem to invite this assumption of discretionary authority by management of non-union organizations. Although many organizations do follow this approach, in practice, as we have seen in Section II, most non-union employers do adopt some type of formal grievance procedure. The reasons they do so derive primarily from three major forces or pressures upon management of non-union organizations.

The first force leading to the adoption of non-union grievance procedures is the threat of union organizing. Virtually all American private sector employers would prefer to operate without the constraints of collective bargaining and many take active steps to manage their human resources in such a way as to reduce the likelihood of union organizing (Kochan, Katz, and McKersie, 1994). Union organizing drives often focus on issues of unfair treatment in the workplace and research suggests that campaigns with a justice focus are more likely to be successful (Bronfenbrenner, 1997). A major reason for this is that union organizers can tout the benefits of having a union grievance procedure, culminating in arbitration before a third-party neutral, to remedy unfair treatment by management. Whereas non-union employees may be skeptical of promises of enhanced wages or job security, which depend to a large degree on the reactions of management, union organizers can more credibly promise to vigorously represent employees through the grievance procedure, whatever management's reaction.

A non-union employer concerned about the threat of union organizing drive can seek to at least partially substitute for the potential benefits of unionization by adopting a non-union grievance procedure. If employees believe that they can get redress for workplace problems through this procedure, then they will see less need for organizing a union to obtain the benefits of a union grievance procedure. Many early non-union grievance procedures were introduced for exactly this reason (Berenbeim, 1980). The non-union arbitration procedure at Northrop was a notable example, where the strong organizing threat of unions in the aerospace industry led the company to adopt a procedure that closely paralleled union procedures, including the critical final arbitration step (Westin and Felieu, 1988). In practice, most non-union organizations did not need to go so far in mimicking union grievance procedures to achieve some union substitution effect. Rather, as long as the procedure has some credibility among employees and provides a degree of check on managerial decision-making, it can have the potential to reduce the relative advantage of a union grievance procedure and diminish the strength of the union organizing motivation.

Peer review panel procedures provide a strong example of how employers have adopted more sophisticated union substitution strategies in the design of non-union grievance procedures. A key aspect of justice arguments in union organizing drives is that the union can serve as a check on unilateral management decision-making in the workplace. Peer review procedures address this concern directly by providing non-managerial employees with the majority of votes on the panel deciding grievances. This form of employee involvement in decision-making also has the benefit of avoiding the limitations on employer dominated employee representation schemes in section 8(a)(2) of the US National Labor Relations Act (Colvin, 2003a). Peer review panels are a relatively time and effort intensive procedure for dealing with grievances and many managers are reluctant to turn over such important decision-making functions to low-level employees (Colvin, 2004a). As a result, research findings suggest that adoption of peer review procedures is more likely in organizations that are subject to stronger union organizing threats, such as in industries like telecommunications and autos, where American unions retain greater strength (Colvin, 2003a).

The second major force leading to the adoption of non-union grievance procedures is the threat of litigation. A key factor in the relatively widespread adoption of non-union grievance procedures in the United States is the unique nature of the American employment law system and the pressures it places on employers. Prospects for employees bringing an employment lawsuit through the American court system are characterized by both relatively low probabilities of success and the chance of relatively large rewards where successful. American employment law continues to be founded on the basic principle of employment at-will under which an employer can terminate an employee for good reason, bad reason, or no reason at all without any obligation to provide prior notice or severance. In order to bring a successful employment lawsuit it is necessary to fall under one of the exceptions to this rule. Courts in most states recognize a limited number of common law exceptions to the at-will rule, such as the public policy exception which has been invoked where the termination violates some strong principle of public policy. In practice, this exception has been limited to unusual situations such as where the employee has been terminated for refusing to commit a crime.

A broader set of exceptions to the at-will rule comes from the various employment statutes enacted by state and federal governments. The prohibitions in the National Labor Relations Act on disciplining or dismissing an employee based on union organizing activity were among the first of these exceptions. The largest category of exceptions in recent years has come from the broad range of anti-discrimination legislation enacted from the 1960s through the present. American anti-discrimination law now bars employment decisions being based on factors such as race, gender, religion, national origin, age, disability, and in some states sexual orientation or smoking. To be successful in the courts, however, it is necessary that employees be able to prove that an adverse employment decision was based on one of these prohibited grounds, which is often a challenging task.

The litigation process in the courts can be both time consuming and expensive, with cases on average taking almost two years to get to trial (Eisenberg and Schlanger, 2003). Research suggests that employment discrimination litigation is less likely to be successful at trial than other plaintiffs and more likely to have awards in their favor overturned on appeal (Clermont and Schwab, 2004). Despite these substantial barriers to bringing a claim, employees who are ultimately successful in the American courts can win substantial amounts of damages. A study of employment discrimination cases in the federal courts found a median award amount of $110,000 and a mean award of $301,000, with a skewed distribution of outcomes including a number of very large awards of over a million dollars (Eisenberg and Schlanger, 2003). Research on employment decisions in the California state courts found an even higher median damage award of $296,991 (Oppenheimer, 2003).

The picture that emerges of employment litigation in the United States is of a high risk, high reward system for employees. For organizations facing the threat of litigation, this means that despite the relative employer-favorability of the at-will rule, they are subject to the pressures of a slow-moving, highly uncertain legal process and the risk of a large damage award from the occasional lawsuit that is successful. How do non-union grievance procedures help in this situation? The most direct way in which grievance procedures can prevent lawsuits is by resolving conflicts in the workplace before they can develop into legal cases. This can occur directly through providing the employee with a remedy for unfair treatment in the workplace. It may also occur more indirectly by allowing the employer to identify and deal with problematic managers or policies that could be the potential cause of future lawsuits (Colvin, 2004a).

Another reason that employers may have adopted non-union grievance procedures in response to the expansion of employment laws is the normative influence of the due process models established by the legal system (Edelman, 1990; Sutton, Dobbin, Meyer, and Scott, 1994; Sutton and Dobbin, 1996). Institutional theory researchers have argued that the uncertainty of the legal environments influenced organizations to adopt procedures that would provide signals of compliance by appearing to provide due process for employees (Edelman, 1990; Edelman, Uggen, and Erlanger, 1999). Professionals in fields such as law and human resource management are argued to have played particularly important roles in structuring and encouraging organizations to conform to these normative influences (Edelman, Abraham, and Erlanger, 1992). Research from this perspective found associations between changes in the employment law environment and the expansion over time of the adoption of non-union grievance procedures (Edelman, 1990; Sutton et al., 1994; Sutton and Dobbin, 1996).

Whereas institutional theory researchers have emphasized the more indirect, normative influences emanating from the employment law environment, in the last two decades the legal system has provided more direct, concrete incentives for the adoption of non-union grievance procedures, particularly for those using arbitration. In a 1991 decision, *Gilmer v. Interstate Johnson/Lane*, the Supreme Court for the first time held that a legal claim based on an employment statute could be arbitrable under an arbitration agreement. The Gilmer decision held out the possibility to employers of establishing non-union arbitration procedures for their workforces that would divert legal claims out of the courts and into a private arbitration procedure designated by the employer (Stone, 1999; Colvin, 2003a). In a 2001 decision, *Circuit City v. Adams*, the Supreme Court confirmed that an arbitration agreement that was part of an employment contract would be enforceable under the *Federal Arbitration Act*.

The result of these decisions is that an American employer can require its non-union employees to sign an agreement to arbitrate any potential legal claim against the company, including statutory claims such as those under the anti-discrimination laws, as a mandatory term and condition of employment. Based on American arbitration law, decisions by these private employment arbitrators cannot be reviewed by the courts apart from in very narrow circumstances such as fraud or misconduct by the arbitrator.

From being a relatively rare phenomenon at the beginning of the 1990s (Feuille and Chachere, 1995), non-union arbitration expanded rapidly in the 1990s and 2000s (Colvin, 2003a; Lewin, 2008) as employers saw it as an opportunity to escape from the risks and uncertainty of the public court system. Research has found that organizations were more likely to adopt non-union arbitration procedures where they were more exposed to potential litigation threats (Colvin, 2003a). An interesting side effect of the expansion of non-union arbitration is that many employers used the occasion of introducing arbitration as an opportunity to review and upgrade other aspects of their non-union grievance procedures (Colvin, 2004a). The result is that the shift in the law of arbitration had an indirect effect of producing a more general expansion of grievance procedures.

Union organizing and litigation threats represent external forces exerting pressure on organizations. In addition to these external factors, organizations also adopt non-union grievance procedures based on internal considerations related to their human resource strategies. Driving these internal motivations is the idea that enhancing fair treatment of employees will produce tangible benefits for the organization.

One major research perspective suggesting the value of adopting non-union grievance procedure is organizational justice theory. Organizational justice theory argues that the degree to which employees perceive organizational decisions as either having or lacking justice will affect important attitudinal and behavioral outcomes. Justice theory argues that there are multiple dimensions of justice perceptions, including procedural, distributive, and interpersonal justice (Colquitt, 2001). The identification of the importance of procedural justice perceptions has particular relevance to the adoption of non-union grievance procedures, since they provide mechanisms specifically designed to provide employees with enhanced procedural fairness in challenging organizational decisions (Sheppard, Lewicki, and Minton, 1992; Folger and Cropanzano, 1998). In a relatively direct test of this premise, Olson-Buchanan (1996) conducted an experimental study in which she found that availability of access to a grievance procedure that enhanced procedural justice increased employee willingness to continue working for the organization.

Another theoretical perspective supporting internal organizational motivations for adopting procedures is exit-voice theory, originally developed by Hirschman (1970) and most famously adapted to the labor relations setting by Freeman and Medoff (1984). Exit-voice theory argues that when confronted with deterioration in their employment situation, employees have two potential options: exit, usually involving quitting; and voice, giving expression to the dissatisfaction in hopes of remedying the situation. To the degree that voice options are enhanced, use of exit will be decreased, thereby saving the employer such costs of turnover as loss of existing employee skills and experience and the need to recruit, select, and train new employees. In their formulation, Freeman and Medoff primarily focused on the voice function of unions, but also acknowledged that non-union grievance procedures could potentially provide a similar voice function. Subsequent research on employee turnover in the telecommunications industry evidence found that in addition to the well-established exit-voice relationship in unionized workplaces, non-union grievance procedures in the form of peer review panels were also associated with lower quit rates (Batt, Colvin, and Keefe, 2002).

The degree to which organizations adopt non-union grievance procedures in order to enhance employee commitment and reduce turnover is likely to depend on the overall human resource strategy followed by the organization. Human resource strategies premised on fostering high levels of employee skill, commitment, and participation in the workplace depend to a greater degree on having a relatively stable, experienced workforce and are more likely to be undermined by employee perceptions of injustice in organizational decision-making. Some studies have found positive associations between high performance or high commitment work systems and the adoption of non-union grievance procedures (Huselid, 1995; Colvin, 2004b). The nature of the work system may also influence the structure of the grievance procedure that is adopted, such as a positive association between the use of self-managed work teams and the adoption of peer review procedures which similarly rely on group employee involvement in decision-making (Colvin, 2003a).

PROCEDURE USAGE

What do we know about how non-union grievance procedures operate? There is a surprisingly small body of research that has attempted to answer these questions. One reason for the limited extent of research in this area is the difficulty in gaining access to organizations to gather data on what are from an employer's perspective private, internal procedures. Although understandable from an employer's viewpoint, this private structure for dispute resolution is more problematic from a public policy perspective when we consider that among the conflicts resolved through these procedures are disputes over workplace discrimination, sexual harassment, and other issues that implicate public statutory rights. The result of the difficulties in gaining access to organizations to conduct research in this area is that we may be seeing a biased sample in which companies that operate procedures feature relatively high degrees of fairness, and due process pro-tections are more willing to provide access to researchers. This could create a more posi-tive picture of procedures than would be reflected in a more comprehensive sample of organizations. With that proviso in mind, what does the existing research tell us?

Some of the earliest systematic research on non-union grievance procedures was con-ducted by David Lewin in the 1980s. Lewin (1987) gathered data on the operation of procedures in a set of non-union organizations that had relatively well-developed for-mal processes for dispute resolution. The companies Lewin examined all had multi-step procedures featuring appeals to successively higher levels of management, but differed in the final step of the procedure with one company having the VP of HR as the final decision-maker, another with the CEO as the final step, and a third with arbitration by an outside third-party neutral as the final step.

The findings of this study indicated both commonalities and differences across organizations. Grievance rates were relatively similar across the companies—around 4–6 grievances annually per 100 employees, a rate about half of that found in typical American unionized workplaces. Rates of appeal dropped with each successive step in the procedures, with few grievances going beyond the second step involving review by a mid-level functional or HR manager. Among grievances that did proceed farther, the highest appeal rate to the final step was in the company which used arbitration as its last stage, which had an average of 0.4 grievances going to the final step annually per 100 employees compared to an average of only 0.1 final step grievances in the other compa-nies (Lewin, 1987). This finding suggests that the use of third-party decision-makers in the procedure may have a substantial effect in encouraging usage by employees.

In addition to the question of grievance rates, Lewin also examined employee win rates in these procedures. A striking finding was that win rates were relatively simi-lar across all companies and steps of the procedures. Employee win rates ranged from 40–50% of grievances in all three companies in the first three steps of the procedures (Lewin, 1987). Employee win rates did go up to 50–65% in the final step of each of the procedures, but overall the noteworthy finding is the similarity of outcomes. One expla-nation that may account for this finding is that employees are rational actors in deciding to file a grievance and managers are likewise rational in deciding whether to resolve a matter before the next step in the procedure. Employees may be reluctant to file griev-ances where they have relatively low chances of winning, either out of unwillingness to expend the effort of pursuing a grievance or out of fear of retaliation from managers for becoming a troublemaker. Conversely in situations where the employee has a relatively strong grievance with a high probability of success, then managers will have a greater incentive to resolve the matter informally before it consumes time and creates embar-rassment by becoming a formal grievance. The result is the grievances most likely to be pursued are those in the middle, where there is some prospect of success but not a high certainty that the employee will be successful. This prediction corresponds to the find-ing of mid-range employee win rates.

In a subsequent study, I investigated the question of whether use of non-managerial decision-makers in procedures affected usage and outcomes across a broader sample of organizations (Colvin, 2003b). In a sample of 180 establishments in the telecommunications industry, I found that that grievance rates were significantly higher in non-union procedures that included either arbitration or peer review. Whereas the annual rate of grievances of disciplinary decisions was only 1.3 per 100 employees under procedures with managerial decision-makers, the rate was 2.9 per 100 employees under peer review procedures, and 3.2 per 100 employees under procedures with arbitration as the final step (Colvin, 2003b). To account for variation in the underlying level of workplace conflict, I also calculated the percentage of all disciplinary decisions that were appealed. The results were similar, with 11% of disciplinary decisions being grieved under procedures with managerial decision-makers, 30% of decisions being grieved under peer review procedures, and 34% being grieved under procedures with arbitration as the final step (Colvin, 2003b). As suggested by Lewin's findings, employee win rates did not much vary by type of procedure, averaging 30–45%; however, the influence of the nature of the procedure on the likelihood of appealing a decision made a bigger difference. Overall in establishments that had only managerial decision-makers in their procedures, on average only 2.7% of disciplinary decisions were successfully reversed through filing grievances. By contrast, 9.9% of disciplinary decisions were successfully appealed under peer review procedures and 11.1% under procedures with arbitration as the final step (Colvin, 2003b). These differences indicate that employees are more willing to bring grievances where the procedures provide the due process protection of non-managerial decision-makers and this ultimately produces more cases in which the employee is successfully able to achieve a change in the decision being challenged.

Procedure structure is only part of what determines usage of non-union grievance procedures. Another important factor is the nature of the workplace employment system. Organizations with work and human resource systems that invest more heavily in employees and provide employees with greater involvement in workplace decision-making are more likely to provide employees with more effective grievance procedures and reduced levels of workplace conflict (Colvin, 2004a). In a recent study, I examined the impact of variation in the structure of procedures and in the nature of work and human resource systems on workplace dispute resolution outcomes (Colvin, 2013). Establishments that had non-union grievance procedures with more due process protections, including steps with non-managerial decision-makers, had higher employee grievance rates and a greater likelihood of appealing disciplinary decisions. However, the use of high involvement work systems, including employee participation systems such as teams and high levels of employee training and skills, had an even stronger impact on workplace dispute resolution, including associations with greater due process protections in procedures, reduced levels of workplace conflict, and lower grievance rates. There is an element of complementarity in these findings. Ideally, employees should prefer effective grievance procedures that they do not need to use too frequently due to fewer adverse decisions in the workplace. The combination of high involvement work systems that reduce underlying levels of conflict, and non-union grievance procedures with stronger due process protections that are more effective at resolving conflicts that do arise, appear to provide this desirable combination of circumstances.

IMPACTS ON EMPLOYEES AND THE WORKPLACE

So far the discussion has focused on how non-union grievance procedures operate in different organizations. But what does research tell us about the individual employee experience of using non-union grievance procedures?

Organizational justice theory suggests that to the degree that non-union grievance procedures enhance perceptions of justice in the workplace, we should see positive individual level attitudinal and behavioral responses from employees (Sheppard et al., 1992; Folger and Cropanzano, 1998). Research in this area has divided employee justice perceptions into separate constructs measuring perceptions of procedural justice, distributive justice, and interpersonal justice (Colquitt, 2001). An important finding from this line of research is the greater importance of procedural justice perceptions over distributive justice perceptions in shaping attitudinal and behavioral outcomes. For grievance procedures, the implication is that we should anticipate that to the degree they provide enhanced procedural fairness in workplace decisions, they should produce positive outcomes beyond the degree to which they produce decisions favorable to employee grievants. The organizational justice theory-based propositions about the positive effects of non-union grievance procedures were tested in an experimental study by Olson-Buchanan (1996). She found that subjects who were given access to a grievance procedure were more likely to be willing to continue working for the organization.

Exit-voice theory provides similar predictions of positive effects from the adoption of non-union grievance procedures. More specifically, exit-voice theory suggests that greater availability of voice options to remedy dissatisfaction with conditions should lead to reduced recourse to the exit option (Hirschman, 1970). In the workplace context, the classic example of this was the finding that the availability of the voice mechanism of union representation and grievance procedures was associated with lower rates of exit as seen in voluntary turnover or quit rates (Freeman and Medoff, 1984; Batt et al., 2002). The direct applicability of this to grievance procedures was shown in a study by Rees (1991) which found that teacher quit rates were lower in school districts where the union contracts included stronger grievance procedures. Relatively little research has tested this proposition in the non-union setting. One study that tested it in the telecommunications industry found some weak evidence that non-union peer review procedures are associated with lower quit rates, but no evidence for other types of non-union grievance procedure (Batt et al., 2002).

A darker perspective on the workplace impact of non-union grievance procedures is suggested by research looking at retaliation against employees who use these procedures. A number of studies of unionized workplaces have found that employees who file grievances are subject to lower performance evaluations, greater likelihood of subsequent exit from the organization, and other negative outcomes (Klaas and DeNisi, 1989; Boroff and Lewin, 1997; Lewin and Peterson, 1999). Similarly, in the non-union sector, Lewin (1990) found that in an organization with a non-union grievance procedure, employees who filed grievances were more likely to have negative performance evaluations in subsequent years. If these negative outcomes reflect retaliation against the employee for using the grievance procedure, then this has the potential to undermine the effectiveness of the procedure and discourage future use. However, it is difficult for research to identify the degree to which negative outcomes for grievance filers reflect actual retaliation or a post-grievance deterioration in the employee's performance, or commitment to the organization. By contrast, in a study that controlled for the perceived mistreatment experienced by the employee, Boswell and Olson-Buchanan (2004) found that grievance filers did not have significantly worse exit and neglect related attitudes and intentions. While further research on this question would be valuable, it is clear that the potential for retribution is a danger for non-union grievance procedures and one that it would be well advised for organizations to guard against.

CROSS-NATIONAL VARIATION IN NON-UNION GRIEVANCE PROCEDURES

So far the discussion has focused on research on non-union grievance procedures in the United States. This reflects in part the reality of the large non-union sector of the American workforce and the high degree of experimentation and innovation by American organizations in this area. The result is that the major body of the research on this topic has used American organizations as its setting. However, many other countries now have sizable and growing numbers of workers who are not represented by unions.

What do we know about grievance procedures for these non-union workers outside of the United States? Non-union grievance procedures have not been a major phenomenon in the coordinated market economies (Hall and Soskice, 2001), such as Germany, France, and most of continental Europe. In particular, nations where collective bargaining is centralized and contract coverage extended to most of the workforce lack the defined non-union sector that has been the center of innovation in grievance procedures. In addition, many of these countries have public employment dispute resolution procedures that are used with much higher frequency by workers than the more complex and expensive American litigation system. For example, in Germany and France, the percentage of the workforce submitting an employment claim through their respective public procedures was 1.5% and 0.7% in 2002 respectively (Gibbons, 2007). By contrast, in the liberal market economies, particularly the Anglo-American countries, the large and growing non-union sector has seen greater variation and innovation in employment relations practices including non-union grievance procedures (Colvin and Darbishire, 2012).

Among the liberal market economies, Canada provides the closest comparator to the United States given the two nations' high levels of economic and cultural integration. A long line of research has noted that, despite these similarities, the relatively more labor favorable legal regime in Canada has produced a much higher union representation rate of just under 30%, compared to around 12% in the United States (Godard, 2003). However, this still means that over 70% of the Canadian workforce is in the non-union sector. Non-union grievance procedures are widespread in Canada as in the United States. In a comparative study of organizations in the American state of Pennsylvania and the Canadian province of Ontario, I found that while 60% of American organizations had adopted non-union grievance procedures, some 46% of Canadian organizations had also adopted non-union grievance procedures (Colvin, 2006). Interestingly, despite Canada following a just cause standard for dismissals compared to the American employment at-will rule, the higher adoption rate for non-union grievance procedures in the United States was in part a result of greater concerns about litigation among the American organizations. What this likely reflects is the greater uncertainty and risk created by the high damages and variability of outcomes in the American litigation system compared to a more employee favorable but relatively predictable employment law regime in Canada (Colvin, 2006). Among Canadian organizations, the predictors of non-union grievance procedure presence are similar to those found in the United States. Analysis of data from the Canadian Workplace and Employee Survey (WES) showed that presence of non-union grievance procedures was associated with the use of high involvement work organization practices (Colvin, 2004b).

Other liberal market economies have substantial non-union sectors, but it is not evident that patterns of development of procedures parallel the North American experience. A survey of non-union multinationals in the Republic of Ireland found that almost all had some type of formal conflict management procedures, but relatively few of these companies used more advanced ADR procedures such as arbitration, peer review, or ombudspersons (Doherty and Teague, 2011). Relatedly, in a study of Irish commercial enterprises, Roche and Teague (2012) found that innovations in ADR procedures were more likely where unions were recognized as compared to non-union settings. This was true for individually focused ADR procedures, such as using review panels or external experts to resolve grievances and group focused ADR procedures such as assisted negotiations and external arbitrators. The one exception to this pattern was that brainstorming problem solving procedures were more common in non-union enterprises. Overall however, Roche and Teague conclude that "[i]n the USA, firms adopting ADR-inspired conflict management practices are doing so to address individual-based disputes and grievances, and as part of more general union substitution strategies, whereas in Ireland innovating firms tend more commonly to be unionized and are focusing on group-based conflict management" (2012: 545).

Evidence from the United Kingdom suggests that the expansion of non-union workplaces in that country is producing a shift in the mode of expression of conflict.

Analyzing data from the 2004 Workplace Employment Relations Survey, Dix, Sisson, and Forth (2009) find that while rates of industrial action are much lower in non-union workplaces, claims to employment tribunals are higher where there are non-union voice mechanisms or no voice mechanism than where there are union voice mechanisms in the workplace. Interestingly in their results, the proportion of workplace with non-union voice mechanisms experiencing grievances was relatively similar to the proportion of workplaces with union voice mechanisms with grievances, 40% versus 45% respectively (Dix et al., 2009).

At the level of public policy, the United Kingdom undertook a more direct approach to encouraging the expansion of workplace grievance procedures with the enactment of a statutory dispute resolution procedure in 2004. The 2004 Act required organizations to follow a three-step procedure for discipline and workplace grievances, involving: the disciplinary decision or grievance being put in writing; a meeting being held to discuss the issue; and a procedure for the employee to appeal the decision (Harris, Tuckman, and Snook, 2012). Failure to follow the statutory grievance procedure would result in a dismissal being presumed to be unfair, and failure of the employee to first pursue the claim through the procedure would result in the subsequent dismissal of an employment tribunal claim. Problems with excessive formalization of processes and an emphasis on procedure over the substance of employment claims quickly led to pressure on the British government to revisit the statutory procedure requirement, which appointed an independent review commission (Harris et al., 2012). This resulted in the Gibbons (2007) report, which recommended the repeal of the statutory grievance procedure requirement. The statutory procedure provisions were repealed in 2009 and replaced by a more flexible approach in which the Advisory, Conciliation and Arbitration Service (ACAS) developed a new Code of Practice on Disciplinary and Grievance Procedures to serve as guidelines for organizations but without the previous preclusive effect on claims. As yet it is unclear what the effect of these shifts in public policy has had on the incidence of grievance procedures in the UK, particularly in workplaces where unions are not recognized.

CONCLUSION

When we survey the landscape of employment relations, it is clear that non-union grievance procedures have become an important institution in the workplace. Most notably in the United States, with its largely non-union labor force, non-union grievance procedures are the primary structure for most employees for addressing conflict in the workplace. Although still limited in extent, current research in this area allows us to identify some key features of this phenomenon. First, non-union grievance procedures are characterized by a high degree of diversity in their incidence, origins, structure, and operations. Rather than a uniform system of conflict management of the type we see in union grievance procedures or public dispute resolution systems, non-union grievance procedures are idiosyncratic to the individual organization and vary widely in their key features. Much as we have seen growing variation in patterns of human resource practices between organizations and widening income inequality across the economy, so also in the rise of non-union grievance procedures are we seeing rising inequality in access to justice in the workplace.

Second, research indicates that the nature of non-union grievance procedures matters for important employee and workplace outcomes. Many non-union grievance procedures are relatively simple structures with only managerial decision-makers and low levels of usage by employees. But we have also seen the expansion of procedures that use non-managerial decision-makers, such as peer review panels and outside neutral mediators and arbitrators, and these procedures are used more frequently by employees with greater levels of success in challenging workplace decisions. Third, non-union grievance procedures do not exist in isolation within the organization. Research in the United States has shown that the expansion and quality of non-union grievance procedures are highly influenced by the nature of external institutional pressures from the legal system and from union organizing threats. Looking across countries, the public policy environment is a key determinant of whether or not non-union grievance procedures are likely to develop as a significant phenomenon in nations other than the United States.

What are the important unanswered questions about non-union grievance procedures? One of the most significant is the basic question of what is the distribution of procedures. Research in the United States suggests that more than half of non-union organizations have some type of formal procedure and that there is wide variation in the nature and structure of these procedures. However, we lack good data on the exact distribution of different types of procedures and how this distribution has changed over time. Data on non-union grievance procedures from other countries are generally even more limited. Systematic national level survey data would allow us to understand the incidence and structure of procedures, as well as to investigate further questions such as the factors that determine the types of procedures that are adopted.

A second area in need of further research is the question of what impacts non-union grievance procedures have in the workplace. Research suggests some positive impacts in the ability of employees to challenge unfair decisions and in the enhancement of organizational justice perceptions. However, among the most troubling of existing research findings is Lewin's (1990) identification of retaliation against both grievance filers and supervisors of grievants. It suggests the importance of identifying how frequent is retaliation and what factors lead to retaliation or what policies or practices might be effective in preventing retaliation. Furthermore, we know little about the potential indirect effect of non-union grievance procedures in the workplace. Does the potential for having their decisions reviewed through procedures cause managers to be more careful and prudent in their workplace decision-making? Do employees engage in positive workplace behaviors because they perceive that non-union grievance procedures protect them from unfair adverse decisions?

Last, relatively little attention has been paid to the question of representation in non-union grievance procedures. One of the main contrasts to grievance procedures in unionized workplaces, where the union provides employees with an institutional structure for representation, is that in non-union procedures the employee is typically unrepresented. He or she must file and present the grievance on his or her own. This may be a daunting task for many employees and hinder effective use of the procedure. Although notionally an employee might hire an attorney to provide representation, in practice this is likely to be prohibitively expensive and management may not allow an outside representative to participate in the process. In some organizations, human resource managers may serve as representatives of employee grievants and partially fill this gap (Colvin, 2004a). However, this creates a natural conflict of interests since they remain employees of the company and so this may only be effective where the issues involved are more lateral conflicts in the workplace and do not implicate hierarchical conflicts with the employer or external rights. More broadly, the question of how to provide effective representation for non-union employees is one that challenges both the operation of non-union grievance procedures and that of employment relations more generally in the non-union workplace.

REFERENCES

Batt, R., Colvin, A., and Keefe, J. 2002. "Employee Voice, Human Resource Practices, and Quit Rates: Evidence from the Telecommunications Industry." *Industrial and Labor Relations Review*, 55(4): 573–94.

Berenbeim, R. 1980. *Nonunion Complaint Systems: A Corporate Appraisal*. New York: The Conference Board.

Bingham, L. B. and Chachere, D. R. 1999. "Dispute Resolution in Employment: The Need for Research." In E. Eaton and J. H. Keefe (eds), *Employment Dispute Resolution and Worker Rights in the Changing Workplace*. Champaign, IL: Industrial Relations Research Association, 95–135.

Boroff, K. E. and Lewin, D. 1997. "Loyalty, Voice, and Intent to Exit a Union Firm: A Conceptual and Empirical Analysis." *Industrial and Labor Relations Review*, 51(1): 50–63.

Boswell, W. R. and Olson-Buchanan, J. B. 2004. "Experiencing Mistreatment at Work: The Role of Grievance-Filing, Nature of Mistreatment, and Employee Withdrawal." *Academy of Management Journal*, 47: 129–39.

Bronfenbrenner, K. 1997. "The Role of Union Strategies in NLRB Certification Elections." *Industrial and Labor Relations Review*, 50(2): 195–212.

Clermont, K. M. and Schwab, S. J. 2004. "How Employment Discrimination Plaintiffs Fare in Federal Court." *Journal of Empirical Legal Studies*, 1(2): 429–58.

Colquitt, J. A. 2001. "On the Dimensionality of Organizational Justice: A Construct Validation of a Measure." *Journal of Applied Psychology*, 86: 386–400.

Colvin, A. J. S. 2003a. "Institutional Pressures, Human Resource Strategies, and the Rise of Nonunion Dispute Resolution Procedures." *Industrial and Labor Relations Review*, 56(3): 375–92.

Colvin, A. J. S. 2003b. "The Dual Transformation of Workplace Dispute Resolution." *Industrial Relations*, 42(4): 712–35.

Colvin, A. J. S. 2004a. "Adoption and Use of Dispute Resolution Procedures in the Nonunion Workplace." In D. Lewin and B. E. Kaufman (eds), *Advances in Industrial and Labor Relations*, vol.13. Bingley, UK: Emerald, 69–95.

Colvin, A. J. S. 2004b. "The Relationship between Employee Involvement and Workplace Dispute Resolution." *Relations Industrielles [Industrial Relations]*, 59(4): 671–94.

Colvin, A. J. S. 2006. "Flexibility and Fairness in Liberal Market Economies: The Comparative Impact of the Legal Environment and High Performance Work Systems." *British Journal of Industrial Relations*, 44(1): 73–97.

Colvin, A. J. S. 2007. "Empirical Research on Employment Arbitration: Clarity amidst the Sound and Fury?" *Employee Rights and Employment Policy Journal*, 11(2): 405–47.

Colvin, A. J. S. 2012. "American Workplace Dispute Resolution in the Individual Rights Era." *International Journal of Human Resource Management*, 23(3): 459–75.

Colvin, A. J. S. 2013. "Participation versus Procedures in Non-union Dispute Resolution." *Industrial Relations*, 52(Suppl. 1): 259–83.

Colvin, A. J. S. and Darbishire, O. R. 2012. "International Employment Relations: The Impact of Varieties of Capitalism." In G. Stahl et al. (eds), *Handbook of International Human Resource Management Research*. 3rd edn. Cheltenham, UK: Edward Elgar, Ch. 4, 52–75.

Colvin, A. J. S., Klaas, B., and Mahony, D. 2006. "Research on Alternative Dispute Resolution Procedures." In D. Lewin (ed.), *Contemporary Issues in Employment Relations*. Champaign, IL: Labor and Employment Relations Association, Ch. 4, 103–47.

Cooper, L. J., Nolan, D. R., and Bales, R. A. 2000. *ADR in the Workplace*. St. Paul, MN: West Group.

Delaney, J. T., Lewin, D., and Ichniowski, C. 1989. *Human Resource Policies and Practices in American Firms*, BLMR #137. Washington, DC: US Department of Labor.

Dix, G., Sisson, K., and Forth, J. 2009. "Conflict at Work: The Changing Pattern of Disputes." In W. Brown et al. (eds), *The Evolution of the Modern Workplace*. Cambridge, UK: Cambridge University Press, Ch. 8.

Doherty, L. and Teague, P. 2011. "Conflict Management Systems in Subsidiaries of Non-Union Multinational Organizations Located in the Republic of Ireland." *International Journal of Human Resource Management*, 22(1): 57–71.

Edelman, L. B. 1990. "Legal Environments and Organizational Governance: The Expansion of Due Process in the American Workplace." *American Journal of Sociology*, 95(6): 1401–40.

Edelman, L. B., Abraham, S. E., and Erlanger, H. S. 1992. "Professional Construction of Law: The Inflated Threat of Wrongful Discharge." *Law and Society Review*, 26(1): 47–83.

Edelman, L. B., Uggen, C., and Erlanger, H. S. 1999. "The Endogeneity of Legal Regulation: Grievance Procedures as Rational Myth." *American Journal of Sociology*, 105(2): 406–54.

Eisenberg, T. and Schlanger, M. 2003. "The Reliability of the Administrative Office of the U.S. Courts Database: An Initial Empirical Analysis." *Notre Dame Law Review*, 78: 1455–96.

Ewing, D. W. 1989. *Justice on the Job: Resolving Grievances in the Nonunion Workplace*. Boston, MA: Harvard Business School Press.

Feuille, P. and Chachere, D. T. 1995. "Looking Fair or Being Fair: Remedial Voice Procedures in Nonunion Workplaces." *Journal of Management*, 21(1): 27–42.

Feuille, P. and Delaney, J.T. 1992. "The Individual Pursuit of Organizational Justice: Grievance Procedures in Nonunion Workplaces." In G. R. Ferris and K. M. Rowland (eds), *Research in Personnel and Human Resource Management*. Stamford, CT: JAI Press, 187–232.

Folger, R. and Cropanzano, R. 1998. *Organizational Justice and Human Resource Management*. Thousand Oaks, CA: Sage.

Freeman, R. B. and Medoff, J. L. 1984. *What Do Unions Do?* New York: Basic Books.

General Accounting Office 1997. *Alternative Dispute Resolution: Employers' Experiences with ADR in the Workplace*, GAO/GGD-97-157 ADR in the Workplace. Washington, DC: GAO.

Gibbons, M. 2007. *Better Dispute Resolution: A Review of Employment Dispute Resolution in Great Britain*. London: Department of Trade and Industry, HMSO.

Godard, J. 2003. "Do Labor Laws Matter? The Density Decline and Convergence Thesis Revisited." *Industrial Relations*, 42(3): 458–92.

Hall, P. and Soskice, D. (eds) 2001. *Varieties of Capitalism: The Institutional Foundations of Comparative Advantage*. Oxford: Oxford University Press.

Harris, L., Tuckman, A., and Snook, J. 2012. "Supporting Workplace Dispute Resolution in Smaller Businesses: Policy Perspectives and Operational Realities." *International Journal of Human Resource Management*, 23(3): 607–23.

Hirschman, A. O. 1970. *Exit, Voice, and Loyalty*. Cambridge, MA: Harvard University Press.

Huselid, M. A. 1995. "The Impact of Human Resource Management Practices on Turnover, Productivity, and Corporate Financial Performance." *Academy of Management Journal*, 38(3): 635–72.

Klaas, B. S. and DeNisi, A. S. 1989. "Managerial Reactions to Employee Dissent: The Impact of Grievance Activity on Performance Ratings." *Academy of Management Journal*, 32(4): 705–18.

Kochan, T. A., Katz, H. C., and McKersie, R. B. 1994. *The Transformation of American Industrial Relations*. Ithaca, NY: ILR Press.

Kolb, D. M. 1987. "Corporate Ombudsman and Organization Conflict Resolution." *Journal of Conflict Resolution*, 31(4): 673–91.

Lewin, D. 1987. "Conflict Resolution in the Nonunion Firm: A Theoretical and Empirical Analysis." *Journal of Conflict Resolution*, 31(3): 465–502.

Lewin, D. 1990. "Grievance Procedures in Nonunion Workplaces: An Empirical Analysis of Usage, Dynamics, and Outcomes." *Chicago-Kent Law Review*, 66(3): 823–44.

Lewin, D. 2008. "Employee Voice and Mutual Gains," Proceedings of the 60th Annual Meeting of the Labor and Employment Relations Association (LERA), Jan., New Orleans, LA: 61–83.

Lewin, D. and Peterson, R. B. 1999. "Behavioral Outcomes of Grievance Activity." *Industrial Relations*, 38(4): 554–76.

Lipsky, D. B., Seeber, R. L., and Fincher, R. D. 2003. *Emerging Systems for Managing Workplace Conflict*. San Francisco, CA: Jossey-Bass.

Olson-Buchanan, J. B. 1996. "Voicing Discontent: What Happens to the Grievance Filer after the Grievance?" *Journal of Applied Psychology*, 81(1): 52–63.

Oppenheimer, D. B. 2003. "Verdicts Matter: An Empirical Study of California Employment Discrimination and Wrongful Discharge Jury Verdicts Reveals Low Success Rates for Women and Minorities," *UC Davis Law Review*, 37: 535–49.

Rees, D. I. 1991. "Grievance Procedure Strength and Teacher Quits." *Industrial and Labor Relations Review*, 45(1): 31–43.

Roche, W. K. and Teague, P. 2012. "Human Resource Management and ADR Practices in Ireland." *International Journal of Human Resource Management*, 23(3): 528–49.

Sheppard, B. H., Lewicki, R. J., and Minton, J. W. 1992. *Organizational Justice: The Search for Fairness in the Workplace*. New York: Macmillan.

Stone, K. V. W. 1999. "Employment Arbitration under the Federal Arbitration Act." In A. E. Eaton and J. H. Keefe (eds), *Employment Dispute Resolution and Worker Rights in the Changing Workplace*. Champaign, IL: Industrial Relations Research Association, Ch. 2, 27–65.

Sutton, J. R. and Dobbin, F. 1996. "The Two Faces of Governance: Responses to Legal Uncertainty in U.S. Firms, 1955 to 1985." *American Sociological Review*, 61(5): 794–811.

Sutton, J. R., Dobbin, F., Meyer, J., and Scott, W. R. 1994. "The Legalization of the Workplace." *American Journal of Sociology*, 99(4): 944–71.

Westin, A. F. and Felieu, A. G. 1988. *Resolving Employment Disputes without Litigation.* Washington, DC: Bureau of National Affairs.

Wheeler, H. N., Klaas, B. S., and Mahony, D. M. 2004. *Workplace Justice without Unions.* Kalamazoo, MI: Upjohn Institute.

CHAPTER 9

··

WORKPLACE MEDIATION*

··

PAUL L. LATREILLE AND RICHARD SAUNDRY

INTRODUCTION

THE challenges faced by organizations in resolving conflict at work, and in particular concerns over the cost of managing individual employment disputes and the threat of litigation, have focused attention on alternative systems of dispute resolution. Prominent among these has been mediation. Although the concept has been in existence and practiced in a variety of forms for centuries (Wall and Lynn, 1993; Griffiths, 2001), academic and policy interest in its application to the workplace is more recent and largely stems from dissatisfaction with conventional rights-based disputes procedures viewed as cumbersome, inefficient, and adversarial (Pope, 1996; Reynolds, 2000).

Mediation's supporters suggest that it is more likely to restore the employment relationship and potentially offers significant financial savings compared with often lengthy traditional grievance and disciplinary processes (Goldberg, 2005). They believe that it also delivers sustainable outcomes and high rates of dispute resolution and satisfaction among the parties (McDermott et al., 2000; Bingham et al., 2002; Latreille, 2011). Cases that might otherwise result in long-term absence and litigation are resolved relatively quickly (Corby, 1999; Kressel, 2006). Furthermore, mediation is believed to trigger the development of improved conflict-handling skills (Anderson and Bingham, 1997; Kressel, 2006), enhance employer-employee relationships (Seargeant, 2005) and develop organizational culture (CIPD, 2007).

This chapter therefore examines a number of key questions. What is workplace mediation and what are its perceived benefits? What factors shape the effectiveness of mediation? To what extent does mediation offer a way to shape the culture of conflict

---

* The authors would like to acknowledge the valuable input and advice of Lisa Banks and Virginia Branney in developing aspects of this chapter.

management? What, if any, are the broader implications of the extension of mediation for employment relations and the regulation of work?

The chapter is structured as follows. Firstly, it examines definitions of mediation and the different styles that have been adopted. Then the diffusion of workplace mediation is assessed, its perceived benefits are examined, and some of the difficulties associated with evaluating the success of mediation initiatives are highlighted. Finally, the broader implications of mediation for conflict management and employment relations are explored.

Defining and Conceptualizing Workplace Mediation

Workplace Mediation—A Definition

Defining mediation is not straightforward as there is no overarching theory of mediation (Bellman, 1998) and some debate between those who emphasize the role played by mediation in shaping and improving decision-making (i.e. Boulle and Nesic, 2001) as opposed to commentators who identify its impact on dispute resolution. For example, Wall and Lynn (1993: 161) simply define mediation as "third-party assistance to two or more interacting parties." From this perspective, mediation would cover a wide range of employment relations exchanges and processes including informal discussions facilitated by line managers or HR practitioners (see Latreille, 2011).

Perhaps more usefully, Moore (2003: 15) defines mediation as: "the intervention in a negotiation or a conflict of an acceptable third party who has limited or no authoritative decision-making power, [and] who assists the involved parties to voluntarily reach a mutually acceptable settlement of the issues in dispute."

This not only identifies the goal of mediation as dispute settlement but also contrasts mediation with conventional dispute resolution processes within which managers, adjudicators or arbitrators retain decision-making authority.

However, even this approach is somewhat prescriptive, implying a linear model of dispute resolution in which the parties move from conflict to consensus as the mediation process unfolds. This underplays the complexity of mediation, the impact of contextual factors (Jones and Bodtker, 2001; Bowling and Hoffman, 2003; Kressel, 2007), and perhaps most importantly the fact that mediation is shaped by power relations both inside and outside the mediation process (Karambayya et al., 1992; Wiseman and Poitras, 2002).

Mediation styles—Facilitation to Transformation

Nonetheless, there is growing recognition of the context specificity of mediation approaches (Bush and Folger, 2005). Consequently it is possible to identify a number of different mediation "styles" (for a detailed review, see Banks and Saundry, 2010). Most workplace mediators adopt a problem-solving approach (Anderson and Bingham, 1997). The evaluative style has its roots in labor-management disputes and is often employed within litigation where mediators seek to ensure that participants are realistic about their relative bargaining positions and accordingly encourage settlement. In contrast, facilitative mediation stresses the importance of recognizing the needs and interests of disputants in order to identify areas for agreement that will be sustainable in the future (Alberts et al., 2005). However, critics suggest that facilitative mediation fails to give sufficient attention to the underlying issues that lead to conflict (Kressel, 2007). Consequently, Kressel argues that mediators need to be more strategic and even depart from a neutral position in order to direct participants to the roots of the dispute.

A radical alternative is provided by transformational mediation (Bush, 2001; Hallberlin, 2001) in which the parties are encouraged to set the agenda, thus exercising control of the process as well as the outcome. While settlement may be reached, it is not the main focus or objective (Bingham and Novac, 2001). Instead, the aim is to empower the parties, restoring their self-confidence and their responsiveness to others. Narrative mediation also moves the emphasis away from problem-solving by re-focusing the "conflict story" in an attempt to establish a basis of respect and equity on which the parties can build a working relationship (Winslade, 2006: 511). However, it could be argued that, in the workplace, the importance of settling the dispute and getting the parties "back to work" makes more relational approaches difficult to justify (McDermott et al., 2001).

Overall, while the facilitative approach is most commonly used for workplace disputes (Herrman et al., 2003; Mareschal, 2005), no single style has become predominant. Indeed, a transformative approach is used in one of the most significant workplace mediation schemes extant—the US Postal Service's Redress scheme (Bingham, 2004). In fact, it could be argued that imposing clear distinctions between mediation styles fails to reflect the fact that mediators may use a range of different approaches within the same case (Riskin, 2003). Furthermore, it provides an essentially static conception of mediation that underplays the extent to which mediation is shaped by the dynamic interplay between the parties, the mediator and the mediation context (Picard, 2004).

Mediation—Principles and Practice

In practical terms, mediations vary in their arrangements. However, they will typically begin with individual meetings between each party and the mediator (referred to as caucuses) at which the parties are able to explore their views of the dispute. This will be followed, unless the relationship is particularly adversarial, with a joint meeting between the parties at which the mediator explains the process of mediation and allows each side an opportunity to set out their perspective without interruption. With the help of the mediator, the parties then proceed to explore the underlying reasons for the dispute. Through techniques such as listening, questioning, summarizing, acknowledging, mutualizing, and reframing (Wall, 1981; Brown and Mariott, 1999), the mediator will seek to establish common ground and hence develop possible solutions to the dispute, or at least a way forward. This may be recorded in the form of an agreement. As the above might suggest, while often described as "informal," mediation is highly structured, albeit still in a flexible manner without the same concern with evidence and reporting that typifies discipline and grievance processes.

The course of mediation, which will often be non-linear, not only relies heavily on the skills of the mediator (see Brown and Mariott, 1999) but also on their style and approach as described above. Nonetheless, a number of key principles tend to underpin mediation practice. Firstly, mediation processes are generally accompanied by assurances of confidentiality. This, it is argued, protects the parties and provides an environment within which individuals can express themselves freely. However, not only may confidentiality be difficult to maintain within a working environment, but it brings with it potential dangers. Confidentiality may restrict the extent to which organizations can learn from disputes to review and improve workplace practice (Fox, 2005). More seriously, it may obscure serious and/or persistent misconduct, preventing the organization from taking appropriate disciplinary action (Anderson and Bingham, 1997). Moreover, organizations may be able take advantage of this lack of transparency to present management failure as interpersonal conflict (Bush and Folger, 2005).

Secondly, it is argued that participation in mediation should be voluntary, and that for mediation to have any chance of a successful outcome, parties must be willing and committed to seeking a resolution (Seargeant, 2005), i.e. participating in "good faith." However, the empirical evidence in relation to this is not altogether clear. For example, Brett et al. (1996) found similar settlement and satisfaction rates for both voluntary and mandated mediation and argue that while forcing parties to settle is inconsistent with mediation, compelling participation is not. While this may be true of court ordered mediation, to which they refer, it is possible that individuals forced to undertake workplace mediation by their manager may be reluctant to engage fully with the process. Moreover, even in cases in which there may be no overt compulsion, individuals may feel obliged to take part in mediation, fearing reputational damage or other ramifications if they refuse (see Latreille, 2011). This may be particularly true for managers who could feel under compulsion to be seen to embrace organizational policies and values.

Thirdly, in some contexts (for example the UK), representation within mediation is seen as neither desirable nor necessary. According to the UK's Advisory, Conciliation and Arbitration Service (ACAS), "the focus of mediation is the resolution of the dispute by participants themselves and to maintain as much informality for the process as possible" (ACAS/TUC, 2010: 3). It could also be argued that representatives could shape the perceptions of participants, obstructing compromise and potential resolution. Conversely, representatives could be crucial in addressing power imbalances between workers and their managers (Dolder, 2004). For example, McDermott et al. (2000) found that participants with representation were more satisfied with the fairness of the process. Indeed, evidence from the USPS's Redress scheme suggests that settlement rates are higher where parties are represented, particularly when that representation is provided by trade unions or professional associations (Bingham et al., 2002; Bingham and Pitts, 2002).

BENEFITS AND EVALUATION

Trends in the Incidence of Workplace Mediation

Determining the incidence of mediation is a difficult exercise. As with technological change, its diffusion includes both inter- and intra-organizational dimensions, the latter in particular being externally unobservable and often regarded as commercially sensitive. In relation to the former, there are survey data for particular sectors and economies, and evidence of increasing incidence. For example, two surveys of US Fortune 1000 companies in 1997 and in 2011 show that the use of mediation in the employment context in the previous three years had risen from 78.6% to 85.5% (Stipanowich and Lamare, forthcoming; see also Lipsky et al., 2012 for a discussion of the factors driving adoption). While the 2011 survey does not reveal the actual number of mediations, half of these firms reported "always" or "frequently" using voluntary mediation in employment disputes aside from court-mandated procedures, suggesting that significant numbers of mediations take place, at least within such very large organizations.

In the UK there is also evidence of an upwards trend in the spread of mediation across organizations. Surveys of their members conducted by the CIPD, claim that the percentage of responding organizations that had used mediation to resolve work problems rose from 42.7% in 2008 to 57.3% three years later (CIPD, 2008, 2011). Strikingly, the figure was substantially higher among public sector employers at 82.8%, consistent with data from Australia (Van Gramberg, 2002) and the US (Bingham and Chachere, 1999) that such organizations are early adopters of mediation. In the UK this partly reflects a strong policy steer towards using such forms of dispute resolution including the ADR Pledge launched in 2001 (now superseded by the Dispute Resolution Commitment) which committed government departments to using such processes, including mediation.

However, other evidence suggests a much lower level of use. Research undertaken by ACAS found that just 5% of private sector businesses had used mediation, falling to a mere 4% in SMEs (Williams, 2011). In addition, data from the WERS 2011 survey found that mediation had been used to resolve a dispute in the previous 12 months in just 7% of private and public sector workplaces (Van Wanrooy et al., 2013).

One possible explanation for the discrepancy in the evidence on mediation use may be definitional. Where survey respondents self-define mediation, this will typically include relatively informal facilitated discussions as well as structured processes involving a neutral, trained mediator.

As regards intra-organizational diffusion, such sketchy evidence as there is concerning uptake suggests relatively modest numbers of mediations in UK workplaces. The CIPD samples comprise mainly larger organizations, and in 2008, an average of just 3.42 mediations in the previous 12 months was reported. Case study evidence reviewed by Latreille (2011) suggests that despite the presence of disputes, low mediation volumes are an issue, especially for in-house schemes where there are accordingly few opportunities for mediators to maintain and develop their skills.

Outside the UK and the US, the evidence is more uneven. Nonetheless, there are signs that the use of mediation across EU states is increasing, covering 19 countries including Austria, Belgium, Bulgaria, Cyprus, Estonia, Finland, Germany, Hungary, Ireland, Latvia, Luxembourg, the Netherlands, Norway, Portugal, Romania, Slovakia, Slovenia, and Spain (Eurofound, 2010). Australasia has also been a focus of mediation activity. For Australia, Van Gramberg (2006) found around half the employers responding to her 2001 survey in Victoria had used mediation in the past. Although later data are not available, as Forsyth (2012: 484) describes, there is evidence of a rise in the inclusion of clauses in workplace agreements and "anecdotal reports of an increasing propensity of employers to utilize workplace mediation". Furthermore, in New Zealand, the use of mediation appeared initially to increase in the wake of the introduction of the Employment Relations Act 2000, but Woodhams, reporting in 2007, suggested that mediation volumes had leveled out with "no evidence of a changing trend" (8).

Mediation—Cost and Efficiency—The Business Case

The increased interest in the use of mediation described above has largely been driven by employing organizations searching for more efficient and effective ways to resolve workplace disputes. It is argued that mediation can be conducted more quickly and at a lower cost than conventional grievance or disciplinary procedures. Significantly, mediation offers financial savings (Goldberg, 2005; Kressel, 2006) compared to conventional dispute procedures. Swift and sustainable resolutions promise to reduce the possibility of long-term absence, make resignations less likely, and minimize the number of cases that reach litigation. In addition, mediation can be organized and conducted relatively quickly and tends to involve significantly less management time than traditional approaches (Corby, 1999; Bingham and Pitts, 2002). While there is a dearth of authoritative data to verify this (Latreille, 2011), one estimate (for the UK) suggested that the average cost of management, union, and witness time in handling an issue through conventional (grievance or fair treatment) procedures was more than five times the direct cost of mediation (Saundry et al., 2013). Furthermore, it is argued that mediation is more likely than conventional procedures to deliver sustainable resolutions, thus maintaining existing employment relationships. This is partly due to the fact that mediation can be used to address emerging conflicts at a relatively early stage, although it is also often used following more adjudicative processes to facilitate a return to parties working together.

Mediation also provides opportunities for staff wishing to progress grievances in a less confrontational manner (Fox, 2005) and for dealing with problems that are otherwise not amenable to resolution through formal procedures (Montoya, 1998; CIPD, 2004). Accordingly, those employees who would normally avoid conflict may be more likely to voice their concerns rather than exiting the organization (Barsky and Wood, 2005). For example, Gazeley (1997: 623) argues that mediation can be cathartic and "offers the chance to educate the participants about their differing perspectives; mediation permits this healing which cannot be achieved through monetary awards or defense verdicts."

Thus, part of the logic for mediation is undoubtedly an attempt to re-establish working relationships where employment is ongoing.

Furthermore, mediation also provides individuals with the opportunity to have "their day in court," while allowing them to express their feelings in a relatively safe and secure environment (Singletary et al., 1995; Sulzner, 2003; Seargeant, 2005). Importantly, while conventional approaches tend to focus on apportioning blame, mediation emphasizes the importance of seeking a jointly agreed resolution (Pope, 1996; Reynolds, 2000). Consequently, Shapiro and Brett (1993) argue that participants find mediation more satisfying than traditional methods and are thus more likely to uphold any agreement reached.

Certainly, there is a broad range of evidence that points to high rates of resolution and satisfaction among the parties to mediation. Evaluations of a number of major mediation programs in the US reveal consistently high levels of participant satisfaction with both process and outcome. For example, Bingham et al.'s (2009) analysis of the USPS Redress scheme found that over 90% of participants were satisfied with the medi-ation process, while 64% of employees and 70% of supervisors reported satisfaction with the outcome. Moreover, the number of informal complaints filed fell by 30% from their peak before the introduction of Redress. High levels of approval were also found in relation to mediation within the US Equal Employment Opportunity Commission (EEOC) (McDermott et al., 2000) and the Massachusetts Commission Against Discrimination (MCAD) (Kochan et al., 2000). In New Zealand, the Department of Labour has reported consistently high settlement rates in recent years—in 2011/12, it mediated in 5,850 cases with a settlement rate of 81% (Department of Labour, 2012). In the UK, CIPD data reveal resolution rates (full or partial) of around 90% in the most recent case and correspondingly positive attitudes among employers (CIPD, 2008). But, as Latreille (2010) documents using the same data, significantly less sanguine views were expressed where the most recent mediation did not result in resolution—arguably representing a further dimension of Feuille and Kolb's (1994) notion of media-tion "fragility."

Measuring the Success of Mediation—An Inexact Science

There are clear difficulties with assessing the benefits of mediation. By its nature, there is no single, ready-to-use index of success in mediation (Urwin et al., 2010). Nonetheless, the easiest and arguably "the ultimate criterion of effectiveness" (Kochan and Jick, 1978: 211), albeit still imperfect, is the rate of settlement. Even here matters are less than straightforward. For instance, as Mack (2003) notes, cases might have been resolved without mediation.

In addition, measuring success in terms of dispute settlement is too simplistic (Greig, 2005). Partial settlements in complex cases can have long-lasting organizational benefits (Fox, 2005). Instead, Mareschal (2005) argues that mediation success should be viewed as a continuum measured against factors such as reaching agreement and narrowing the number of issues in dispute, whilst Hoskins and Stoltz (2003: 347) contend that as change often occurs in the months following the mediation, mediators should view agreement as a step "along a path of development." Importantly, transformative mediation measures success not in terms of settlement but the parties' level of participation and recognition of each other (Bush, 2001; Bingham, 2003). Thus, meaningful comparisons between studies of mediation are problematic and data need to be treated with caution.

This difficulty in evaluating success rates is compounded by a number of factors. Participants' expectations, understanding, and attitude towards mediation will influence the nature of, and satisfaction with, the eventual outcome (Silberman, 1989; McDermott et al., 2000). Moreover, in workplace mediation, the mediator normally has the final decision as to whether a case is suitable. Consequently, mediation takes place when it is most likely to be successful (Greig, 2005).

Also, as Mack (2003: 21) notes, there are substantial difficulties in identifying a suitable control group. Many studies focus only on those participating in mediation (e.g. Wood and Leon, 2006), or compare, in a sometimes simplistic manner, outcome measures between mediated and non-mediated (adjudicated) disputes. This means that the counterfactual is likely to be incorrectly measured. The key problem here is that where the parties exercise any choice over whether or not mediation is taken up, the issue of sample selectivity emerges: parties/disputes where individuals select into mediation are likely to differ systematically from those where they do not (see Chapter 16).

Furthermore, comparing the effectiveness of mediation with that of more traditional dispute resolution processes is problematic (Mahoney and Klass, 2008) since participants are unlikely to have experienced mediation and grievance processes simultaneously. Many of the empirical studies of mediation consider short-term measures of success and have little to say about the sustainability of settlements or the resilience of participants' views. For example, it is possible that satisfaction levels might change if problems persist in ongoing relationships. Examining longer-term outcomes is argued to be especially important where there is a potential power imbalance between the parties (Wade, 1998). However, there is a notable dearth of longitudinal empirical studies of the impact of workplace mediation.

Mediation—Factors Shaping Effectiveness

Despite these difficulties, the empirical literature has identified a number of key drivers of mediation effectiveness. Firstly, the timing of referral is argued to be crucial. While policy discussion of mediation has characterized it as a form of early resolution (see Gibbons, 2007, in the case of the UK), some of the UK evidence suggests it is still seen as a "last resort" (CIPD, 2008). Mack (2003) argues that the "ripeness" of a dispute for mediation (Astor and Chinkin, 2002: 280; Sourdin, 2002: 110–13) is a complex matter. For example, an early referral may enable resolution before the positions of the parties have hardened; too early, however, and parties will not see the necessity to enter mediation. In fact, mediation may be seen to constitute escalation of a dispute and undercut attempts by supervisors and line managers to address the issue informally by other and more direct means (Wall et al., 2001; Greig, 2005).

Secondly, the skills and strategies employed by the mediator are crucial in determining outcomes. For example, their ability to establish rapport and trust (Kressel and Pruitt, 1985), gain the confidence of the parties (Goldberg and Shaw, 2007), and their level of empathy with the disputants (Poitras, 2009) are all seen as important. For some, this is inevitably linked to the extent to which they are seen as impartial. This in turn raises questions over the use of mediators external to the organization versus in-house specialists. While the latter may benefit from an understanding of the environmental context of disputes, it may be more difficult for them to establish credibility. For example, the USPS decided to use external "neutral" mediators in their Redress scheme after pilot exercises had revealed higher rates of settlement and satisfaction when compared to internal mediators (Nabatchi and Bingham, 2010). Against this, Latreille's (2011) review of UK practice found that the use of external mediators could be more costly, subject to time delays, and was associated by parties with formalization of the dispute. Latreille (2011) also finds that resolution rates are lower among externally mediated cases, possibly reflecting that this option typically occurs later, when positions have become more intractable.

Thirdly, a variety of case and party characteristics has been found to impact quite consistently on mediation settlement. A prominent feature is the commitment of the parties to the process (Hiltrop, 1989), which in turn underpins arguments that participation in workplace mediation should be essentially voluntary. Relatedly, Poitras (2007) has argued that mutual acceptance of responsibility may be important both in developing trust and in getting the parties to focus on cooperation. More generally, the outcome may depend on the level of negotiation and conflict management skills of the disputants themselves (Wall and Dunne, 2012). Crucial too are the parties' expectations of mediation (Guthrie and Levin, 1998; Herrman et al., 2003): satisfaction is likely to be lower where parties' expectations about what it may deliver are misconceived or unrealistic; thus, preparation for, and the introduction to, mediation are key.

MEDIATION AND WORKPLACE RELATIONS— BROADENING THE DEBATE

Transforming the Culture of Conflict Management?

At a broader level, the introduction of in-house mediation schemes may have an impact beyond the specific disputes that are mediated. Those parties directly involved within mediation may change the way that they deal with disputes. For example, the literature suggests that for managers, mediation training can improve their ability to handle workplace conflict (Bingham, 2004), enhance their reputation (Reynolds, 2000) and enable them to gain "knowledge or resources that can greatly expand the opportunities for creative problem solving" (Kressel, 2006: 747). Seargeant's (2005) evaluation of mediation in small firms in the UK found evidence of a sustained improvement in employer-employee relationships. Similarly, the UK government claim that the extension of mediation can help to develop organizational culture and high-trust relationships (BIS, 2011).

In the US, culture change has been linked to the use of transformative mediation which, it is argued, can improve workplace environments by developing the communication and conflict management competencies of participants (Bush and Folger, 2005). The foremost example of this is the introduction of the Redress program by the US Postal Service, which looked to transformative mediation as a way of addressing labor-management conflict that had become deeply embedded within the organization. A detailed, longitudinal study of the Redress initiative found that supervisors who underwent mediation training and/or mediation "listen more, are more open to expressing emotion, and take a less hierarchical top-down approach to managing conflict" (Bingham et al., 2009: 43). Furthermore, it is argued that, over time, Redress improved the organizational climate, reducing the number of formal discrimination complaints and stimulating early resolution. In the UK, Saundry et al.'s (2013) case study of the introduction of mediation at a public health organization focused on the way in which high-trust relationships between key actors within conflict resolution could be built, particularly between managers and trade union representatives. This research argued that the introduction of mediation was not a simple panacea for workplace conflict but could provide a conduit through which workplace relations and the way in which conflict was managed could be reframed.

It is also argued that these wider benefits are more likely to be realized when organizations introduce complementary ADR practices (Bendersky, 2003) as part of an overall strategic approach. The suggestion that organizations should develop integrated conflict management systems (ICMS) has gained widespread support in the US (Ury et al., 1988; Lynch, 2001, 2003; Lipsky et al., 2003; see also Chapter 12 in this volume). For example, Lipsky et al. (2003) have argued that this approach has the potential to transform organizations rather than simply manage disputes.

However, there is as yet little robust evidence as to the extent to which organizations have adopted transformative approaches to mediation as part of an integrated conflict management strategy (but see Roche and Teague, 2011). Crucially, Lipsky et al. (2003:125) also argue that "organizational culture, which reflects the values, experiences, and belief structures of the organization's decision makers plays a critical role" in providing an environment in which integrated approaches can be introduced. Therefore, one might question whether mediation as part of a conflict management system can have a transformative effect unless a conducive organizational culture already exists.

Furthermore, assessing the general impact of mediation is challenging. In particular, it is difficult to isolate the effect of mediation from other initiatives and contextual factors. This is particularly the case with broader measures of conflict such as staff absence and turnover. Importantly, the link between improved systems of conflict management and the incidence of individual employment disputes is not straightforward. For example, it could be argued that a successful mediation scheme could increase employee confidence in dispute resolution and therefore make them more likely to report problems and make complaints. High volumes of "complaints" may not necessarily indicate high levels of conflict but could be an indicator of employees' faith in the system (Olson-Buchanan and Boswell, 2008).

Efficiency, Power and Justice

Any evaluation of the significance of workplace mediation inevitably rests on the way in which the employment relationship, and specifically power and conflict, is conceptualized. However, the discussion above, like much academic and policy debate over workplace mediation, is characterized by a functionalist and managerialist approach whereby mediation is viewed as a solution to the "problem" of conflict and its attendant costs, and which must be eliminated. This unitarist approach exhibits a preoccupation with the efficiency of dispute resolution (Budd and Colvin, 2008) while underplaying the extent to which mediation reflects dynamics of power and control, and how the competing interests of organizational actors are affected by and played out within mediation. The operation of power relations is central to understanding workplace mediation in three distinct ways: within the mediation process itself; between individuals subject to mediation and their colleagues; and in the interplay between mediation and collective employment relations.

Mediation research tends to focus on power asymmetries within the process and particularly between disputants resulting from differences in grade or communication skills (Tillett, 1999). In such cases, the stronger party may simply refuse to participate (Wiseman and Poitras, 2002) or the weaker party may feel too intimidated to contribute. Agusti-Panareda (2004) argues that mediation should not be ruled out in such instances as the process protects the disputants. Moreover, Gewurz (2001) contends that it may possible to moderate mediation style in order to address power imbalances. However, this arguably threatens the impartiality of the mediator and presumes that he or she is also not subject to the exercise of power. If one considers that many mediations are carried out by external providers, contracted by the organization, this is questionable at best. Moreover, Bollen et al. (2010: 632) speculate that mediators may "reinstall" power dynamics—for example being pressured by the "more powerful party to speed up the process [rather] than [attending] to the need of the less powerful party to vent opinions and emotions." Nonetheless it is also important to note that participants' perceptions of procedural and interpersonal justice influence their satisfaction with outcomes—in short, employees who believe the process used to arrive at a decision was fair (procedural justice) are more likely to view the outcome positively (Nesbit et al. 2012) even when there is no resolution (Kressel and Pruitt, 1985).

But perhaps more importantly, the literature tends to neglect power relations between employer and employee outside the mediation room. Mediation is ultimately a management process, potentially perceived as organizationally aligned and, from a radical perspective, may be seen as a means of controlling dissent and asserting control. As Sherman (2003) argues, mediators cannot change the fundamental power relationship that exists between parties, nor can they protect the weaker party outside the mediation session. Those power relations are inevitably underpinned by the organizational context within which mediation takes place and are also reflected in the way in which managers interact with the mediation process.

Organizational imperatives to resolve issues quickly in order to avoid cost, disruption, and/or negative public relations may not only pressure parties into agreeing to mediation but also implicitly coerce both mediator and disputants to settle (Coben, 2000). Perhaps more fundamentally, it could be argued that the mediation process effectively internalizes workplace conflict, recasting issues of unfair treatment through a unitarist lens into interpersonal clashes or communication breakdown. In short, responsibility for conflict is shifted from the manager to the managed. As such, mediation could constitute a form of self-discipline (Edwards, 2000) whereby legitimate resistance is stifled and employer control is reinforced (Colling, 2004).

Perhaps for this reason, some argue that mediation is unsuitable in cases involving overt bullying, harassment, and other situations where formal sanctions should be used (Bellman, 1998; La Rue, 2000). Indeed, Mareschal (2002: 1262) argues that "victims of discrimination should not have to 'negotiate' for the enforcement of civil rights granted by law." However, others contend that early mediation may be useful in resolving disputes that would alternatively develop into cases where formal sanctions would be unavoidable by highlighting the "unconscious and subtle discrimination or 'micro-inequities' that often serve as the basis for many, if not most, claims of workplace discrimination" (Stallworth et al. 2001: 37).

Mediation—Reinforcing or Challenging Managerial Control?

This has wider implications. In the UK, Colling (2004: 572) has argued that the extension of mediation is an integral part of a process of privatization whereby dispute resolution has been progressively transferred from the state to the workplace but "without the democratic and collective elements of socialized systems." In the US, the rise of ADR has generally mirrored the erosion of collective labor regulation (Colvin, 2003) with some employers using practices such as mediation as a substitute for trade union voice (Olson-Buchanan and Boswell, 2008) and possibly a union avoidance tactic (Lipsky and Seeber, 2000). At best, the role of unions has tended to be limited to a consultative role as employers seek to win support for mediation among the workforce. Unions are thus a means to an end rather than an integral part of the process. Therefore it may be argued that mediation provides a means to chip away at the equity and employee voice afforded by union involvement in dispute resolution processes in an attempt to increase speed and reduce costs. Unions may accordingly view mediation with scepticism, as "a way of undermining the role of the union in representing members with individual problems at work" (Bleiman, 2008: 17) or subverting the grievance process itself (Gourlay and Soderquist, 1998). Mediation's focus on "interests" may also be uncomfortable for union officials more accustomed to pursuing the "rights" of their members, not least since mediation does not establish precedent. Moreover, since both proceedings and outcomes are typically confidential, such privatization may inhibit system change and circumscribe union organizing opportunities (Bleiman, 2008).

However, this view assumes that existing conventional procedures, involving adjudication or litigation, provide workers with access to both organizational and civil justice. In fact, it could be argued that mediation can be seen as challenging the managerial authority implicit in most conventional disputes procedures. Whereas in most circumstances managers not only have authority over their subordinates but also unilateral decision-making power in disciplinary and grievance cases, they have no direct authority within the mediation process; issues that would normally be subject to managerial prerogative become open to joint resolution. Interestingly, Bingham et al. (2009) point out that under the Redress scheme over 90% of equal employment opportunity (EEO) cases were decided in favor of the supervisor (Bingham and Novac, 2001).

In the US there is tentative evidence of public sector unions seeking to extend their influence by embracing alternative forms of dispute resolution (Robinson et al., 2005), while Lipsky and Seeber (2000:45) contend that for some unions this "can extend the authority and influence of a union into areas normally considered management prerogatives." At the same time, Saundry et al. (2013) have argued that active involvement in mediation potentially offers trade unions and their members an ability to shape the resolutions of individual employment disputes as opposed to relying almost exclusively on the enforcement of individual employment rights to challenge managerial control. As Bleiman (2008) argues, unions may have an important role to play, securing the "informed consent" that is fundamental to mediation uptake and success, ensuring that mediation is demand led rather than supply (i.e. HR) pushed. The potential of improved relationships with management combined with a focus on resolution as opposed to procedure, also offer unions the chance to re-establish important informal processes of resolution in relation to a wide range of issues, including disciplinary cases.

In this context, it is interesting to note that a succession of studies have found line managers to view mediation not as a way of asserting control but as a threat to their authority (Seargeant, 2005; Saundry and Wibberley, 2012). The potential resistance of line managers to workplace mediation underlines the importance of examining mediation through a lens that accepts that the management of individual conflict is itself contested and reflects the balance of workplace power.

CONCLUSION

There is little doubt that interest in workplace mediation, from practitioners, policymakers, and scholars, has grown significantly in recent years. While the precise trajectory of mediation has depended to some degree on its relationship to national regulatory and institutional contexts, it has generally been seen as an antidote to a growing "problem" of embedded organizational grievance cultures and the greater use of litigation to resolve individual employment disputes. This has been aided by an increasingly persuasive evidence base that has pointed to high rates of resolution and participant satisfaction, and substantive benefits over conventional disputes procedures.

Accordingly, the case for mediation has been largely framed in terms of increasing the efficiency of dispute resolution as opposed to concerns over equity and justice. Indeed, critics have suggested that mediation essentially masks the coercive reality of work relations—neglecting power asymmetries and shifting the responsibility for conflict onto the shoulders of those subject to ill and unfair treatment. From this perspective, the promotion of mediation as an alternative to traditional grievance and disciplinary procedures and as an approach that prioritizes conflict resolution over adjudication, represents an attempt to limit the ability of workers to challenge managerial prerogative and enforce their rights.

However, this not only assumes that conventional workplace processes afford individual employees an opportunity to assert and enforce their rights but also suggests a false dichotomy between justice on the one hand and conflict resolution on the other. In contrast, it could be argued that in-company mediation represents a shift away from the managerial prerogative inherent in adjudicative procedures towards a measure of joint regulation. Furthermore, it could be claimed that resolution is not achieved at the expense of procedural justice but is a function of the extent to which participants feel that their interests have been acknowledged and they have been fairly treated.

It is perhaps significant that a major barrier to the extension of workplace mediation is the view of line managers who see its use either as an indication of their own failure or as a threat to their authority. In addition, despite the exhortations of scholars to organizations to adopt mediation as part of an integrated approach to conflict management, doubts remain as to whether conflict is viewed as a strategic matter, and mediation accordingly perceived as simply an additional tool in the conflict management box. Perhaps part of the problem for this lies in a tendency to conceptualize mediation as a management construct that can be applied to the pathogen of workplace conflict and can help to reassert managerial control over dispute resolution. However, the authors would suggest that such a view minimizes the wider significance of mediation. This does not lie in its role as a system of dispute resolution but on the fact that mediation is fundamentally based on an acceptance of the legitimacy of conflict. Accordingly, it has the potential to reframe attitudes to workplace conflict and re-open informal channels of dispute resolution.

References

ACAS/TUC 2010. *Mediation—A Guide for Trade Union Representatives*. London: ACAS/TUC.

Agusti-Panareda, J. 2004. "Power Imbalances: Questioning." *Dispute Resolution Journal*, 59(2): 101–23.

Alberts, J., Heisterkamp, B., and McPhee, R. 2005. "Disputant Perceptions of and Satisfaction with a Community Mediation Program." *International Journal of Conflict Management*, 16(3): 218–44.

Anderson J. and Bingham L. B. 1997. "Upstream Effects from Mediation of Workplace Disputes: Some Preliminary Evidence from the USPS." *Labor Law Journal*, 48: 601–15.

Astor, H. and Chinkin, C. 2002. *Dispute Resolution in Australia*. Sydney: LexisNexis Butterworths.

Banks, L. and Saundry, R. 2010. "Mediation—A Panacea for the Ills of Workplace Dispute Resolution? A Comprehensive Review of the Literature Examining Workplace Mediation." iROWE Discussion and Policy Paper, No.1.

Barsky, A. and Wood, L. 2005. "Conflict Avoidance in a University Context." *Higher Education Research and Development*, 24(3): 249–64.

Bellman, H. 1998. "Some Reflections on the Practice of Mediation." *Negotiation Journal*, 14: 205–10.

Bendersky, C. 2003. "Organizational Dispute Resolution Systems: A Complementarities Model." *Academy of Management Review*, 28(4): 643–56.

Bingham, L. B. 2003. *Mediation at Work: Transforming Workplace Conflict at the United States Postal Service*. Arlington, VA: IBM Center for The Business of Government (Human Capital Management Series).

Bingham, L. B. 2004. "Employment Dispute Resolution: The Case for Mediation." *Conflict Resolution Quarterly*, 22(1–2): 145–74.

Bingham, L. B. and Chachere, D. R. 1999. "Dispute Resolution in Employment: The Need for Research." In A. E. Eaton and J. H. Keefe (eds), *Employment Dispute Resolution and Worker Rights in the Changing Workplace*. Champaign, IL: Industrial Relations Research Association, 95–136.

Bingham L. B. and Novac, M. 2001. "Mediation's Impact on Formal Discrimination Complaint Filing: Before and After the REDRESS Program and the United States Postal Service." *Review of Public Personnel Administration*, 21(4): 308–31.

Bingham, L. B. and Pitts, D. 2002. "Highlights of Mediation at Work: Studies of the National REDRESS Evaluation Project." *Negotiation Journal*, 18: 149–60.

Bingham L. B., Hallberlin, C., Walker, D., and Chung, W. 2009. "Dispute System Design and Justice in Employment Dispute Resolution: Mediation at the Workplace." *Harvard Negotiation Law Review*, 14: 1–50.

Bingham, L. B., Kim, K., and Raines, S. 2002. "Exploring the Role of Representation in Employment Mediation at the USPS." *Ohio State Journal on Dispute Resolution*, 17(2): 341–77.

Bleiman, D. 2008. "Should I Try Mediation?" *A Discussion Paper for Trade Union Members*, Mimeo <http://digitalarchive.gsu.edu/cgi/viewcontent.cgi?article=1018&context=colpub_seedgrant > accessed 7 Aug. 2013.

BIS (Department of Business, Innovation and Skills) 2011. *Resolving Workplace Disputes: A Consultation*. London: BIS.

Bollen, K., Euwema, M., and Müller, P. 2010. "Why are Subordinates Less Satisfied with Mediation? The Role of Uncertainty." *Negotiation Journal*, 26(4): 417–33.

Boulle, L. and Nesic, M. 2001. *Mediation: Principles, Process, Practice*. London: Butterworths.

Bowling D. and Hoffman D. 2003. *Bringing Peace Into The Room: The Personal Qualities of the Mediator and their Impact on the Mediation*. San Francisco: Jossey Bass.

Brett, J., Barsness, Z., and Goldberg, S. 1996. "The Effectiveness of Mediation: An Independent Analysis of Cases Handled by Four Major Service Providers." *Negotiation Journal*, 12: 259–69.

Brown, H. J. and Mariott, A. 1999. *ADR Principles and Practice*. London: Sweet and Maxwell.

Budd, J. and Colvin, A. 2008. "Improved Metrics for Workplace Dispute Resolution Procedures: Efficiency, Equity, and Voice." *Industrial Relations*, 47(3): 460–79.

Bush, R. 2001. "Handling Workplace Mediation: Why Transformative Mediation?" *HOFSTRA Labor and Employment Law Journal*, 18(2): 367–74.

Bush, R. and Folger J. 2005. *The Promise of Mediation: Responding to Conflict through Empowerment and Recognition*. San Francisco: Jossey Bass.

CIPD (Chartered Institute of Personnel and Development), 2004. *Managing Conflict at Work*. London: CIPD.

CIPD, 2007. *Managing Conflict at Work*. London: CIPD.

CIPD, 2008. *Workplace Mediation—How Employers Do It*. London: CIPD.

CIPD, 2011. *Conflict Management*. London: CIPD.

Coben, J. 2000. "Mediation's Dirty Little Secret: Straight Talk about Mediator Manipulation and Deception." *Journal of Alternative Dispute Resolution in Employment*, 2(4): 4–7.

Colling, T. 2004. "No Claim, No Pain? The Privatization of Dispute Resolution in Britain." *Economic and Industrial Democracy*, 25(4): 555–79.

Colvin, A. 2003. "Institutional Pressures, Human Resource Strategies and the Rise of Non-union Dispute Management Procedures." *Industrial and Labor Relations Review*, 56: 275–391.

Corby, S. 1999. *Resolving Employment Rights Disputes through Mediation: The New Zealand Experience*. London: Institute of Employment Rights.

Dolder C. 2004. "The Contribution of Mediation to Workplace Justice." *Industrial Law Journal*, 33(4): 320–42.

Department of Labour 2012. *New Zealand Thriving through People and Work—Annual Report for the Year Ended June 30, 2012*. Wellington: Ministry of Business, Innovation and Employment.

Edwards, P. 2000. "Discipline: Towards Trust and Self-discipline?" in S. Bach and K. Sisson (eds) *Personnel Management: A Comprehensive Guide to Theory and Practice in Britain*, 3rd edn. Oxford: Blackwell, 317–39.

Eurofound 2010. *Individual Disputes at the Workplace: Alternative Disputes Resolution*. Dublin: European Foundation for the Improvement of Living and Working Conditions.

Feuille, P. and Kolb, D. M. 1994. "Waiting in the Wings: Mediation's Role in Grievance Resolution." *Negotiation Journal*, 10: 249–64.

Forsyth, A. 2012. "Workplace Conflict Resolution in Australia: The Dominance of the Public Dispute Resolution Framework and the Limited Role of ADR." *International Journal of Human Resource Management*, 23(3): 476–94.

Fox, M. 2005. "Evaluation of the ACAS Pilot of Mediation and Employment Law Visits to Small Companies." *ACAS Research Paper*, 05/05.

Gazeley, B. J. 1997. "Venus, Mars and the Law: On Mediation of Sexual Harassment Cases." *Willamette Law Review*, 33: 605–45.

Gewurz, I. 2001. "(Re)designing Mediation to Address the Nuances of Power Imbalance." *Conflict Resolution Quarterly*, 19(2): 135–62.

Gibbons, M. 2007. *A Review of Employment Dispute Resolution in Great Britain*. London: DTI.

Goldberg, S. 2005. "How Interest based Grievance Mediation Performs in the Long Term." *Dispute Resolution Journal*, 60(4): 8–15.

Goldberg, S. B. and Shaw, M. L. 2007. "The Secrets of Successful (and Unsuccessful) Mediators Continued: Studies Two and Three." *Negotiation Journal*, 23(4): 393–418.

Gourlay, A. and Soderquist, J. 1998. "Mediation in Employment Cases is Too Little Too Late: An Organizational Conflict Management Perspective on Resolving Disputes." *Hamline Law Review*, 21: 261–86.

Greig, M. 2005. "Stepping into the Fray: When do Mediators Mediate?" *American Journal of Political Science*, 49(2): 249–66.

Griffiths, The Rt. Hon. Lord 2001. "Foreword" to Boulle, L. and Nesic, M. (2001) *Mediation*. London: Butterworths.

Guthrie, C. and Levin, J. 1998. "A 'Party Satisfaction' Perspective on a Comprehensive Mediation Statute." *Ohio State Journal on Dispute Resolution*, 13(3): 885–907.

Hallberlin, C. 2001. "Transforming Workplace Culture through Mediation: Lessons Learned from Swimming Upstream." *HOFSTRA Labor and Employment Law Journal*, 18(2): 375–84.

Herrman, M., Hollet, N., Eaker, D., and Gale, J. 2003. "Mediator Reflections on Practice: Connecting Select Demographics and Preferred Orientation." *Conflict Resolution Quarterly*, 20(4): 403–27.

Hiltrop, J. M. 1989. "Factors Associated with Successful Labor Mediation." In K. Kressel and D. Pruitt (eds), *Mediation Research: The Process and Effectiveness of Third Party Intervention*. San Francisco: Jossey-Bass, 213–40.

Hoskins, M. and Stoltz, J. 2003. "Balancing on Words: Human Change Process in Mediation." *Conflict Resolution Quarterly*, 20(3): 331–49.

Jones, T. and Bodtker, A. 2001. "Mediating with Heart in Mind." *Negotiation Journal*, 17: 217–44.

Karambayya, R., Brett, J., and Lyle A. 1992. "The Effects of Formal Authority and Experience on Third-party Roles, Outcome and Perception of Fairness." *Academy of Management Journal*, 35: 426–38.

Kochan, T. and Jick, T. 1978. "The Public Sector Mediation Process: A Theory and Empirical Examination." *Journal of Conflict Resolution*, 22(2): 209–40.

Kochan, T., Lautsch, B., and Bendersky, C. 2000. "An Evaluation of the Massachusetts Commission Against Discrimination Alternative Dispute Resolution Program." *Harvard Negotiation Law Review*, 5: 233–74.

Kressel, K. 2006. "Mediation Revisited." In M. Deutsch and P. Coleman (eds) *The Handbook of Constructive Conflict Resolution: Theory and Practice*. San Francisco: Jossey Bass.

Kressel, K. 2007. "The Strategic Style in Mediation." *Conflict Resolution Quarterly*, 24(3): 251–83.

Kressel, K. and Pruitt, D. 1985. "The Mediation of Social Conflict." *Journal of Social Issues*, 41(2): 1–10.

La Rue, H. 2000. "The Changing Workplace Environment in the New Millennium: ADR is a Dominant Trend in the Workplace." *Columbia Business Law Review*, 2000(3): 453–98.

Latreille, P. L. 2010. "Mediating Workplace Conflict: of Success, Failure and Fragility." ACAS Research Paper, 06/10.

Latreille, P. L. 2011. "Workplace Mediation: A Thematic Review of the ACAS/CIPD evidence." ACAS Research Paper, 13/11.

Lipsky, D. and Seeber, R. 2000. "Resolving Workplace Disputes in the United States: The Growth of Alternative Dispute Resolution in Employment Relations". *Journal of Alternative Dispute Resolution*, 2(3): 37–49.

Lipsky, D., Seeber, R., and Fincher, R. 2003. *Emerging Systems for Managing Workplace Conflict: Lessons from American Corporations for Managers and Dispute Resolution Professionals*. San Francisco: Jossey-Bass.

Lipsky, D. B., Avgar, A. C., Lamare, J. R., and Gupta, A. 2012. "The Antecedents of Workplace Conflict Management Systems in U.S. Corporations: Evidence from a New Survey of Fortune 1000 Companies" Mimeo.

Lynch, J. 2003. *Are Your Organization's Conflict Management Practices and Integrated Conflict Management System?* <http://www.mediate.com//articles/systemsedit3.cfm> accessed 24 Jul. 2013.

Lynch, J. F. 2001. "Beyond ADR: A Systems Approach to Conflict Management." *Negotiation Journal*, 17(3): 207–16.

McDermott, P., Obar, R., Jose, A., and Bowers, M. 2000. *An Evaluation of the Equal Employment Opportunity Commission Mediation Program*. US Equal Employment Opportunity Commission <http://www.eeoc.gov/eeoc/mediation/report/> accessed 24 Jul. 2013.

McDermott, P., Obar, R., Jose, A., and Polkinghorn, B. 2001. *The EEOC Mediation Program: Mediators' Perspective on the Parties, Processes and Outcome*. US Equal Employment Opportunity Commission. <http://www.eeoc.gov/eeoc/mediation/mcdfinal.html> accessed 24 Jul. 2013

Mack, K. 2003. *Court Referral to ADR: Criteria and Research*. Australia: National ADR Advisory Council and Australian Institute of Judicial Administration.

Mahoney, D. and Klass, B. 2008. "Comparative Dispute Resolution in the Workplace." *Journal of Labor Research*, 29: 251–71.

Mareschal, P. 2002. "Mastering the Art of Dispute Resolution: Best Practices from the FMCS." *International Journal of Public Administration*, 25: 1351–77.

Mareschal, P. 2005. "Building a Better Future through Mediation: Insights from a Survey of FMCS Mediators." *Journal of Collective Negotiations*, 30(4): 307–23.

Montoya, J. 1998. "Let's Mediate: A Whole New Ball Game for the EEOC?" *Employee Relations Law Journal*, 24(2): 53–71.

Moore, C. 2003. *The Mediation Process: Practical Strategies for Resolving Conflict*. San Francisco: Jossey Bass.

Nabatchi, T. and Bingham, L. B. 2010. "From Postal to Peaceful: Dispute Systems Design in the USPS REDRESS® Program." *Review of Public Personnel Administration*, 30(2): 211–34.

Nesbit, R., Nabatchi, T., and Bingham, L. B. 2012. "Employees, Supervisors, and Workplace Mediation Experiences of Justice and Settlement." *Review of Public Personnel Administration*, 32(3): 260–87.

Olson-Buchanan, J. and Boswell, W. 2008. "An Integrative Model of Experiencing and Responding to Mistreatment at Work." *Academy of Management Review*, 33(1): 76–96.

Picard, C. 2004. "Exploring Integrative Framework for Understanding Mediation." *Conflict Resolution Quarterly*, 21(3): 295–311.

Poitras, J. 2007. "The Paradox of Accepting one's Share of Responsibility in Mediation." *Negotiation Journal*, 23(3): 267–82.

Poitras, J. 2009. "What Makes Parties Trust Mediators?" *Negotiation Journal*, 25(3): 307–25.

Pope, S. 1996. "Inviting Fortuitous Events in Mediation: The Role of Empowerment and Recognition." *Mediation Quarterly*, 13(4): 287–95.

Reynolds, C. 2000. "Workplace Mediation." In M. Liebmann (ed.) *Mediation in Context*. London: Jessica Kingsley.

Riskin, L. 2003. "Decision Making in Mediation: The New Old Grid and the New Grid System." *Notre Dame Law Review*, 79(1): 1–53.

Robinson P, Pearlstein A, and Mayer, B. 2005. "DyADS: Encouraging 'Dynamic Adaptive Dispute Systems' in the Organized Workplace." *Harvard Negotiation Law Review*, 10: 339–82.

Roche, W. K. and Teague, P. 2011. "Firms and Innovative Conflict Management Systems in Ireland." *British Journal of Industrial Relations*, 49: 436–59.

Saundry, R. and Wibberley, G. 2012. "Mediation and Informal Resolution—A Case Study in Conflict Management." ACAS Research Paper, 12/12.

Saundry, R., McArdle, L. and Thomas, P. 2013. "Reframing Workplace Relations? Conflict Resolution and Mediation in a Primary Care Trust." *Work, Employment and Society*. 27(2): 221–39.

Seargeant, J. 2005. "The ACAS Small Firms Mediation Pilot: Research to Explore Parties' Experiences and Views on the Value of Mediation." ACAS Research Paper, 04/05.

Shapiro, D. and Brett, J. 1993. "Comparing Three Processes Underlying Judgments of Procedural Justice: A Field Study of Mediation and Arbitration." *Journal of Personality and Social Psychology*, 55(6): 1167–77.

Sherman, M. 2003. "Mediation, Hype and Hyperbole: How Much Should We Believe?" *Dispute Resolution Journal*, 58(3): 43–51.

Silberman, A. 1989. "Breaking the Mould of Grievance Resolution: A Pilot Program in Mediation." *Arbitration Journal*, 44(4): 40–5.

Singletary, C., Shearer, R., and Kuligokski, E. 1995. "Securing a Durable Mediation Agreement to Settle Complex Employment Disputes." *Labor Law Journal*, 46: 223–7.

Sourdin, T. 2002. *Alternative Dispute Resolution*. Sydney: Law Book Company.

Stallworth, L., McPherson, T., and Rute L. 2001. "Discrimination in the Workplace: How Mediation Can Help." *Dispute Resolution Journal*, 56(1): 35–44.

Stipanowich, T. and Lamare, J.R. (forthcoming. "Living with "ADR": Evolving Perceptions and Use of Mediation, Arbitration and Conflict Management in Fortune 1000 Corporations." *Harvard Negotiation Law Review*.

Sulzner, G. 2003. "Adjudicators (Arbitrators) Acting as Mediators: An Experiment in Dispute Resolution at the Public Service Staff Relations Board of Canada." *Journal of Collective Negotiations in the Public Sector*, 30: 59–75.

Tillett, G. 1999. *Resolving Conflict: A Practical Approach*. 2nd edn. Oxford: Oxford University Press.

Urwin, P., Karuk, V., Latreille, P., Michielsens, E., Page, L., Siara, B., Speckesser, S. with Chevalier, P. A., and Boon, A. 2010. "Evaluating the Use of Judicial Mediation in Employment Tribunals." *Ministry of Justice Research Series*, 7/10.

Ury, W., Brett, J. M., and Goldberg, S. B. 1988. *Getting Disputes Resolved: Designing Systems to Cut the Costs of Conflict*. San Francisco: Jossey-Bass.

Van Gramberg, B. 2002. "Employer Demand for Mediation." *Refereed Proceedings of the 16th Conference of the Australia and New Zealand Academy of Management*, La Trobe University, Beechworth, 4–7 Dec.

Van Gramberg, B. 2006. *Managing Workplace Conflict: Alternative Dispute Resolution in Australia*. Sydney: The Federation Press.

Van Wanrooy, B., Bewley, H., Bryson, A., Forth, J., Freeth, S., Stokes, L., and Wood, S. 2013. *The 2011 Workplace Employment Relations Study: First Findings*. <https://www.gov.uk/government/uploads/system/uploads/attachment_data/file/175479/13-535-the-2011-workplace-employment-relations-study-first-findings1.pdf> accessed 24 Jul. 2013.

Wade, J. 1998. "Current Trends and Models in Dispute Resolution Part II." *Australasian Dispute Resolution Journal*, 9: 113–28.

Wall, J. 1981. "Mediation: An Analysis, Review and Proposed Research." *Journal of Conflict Resolution*, 25: 157–80.

Wall, J. and Lynn, A. 1993. "Mediation: A Current Review." *Journal of Conflict Resolution*, 37(1): 160–94.

Wall, J., Stark, J., and Standifer, R. 2001. "Mediation: A Current Review and Theory Development." *Journal of Conflict Resolution*, 45(3): 370–91.

Wall, J. A. and Dunne, T. C. 2012. "Mediation Research: A Current Review." *Negotiation Journal*, 28(2): 217–44.

Williams, M. 2011. "Workplace Conflict Management: Awareness and Use of ACAS Code of Practice and Workplace Meditation—A Poll of Business." ACAS Research Paper, 08/11.

Winslade, J. 2006. "Mediation with a Focus on Discursive Positioning." *Conflict Resolution Quarterly*, 23(4): 501–15.

Winslade, J. and Monk G. 2000. *Narrative Mediation*. San Francisco: Jossey Bass.

Wiseman, V. and Poitras, J. 2002. "Mediation Within a Hierarchical Structure: How Can It be Done Successfully." *Conflict Resolution Quarterly*, 20(1): 51–65.

Wood, D. and Leon, D. 2006. "Measuring Value in Mediation: A Case Study of Workplace Mediation in City Government." *Ohio State Journal on Dispute Resolution*, 21(2): 383–408.

Woodhams, B. 2007. *Employment Relationship Problems: Costs, Benefits and Choices*. Wellington: Department of Labour.

CHAPTER 10

THE ORGANIZATIONAL OMBUDSMAN

MARY ROWE AND HOWARD GADLIN

THIS chapter discusses the organizational ombudsman in the context of conflict management systems. The organizational ombudsman is different from other conflict managers, designated in a way that may be unique in modern organizations.

The first section describes the unusual role of the organizational ombudsman (OO), as it is understood in the US and in some other countries around the world. It presents in two ways the rationale why an OO is seen as valuable and effective: 1) by strengthening the conflict management system itself, and 2) by direct contributions to stakeholders. In addition, the first section addresses the question: "Is the OO *part* of a conflict management system or does the OO *work with* a system?"

The second section examines the origins of organizational ombudsmen, examines variations in how OOs operate, and presents some of the challenges faced by OOs in working to the code of ethics and standards of practice governing their roles.

The third section looks in more detail at the actual work of ombudsmen and the competencies required to do this work.

The fourth section examines more of the challenges and dilemmas of the OO role and identifies issues to be addressed as the field continues to develop.

ORGANIZATIONAL OMBUDSMEN AND CONFLICT MANAGEMENT SYSTEMS

The organizational ombudsman is an odd duck—perhaps the only professional manager within an organization whose role does not include "representing" the organization. The ombudsman is meant to be independent while being a part of the organization. (Indeed, the OO's effectiveness derives in significant ways from being an insider.) The OO shares with others a commitment to the mission and values of the organization the OO serves, yet the OO's loyalty to the organization has to be subservient to principles of fairness and impartiality.

An organization that establishes an OO has hired a professional who may critique managerial policies and the actions of managers and employees. The OO may question both leaders and employees if they do not honor the organization's values or properly implement its policies and procedures. Although in the broadest sense the OO contributes to the management of conflict in an organization, the OO's focus is not primarily on *containing* conflict, in the manner of most other units that address conflict in an organization. Rather the OO is concerned that most conflict should be productive for the organization. The OO endeavors to foster an organizational climate such that all issues of concern to employees and management can be brought to attention safely.

In most organizations conflict is seen primarily as something that interferes with efficient functioning and therefore has to be "managed." Some organizations have an intentionally designed "conflict management system" that is at least somewhat structured and coordinated (Rowe, 1984; Ury, Brett and Goldberg, 1988; Rowe, 1996; Gosline et al., 2001; Lipsky, Seeber, and Fincher, 2003).

Line management usually plays a central role—working in conjunction with staff offices such as Human Resources, employee assistance programs, compliance offices— and with unions, if any—to manage issues that arise. In many organizations, while there is not a formally designated conflict management system for managing conflicts, some of the same offices may exist and work independently. In this latter case there may be little coordination among offices dealing with conflict, or there may be a kind of "de facto system." An ombuds office may be included in a conflict management system by design. It may also participate in a de facto system, but it may have been created with little attempt at coordination.

What is an ombudsman office and how does an ombudsman office fit, in the context of an actual or de facto conflict management system? The International Ombudsman Organization—the largest association of OOs—defines an Organizational Ombudsman as "an individual who serves as a designated neutral within a specific organization and provides conflict resolution and problem-solving services to members of the organization (internal ombudsman) and/or for clients or customers of the organization (external ombudsman)."

The organizational ombudsman (OO) office is configured differently from all other offices. In the US it is designated as independent, neutral, and confidential[1]. It is also explicitly designated as informal—that is, without management power or decision-making authority. In Canada it is designated as independent, impartial, confidential and accessible, and also does not make management decisions[2]. Both sets of OOs in North America lay great emphasis on fairness.

The OO works *with* the conflict management system, but ideally reports directly to the CEO or Board of Directors; the office functions independently from all ordinary line and staff structures. People's opinions differ as to whether working with a conflict management system makes an OO office *part* of a conflict management system. Many OOs in North America work within a framework of professional standards promulgated by the relevant professional association, as noted above. However, there are no standards, beyond the emphasis on independence, that speak directly to the question of how an OO liaises with a conflict management system.

Figure 10.1 presents one way of understanding how the OO office fits in by showing the various components of a conflict management system. In the language of negotiation theory, conflicts can be resolved on the basis of interests, rights, and various sources

ANALYZING YOUR CONFLICT MANAGEMENT SYSTEM

Some Conflict Management Options

Interest-based | Rights-and-power-based

Column headings (left to right):
delivering respect, affirming feelings · active listening, probing respectfully · providing information, one-on-one · receiving information, one-on-one · reframing issues, illuminating context · helping develop and evaluate options · offering referrals to other resources · coaching, helping people help themselves · offering shuttle diplomacy · looking into a problem informally · facilitating a generic approach · identifying/communicating patterns of issues · communicating "new" issues · conflict management/team coordination · working for systems change · following up with stakeholders · informal conflict system coordination · accompanying/representing another · acting as advocate or witness · pursuing formal investigations · keeping case records/compliance reports · formal decision-making, adjudication/arbitration · enforcing managerial decisions · dealing with formal appeals

Some Conflict Management Offices

- Affirmative Action
- Affinity Groups/Networks
- Audit
- Conflict Coaches/Counselors
- Conflict Management System Office/Coordinator/Steering Committee
- Disabilities
- Disciplinary Office/Internal Affairs
- Email/Online Harassment Officers
- Employee Assistance/Social Workers
- Environmental Hazards/Waste Hazards
- Equal Opportunity
- Ethics/Compliance
- Graduate Students Deans/Advisors
- Hot Lines/Advice Lines/Idea Lines
- Human Resources/Human Capital
- Human Rights/Civil Rights
- Human Subjects/Animal Care
- Inspection/Inspectors General
- I.P./Patents/Copyrights
- Legal Counsel/General Counsel
- **Line Management relevant to issue**
- Mediation Program
- Medical/Nursing/Fitness for Duty
- Mentors/Peer Advisors
- Model Workplace
- Mortality/Morbidity
- **Ombudsman Office**   x x x x x x x x x x x x x x x x x x x x x
- Patient Ombudsman/Advocate
- Quality Assurance Circles/Monitors
- Race Relations/Cultural Relations
- Religious Counselors/Chaplains
- Residence Advisors/Managers
- Risk Management
- Safety/EH&S Working Groups
- Security/Campus Police
- Sexual/Racial Harassment Advisors
- Staff Associations
- Undergraduate Dean/Advisors/Council
- Unions, Stewards, Union Officials
- Work/Family/Personal Life Programs
- Working Groups/Councils

Adapted and revised from a chart by Mary Rowe and Brian Bloch 14 Harv. Negot. L. Rev. 239 (Winter 2009)

FIGURE 10.1 Components of an Organizational Conflict Management System

Source: Adapted and Revised, from a Chart, "Analyzing your Conflict Management System," by Mary Rowe and Brian Bloch, *Harvard Negotiation Law Review*, 239, (Winter, 2009).

of power. Many staff offices that address employee issues and concerns are oriented primarily toward legal rights and positional power. This is especially true for compliance offices. Many line and staff managers are oriented first towards the legal rights of the organization as represented by the authority of management. The authority and interests of management may be placed before the rights and interests of employees, students, trainees, and clients or customers. A conflict management system may also interact directly with entities like unions and staff associations—advocates that focus on the interests and rights of their constituencies. These latter entities may use their power to attempt to counterbalance or check the authority of management.

Thousands of organizations in North America have employee assistance, health care, chaplains, and counseling offices that serve the interests of their clients outside the realm of formal conflict management. Some organizations have sanctioned affinity groups and networks serving their members. (Few organizations have all of these, but many have one or another.) These function as informal entities in the conflict management system.

Figure 10.1 shows a way to analyze a specific conflict management system. All the offices that provide conflict management can be located, together with the functions provided by each. (Of course one would add in any other offices and/or functions provided in a particular conflict management system.) Analysis of the functions that are provided will illuminate strengths and lacunae in any conflict management system.

Figure 10.1 also serves to demonstrate the functions of an OO in the context of a conflict management system. The check marks for OOs in Figure 10.1 illustrate the fact that OOs offer all the informal conflict management functions listed there.

OOs differ from all the other entities in Figure 10.1 in their eclectic orientation towards referrals, support, and service to *all* the entities that are part of the relevant conflict management system—OOs interact with all the other entities as well as with all members of the organization. OOs are typically focused first on interests, and, as neutral or impartial practitioners, they are mindful of the interests of all stakeholders involved in a specific concern. However, OOs must also be attentive to and express a strong concern about legal and moral rights—again of all stakeholders. OOs regularly offer referrals to the rights- and power-based options in Fi gure 10.1, as well as offering interest-based options. Above all they focus on fair process, whether formal or informal.

The OO office must be and appear to be impartial. Many OOs endeavor to use impartial language, for example avoiding words like "client." Although OOs are committed to impartiality, they are also acutely aware of differences in power and areas of inequality within their organizations, and the impact of these on interactions in the organization.

OOs assert that they do not "represent" people who come to them, nor do they represent the organization. Typically they keep no case records for their organizations—in part because there are limited legal protections for ombudsman confidentiality. (There are no OO case records that can be used for administrative decision-making, or used during formal proceedings, or for reports to government agencies.)

Most OO programs were mandated from the beginning not only to address individual complaints, grievances, and conflicts, but also to bring systemic issues to attention. OOs are meant to illuminate aspects of the organization's policies, procedures, structure, and culture that regularly elicit grievances and complaints, exacerbate tensions and conflicts, and undermine the organization's efforts to fulfill its mission and accomplish its goals. (They do this in the traditional manner of ombudsmen, by "reason and persuasion;" as noted earlier, by their terms of reference, OOs have no decision-making power.)

In broadest terms this latter function is sometimes described as offering "upward feedback" to the leadership, but there is variation in how different organizations and different OOs interpret upward feedback. Some OOs compile statistics that give a quick overview of problems reported from within the organization. The data may illuminate divisions or cohorts within which certain categories of issues are most prominent.

For other OOs, identifying systemic problems entails much more than a statistical account of woes and worries. Rather, it requires assertively, but tactfully, working directly with problematic units and with management or, if management is unresponsive, upper leadership, until relevant managers acknowledge and take action to study or address the issues.

Organizations and OOs differ in the extent to which OO reports are made public. Some OOs present a periodic report to the entire organization summarizing, in broad terms, the number and types of OO cases. They may discuss those numbers with respect to the context in which they occur. These reports may offer critical reflections on the state of the organization as a workplace. Other OOs periodically make oral or written reports to all senior officers. In Canada an OO may also issue a public report about a given problem.

In addition to written reports—or instead of such reports—there are other (possibly more effective) ways in which OOs provide systemic feedback within a particular unit of the organization. This feedback includes frequent face-to-face meetings held by the OO with the unit or with the leadership of a unit. For example, a department having serious internal conflicts and tensions about racial differences among staff might ask for the OO's assistance to help understand and address those issues. Worried about how the mere fact of these problems might be seen by upper management, department heads may turn to the OO precisely because the OO is confidential and does not conduct formal investigations, or issue public reports and recommendations. OOs who take on such matters are bumping against the boundaries of organizational development specialists—as with every other sort of intervention, this can be a source of discussion within the OO field.

The Structural Rationale for an OO

The structural rationale for an OO office includes informal and often invisible coordination of the conflict management system, checks and balances, backup, fail-safe, and support to organizational learning—strengthening the whole conflict management system. One of the purposes of both OOs and conflict management systems is to provide a coordinated, strategically oriented context for organizational improvement. Organizational problems, conflicts, and grievances may then be seen as more than annoyances; rather they provide opportunities for organizational learning. However, it is very challenging to maintain a truly coordinated conflict management system. (Although one of the authors proposed and described the concept of an *integrated* conflict management system, an "ICMS," in a number of papers in the 1980s and 1990s (e.g., Rowe, 1984, 1990, 1993, 1996) we have come to believe that real integration is very difficult).

The OO can and does help in informal *coordination*, but even this task is never-ending. This is true for at least three reasons: 1) many organizations function with independent divisions, dispersed outposts, and sub-units; 2) there is no common language about conflict, and managers have varied views and also change frequently; and 3) offices within a conflict management system have different missions. These points are discussed in order below.

In sizable organizations there are very few offices that are aware of the full range and depth of concerns that arise within—and also across—the different units and silos of the organization. Line management in each locale is structured around somewhat different goals. Almost all staff offices are specialized. It is often a struggle for line and staff managers to communicate effectively even about their achievements, let alone about problems and conflict.

Even though budgets provide one common language—the language of money—within an organization, there is no common language for describing or managing people conflicts. Within organizations information is often filtered according to status and expertise within the organization. Top leaders are broadly insulated from learning about conflicts and problems. People with special expertise often assume that only colleagues with the same expertise can understand their concerns.

Ombuds offices can "hear" across the entire organization, across virtually all boundaries. Because of the standards of "confidentiality, neutrality, independence, and informality," successful OO offices are one of the few places where people from anywhere in the organization feel relatively free to come to speak, at any time, about any issue.

Employees (and managers) differ greatly in how they perceive conflict—even before they walk in to work. Once inside, they are typically very much influenced by their work context, and especially by their perceptions of their local superior. Local bosses, in turn, vary greatly. Add all this together and there are many points of view *about* conflict—and no common language.

Therefore, one task for OOs is to help people not just to deal with their conflicts but also with their different views about conflict. As examples, mild conflicts may be formidably presented as "grievances," for example, in organizations with strong grievance procedures where it is known that being the object of a grievance can create difficulties for a disliked manager. On the flip side, conflicts may be ignored because they are embedded in age-old customs—like hazing, and racist jokes and jibes—that are simply taken for granted within the organization. OOs endeavor to help with different views about conflict, for example by offering a range of options for people with different views.

A third reason why it is difficult to keep a conflict management system coordinated is that the different managers within the conflict management system are focused on their own missions and their own goals, principles, and methods. For example, general counsel and compliance offices are oriented toward resolving conflicts—and keeping records—in a formal way focused on rights and power. Employee assistance programs, health-care practitioners, counselors, chaplains, and affinity groups, where they exist, work informally and are more focused on the individual interests of those whom they serve.

It is conceptually and legally uncomfortable for confidential offices to report to a compliance office and an ICMS ought not be configured in this way. (An ombuds office cannot, of course, report to any compliance office and still be "independent.") It is also obviously not appropriate for an informal practitioner to supervise an ICMS with compliance units. This dilemma is a major issue as one thinks about the concept of an *integrated* conflict management system. However, it is possible to think about a *coordinated* conflict management system.

OOs, as neutrals, work daily with all line and staff offices—endeavoring to be knowledgeable and respectful about the roles and values of each. OOs will search for, help to develop, and offer or refer to appropriate dispute resolution options, whether formal or informal, within the conflict management system of the organization (Gadlin, 1987). The concept of "appropriate" usually captures the ideas that the options are appropriate for the values of the persons with concerns, appropriate for the context, and also perceived to be fair.

OOs endeavor to consider the interests of every stakeholder in a concern. In this way they consider and complement the roles of line management and relevant staff offices. In addition, by being mindful of and introducing the perspectives of all parties to a problematic situation, OOs can provide checks and balances. If a manager needs particular support an OO can provide some back-up assistance. If some part of the conflict management system is failing to respond to a problematic situation, an OO can sometimes step in and alert senior managers, as a fail-safe. OOs can help the organization learn from any problem—and from any innovation—that is brought to them. As impartial and non-aligned parties, they can help keep the organization accountable—and better oriented—to its own mission and rules.

OO offices can offer a degree of consistency and stability to a conflict management system. OOs offer consistent language, understanding of policies, and ways of thinking about available options. Some OOs have also taken a leading role in forming institutional conflict management system steering committees. These informal but long-lasting groups bring together representatives from the major conflict management system offices (including the OO office) for monthly discussions—to communicate about conflict, problem prevention, and options for conflict management.

In this way, on a daily, even hourly basis, OOs serve as informal coordinators for a conflict management system. There is disagreement within the ombudsman profession about whether OOs compromise their independence in this informal and often invisible role. Some OOs see constant, de facto coordination to be a quasi-managerial function, as part of the conflict management system. Some see it as the sum of individual acts of support to the conflict management system and its people, and therefore completely compatible with OO independence. The final section below examines more closely how OOs operate and interact within their organizations.

The Outcomes Rationale for an OO

The direct contributions to stakeholders derive from an OO office being—and being seen to be—safe, accessible, and credible. The usefulness and effectiveness of an OO are methodologically difficult to measure—in part because of near absolute confidentiality and the lack of records—but elements of OO effectiveness can be described.

All organizations need mechanisms whereby mistakes, omissions, problems, conflicts, and wrongdoing can be identified and addressed. Virtually all surveys about violations show that many managers and employees frequently see or hear about serious infractions of policies, rules, and laws—and about acts of omission and commission against the organizational mission. However, in Rowe, Wilcox, and Gadlin (2009) it is noted that many people do not act on the spot or come forward in a timely manner when they perceive unacceptable behavior. They may fear loss of relationships, loss of privacy, retaliation, or just "bad consequences." People may worry about being seen as a troublemaker. Many do not feel sure of themselves. Many feel they do not have "enough evidence" to act.

OOs try to establish themselves as zero barrier offices (Rowe and Bendersky, 2002). OOs endeavor to be "safe, credible and accessible" for all (Rowe and Baker, 1984). They regularly hear more than employee hotlines about unacceptable behavior. OOs also endeavor to be accessible to all, in person, by phone, email, intranet systems, and letter. Most OOs will accept visits from groups, most will accept anonymous communications, and many will interact with people who remain anonymous, in order to be and appear to be "safe." OOs try to find acceptable and credible options, to deal with all concerns, while protecting the confidentiality of those with whom they interact.

The credibility of OOs is methodologically difficult to measure. It is useful to think about credibility in terms of trust, and in terms of demonstrable usefulness of the OO office. Trust is perhaps most easily measured by whether people seek out the office and the issues that are presented. At professional gatherings and in surveys most OOs report that they are swamped with work. OOs receive a very wide range of issues—ideally from every demographic and geographic group of employees in the organization. In unionized workplaces if the OO hears issues covered in the bargaining agreement, they have usually been referred through the union; if not, the OO refers the person raising the issue to the union.

"Word of mouth" is a typical mode of referral to an OO office, suggesting that most OO offices are reasonably trusted to be confidential, independent, and impartial. In some organizations with very diverse populations, people from some cultural/ethnic backgrounds may be reluctant to contact an OO. In this case OOs hopefully will review the distribution of those who use their office to understand if specific cohorts and sub-populations are under-represented and take steps to reach those groups. In most ombudsman programs managers frequently call the office for consultations—for their own issues and those of their supervisees. While no systematic data can be cited, OOs appear to the authors to receive by far the widest range of issues, and of cohorts, of any conflict management office.

Because OOs can receive calls from the whole organization, they are often seen to be a good place to start for multi-issue, multi-regulation, multi-cohort problems that have roots and branches across organizational boundaries. Because OOs are relatively senior professionals, they bring high-level skills to each concern, like having the most senior internist serve in the emergency room in a hospital. In addition most OOs acknowledge contacts within a day or so; they are unusually responsive and also expeditious for people in a hurry. OOs frequently help people with "red tape."

It may be that one reason for the credibility of OOs is that they are constantly "tutoring." People facing a problematic situation often can only think of one way to address it; OOs typically help people identify and consider a wider variety of options. Another contribution of the OO is to help people who are fixed in their views to be more appreciative of the perspectives of those with whom they disagree or are in conflict. It is, by definition, hard to get someone with rigid ideas to hear another point of view. Opposing arguments from opponents often just strengthen the original belief. Experience suggests that respectful questions and facts from a relatively high-level neutral—one who has no stake in the matter at hand—can sometimes help a person to gain perspective.

OOs are not universally successful. Many must work hard to be a significant resource for people in the very top leadership positions in organizations. Current OO programs primarily address the concerns of people below the top leadership. Certainly many organizational leaders rely on upward feedback from OOs and some will ask an OO for further perspectives on particular issues about which the OO is knowledgeable. But when it comes to conflicts between top leaders, or addressing major policy decisions, the OO typically is an underutilized resource.

Measuring the effectiveness of OOs is methodologically very difficult (Rowe, 2010a). Many of the benefits (and costs) are subjective. OOs will not always be able to help each person who calls them either in terms of the outcome desired or even a fair process. By the same token, it is not accurate that every case will be cost-effective for the employer. Many of the matters that come to an OO are not "important" from a narrow cost-effectiveness perspective. However, the high traffic in many OO offices helps constituents to know that a zero barrier office exists when delicate problems do arise. Satisfaction surveys regularly show high levels of gratitude and satisfaction from most stakeholders—although the authors know from their own practice and from colleagues that there are always stakeholders who are disappointed.

It is likely that most OO offices at least cover their costs, in objective terms. Many OOs have put forward metrics that suggest their value (Rowe, 2010a). In particular, an OO that has been in place for any length of time will be able to point to very serious cases of unacceptable behavior that have been forestalled, or identified and dealt with, because of calls to the OO. Usually the most serious cases are known to senior managers, so there is no question about breaching confidentiality. Many OOs can point to having helped effectively with one or several cases each year, each of which would otherwise have entailed costs in excess of the cost of the office. Significant savings—in terms of money, reputation, and image, and savings in human costs—are usually easy to discuss.

Dozens or hundreds of cases will show that red tape has been dealt with, and that unfair processes have changed (Rowe, 2012a).

To sum up, the authors believe that the growth of the OO role is attributable in part to the effectiveness of the function. To understand the role more fully, the social and political context that influenced the emergence of OOs is examined.

Genesis and Development of the Organizational Ombudsman Role

Informal mechanisms for addressing dissatisfactions, conflicts, and grievances have existed for centuries in a wide range of cultural and economic contexts. Here and there, some of these mechanisms looked something like the modern organizational ombudsman, albeit with different titles. However, most histories of the modern ombudsman role take special note of the Swedish Parliament's establishment of the role and use of the word in 1809. Parliament intended to provide a means whereby citizens could pursue complaints and grievances against the administrative and executive branches of the government. It established the classical ombudsman.

Modern intra-organizational roles like those of an OO, but with various titles, appeared spontaneously, on an occasional basis, throughout the 20th century. In addition, beginning in the 1960s in North America, the classical ombudsman concept was explicitly adapted for organizations in many sectors—universities, corporations, non-profit, and government agencies. An intra-organizational version of the role emerged, to allow people to raise issues and concerns in their lives as employees, managers, and students, rather than as citizens.

Although many organizations had various informal means by which internal issues could be addressed, the incorporation of informal functions under a unifying concept—"the ombudsman"—has strongly facilitated a wider use of those informal functions. From the 1960s two contributing influences converged to create conditions in which the OO adaptation was able to develop relatively quickly in the US. At the individual level there was more attention to autonomy, authenticity, dissent, self-expression, self-determination, and personal gratification. At the social/cultural level, attention was paid to issues of justice, civil rights (racial and gender), social equality, anti-authoritarianism, protest, counter-cultural formations, and alternatives to formal, authoritative, bureaucratic processes. Diversity issues became important in the Second World War. Immigration, internal migration, and other developments in the workforce in the post-war years brought unprecedented diversity by race, religion, nationality, gender, age, disability, and class. The post-war years also brought waves of regulation about safety, civil rights, and the use of public money.

As these social currents and legal requirements intersected within organizations they produced change and increased reflection. Organizational leaders and managers were searching for ways to maintain organizational authority and control, to comply with new laws—and to respond to pressures for expanded rights and increased opportunities for disagreement, dissent, and autonomy. This was also a time of extraordinary interest in entrepreneurship. Organizational leaders were seeking ways to foster discussion, creativity, innovation, and "intrapreneurship" within the organization. Not surprisingly, some of the same organizations that were fostering innovation were among the pioneers in developing internal ombudsman-like programs—the Control Data Corporation, Bell Labs, and MIT were notable examples.

Challenges to authority and bureaucracy, and increased oversight by government agencies, led a wide range of organizational leaders to rethink the structure of work groups and authority. Control and orderliness were no longer associated just with the structure and assertion of positional power. Creating conditions in which autonomy and participation could flourish, and where individual rights and interests were honored, became a way of maintaining control and complying with the law. Fewer layers of management were more cost-effective—and more democratic. Flattening hierarchies, collaborative workgroups, and cross-cultural, cross-functional, self-governing teams paralleled the rise of the organizational ombudsman. All were contributors to the movement away from authoritarian, hierarchical organizational structures.

Alternative Dispute Resolution and Appropriate Dispute Resolution

Various challenges to authority and concerns about cost that characterized the period from the 1960s were also evident in the emergence of mediation, and the broader field of alternative dispute resolution (ADR). There emerged some "competition" between formal and informal justice systems.

The formal judicial system, where authoritative third parties rendered binding decisions grounded in the law, was seen by some people as one of the agencies within society wherein power inequalities were replicated. Women and people of color were well represented among those raising questions about the formal systems. (These formal systems were built around "due process," they followed clear rules and procedures: the rules of evidence, representation, impartiality, and disinterestedness of deciders, equal access to information by all and from all parties, and possible appeals.) This questioning of the role and impact of formal justice systems was somewhat ironic since the formal justice system, structured around due process, had earlier been considered among the cornerstones of social equality especially when the issues were related to class, race, and gender (Menkel-Meadow, 2012).

By comparison, advocates of the burgeoning alternative dispute resolution movement linked equality to an anti-authority stance and an emphasis on individual autonomy. They promoted "informal" justice by emphasizing "direct party empowerment and participation" in "case presentation and resolution." The focus in informal justice was on self-determination, and future-oriented problem solving. Mediators sought solutions on the basis of needs and interests rather than rights and legal claims (Menkel-Meadow,

2012). As the differences between ADR and the formal system were being defined, some of its corporate proponents were moving to incorporate ADR into conflict management systems. This was done by claiming the advantages of ADR: cost effectiveness, efficiency, legitimacy, flexibility, and confidentiality (including protecting the image of the organization). These qualities were also attractive to overburdened court systems many of which were open to experimenting with mediation programs.

In many ways the organizational ombudsman field grew rapidly because it caught the ADR wave—while simultaneously providing an alternate path for some of the strengths and processes of formal grievance procedures and the formal justice system. Rather than lining up with one side or the other, or even addressing the tensions between formal and informal approaches to dispute resolution, the OO field affirmed the value of both. While the legal and ADR professions then got somewhat caught up in competitively debating the disadvantages and advantages of the two approaches, organizational ombudsmen were embracing both. OOs emerged offering *appropriate dispute resolution* options for the choice of disputants.

OOs did not present themselves as a venue for providing formal justice. (OOs do not conduct hearings or render, affirm, or overturn decisions.) However, they became a resource to which members of an organization could turn when they felt the organization's formal grievance channels were not being implemented fairly or—much more common—when formal channels were inadequate to address key issues within the organization. This was especially true with respect to issues for which there were no formal policies or laws.

OOs frequently found themselves asking for formal policies that seemed to be needed for "new" issues. Examples early on included academic misconduct at universities, abrogations of corporate commitments of a kind that are now called "waste, fraud, and abuse," unanticipated varieties of safety problems, and all the varieties of harassment and bullying (Rowe, 2010b). By affirming, rather than challenging, formal justice systems, while also offering alternatives to them, organizational ombudsmen presented themselves as a complement to the organization's traditional lines of authority and status. The role of OO was structured from the start within the organization, although independent of, other major components of the conflict management system. In many milieux the organizational ombudsman role was not seen as a challenge to the authority of organizational leadership. Especially within the US, it was often on management initiative that the ombudsman program was developed.

In some organizations, in the early days of organizational ombudsmen, the establishment of an ombudsman program was discussed as a counter to movements towards unionization. It should be noted, however, that the situation has changed somewhat and there are instances where unions are partners in the creation of conflict management programs, e.g., in government agencies in Ontario, Canada (Lynch, 2010).

Whatever the motivations behind the development of organizational ombudsman programs, their establishment is either implicitly or explicitly an acknowledgment that the complexities of bureaucratic organizations call for programs and processes whereby inconsistencies, inefficiencies, rigidities, favoritism, newly configured indignities, and other forms of unfairness—and illegal behavior—can be surfaced and addressed. The establishment of an OO tacitly acknowledges that the formal procedures and processes of an organization can be unfair, slow or otherwise poorly administered (Gadlin et al., 2000).

In addition, in every organization, there are—for both individuals and groups—many issues and conflicts for which there cannot, realistically, be rules, regulations, or policies. These issues and conflicts nonetheless may need to be addressed. Organizational ombudsmen have often established their value by providing options for redress in matters for which there are no useful formal mechanisms—or in the many cases where there never would be sufficient evidence for formal grievance or complaint (Rowe, 1990, 2010a).

In an era where the very legitimacy of authority was being challenged on numerous fronts, the establishment of ombudsman programs that actually offer a path to questioning authority has served to enhance the legitimacy of that authority. This enhanced legitimacy and relatively swift responsiveness have sometimes improved morale and have served also to help some organizations retain top professionals. Even if they did not always employ the term "procedural justice," ombudsman programs heightened employees' and managers' sensitivity to such matters. Research has demonstrated that procedural justice (enhanced by swift responsiveness) is critical to employees' identification with their organization and acceptance of the legitimacy of its leadership (De Cremer and Tyler, 2007; Blader and Tyler, 2009).

Variations in Practice

Above, the organizational ombudsman concept and role was presented as if there were unanimity of opinion among OOs about the role. In reality the situation was—and remains—more diverse. Initially there were no professional organizations and no sense of common standards. Once professional associations began to form, significant differences appeared among the members.

Many OOs were solo practitioners who had tailored their ombudsman role to the idiosyncratic requisites and culture of their organizations. Different sectors—academic, corporate, governmental, international, and NGOs—each had their own demands and peculiarities. To make matters even more complicated, some divisions in the larger dispute resolution field (between formal and informal approaches to justice) were also replicated among the OOs. There were some OOs who were affiliated with the ADR movement, others who saw OOs as more akin to the formal justice system. Some were inspired by the concept of social justice, and still others were tuned to organizational and inter-personal power dynamics, and less focused on questions of rights and interests.

Among the factors that inclined OOs in one direction or another was their prior field of experience—senior line manager vs staff, high-tech professional vs social worker vs lawyer vs psychologist vs HR specialist vs academic—not to mention personal dispositions and skills. (In the early days surveys suggested that virtually all OOs had been selected on the basis of personal attributes—characteristics such as being trusted by the CEO, patience, fairness, objectivity, and empathy—rather than on the basis of formal training or previous work experience (Rowe and Ziegenfuss, 1993).)

There have been national differences as well. OOs in Canada, Europe, Africa, Asia, Australia, and South America have had their own customs and sensibilities. Pioneer OOs in South Africa, Japan, and New Zealand seem to us more like the US model; some in South America are developing somewhat different models.

In Canada and Europe some ombudsmen, especially in the academic world, developed the internal ombudsman role explicitly as an adaptation of the classical ombudsman role. These "neo-classical" ombudsmen proliferated in Scandinavia and were being created within many of the provinces of Canada and a few states and cities in the US. On the other hand, although they saw their responsibilities as including the conduct of formal investigations and issuance of reports and recommendations, Canadian and European ombudsmen in organizations were not confined to classical functions. They incorporated into their practices many of the same interest-based approaches to addressing issues and resolving conflicts, as did their US counterparts. In addition, some classical ombudsmen in Europe have reported that they have done the same (Luigi Cominelli, 2004).

In the US, from 1970 on, most OOs were careful to differentiate themselves from the classical ombudsman model. For one thing, some offices had been created with no reference to the classical ombudsman. They were spontaneously invented as independent, confidential, informal, internal neutrals and originally with different titles. There have been many of these OO-like offices around the world with different names, like the Registrars and Partners Counsellor of John Lewis in the UK, which were established in the first half of the 20th century. Other examples include the wide variety of "organizational troubleshooters" described by Ziegenfuss (1988).

Concerned about maintaining independence from formal processes and managerial responsibilities, and determined to avoid being subpoenaed by complainants— or forced by their organizations to breach confidentiality—OOs in the US eschewed formal investigations, fact-finding, and case records. Some avoided making public recommendations. At most they might acknowledge that in the face of a complaint they would "look into" the complaint while never fully spelling out what constituted "looking into" something. In the very rare circumstances (now contrary to IOA Standards of Practice) where an OO did conduct a formal investigation it would be clearly described as an exception to the rule, and the reasons for the exception would be explained.

IOA Standards of Practice are now widely shared and there is an IOA Certification program, but there is no precise standardization of practice within the US. Some US OOs still feel somewhat akin to the ADR movement and many provide conflict resolution services such as facilitation and mediation from within their offices. Others limit themselves to coaching and helping those who visit them to explore and analyze various

Locations: Africa, Asia, Australia, Canada, Central America, Europe, New Zealand, South America, United Kingdom, United States.

Sectors: Aerospace, agriculture, business services and consulting, consumer goods retail and wholesale, financial, health care, pharmaceutical, high-tech, IT, manufacturing, oil and gas and other energy, R&D, telecommunications; a wide range of academic institutions, including school systems; federal, state and local government, quasi-government organizations, other not-for-profit, multi-national and international organizations; numbers growing, albeit slowly—about one in six of the Fortune 500 companies.

Length of Cases: Varies from OO to OO; 15% to 40% of all cases take less than an hour; at least 5% take more than 100 hours; 55 to 80% of all cases are in-between.

Common Topics of cases: Compensation and benefits; evaluative relationships; peer and colleague relationships; career progression and development; legal, regulatory, financial and compliance, safety, health and physical environment; service and administrative; strategic and mission related; values, ethics and codes of conduct.

Issues reported as more numerous in recent years: Multigenerational issues, cases with more than three issues, multi-ethnic, multi-language and multi-race issues; complex gender issues; bullying; cross-organizational, multi-cohort, multi-unit and multi-country issues; cases with multiple sets of relevant rules, codes, contracts or regulations; multiple offices involved in solutions; complaints about other offices in the organization; cases lasting longer than six months; and single cases becoming the impetus for a systemic response in a department, division or college, or for a systemic response organization wide. (Only those cases including groups were reported to be "much the same," year to year.)

The *significance* of certain issues has been reported to be somewhat higher in recent years, especially in academia. These include: impact on the financial health of the organization, reputation of the organization, safety and security of the organization, personal relationships, and the job security, reputation, and health of individuals. Many OOs reported more discussions with compliance offices within the organization.

Source: IOA Compensation and Practice Survey, 2010, available to IOA members at http://www.ombudsassociation.org/members-only/business-planning-and-policy-documents/member-surveys

FIGURE 10.2 Organizational Ombudsmen—A Brief Overview

Source: International Ombudsman Association Compensation and Practice Survey, 2011.

options. They provide comfort and guidance, help to clarify policies and rules, and refer people to relevant organizational processes.

Other differences include the preferred level of dealing with issues. Some OOs hover safely at the level of individual cases, and others use experience with individual cases as an entrée into systemic and policy issues within the organization. Many OOs deal with very complex problems.

Figure 10.2 provides facts from a 2010 International Ombudsman Association survey. Figure 10.2 does not include the number of OOs around the world in this century. There are many hundreds, but it is not possible to provide an exact number. Some organizations have internal "Ombudsman" offices that do not function as Standards of Practice organizational ombuds. And, conversely, some organizations have senior managers who *do* function as neutral, independent, confidential, and informal conflict experts—thus practising to the IOA Standards of Practice—but with different titles.

Competencies and Functions of Organizational Ombudsmen

It is now well established that human beings make decisions quickly, often without knowing it, on the basis of intuitive understanding, modulated and informed by the slower processes of cognitive thought (Kahneman, 2012). Ideas like "trust" and "interpersonal chemistry" and "the perception of fairness" now share center stage in decision-making with "reason" and "rational choice" and "delivering justice." This approach to understanding decision-making—inspired by research in social psychology and neuroscience—illuminates the importance of providing options in a conflict management system. An effective system requires options that can support responsible and effective problem solving and decision-making on the basis of both "trust" *and* "rational choice." An OO needs to have skills in each domain of decision-making, and to understand how each domain works. The OO needs to try to understand his or her own decision-making processes and to understand those of all stakeholders in the conflict management system.

The first task for an organizational ombudsman is to build enough of a relationship with each stakeholder and stakeholder group to be perceived as fair, safe, accessible, and credible. The second task is to help all managers and employees actually to *understand* the organization's conflict management system, its options and its resources. (This is the task that develops into de facto, informal coordination of a conflict management system.)

Many employees and managers move around constantly. Few people listen well. Few managers respond promptly to calls for help—in fact few managers respond in a timely way to any communication. People joke, "Nobody reads the rules any more." Very few people understand any organizational conflict management system in its entirety. Few people understand their options. In this context, for many OOs around the world, the most basic functions of an OO include:

- delivering respect, for example affirming the feelings of each person involved in a concern, while staying explicitly neutral on the facts of a case, responding as quickly as possible when called, endeavoring to build some degree of relationship
- active listening, probing respectfully, serving as a sounding board
- providing and explaining information, one on one, for example about policies and rules, and about the *context* of a concern
- receiving vital information, one on one, for example from those reporting unacceptable behavior, criminal and safety violations, and the like
- reframing issues, illuminating the context, and facts and feelings, that might have been overlooked
- helping to develop options, and then helping to evaluate the pros and cons of all the choices for the issues at hand.

In their direct work with those who call upon the office, the OO's orientation is to work with callers to develop some of the skills the callers will need to deal with their issues in context. OOs provide "just-in-time" support in learning about effective negotiation, one on one, in a way that is tailored to individual needs. These functions include:

- offering the option of referrals to other resources—including "key people" in the relevant department, managers and compliance offices, and all relevant support services
- helping people help themselves to use a direct approach, for example helping people to collect and analyze their own information, helping people to draft a letter about their issues, coaching and role playing to help people learn to negotiate and to engage in problem-solving. This is the function of teaching people "how to fish" rather than "giving them a fish."

Often those who come to the OO do not want or need direct intervention from the OO, or at least not initially. However, there are many situations where an OO may also offer, or be asked, to play a role. Except in the very rare case where the OO judges there is imminent risk of serious harm, and that there are no other options, this would be done only with permission from the person who asks for help—and of course the OO also has to agree to act. These functions include:

- offering shuttle diplomacy, for example helping employees and managers to think through proposals that may resolve a dispute in a fair way, and facilitating discussions, in a back and forth process; helping a manager to review or reformulate a decision
- offering mediation inside the organization, bringing various people together
- "looking into" a problem informally, for example checking for new policies, or resource constraints, checking unobtrusively with staff offices to find out if others have heard about a certain kind of issue
- facilitating a generic approach to an individual problem, for example asking for the law proscribing uncompensated overtime to be enforced throughout a whole division. This may lead to a fair outcome while protecting the identity of an individual who came forward.

Information from repeated ombudsman association surveys shows that an OO may spend 20–40% of his or her time serving the whole organization and its conflict management system. These functions include:

- providing early warning of issues that are "new" and potentially disruptive to the organization, by getting back to relevant managers in a manner consonant with confidentiality, when the OO sees something unexpected and potentially disruptive
- identifying and communicating about *patterns* of issues, for example reporting to each senior officer on a regular basis about what comes to the OO office about his or her domain; writing specific and/or annual reports

- working for systems change, for example suggesting new policies, procedures, and structures, and participating in relevant training about conflict management; serving as a resource person to policy committees; helping to spread good ideas that have popped up somewhere in the organization
- following up on a case with relevant stakeholders, and following up on recommendations made by the OO
- helping informally, and often invisibly, to connect and coordinate all the elements of the conflict management system—in the context of thousands of daily communications with employees and managers. OOs support all cohorts to understand and use all the resources and options in the system.

There are conflict management functions that an OO does not undertake. The functions that follow help to distinguish OO offices from all other line and staff managers. These include:

- keeping case records for the organization or for compliance purposes (as distinguished from keeping identity-free statistics for feedback to senior officers)
- pursuing formal investigations for the purpose of managerial decision-making and administrative action
- acting as advocate or witness in a formal adjudicatory process (as distinguished from advocacy for a fair process) for any stakeholder in the conflict management system
- accompaniment or representation of any party in a formal conflict management process
- dealing with formal appeals
- making managerial decisions about a grievance or conflict (except in the very rare case of imminent risk of serious harm, where there appear to be no other options)
- acting as an arbitrator or judge.

Challenges and Dilemmas

Some variations in OO practice can be understood in relation to the major developments that helped to foster the role: controversy about how formal and informal systems contribute to justice and problem-solving, and efforts to help organizations make sense of and adapt to changing notions of authority, leadership, hierarchy, diversity, bureaucracy, and government oversight (Gadlin, 2010).

From the beginning the OO role has been subject to contradictory obligations and responsibilities. Noriko Tada likens the Japanese OO to a kabuki "Kuroko" actor: a "visible invisible" on the stage. The Kuroko dresses all in black. He does not show his face, and is not formally part of the action, but without the Kuroko things do not work efficiently—and sometimes not at all (Tada, 2012). Brian Bloch, from his many years as an

OO in India, reflects on the Hindu concept of Achintya Bheda Abheda: "an inconceivable oneness and difference" (Bloch, 2012). The OO must consider the rights and interests of all the stakeholders—independent—yet part of the organization. The OO can also be seen as an oxymoronic "inside outsider" (Gadlin, 2000).

Because they report to senior leadership and therefore are likely to desire the approval of "the boss," OOs can be vulnerable to the influence of the senior leader. However, access to that leader also provides the chance to influence her or him. Most OOs report that their access to the top contributes significantly to their credibility. This credibility is amplified by their insider status. It is understood that they have an up-close understanding of the entire organization, the internal culture and politics of the organization. They know the key players for just about every matter than can arise (Tada, 2012). While it is possible for a long-term OO to become inured to the particular injustices and abuses tolerated in their organizations, they are also likely to be able to see through the pretenses and subterfuges by which abusive or overbearing managers maintain their organizational empires.

From the perspective of any of the sophisticated frameworks from which we now understand organizational dynamics—systems theory, network theory, complexity theory—it is difficult to believe that an effective OO can really be independent in the full sense of that term.

In a similar way the second of the four pillars of ombudsman work, neutrality, is also problematic. First, there is the question of whether in fact *anyone*, no matter how strong his or her reputation for fairness, can actually claim to be either neutral or impartial. The term "neutrality" as used by OOs usually includes impartiality. Neutrality also refers to structural factors—not being part of the management team or any other organizational unit—while impartiality refers to how the OO conducts himself or herself in relation to individuals and groups, not advocating for or preferring one party. Impartiality involves an absence of bias. The OO can try to be both neutral and impartial (Gadlin and Pino, 1997).

However, the vast literature on unconscious bias demonstrates quite clearly that the ideal of being without bias is, in any literal sense, unattainable. Most OOs are scrupulous in their efforts to be equally fair and even-handed, in their treatment of each person with whom they interact, but too much is known about the influence of unconscious factors to have confidence that any given OO can actually ward off the influences of unconscious biases.

Recently some OOs have preferred the term multi-partiality because it acknowledges that in establishing a credible trusting relationship with various parties to a conflict, it is necessary to appreciate each of their perspectives, and to establish a supportive relationship concerned with the interests of all. Whereas impartiality connotes equidistance, multi-partiality connotes being comparably understanding of each party. Others would suggest that it is possible to affirm or at least understand the *feelings* of each party while staying explicitly neutral about the *facts* of a case.

One could argue that the OO is unbiased in the sense of not having a particular interest in the outcome of a particular case. But the OO's commitment to fair process means that the OO must be concerned with the process by which a particular case is resolved. Although a rule or process by itself might be fair, the OO may raise questions about unfair implementations of rules. And the OO must make judgments about fairness in order to decide whether or not to proceed with a case.

Neutrality is equally problematic because, in addition to implying a lack of having a personal stake in an outcome, it also suggests not taking sides. But *not* taking sides—in organizations in which people differ significantly in formal power and status, not to mention different degrees of informal power and influence within the culture and politics of the organization—is more easily imagined than achieved. There are OOs who believe that they come closest to true neutrality by having no direct impact on the outcome of a situation, and who believe that they are mere facilitators of processes in which people develop and enact the resolution to their problems or conflicts. These practitioners may be vulnerable to the accusation that their existence simply ratifies pre-existing power discrepancies—that they are sanctifying organizational injustices that are incorporated into the organizational structure—and that this itself is a "bias."

The challenge of OO neutrality gets more complicated when the ombudsman's role regarding organizational change is considered. In addition to handling individual cases the OO has a responsibility to identify and bring to management systemic problems within the organization. Of course identifying a problem is a necessary first step in addressing it and therefore OOs may feel comfortable describing themselves as change agents within an organization. But an OO who has identified a problem usually has special insights that derive from working with the cases that exemplify the problem. Because of this understanding of the problem the OO may be asked to participate in the committee charged with rectifying it. The OO may therefore be invited into quasi-managerial functions—formulating a new policy (e.g. parental leave, research integrity), developing a program (e.g. to reduce racial tensions), creating ways to address negative features of organizational culture (e.g. bullying).

Although some OOs, concerned with maintaining independence and fostering neutrality, might refuse to participate in such activities, OOs still have responsibility for raising a problem in the first place. And raising a problem is never a neutral act, even if it is framed in the most neutral way possible.

Some argue that there is an alternative: to be a "resource" for a remedial task force though never a named member. But just "not being named" hardly means "not having an impact," though this stance seems better than joining a committee. Simply put, there is no perfect way to be an independent neutral. Almost any organizational change has an impact on the distribution of power and within the organization and in being involved in such change the impact of the OO's actions are not distributed evenly no matter how even-handed the OO has been in identifying, naming, and addressing an issue. From the perspective of systems theory, there is no such thing as neutrality. Things unfold differently when the OO is involved than they would have if the OO has not been involved.

CONCLUSION

The intra-organizational ombuds role has old roots in many cultures. In the modern world the role is configured in a way that may be unique in conflict management as an "inside outsider," and "invisibly visible" conflict expert.

OOs can hear from everyone in an organization, across all the boundaries of geography, demography, rank, status, and expertise. OOs can offer all interest-based conflict management options, and refer to all rights-based formal channels. The OO may earn its keep by strengthening, and informally coordinating, the entire conflict management system of an organization. The OO also earns its keep by offering effective options to the individual employees and managers who call upon it.

Organizational ombuds appear to be proliferating in part because of demonstrable effectiveness. The idea of an OO also spread faster because it accommodated the essential spirit of ADR while avoiding the controversies between ADR and justice delivered by the courts. Rather than lining up with one side or the other, or even addressing the tensions between formal and informal approaches to dispute resolution, the OO profession affirms the value of both. OOs endeavor to foster *appropriate* dispute resolution rather than stereotypical "ADR."

The OO profession is built on independence, confidentiality, neutrality, and informality. The individual OO continually faces dilemmas—the struggles to be impartial, to try to be neutral while fostering fair processes, and the challenge of practice as an independent professional, while earning trust within the organization. OOs have to take great care to maintain confidentiality, and to remain reasonably outside the sphere of managerial decision-making.

The OO role itself, however, appears to be robust. Organizational ombudsmen typically support the lives of hundreds of employees and managers, students and others, while earning generally high satisfaction ratings. OO appear to deal with the widest range of concerns and conflicts within organizations and are one of the few offices that deal with the entire organization. OOs regularly help to surface illegal and otherwise unacceptable behavior and occasionally offer early warning of "new" issues. Ombudsmen regularly help people with concerns to learn how to deal directly with those concerns, and regularly work hard on systems improvements as well as acting as informal intermediaries.

While the contributions of OOs seem appreciated within those organizations that have one, it is not generally seen as essential. "Essential" offices are usually unambiguously designed to serve the needs of management whereas the OO by definition is independent and neutral. In organizations where the OO plays an important role it is often because that particular OO has earned trust with leaders and throughout the organization. Whether OOs will come to be seen as essential for competitive organizations will depend on OOs expanding their conception of the role in an effective way, and on organizations moving further toward becoming learning organizations.

Notes

1. <http://www.ombudsassociation.org/about-us/code-ethics> and <http://www.ombudsas sociation.org/about-us/mission-vision-and-values/ioa-best-practices-standards-practice> accessed 23 Sept. 2013.
2. <http://www.uwo.ca/ombuds/SoPJune2012EF.pdf>.

References

Blader, S. and Tyler, T. R. 2009. "Testing and Exploring the Group Engagement Model." *Journal Applied Psychology*, 94: 445–64.

Bloch, B. 2012. Ombudsman with the Special Trustee for American Indians in the Department of the Interior, and Co-director and Organizational Ombudsman of ISKCONResolve, personal communication.

Bloch, B. and Miller, D. 2009. "Analyzing Your Conflict Management System --A Supplemental Chart." A Series of Six Articles. *Harvard Negotiation Law Review*, Winter. <http://www.hnlr. org/?page_id=35%3E>.

Cominelli, L. 2004. Assistant Professor of Sociology of Law at the University of Milan, personal communication.

David B. Lipsky, Ronald L. Seeber, and Richard D. Fincher. 2003. *Emerging Systems for Managing Workplace Conflict: Lessons from American Corporations for Managers and Dispute Resolution Professionals*. San Francisco, CA: Jossey-bass.

De Cremer, D. and Tyler, T. R. 2007. "The Effects of Trust and Procedural Justice on Cooperation." *Journal Applied Psychology*, 92: 639–49.

Gadlin, H. 1987. "Dispute Resolution and the Ombudsman: Rethinking Ombudsman Effectiveness." Society for Professionals in Dispute Resolution, New York, Oct.

Gadlin, H. 2010. "I Was Just Thinking about Fairness." *Journal of the International Ombudsman Association*, 4(1): 39–44.

Gadlin, H. 2012. "Some Thoughts on Informality." *Journal of the International Ombudsman Association*, 5(1): 31–6.

Gadlin, H. and Pino, E. 1997. "Neutrality: A Guide for the Organizational Ombudsperson." *Negotiation Journal*, 13(1): 17–37.

Gadlin, H., Stieber, C., Bauer, F., Shelton, R. L., and Wagner, M. 2000. "The Many Different, and Complex roles Played by Ombudsmen in Dispute Resolution." *Negotiation Journal*, 16(1): 37–114.

Kahneman, D. 2012. *Thinking, Fast and Slow*. New York: Farrar, Straus and Giroux.

Lynch, J., Q.C. 2010 *Chief Commissioner of the Canadian Human Rights Commission*, Canada, personal communication.

Menkel-Meadow, C. 2012. "Informal, Formal, and 'Semi-Formal' Justice in the United States." In D. Maleshin (ed.), *Civil Procedure in Cross-Cultural Dialogue: Eurasia Context*, 90–110. Moscow: Statut Publishing House.

Rowe, M. 1984. "The Non-Union Complaint System at MIT: An Upward-Feedback Mediation Model." *Alternatives to the High Cost of Litigation*, 2(4): 10–18.

Rowe, M. 1990. "People Who Feel Harassed Need a Complaint System with both Formal and Informal Options." *Negotiation Journal*, 6(2): 161–72.

Rowe, M. 1993. "The Post-Tailhook Navy Designs an Integrated Dispute Resolution System." *Negotiation Journal*, 9(2) 203–13.

Rowe, M. 1996. "Specifications for an Effective Integrated Complaint System." In Bernice R. Sandler and Robert J. Shoop (eds), *Sexual Harassment on Campus*. New York: Simon and Schuster, Allyn and Bacon.

Rowe, M. 2010a. "Identifying and Communicating the Usefulness of Organizational Ombuds, with Ideas about OO Effectiveness and Cost-Effectiveness." *Journal of the International Ombudsman Association*, 3(1): 9–23.

Rowe, M. 2010b. "The Several Purposes of the Crystal Ball." *Journal of the International Ombudsman Association*, 3(2): 60–5.

Rowe, M. and Baker, M. 1984. "Are You Hearing Enough Employee Concerns?" *Harvard Business Review*, 62(3): 127–36.

Rowe, M. and Bendersky, C. 2002. "Workplace Justice, Zero Tolerance and Zero Barriers: Getting People to Come Forward in Conflict Management Systems." In T. Kochan and R. Locke (eds), *Negotiations and Change, From the Workplace to Society*. Ithaca, NY: Cornell University Press.

Rowe, M., Wilcox, L., and Gadlin, H. 2009. "Dealing With—Or Reporting—'Unacceptable' Behavior." *Journal of the International Ombudsman Association*, 2(1): 52–64.

Rowe, M. and Ziegenfuss, J. T. 1993. "Corporate Ombudsmen: Functions, Caseloads, Successes and Problems: A Survey of 55 Corporate Ombudsmen." *Journal of Health and Human Resources Administration*, 15(3): 261–80.

Society of Professionals in Dispute Resolution. 2001. "Designing Integrated Conflict Management Systems: Guidelines for Practitioners and Decision Makers in Organizations." *Cornell Studies in Conflict and Dispute Resolution*, 4. Ithaca, NY: Cornell/PERC Institute on Conflict Resolution and Washington, DC: Association for Conflict Resolution. <http://digitalcommons.ilr.cornell.edu/icr/2>

Tada, N. 2012. "Informality for a Organizational Ombudsman in Japan," *Journal of the International Ombudsman Association*, 5(1): 23–6.

Ury, W., Brett, J., and Goldberg, S. 1988. *Getting Disputes Resolved*. San Francisco: Jossey-Bass.

Ziegenfuss, J. 1988. *Organizational Troubleshooters: Resolving Problems with Customers and Employees*. San Francisco: Jossey-Bass.

CHAPTER 11

LINE MANAGERS AND WORKPLACE CONFLICT

JOHN PURCELL

INTRODUCTION

CONFLICT in organizations is inevitable. Line managers are at the heart of most workplace conflict, whether causing it, experiencing it, dealing with it, or coping with its consequences. The managerial dilemma of seeking and maintaining control of the work process through employees, who will have their own goals and needs and are able to choose, in all but the most regulated jobs, how they perform the work, is the central task of the line manager. The relationship is characterized by "vulnerability and risk" (Whitener et al., 1998: 525) since there are few certainties and managers have to make a succession of choices in the way work is allocated, tasks are to be performed, employees rewarded or punished, and when to intervene or let things pass. If the worker is to be disciplined is this because of a lack competence such that the job cannot be done well enough or fast enough, or is this failure a question of conduct where the individual chooses, for one reason or another, not to do what is required? It may be easier to do nothing and let the problem solve itself, but here there is always the danger of the "sucker's payoff" (Whitener et al., 1998: 524) where the manager is exploited or embarrassed. "Managers often face such dilemmas and exhibit this fear; concerns about gullibility and embarrassment often underlie managers' reluctance to trust" (Whitener et al., 1998: 524). Where trust is lacking in the manager–employee relationship the potential for conflict grows considerably. The urge is to increase monitoring and surveillance to ensure compliance but simultaneously to doubt some of the evidence, what Luhmann (1979) described as "relying more and more on less and less" in a cycle of low trust. While the differing personal attributes of managers help to explain why some managers get caught in this low trust, conflict-riddled relationship, the key variance is most likely to be found in organizational characteristics. Some organizations are "hotspots" where the ill-treatment of employees is much more pronounced than in others (Fevre et al., 2011a).

In this chapter the prevalence of workplace conflict needs to be examined as far as this is possible given chronic problems of under-reporting. Conflict needs to be contextualized to find where it is most likely to occur and to begin to identify the organizational characteristics of high-conflict organizations. The changing roles of line managers, and the pressures they are under, need to be scrutinized in order to appreciate why managerial conduct is central to both the causes and solutions of workplace conflict. It is very easy to exaggerate the "problem" of conflict. The majority of the 3,979 respondents to the British Workplace Behaviour Survey (BWBS), conducted by Fevre and his colleagues in 2008, did not report unreasonable treatment, denigration, or disrespect and very few had experienced actual violence (Fevre et al., 2011a). This leads to the question: what are the managerial behaviors that reduce or limit the extent of conflict in the workplace?

The Extent of Conflict Involving Line Managers

Conflict in the workplace can take many forms and be between the manager and subordinate employee, between individual workers, and between employees and clients or customers. Usually it is an individual event, but at times collective conflict can erupt expressing difficulties in the wider employment relationship. Here managerial roles will be different, with the manager having to deal with forms of industrial action such as overtime bans or walkouts. The best evidence of individual conflict comes from the BWBS, which looked at a wide range of workplace experiences that could lead to accusations of bullying and harassment. After careful cognitive testing of the way people interpret the terms used in the questionnaire, 21 areas were identified and used in the questionnaire administered on a face-to-face basis (Fevre et al., 2011b). These were then grouped into three broad categories: unreasonable treatment (experienced by 47% of respondents), denigration and disrespect (experienced by 40%) and actual violence, which happened to 5% of those responding.

Breaking down the responses to individual items is revealing. The most common form of unreasonable treatment was being given an unmanageable workload or impossible deadlines. This was reported by 29.1% of the respondents. Interestingly, managers were more at risk of being given too much to do, or insufficient time to do it, than others. This helpfully reinforces the point that the line manager role is both that of a boss and a subordinate under the command of more senior managers. They can be the cause of conflict, the recipients of conflict, and the persons responsible for seeking to resolve conflict. The second most-frequent complaint (27%) under the generic category of "unreasonable treatment" was "having my opinions ignored", while 20% complained that their employer did not follow proper procedures. Just over 1 in 6 complained that someone was continually checking up on them or their work when it was not necessary. Overall around two-thirds of the incidents were blamed on "employers, managers and supervisors."

Incidents of "denigration and disrespect" are more likely to be blamed on co-workers and clients or customers than on managers, although around two-fifths of cases were attributed to managerial misconduct. The most commonly reported problem in this category was "being shouted at or someone losing their temper with you" (23.6%), while slightly less (22.3%) reported "being insulted or having offensive remarks made about you."

The incidence of actual violence, experienced by 4.9% of employees, is higher than previous estimates of around 0.9% of working adults reporting violence (Jones et al., 2010: 163). In the majority of cases (78%) this violence was carried out by clients or customers or by people more loosely defined as "members of the public." Employers, meaning managers of various levels, were accused as the perpetrators in 9% of cases. Again, managers could themselves be the victims of violence in the workplace, usually from outsiders (Jones et al., 2010: 171) and were more likely to witness violence than other staff. "This may happen because more junior staff call in managers to deal with difficult situations" (Fevre, 2011a: 19).

More recent evidence of workplace conflict comes from the 2011 CIPD Outlook structured survey of 2,068 employees in the UK (CIPD, 2011). The survey is repeated on a quarterly basis allowing for some form of trend comparison. For example, "the proportion of staff saying they are under pressure at work either every day or once or twice a week, has edged up ... since the last quarter of the previous year, with 42% saying they are under excessive pressure" (CIPD, 2011: 8). The increase in pressure at work was especially notable in the public sector. The BWBS reports that incidents of mistreatment are more often found in the public sector than elsewhere. It was in the public sector, too, that respondents to the CIPD report were more likely to say that it was probable or very probable that they could lose their job as a result of the economic downturn (29% compared with 17% of those in the private sector). The reported incidents of redundancy were, at 57%, much higher than in the private sector where the rate was 37% (CIPD, 2011: Table 16). It was in the public sector, too, that reported incidents of workplace conflict were at their highest and had grown in the recession. An increase of conflict at work between colleagues was reported by 28% of public sector respondents compared with 17% of private sector workers. An increase in bullying by line managers was noted by a quarter of public sector respondents but only 17% of those in the private sector. Meanwhile, stress levels have shot up in the public sector (71%) compared with exactly half in the private sector. The autumn 2012 CIPD employee outlook survey assesses the relationship between levels of employee engagement and exposure to excessive pressure at work. Over half of the 15% who suffered excessive pressure every day were disengaged. By comparison, of the 22% who said they rarely experienced excessive pressure, only 6% were disengaged (CIPD, 2012:17).

There was a strong correlation in the BWBS between those who claimed to have experienced some form of workplace conflict in the shape of bullying and harassment and reported incidents of changes in work organization. Twenty percent reported that "I have less control over my work now than I had a year ago" while a quarter said that "the pace of work at my current job is too intense." Over half reported that "the pace of work has increased over the past year or so." Two-fifths said that "the nature of my work over the last year or so has changed (Fevre et al., 2011a: 169). It was in these circumstances that respondents were much more likely to report that they had been badly treated at work. While it may well be the case, as reported by Hodson (2001: 94) from his ethnographies, that a major cause of abusive behavior is poor management and that direct physical or verbal abuse "occurs across a range of workplaces," the pressures leading to such incidents go beyond the particular pressure felt by an individual manager "on a bad day at the office" to wider organizational and environmental features such as the recession giving rise to increasing pressure at work.

This is reflected in a 15% rise in the number of individuals taking a case to an Employment Tribunal in 2008/9 compared with the previous year. This is considered by Podro (2010: 6) to be "an underestimate of individuals affected by the recession and choosing to take their employer to tribunal." She reports an increase in the number of calls to the Acas Helpline relating to topics of discipline, dismissal, and grievance, from 25.9% in 2008 to 30.6% in 2009. Helpline advisers have also reported an increase in calls related to bullying and harassment, and stress. She quotes one Helpline adviser.

> "From the calls I have taken people are taking more sick days off due to being bullied by managers and being more stressed by being put under increased pressure due to reduced staffing levels". Another adviser noted: here is a cascade of stress down the management chain. The MD shouts at senior management who takes it out on the line manager which in turn affects employees. The uncertainty in companies is leading to more problems between colleagues. It is not necessarily getting raised with employers as people are scared to be seen as making a fuss and problems can escalate quickly.
>
> (Podro 2010: 8)

The evidence is also clear that in a recession levels of labor turnover fall. Podro (2010: 7) cites CIPD data that the turnover rate of 15.7% in 2009 was notably lower than the 17.3% the previous year. Absenteeism rates also fell. In the classic, and much cited, study by Hirschman (1970) individuals are seen to choose either to exit or to stay to seek ways in which the organization can be improved. This both reflects and reinforces loyalty. In cases of recession-induced staying, the outcome is more likely to be resentment than working positively. This will certainly breed latent conflict which may flare up from time to time. In these circumstances the only type of commitment shown by the employee is likely to be "continuance commitment" (Meyer and Allen, 1991). This is not really commitment at all, and is the antithesis of "affective commitment," which expresses a psychological bond between the individual and the organization. The individual with continuance commitment is trapped and feels unable to move or leave.

THE DISTRIBUTION OF WORKPLACE CONFLICT

The results of the BWBS survey of ill-treatment point to a number of workplace characteristics associated with a higher incidence of poor behavior and conflict. The authors
found that "unreasonable treatment was more common among full-time, well-paid professional, associated professionals and technical jobs in organizations of between 250
and 500 employees that were part of larger organizations" (Fevre and Lewis, 2012: 30).
They go on to note that this is the sort of workplace "where one would expect to see the
existence of professional HR, good policies, potentially well-trained management and
trade union representatives." This confounds the normal biases that such professionally
managed firms are bastions of good practice and that autocracy is most likely to be found
in small, owner-managed firms. Such stereotypes are subject to critical appraisal by
Edwards (2012: 141–142) who suggests that small firms tend to "eschew formal systems
of monitoring and supervision, which means there remains a degree of dependence on
employees... which creates space for organizations based on informal principles rather
than autocracy." These informal principles involve flexible ways of achieving negotiated
order relying on personal connections. Edwards (2012: 142) suggests that it may be the
case that autocracy is most likely in larger, less-personalized, and more Taylorized workplaces. The BWBS data confirms this.

The type of people most likely to report ill-treatment were those with disabilities or
long-term health conditions, often because of the manner in which employers dealt
with sickness absence. However, "the most common reason for ill-treatment lay not in
individual characteristics but in the characteristics of the workplace. Employees who
felt they had less control over their work had an increased risk of seven out of eight types
of unreasonable treatment" (Fevre and Lewis, 2012: 31). This also applied to those who
had experienced changes in work or work pace. "The biggest risk factor, however, was
working in a place where the fairness and respect score was low" (Fevre and Lewis, 2012:
31). This index is created by combining the responses to questions concerning: whether
the needs of the organization always came before the needs of people; whether their
work required them to compromise their principles; and whether people were treated as
individuals. These reflect fundamental attributes of management style or organizational
culture that can be significantly disrupted as a result of ownership changes (Boxall and
Purcell, 2011: 182–4, 299–303).

Fevre et al. (2011a: 25) provide material from case studies collected to complement
the BWBS.

> In a large financial services company, reports of highly aggressive behavior from
> managers were common, including shouting and swearing, public humiliation
> in meetings, and receiving offensive emails and telephone texts relating to perfor-
> mance. Several employees referred to the practice of the ritual shaming by regional
> managers intended not only to punish but to humiliate publically.... Employees told

us that the company had changed from caring for customers and ensuring products and service fitted client needs, to a culture where selling was the predominant driving force. This caused real problems for some staff.

A second case study in an NHS hospital trust reveals the relationship between intensive work and ill-treatment.

> Clinical overbooking to reduce waiting times, constant changes to shift patterns, covering for sick colleagues and increased weekend working left many employees struggling to cope. Work pressures and resulting feelings of stress were felt by employees at all levels and grades, including managers. The constant feeling of being checked upon by managers who themselves were being audited because of a budgetary deficit led many employees to take time off with ill health. The working environment of much of the organization seemed to function as a "pressure cooker" where tempers fray, insults are traded, and intimidation is practiced. Employees of all ages...appeared to be on the receiving end of ill-treatment with aggressive behavior being seen as commonplace. Shouting and loss of temper amongst colleagues was widely reported and swearing and finger pointing seemed to be a quite common occurrence...These situations led people feeling too intimidated to respond and they found it difficult to understand why they were receiving insults and threats.
>
> (Fevre et al., 2011a: 27)

Both of these accounts illustrate the problem of work intensification. Edwards (2005: 394) summarizes the classic characteristics.

> Work schedules are increasingly diverse, and workers asked to perform them have a very wide range of expectations of work. Cost pressures are often substantial. The upshot is that workers are controlled more tightly than in the past. Studies point to an increase in the use of systems of performance monitoring and to growing worker awareness of the pressures to perform, and there is clear evidence of an intensification of work effort...The implication here is that managerial power has reduced the ability of workers to engage in "undisciplined" behaviour.

Line managers are in the front line of performance monitoring and exerting pressures to perform. In doing so they are responding to the very same pressures that they experience from senior managers.

The "Problem" of Line Managers

Line managers are now much more involved in the management of employees than they were. There are a number of linked aspects to this expanded role. In the 1990s the trend was "to return HRM to the line" (McGovern et al., 1997). This movement, which continues, involved making line managers more responsible than they previously had been for the enactment of HR policies and practices. It is a misnomer to refer to this as "returning HR to the line" since what it really entails is the spreading of practices such as appraisal and performance management, previously limited to higher echelons, to all or most of the work force. At the same time, partly in response to the growing volume of individual rights enshrined in legislation, line managers took on more responsibility for the application of policies on discrimination, flexibility, and grievance and disciplinary matters, as well as selection. This was inevitable since it is only the manager with direct responsibility for a team of employees who is able to make the micro-level decisions in these matters and deal with the conflicts that can arise in their application. It may be that decisions can be escalated up the chain of command but, from the employees' perspective, it is the line manager who embodies the organization. If perceived organizational support is crucial for reciprocation through effort and good work then this is triggered by line managers in what is known as "leader–membership exchange" (Uhl-Bien et al., 2000: 138). It is "the key relationship that affects trust throughout the organization" (Sanders, 2012: 3).

There are a number of problems associated with this greater line management responsibility for the application and management of employment issues. First, there is clear evidence that this growth in the line manager's role was achieved by adding responsibilities to an already complex set of duties (Hales, 2005) leading to role overload. Second, one consequence of this overload is that it is often the case that what ought to happen does not take place, such as performance appraisals, team briefing, and dealing effectively with grievances. There is often a clear difference "between espoused and enacted HR practices with the gap often explained by line managers' lack of training, lack of interest, work overload, conflicting priorities and self-serving behaviour" (Purcell and Hutchinson, 2007: 5). What this means is that there is often "a strong disconnect between the 'rhetoric' of human resource management as expressed by the HR department and the reality as experienced by employees" (Truss, 2001: 1143). Third, line managers may give a low priority to dealing with employment issues. One study (McGovern et al., 1997: 21) asked line managers to "rank in order what motivates you to be involved in personnel activities." The first ranked answer was "personal motivation" as opposed to targets, company values, career advancement, and other possible reasons. In other words, the attention line managers give to HR issues is discretionary and for some it is something best avoided. Fourth, line managers often complain of a lack of support from senior managers making the role harder still (Hutchinson and Purcell, 2010). This reluctance was magnified when issues involved legal complexities where they lacked both specialist knowledge and time to devote to issues seen as "too hot to handle" (Harris, 2005: 81).

Part of the difficulty for line managers is to know the limits of their authority. When should a matter be referred to senior managers? Sometimes an enthusiastic manager can make a decision about how to handle a particular issue only to find the approach taken was not supported, or may even have been undermined by the HR or senior line manager. This ambiguity in the line managers' role is confirmed by Workplace Employment Relations (WERS) research which shows that "three-quarters of line managers in Britain could not make final decisions" on any of the fifteen potential "job duties" in employment (Kersley et al., 2006: 54). For example, in handling their equal opportunities job duties, line managers in branch sites were supposed to follow policy in three-quarters of cases and/or consult others before making a decision in two-thirds of such workplaces (Kersley et al., 2006: 55). In dealing with the classic conflict areas of discipline and grievances, over half of "local" managers had to consult other managers before making a decision and three-quarters were required to follow a policy or procedure (Kersley et al., 2006). This may seem sensible but, as noted, there is often a big gap between espoused and enacted practices.

One aspect of the problem, as research in Ireland (Teague and Roche, 2012) has shown, is that line managers commonly receive no training in "people management," nor do these duties form part of any assessment of their competence as line managers. Not surprisingly, many line managers were seen by their managers as lacking in confidence when handling workplace conflict. In their survey of 360 enterprises in 2008, with the respondent being the person most familiar with handling conflict, Teague and Roche reported that three-quarters agreed or strongly agreed with the statement that "line managers and supervisors are required to conduct regular face-to-face meetings with employees to gauge areas of concern to them and resolve problems." A similar high proportion reported that in their organizations "line managers and supervisors are specifically and formally enabled to resolve employee problems quickly and informally whenever possible." And yet, despite this formal duty placed on line managers in conflict management, almost half of the respondents said that "in practice, line managers and supervisors lack the confidence to resolve workplace conflict and rely on HR managers or other senior managers" (Teague and Roche, 2012: 242). Edwards (2005: 391) reports very similar findings from a survey in the early 1990s concerning line managers conducting return-to-work interviews with workers who had been absent. Half did not do so. The policy was often a case of "pass the baton" according to case studies conducted by Dunn and Wilkinson (2002: 238). Very little appears to have changed, apart from growing role overload, since Child and Partridge's classic study in 1972 of "the lost managers."

Summarizing the evidence, Teague and Roche (2012: 243) pointed to the "asymmetric characteristics" of a sizeable number of firms: "conflict management responsibilities are delegated to line managers; inadequate support structures are put in place to help them perform this role; and the capacity of line managers to perform their conflict-management duties with confidence and without a high reliance on other executives seems to be in considerable doubt."

Acas (2010: 8) noted that it is line managers who bring the employment policies, designed by professional HR departments, "to life" in daily application. "Unfortunately it is also line managers who are most often implicated in areas of poor employment practice which come to Acas' attention through individual conciliation linked to applications to employment tribunals." Weaknesses in the management of workplace conflict can most often be traced back to line manager neglect or confusion. This is often exacerbated by senior managers setting tough performance targets and monitoring systems while failing to give support to the people management part of the front-line manager's job. It is rare to find employers deliberately flouting recognized practice in dealing with conflict, leading to the conclusion that managerial problems in this area are the product of neglect. One element of this is that most line managers are appointed to their jobs because of their technical or professional skills related to the commercial objectives of the firm rather than for their people management skills. Not surprisingly they often lack competence in people management and the confidence to do what is required.

This was all too evident in a study of ward managers in five NHS Acute hospitals between 2005 and 2008 (Hutchinson and Purcell, 2010). Almost all of the 117 ward managers interviewed said that "my job requires me to work very hard," while four-fifths complained that they "never seem to have enough time to get my work done." An equal number reported that their job was stressful (Hutchinson and Purcell, 2010: 366). All of the ward managers were required to perform clinical duties as senior nurses and this work took precedence. The time allocated to management work was typically one day a week, or, in one case, half a day. A number of the managers commented that "management work" was what they took home with them at the end of a shift.

All of those who reported that they experienced problems in performing people management roles, as virtually all did, were asked an open question to identify the barriers that prevented them from performing their people management roles effectively. Six interlinked issues emerged: heavy workloads and stress; role conflict and ambiguity; a general lack of resources; inadequate training; and lack of support from senior managers, and from HR (Hutchinson and Purcell, 2010: 367). The lack of training was a particular difficulty.

> A significant proportion (37%) claimed not to have received any management training. None of the trusts appeared to have a formalized approach to developing managerial skills, and training tended to be conducted in an *ad hoc* and reactive way... Even when structured training was available, financial constraints and releasing managers often prevented access to this type of training.

The study also interviewed senior managers and the HR director in these five Acute Hospital Trusts. None of the senior managers questioned the clinical ability of their ward managers, but there was a widespread perception that some lacked the necessary skills and competencies in people management.

> All trusts admitted to selecting managers almost exclusively on their clinical ability and giving "management" skills a low priority while at the same time recognizing that a good clinician does not necessarily make a successful manager. Although there was awareness of the potential for role conflict, resource constraints and heavy workloads, few senior managers questioned the impact this might have on the ability of ward managers to manage effectively.

> (Hutchinson and Purcell 2010: 369–70).

While ward managers frequently complained of lack of support from senior managers, this was not recognized by the senior managers themselves. In their view, the HR function provided adequate advice and guidance. This view was certainly not shared by the ward managers. Senior managers did not see the problems ward managers had as systemic but, by implication, it was the fault of the managers themselves. They often complained that the ward managers "went native" by putting the needs of their ward and their staff ahead of a requirement to operate for the corporate interests of the Trust as a whole.

Improving the Capacity of Line Managers to Reduce and Manage Workplace Conflict

Line managers have conflicting roles, and priority is nearly always given not to people management but to production or service, quality, and quantity, meeting targets, responding to crises, and satisfying senior management, who often have their own targets. In these circumstances advice on how to improve line managers' capability and conduct in managing workplace conflict can easily slip into "optimistic aspirations" or unrealistic, somewhat pious, exhortations of what should be done as exemplars of best practice. The issue of line managers' handling of workplace conflict is best understood not as an individual characteristic (some managers are better than others) but deriving from organizational attributes. These concern questions about culture as in "a culture of bullying," excessive pressure and stress, problems with procedures and rules, lack of training, poor selection criteria, and most obviously a lack of trust at all levels of the firm. Evidence of poor management and the experience of workplace conflict is not widespread, with less than half of employees reporting ill-treatment. It is appropriate now to focus on the sort of behaviors, systems, and procedures that well-managed firms appear to be able to adopt. The one caveat in doing so is the need to bear in mind that it is often hard to change organizational behavior. "Path dependency" means that certain styles of behavior becomes embedded, and unless a major shock is experienced, it is very difficult to change. One need only look at banks and finance companies to see how a fixation on bonuses linked to product innovation and selling is proving so hard to eradicate despite widespread condemnation of this form of short-termism. The example given above of the financial services company is not unusual (see the *Guardian*, 3 November 2012 for an example of the high street bank, NatWest, selling payment protection insurance policies in the early 2000s).

Trust is fundamental in the line manager–employee relationship since in the exchange relationship trusting behavior by the manager comes to be reciprocated by commitment and engagement by the employee (Boxall and Purcell, 2011: 224). As we have seen, this "leader–member exchange" is not restricted to the individual relationship but spills over into wider organizational commitment since, for many, their line managers are the embodiment of the organization. To trust is to take a risk in the behavior of others and to expose yourself to a form of dependency on others. "It requires hope for the future and expectations of the conduct of others" (Purcell, 2012: 10). Research sponsored by the CIPD identifies four types of trusting behavior of "leaders," like line managers. There is a requirement to be able to do the right thing or best thing, that is, to be recognized as having competence and ability. There is a need is to be guided by some principles of benevolence or well-meaning especially in treating others with respect, and to have integrity and honesty. There is also a requirement to be predictable (Searle, Hope-Hailey, Dietz, 2012). It is trust that provides the linkage with employees' perceptions of organizational justice: procedural, distributive, interactional, and informational. An occupational analysis of factors associated with high levels of organizational commitment by Purcell and his colleagues (2009: 102), using WERS data, found that "trust in management" was the dominant factor for each of the eight major occupational groups studied. Interactional justice most obviously concerns line managers since it rests on the way line managers tell their staff about decisions. It is sometimes included within procedural justice that "concerns the way in which decisions are taken, information collected, the openness of the process and the extent to which people's views are taken into account" (Purcell, 2012: 9). Research on employee engagement shows that procedural justice judgments play a major role in shaping people's reactions to their personal experience (Tyler and Blader, 2003: 350). The focus on procedural justice also draws attention to the way managers manage: the way they treat people with respect, the transparency of their decisions and their openness to employee views and voice.

Whitener et al. (1998: 516) define managerial trustworthy behavior as:

> volitional actions and interactions performed by managers that are necessary though not sufficient to engender employees' trust in them...managers initiate and build relationships by engaging in trustworthy behaviour as a means of providing employees with social rewards....Managers who engage in this behaviour will increase the likelihood that employees will reciprocate and trust them.

Five categories of behavior are identified (Whitener et al., 1998: 516–18) as required for the generation of trust. These are behavioral consistency, behavioral integrity (telling the truth and keeping promises), communication (timely, accurate information, explanations for decisions and openness), demonstration of concern (consideration for needs, protecting employee interests, refraining from exploiting others).

The final item is "sharing delegation and control," which raises some fundamental issues about the nature of management. The authors note that actions to delegate and share control "may conflict with a manager's ability to directly control an employee's actions" (Whitener et al., 1998: 518). There is considerable research evidence that shows that levels of job satisfaction and organizational commitment are associated with job autonomy and job challenge, while the antithesis of routine, closely controlled and monitored work is linked with work-related stress. To have job autonomy in the performance of challenging work nearly always requires the manager to delegate some control and trust the person to perform without close surveillance. This would then also require some form of participation in decisions concerning the job. Whitener et al. (1998: 517) summarize the evidence.

> The extent to which managers involve employees influences the development of trust. Driscoll (1978) has found that employees' trust is higher when they are satisfied with their level of participation in decisions; it is also higher when employees can determine their work roles (Deci, Connell and Ryan 1989).... When managers share control, they demonstrate significant trust in and respect for their employees (Rosen and Jerdee 1977).

There are strong links to employee engagement, especially engagement with the job. "Job engagement is associated with a sustainable workload, feelings of choice and control, appropriate recognition and reward, a supportive work community, fairness and justice and meaningful and valued work" (Saks, 2006: 603). For Saks the policy implications that flow from this diagnosis are "training for line managers and job design interventions" to build autonomy, challenge, and variety.

Not all jobs, nor all work settings, allow employees to have high autonomy and delegated authority. The critical issue seems to be the extent to which the organization requires high control and close monitoring of employees. This may derive from the nature of the work itself but it is more likely to be the product of choices, often at the subconscious level, that senior and line managers make about work organization and the managerial role. This would include choices made in HR, or by HR managers, concerning the nature of rewards and monitoring of employees at work. As Edwards (2005: 385) puts it, "workplace relations turn on the relationship between control and autonomy." Studies in call centers have shown how close surveillance of employees is more likely at the lower-skilled end where calls are of short duration, measured in seconds. The contrast is with business-to-business call centers where the call duration is up to the employee, and often lasts for twenty minutes. Employees are measured on outcomes, like sales, with only light surveillance of their conduct (Batt, 2002). This is an illustration that "it is increasingly common for organizations to combine autonomy in the conduct of tasks with clear performance standards for their completion" (Edwards, 2005: 385). At the lower end of call centers, taking mainly inbound, short duration, transactional calls, job autonomy is low and management control is high, combining to produce a hire and fire, formal discipline workplace, for as long as there is a ready labor supply. However, the higher end of long duration, outbound calls with customer service officers having higher levels of education, meets the mix of job autonomy with an emphasis on performance standards.

This has led Edwards and his colleagues (Collinson, Rees, and Edwards, 1998) to propose the "disciplined worker hypothesis." The paradox seemed to be that workers who were closely monitored as part of a quality program, as in "total quality management," were more likely to accept "the discipline and purpose of a quality management system and the performance standards that go with it" (Collinson, Rees, and Edwards,

1998: 387). The system of management was seen to be legitimate and performance measures were fair and objective. In other words, questions of relative autonomy and participation in decision-making, heralding higher levels of trust and lower levels of workplace conflict, do not require management by exception, where the manager leaves the employee alone and only intervenes when asked to in order to resolve a problem. Managing in circumstances of strong performance controls but mixed with high levels of individual autonomy can equally be associated with low levels of workplace conflict provided the manager is participative, provides information, shows respect, is consistent, and has integrity. It is no longer quite so straightforward to suggest, as Creed and Miles (1996) did, that "high control organizations, with a high degree of centralization and formalization and a primary focus on efficiency, will constrain or impede the development of trustworthy behaviour such as delegation and control" (cited by Whitener, 1998: 519).

Mutual trust between line managers and employees, and between line managers and their superiors, is a necessary prerequisite for successful conflict management since it is likely to reduce the level of conflict such as the type of unsatisfactory conduct recorded by the BWBS. The generation of trust is not, of itself, sufficient. There is a need for "due process." It has been noted, for example, that appraisal systems based on due process, such as adequate notice, fair hearing and judgments based on evidence, led to managers communicating more openly and allowing more employee participation. It also encouraged consistency toward all subordinates (Folger, Konovsky, and Cropanzano, 1992). However, it is well known that appraisals often do not take place. In very large organizations, such as the NHS, getting two-thirds of staff appraised is considered a success. The requirement is not just to have an effective "due process" based procedure for performance management as well as grievance and discipline, but for it be embedded as part of the way the organization performs. Roche and Teague (2012: 235) cite Rowe (1997) "who contends that conflict management systems must be embedded in line management and team management rather than based primarily in staff offices such as HR or a legal department." But this, as they suggest, is a very broad-brush statement. It is one thing "for nearly all the contributors to the theory of conflict management systems… to envisage that conflict management will… become embedded in organizational processes and thereby in the routine practice of management." But the evidence cited above would suggest that what ought to happen often does not. Much emphasis is placed on the need for training and for the manager's handling of workplace conflicts to be included within performance appraisals.

The approach of the UK government has been to link the use of alternative dispute resolution (ADR) procedures to the adoption of a revised Acas Code of Practice on Discipline and Grievance in 2010. This codifies due process principles in dealing with conflict between an employee and a manager through the use of disciplinary and grievance procedures. If a case subsequently comes to an employment tribunal the sum awarded can be increased or decreased by up to 20% if the Code has not been followed. The aim is for this to be an incentive for organizations to improve the handling of conflicts at the line manager level. In effect Acas, through its Code of Practice, is advocating a rights-based approach to conflict management. This classically involves a written, multi-step procedure where the issue can rise up the management hierarchy if not resolved lower down, but with emphasis given to seeking to resolve the matter at the earliest stage at the level of the immediate line manager.

Part of a rights-based approach is the right of an individual to be accompanied at a disciplinary or grievance hearing. Where unions are present, and especially where they are recognized, this will be a union officer or lay official like a shop steward. There is a particular irony in this. The presence of a union representative at a place of work is associated with higher levels of conflict being expressed and with lower levels of trust reported by both managers and employees. However, the conflicts expressed are more likely to be satisfactorily resolved (Bryson, 2004; Bryson and Freeman, 2007). Employee representation is an important feature of conflict management. The quality of the relationship between the line manager and the employee representative is important since it allows for informality around the edges of a formal procedure.

CONCLUSION

There would appear to be universal agreement that workplace conflict is best resolved early and as near as possible to the source of the problem. The involvement of senior managers, HR professionals, and, even worse, lawyers and other external parties, tends to polarize the issue and lead to defensive behavior especially if there is likelihood of the matter ending up in an employment tribunal or labor court. Early resolution places the responsibility for dealing with conflicts on line managers. It is curious, then, that research on line managers over many years has identified problems with their capability and competence in dealing with people management issues. The cumulative effect of a being promoted to a line manager because of technical competence, lack of training, an over-burdened job, conflicting roles and ambiguity, lack of support from senior management, performance targets that neglect people management issues, and often a strong inclination to avoid dealing with conflict, combine to significantly reduce managerial effectiveness. It is not surprising, given the pressures that many managers are under and the ubiquity of performance management systems, targets, and monitoring, that line managers often report stress. This contributes to the problem that line managers experience conflict in their relationships with senior staff and are often the cause of conflicts that they are responsible for handling. Cost pressures and time constraints in the recession add further to managerial workloads.

It is much too simplistic to blame line managers for these difficulties, as senior managers are prone to do. The evidence is of systemic failures and destructive organizational cultures and modes of behavior that can entrap the manager and make it very difficult to modify accepted patterns of behavior. It becomes hard to build personal relationships, especially when line managers often move from one position to another. Personal relationships take time to develop and are the bedrock of trust. It is trust that reduces the probability of conflict erupting while making its resolution easier when it does occur. Where there is trust it is also much easier for due process to take place so that conflict is handled in a transparent way and not buried or ignored.

Organizations vary considerably in the way people management becomes a priority or is relegated to an administrative necessity. All organizations have cultures that, at their simplest, are talked about as "the way we do things here." It is these priorities, cultures, and the business goals they support that set the parameters for line managers. There is a great deal more that employers, and governments, could do to improve line management capabilities in people management in general and conflict management in particular, but it will never be sufficient until rather deeper changes at the organizational level are embedded to help build trust and due process.

REFERENCES

Acas, 2010. "Building Employee Engagement." Policy discussion paper. London, Acas.

Batt, R. 2002. "Managing Customer Services, Human Resource Practices, Quit Rates, and Sales Growth." *Academy of Management Journal*, 45: 587–97.

Boxall, P. and Purcell, J. 2011. *Strategy and Human Resource Management*. 3rd edn. Basingstoke: Palgrave.

Bryson, A. 2004. "Managerial Responsiveness to Union and Non-union Worker Voice in Britain," *Industrial Relations*, 43(1): 213–41.

Bryson, A. and Freeman, R. 2007. "What Voice do British Workers Want?" In R. Freeman, P. Boxall, and P. Haynes (eds) *What Workers' Say: Employee Voice in the Anglo-American Workplace*. Ithaca, NY: Cornell University Press.

Child, J. and Partridge, B. 1972. *The Lost Managers: Supervisors in Industry and Society*. Cambridge: Cambridge University Press.

CIPD 2011. "*Employee Outlook*." Part of the CIPD outlook series. London: CIPD.

CIPD 2012. *Employee Outlook*. Autumn. London: CIPD.

Collinson, T., Rees, C., and Edwards, P. 1998. "Involving Employees in Total Quality Management." *DTI Employment Relations Research Series 1*. London: DTI.

Creed, W. and Miles, R. 1996. "Trust in Organizations: A Conceptual Framework Linking Organizational Forms, Managerial Philosophies, and the Opportunity Costs of Controls." In R. Krammer and T. Tyler (eds), *Trust in Organizations: Frontiers of Theory and Research*. Thousand Oaks, CA: Sage, 16–38.

Deci, E., Connell, J., and Ryan, R. 1989. "Self-determination in a Work Organization." *Journal of Applied Psychology*, 74: 580–90.

Driscoll, J. 1978. "Trust and Participation in Organizational Decision Making as Predictors of Satisfaction." *Academy of Management Journal*, 21: 44–56.

Dunn, C. and Wilkinson, A. 2002. "Wish You Were Here: Managing Absence." *Personnel Review*, 31(2): 228–46.

Edwards, P. 2005. "Discipline and Attendance: the Murky Aspect of People Management." In S. Bach (ed.), *Managing Human Resources: Personnel Management in Transition*. 4th edn. Oxford: Blackwell, 375–97.

Edwards, P. 2012. "Employment Rights in Small Firms." In L. Dickens (ed.), *Making Employment Rights Effective: Issues of Enforcement and Compliance*. Oxford: Hart Publishing, 139–58.

Fevre, R. and Lewis, D. 2012. "Why Ill-treatment at Work is So Hard to Change." *People Management*, Jun., 30–5.

Fevre, R., Lewis, D., Robinson, A., and Jones, T. 2011a. *Insight into Ill-treatment in the Workplace: Patterns, Causes and Solutions*. Cardiff School of Social Sciences <http://tinyurl.com/socsi-insight>.

Fevre, R., Robinson, A., Jones, T., and Lewis, D. 2011b. "Researching Workplace Bullying: The Benefits of Taking an Integrated Approach." *International Journal of Social Research Methodology*, 13(1): 71–85.

Folger, R., Konovsky, M., and Cropanzano, R. 1992. "A Due Process Metaphor for Performance Appraisal." In B. Shaw and L. Cummings (eds) *Research in Organizational Behaviour*, 14: 129–77. Englewood Cliffs, NJ: Prentice-Hall.

Hales, C. 2005. "Rooted in Supervision, Branching into Management: Continuity and Change in the Role of the Front-line Manager." *Journal of Management Studies*, 42: 471–506.

Harris, L. 2005. "Employment Law and Human Resourcing Strategies." In J. Leopold, L. Harris, and T. Watson (eds), *The Strategic Management of Human Resources*. Harlow: Pearson Education.

Hirschman, A. 1970. *Exit, Voice, and Loyalty: Responses to Decline in Firms, Organizations and States*. Boston MA: Harvard University Press.

Hodson, R. 2001. *Dignity at Work*. Cambridge: Cambridge University Press.

Hutchinson, S. and Purcell, J. 2010. "Managing Ward Managers for Roles in HRM in the NHS: Overworked and Under-resourced." *Human Resource Management Journal*, 20(4): 339–76.

Jones, T., Robinson, A., Fevre, R., and Lewis, D. 2010. "Workplace Assaults in Britain: Understanding the Influence of Individual and Workplace Characteristics." *British Journal of Criminology*, 51: 159–78.

Kersley, B., Alpin, C., Forth, J., Bryson, A., Bewley, H., Dix, G., and Oxenbridge, S. 2006. *Inside the Workplace: Findings from the 2004 Workplace Employment Relations Survey*. London: Routledge.

McGovern, F., Gratton, L., Hope-Hailey, V., Stiles, P., and Truss, K. 1997. "Human Resource Management on the Line?" *Human Resource Management Journal*, 7(1): 12–29.

Meyer, J. and Allen, N. 1991. "A Three-component Conceptualisation of Organizational Commitment." *Human Resource Management Review*, 1: 61–98.

Podro, S. 2010. "Riding Out the Storm: Managing Conflict in the Recession and Beyond." *Acas Discussion Paper*. London: Acas.

Purcell, J. 2012. "The Limits and Possibilities of Employee Engagement." *Warwick Papers in Industrial Relations Number 96*. Coventry: Industrial Relations Research Unit, University of Warwick.

Purcell, J. and Hutchinson, S. 2007. "Front-line Managers as Agents in the HRM-performance Causal Chain: Theory, Analysis and Evidence." *Human Resource Management Journal*, 17: 3–20.

Purcell, J., Kinnie, N., Swart, J., Rayton, B., and Hutchinson, S. 2009. *People Management and Performance*. London: Routledge.

Roche, W. and Teague, P. 2012. "Do Conflict Management Systems Matter?" *Human Resource Management*, 51(2): 231–58.

Rosen, B. and Jerdee, T. 1977. "Influences of Subordinate Characteristics on Trust and Use of Participative Decision Strategies in a Management Simulation." *Journal of Applied Psychology*, 62: 628–31.

Rowe, M. 1997. "Dispute Resolution in the Non-union Environment: An Evolution toward Integrated Systems for Conflict Management?" In S. Gleason (ed.), *Frontiers in Dispute Resolution in Labor Relations and Human Resources*, 77–106. East Lansing, MI: Michigan State University Press.

Saks, A. 2006. "Antecedents and Consequences of Engagement." *Journal of Managerial Psychology*, 21(7): 600–19.

Sanders, D. 2012. "Placing Trust in Employee Engagement." *Employment Relations Comment*, Nov. London: Acas.

Searle, R., Hope-Hailey, V., and Dietz, G. 2012. *Where has All the Trust Gone?* London: CIPD.

Teague, P. and Roche, W. 2012. "Line Managers and the Management of Workplace Conflict: Evidence from Ireland." *Human Resource Management Journal*, 22(3): 235–51.

Truss, K. 2001. "Complexities and Controversies in Linking HRM with Organizational Outcomes." *Journal of Management Studies*, 38: 1121–49.

Tyler, T. and Blader, S. 2003. "The Group Engagement Model: Procedural Justice, Social Identity, and Cooperative Behaviour." *Personality and Social Psychology Review*, 7(4): 349–61.

Uhl-Bien, M., Graen, G., and Scandura, T. 2000. "Indicators of Leader–member Exchange (LMX) for Strategic Human Resource Management Systems." *Research in Personnel and Human Resources Management*, 18: 137–85.

Whitener, E., Brodt, S., Korsgaard, M. A., and Werner, J. 1998. "Managers as Initiators of Trust: An Exchange Relationship Framework for Understanding Managerial Trustworthy Behaviour." *Academy of Management Review*, 23(3): 513–30.

CHAPTER 12

CONFLICT MANAGEMENT SYSTEMS

WILLIAM K. ROCHE AND PAUL TEAGUE

INTRODUCTION

ONE of the most influential concepts in the recent literature on conflict management is that of conflict management systems comprising multiple, complementary conflict management practices, pivoted mainly around alternative dispute resolution practices concerned to promote "interest-based" approaches to conflict resolution. The literature on this important concept remains primarily prescriptive, although some empirical work has sought to establish the incidence and outcomes of conflict management systems. This chapter reviews the concept of conflict management systems, considers the evidence available on the antecedents and incidence of such systems, and considers the outcomes associated with the conflict management systems paradigm. The chapter concludes by presenting the authors' assessment of current priorities in the study of conflict management systems.

THE FEATURES OF CONFLICT MANAGEMENT SYSTEMS

Since the 1980s an influential strand in the literature on conflict management in organizations has pointed to the supposed superior features and effects of conflict management systems. An earlier strand of the conflict resolution literature had canvassed the idea of a systems theory. But this early version of systems theory was concerned with the operation and effects of classical grievance procedures in unionized firms, taking systematic account of external and internal influences on their operation and outcomes (Lewin, 1999). The newer theory of conflict management systems is distinct in proposing a series of generic design principles for conflict management in unionized and non-union firms that depart significantly from classical approaches to managing conflict. Indeed Lipsky and his colleagues (2003: 5) refer to conflict management systems as a "new paradigm for organizations." Bingham and Chachere (1999: 95) refer to the area as a "new field of practice and scholarly inquiry," and Costantino and Sickles Merchant (1996: xiv) make reference in the same context to the emergence of "next generation conflict management systems."

The core claims of conflict management systems theory were originally developed in Ury, Bret and Goldberg's 1988 text (reissued in 1993), *Getting Disputes Resolved: Designing Systems to Cut the Costs of Conflict*—a book described by subsequent contributors as "revolutionary" (Costantino and Sickles Merchant, 1996: 44). Much of the subsequent literature can be seen as a series of attempts to refine and develop this basic paradigm.

Work by Ury et al. on the development of the conflict management systems concept can be seen as an extension of Ury's earlier highly influential work on the theory of "principled negotiation" and the associated idea of interest-based approaches to conflict resolution (Ury and Fisher, 1981). A further feature of the work of Ury and his colleagues on conflict management systems is the degree to which the ideas proposed were based on the authors' experience in reforming dispute resolution systems in the US coal mining industry, a unionized sector with a tradition of adversarial industrial relations. Subsequent developments and refinements to the conflict management systems concept tended to have rather little to say about collective disputes or working with trade unions.

In *Getting Disputes Resolved*, Ury et al. (1993: ch. 1) proposed a theory of "dispute systems design" based on a distinction between three primary methods of dispute resolution and six principles for establishing dispute resolution procedures. With respect to the three primary methods, disputes, they suggested, may be handled through "power-based methods," such as strikes, lockouts, or other coercive sanctions. They may be handled through "rights-based methods," where the parties seek a resolution on the basis of rules or principles, such as those set down in contracts, collective agreements, or in company policies, in legislation enshrining employment rights, or in social norms and conventions. Examples of these methods are provided by the operation of traditional grievance procedures, arbitration, and the adjudication of grievances and disputes by the civil courts or by administrative agencies. Disputes may also be addressed on the basis of "interest-based methods," where the parties seek to identify and accommodate their underlying needs or "interests" through joint problem solving and associated techniques for arriving at mutually satisfactory outcomes. An interest-based approach involves practices such as mediation, facilitation, and joint problem solving.

Ury et al. advocate the primacy of interest-based over other methods of managing workplace conflict on the grounds that interest-based methods are less costly and more satisfactory or versatile than either rights-based or power-based methods by being capable of addressing more of the concerns of disputants and at lower cost (Ury et al., 1993: ch. 1). The overall cost of disputes is seen to comprise a series of interrelated elements that are seen to co-vary: transaction costs (time, money, and opportunity costs arising from disputes), satisfaction with conflict outcomes, effects on relationships between the parties in dispute, and the likelihood of conflict recurring. However, it is recognized that interest-based methods may not always be optimal or effective. For example, rights- or power-based approaches may be required to bring a party to the negotiating table and to engender a willingness to proceed on an interest-based basis. Parties may have such divergent perceptions of rights or power resources that interest-based approaches are not feasible. Interests may be seen to be so divergent that only other methods of resolving disputes are countenanced, and where matters of public interest may be involved in disputes, only rights-based adjudication can serve a societal interest in establishing the outcome (Ury et al., 1993: 15–17). As a result, dispute resolution systems need to be designed to provide rights-based and power-based methods as "backups" to interest-based methods and for these to be designed to involve the lowest costs possible.

Here the distinction between three primary dispute resolution methods links forward to Ury et al.'s six principles for designing and operating dispute resolution procedures (1993: ch. 3). The first principle involves a preference for dispute management that puts the emphasis on interests and associated dispute resolution practices and for settling grievances and disputes wherever possible informally and at the lowest possible level. This principle informs the creation of multi-step dispute resolution procedures, with "multiple points of entry" for parties with a grievance, reinforced by confidence on the part of grievants or disputants that they will not suffer retaliation. It also implies that managers must be delegated the authority to resolve conflict and that provision should be made for informal as well as formal contacts between the parties to a grievance or dispute. Those involved in dispute resolution should also be trained and skilled in the use of interest-based methods such as mediation (Ury et al., 1993: 43–47).

The second principle involves the provision of so-called "loopbacks," whereby the parties to a grievance or dispute are not constrained to move in a linear fashion through the typical steps in a traditional formal dispute resolution system, but can opt to return from rights-based or power-based methods to interest-based or more informal methods. Loopbacks can be facilitated by information provision and fact finding and by such techniques as "advisory arbitration" or "mini-trials." Loopbacks from power-based methods comprise mechanisms such as "cooling off periods" and the provision of additional mediation or conciliation prior to power being exercised.

The third and related principle involves the provision of "low-cost" rights- and power-based "backups" to a primarily interest-oriented process. These might include various forms of arbitration, short work stoppages or "symbolic strikes," and "rules of prudence" focused on limiting the cost and damage of using power-based methods.

The fourth principle of conflict management systems design involves consultation with affected parties in designing dispute resolution processes and systems and the use of post-dispute feedback to bring about ongoing improvement in processes and systems.

The fifth principle echoes classical dispute resolution processes in proposing that dispute resolution processes be arranged in a "low-to-high-cost sequence" involving the use of methods such as negotiation, mediation, or conciliation before arbitration or other forms of adjudication or prior to contests of power. Here, however, the sequence also involves harnessing interest-based methods before the alternatives are brought into use.

The sixth principle advocates finding ways of fostering the motivation, skills, and resources necessary to support the effective use of the procedures and processes put in place in a conflict management system.

Ury et al.'s model is generic in the sense that it covers the design of conflict management or dispute resolution systems as they might apply to grievances between individuals and their managers, between unions and employers, and between groups of employees and management outside collective bargaining. Indeed the text is peppered with references to disputes of other kinds in schools and families, between nations, between corporations, and between corporations and their customers or clients. The theory overlaps in important ways with classical approaches and procedures for conflict management; for example, in advocating formal multi-step procedures, in emphasizing the informal resolution of conflict at the lowest organizational level, and in endorsing established mechanisms such as mediation, arbitration, cooling-off periods and the like. The ways in which the theory departs from classical approaches to managing grievances and disputes also bear emphasis. First, interest-based methods and associated ADR practices are assigned primacy. Second, the theory departs from the linear, step-wise approach to conflict management associated with classical practice. In classical dispute or grievance procedures conflict was first expected to be handled directly and informally between the disputants, and then, if it proved incapable of resolution at this level, to be moved onwards or upwards in a linear manner through successive stages of procedure involving increased investments of time and expertise by progressively higher levels of management. In unionized firms, where individual grievances or collective disputes have arisen, the same procedures usually also involved progressively more senior union representatives. In either non-union or unionized firms, traditional grievance and dispute resolution might perhaps culminate in arbitration or some related method of adjudication, or possibly in litigation. In contrast, in conflict management systems, disputants may opt to address their concerns through interest-based options or be permitted to move forward between these and rights-based options, or to loop back from rights-based to interest-based options in their search for an effective way, or series of ways, of resolving their disagreement. Finally, stakeholders in conflict management systems are expected to be formally involved in the design and evaluation of dispute resolution processes in order to ensure that these are seen to be legitimate, fair, and worthy of confidence on the part of all organizational stakeholders. In Ury et al.'s study the conflict management system was designed primarily to change aspects of the operation of the grievance procedure under the collective bargaining contract (Ury et al., 1993: chs 5–7). Other innovations, such as the use of "preventive communication" surrounding impending changes in working conditions, were also introduced. However, the parties directly involved in the coal mines appear not to have countenanced the extension of the principles behind conflict management systems to conflict in general or to the negotiation or renewal of collective agreements.

Rowe (1997) and also Rowe and Bendersky (2003) elaborated on aspects of this model primarily in the context of the management of conflict involving individuals or involving groups outside the collective bargaining process. Conflict management systems, it was contended, should be open to all categories of employees and encompass virtually any concern of employees, whether as individuals or as members of teams (Rowe, 1997: 88). Rowe advocates the provision of multiple interest-based and rights-based options, less in accordance with the principle of the low-cost to high-cost rankings of different options, as proposed by Ury et al., than on the grounds that employees have different preferences with respect to conflict resolution that needed to be accommodated by multiple and different processes and options. In this way the principle of "redundant resources" ought to be enshrined in the design of conflict management systems by providing for multiple and overlapping ways of resolving conflict (Rowe, 1997: 83–86). Like Ury et al., Rowe believes that most employees, given the choice, would opt for interest-based options for resolving workplace problems.

Apart from providing for "loopback" options of the kind proposed by Ury et al., and for "loop forward" options, which allow persons involved in conflict to skip steps or levels in a procedure, Rowe stresses the importance of allowing for "parallel options" wherein the same problem might be addressed simultaneously through different processes (1997: 88; Rowe and Bendersky, 2003: 126–8). "Multiple access points" or "fair gatekeepers" to processes are also advocated—"ombudspersons" being seen as among the pivotal gatekeepers in conflict management systems (Rowe, 1997: 88). Specialists like ombudspersons could also play "multiple roles": acting as mediators prior to problems being considered by peer review panels, while also coordinating these panels. However, mediation could also be provided by external and neutral "fact-finders" otherwise also engaged to provide informational or technical assistance to the parties involved in a dispute or grievance (Rowe, 1997: 95). Finally, echoing Ury et al., Rowe emphasizes the importance of involving organizational stakeholders in the design, oversight, monitoring, and evaluation of the system (1997: 88 and 95).

Costantino and Sickles Merchant (1996: 44) in the influential text *Designing Conflict Management Systems*, openly acknowledge their indebtedness to Ury et al., but claim to revise and extend conflict management systems theory through the application of organizational development principles. They claim that pre-existing theory had failed adequately to address the underlying causes of conflict and emphasize the importance of providing for "preventive ADR options," such as consensus building, partnership, and training in joint problem solving (1996: 38–9). According to Costantino and Sickles Merchant "organizational dynamics" had also been inadequately considered by earlier contributors, including the need to make provision for "incentive and reward structures" to support conflict management systems (1996: 50). These include rewards like recognition, involvement, and participation in the design of systems—such participation is seen as a reward in its own right—and performance pay, linked to managers' effectiveness in handling ADR (1996: ch. 11). More generally, Costantino and Sickles Merchant claim that the systematic involvement of organizational stakeholders, through the application of "interest-based conflict management design principles," should be provided for in the creation of dispute resolution systems, in their ongoing evaluation and continuous improvement (1996: 53–9).

Some of these ideas were present, though perhaps in a more muted way, in Ury et al. and they again appear in Slaikeu and Hasson (1998). The key refinement here is a definition of best-practice systems design that appears to envisage a typical but nonmandatory linear sequence in dispute resolution beginning with "individual initiative," followed by negotiation, mediation, an appeal to "higher authority," via a rights-based option, and failing all these, resort to force or power (Slaikeu and Hasson, 1998: 47 and see also Conbere, 2001: 222–3). Lipsky et al. (2003) in another canonical text *Emerging Systems for Managing Workplace Conflict*, again echo and endorse the received postulates of earlier contributors. The concept of "multiple access points" is extended to include the supervisors, trade union stewards, workplace leaders, and others, who may act as gatekeepers facilitating individuals or groups in accessing the multiple options of the conflict management system (2003: 14). Lipsky et al. also develop Rowe's original emphasis on providing for fairness in conflict management systems by stressing the importance of allowing people to be accompanied by an ally or advocate when engaged in seeking a solution to a problem or redress for a grievance. To this principle Lipsky et al. add other principles of a "fair conflict management system" that include a right to privacy and confidentiality, the "neutrality of neutrals" (mediators, arbitrators, fact-finders, etc.) and the prohibition of reprisal or retaliation (2003: 18). "Support structures" for conflict management systems are conceived to be a critical facet of the overall "organizational infrastructure" in firms practicing conflict management. While this concept is elaborated in general terms, the provision of training in conflict management skills and the accountability of managers for conflict management, through the routine use of such mechanisms as performance management, are seen as facets of a supportive "organizational infrastructure" (Lipsky et al., 2003: 17–19). Some contributors seek to distinguish between conflict management systems and "integrated conflict management systems," the basis of the distinction being that integrated conflict management systems seek to build effective conflict management into an organization's routine operations, promoting competence in dealing with conflict throughout the organization (Society of Professionals in Dispute Resolution, 2001: 8–9; Lipsky and Seeber, 2006: 372–3.)

Standard desiderata for the design of conflict management systems stress the importance of providing for fairness, particularly procedural fairness. Conflict management systems that are considered procedurally fair normally exhibit two features. One is that all aspects of the system are pre-fixed and pre-announced. The other is that these arrangements are applied transparently and consistently. In practice, this usually involves a series of "due process" provisions such as the provision of fair, impartial and neutral fact-finding and adjudication, guarantees of confidentiality for grievants, sanctions against retaliation, allowing people pursuing grievances to be supported by persons or advocates of their choice, and sometimes building a right of appeal into conflict management systems. These due process principles are followed to varying degrees in practice (Lipsky and Seeber, 2006: 376–7).

INDIVIDUAL GRIEVANCES, CONFLICT IN GROUPS, AND COLLECTIVE BARGAINING

Ury et al.'s seminal text focused in the main on individuals pursuing grievances with trade union support through procedures established under collective bargaining contracts. Sometimes grievances had more general import, such as where the skills and qualifications for particular jobs were at issue. Subsequent refinements of the concept have tended to remain biased towards individual grievances, while mainly dealing with grievances that arise outside the ambit of the collective bargaining process or collectively agreed procedures. Sometimes grievance handling has been considered in the context of statutory employment rights. The individual bias of the literature has meant that the workings and outcomes of ombudspersons, mediators, review panels, arbitrators, and the like and their interrelations have received the greatest level of attention in the literature (see Rowe, 1997; Bingham and Chachere, 1999; Bingham, 2004; Lynch, 2001; and Bingham et al., 2009).

Conflict involving groups and conflict arising in the context of management-union relations and collective agreements have however been covered by some contributors. Several contributors have focused on what they see as the pivotal role of conflict management systems and associated ADR practices in team-based work settings (Bendersky, 2003: 643; Rowe and Bendersky, 2003: 121–2; Lipsky et al., 2004: 68). Bendersky claims that team-based forms of work organization, involving delegated authority, have given rise to new types of conflicts, as workers become more interdependent and also more involved in decision-making (2003: 643). Lipsky et al. claim that the delegation of responsibility for controlling work to teams has created pressure for delegating authority for preventing or resolving disputes to members of teams (2004: 68). The idea that ADR practices can support new forms of work organization based on team working is elaborated at length by Kaminski (1999), who considers ADR practices in the context of new forms of collective bargaining based on employer-union partnership arrangements and associated problem solving and interest-based bargaining techniques. Lynch (2001: 213) extends her discussion of conflict management systems to encompass innovations in relations between managers and unions. Cutcher-Gershenfeld's (2003) extended theoretical discussion of interest-based bargaining is also conducted in the context of the rise of ADR practices more generally.

McAndrew's studies of innovations in collective bargaining arrangements in the New Zealand police have shown how mediators had been empowered to act also as arbitrators (collective "med-arb") in the context where the use of interest-based bargaining has been increasing (McAndrew, 2003, 2012, this volume). Studies of collective bargaining and dispute resolution in the UK have also identified moves in some areas towards joint fact-finding initiatives and the use of external mediators or facilitators early in cycles of negotiating activity—so-called "assisted negotiations"—with a view to avoiding deadlock or triggering disputes (Kessler and Dickens, 2008; Dix et al., 2009).

Innovations of this kind—all pertaining in one way or another to the domain of group and collective bargaining conflict—have yet to be systematically considered in theoretical writings on conflict management systems. The parallels with innovations in individual grievance handling nevertheless appear strong. For example, in "assisted negotiations" facilitators or mediators may be used early in a negotiating cycle to prevent deadlock—thus inverting the traditional principle of resorting to third parties only when deadlock has already arisen. The use of mediators in the negotiating process, sometimes with the possibility that mediators may provide indicative or advisory arbitration decisions or even fully-fledged arbitration (the "med-arb" mechanism), again parallels developments in individual grievance handling in the conflict management systems literature. More generally, the use of interest-based bargaining represents a means of elevating interest-based processes and mechanisms over rights-based or power-based processes and mechanisms in collective bargaining. Notwithstanding these developments and innovations in collective bargaining and associated dispute resolution procedures, the individual grievance handling bias of the literature on conflict management systems remains. The supposed affinity between the conflict management systems approach and team working, noted by several prominent contributors, remains relatively under-developed both theoretically and empirically, although Bendersky and Hays have been doing interesting work on conflict in groups and teams (see Bendersky and Hays, 2012). The new interest from the 1990s in interest-based bargaining and multiple parallel techniques for collective bargaining and conflict resolution still finds little resonance in texts on the conflict management systems approach.

MANAGERS AND CONFLICT MANAGEMENT SYSTEMS

As has been seen, the theory of conflict management systems envisages a series of specialist roles associated with specific conflict resolution options (ombudspersons, facilitators, mediators, fact-finders, arbitrators, etc.). These roles are pivotal to the use of practices and to the operation of mechanisms that exist outside the formal managerial and work processes of organizations. In this way these roles and their associated practices and mechanisms can be seen as involving a distinct organizational subsystem or architecture for conflict management in their own right. However, nearly all contributors in one way or another envisage that, to be effective, conflict management systems need to become embedded in mainstream organizational processes and systems and thereby in the routine practice of management. Ury et al. were clear from the start that effective conflict management systems required active sponsorship by senior managers, symbolized by their willingness routinely to engage with employees individually and collectively to listen to concerns and try to understand them. They were equally clear that for conflict management systems to function effectively, line managers and supervisors needed training in conflict handling, especially through interest-based techniques, and that performance management systems needed to take account of managers' proficiency in managing conflict and handling grievances (Ury et al, 1993: chs 5–7).

Curiously, what is envisaged of managers, especially line managers and supervisors, is often dealt with in very general or broad-brush terms in the subsequent literature. There is a tendency to equate management involvement with the "informal" phase of conflict management, where the parties deal with each other directly. This, however, seems unhelpful in that effective management engagement is also seen, as discussed, to require formal organizational systems that incentivize managers to resolve conflict, and because managers are also commonly expected to play a proactive role in conflict resolution and prevention.

Rowe (1997: 87) contends that conflict management systems must be "embedded in line management and team management rather than based primarily in staff offices such as HR or a legal department." Some contributors equate line involvement in conflict management with a "proactive approach" in which potential flashpoints are anticipated rather than simply made subject to "reactive" interventions (Rowe, 1997: 87; Lynch, 2001: 208–209; Lipsky et al., 2003: 18–19) Echoing and extending the long-established principle that disputes are best settled at the lowest possible level in organizations, Lipsky et al. (2003: 9) stress the need to spread the responsibility for conflict and its resolution to the "lowest level of the organization," which must encompass line managers and supervisors (as well as employees as potential grievants or disputants). Costantino and Sickles Merchant (1996: 130–1) articulate the same point as the "principle of subsidiarity" in designing conflict management systems: an injunction that disputes should be resolved at the lowest possible organizational level.

The literature repeats the need for training in appropriate conflict handling skills (Costantino and Sickles Merchant, 1996: ch. 8; Lewin, 1999: 144–5; Lipsky et al., 2003: 14–19). Lynch observes that an "integrated system" gives managers the skills to resolve conflict and also holds them accountable for doing so (2001: 212). Conbere (2001: 233) goes considerably further in considering whether investment in line management training may be more significant with respect to positive outcomes than the formal conflict management mechanisms that preoccupy the literature on conflict management systems. What might be described as a "proto-systems" classic, Ewing's *Justice on the Job* (1989) considers line managers and supervisors as the most significant influence on the effectiveness of conflict management and dispute resolution. This view is conveyed by a figure representing a "system for complaint resolution" as a triangle in which complaint handling by supervisors makes up the greatest amount of the area enclosed by the sides, while the complaint-handling activities of employee relations managers and other conflict resolution specialists (investigators, tribunal members, etc.) represent a relatively small area enclosed within the apex of the triangle (Ewing, 1989: 6).

In conclusion, line managers and front-line managers or supervisors are commonly regarded as key actors and sometimes the primary management actors in conflict management systems. Effective line management engagement is seen to include anticipating and precluding conflict, being formally capable of resolving disputes directly, being in receipt of training in conflict management and being held accountable for performance.

SYSTEMS EFFECTS AND COMPLEMENTARITIES

Here the focus is on empirical research testing aspects of the conflict management systems theoretical and prescriptive literature, mindful that related bodies of research, some reported elsewhere in this volume, deal with the effects of various component practices associated with conflict management systems, for example non-union grievance systems, mediation or organizational ombudsmen.

Why should "systems" of conflict management practices be expected to have superior outcomes to either traditional approaches to dispute resolution (built primarily around rights-based and power-based methods) or to more ad hoc and limited combinations of power-based, rights-based, and interest-based mechanisms? The hypothesized systems effects of conflict management systems are handled in different ways in the literature and with lesser or greater degrees of explicitness and theoretical formality. For some contributors the idea of a system is used in little more than a metaphorical way to denote obvious interrelationships between different conflict management practices (for example in Costantino and Sickles Merchant, 1996: 21–6). For Ury et al. (1993) the fundamental principle or mechanism involved in the effectiveness of conflict management systems is the substitution of low-cost for high-cost methods of dispute resolution—where cost is understood in the multidimensional sense outlined above—conflict management practices are arrayed in a low-to-high-cost sequence, and they expand interest-based options at all levels of procedures. For others the underlying premise appears to be that systems involving more interest-based conflict management practices are superior to systems with fewer, provided that they coexist with rights-based and low-cost power-based fallbacks. The key premise here is that systems, with built-in redundancy, work effectively by catering for different preferences on the part of grievants and disputants regarding the means for resolving disputes and the appropriateness of alternative methods for addressing different issues (Rowe, 1997).

For yet other contributors, the availability of conflict management options of different kinds in a system may have distinctive effects because each type of practice is rendered more effective by the presence in the system of other types of practices. Thus Conbere contends (2001: 231) that a "law of interaction" arises in conflict management systems whereby a "conflict management system involves cross-dependencies or synergies between different units in the system" (Conbere, 2001). This basic idea is developed most fully and formally in Bendersky's "complementarities model" of conflict management systems (Bendersky, 2003, 2007). Bendersky's direct focus is on the effects of what she terms "dispute resolution systems" on employees' attitudes and behavior: attitudes with respect to conflict, reducing "conflict avoidance" behavior and increasing direct efforts to resolve conflicts. She adds to the established distinction between rights-based and interest-based processes, the concept of "negotiated processes" which relates to the direct efforts of disputants to resolve their differences (Bendersky, 2003: 643). Bendersky's contention is that when introduced in tandem, all three types of dispute resolution processes may complement each other in the specific sense that the effectiveness of each type is increased (or the weaknesses of each type are mitigated) by the presence in the system of the other types. Important also, she contends, is that disputes may not commonly align with each type of process because disputes may be multidimensional—some aspects suited to rights-based determination and others to negotiated or interest-based resolution. Here it is not so much "redundancy" and related properties of systems that matter as much as operating at least some interest-based, rights-based, and negotiated processes in tandem. A "complementary dispute resolution system" is defined in terms of the following features: 1) individuals can use any process to address any kind of conflict, 2) the same conflict can be addressed through multiple processes, and 3) the limitations of each type of process are mitigated through allowing for interactions with the other processes in the system (Bendersky, 2003: 647).

For Bendersky rights-based processes systematize and formalize dispute resolution and the parties become accountable for implementing settlements. Their limitation is that they are best suited to addressing violations in contracts. But this weakness can be mitigated by the presence of interest-based and negotiated processes. Interest-based processes promote information exchange between the parties in a dispute to reveal their underlying interests—through a process that may be facilitated by mediators—and this can encourage settlements. The potential limitations of these processes reside mostly in the possibility that mediators may not possess expertise on the issues in dispute and that some disputes may involve matters of public interest that some disputants may seek to have determined by rights-based and public forums. Negotiated processes are deemed to be the least costly and most efficient, but the danger with these arrangements is that power or skill differences between the parties in dispute may deter the weaker party from using them. These weaknesses may be mitigated by the availability of both rights-based and interest-based processes provided that the interactions between the two produce complementarity effects (Bendersky, 2003: 645-7). Dispute resolution systems where some design flaw prohibits the emergence of complementarities are termed "parallel dispute resolution systems" by Bendersky (2003: 644). Such systems are considered suboptimal and result in more limited outcomes. Below, when the outcomes of conflict management systems are discussed, the empirical evidence for complementarities or system effects of these kinds is reviewed.

Antecedents and Prevalence of Conflict Management Systems

Ury et al. (1993: 65–8) pointed to three antecedent conditions for the emergence of conflict management systems: crisis or "acute distress" in prevailing conflict management procedures, organizational insiders who may promote better ideas for managing conflict, and the establishment *de novo* of new approaches in organizations seeking to establish positive relations with their workforces. In the case of US coal mining during the 1980s, especially the case of Caney Creek Mine studied intensively by Ury and his colleagues, crisis and possible closure was the key triggering factor in the emergence of more systemic approaches to conflict resolution (Ury et al., 1993: ch. 6). In spite of the breakthrough at this and other mines and the parties' willingness to modify the industry-level procedural agreement on dispute resolution to permit the use of interest-based options, there was little evident diffusion of the new paradigm throughout the industry. Much of the subsequent literature addresses antecedents of conflict management systems in organizations in highly general terms and without making much of a distinction, or any at all, between influences on the uptake of conflict management systems and influences on the adoption of ADR practices in general. Lipsky et al. (2003: 68), Bendersky (2003: 643) and Rowe and Bendersky (2003: 121–2) all contend that the advent of conflict management systems and associated ADR practices reflects a move away from hierarchical organizations towards flatter team-based structures. Growing workforce diversity and the expanding body of employment rights are also seen as external pressures for the adoption of conflict management systems (Bendersky 2003: 643). Lipsky et al. highlight an explosion in litigation and increasing dissatisfaction with the US judicial system, including concern with excessive costs and delays, as important drivers of conflict management systems. Secular trends such as globalization, deregulation, declining union density, and the professionalization of human resource management are also identified as important antecedents (Lipsky et al., 2003: chs 2 and 3).

Lipsky et al. (2012) have conducted the first systematic empirical study of the antecedents of conflict management systems based on a survey of a sample of 360 Fortune 1,000 companies in the US in 2010–11. The survey uses a series of proxy measures to identify the existence of conflict management systems and to distinguish these from the use of ADR practices. The most comprehensive of these is whether firms possessed an office or function dedicated to the management and administration of the firms' dispute resolution system, or employed an ombudsman for handling disputes. The presence of either of these was regarded as indicating that firms had at least a key component of a conflict management system in place.

A quantitative analysis revealed that firms adopting a strategic conflict management orientation, focused on improving employment relationships, were more likely to have established a conflict management system, indicating for the authors that firms' decisions to adopt conflict management systems reflected strategic choices rather than responses only to push and pull factors in firms' external and internal environments (Lipsky et al., 2012: 33). The study also established that firms committed to ADR (as reflected in the proportion of their workforce involved in ADR programs) were more likely to have developed conflict management systems. Firms with a high commitment to corporate social responsibility and thus to advancing the interests of a broad set of external and internal stakeholders were also found to be more likely to have developed conflict management systems. Union status was not found to be a significant influence (Lipsky et al., 2012: 34).

In a study of practices for managing group and collective conflict in firms with fifty or more employees in Ireland, Roche and Teague (2011) identified a pattern through empirical modeling that resembled the sets of practices associated with conflict management systems. The adoption of this conflict management system was associated with a more general commitment to human resource management and a more proactive approach to conflict management than in firms adopting a traditional conflict management approach. The firms in question were also significantly more likely to be indigenous employers rather than multinationals (Roche and Teague, 2011).

Studies of organizations in different countries are also helpful in identifying some of the antecedents of conflict management systems. The conflict management system developed by the Royal Canadian Mounted Police (RCMP) during the 1990s was influential as a paradigm for leading-edge practice in conflict management. The RCMP system focused on interest-based grievance resolution, with rights-based backup procedures, in an organization where union representation was prohibited. Deukmedjian (2003: 323–5) discussed the background to the advent of the new conflict management system as reflecting the external ascendancy of neoliberalism, with its emphasis on self-government, self-determination, and new ways of addressing conflict in general. Within policing, the related development of community policing prioritized local partnerships and consultation and new problem-solving competencies on the part of police officers. With these new developments came an emphasis among senior officers on the use of extrajudicial processes and forms of ADR for resolving conflict both publicly and organizationally. These new approaches were championed by a new police commissioner. A pay freeze had also led demoralized police officers to overload the established grievance systems with complaints, building up further pressure for change and innovation.

In the New Zealand police force, where police officers are unionized but strikes are prohibited, McAndrew (2003) describes the emergence of a conflict management system combining information gathering and informal negotiation with mediation, indicative decisions by an arbitrator, and interest-based bargaining. The spur to these innovations was an economy-wide movement towards enterprise bargaining, resulting in police pay and conditions being determined in a different and more traditional

CONFLICT MANAGEMENT SYSTEMS 263

manner than the rest of the state sector. During cycles of difficult pay negotiations, the parties reached the view that collective bargaining and dispute resolution processes were unsatisfactory and confusing (McAndrew, 2003: 739). This shared sense of the inadequacy of the existing system spurred innovations in dispute resolution, the success of which led to further incremental innovation and the gradual emergence of a conflict management system for handling collective disputes.

From these two cases it appears that conflict management systems may develop when sets of antecedent conditions are found that may include disjunctures in the external environment, new internal pressures, shared dissatisfaction with the adequacy of existing procedures, and possibly also changes in organizational leadership.

Other studies taking account of developments in public agencies mention specific measures such as the effects in the US of the Clinton–Gore initiative to support partnership working on the adoption of conflict management systems in federal agencies, as well as the influence of the "reinventing government" movement on public management and governance (Costantinou and Sickles Merchant, 1996: 53). President Clinton's 1991 Executive Order on Labor-Management Partnerships required federal agencies to train employees in ADR and promoted an increase in its use (Administrative Conference of the United States, 1995: 22). A series of further administrative and regulatory developments also promoted the growing use of ADR and the development of conflict management systems. The Administrative Dispute Resolution Act 1990 mandated federal agencies to use ADR to resolve many types of disputes. The Equal Opportunities Commission also issued a series of regulations promoting and requiring the use of ADR by federal agencies in equal opportunities disputes (US Equal Opportunities Commission, 2004).

Turning to the prevalence of conflict management systems of different kinds, the international evidence here is limited and in various ways also problematic. The most detailed studies are those undertaken by Lipsky et al., based on surveys of Fortune 1,000 firms in the US in 1997 and 2010–11 (Lipsky et al., 2003, 2012). Lipsky et al. estimated that around 17% of these firms had adopted conflict management systems by 1997 (Lipsky et al., 2003: 126). In 2010–11—when a different method of estimation was used—this had risen to about 33% (Lipsky et al., 2012: 24–5). Some major US and international companies were prominent among firms with conflict management systems, including Coca-Cola, Macy's, General Electric, and Prudential.

The evidence available on other countries suggests that conflict management systems have yet to cross either the Atlantic or Pacific to any significant degree. In New Zealand conflict management procedures combining interest-based and rights-based options are becoming more common, shifting the emphasis away from a traditional reliance on rights-based options. Similar developments are evident in areas of the public service. The use of interest-based options in renewing collective bargaining contracts is more limited (see Rasmussen and Greenwood in this volume). In the case of Ireland, there appears to have been more experimentation with interest-based forms of ADR in group and collective bargaining disputes than in the handling of individual grievances (Roche and Teague, 2012a). In the Irish study that sought to portray different approaches to managing collective bargaining by deploying empirical modeling, Roche and Teague (2011) identified an approach, labeled a "hybrid ADR system," with some similarities to the conflict management systems model that was used by 5% of firms with fifty or more employees. A study of conflict management systems in eighty-three non-union multinational firms in Ireland reports modest usage of conflict management practices ranging from interest-based options (mediation and facilitation, hotlines, open-door policies, and ombudsmen) to rights-based options (peer and management review and arbitration). Some 25% of the firms surveyed are seen to use a wide range of these practices (Doherty and Teague, 2012: 8–9). The reasons given for the limited prevalence of conflict management systems include low demand for such systems and a concern by local subsidiary managers that initiating innovation in the area of conflict management would sit uneasily with parent firms' emphasis on harmonious HR policies and might thus compromise career progression (Doherty and Teague, 2012: 16–29).

In the case of public sector agencies, by the mid-1990s ADR was most widely used in US federal agencies for resolving workplace grievances and disputes. Among the areas now covered by ADR practices were the handling of individual grievances, the resolution of equal opportunities complaints, and the use of interest-based bargaining and assisted negotiations in industrial relations and collective bargaining (Administrative Conference of the United States, 1995: 22–4). A review of 25 years of development in ADR in federal agencies concluded that the increased prevalence of integrated conflict management systems combining interest-based and rights-based practices was one of the most significant developments in conflict management (Gadlin, 2012: 1–2). Conflict management systems are reported as being widespread across federal agencies (see US Office of Personnel Management, 2002). Conflict management systems have also been established in US-headquartered international agencies, such as the World Bank. Scandals and workforce grievances in the United Nations have promoted attempts to develop a more robust internal justice system in the agency, comprising an ombudsman, a series of ADR practices, and dispute tribunal (UN General Assembly, 2006: 12; Borger, 2012).

The durability of conflict management systems and related innovations is also an important issue and again limited data are available. Lipsky et al. (2012) suggest in the case of the US that, like ADR, practices in general conflict management systems are well embedded in major companies and seem set to remain a key feature of conflict resolution for the foreseeable future. In the case of the public sector the picture appears less clear. The influential RCMP conflict management system attenuated significantly following a promising start. The system appears to have lost momentum and organizational supports when new leaders took command and pursued different priorities to their predecessors. Assessments of innovations in the RCMP during the 1990s, including ADR, concluded that many had a limited institutional lifespan (see Murphy and McKenna, 2007: 15). Studies of the operation of the conflict management system found that it had low credibility, especially among those who had participated in it, and that it was impaired by problems of perceived partisanship and by poor training (Robichaud et al., 2008: 17–18). The grievance and ADR process was adjudged within the organization as of high importance but as failing to meet expectations (Duxbury, 2007: 26). A significant backlog of grievance cases again built up with long delays in grievance resolution. A major review of governance and culture in the RCMP reported that a high level of dissatisfaction existed with how people were managed. The length of time required for grievance resolution was criticized. While no explicit analysis was undertaken of the operation of ADR practices and their alignment with rights-based processes, the report advocated strengthening the independence and stature of rights-based tribunals for adjudicating on grievances and disciplinary issues (Government of Canada, 2007).

The med-arb model in the New Zealand police has also faced significant challenges but remains intact. The main challenges have arisen in the external political and economic environment. The government sought to regain control over police pay fixing, with its potential to set bargaining headlines, by offering police officers a limited right to undertake industrial action in return for the discontinuance of the conflict management systems model. The proposal was rejected by the police union. The advent of recession and fiscal consolidation have made for a more difficult pay bargaining environment, shifting the center of gravity in the model away from negotiation and mediation towards arbitration (McAndrew, 2012, and in this volume).

Outcomes of Conflict Management Systems

The mainly theoretical and prescriptive studies that dominate the literature commonly claim, sometimes using quite portentous language, that conflict management systems are significantly more effective than conventional dispute resolution practices. Few advance explicit or specific claims as to the expected outcomes and fewer still support these with empirical data (see esp. Costantino and Sickles Merchant, 1996; Rowe 1997; Lipsky et al., 2003). In the studies that do advance claims regarding outcomes it is possible to distinguish claims regarding outcomes relevant to employers, outcomes relevant to employees, and outcomes relevant to employees that are seen to mediate outcomes relevant to employers. Some of these claims are carried over from the general literature on ADR practices, or from research on specific ADR practices. Although conflict management systems are widespread across US federal agencies, independent studies of the operation and outcomes of federal conflict management systems remain few.

Employer Outcomes

Ury et al.'s classic (1988: chs 5–7) suggested that innovations in conflict management in some coal mines had reduced the incidence of wildcat strikes and arbitration. Conflict management systems have also been seen as contributing to improved productivity

(Bingham and Chachere, 1999: 98–9; Conbere, 2001: 233; Lynch, 2001: 214). They are claimed to have been instrumental as well in "dramatically reducing the costs of conflict" (Lynch, 2001: 214), in facilitating significant organizational change (Lynch, 2001: 214), in being associated with better employment relations (Bingham and Chachere, 1999: 98–9), and in also being associated with higher organizational morale and loyalty (Bingham and Chachere, 1999: 98–9). Links with lower absenteeism, lower voluntary turnover or "quit rates" are also posited (Bingham and Chachere, 1999: 99; Lipsky and Avgar, 2004: 191). Links are also sometimes made with union avoidance (Bingham and Chachere, 1999: 100; Lipsky and Avgar, 2004: 181).

In a test for complementarities in conflict management systems, Roche and Teague (2012b) report firm-level survey data for Ireland that examines whether conflict management systems positively affected a series of employer-relevant outcomes including relative labor productivity and capacity to handle change, rates of voluntary turnover and absence, and the employment relations climate. Various possible types of complementarities were tested for. These included whether more interest-based practices for managing individual and group conflicts were associated with the increasing marginal effectiveness of conflict management systems, provided that they were accompanied by rights-based options; whether the same sets of practices were more effective when each occurred in combination with the other (i.e. individual and collective practices *both occurring* in the conflict management system). No evidence of either set of complementarities could be found. A test of a derivative form of Bendersky's model examined whether organizational outcomes were superior where interest-based and rights-based practices coexisted, irrespective of the number of practices of either type that were present (Roche and Teague, 2012b: 251–2). Again no evidence could be found for the type of complementarities posited in this model. The only feature of conflict management systems found to have significant and consistent effects on the outcomes examined (absence rates excepted) was proactive line and supervisory management engagement in conflict resolution (Roche and Teague, 2012b, 2012c).

Employee Outcomes

Employee outcomes associated with conflict management systems include contributing to perceptions of "procedural justice," satisfaction with substantive outcomes of conflict resolution procedures as well as with procedures themselves, a better capacity to resolve "destructive conflict," higher work satisfaction, higher organizational identification and commitment, and more productive working (Conbere, 2001: 233; Lynch, 2001: 214; Bendersky, 2003: 649–52) Some of these employee outcomes may also be viewed as influences that mediate hypothesized employer outcomes like higher productivity (Conbere, 2001: 233).

Bendersky (2007) presents a test of what might be viewed as a reduced-form version of her complementarities model in a Canadian government agency that operated three different dispute resolution system models. Her focus is on how complementary conflict management practices might affect employee outcomes. The first dispute resolution system, operated in two research sites, involved a rights-based grievance procedure alone. The second involved such a procedure in addition to a three-day interest-based training workshop for employees, and the third involved these two components plus an interest-based neutral who coached disputants in dispute resolution options and provided ongoing education in dispute resolution. The claim that to compare workplaces that were otherwise similar meant that the three-component system could only be validly compared with one of the rights-based only workplaces and the two-component system with the other, limits the inferences that can be drawn from the analysis. Bendersky found that the three-component dispute resolution system was associated with consistently more positive conflict-related employee attitudes and behavior than the one single-component dispute resolution system workplace with which comparison was made. There was also less "conflict avoidance behavior" (or more conflict resolution behavior on the part of individuals). The three-component system site also performed better than the single component (rights-procedure only) site with which comparison was made in respect of employees' use of multiple conflict resolution avenues—though this seems something of a straw man comparison, as the three-component system site was set up to provide multiple avenues. The two-component dispute resolution system was found to be negatively associated with conflict-related attitudes and behavior, as compared with the one workplace with the single-component dispute resolution system with which comparison was made (Bendersky, 2007: 215–17). Bendersky (2007: 220) interprets the results as "consistent with the complementarities model." The effects of the three-component model appear obviously so. The negative results for the two-component model are seen to reveal the "detrimental effects of implementing a subset of components"—something that seems to extend the theory in a significant and for practical purposes rather ominous direction (Bendersky, 2007: 221).

In respect of public agencies, while conflict management practices in the United Nations have increasingly come to resemble the features of a conflict management system, the agency has been dogged by high-profile grievances, especially surrounding its alleged failure to protect whistleblowers (Borger, 2012). The US Federal Transport Security Administration (TSA) operated an integrated conflict management system that has been regarded by some commentators as a model system (see Gadlin, 2012: 2). However, an audit of the TSA was critical of how employees' concerns continued to be handled, noting in particular that the level of grievances filed in the agency was above average for comparable bodies, and attributing this to the agency's failure to provide sufficient conflict management tools and clear guidance on the structures, authorities, and oversight responsibilities of three major components of conflict management in the workplace: the office of the ombudsman, the integrated conflict management system, and a national advisory council through which staff provide advice to senior management on workplace issues (Department of Homeland Security, Office of Inspector General, 2008). As discussed above, follow-up studies of the conflict management system in the Royal Canadian Mounted Police reported no positive effects of the attenuated system in existence by the early 2000s. The system appears to have become more a source of dissatisfaction than the contrary. The conflict management system in the World Bank comprises an ombudsman, augmented by regionally based "respectful workplace advisers," a panel of mediators (mainly internal), who mediate in grievances as well as engaging in group facilitation, and a peer review process. Users register a high overall level of satisfaction with the system (World Bank 2010a, 2010b, 2011). The major problem confronted in operating the system was that peer review had evolved into a quasi-judicial process, with extensive involvement by lawyers and adversarial hearings. This led to the revision of the peer review process, curtailing the role of lawyers, who are no longer permitted to attend hearings or draft submissions. Cases are now resolved in a more straightforward manner, with the emphasis on resolving grievances rather than on adjudication (World Bank, 2010b).

PRIORITIES FOR RESEARCH AND PRACTICE: FOCUSING ON BASIC QUESTIONS AND ISSUES

The concept of conflict management systems is one of the major innovations in the theory of conflict resolution in organizations in recent decades. The concept and associated ideas represents a sophisticated and generally persuasive body of thought, which helps to explain the influence it has exerted and continues to exert on innovation and practice in the field, especially in the US. So dominant has the paradigm become in addressing the design features of an effective approach to conflict management in organizations that for some it has become more apt to speak of "appropriate dispute resolution" than alternative dispute resolution—implying that ADR-oriented systems have become something of a new orthodoxy (Gadlin, 2012: 4). Yet the prescriptive literature advocating the advantages and outcomes of conflict management systems continues on the whole to rely on little more than anecdotal evidence or even on unsubstantiated conjectures. The criticism long ago advanced that there were "few measurable data documenting hard savings or substantive impact of conflict management systems" (Administrative Conference of the United States, 1995: ix) is echoed in recent critical assessments (Department of Homeland Security Office of Inspector General, 2008). Academic commentators are correct in their criticism that "models and theory have lacked the rigorous empirical examination and development that result from disciplined theory or model building" (Bingham and Conbere, 2001: 226) and in their call for "more rigorous models requiring more sophisticated statistical techniques" (Lipsky and Avgar, 2004: 184–6). In the few studies to date where such strictures have been followed in tests for complementarities (Bendersky, 2007; Roche and Teague, 2012b), the results have been mixed.

More empirical case studies of the operation and outcomes of different conflict management systems are also required and these need to move away from being proffered as exemplary illustrations and instead report more objectively on the features, operation, and outcomes of conflict management systems of different types, operating in different contexts. More survey-based studies are also required to establish the incidence of conflict management systems, as distinct from different ADR practices, trends in the pervasiveness of the conflict management systems in organizations, and the durability of conflict management systems. In addition, the bias of the conflict management systems literature towards individual grievance handling needs to be corrected through more studies of the application of the conflict management systems approach to the handling of group and collective conflict. Finally, there needs to be more investigation of the possible "spillback" dynamics of conflict management systems. Most credible research on the incidence of conflict management systems suggests that they commonly represent a "spillover" from the use of a high commitment approach to the management of people. Yet few studies have sought to find out whether the operation of conflict management systems spill back and impact on the architecture of the organization or the behavior of managers or employees. One exception is an interesting study by Gadlin and Sturm (2007) which suggests that the adoption of a systematic approach to conflict management spills back to improve change management processes within organizations. Further studies of this kind would be useful.

Somewhat ironically, therefore, despite the novelty and influence of the conflict management systems concept, the work that needs to be done and the questions and issues that continue to arise remain quite basic and fundamental: why are these systems adopted, how pervasive have they become, how durable do they seem to be, how do they operate and what are their outcomes? Only when these questions are rigorously addressed can a fuller assessment be made of this important area of theory and practice in the field of conflict resolution.

References

Administrative Conference of the United States, 1995. *Towards Improved Agency Dispute Resolution: Implementing the ADR Act*. Washington, DC: Administrative Conference of the United States.

Bendersky, C. 2003. "Organizational Dispute Resolution Systems: a Complementarities Model." *Academy of Management Review*, 28(4): 643–56.

Bendersky, C. 2007. "Complementarities in Organizational Dispute Resolution Systems: How System Characteristics Affect Individuals' Conflict Experiences." *Industrial and Labor Relations Review*, 60(2): 204–24.

Bendersky, C. and Hays, N. A. 2012. "Status Conflict in Groups." *Organization Science*, 23(2): 323–40.

Bingham, L. B. 2004. "Employment Dispute Resolution: the Case for Mediation." *Conflict Resolution Quarterly*, 22(1): 45–74.

Bingham, L. B. and Chachere, D. R. 1999. "Dispute Resolution in Employment: The Need for Research." In A. E. Eaton and J. Keefe (eds), *Employment Dispute Resolution and Worker Rights*. University of Ilinois, Champaign-Urbana: Industrial Relations Research Association, 95–136.

Bingham, L. B., Hallberlin, C. J., Walker, D., and Chung, W. T. 2009. "Dispute System Design and Justice in Employment Dispute Resolution: Mediation at the Workplace." *Harvard Negotiation Law Journal*, Winter: 1–37.

Borger, J. 2012. "UN Tribunal Finds its Ethics Office Failed to Protect Whistleblower from Reprisals." *Guardian*, 28 June.

Conbere, J. P. 2001. "Theory Building for Conflict Management System Design." *Conflict Resolution Quarterly*, 19(2): 215–36.

Costantino, C. A. and Sickles Merchant, C. 1996. *Designing Conflict Management Systems*. San Francisco, CA: Jossey-Bass.

Cutcher-Gershenfeld, J. 2003. "How Process Matters: A Five-Phase Model for Examining Interest-based Bargaining." In T. A. Kochan and D. Lipsky (eds), *Negotiations and Change: From the Workplace to Society*. Ithaca: Cornell University Press, 141–60.

Department of Homeland Security, Office of the Inspector General 2008. *Transportation Security Administration's Efforts to Proactively Address Employee Concerns*. Washington, DC: US Department of Homeland Security.

Deukmedjian, J. (2003). "Reshaping Organizational Subjectivities in Canada's Police Force: The Development of RCMP Alternative Dispute Resolution." *Policing and Society*, 13(4): 331–48.

Doherty, L. and Teague, P. 2012. "Conflict Management Systems in Subsidiaries of Non-Union Multinational Organizations Located in the Republic of Ireland." *International Journal of Human Resource Management*, 22(1): 57–71.

Duxbury, L. 2007. *The RCMP: Yesterday, Today and Tomorrow: An Independent Report Concerning Workplace Issues at the Royal Canadian Mounted Police*. <http://dispersingthefog.com/report-2.pdf>.

Dix, G., Sisson, K., and Forth, J. 2009. "Conflict at Work: The Changing Pattern of Disputes." In W. Brown, A. Bryson, J. Forth, and K. Whitfield (eds), *The Evolution of the Modern Workplace*. Cambridge: Cambridge University Press, 176–200.

Ewing, D. E. 1989. *Justice on the Job: Resolving Grievances in the Nonunion Workplace*. Boston, MA: Harvard Business School Press.

Gadlin, H. 2012. "Remarks of Howard Gadlin, Ombudsman and Director of the Centre for Cooperative Resolution, National Institute of Health." Administrative Conference of the United States/Department of Justice Symposium, 19 Mar. <http://www.acus.gov/wp-content/uploads/downloads/2012/07/E-ACUS-DOJ-Symposium-Gadlin-Remarks.pdf> accessed 23 Sept. 2013.

Gadlin, H. and Sturm, S. P. 2007. Conflict Resolution and Systemic Change. *Journal of Dispute Resolution*, 50(1): 1–65.

Government of Canada, 2007. *Rebuilding the Trust: Task Force on Governance and Cultural Change in the RCMP*. Ottawa: Government of Canada.

Kaminski, M. 1999. "New Forms of Work Organization and their Impact on Collective Bargaining." In A.E. Eaton and J. Keefe (eds), *Employment Dispute Resolution and Worker rights*. University of Ilinois, Champaign-Urbana: Industrial Relations Research Association, 219–46.

Kessler, I. and Dickens, L. 2008. "Dispute Resolution and the Modernization of the Public Services." *Journal of Industrial Relations*, 50(4): 612–29.

Lewin, D. 1999. "Theoretical and Empirical Research on the Grievance Procedure and Arbitration: a Critical Review." In A.E. Eaton and J. Keefe (eds), *Employment Dispute Resolution and Worker Rights*. University of Ilinois, Champaign-Urbana: Industrial Relations Research Association, 137–86.

Lipsky, D. B. and Avgar, A. C. 2004. "Commentary: Research on Employment Dispute Resolution: Toward a New Paradigm." *Conflict Resolution Quarterly*, 22(1–2): 175–89.

Lipsky, D. B., Avgar, A., Ryan Lamare, J., and Gupta, A. 2012. "*The Antecedents of Workplace Conflict Management Systems in US Corporations: Evidence from a New Survey of Fortune 1,000 Companies*." Ithaca: ILR School, Cornell (draft paper).

Lipsky, D. B., Seeber, R., and Fincher, R. B. 2003. *Emerging Systems for Managing Workplace Conflict: Lessons from American Corporations for Managers and Dispute Resolution Professionals*. San Francisco, CA: Jossey-Bass.

Lynch, J. F. 2001. "Beyond ADR: A Systems Approach to Conflict Management. *Negotiation Journal*, 17(3): 207–16.

McAndrew, I. 2003. Final Offer Arbitration: A New Zealand Variation. *Industrial Relations*, 42(4): 736–44.

McAndrew, I. 2012. "Collective Bargaining Interventions: Contemporary New Zealand Experiments." *International Journal of Human Resource Management*, 23(3/4): 477–94.

Murphy, C. and McKenna, P. 2007. *Rethinking Police Governance, Culture and Management: A Summary Review of the Literature*. <http://www.publicsafety.gc.ca/cnt/cntrng-crm/tsk-frc-rcmp-grc/_fl/archive-rthnk-plc-eng.pdf>.

Robichaud, D., Benoit-Barne, C., and Basque, J. 2008. *Rebuilding Bridges: Report on Consultation of Employees and Managers of the Royal Canadian Mounted Police—C Division*. Université de Montréal: Research Group on Language, Organization and Governance.

Roche, W. K. and Teague, P. 2011. "Firms and Innovative Conflict Management Systems in Ireland." *British Journal of Industrial Relations*, 49(3): 436–59.

Roche, W. K. and Teague, P. 2012a. "Human Resource Management Practices and ADR in Ireland." *International Journal of Human Resource Management*, 23(3–4): 528–49.

Roche, W. K. and Teague, P. 2012b. "Do Conflict Management Systems Matter?" *Human Resource Management*, 51(2): 231–58.

Roche, W. K. and Teague, P. 2012c. "Line Managers and the Management of Workplace Conflict: Evidence from Ireland." *Human Resource Management Journal*, 22(3): 235–51.

Rowe, M. 1997. "Dispute Resolution in the Non-union Environment: an Evolution Toward Integrated Systems for Conflict Management?" In S. Gleason (ed.), *Frontiers in Dispute Resolution in Labor Relations and Human Resources*. East Lansing: Michigan State University Press, 79–106.

Rowe, M. and Bendersky, C. 2003. "Workplace Justice, Zero Tolerance and Zero Barriers." In T. A. Kochan and D. Lipsky (eds), *Negotiations and Change: From the Workplace to Society*. Ithaca: Cornell University Press, 117–40.

Slaikeu, K. and Hasson, R. 1998. *Controlling the Costs of Conflict*. San Francisco, CA: Jossey-Bass.

Society of Professions in Conflict Resolution, 2001. *Designing Integrated Conflict Management Systems: Guidelines for Practitioners and Decision Makers in Organizations*. Ithaca: Cornell Studies in Conflict and Dispute Resolution.

UN General Assembly 2006. *Report of Redesign Panel on the United Nations System of Administration of Justice*. New York. United Nations.

US Equal Opportunities Commission 2004. *ADR Report: Part II—The Best Practices in Alternative Dispute Resolution 2003–2004*.<http://www.eeoc.gov/federal/adr/adr_report_2004/adrii.html> [accessed 9/23/13].

US Office of Personnel Management 2002. *Alternative Dispute Resolution: A Resource Guide*. <http://mtweb.mtsu.edu/cewillis/2006%20ADR%20Spetrum.html> accessed 23 Sept. 2013.

Ury, W. L., Brett, J. M., and Goldberg, S. B. 1993. *Getting Disputes Resolved: Designing Systems to Cut the Costs of Conflict*. Cambridge, MA: The Program on Negotiation at Harvard Law School. First published (1988) by Jossey-Bass, San Francisco, CA.

Ury, W. L. and Fisher, R. (1981). *Getting to Yes: Negotiating Agreement without Giving In*. New York: Penguin.

World Bank, 2010a. *Ombuds Services and Respectful Workplace Advisors Program: Annual Report for 2010*. Washington, DC: The World Bank.

World Bank, 2010b. *Mediation Services; Annual Report for 2010*. Washington, DC: The World Bank.

World Bank, 2011. *Peer Review Services: Annual Report for 2010*. Washington, DC: The World Bank.

PART 3

....

EXEMPLARS AND

INNOVATORS

....

Introduction to Part 3

WILLIAM K. ROCHE, PAUL TEAGUE, AND ALEXANDER J. S. COLVIN

Approaches to conflict management vary widely across organizations and the field is continuing to evolve. The contributors to this section describe a series of different leading examples of innovative approaches to conflict management.

An important question is whether best practice models exist in conflict management. In other fields of management practice there has been a tendency to fixate on leading examples of organizational innovations as best practices to be followed by organizations in general. For example, recent decades saw varied efforts to identify key examples of high performance work system models to be emulated. In the area of conflict management, there is a similar tendency to look to leading exemplars for best practice models to be emulated. However, it is important to recognize that different approaches to conflict management often reflect the specific environments and institutional contexts in which they are developed. In identifying innovations to follow, it is important to focus not just on the practices utilized but also the context in which they are employed.

The contributions in this section provide four examples of conflict management innovators from contrasting settings. Two of the examples are from the United States, with its unique legal and labor relations environments. Whereas Bingham's chapter focuses on systems for the resolution of individual employment rights disputes in the quasi-public organizational setting of the US Postal Service (USPS), Eaton and Kochan look at the resolution of collective bargaining conflicts in the private sector setting of the Kaiser Permanente health care organization. The first non-US example, McAndrew's chapter on med+arb in the New Zealand police, illustrates an innovation in resolution of public sector collective bargaining disputes. By contrast, the final example, Urwin and Latreille's chapter on judicial mediation in UK employment tribunals explores an innovation within the context of a public employment dispute resolution system. Each of these contributions illustrates ways in which conflict management innovations have developed in these contrasting organizational and institutional settings.

Lisa Amsler provides a detailed evaluation of one of the largest scale organizational innovations in conflict management, the USPS "REDRESS" equal employment dispute mediation program. This program was noteworthy both for its widespread implementation of an innovative dispute system design and its systematic efforts to evaluate the operation and effect of the program, conducted in collaboration with Professor Amsler and her colleagues at Indiana University. A striking feature of the development of the REDRESS program is that a series of three different experimental programs were tried and evaluated before the implementation of a final national dispute system. Not all organizations may have the resources and sustained commitment to be able to engage in this level of experimentation in the dispute system design process, but the USPS experience demonstrates its value where it is undertaken.

A noteworthy feature of the final national REDRESS program is that it used an explicit transformative mediation model. This provides a valuable opportunity to see the impact of a large scale test of the effects of this particular model of mediation practice. The overall results of the evaluation of the USPS program are positive. The system was designed to minimize the problem of pro-employer bias, which is a particular danger in the United States due to the employer driven nature of US employment relations. Evaluation of the program also produced an important finding that disputant satisfaction with disputant–disputant interpersonal interactions was a strong predictor of both perceptions of organizational justice and also settlement. This finding reinforces the driving principle in transformative mediation of the importance of empowering disputants to be able to resolve disputes themselves.

Adrienne Eaton and Thomas Kochan provide a detailed description and analysis of the labor-management partnership at Kaiser Permanente, currently the largest private sector partnership initiative in the United States. Labor-management partnership efforts have had a mixed history in the US, characterized by many promising initiatives that failed to endure. By contrast, the partnership at Kaiser Permanente began in the late 1990s and has continued to the present day. This success is despite the challenges on the labor side of trying to coordinate across some twenty-eight local unions and an array of different national unions. Recently the partnership has had to endure an inter-union competition for membership between the Service Employees International Union (SEIU) and a break-away rival, the National Union of Health Care Workers (NUHW).

Despite the challenges it has faced, the labor-management partnership at Kaiser Permanente has endured through a series of rounds of national negotiations. The national level negotiations have been conducted using an Interest-Based Bargaining (IBB) approach. This is supported by decentralized labor-management task groups focused on specific issues. The partnership has extended down to the workplace level with a joint effort to expand cross-functional "unit based teams". It has also expanded the substantive agenda for bargaining, with a notable recent focus on the issue of promoting a healthier workforce. Overall Kaiser Permanente is an important counter-example to the generally dismal picture that is often drawn of the state of labor-management relations in the United States.

Ian McAndrew's study of conflict resolution in the New Zealand police explores the use of mediation and arbitration in an unusual "med+arb" model to resolve interest disputes between the police force and the union representing police officers. In New Zealand as in other countries, police are barred from striking and instead arbitration is available for resolution of bargaining disputes over wages and conditions of employment. In the New Zealand process, both a mediator and an arbitrator are appointed by the Department of Labour in the event of a police bargaining dispute and then bargaining continues in the presence of the mediator and often the arbitrator as well. This provides an interesting structural contrast to other systems, such as those commonly used in North America, where the interventions of the mediator and the interest arbitrator are kept separate and the interest arbitration hearing is divorced from the bargaining process.

McAndrew finds that the New Zealand police med+arb model has been successful in encouraging voluntary settlements between the parties. It has not shown evidence of a narcotic effect of the parties becoming dependent on the intervention of the arbitrator. Wage increases have been moderate under this system, belying concerns about the loss of government control of police remuneration. One danger that the New Zealand police med+arb model avoids is the chilling of settlement negotiations by the arbitrator being privy to compromise offers. It does this by having the arbitrator present for the formal negotiations, but not the mediators caucusing with each party. Among the limitations of this model are that it is relatively time and resource intensive and is relatively conservative in its outcomes. There is also a concern that the influence of mediation has been diminishing over time and McAndrew suggests the potential value of a return to a more proactive role for mediation in the process.

Peter Urwin and Paul Latreille examine the use of ADR techniques in the context of a public employment dispute resolution procedure. The UK Employment Tribunal (ET) system is itself a form of ADR procedure when contrasted with conflict resolution through the general court system. However, in recent years it has had to deal with the challenges of handling steadily rising numbers and increased complexity of cases. In the initiative examined by Urwin and Latreille, judges undertook facilitative mediation of ET claims in three regions of the UK for a one year period. This judicial mediation pilot program was evaluated using surveys of both claimants and employers who were parties to the claims, including both claims that were mediated and claims that were not mediated.

One contrast that emerged in the evaluation of the program is that employers viewed judicial mediation more favorably than did complainants. Mediation did have a positive effect of reducing recourse to tribunal hearings, but interestingly this effect was concentrated among female claimants. Overall however, effects on resolution rates were not statistically significant and the program created additional costs. Despite this, the program was later extended nationally, potentially providing future opportunities to evaluate the wider impact of judicial mediation.

In examining exemplars of innovative practices, there is a danger of analyzing the cases through rose-tinted lenses, focusing only on the positive lessons to be learned. Certainly there are important positive lessons to be taken from these four cases. The USPS REDRESS program and the judicial mediation of ET claims examples illustrate the value of careful evaluation of innovative programs including extensive data collection. Mediation is a central component of ADR practice and three of our four examples feature it. The relative advantages of different styles of mediation has been an important topic in the literature and it is worth noting the more strongly positive results from the transformative mediation model used in the USPS REDRESS program compared to the less evident benefits of the evaluative mediation practiced in the UK ET judicial mediation program.

In addition to the positive lessons, challenges and barriers encountered in developing conflict management systems can often be equally or more informative. Balancing the interests of multiple parties can often be a particularly challenging task in conflict management, yet the Kaiser Permanente example points to possibilities for how a comprehensive labor-management partnership approach can overcome this difficulty, even in the context of strong intra-party conflicts on one side. Another issue that can plague conflict management systems is neglect and disuse. McAndrew's study of the New Zealand police system raises important cautionary flags about the danger of declining use of the mediation component of that system and the need to take an ongoing proactive approach to conflict management. Although none of these exemplars of conflict management indicates a single, universally applicable approach to developing a conflict management system, the innovations they present do suggest a set of approaches that can be drawn upon to guide developments in a range of different organizational settings and institutional contexts.

CHAPTER 13

USING MEDIATION TO MANAGE CONFLICT AT THE UNITED STATES POSTAL SERVICE

LISA BLOMGREN AMSLER

THE United States Postal Service (USPS) REDRESS© program (Resolve Employment Disputes Reach Equitable Solutions Swiftly) shows how mediation can help manage workplace conflict in a large, unionized organization. By 2000, REDRESS© was the world's largest employment mediation program. Its design and institutionalization is the product of a rare confluence of factors: a huge employer with substantial workplace conflict; a hurting stalemate that made the organization ripe for change; dedicated and visionary champions; consistent working conditions across thousands of locations; pragmatic experimentation with program design; a data-driven environment; and a rare investment in systemic, continuous evaluation to ensure program accountability.

The program had its limits: it applied only to complaints of discrimination, not workplace conflict generally, so it was embedded in the silo of Equal Employment Opportunity (EEO) offices within the USPS. However, the twelve-year research collaboration between the USPS and Indiana University's School of Public and Environmental Affairs (IU) gave the field of conflict management its most comprehensive quantitative evaluation of an employment mediation program's organizational impact to date.

Adapting the analytic framework for dispute system design (DSD) proposed by Smith and Martinez (2009), this chapter will describe the program's stakeholders and context; goals; designs, structure, and resources; and success and accountability. It will conclude with lessons that the USPS experience teaches us about conflict management and organizational justice.

USPS Stakeholders and Context

The USPS is a semi-independent establishment, at the same time public and private, with a unique legal framework. It is not an executive branch agency of the United States federal government supported by taxpayer dollars. Since the Postal Reorganization Act of 1970, the USPS has supported itself through the sale of postal products like postage stamps. It is more akin to UPS (United Parcel Service) and FedEx (Federal Express), two large private parcel delivery corporations. As an establishment that serves every community in the United States and reaches internationally, its external stakeholders include the public and every organizational form it takes, private, nonprofit, or public, and their elected representatives.

It is also a large, civilian, unionized employer. The National Labor Relations Board, which primarily oversees private sector labor relations, has jurisdiction over the USPS, not the Federal Labor Relations Authority that oversees federal agencies and their employees. The USPS has at least seven collective bargaining units (including clerks, postal workers, rural, and other letter carriers). Thus, its internal stakeholders include employees, their elected representatives and union leadership, managers in each region and function (the law department, operations, supply chain management, human resources, labor relations, EEO, contracting, etc.), senior leadership, Board of Governors, Postal Regulatory Commission, and contractors, among others.

At the inception of its mediation program in 1994, the USPS had over 800,000 employees and was one of the world's largest civilian employers. The USPS created REDRESS© for individual employee complaints of discrimination arising under federal Equal Employment Opportunity (EEO) laws, including Title VII of the Civil Rights Act of 1964 (42 U.S.C. Sec. 20003, *et seq.*), Americans With Disabilities Act (42 U.S.C. Sec. 12101, *et seq.*), and Age Discrimination in Employment Act (29 USC. Sec. 621, *et seq.*). Under relevant law pertaining to federal employers, the USPS addressed EEO complaints internally for the first two stages: inquiring into an informal complaint and investigation of a formal complaint. Thereafter, the case went to the EEOC. This was part of its legal and regulatory context.

At the time the USPS considered using mediation for EEO complaints, like all other employers in the United States, it was subject to *Alexander v Gardner Denver* (415 U.S. 36, 1974). This case carved out an exception from the scope of mandatory bargaining in labor relations; it permitted employees subject to a collective bargaining agreement to pursue an EEO claim outside the negotiated grievance-arbitration procedure, reasoning that Congress provided for cooperation and voluntary compliance as the preferred means to resolve EEO complaints. It provided a conciliation procedure in Title VII (p. 44). Thus, in 1994, the USPS had a legal right unilaterally to structure a voluntary dispute resolution program for EEO complaints.

A key set of internal stakeholders was the Law Department of the USPS. It was responsible for representing the organization in all litigation arising from workplace conflict.

Increasing caseload with constrained resources demanded new thinking. REDRESS© had substantial champions in the Law Department's General Counsel Mary Elcano, Managing Counsel Karen Intrater, and Chief ADR Counsel and National Program Manager Cynthia Hallberlin.

Goals: Addressing a Massive Stream of Disputes

The USPS created its mediation© program in the context of a larger system containing multiple streams of workplace disputes that affected both internal and external stakeholders. Employees could raise issues under one of several collective bargaining agreements, the EEO complaint process, the Merit Systems Protection Board (5 U.S.C. 7701, *et seq.*), the National Labor Relations Board, statutory workers compensation, a non-union administrative grievance procedure, or an employee assistance plan, and sometimes under more than one of these systems simultaneously.

When the Law Department conceived REDRESS©, there was a substantial grievance-arbitration case backlog under the union contracts, with over 38,000 cases awaiting arbitration that were taking a year or longer to be resolved (1992 data from GAO, 1994a). In fiscal 1994, the organization's over 800,000 employees filed over 61,000 grievances that were not settled on the shop floor (GAO, 1994a). A government interview study revealed that reasons included an "autocratic management style, adversarial employee and union attitudes, inadequate and inappropriate performance management systems, and the nature of the work", which was increasingly mechanized, regimented, routine, and production-oriented (GAO 1994a: 2–3; see also 1994c and 1994d).

There were also a growing number of EEO complaints (GAO, 1998); processing time had increased and the capacity of EEOC staff to handle cases had not. In 1994, USPS employees filed almost 25,000 complaints alleging discrimination; by 1997, the number of complaints approached 28,000 annually (GAO, 1998). Of the 34,262 federal sector EEO cases for fiscal year 1997, 13,549 or over 39% involved the USPS (Bingham and Napoli 2001). In 1998, USPS employees represented 32% of the federal workforce but were responsible for 51% of EEO complaints, 47% of hearing requests, and 47% of appeals (Nabatchi and Stanger, 2012).

A tragic 1991 shooting of five co-workers by a employee at the Royal Oak, Michigan, post office followed other incidents of violence in the 1980s (GAO, 1992a and 1992b); as a result, the phrase "Going Postal" became associated with workplace conflict at the USPS. A rigorous analysis by a blue ribbon commission found that there was no statistically significant difference between the level of workplace violence at the USPS compared to other employers (Califano et al., 2000); the commission found workplace violence was actually slightly lower at the USPS overall. The USPS adopted a zero tolerance policy for verbal threats of violence so rigorous that it was later made an exception to mediator confidentiality in the REDRESS© program. However, this created a context in which the public perception and the reality of caseloads together demanded a different approach to conflict at work.

Designs, Structure, and Resources

The USPS engaged in a giant experiment, one only possible because it was large and had consistent working conditions at each of its over 31,000 locations in the United States. Multiple locations allowed for natural quasi-experiments. It had a tradition of pilot programs. It had used mediation by the Federal Mediation and Conciliation Service in various contexts and mediation by union–management pairs in one collective bargaining agreement (GAO, 1997a: 23). Moreover, during the design period from 1994 to 2000, the economics of the USPS were relatively stable, unlike the financial stress facing the agency two decades later when email had significantly eroded income from first class mail. The prospect of transaction cost savings through better conflict management in such a large organization justified the resources that it devoted to this new system (Bingham, 2002c). These resources were relatively minor in relation to the size and scope of the USPS. During the design period, each of its thirty or more regional managers had responsibility for the economic equivalent of Fortune 1000 or Fortune 500 companies.

However, the USPS was both a disputant and at the same time it controlled dispute system design (Bingham, 2002a, 2002b, 2008–9). In the United States, the power to design employment conflict management systems is not equally distributed. Control over DSD derives from law and contract. It stems from both legal and economic power. Designers exercise that power directly or as agents for an organization. For example, federal courts have the power to control design for their Alternative Dispute Resolution (ADR) systems under the Alternative Dispute Resolution Act of 1998. While they administer court-connected ADR systems for disputes on their dockets, the courts themselves are third parties; they are not disputants in these cases. Sometimes, parties have balanced bargaining power, which gives them mutual or shared control over DSD. This enables them to negotiate systems for their own benefit through arms length contracts. For example, Fortune 500 companies may negotiate DSDs into supply or other commercial contracts. Labor unions and management negotiate DSDs in their grievance procedures. In these cases, both law and economic power give them shared control over DSD.

In the United States, the existing legal framework also gives private and nonprofit sector companies the power to design and effectively impose systems for those with little economic or bargaining power, for example, their employees and consumers, through contracts of adhesion. A corporation can abuse this power. For example, it may internally manage its binding arbitration program to disadvantage its employees or customers through unconscionable contracts. Employers have been known to set up the equivalent of kangaroo arbitration panels of former managers. Control over DSD shapes the resulting procedures. It determines in part who sets the goals and makes design choices.

The USPS initially adopted mediation effective in autumn 1994 as part of a negotiated settlement to a class action discrimination suit in the Panhandle of Florida. Union leaders, employee lawyers, and the USPS law department represented internal stakeholders in settlement negotiations. In this and subsequent design changes, the USPS consulted with internal stakeholders and focus groups. However, because of *Gardner-Denver*, it never negotiated with unions over the structure and content of REDRESS©; with seven different bargaining units, it would have been difficult to negotiate. Thus, the USPS exercised effective unilateral control over DSD for REDRESS©. However, that control was constrained by law; the USPS could not mandate that all EEO complainants use ADR. Thus, it had to design a program that employees would want to use. It had to consider the incentive structure within the organization (Nabatchi and Bingham, 2010).

Enduring Design Elements: Each of the REDRESS© experiments contained certain basic structural features:

- To be eligible, an employee must file an informal complaint of discrimination in employment with the USPS EEO office.
- Mediation is offered to almost all EEO complainants, with limited exceptions.
- Mediation is voluntary for the complainant.
- Mediation is mandatory for the respondent supervisor, who is an agent of the USPS as employer.
- A mediation session is scheduled promptly, generally within a month of a request.
- If they choose to bring a representative, complainants may bring any they choose, whether lawyer, union representative, co-worker, friend, or family member.
- The respondent is accompanied by or has immediate access to a management representative with authority to authorize a settlement.
- Mediation sessions occur in a private location at the workplace during working time for which participant employees are paid.
- If the employee is a member of a bargaining unit, that union has the right to review the settlement to ensure it is consistent with the contract.
- The mediator distributed exit surveys and completed a report.

First Experiment—The Panhandle Pilot: During the early pilot phase of the program from 1994 to 1997, the USPS used facilitative, outside neutral mediators trained by the Justice Center of Atlanta (JCA). The traditional facilitative mediator uses interest-based negotiation, asks problem-solving questions, brainstorms solutions, and uses reality-testing techniques. Primm (1993), the founding director of JCA, described indicators of success to be resolution, implementing agreements, satisfaction, and progress in understanding how the conflict occurred.

In 1996, IU conducted qualitative, exploratory, open-ended interviews of 42 employees and supervisors who had participated in facilitative mediation. This was a representative sample of 15% of the participants in the Florida Panhandle pilot to that date. Researchers found that participants, both supervisors and employees, said that they listened to each other in the mediation (Anderson and Bingham, 1997: 606–7). This may sound trivial, but it was actually a significant change in the culture for managing conflict at the USPS at the time. That culture was command and control or paramilitary. For example, one interviewee was a supervisor who described how a grievance on the shop floor would routinely escalate into a screaming match. The supervisor said he would interrupt the employee if he thought the employee had said something that was not true; he did not want to appear to have admitted the USPS did something wrong. The employee repeated the claim, and the supervisor again contradicted it, each raising their voice in turn until impasse. The supervisor reported that, through mediation, he learned it was more effective simply to listen to the grievant without interruption. He felt mediation was teaching him conflict management skills. Moreover, these skills allowed disputants to resolve conflict upstream, earlier in the life of the dispute.

The second study of the pilot used exit surveys to compare employee and supervisor perceptions of procedural justice (Bies, 1987; Bingham, 1997). IU exit surveys employed five-point Likert scales (five as very satisfied) about satisfaction with process (the fairness, information, opportunity to present views, control, treatment, understanding, and participation in the process with a 35 point maximum); satisfaction with the individual mediator (preparation, respect, knowledge, impartiality, performance, skill, and fairness, a 35 point maximum); and satisfaction with the outcome (outcome, speed, outcome relative to expectations, control, and long-term effects of mediation, a 25 point maximum). It found both employees and supervisors were highly and similarly satisfied with the JCA facilitative mediation process and its mediators. For the process index, the employee average was 30.9; supervisors' average was 32.2. For the mediator index, employees' average was 31.8; supervisors' was 32.9. This was important to the USPS as an organization, because it provided outside validation that employees and supervisors judged the system to be fair. Although employees were statistically significantly less satisfied than supervisors with outcome (employees' average 18.5 to supervisors' 20.2), this result was consistent with both common sense and procedural justice literature. Complainants' expectations are disappointed, while respondents are relieved the case is resolved.

Second Experiment—Inside and Outside Mediators: During 1994–7, the USPS law department experimented with two program designs to determine whether using federal employees as mediators was feasible. One design was an early pilot similar to the current federal Shared Neutrals program, in which federal employees, trained as mediators, cross agency boundaries to mediate employment disputes at no cost. The USPS used Veterans Affairs (VA) mediators and provided the VA with mediators for its cases. Due to the low number of cases mediated, there were no usable data from this experiment.

A second experiment used USPS employees as inside neutral mediators. The USPS provided both inside and outside neutral mediators training in the facilitative style by the JCA. The pilot program took place in upstate New York. The DSD was the same in both inside and outside neutral programs apart from the source of the mediator. However, there was selection bias in favor of inside mediators: cases were not randomly assigned nor were all cases mediated. Instead, EEO ADR specialists referred inside neutrals cases they felt were more likely to settle.

Bingham et al. (2000: 14) compared inside and outside mediators using analyzes of variance on each of the process, mediator, and outcome procedural justice indices in the standard exit survey. They found statistically significant differences in perceptions of the mediator and outcome. The inside neutral mean process index was 30.51 while outside was 31.78 (marginally significant at .07 level); the inside mediator index was 22.98 and outside 24.23 (significant at .01 level); and the inside mediator outcome index was 18.39 while outside was 19.98 (significant at the .05 level). Also, outside mediators resolved more cases fully or partially (75%) than insiders (56%). Employees were less satisfied with the fairness and impartiality of inside mediators. One possible explanation was perceived bias: as fellow employees, inside mediators were more subject to USPS control. Another possible explanation is that they were less skilled. However, the selection bias by EEO ADR specialist meant the insiders had easier cases; moreover, they knew the USPS as an organization far better than any outsider could. These two factors would tend to cancel out any difference in skill between inside and outside neutrals.

One important design feature is that employees did not have a choice between inside or outside neutral designs. Contrast, for example, an ombuds program; the ombuds uses conflict coaching to help employees determine the best way or process to proceed. Instead, the USPS implemented inside and outside neutral designs in different geographical locations to allow for a natural experiment. If employees had been permitted to choose, there might not have been a difference in satisfaction. They might have been predisposed to be satisfied with their choice.

Third Experiment—the National Model Using Transformative Mediators: From 1994 to 1997, the USPS expanded pilot programs from the Panhandle to 25 cities, all using JCA facilitative mediators. During this period, mediator practices varied widely. Robert A. Baruch Bush and Joseph P. Folger published their first edition of *The Promise of Mediation* (1994) advocating for a different model of practice, transformative mediation. Bush and Folger described evaluative mediators as subject matter experts who would provide an opinion on the substantive, legal merits of a discrimination complaint. They were termed "directive" in that they used pressing tactics with the disputants with the primary goal in mediation as settlement. In contrast, they described a facilitative mediator as one who used problem-solving and interest-based negotiation strategies. All mediators used active listening and communication skills including reframing. Bush and Folger saw the primary goal of both evaluative or directive and facilitative mediators as settlement.

In contrast, Bush and Folger argued for a new model: transformative mediators. In their view, mediators should seek to foster communication between the disputants, empower them, and help them recognize each other's perspectives. Empowerment and recognition might naturally lead to settlement, but it was merely a byproduct, not the primary goal. Transformative mediators would help disputants identify resources and information they needed to make decisions. They would never evaluate the merits of a claim or its legal strengths and weaknesses. It would be inappropriate for them to give an opinion on the likely outcome before an administrative law judge or in court. The USPS began to consider the transformative model as an alternative (Hallberlin, 2001). USPS Law Department system designer Cynthia Hallberlin joined Bush and Folger's Transformative Training Design Consultation Project in 1996 (Hallberlin, 2001).

In 1997, IU presented Florida Panhandle pilot survey data (Bingham, 1997) and interview results (Anderson and Bingham, 1997) to the Postmaster General and Management Committee. The USPS leadership decided to roll out the REDRESS® program nationally, taking it from 25 cities to every village and hamlet in the United States where there was a post office. This policy decision dictated a single, national, consistent dispute system design.

USPS Law Department system designer Cynthia Hallberlin argued that the transformative mediation model was better in principle. USPS's goal was to move conflict management upstream to foster individual learning of better communication skills. Transformative mediation's focus of party empowerment and recognition was consistent with this goal.

Moreover, the transformative model provided a check on USPS control over DSD. By federal law, the USPS could not legally mandate that employee complainants participate in mediation; REDRESS® had to be voluntary for the complainant, although not for respondent supervisors who had an incentive to avoid participating (Nabatchi and Bingham, 2010). When EEO cases were handled through the traditional adversarial administrative process, the USPS prevailed in over 95% of all EEO complaints, either on the merits or because employees failed to pursue them. In other words, in 95% of all cases, if the mediator had discretion to give an opinion on who would likely prevail, that mediator would probably tell complainants they had a weak case. Moreover, other federal agencies had put out requests for proposals (RFP) seeking mediators; one RFP required that mediators demonstrate an 80% or higher settlement rate. This created an incentive for mediators to press employees to drop their cases to achieve a high personal settlement rate and get repeat business from the agency paying the bills.

Although by this point all the mediators were contractors and not USPS employees, the USPS was selecting mediators for its roster, training them, assigning them to cases, and paying them. Employees could quite reasonably conclude that mediators who expressed opinions on case merits were biased in favor of the USPS. If they did conclude that mediators were biased, they would return to the shop floor and advocate against other employees using the REDRESS® program. The program was voluntary; the USPS could not force complainant employees to use it. Therefore, the system would fail in its chief goal to help employees and supervisors learn how better to manage conflict.

In contrast, transformative mediators are ethically prohibited from opining on the merits of a claim, even when the parties ask them to. Together, Hallberlin, Bush, and Folger collaborated on developing uniform, consistent training for the final REDRESS® national program. The USPS rolled it out over an eighteen-month period beginning in January 1998. It used a Train-the-Trainers model; selected mediators were trained in the transformative model and invited to train other mediators as the USPS identified them for the national roster. Initially, the USPS identified 3,000 mediators nationally. The USPS did not limit the roster to mediators who were lawyers with substantive employment law expertise since mediators were not expected to evaluate cases. Instead, the roster included mediators from psychology, counseling, and social work, as well as teachers, academics, human resource professionals, and retirees from these professions. Many of the mediators had extensive experience in family and domestic relations practice (Gann and Hallberlin, 2001).

As a way of maximizing USPS resources, mediators were trained for free in exchange for agreeing to mediate one case *pro bono*. EEO ADR specialists observed mediators to ensure that they practiced in the transformative model (Gann and Hallberlin, 2001). Over time, based on observations, the USPS culled the roster and reduced it to 1,500 experienced mediators. National outreach produced a roster comprised of 44% women and 17% minorities, reflecting a fairly high level of racial diversity. In a sample of 671 active mediators, 570 were Caucasian, 77 were African-American, 4 were Asian-American, 3 were Native American, and 17 were Latino. This yielded the most demographically diverse mediator roster in use at the time.

Indiana University conducted an email survey of EEO ADR Specialists, whose job it was to administer and manage the mediation program in each geographic district, to determine if they could identify whether mediators on the national roster were engaged in behaviors that were transformative or evaluative (Nabatchi and Bingham, 2001). In general, specialists' descriptions of observed behaviors were consistent with the transformative model. IU also sent a survey to the 3,000 mediators on the initial USPS roster and asked the mediators to complete two tasks: to identify mediator statements as reflecting a more or less transformative mediation session, and to categorize mediator tactics as transformative, evaluative or as neither (Nabatchi et al., 2010). These results generally supported a conclusion that mediators had cognitive comprehension of the transformative mediation model.

Success and Accountability: Evaluating the Final National DSD of REDRESS©

Evaluation is a critical early component of a comprehensive DSD. It provides transparency and accountability to stakeholders. Stakeholders include the people and organizations that create, host, use, and are affected by a DSD. Evaluation of how a system functions can engender trust in the system, which can in turn enhance its use. Evaluation also provides a feedback loop for improving the system. Without a comprehensive, longitudinal view of the system and its outcomes, it is hard to justify the investment of resources a DSD requires.

From the inception of the first pilot program in 1994, the USPS incorporated an evaluation system into the design of the REDRESS© program to make it accountable within the organization. The Law Department knew that USPS management was numbers driven. Many managers had MBAs. In order for the program to have a future, it needed to demonstrate its impact. The USPS and IU collaboratively designed a system for continuous data collection that became part of each experiment with design and ultimately part of the national program. That system had the following components:

- Mediators distributed a confidential Exit Survey to each participant and their representatives. There were no identifying numbers on the survey.

- The Exit Survey contained: the zip code of the mediation; procedural and organizational justice items measuring satisfaction with process, mediator, and outcome; an item about whether there was full, partial, or no resolution; and later transformative indicators. It contained no demographic information due to concerns about discovery for use in class action litigation.
- Participants were invited to complete the exit surveys on work time and mail them to IU postage prepaid in printed addressed envelopes.
- As a condition of getting paid, the mediator completed a Mediator Report on: who attended the mediation; whether there was a full, partial, or no settlement; and how many exit surveys were distributed.

Indiana University received the confidential surveys and entered them into an Access database for analysis. IU prepared bi-annual reports by zip code cluster showing satisfaction with various aspects of the mediation. There were 85 zip code clusters. USPS program managers used the basic descriptive satisfaction data to manage program performance and consistency. By the time the national program achieved full implementation, the USPS was conducting about 15,000 REDRESS© mediation cases a year. Generally, each mediation session had four participants (each disputant and their representative). Eventually, by the close of 2006 when data collection ceased, the exit survey database had over 270,000 surveys.

In addition to this basic system, researchers triangulated data sources. IU collected archival data on EEO informal and formal complaint filing rates; administered a survey to the mediator roster; conducted an email survey of USPS EEO ADR Specialists; and conducted a qualitative panel study with interviews in 1998 and 2000 of a sample of USPS employees in New York, Cleveland, and San Francisco.

For the final national REDRESS© DSD, IU redesigned the exit survey to include new indicators intended to capture elements of the transformative mediation model such as empowerment, recognition, and directive/evaluative mediators (Nabatchi et al. 2007). Items addressed mediator tactics (e.g. the mediator told you who would win this case in court; the mediator helped the other person understand your viewpoint). Others concerned the interpersonal communication between the disputants: (e.g. the other person listened to your views; the other person learned something new about your point of view). Researchers used the exit survey dataset to examine a series of organizational justice questions.

The first study examined the procedural justice indicators of satisfaction with the process, mediators, and outcome. The national model using transformative mediation generally produced the same pattern of procedural justice results as the facilitative style (Moon and Bingham, 2007; Bingham et al., 2009). Specifically, in the analysis of over 81,000 exit surveys completed between 1998 and 2003 (i.e. the transformative period), both employees and supervisors were equally and highly satisfied with the mediation process (the mean employee process index was 31.49 and supervisor process index was 31.79 out of a maximum of 35; Moon and Bingham, 2007: 49). These were comparable to the facilitative model results with a small sample of only 78 employees and 100 supervisors (Bingham, 1997).

Internal stakeholders considered it an important indicator of fairness or absence of bias in the system that both complainants and supervisors be equally satisfied with the mediation process and the mediators. IU conducted a final comprehensive analysis of complete national program data on the transformative model, not including earlier facilitative data, using percent satisfied or highly satisfied on indices of process, mediators, and outcome (Bingham, et al., 2009. Complainants were on average 91.2% and supervisors 91.6% satisfied or highly satisfied with process. Complainants were 96.5% and supervisors 96.9% satisfied or highly satisfied with the mediators. Complainants were 64.2% and supervisors 69.5% satisfied or highly satisfied with the outcome. This was consistent with the facilitative mediation results (Bingham, 1997). It was also consistent with basic procedural justice findings that both complainants and supervisors generally are satisfied with the process; however, the complaining party is generally somewhat less satisfied with outcome.

Evaluating Systemic Impact on the USPS as an Organization

In two other studies of the final national program model, researchers attempted to measure the impact of the program on the USPS as an organization. Researchers used archival EEO informal and formal case filing data to examine formal complaint filing rates before and after the USPS rolled out the national transformative model of REDRESS© (Bingham and Novac 2001). The USPS maintained data by geographic district zip code and monthly accounting period that included informal EEO complaints, formal EEO complaints, and the number of employees in that region. In addition, researchers created a dummy variable for the accounting period in which REDRESS© achieved full implementation in that geographic district. Researchers conducted a multivariate regression with control variables for number of informal complaint cases, employee census, and the dummy variable for REDRESS© implementation date over a five-year period. The dependent variable was the number of formal EEO complaints. It took eighteen months to complete the roll out, providing variability for date of implementation. Researchers found that implementation of the mediation program correlated with a substantial drop (more than 25%) in formal EEO complaints (Bingham and Novac 2001). There were no exogenous factors at work during the period, and economic conditions were stable. This trend suggested that mediation had a positive impact on the USPS system for addressing complaints of discrimination, in that complaints were resolved through mediation at the informal stage and did not reach the formal stage.

In the second study, researchers conducted exploratory research entailing qualitative interviews of a total random sample of over 200 employees in three cities (New York, Cleveland, and San Francisco) before and after implementation of the national transformative mediation model (Bingham et al., 2009). Perceptions of the EEO program appeared to improve after REDRESS©. Those reporting they were satisfied or highly satisfied with the EEO process improved from 25% to 35% and satisfaction with the fairness of the process improved from 20% to 44%. However, satisfaction with the fairness of the union contract grievance procedure process declined slightly from 47% to 38%. These results were at best suggestive of how experience with mediation might change the overarching system within which the mediation program was embedded. The sample was too small to allow for generalizable findings.

Over the period from 1994 to 2006 when data collection ceased, the rate at which disputants resolved their own case after mediation was scheduled, but before it actually took place, gradually increased from 2% to 14%. Controlling for changes in the size of the workforce, by 2006 USPS internal data suggested that informal EEO complaint filings dropped 30% since their peak before the USPS implemented REDRESS©. Moreover, there was a change in the composition of the complainant pool. By 2006, the complaints were coming from 40% fewer people; this meant that the people filing complaints were more likely to be repeat filers. The national evaluation terminated at the end of 2006 and there are no further data on program performance.

Lessons Learned about Conflict Management and Organizational Justice

A fundamental goal of any system for managing conflict is justice; however, justice can take many forms in dispute systems (Bingham, 2008–9). There are varieties of fairness, not simply what a court in a given jurisdiction would determine. These varieties of justice relate to the outcomes of the process, party voice and control over process, impacts on organizations and their members, and impacts on communities. Substantive and distributive justice reflect the justice of an outcome produced by a decision process, that is, whether it fairly distributes something tangible or fairly enforces rights or obligations. Procedural justice concerns fair process, including opportunities for participants to exercise voice and control and participants' perception of fairness in these processes. Traditional principles of procedural justice in social psychology include voice, opportunity to be heard, and the basis for decisions, dignified and respectful treatment of participants, and impartiality and trustworthiness of the decision-maker (Lind and Tyler, 1988).

Organizational justice is a variant of procedural justice that is geared to the context of employers, whether public, private, or nonprofit. This dimension of justice reflects the quality of treatment for someone engaged in an organization's processes, and includes both interpersonal and informational aspects. Employees who experience greater organizational justice exhibit better organizational citizenship behaviors like reduced absenteeism and greater loyalty. All varieties of justice address how people function in relation to each other. However, within a community there are varieties of justice that relate to intentional harm. These include both retributive and deterrent justice in criminal law. Restorative justice aims to reintegrate an offender into the community. Transitional justice has the goal to establish rule of law and democracy in a post-conflict society. Communicative justice describes idealized speech or undistorted communication.

The conversation about justice seems absent from much of the work on dispute system design and organizational conflict management. Of these varieties of justice, procedural and organizational justice provided the primary frame for the IU evaluation of REDRESS©. The USPS did not examine distributive justice in terms of systematic patterns in the outcomes of mediation. The median distributive economic value of settlements reported in exit surveys was zero; about a third of the settlements contained commitments to communicate in future with mutual respect. Other substantive outcomes included: retrospective granting of leave; providing access to overtime; opportunities for details to higher rated positions; and adjustments in discipline. Some complainants observed in the comment section of exit surveys that they wanted supervisors punished for their behavior; however, REDRESS© was not designed to provide retributive or deterrent justice for poor behavior at the workplace. At best, it was an effort to restore relations in the workplace community, one mediation case at a time.

The chief lessons learned in the grand USPS experiment with mediation concern organizational justice (Sheppard et al., 1992). Organizational justice explores how employees' perceptions of fairness impact behavior within organizations (Greenberg, 1987). Organizational justice researchers have identified four factors of organizational justice: distributive, procedural, informational, and interpersonal dimensions to explain perceptions of fairness with organizational processes (e.g. Colquitt, 2001; Colquitt et al., 2001). While some scholars have explored disputants' perceptions of distributive and procedural justice in third-party dispute processes, such as mediation, arbitration, and non-union grievance systems (e.g. Austin and Tobiasen, 1984; Lind and Tyler, 1988; Shapiro and Brett, 1993; Tyler et al., 1996; Bingham, 1997; Blancero et al., 2010; Bingham, 1997), no one has examined all four factors of organizational justice in the context of workplace mediation.

Much organizational justice research looks at the relation between a disputant and a neutral or higher level decision-maker, not at the relation to the other disputant (e.g. Colquitt, 2001; Colquitt et al., 2001). This work on organizational justice explains perceptions of fairness in a two-way relationship, where one decision maker (i.e. a supervisor or management) holds authority and control over some kind of subordinate (i.e. an employee or labor). Most organizational justice research involves "an employee and a supervisor, where the supervisor is identified as the relevant authority figure" (Nabatchi et al., 2007: 152) and the supervisor is acting as an agent for the organization responsible for implementing policies and/or making decisions.

This is not the same role as a mediator at the workplace. The mediator is not applying organizational policies or deciding disputes as a management step in a grievance procedure. The mediator is attempting to help parties communicate. Particularly in transformative mediation, disputants' satisfaction with their own interactions (i.e. disputant–disputant) in theory should be an important factor in perceptions of organizational justice. This suggests a need to adapt organizational justice scales and measures to the different triadic structure of mediation. The REDRESS© exit survey database allowed IU to explore these questions.

Using confirmatory factor analysis to examine exit surveys, researchers found that a six-factor model for organizational justice best fit the data (Nabatchi et al., 2007). Factors differed little for employees and supervisors. The six factors included:

1. *Distributive justice*, which captures a disputant's perception of the fairness of the distribution or allocation of outcomes.
2. *Procedural justice-process*, which captures a disputant's perception of the fairness of the rules and procedures that regulate the mediation process.
3. *Procedural justice-mediator*, which captures a disputant's perception of the fairness of the mediator's performance as a professional.
4. *Informational justice*, which captures a disputant's perception of fairness of the enactment and explanation of decision making procedures.
5. *Disputant–mediator interpersonal justice*, which captures a disputant's satisfaction with the way s/he was treated by the mediator in their interactions with each other during the mediation process.
6. *Disputant–disputant interpersonal justice*, which captures a disputant's satisfaction with the way s/he was treated by the other disputant in their interactions with each other during the mediation process. (Nabatchi et al., 2007: 152–4)

This last factor indicates that disputant satisfaction with their own interactions (i.e. disputant–disputant) is an important factor in the perceptions of organizational justice.

However, would disputant–disputant interpersonal justice contribute to settlement? Nesbit et al. (2012) found that it did. Researchers drew a sample of 4,240 paired REDRESS© exit surveys in which complainants and respondents on the same case were matched through an examination of mediator code, zip code, and date of mediation (Nesbit et al., 2012). Matching employee with supervisor exit surveys in a sample, researchers found that disputant–disputant interpersonal justice, and a separate corroboration variable (identifying when employees and supervisors in the same case agreed that they listened to each other) were strong predictors of settlement for both employees and supervisors.

This finding is important for designing employment conflict management systems. It suggests that, despite the fact that settlement is not its goal, transformative mediation may foster settlement better than evaluative mediation. Moreover, the findings suggest that we need to adjust our concept of the determinants of organizational justice when designing conflict management programs.

Voice matters; providing voice in a safe environment that permits disputants to discuss their differences can have a positive impact on organizations.

Conclusion

The USPS created REDRESS© in a unique set of circumstances and for a unique employer. However, its model is easily transferable to other settings. Arguably, mandatory or adhesive employment arbitration systems seek to manage risk, avoid the outlier jury award, and achieve distributive justice in a way that is more accessible or cost effective than litigation. In comparison, voluntary employment mediation can contribute to organizational health by providing opportunities for multiple forms of justice. Mediation programs can provide procedural justice, organizational justice, and distributive justice. They can provide voice and treat people with respect. They can permit disputants to reconcile. They can right a wrong in a way that provides disputants with what they want and need rather than what a court determines they are entitled to. They can do this in a way that fosters individual disputant self-determination and restores the relationship between co-workers, and between disputants and the organization.

However, in order to have these benefits, mediation programs need to avoid both the appearance and reality of pro-employer bias. In the United States, employers have almost complete control over the design of a conflict management system or dispute system design in the absence of a union. The temptation to design a system so as to maximize employer benefit and minimize risk can easily result in a system that is skewed in the employer's favor. The system requires structures that provide checks and balances against bias. In the case of REDRESS©, the USPS tried to achieve this by using transformative mediation. By avoiding mediator evaluation of the merits or strengths and weaknesses of cases, the USPS kept the focus in the mediation session on empowering the disputants and helping them understand each others' views and perspectives on the conflict. While mediators undoubtedly departed from the purest form of transformative mediation practice, the existence of a set of standards may have helped deter abuses like pressing employees to drop their cases in order to improve the mediator's personal settlement rate.

The shift from collective bargaining rights to individual employee rights has brought with it the need for new systems of employee voice to manage workplace conflict. Employment mediation can serve a key role in these new systems.

REFERENCES

Anderson, J. F. and Bingham, L. B. 1997. "Upstream Effects from Mediation of Workplace Disputes: Some Preliminary Evidence from the USPS." *Labor Law Journal*, 48: 601–615.

Austin, W. G. and Tobiasen, J. M. 1984. "Legal Justice and the Psychology of Conflict Resolution." In. R. Folger (ed.), *The Sense of Injustice: Social Psychological Perspectives*. New York: Plenum Press, 227–74.

Bies, R. J. 1987. "The Predicament of Injustice: The Management of Moral Outrage." In L. L. Cummings and B. M Staw (eds.), *Research in Organizational Behavior*. Greenwich, CT: JAI Press, 9: 289–319.

Bingham, L. B. 1997. "Mediating Employment Disputes: Perceptions of REDRESS at the United States Postal Service." *Review of Public Personnel Administration*, XVII(2): 20–30.

Bingham, L. B. 2002a. "Why Suppose? Let's Find Out: A Public Policy Research Program on Dispute Resolution." *Journal of Dispute Resolution*, 1: 101–26.

Bingham, L. B. 2002b. "Self-determination in Dispute System Design and Employment Arbitration." *University of Miami Law Review*, 56(4): 873–908.

Bingham, L. B. 2002c. "The Next Step: Research on How Dispute System Design Affects Function." *Negotiation Journal*, 18(4): 375–9.

Bingham, L. B. 2008–9. "Designing Justice: Legal Institutions and Other Systems for Managing Conflict." *Ohio State Journal on Dispute Resolution*, 24(I): 1–50 (lead article).

Bingham, L. B., Hallberlin, C. J., Walker, D. A., and Chung, W. T. 2009. "Dispute System Design and Justice in Employment Dispute Resolution: Mediation at the Workplace." *Harvard Negotiation Law Review*, 14: 1-50 (lead article).

Bingham, L. B. and Napoli, L. M. 2001. "Employment Dispute Resolution and Workplace Culture: The REDRESS™ Program at the United States Postal Service." In M. Breger and J. Schatz (eds.), *The Federal Alternative Dispute Resolution Deskbook*. Washington, DC: The American Bar Association, 507–26.

Bingham, L. B. and Novac, M. C. 2001. Mediation's Impact on Formal Complaint Filing: Before and After the REDRESS™ Program at the United States Postal Service." *Review of Public Personnel Administration*, 21(4): 308–31.

Bingham, L. B. and Pitts, David W. 2002. "Research Report: Highlights of Mediation at Work: Studies of the National REDRESS® Evaluation Project." *Negotiation Journal*, 18/2: 135–146.

Bingham, L. B., Chesmore, G., Moon, Y., and Napoli, L. M. 2000. "Mediating Employment Disputes at the United States Postal Service: A Comparison of In-house and Outside Neutral Mediators." *Review of Public Personnel Administration*, XX(1): 5–19.

Bingham, L. B., Kim, K., and Raines, S., and Summers, C. W. 2002. "Exploring the Role of Representation in Employment Mediation at the USPS." *Ohio State Journal of Dispute Resolution*, 17(2): 341–77.

Blancero, D. M., DelCampo, R. G., and Marron, G. F. 2010. "Just Tell Me! Making Alternative Dispute Resolution Systems Fair." *Industrial Relations*, 49: 524–43.

Bush, R. A. B. and J. Folger. 1994. *The Promise of Mediation: Responding to Conflict Through Empowerment and Recognition*. San Francisco: Jossey-Bass Publishers.

Califano, Joseph A., Fraser, D. A., Hamburg, B. A., Hamburg, D. A., Robson, J. E. and Zoellick, R. B. 2000. *Report of the United States Postal Service Commission on a Safe and Secure Workplace*. New York, NY: National Center on Addiction and Drug Abuse at Columbia University. Accessed at <http://permanent.access.gpo.gov/lps12068/33994.pdf>.

Colquitt, J. A. 2001. "On the Dimensionality of Organizational Justice: A Construct Validation of a Measure." *Journal of Applied Psychology*, 86(3): 386–400.

Colquitt, J. A., Conlon, D. E., Wesson, M. J., Porter, C., and Ng, K. Y. 2001. "Justice at the Millennium: A Meta-analytic Review of 25 Years of Organizational Justice Research." *Journal of Applied Psychology*, 86: 425–45.

Gann, T. G. and Hallberlin, C. J. 2001. "Recruitment and Training of Outside Neutrals." In Marshall J. Breger et al. (eds.), *The Federal Administrative Dispute Resolution Deskbook*, 623–7. Washington, DC: American Bar Association.

Government Accountability Office, US (GAO, formerly US General Accounting Office) 1992a. *USPS Crisis Management*. Washington, DC: US Government Printing Office, GAO/GGD-92-4R.

Government Accountability Office (GAO) 1992b. *Royal Oak Tragedy*. Washington, DC: US Government Printing Office, GAO/GGD-92-29R.

Government Accountability Office (GAO) 1994a. *U.S. Postal Service: The State of Labor-Management Relations*. Washington, DC: US Government Printing Office, GAO/GGD-95-46.

Government Accountability Office (GAO) 1994b. *Postal Service: Role in a Competitive Communications Environment*. Washington, DC: US Government Printing Office, GAO/GGD-94-162.

Government Accountability Office (GAO) 1994c. *United States Postal Service: Labor Management Problems Persist on the Workroom Floor, Vol. I*. Washington, DC: US Government Printing Office, GAO/GGD-94-201A.

Government Accountability Office (GAO) 1994d. *United States Postal Service: Labor Management Problems Persist on the Workroom Floor, Vol. II*. Washington, DC: US Government Printing Office, GAO/GGD-94-201B.

Government Accountability Office (GAO) 1997a. *United States Postal Service: Little Progress Made in Addressing Persistent Labor–Management Problems, Vol. I*. Washington, DC: US Government Printing Office, GAO/GGD-98-1.

Government Accountability Office (GAO) 1997b. *United States Postal Service: Little Progress Made in Addressing Persistent Labor–Management Problems, Vol. II*. Washington, DC: US Government Printing Office, GAO/GGD-98-7.

Government Accountability Office (GAO) 1998. *Equal Employment Opportunity: Rising Trends in EEO Complaint Caseloads in the Federal Sector*. Washington, DC: US Government Printing Office. GAO/GGD-98-157BR.

Government Accountability Office (GAO) 1999. *Equal Employment Opportunity: Complaint Caseloads Rising, with Effects of New Regulations on Future Trends Unclear*. Washington, DC: US Government Printing Office. GAO/GGD-99-12B.

Greenberg, J. (1987). "A Taxonomy of Organizational Justice Theories." *Academy of Management Review*, 12(1): 9–22.

Hallberlin, C. J. 2001. "Transforming Workplace Culture Through Mediation: Lessons Learned from Swimming Upstream." *Hofstra Labor and Employment Law Journal*, 18: 375–383.

Lind, E. A. and. Tyler, T. R. 1988. *The Social Psychology of Procedural Justice*. New York, NY: Plenum Press.

Moon, Y. and Bingham, L. B. 2007. "Transformative Mediation at Work: Employee and Supervisor Perceptions on USPS REDRESS Program." *International Review of Public Administration*, 11(2): 43–55.

Nabatchi, T. and Bingham, L. B. 2001. "Transformative Mediation in the United States Postal Service REDRESS™ Program: Observations of ADR Specialists." *Hofstra Labor & Employment Law Journal*, 18(2): 399–427.

Nabatchi, T. and Bingham, L. B. 2010. "From Postal to Peaceful: Dispute Systems Design in the United States Postal Service REDRESS Program." *Review of Public Personnel Administration*, 30(2): 211–34.

Nabatchi, T., Bingham, L. B. and Good, D. H. 2007. "Organizational Justice and Workplace Mediation: A Six Factor Model." *International Journal of Conflict Management*, 18(2): 148–76.

Nabatchi, T., Moon, Y. and Bingham, L. B. 2010. Evaluating Transformative Practice in the USPS REDRESS Program. *Conflict Resolution Quarterly*, 27(3): 257–89.

Nabatchi T. and Stanger, A. 2013. Faster? Cheaper? Better? Using ADR to Resolve Federal Sector EEO Complaints. *Public Administration Review*, 73(1): 50–61.

Nesbit, R., T. Nabatchi, and L. B. Bingham 2012. "Employees, Supervisors, and Workplace Mediation: Experiences of Justice and Settlement." *Review of Public Personnel Administration*, 32(3): 260–87.

Primm, E. 1993. "The Neighbor Justice Center Movement." *Kentucky Law Journal*, 81: 1067–83.

Shapiro, D. L. and Brett, J. M. 1993. "Comparing Three Processes Underlying Judgments of Procedural Justice: A Field Study of Mediation and Arbitration." *Journal of Personality and Social Psychology*, 65: 1167–77.

Sheppard, B. H., Lewicki, R. J., and Minton, J. W. 1992. *Organizational Justice: The Search for Fairness in the Workplace*. New York, NY: Lexington Books.

Smith, S. and Martinez, J. 2009. "An Analytic Framework for Dispute Systems Design." *Harvard Negotiation Law Review*, 14: 123–69.

Tyler, T. R., Degoey, P., and Smith, H. J. 1996. "Understanding Why the Justice of Group Procedures Matter: A Test of the Psychological Dynamics of the Group-value Model." *Journal of Personality and Social Psychology*, 70: 913–30.

CHAPTER 14

THE EVOLUTION OF A LABOR-MANAGEMENT PARTNERSHIP

The Case of Kaiser Permanente and the Coalition of Kaiser Permanente Unions

ADRIENNE E. EATON AND THOMAS A. KOCHAN

INTRODUCTION

IN May 2012, elected delegates of the unions affiliated with the Coalition of Kaiser Permanente Unions (the "Coalition") came together to discuss and vote on the latest and newly bargained national collective bargaining agreement that would cover approximately 100,000 workers at the largest health maintenance organization (HMO) in the US. One after another, rank and file union representatives who were involved in the negotiations rose to extol the virtues of the interest-based bargaining process used to reach the new agreement. A worker who had served on the task force focused on employee benefits reported that the "process really worked and it was a great experience." Others were more specific. "Interest-based problem solving is a really good technique we use in the [labor–management] partnership. It's actually one of the fundamental tools because it allows people to see that once you separate the two—management and labor—and allow them to surface their interests, they come together and we look for their common interests," said an optometrist from Kaiser's Northern California region. A nurse from the Southern California region reported, "Coming into this, we could have been very adversarial and not really known what the other side was thinking, but with interest-based meetings, the common issues committee developing those, it really made a difference in understanding that we were all geared toward the same end."[1] In praise rarely heard about labor negotiations, another RN from the Southern California region said, "It was one of the best experiences of my life!" Over the course of the next day, the delegates went on to give their enthusiastic endorsement to the new contract.

In an era of often intense labor–management conflict, with entire states eliminating collective bargaining rights for public sector workers and concessionary agreements being negotiated in a wide array of industries and sectors, how did Kaiser Permanente (KP or just "Kaiser") and the union coalition end up in this place? This chapter provides an overview of the KP labor–management partnership (LMP) from its inception in 1997 to the present day. It both radically condenses the story told in our 2009 book, *Healing Together: The Labor–Management Partnership at Kaiser Permanente* and updates that story. It concludes with a discussion of the challenges ahead for the partnership.

BACKGROUND

Kaiser Permanente is an integrated health insurer and provider of health care. The name brings together the Kaiser Health Plan (the insurance business), the Kaiser Foundation Hospitals (regionally based, non-profits) and the Permanente Medical Groups (for-profit physician practices). Kaiser operates in eight semi-autonomous regions serving over nine million "members," the term used within Kaiser to describe insurance subscribers.[2] The vast majority of these members reside in California where Kaiser operates dozens of hospitals. With the exception of the northwest (with just one), the other regions do not operate hospitals. Taken as a whole, KP operates over 600 medical offices in its various regions, and employs over 16,000 physicians and approximately 173,000 other employees, of whom about 100,000 are members of the 28 union locals that are part of the union Coalition and party to the labor–management partnership. (There are additional unions representing segments of the Kaiser workforce who are not part of the LMP, a phenomenon discussed in additional detail later in the chapter.) The 28 local unions involved in the Coalition are affiliated with an array of national unions, including affiliates of the AFL-CIO and Change to Win. The umbrella organizations include: the American Federation of State, County and Municipal Employees (through its nursing affiliate, UNAC); the American Federation of Teachers (through its healthcare affiliate, OFNHP); the International Brotherhood of Teamsters; the International Federation of Professional and Technical Employees; the International Longshore and Warehouse Union; Office and Professional Employees International Union; the Service Employees International Union; the United Food and Commercial Workers; and the United Steel Workers. It is worth noting that KP is sometimes referred to as the "HMO that labor built" because of the labor movement's role in supporting the establishment and growth of the organization, especially in its early years.[3]

Origins of the Labor Management Partnership

Despite its reputation as the "HMO that labor built" and a decades-long history of mostly positive labor–management relations, when Kaiser began facing serious competitive pressures for the first time in the 1980s, it resorted to the kind of aggressive labor cost cutting typical of US corporations. This included outsourcing work, closing facilities, and the pursuit of collective bargaining concessions from its many unions. In turn, and not surprisingly, Kaiser workers and their unions responded in kind, conducting numerous strikes in the 1980s and 1990s.

At the time, collective bargaining at KP was highly decentralized: the various local unions bargained their own contracts, sometimes multiple contracts for different bargaining units. There was little coordination among the locals either across or even within the various internationals. This made the unions particularly vulnerable to KP's concessionary campaign. The unions began to see that they needed to come together for the first time, to plan resistance. This process began with the Service Employees International Union (SEIU). SEIU was the international union with the largest number of members working for Kaiser and both national and local union leaders were concerned about the deteriorating situation at Kaiser. The union convened meetings of leaders at locals with Kaiser members, meetings that went on for a couple of years. By 1994, then SEIU President John Sweeney asked the Industrial Union Department (IUD) of the AFL-CIO to pull together all of the Kaiser unions to begin to coordinate bargaining. Throughout 1995, the unions began meeting, starting with an international presidents' group, then moving on to a delegates meeting and later a Steering Committee consisting of local presidents.

At these meetings, the unions began to develop both strategies and structures for joint action. Very early on in the process, this took two tacks that came to be known as Plans A and B: one an adversarial corporate campaign approach, and the other a partnership approach. The two were entwined; union leaders felt it was necessary to demonstrate their willingness and ability to hurt Kaiser via a strategic campaign, but at the same time were concerned about inflicting permanent damage on a heavily unionized employer. Pete deCicco, then Secretary-Treasurer of the IUD, was interested in a partnership approach based, in part, on his own experience with job enrichment at General Electric in Lynn, Massachusetts, when he was an IUE business agent. DeCicco and others conceived of the partnership approach as not just an alternative labor relations strategy, but also an alternative business strategy that would emphasize a high road, quality of care focus rather than the low road the unions felt KP was pursuing.

Importantly, Kaiser management was having a similar conversation. They were worried about the impact of repeated strikes and the prospects of more trouble as the unions began to band together. It was in this context that union and management leaders met, along with then director of the Federal Mediation and Conciliation Service,

John Calhoun Wells, at the Dallas airport in December 1995 where union leaders were surprised by the conciliatory and partnership-oriented opening talk by KP CEO, David Lawrence. This meeting established that there was strong interest, though not unanimity, on both sides of the labor–management divide in a more collaborative approach. The Dallas meeting began a period of intense negotiations, facilitated by John Stepp and Tom Schneider of Restructuring Associates, Inc. (RAI) and other mediators, that took place throughout 1996 and into 1997 and resulted in a written partnership agreement.

EARLY YEARS

Early on, the parties created a joint governance structure for the partnership. At the top of that structure sat the Senior Partnership Committee (or Council as it later became titled), co-chaired by Peter diCicco, who had become the Executive Director of the Coalition of Kaiser Permanente Unions, and Gary Fernandez, Kaiser's senior vice-president in charge of the partnership. There were approximately 50 members of this group drawn from local or regional labor and management leadership. The group met four times a year to share reports and coordinate partnership activities. Below this sat similar joint leadership structures at the regional and at the service area or local facility levels. It is important to note that the lower you went down into the organization, the less consistently you would find functioning partnership structures at this time: some facilities might have a regularly meeting local steering committee and lots of partnership activities and others might have nothing.

The parties also built a staff structure in these early stages, known then and now as the Office of Labor–Management Partnership (OLMP). The OLMP staff included internal consultants, half drawn from management and half from labor. Kaiser itself funded these positions. The union coalition funded separate staff positions—a very few at the start but which have grown in number considerably over time.

The parties faced some early challenges to their budding relationship related to security for both the unions and their members. While the original partnership agreement had called for employment security for union workers, there was lack of clarity about what was intended and some contentious redeployments of covered employees had taken place. The Senior Partnership Council and other leaders worked through the issue and reached a five-page, more detailed agreement around employment security in fall of 1999. This agreement provided an important foundation to guide staffing decisions through later budgetary crises and the implementation of a major program of technological change—the implementation of a new electronic medical records system. Tensions around management's response to union organizing and inadequate management neutrality language in the initial partnership agreement similarly led to a more detailed agreement on this issue, also in 1999.

In this same timeframe, two very exciting and intense partnership projects provided the parties with the kind of early "wins" that partnerships typically require for sustenance. One of these involved the opening of a new hospital in the Southern California region. A joint labor–management team used partnership principles to design a more patient-centered facility and open it in a more accelerated timeframe than was typical (8 months versus 2 years). The hospital initially performed highly on important metrics and the participants built trust and a good story of how to work together. The second project involved a joint redesign of an existing facility, the Optical Lab in Northern California, which management had originally slated for closure. Using interest-based problem-solving methods, the parties were able to identify ways to reduce costs, increase revenues, and improve quality and service sufficiently to save the facility. Again, the individual labor and management representatives involved experienced the process as a transformative one.

FIRST INTEREST-BASED BARGAINING NEGOTIATIONS

The labor–management relationship and ultimately the partnership took another step forward in 2000 when the parties negotiated a first time ever national agreement *and* did it using Interest-Based Bargaining (IBB). Bargaining over a new labor contract often presents significant challenges to labor–management partnerships as the "rules of engagement" and modes of interacting are frequently in contradiction. The Kaiser partnership had faced an early challenge when local bargaining in the Northwest region led to a strike in 1997. This helped convince the partnership leaders that a different approach was needed. Labor was also pushing for a unified, national negotiation process, an idea initially rejected but eventually accepted by management leaders after a mediator helped the parties carefully design a complex negotiation process that created safeguards and opt outs if either party felt it was headed off the rails.

The process, which has been used in the other episodes of comprehensive national bargaining at KP ever since, involved decentralized task groups of labor and management representatives, using IBB methods to develop recommended solutions in various issue areas. In 2000 there were seven task groups focusing on wages, benefits, work–life balance, performance and workforce development, quality and service, employee health and safety, and work organization and innovation. About 300 people participated in these groups. The recommendations went forward to a joint negotiating body called the "Common Issues Committee." Although the CIC process was rockier than the task group process, and at times resembled more traditional, positional bargaining, an agreement was reached that was ratified by 93% of the union members voting.

INTER-REGNUM

Despite successful national negotiations, the early wins and the infrastructure development, the partnership was still diffusing slowly. In 2001, internal Kaiser employee surveys indicated that 18–29% of partnership union-represented employees reported personal involvement in the partnership.[4] While the interaction between labor and management leadership was improving, there was real frustration throughout the organization at the difficulties in moving the partnership to the frontline workforce, a movement that would be necessary, all agreed, to achieve the kinds of organizational performance improvements that everyone hoped for.

There was also substantial variation in the intensity of partnership activity across both time and space. A particular hospital in California might have a very high level of partnership activity with union leaders integrated into managerial leadership groups and multiple labor–management committees meeting on a wide variety of projects including initiatives of strategic importance to the organization, while another hospital in the same region might have very little partnership activity and extremely hostile labor–management relations. Even the first hospital might not look the same after a year or two—if a key manager or union leader changed and commitment to partnership declined, partnership activity could fall off considerably.

SECOND IBB NEGOTIATIONS

The parties went into the second round of national negotiations in 2005 facing these and other challenges. The other challenges came from both sides of the traditional labor–management table. On the management side, while Kaiser had experienced financial ups and downs overall, some of the regions outside of California were struggling (and continue to do so today) and the organization's leadership worried about the state of the nation's health care system and the constant downward pressures on costs from their insurance customers. The leadership of Kaiser's Southern California region was also fixated on solving a chronic attendance problem. Meanwhile, SEIU, the largest of the Kaiser unions, was threatening to leave the AFL-CIO and take other affiliates—including some involved in the Kaiser coalition—with it. In addition, as part of SEIU's internal restructuring, the large southern and northern California locals had merged, putting intense pressure on the union's local and national leadership to deliver real gains for members in order to demonstrate the value of the restructuring. A survey of the parties, done shortly after bargaining concluded, shows that while the parties had some overlapping priorities for the negotiations, there were also substantial differences (Kochan et al., 2009: 100). The most salient of these involved regional differences. Management was interested in an agreement that reflected the different health care and labor markets in the different regions while labor placed a high priority on reducing wage differentials across regions. Labor was also keenly interested in increasing management accountability for the partnership; management, not so much.

Despite the gaps in the parties' respective hopes for the focus and outcome of bargaining, they were once again successful in negotiating a new agreement. It is also clear that labor was much happier with the outcome than management. The process itself resembled the 2000 process. Task groups were used again; they met for fifteen days stretched over four months. This time there were eight such groups: attendance, benefits, performance-based pay, performance improvement, service quality, scope of practice, work–life balance, and workforce development. The topics these groups worked on reflected the agendas of the different parties and, to an even greater degree than in 2000, are remarkable in the history of US collective bargaining. All but one of the groups made extensive use of the interest-based process. The one that reverted to more traditional bargaining, at least in the eyes of many of the participants, was the benefits group. The union representatives to this group were looking to maintain benefit levels generally and to eliminate regional differences in benefits through bringing the lower regions up. Management resisted the latter goal and was interested in introducing a defined contribution pension plan for the first time, but as a supplement to rather than a substitute for the traditional defined benefit pension. Although a more traditional process was used, even this group was able to issue a set of joint recommendations. The recommendations from all the task groups were again forwarded to the Common Issues Committee for the final stages of the negotiations process.

The concluding phase of the negotiations, the work of the Common Issues Committee, was hardly smooth sailing. Reaching consensus on the task group recommendation on attendance proved difficult and ate up a lot of time, which in turn put pressure on the parties to fashion a settlement on economic issues. Here again, the process become much more positional and traditional. Many members of the management team had not been through traditional bargaining before and as the process and the related behaviors on the labor side of the table became more traditional, they became upset. At the same time, and probably not surprisingly given the organizational complexities on both sides of the table, the intra-organizational bargaining processes became very intense and difficult. On the management side, this largely took the form of conflict between the lead negotiators and organizational leadership who were not at the table. Indeed, management stepped to the brink of abandoning national bargaining for a return to decentralized local bargaining and probably some accompanying labor unrest, but backed away. As is often the case in traditional bargaining, much work at this stage was actually done in sidebars with a single management and labor leader or a very small group of leaders. One such sidebar led to a proposed solution of equity adjustments across regions and a mid-contract reopener. This caused the union team to explode internally—in particular, with non-SEIU unions blowing up at SEIU. In the end, the union coalition was able to reallocate the money that KP management had placed on the table in ways that were viewed as more equitable and most union leaders felt that SEIU had used its considerable bargaining power for the collective good rather than its own narrower interests.

2005–9

While the economic issues had created most of the fireworks in the negotiation process, the new agreement also dealt with two nagging problems: the lack of focus on performance improvement and the failure to move the partnership in any broad and sustained way to the frontlines. The new agreement contained significant new language on performance improvement. This excerpt from the 2005 agreement provides a sense of the breath of the parties' vision:

> The parties are dedicated to working together to make Kaiser Permanente the recognized market leader in providing quality health care and service. This can be accomplished through creating a service culture, achieving performance goals, developing the Kaiser Permanente workforce, increasing employee satisfaction, promoting patient safety programs and focusing attention on employee health and work-life personal-life balance. The goal is to continually improve performance by investing in people and infrastructure, improving communication skills, fostering leadership, and supporting involvement in the community.[5]

It also called for the implementation of Unit-Based Teams (UBTs) throughout the organization. UBTs are discussed further in the next section.

2009–Present

How has the partnership fared since 2009? The good, maybe even remarkable, news is that it survived an escalating inter-union battle for members between the SEIU and a rival National Union of Health Care Workers (NUHW) created by Sal Rosselli, a former SEIU leader who broke away from SEIU after the national union put his California local in trusteeship. It also continued to use interest-based negotiations processes to negotiate a wage reopener in 2010 and, as described in the opening paragraph, a contract renewal in 2012. Perhaps the most notable achievement in recent years has been the adoption and spread of frontline work teams the parties call "Unit Based Teams" (UBTs). Yet significant challenges lie ahead as the inter-union conflicts continue and as the parties search for ways to adapt to a changing health care policy environment.

The Inter-union Battle and its Effects

In January 2009, the SEIU placed its California local union, with 60,000 Kaiser members, in trusteeship for alleged mismanagement of union funds. This was the culmination of months, actually years, of sparring over union strategy between SEIU President Andrew Stern and Sal Rosselli, president of SEIU's very large, consolidated health care union local in California, UHW (United Healthcare Workers—West). Rosselli objected to, among other things, the national union's pursuit of collective bargaining agreements that focused more on getting firms to accept the union in previously unorganized settings than negotiating strong initial contracts. While this was the key substantive issue in the debate, deep interpersonal differences between these two leaders were also at the heart of their rift. In response to the trusteeship, Rosselli resigned from SEIU and started building NUHW, and began aggressive efforts to convince Kaiser workers to switch to his union. Union petitions for elections to represent these workers were filed and although NUHW failed to win an election with the largest units, it did win three small units and challenged the legality of the overall election results by arguing that SEIU committed a range of unfair labor practices and also argued that Kaiser management took actions that "favored" the SEIU partnership union—an act that is illegal under the US National Labor Relations Act. The National Labor Relations board ruled that some of the NUHW claims were valid and thus ordered the election be rerun. The election was held in April, 2013. Once again SEIU won the election by a 57% to 43% margin and, therefore, will continue to represent all but a small number of the Kaiser service employees. This is not, however, likely to end the inter-union battles. NUHW will continue its efforts to reach contract settlements in the three bargaining units it represents. It has not been able to do so up to this point, despite the pressures exerted through several one day strikes.

The effect of this on-going battle has been frustrating to Kaiser managers and union leaders who want to continue to move the partnership forward. The internal union fighting and NLRB elections have slowed the implementation of Unit-Based Teams in some areas. NUHW has taken a largely negative posture toward the partnership and SEIU has excluded NUHW from the union coalition and insisted that NUHW be excluded from the partnership. The battle has also led Kaiser management to formalize and tighten its labor relations strategy to focus more attention on complying with doctrines and regulations of the NLRA. Yet support for the partnership remains very strong among senior executives at Kaiser.

2010 and 2012 Contract Negotiations

In 2010 Kaiser and the Coalition negotiated a wage reopener and in 2012 the full contract was up for renegotiation. Both sets of negotiations were preceded by the same extensive amount of information exchange and sharing regarding Kaiser's financial performance and projections, and by engaging large numbers of local union delegates in pre-bargaining conversations. Interest-based negotiations techniques were used in both years, although less extensively in 2010 given that the scope of bargaining was limited to wages. A major debate within management (and with union leaders) occurred in 2010 over whether to address Kaiser's growing concerns over future pension and retiree health care liabilities, however a decision was made to put those aside with a commitment to address them in 2012 negotiations. The pool of union representatives involved in the negotiations process, already large by most standards was also expanded in 2010. Stimulated at least in part by NUHW criticism of a bargaining process that allegedly excluded rank and file members, the unions created an observer status and expanded the Common Issues Committee so as to increase opportunities for rank and file involvement.

The pension issue thus became the central management objective for 2012 and a central issue in bargaining. Some within management describe the results as "outstanding" and some describe them as "a very important first step" in efforts to curb what had been viewed as unsustainable future increases. Essentially the parties capped Kaiser's future liabilities for retiree health care costs by agreeing that employees would absorb cost increases if the overall rate of health care costs rises above a threshold amount. This cap is scheduled to take effect in 2017 although union leaders are clear that they plan to raise the cap when the time for implementation approaches. As long as a cap is in place, however, it gives Kaiser's actuaries the ability to predict its future costs with greater certainty and less money needs to be set aside each year to cover these future costs. All the parties that participated directly in the negotiations over this complex set of issues described it as a good example of the use of interest-based bargaining. Management was clear about its interests: getting control over future cost projections to reduce its open ended responsibilities and thereby lowering the amount it needed to set aside to cover future liabilities. The Coalition was equally clear about its key interest: No cuts in benefits. A benefits' subcommittee used these two interests to explore options and ended with an agreement that achieved both.

One of the most interesting aspects of the 2012 agreement is the emphasis given to promoting a healthy workforce. This too was a keen interest of management. The Coalition shared this interest but was keen on not designing a program or set of incentives or penalties that would apply to *individual* members (the kind of bonuses to stop smoking, for example, that some employers have implemented). The result, labeled "Total Health," is a range of joint education and other programs to promote workforce awareness along with small monetary incentives that would trigger bonuses if certain targets are met *collectively*. Our sense is that this represents the most elaborate set of contract and/or joint union–management provisions on this subject in the country. Further, it is likely to get organizational attention and support in that it is tied into a Kaiser business strategy of improving the health of their insurance customers' workers. Total Health within Kaiser is intended to provide a model for those customers. At the same time, some union delegates reacted negatively to this aspect of the new contract, feeling the program will represent an intrusion into their private lives, a view encouraged by NUHW.[6]

The process used in 2012 was largely similar to that used in earlier bargaining rounds. Observers were again used and many of the union representatives who testified at the May 2012 delegates meeting to the positive experience of IBB and the contract that resulted had occupied the observer role.

Expansion of Unit Based Teams

In 2005, negotiations culminated in a joint commitment to focus on expanding "unit based teams" (UBTs), that is, cross functional teams of frontline employees (nurses, service employees, technicians, physicians, and managers) to focus on Kaiser's core objectives (what they call their value compass) of quality, service, cost control, and a great place to work. Efforts to get this initiative launched floundered for two years during a period of leadership turnover on both the union and management sides of the partnership. Momentum then picked up when the new partnership leaders made this a high priority and UBTs have evolved to become the centerpiece of partnership efforts to improve health care delivery and performance. Annual goals were set in 2005 to increase the numbers of teams, culminating in a goal of 100% coverage by 2010. Given the official achievement of that goal, the new agreement focuses on increasing the effectiveness of UBTs, with targeted percentages at the "high performance" level increasing each year. By June 2012 1,100 teams were operating, covering nearly all of the Coalition members, although only some members were actively engaged as participants. Internal Kaiser analysis of the teams found that those rated 4 or 5 on their 5-point effectiveness scale achieved higher employee satisfaction ratings on Kaiser's "People Pulse" survey. Higher scores on this survey in turn have been shown to be related to higher levels of patient satisfaction and several other quality of care measures.

There remains a great deal of variability in team effectiveness, however. Teams in Northern California are hampered by the fact that the nurses in that region are not part of the Coalition and their leaders actively discourage them from participating in these teams. Although the actual participation by nurses varies, this variation complicates considerably the work of teams in that region and makes managing them more challenging than in settings where the nurses are encouraged by their union to participate.

A study of over a dozen high performing teams drawn from different regions and working in different types of departments including, but not exclusively, patient care, identified several factors that appeared to be associated with success. These include: joint leadership by management and labor representatives; clear "line of sight" from the team's work to important organizational goals; measurement of the team's contribution to those goals and team review of those measures; use of both interest-based problem solving and a Rapid Improvement Model being diffused in the organization; training, facilitation and metrics support; and flexibility in structure, methods, and scheduling (Eaton et al., 2010).

National Health Care Policy and its Effects

The US finally enacted a national health insurance law in 2010 that extends coverage to most of the population. However, it remains highly controversial. The re-election of President Obama greatly increased the likelihood that the law would not be repealed any time soon, although there continues to be resistance to certain aspects of the law from Republican governors of some states. The law poses both tremendous opportunities and challenges to Kaiser and the labor–management partnership. The opportunities lie in the large new pool of potential customers that Kaiser can compete for—essentially a pool of lower income individuals and families. But the payment provisions in the law will put enormous downward pressure on prices for health care coverage, both for the new low income enrollees and for those over the age of 65 covered by the nation's Medicare program. Kaiser cannot hope to compete for these groups without substantially lowering the price of its insurance offerings and services.

This will pose a significant challenge to the partnership. The partnership has done a good job at helping Kaiser achieve incremental changes in practices that gradually improve services, quality, and cost performance. The new price points for these growth opportunities will, however, likely require radical or disruptive changes to lower costs that cannot be achieved with marginal or incremental changes in practices. Whether and how Kaiser and the partnership address the demand for disruptive change will be among the next big challenges the parties face.

Conclusions

The partnership built by Kaiser Permanente and its union coalition has now survived for fifteen years and continues to serve as the nation's largest and most comprehensive labor–management partnership in history. While labor–management partnerships tend to have limited half-lives in the United States, this one has demonstrated an ability to work through the various pivotal events that come along and often lead to the demise of partnerships. For example, in response to a threatened layoff, the parties negotiated a comprehensive employment security agreement, restructured operations and work systems in an optical laboratory that significantly improved performance and avoided closure. They also introduced one of the nation's largest electronic health care systems without laying off any workers, and managed through several leadership successions in both the management and union organizations.

Kaiser was successful in stopping and then reversing the downward spiral in which the parties were caught in the mid-1990s; it has achieved net operating surpluses (as a non-profit it does not earn "profits") in each year since 2000. The partnership produced a decade of labor peace and only recently have work stoppages involving non-partnership unions at Kaiser become a significant problem. Labor relations in the day-to-day functioning of the organization improved markedly, as evidenced by the decline in grievance rates and many examples of the effective use of issue resolution tools developed by the parties. The parties' use of interest-based bargaining in five successive negotiations of national-level agreements represents the largest (in terms of number of workers, geographic scope of operations, and number of unions covered) and the most extensive (in terms of range of issues addressed and numbers of participants involved) application of this process in US labor relations.

The majority of the Coalition members have responded favorably to the partnership. A 2008 survey found that 70% of the union members responding preferred partnership over a more arms-length labor–management relationship. Moreover, union members participating directly in partnership activities reported higher levels of job satisfaction and influence in decision-making than those not participating. The same result was found for those participating in UBTs compared to those not directly involved in these workplace level teams.

Under the partnership, the capacity of employees to influence decisions increased, both at an individual level and collectively, through their unions. Employees and union leaders learned new skills and the new organizational arrangements within and across the unions gave them new capacities for collective action, such as working in coalition and participating in decision-making on topics and processes, including the design and planning of new facilities that heretofore had been out of their reach.

Wages have risen at least in tandem with, and for certain lower paid occupational groups more than, wages of other health care workers across the country while the cuts in health care and pensions experienced by many US workers have been avoided.

The introduction of electronic medical records technologies was actively supported by the partnership. The collectively bargained agreement outlining how workforce issues would be dealt with paved the way for acceptance of this initiative and provided the guidelines for involving workers and union leaders at the local level in fitting the new technologies to their specific circumstances.

Finally, and of particular importance to a labor movement facing continued union decline and continuous conflicts in union organizing drives, Kaiser's unions expanded in tandem with the growth of Kaiser's workforce and organized approximately 8,000 new members. Is this partnership sustainable? Here we are cautiously optimistic, yet, given the long history of labor–management partnerships in the United States, we are also realistic. The partnership faces at least two big challenges.

First, the inter-union rivalries involving SEIU, NUHW, the CNA, and now several other unions continue to frustrate management and divert union attention, resources, and efforts. Whether Kaiser's employees will continue to endorse the partnership and choose partnership unions over rivals that favor a more militant and arms-length strategy remains to be seen. So far the majority has continued to support the partnership in election votes, in ratification of negotiated agreements, in surveys, and in participation in teams. The battle for Kaiser union members will, however, likely continue for some time and with it all the tensions and risks to the partnership.

The second big challenge lies in whether and, if so, how the parties will address the cost pressures and new service modes required to participate in the new national health care legislation. Significant disruptive changes in modes of health care delivery are likely to occur in the US in the near future. Pressures to increase preventive care, coordinated delivery and payment of health care work to Kaiser's advantage since it has years of experience in doing this. Yet its costs are significantly higher than the reimbursement rates for low income and retired patients will allow. Whether the partnership can help respond to the disruptive changes in the health care industry that lie ahead will ultimately determine whether or not the partnership will survive.

Notes

1. Some of these quotes and other interviews could be viewed at <http://www.lmpartnership.org/stories-videos/getting-thumbs> at the time of writing this chapter.
2. The regions are—in order by size of membership: Northern California, Southern California, Colorado, Mid-Atlantic (the Washington, DC, area), Northwest (Oregon and parts of southern Washington), Hawaii, Georgia, and Ohio.
3. For details on that history, see Kochan et al. (2009: 25–30), and Hendricks (1993).
4. The range represents scores in different regions. Mid-Atlantic was the low end and Southern California the high with other regions in between.
5. This language was first included in the National Labor Agreement in 2005 and remained unchanged in 2012. See 2012 *National Agreement: Coalition of Kaiser Permanente Unions and Kaiser Permanente*, p. 12. <http://www.lmpartnership.org/what-is-partnership/national-agreements/2012-national-agreement>.
6. An NUHW flyer posted on the union's website (<http://nuhw.squarespace.com/storage/doc/leaflets/Peer%20Pressure.pdf>) argues "Our personal lifestyles are none of SEIU's business. We're adults, and we shouldn't be punished for making our own decisions about our lives." It goes on to complain that "SEIU will share private, personal information about us with management."

References

Eaton, A., Konitsney, D., Litwin, A. S., and Vanderhorst, N. 2010. "The Path to Performance: A Study of High-Performing Unit-Based Teams at Kaiser Permanente." Publication of the Kaiser Permanent Labor Management Partnership, Dec.

Hendricks, R. 1993. *A National Model for Health Care: The History of Kaiser Permanente*. New Brunswick NJ: Rutgers University Press.

Kochan, T., Eaton, A., McKersie, R., and Adler, P. 2009. *Healing Together: The Labor Management Partnership at Kaiser Permanente*. Ithaca, NY: Cornell University Press.

CHAPTER 15

··

"MED+ARB" IN THE
NEW ZEALAND POLICE

··

IAN McANDREW[*]

INTRODUCTION

··

MANY nations accept that law enforcement personnel are entitled, like other employees, to engage in collective bargaining over their pay and conditions. There are exceptions, perhaps most prominently the Royal Canadian Mounted Police. But even in the roll-back of public worker rights in parts of the United States since 2010, police have usually been the exception who retained their rights. Indeed, there would be few occupations more completely unionized in the Western world than law enforcement, even if many police would not acknowledge their organizations as "unions".

If they were of a collective mind to do so, police could be devastatingly effective in striking to have their way at the collective bargaining table. There have been strikes in the past, including some quite notorious ones, such as those in Boston and London in 1918, and that in Melbourne, Australia in 1923. New Zealand's first police strike was a small affair in Wellington in 1852, and there were quite a number of others to follow. But in more recent times, while there were waves of police strikes in parts of the United States in the 1970s and 1980s, there have been nothing more than sporadic police strikes around the world since then. Demonstrations and lesser forms of job actions have

* The author is indebted to advocates for the New Zealand Police and the New Zealand Police Association involved in collective bargaining, mediation, and arbitration across two decades for their generous involvement in interviews and sharing of information and insights that have informed this study. Thanks are due also to the *Handbook* editors for helpful comments. The author remains responsible for any errors of fact or interpretation.

appeared occasionally, but strikes have been rare. Disinclination among police personnel is a factor, but so too is public policy.

It is widely believed that public safety considerations demand that police officers not be entitled to strike. This notion was most famously expressed by the then-Governor of Massachusetts, Calvin Coolidge, on the occasion of the Boston police strike: "There is no right to strike against the public safety by anybody, anywhere, any time." Even the International Labour Organization accepts that police should be an exception to the otherwise universal principle that workers are entitled to withdraw their labor (ILO 2003: 100).

With bargaining authorized but strikes prohibited, policy-makers have long sought effective alternative impasse procedures in the event of a breakdown in police labor negotiations. Non-coercive measures, such as mediation, conciliation, and fact-finding are often tried and frequently successful, but cannot guarantee a resolution. So governments in many jurisdictions provide some form of binding arbitration for the ultimate resolution of law enforcement collective bargaining disputes.

Since 1990, New Zealand has employed a unique, multi-faceted, party-directed, flexible and constantly evolving system combining negotiation, mediation, and arbitration for the setting of pay and conditions for the national (and only) police force. This chapter first briefly surveys impasse resolution processes relevant to collective disputes before describing the evolution and experience of the New Zealand model, and noting its strengths and limitations.

Dispute Resolution in Collective Bargaining

In collective bargaining regimes, agreements freely reached between the bargaining parties without outside involvement are generally prized as most rewarding and enduring. Beyond that, mediation or conciliation, variously defined, are almost universally available in one form or another to assist bargaining parties who run into difficulties, and they are frequently successful, particularly where the difficulties arise from process miscalculations and where the parties' real bottom line tolerances, once pressed, are not incompatible.

Conciliation and mediation are terms often used interchangeably. However, in New Zealand they are recognized as different processes. Conciliation has a history stretching back to the 1890s in New Zealand and it has historically denoted a more proactive involvement by the neutral in managing the issues under negotiation than would be true in mediation, which tends to be directed more baldly at promoting settlement through compromise. Curiously, in some other countries, these terms have precisely the reverse meanings (Brenninkmeijer et al., 2006: 15). Either way, the assistance to parties in reaching their own settlements through these processes has a long record of success in collective bargaining, including in New Zealand.

In most private sector collective bargaining regimes, only these non-coercive impasse procedures are available. If they fail to produce a result, the bargaining parties are generally left to their own devices. On the other hand, in many public sector jurisdictions, where strikes and other job actions are considered less appropriate, additional impasse procedures are often provided for by statute, particularly for law enforcement and perhaps other public safety workers. These procedures might include additional non-coercive measures like fact-finding, advisory arbitration, or facilitation (McAndrew, 2012), but in many jurisdictions they include binding arbitration in one form or another.

All Australian states and Canadian provinces and a majority of American states (Slater, 2012: 215) provide some form of binding interest arbitration for public sector collective bargaining disputes, more often for police than for any other occupation. Some form of third-party adjudication is generally available in European jurisdictions as well, although there is much less of a history of resort to arbitration in the more political labor relations environment in Europe.

There are a number of "standard" forms of arbitration in use, some involving an integration or interaction with other techniques, principally mediation or conciliation. And there have been some other more exotic variations—most originating in the labor relations arena—either tried or suggested in the never-ending quest to find alternatives to strikes and lockouts and to the perceived deficiencies of conventional arbitration forms. A brief review is in order before presenting the New Zealand med+arb system for police labor–management negotiations, which incorporates ideas from a number of these dispute resolution methods.

Conventional Arbitration

"Conventional arbitration" was the first system of final and binding arbitration used for police collective bargaining impasses and it is still employed in most jurisdictions where arbitration is available. It was much studied in the 1970s and 1980s but has been largely left alone since then. One exception is the comprehensive "long haul" assessment of conventional arbitration under New York State's 1967 Taylor Law by Kochan et al. (2010).

In conventional interest arbitration the parties present evidence and argument to the arbitrator, after which the arbitrator issues a final and binding award setting the terms thus far unresolved between the parties.

The arbitrator is free to make any determination on each of the issues still in dispute, whether that be the final position of one of the parties, or a position between the final positions of the parties, or conceivably even a position outside those parameters. There would ordinarily be criteria, usually set out in statute, to guide or bind the arbitrator. The parties' evidence and argument would be directed at those criteria, and in most regimes the arbitrator would be required to provide some reasoning for his or her award in terms of the applicable criteria.

Conventional arbitration was subject to several early process criticisms. It was said that arbitrators would tend to "split the difference" between the final positions of the parties rather than ruling on the merits. That being so, the availability of arbitration would have a "chilling effect" on the negotiations process, discouraging compromise, as parties held their positions for arbitration. It was also thought that there might be a "narcotic effect" with parties increasingly relying on arbitration to set the terms, directing their strategies to arbitration, and eventually losing the skills and will to freely negotiate agreements together.

There is considerable evidence, including the study by Kochan et al. (2010) to suggest that these concerns were overstated, but they nonetheless have continued to concern some critics and stimulated experimentation with alternative approaches to binding arbitration.

Final Offer Arbitration

"Final offer arbitration" (FOA) was introduced in a handful of North American public sector jurisdictions to address some of the perceived deficiencies of conventional arbitration. In an FOA system, the arbitrator must select the final position of one or the other party and is not entitled to "split the difference" or fashion some other solution of his or her own design. The thinking behind FOA is that the parties will be motivated to compromise in order to win the arbitrator's endorsement of their final position, thereby overcoming the "chilling effect." Ideally, in the process of the parties each positioning themselves as the more reasonable on the applicable criteria, they will sail close enough to see the prospect of a voluntary settlement, and both will view that as preferable to the risk of losing the arbitration ballot. FOA is the system used in professional baseball salary disputes in North America. Hanany et al.'s (2007) analysis in that context demonstrated that risk aversion can be a motivator for parties to reduce their demands and settle during the dispute resolution process rather than take their chances with the arbitrator's decision under FOA.

There are two forms of FOA. In "issue-by-issue FOA," the arbitrator must select the final position of one or the other party on each separate issue in dispute, thereby allowing the arbitrator some room to fashion a compromise where there are several or many issues for resolution in arbitration. A "package FOA" model, on the other hand, has no such soft option. The arbitrator must select the final position across all issues that best fits the applicable criteria, thereby discouraging the parties from taking an adventurous position on even a single issue that might spoil the appeal of the package.

Blending Arbitration with Mediation

Various models have been devised in an effort to combine the persuasive advantages of mediation (or conciliation) with the certainty of binding arbitration. Conventionally in collective bargaining, where arbitration is provided for, the processes are sequential. First, the parties attempt to negotiate an agreement unassisted. In rare instances they may be guided by a conciliator effectively chairing the negotiations; more usually they are initially left to their own devices. Failing agreement, a mediator might enter the negotiations to manoeuvre the parties towards a settlement. Customarily, in arbitration regimes, parties would move into the arbitration phase of dispute resolution only following the failure of mediation. Mediation and arbitration would be provided by separate neutrals, with little interaction between them. It would typically be considered inappropriate for the arbitrator to have access to information imparted to the mediator by the parties in separate caucuses or even jointly.

There are, however, several variations of dispute resolution, tried or advocated for collective bargaining that seek to combine mediation and arbitration. The first is by use of a *tripartite arbitration panel* in lieu of a single arbitrator. As with a single arbitrator, a panel would ordinarily be convened following the failure of mediation. However, the deliberations within a tripartite panel allow the neutral chair an opportunity to mediate further between the representatives of the parties on the panel to try to come up with a unanimous award. The neutral may indicate his or her "leanings" in order to stimulate compromise during this process. Should these efforts at settlement be unsuccessful, the neutral will decide the matter with the support of one or the other of the partisan panel members.

There are other more formal efforts to combine the advantages of mediation and arbitration. Perhaps the best known is *"med-arb,"* a process used in a variety of jurisdictions, including labor and employment relations, but recognized more often for rights disputes than for interest matters such as collective bargaining. As occurs informally in a tripartite panel, in med-arb a single neutral first attempts to mediate a settlement between the parties, but failing that will resolve the matters in dispute by issuing a binding award.

The principal criticism of med-arb is the contended incompatibility of the two roles. Knowing that the neutral may ultimately be making a decision is likely to have a "chilling effect" on the parties in the mediation phase as they position themselves for the arbitration phase. They will not only hold their positions, but they will also be less than fully forthcoming to the neutral. The neutral, thus lacking full knowledge, will be both less effective in mediation than a "pure" mediator and incompletely informed at the arbitration stage. In the unlikely event that a party is fully open with the neutral, then the neutral is likely to have information at the arbitration stage that an arbitrator rightly ought not to have (Dendorfer and Lack, 2007).

"Arb-med" is a process proposed to counter the "chilling effect" of med-arb. Arb-med again involves a single neutral who first hears the evidence and argument of the parties and prepares an award that will bind the parties in the event that a voluntary settlement is not reached, but is sealed pending efforts at settlement. The neutral then attempts to mediate an agreement between the parties. The advantage over med-arb is said to be that the parties can be more open with the neutral during mediation. Unconcerned with positioning themselves for an arbitration outcome that is already locked away, they can

be more settlement-oriented, motivated by the aversion to gambling on the arbitration award (Ross and Conlon, 2000).

"*Mediation-supported arbitration*" (Vipond, 2010; Johnson, 2010) is another variation employed in the Canadian province of British Columbia (BC) for first contract impasses. In the BC process, a mediator called into a bargaining impasse, but unable to resolve it in mediation, is entitled to make a range of recommendations as to either the substance of the issues or the process the parties might follow (strike or lockout, arbitration, or med-arb). The parties have an additional period of 20 days following the recommendations to attempt to resolve matters voluntarily. The parties are free to introduce the mediator's substantive recommendations in arbitration and they are given considerable deference. However, communications during the mediation process are inadmissible in arbitration. The mediator's process recommendations must be approved by the head of the mediation service, but there is a presumption that they will be, absent compelling reasons to the contrary.

Giving the mediator a range of options for making recommendations is intended to allow the mediator to tailor recommendations to the circumstances of the particular dispute. It is also designed to motivate negotiation by creating uncertainty, not only over whether and what substantive recommendations will be issued by the mediator, but also over whether arbitration will actually be available. That the mediator's substantive recommendations are disclosable to the arbitrator is intended to encourage the parties to take the mediation process seriously rather than waiting for arbitration. The deference shown by arbitrators to the mediators' recommendations is likewise intended to motivate the parties to deal in mediation.

Other variations on the theme of integrating mediation and arbitration have been proposed, even if not all have been tested. Goldberg (2003) proposed *post-arbitration negotiation* in which parties have a short period of time to attempt to negotiate an agreement, if necessary with the assistance of a mediator, after the arbitrator has heard evidence and argument and tabled the arbitration award.

Essentially, the parties have the opportunity to agree a better deal for both of them than that represented by the arbitrator's intended award. Failing a full agreement, the arbitrator's award will prevail, in whole, or in respect to the still unresolved matters if partial agreement has been reached. The advantages are said to be that the parties can now negotiate having heard the full thinking of the other party as put in arbitration, rather than just what tends to be positional information put across the table in negotiations, and the parties are also now negotiating against known "BATNAs" (the arbitration award) rather than the uncertain outcomes that prevailed prior to the arbitration award.

Witkin (2010) proposed what he termed "*consensus arbitration*," a process in which the neutral would conciliate negotiations between the parties, issuing "incomplete, preliminary decisions" along the way, essentially pegging some points in place, thereby both disposing of those points and providing foundations and certainty for further negotiations on other points still in play. A partial decision might set a particular direction, endorse criteria for decision making, or set out a framework for determining an issue, inviting the parties to address specifics or negotiate the details. This model, it is said, would provide finality but without isolating the arbitrator; the parties would have the opportunity for significant input in shaping the final award.

Dendorfer and Lack (2007) surveyed several models interacting mediation and arbitration, including med-arb and arb-med. They also advanced the concept of a "*mediation window*" in which the arbitration process would be suspended mid-way for a period of mediation, where a separate neutral would assist the parties in trying to resolve some or all issues in dispute on the basis of what each party had heard from the other in front of the arbitrator. Failing agreement, the mediator would exit and the arbitration process resume towards an eventual binding award.

Dendorfer and Lack (2007) also discussed what they termed "*shadow mediation*," a process in which the mediator observes the arbitration proceedings and either operates in the background or at the call of the parties or the arbitrator (or arbitration panel) to assist the parties in sorting out whole or part or intermediate issues as the matter is developing in arbitration. The arbitrator would not be privy to discussions taking place in mediation and would eventually issue an award covering issues remaining in dispute at that point.

Both the "mediation window" and the "shadow mediation" concepts are familiar in the broad field of employment dispute resolution in New Zealand, though not recognized by those terms. And indeed, many of the concepts and ideas mentioned above have featured at times in the system for fixing pay and conditions for the New Zealand police, which is the focus of the balance of this chapter.

The New Zealand Police Negotiation Model

Private sector labor relations in New Zealand were regulated from 1894 until 1984 by conciliated negotiations and contingent arbitration. Wages and conditions were governed by wide-coverage multi-employer documents negotiated by representative union and employer bodies, with referral to binding determination in the court of arbitration at the election of either party, in the event no agreement was reached. With some exceptions, union–employer negotiations usually took place under the chairmanship of a state conciliator, more active or passive, depending on the inclinations of the parties. In most instances, conciliators guided the parties through discussions of the issues; in some other negotiations, the conciliator might have done little more than take notes. Again, if negotiation and conciliation failed to produce an agreement, either party could apply to the arbitration court to set wages and conditions for workers covered by the document.

The government employment sector was regulated during this period by something akin to a civil service system. The conciliation and arbitration system began to be dismantled from the mid-1980s when government sought to restructure and decentralize private sector wage setting as New Zealand was opened up to the global marketplace. In 1988, government pushed its own employees into "enterprise" collective bargaining and made available arbitration of bargaining impasses if both employer and union elected to forgo strikes and lockouts. The arbitration option had a very short life, being withdrawn for most of the public sector with a change of government in 1990. The exception was the national police force.

Sworn police officers today remain the only occupation for which arbitration of wage and conditions disputes is available. Collective agreements for non-sworn or "civilian" support staff employed by the police service are negotiated by the New Zealand Police Association (NZPA) in conjunction with those for sworn officers, but are not subject to arbitration.

The present med+arb system for police negotiations has been provided for in legislation since 1989 and was updated, although not changed substantially, in a comprehensive review of the Policing Act in 2008. Regulations governing the arbitration elements of the process are set out in a "schedule" or appendix to the Act. Reference to arbitration is by the mediator involved in the dispute.

Generally speaking, the process for police negotiations begins with the parties meeting to bargain informally. Failing agreement, they ask the Department of Labour (DOL), a division of the Ministry of Business, Innovation and Employment (MBIE), to appoint both a mediator and an arbitrator to assist the negotiations, and the bargaining continues at a more formal level, in the presence of the mediator and usually of the arbitrator as well. The neutrals have always been agreed between the parties and all have been experienced in both mediation and arbitration, employed either as adjudicators with the current industrial tribunal, the Employment Relations Authority (ERA), or as mediators with the MBIE/DOL Mediation Service or, in the 1990s, as members of the Employment Tribunal that was the predecessor to both the ERA and the MBIE/DOL Mediation Service.

There are several specifications set out in the schedule to the Policing Act. It provides for a tripartite arbitration body with the chair appointed by the CEO of the DOL and up to two members appointed by each of the bargaining parties—the NZPA and New Zealand Police ("NZ Police" or "the Commissioner"). If the parties do not nominate partisan members, the CEO of the MBIE/DOL may appoint members in addition to the chair or the parties may agree that the neutral arbitrator act alone. The arbitration method is "package FOA" with the arbitration body precluded from fashioning a compromise. The parties present final offers prior to the arbitration hearing but are entitled to modify their final offers following the hearing but prior to a determination by the arbitrating body.

The Policing Act authorizes the bargaining parties to agree alternative arrangements to those set out in the schedule, and indeed the parties have modified their arrangements within the broad med+arb model a number of times over the years, although without departing from the basic framework set out in the statute. The most formal experimentation was with the early development of a document entitled the *Police Negotiations Framework* in the mid-1990s (McAndrew, 2003).

The "Police Negotiation Framework"

The first resort to arbitration between the NZPA and the NZ Police under the new regime took place in 1990. The award was in favor of the Commissioner, but it was agreed that the negotiation experience had been unpleasant for all involved. Negotiations leading to conventional arbitration under the previous model in 1989 had left a similar bad taste and conditioned the environment for 1990 and beyond. In 1993, the NZPA was looking for a substantial pay increase. The negotiations dragged on into 1994. A three-year deal was eventually agreed with significant assistance from the mediator. Arbitration was not required this time around. Still, the NZPA did not achieve what it had set out to achieve regarding police pay and the parties acknowledged that a comprehensive review was appropriate.

The parties were also again unhappy with the process in the 1993–4 negotiations, including the mechanisms available for dispute resolution, and immediately afterwards a joint working party was established to look at how the process could be made more effective. The working party completed its report in 1995. The availability of arbitration was endorsed as necessary in light of the proper prohibition on strikes, but the availability of arbitration was seen as having inhibited bargaining during the 1993–4 round—the "chilling effect." There was also a concern with the confrontational style of the negotiations, and that was also attributed to some extent to the availability of FOA. Mediation, on the other hand, was seen as having been fundamental to the reaching of an agreement. The report was adopted by the parties as the *Police Negotiation Framework* ("*PNF*") within the statutory regime, with the major changes adopted being a more active role for the mediator and having the arbitrator observe the formal bargaining from the outset.

The 1997 negotiations loomed large, with the *PNF* in place and a comprehensive review of police pay having been completed. The Commissioner's view, following from the review, was that police pay was sitting about where it should be relative to the market, and that was the basis of management's position throughout the process.

The negotiations commenced in mid-1997 and continued through February 1998. Both the mediator and the arbitrator sat through all the formal bargaining sessions, and the mediator also met with the parties in informal negotiations and caucuses. When no agreement had been reached by late February, the mediator referred the dispute to the arbitrator, who convened a meeting of the parties to review the procedure for arbitration. It was determined that the arbitrator was to act alone. The *PNF* required that the arbitrator consider information he had acquired during his observation of the negotiations plus any submissions offered by the parties specifically for arbitration, and having regard to the criteria set out in the statute. Under the *PNF*, the arbitrator was required to issue an *interim decision* with supporting reasons, stating which party's present position on the package of issues he would choose.

The arbitrator sent a number of key signals in his interim decision. Only remuneration issues were within the scope of bargaining and arbitration for police at that time. While there were several remuneration issues in play, the arbitrator made it clear that he did not regard all issues as equally compelling, and he singled out base pay rates as the one most influencing his pick between the two packages. He opted for the employer's package.

Under the *PNF*, the parties engaged in further mediated bargaining, with the arbitrator again observing the formal sessions, while his interim decision remained private to the parties for a period of 10 days after its issue. Despite the resumption of mediation, the impasse remained unresolved by mid-July 1998 and was now subject to binding arbitration under the *PNF*. At this stage, the parties had a further opportunity to revise their final offers.

Offers were exchanged and the parties spoke to their proposals in a two-day hearing. Neither party significantly modified its position. The final arbitration decision was issued a month later and adopted the employer's package on the basis that the employer's proposed increases in the base pay rate and the scheduling of those increases best fitted the criteria in the statute. The award also endorsed the concept of "total remuneration" for market comparative purposes, a concept proposed by the employer and arising from the comprehensive salary review undertaken since the last negotiation. The new document was to expire in December 2000. By the time the award was issued, the mediator and the arbitrator had each committed over 20 days to the process.

The parties again turned their attention to the *PNF* at the completion of the 1997–8 negotiations. It was acknowledged that these negotiations were always going to be difficult, with police officers having high expectations around pay, while management's research told them pay levels were about right. In these circumstances, the assessment was that the impasse resolution mechanisms had been fairly effective.

Whether the arbitrator should observe the negotiations had been a contentious issue in the development of the *PNF*, there being fears of both a "chilling effect" and a "narcotic effect." In reflecting on the negotiations, the parties concluded that the presence of the arbitrator had positively affected the behavior of the negotiators, had not been responsible for the dispute ending up in arbitration, and had positively contributed to the arbitrator being fully informed in making his eventual decision. There was some concern at the chilling effect as the prospect of arbitration became more real late in the process, but it was felt that that would occur in any system that offered contingent arbitration. The parties concluded that any chilling effect could not be attributed to the presence of the arbitrator at the negotiations, particularly as efforts at "deal making" were largely done privately between the parties, or with the mediator, but outside the view of the arbitrator.

There was more concern with the chilling effect of the arbitrator's interim decision, with both parties having elected to keep their powder pretty dry until they had seen the arbitrator's initial thinking. Interim feedback from the arbitrator during the mediated negotiation process was considered valuable, but the interim decision as a formal step was seen as having taken on too much significance and as having acted as a barrier to bargaining early on. Some modifications were proposed for a revised *PNF* and these were adopted for the negotiations scheduled in 2000. Since this revision, the parties have paid less conscious attention to the *PNF*, as a document, although its principles and basic framework continue to guide the process.

The revised *PNF* introduced the *information gathering and informal negotiation first phase* preceding the involvement of the neutrals, to give the parties an initial opportunity to reach a voluntary agreement, still recognized as the option to be preferred under ideal circumstances. If agreement is not reached, either party can initiate the second or "formal negotiations" phase by calling for the appointment of both a mediator and an arbitrator. The mediator was expected to actively conciliate the negotiations in the New Zealand tradition, guiding the conversation through the detail of the issues if required, but also to engage in classic mediation intervention techniques, nudging the parties towards an agreement, particularly later in the process.

Under the revised *PNF*, either or both parties could ask the arbitrator to indicate his or her thinking on any aspect of their current position, such indications to be advised to both parties. The arbitrator was free to decline any specific request if he or she considered it premature or unhelpful, but was expected to provide a reasonable level of feedback to guide the parties. If negotiations reached the point of formal referral to arbitration, the arbitrator was charged with convening a tripartite panel, hearing evidence and submissions, and eventually issuing a decision as before. There were, however, to be no more formal interim decisions, as such.

The revised *PNF* was in place for the 2000 negotiations, with the impasse processes taking a slightly different turn. The mediator conciliated the negotiations while the arbitrator observed. The arbitrator's active involvement was limited to one pivotal intervention orchestrated by the mediator which broke a deadlock over the appropriateness of the employer relying on "ability to pay" as a determining criterion on pay. The arbitrator indicated that "ability to pay" would carry some weight, but would not be accorded "trump" status among other criteria set out in the statute. This ruling was instrumental in moving the negotiations forward to an eventual agreement. The mediator was responsible not only for drawing the arbitrator in to rule on the matter, but also in paving the way for the arbitrator's ruling to carry the weight that it did.

Continuing Evolution of the Model

The 2000 agreement was for just one year, as a new Labour government settled into office. The 2001 negotiations settled quickly on an 18-month contract during the informal negotiations between the parties, with little involvement by the mediator and no attendance by the arbitrator.

The 2003 negotiations represented more of a turning point in several respects. A new team was involved representing the Commissioner, with a lead advocate vastly experienced in private sector "deal making" but without previous experience of the police labor relations process. The budget environment, at least in relation to the police, was still relatively bountiful.

The parties settled on a three-year agreement with some notable features. First, the collective agreement had up to this point been essentially limited to remuneration items, not conditions. In 2003, all terms and conditions were included to create a comprehensive collective agreement, as is consistent with private sector industrial practice. As such in the police environment, all matters were from this point forward subject to negotiation and FOA-by-package arbitration.

Second, the parties negotiated a pay structure in which all sworn staff were entitled to annual "competency service increments" ("CSIs"), essentially automatic step increases within range, with those at the top of ranges receiving an equivalent annual lump sum payment. These CSIs were valued at about 1.7% of base on average, and were introduced as an incentive to retain staff, but as an alternative to performance-based incentives. It was anticipated that the cost would be relatively stable assuming turnover in the service stayed at the level it was, with recruits coming into the lower ranges replacing longer serving staff exiting from higher ranges. CSIs were to be in addition to any negotiated "across-the-board" ("ATB") pay increases to reflect cost-of-living and the like.

A third key change across the 2003 and 2006 agreements was the reintroduction of a number of financial allowances and premium payments, some of which had been removed or moved into the base during the 1990s. For the most part, these new forms of remuneration were written into the collective agreement as being outside "total remuneration" for comparative purposes, thereby nullifying to some extent work that police management had done in earlier years establishing labor market relativities. The 2006 agreement was a two year agreement, and a further one year agreement was reached without controversy in 2008.

There were some other developments as well. In 2000, an experienced state mediator, but one with arbitration experience on the Employment Tribunal in the 1990s, had been assigned to the arbitration role. The Employment Tribunal member who had mediated for the parties through the 1990s and continued to do so as a state mediator after 2000, retired and was replaced in the mediation role from 2006 by another experienced state mediator, but one seen as having a less directive mediation style.

In the comprehensive review of the Policing Act that began in 2006 and concluded with the new legislation in 2008, the government floated the idea of authorizing the police to take limited strike action—overtime bans, ticket bans, and the like—but stopping well short of full strikes, in exchange for the police relinquishing access to arbitration. This was an effort by government to retake control of its police payroll, but the NZPA ultimately rejected the idea and the med+arb model came through the statutory review pretty much intact.

Strategy Around a Single Issue

The 2009 negotiations began in an environment conditioned by the election of a new fiscally-conservative government, a tight budget, and an acute awareness of the likely effect on other state unions of any agreement reached or award handed down for police. The immediate players were the same as in recent years, except that a different state mediator—again vastly experienced in both mediation and arbitration but new to the police negotiations—stepped into the arbitration role.

The 2009 negotiations illustrate the med+arb process in practice where a single dominant issue is in play. The negotiations began in May and the parties settled some peripheral issues with the assistance of the mediator. The arbitrator observed the formal negotiations. There was, however, no movement on an ATB pay increase in this phase. The NZPA's position was 2% but the Commissioner was offering nothing. The association also had a contentious overtime proposal on the table as the only other issue unresolved.

At the end of July, the mediator handed the negotiations off to the arbitrator. The parties opted for an arbitration panel, in part because the arbitrator had not been involved in the police negotiations in the past. Each appointed two members to sit with the neutral arbitrator. Nonetheless, the neutral arbitrator was recognized as the pivotal decision-maker on the panel.

The statute provides a list of criteria to be considered by the arbitration body, specific but also open-ended to an extent. The criteria include consideration of recruitment and retention, fairness and equity, any changes over time in the work of police, productivity improvements, and relativities within and without the police service. Importantly for the NZPA, the criteria also include recognition of "special conditions applicable to employment in the Police, including the prohibition on strikes by constables." And following the 2008 statutory revisions, "any other matters that the Commissioner, the appropriate service organisation, or the arbitrating body... considers relevant." "Service organisation" most often refers to the NZPA, although there is another smaller organization representing some higher ranks to which the arbitration provisions also apply. Prior to the 2008 amendments, only the Commissioner could nominate "any other matters."

As the negotiations approached arbitration in 2009, the NZPA was confident that the arbitrator could not, having regard to these statutory criteria, award zero. Tactically, there was no incentive at all for the NZPA to agree to zero. If the troops were to receive no increase, it was better that the arbitrator make that ruling. For management also, if there was to be an ATB increase, it was better that the arbitrator make that call, rather than have the Commissioner do so and suffer the displeasure of the politicians.

The parties exchanged written submissions by early August, with a hearing following before the full arbitration panel. Management supported its zero proposal by reference to the CSI scheme which would see all officers receive either a step increase or a lump sum equivalent in any event. There was little attention to external relativities, in which so much research had been invested in the past, or to the other statutory criteria. With FOA being on a package basis, the NZPA made the tactical decision to withdraw the overtime issue to avoid compromising what it saw as still being an elegant, stand-alone contest between 2% and nothing on the ATB pay issue.

Following the hearing, the parties were invited to revise their final offers on the remaining pay issue before the panel made its decision. The Commissioner revised the police management offer to 1% from the date of agreement or award. As the parties were now two months into the new contract term, this amounted to 1% for 14 months, so something less than an annualized 1%. It could be speculated that 1% backdated might have been more "competitive" with the association's 2% for 12 months offer than was the "something less" than 1%. But it might also be postulated that movement from zero in mediation to 1% in arbitration might be seen by the arbitrator as mere expedience, undermining the integrity of police management's analysis on salaries.

After receiving the final offers, the arbitrator directed the parties back to mediation, but no progress was made. The mediator so informed the arbitrator, who issued her decision adopting the NZPA's final offer of 2% ATB for the 12-month term.

Seeking Systemic Change

By contrast with the highly visible 2009 process, the 2010 negotiations settled quickly and quietly in the informal negotiation phase. It was a two-year deal with a lump sum payment in the first year and a 1.3% ATB pay increase in the second year. The NZPA was also successful in getting some movement on the overtime issue that had been taken off the table the previous year. The Commissioner was seen to take a more active interest in negotiations following the "loss" in arbitration in 2009, and the NZPA leadership perceived that their more ready access to the senior executive floor of Police Headquarters was instrumental in achieving a quick and quiet settlement in 2010.

Concomitantly, there was only minimal involvement by the neutrals in the 2010 negotiations. There is a sense that the parties felt that they had "failed" when forced to resort to arbitration in 2009 and there was additional resolve to reach a voluntary agreement in 2010. The non-interventionist style of the mediator was appropriate to this circumstance, as was the willingness of the Commissioner to be involved. The arbitrator who had served (but not arbitrated) for several years prior to 2009 resumed the role, replacing the 2009 arbitrator, but given her familiarity with the parties and the issues, was not actually required to be in attendance before the parties came to their own agreement.

If 2009 was illustrative of bargaining over a single issue in the context of the med+arb model, 2012 saw the Commissioner attempting to promote a more far reaching agenda through the process. Police management had again experienced a change in labor relations leadership, with a new HR presence recruited from the private sector, but also a resurrection of key personnel who had been involved in the early years of the med+arb process and in the development of the *PNF* and the early NZ Police remuneration and bargaining strategies.

The new team identified what they perceived to be some fundamental strategic imperatives to be addressed in the 2012 negotiations. In retrospect, the concessions made in 2003 were now seen by management as having been, if superficially sensible, strategically unsound. First, it was believed that too many allowances and premiums had been introduced to the remuneration scheme but left sitting outside the definition of "total remuneration" for purposes of comparisons in the marketplace. Some of these allowances were seen by management as inappropriate and they were targeted for removal.

Most were accepted as having some legitimacy but it was felt that they needed to be recognized as a part of remuneration for relativity purposes. The work that had been done on analyzing relativities in earlier years was seen as having been devalued by having a range of payments sitting outside of what was considered comparable remuneration.

Second, the CSI scheme was seen by management as being dysfunctional and financially unsustainable. The CSIs had been introduced in 2003 to replace a performance-based system that had been accepted as not achieving its purpose. In effect, issues around assessing and rewarding performance had been sidetracked by simply having everyone receive an annual CSI. Over time, the scheme had become increasingly more expensive because the CSIs compounded year after year, and because of a decline in the turnover rate of police officers. It was felt by management that CSIs needed to be addressed in 2012 and that the CSI scheme needed to be replaced with an effective performance-based remuneration structure.

These two areas of concern led NZ Police to devise a complex set of proposals to remove some allowances, roll some others into base pay, or at least have them recognized as part of "total remuneration," buy out the CSIs, and eventually introduce a performance-based scheme. Management was prepared to offer the equivalent of three years' CSIs in a lump sum payment plus modest ATB adjustments on a three-year contract, and money was available to invest in that sort of deal.

Police management decided to take what the new HR team considered to be a different, "interest based" approach to the negotiations, seeking to be open with the NZPA negotiating team about the financial hole that past agreements were seen to have created and asking the association to partner with management in resolving the difficulties. This approach was to take the form of extensive briefings to the NZPA team about the financial situation and the comprehensive proposals that the Commissioner was putting forward to address the situation.

In part because of the unfamiliarity of some key figures on the management side with the unique police med+arb process, but also quite deliberately because of the open approach to the negotiations that the management team favored, it was proposed that the initial information exchange and ensuing discussion of the management agenda take place in the "informal negotiation" phase, without either the mediator or the arbitrator in attendance.

While there was some disquiet over this approach, on balance it was felt that having dispute resolution personnel in place would be inconsistent with the open, interest based approach intended. For its part, the NZPA was happy to hear the management briefing without the arbitrator exposed to, and possibly "buying into" the management rationale. The absence of the arbitrator essentially relieved the association team of having to consider and counter the management research and proposal point by point. Instead, the NZPA team could simply sit back initially and assess the scheme as it was presented.

Negotiations began in April 2012 with the sort of extensive briefing intended by NZ Police. Things did not proceed entirely smoothly. There was an appeal for a positive approach, but the NZPA representatives felt that they had always adopted a positive approach characterized by what was good for the police service alongside what was good for the membership; witness a decade of reaching agreements with only one resort to arbitration.

At the same time, the NZPA leadership resented that they had seemingly been involved only at the point that management had completed its research and apparently decided on its intended course of action. As the association characterized it, police management had spent a lot of time and resources coming up with a "radical" plan that they then proceeded to "drop" on the NZPA. And NZ Police's engagement of a "hired gun" to lead the negotiations, despite the presence of a new professional HR director and a respected insider with long experience of police negotiations, was seen as a retrograde step in terms of the relationship between the parties.

The mediator joined the parties for "formal negotiations" after several weeks. But ultimately, the NZPA representatives rejected the comprehensive NZ Police suite of proposals in its entirety, proposing instead a modest ATB increase appropriate, as they saw it, to the tight fiscal environment. By this point it was apparent to the NZPA leadership that the complex and "radical" nature of the NZ Police proposals would make them difficult to sell to the arbitrator, particularly since she had not had the benefit of the initial briefings.

The NZPA negotiating team took the management proposals to membership information meetings around the country, and they were predictably soundly rejected. Given the range of "take aways" in the management offer, there was never much danger of the members buying it at the report back meetings, absent a strong endorsement from the leadership, the positives in the package notwithstanding. On the other hand, the membership was well aware, from internal police communications, association communications, and a fairly transparent government media campaign that the government policy of fiscal restraint extended to law enforcement, as elsewhere. The Commissioner and government ministers were prominent in the media discussing budget cutting, and essentially equating pay increases to job losses, challenging the NZPA to "act responsibly" in the negotiations. In this environment, modest ATB increases were always going to be acceptable to the membership, as long as nothing was lost.

With the NZPA's rejection of the management proposal, and its adoption of a modest ATB proposal, police management was left contemplating arbitration with a very complex, sweeping, claw back proposal—sophisticated to be sure, well researched, imaginatively and professionally presented, and even well-funded, but still complex and far reaching. And potentially competing in arbitration with NZPA's conservative, conventional proposal for modest ATB increases.

There was a belated sense in management that having the arbitrator present, being "educated" from the outset of the negotiations, exposed to the dire straits of state finances and the cost structures and supposed illogic inherent in aspects of the police remuneration arrangements, might have made the prospect of prevailing in arbitration with their complex proposals somewhat more feasible than it now was.

In the final analysis, government ministers preferred that NZ Police put aside the more ambitious agenda for the time being and settle conventionally, which they did, agreeing to zero, 1%, and 1% ATB numbers for a three-year contract. The fact that modest annual increases were available across three years through voluntary settlement served the government cause of keeping any pay adjustments for other public workers to a minimum. But the anticipated difficulty of persuading an arbitrator to adopt a complex, comprehensive pay restructure over a simple succession of modest ATB pay increases was an important consideration in electing to settle rather than taking the matter to arbitration. So while the 2012 outcome was not determined in arbitration, it was certainly determined in the shadow of arbitration. And management was left with a significant agenda for pay restructuring put back on the shelf.

Analysis: the Strengths and Limitations of the med+arb Model

Governments have mixed feelings over arbitration of police labor–management impasses. On the one hand, few politicians want to be seen as being at odds with their police. The police are identified in the public view with order and safety. Police associations and unions often position themselves as champions of public safety, and they generally are reflecting their members' views in doing so. The NZPA is particularly adept at occupying centre stage in all matters to do with law, order, and public safety in New Zealand. Government ministers are happy to steer clear of disputes with the NZPA over pay and conditions, and arbitration allows them to do so.

On the other hand, the availability of arbitration for police remuneration disputes constantly threatens to take adjustments in a significant part of the police budget out of the hands of the government. No government politician likes that loss of control, which is only exacerbated by the "demonstration effect" of any police arbitration award in subsequent negotiations with unions representing other public employees. In addition to these practical political concerns, conventional criticisms of "narcotic" and "chilling" effects and the like remain in circulation.

If the New Zealand police med+arb model has as its objectives promoting voluntary agreements, but guaranteeing finality of outcomes without disruption of police services when voluntary agreement is not possible, it seems to be effective.

Table 15.1 sets out the "bare bones" history of this unique med+arb model since its inception in 1990. In reading the table, pay adjustments, whether percentages on base or lump sum payments in lieu of adjustments to base rates usually occur annually. Just once, in January 2008, there was a half-year adjustment in addition. There have been occasional years without any adjustment. Some significant remuneration "moves," such as the introduction of salary ranges, are also noted in the table.

Table 15.1 NZ Police Remuneration Adjustments, 1990–2014

Year	Process	Term	Remuneration Adjustments
1990	Arbitration	2 years	4%
1992	Mediated negotiation	1 year	0%
1993	Mediated negotiation	3 years	0% + 1.5% + $520 lump sum + 0.6% (and salary ranges introduced)
1996	Mediated negotiation	2 years	2.2%
1998	Arbitration	1½ years	$2000 lump sum + 2.5% (and "total remuneration concept" introduced)
2000	Mediated negotiation*	1 year	3%; *the process included an interim decision on pay criteria by the arbitrator
2001	Informal negotiation	1½ years	2% + 1%
2003	Mediated negotiation	3 years	3% + 2% + 2.5% (and CSIs introduced from 2004)
2006	Mediated negotiation	2 years	4% + 4% + 1% (half year increase)
2008	Informal negotiation	1 year	4%
2009	Arbitration	1 year	2%
2010	Informal negotiation	2 years	$1000 lump sum + 1.3%
2012	Mediated negotiation	3 years	0% + 1% + 1%

Strengths of the Model

What conclusions can be drawn from the evidence? First, there cannot be said to be a significant narcotic effect. Arbitration has decided the outcome of the negotiations on only three occasions across more than two decades. This compares with the parties having reached ten voluntary agreements over that period. Arbitration awards have governed pay for only four and a half years. Aversion to "gambling" on an arbitration award has certainly been a factor, as for example in the 2012 negotiations. A loss in arbitration, as for NZ Police in 2009, appears to heighten the impetus to settle voluntarily in following years. And both parties continue to express a strong preference for reaching negotiated settlements if at all possible.

The table of settlements also indicates that the model has generally produced moderate adjustments in remuneration over the years, particularly under arbitration awards. But even in most years when negotiated settlements are reached, salary adjustments have been moderate. In part this is likely to reflect a concern that if governments feel they have "lost" in arbitration or suffered from the threat of arbitration once too often, they may be tempted to change or even abandon the system. So even in non-arbitration years, negotiations take place in the shadow of arbitration.

Having said that, there is also a sense in the NZPA that, to be effective—including in motivating the parties to reach voluntary agreement most of the time—arbitration actually has to be used once in a while. In that sense, arbitration is analogous to strike action in other industries or occupations.

Occasional resort to arbitration provides credibility to what is the parties' usual aversion to arbitration. It is also arguably necessary in providing credibility to the negotiating teams in relation to their constituents. It puts them in a position to be able to credibly say to the NZPA membership or the police executive in non-arbitration years that the deal on the table is the best deal available, that nothing better would be available in arbitration, and that going to arbitration involves a potential loss, but no potential gain over the deal on offer. So, while there is no evidence of an over-reliance on arbitration, it is always hovering over the negotiations, and there is reason to believe that it has to be and will be used occasionally.

Relatedly, the preponderance of negotiated agreements over time would suggest that the model encourages negotiation under most circumstances, and that there is no debilitating chilling effect. The parties acknowledge that they manage their positions towards arbitration once arbitration becomes likely, but they argue that that is an inevitable feature of any contingent arbitration system.

The formal "interim decision" issued by the arbitrator in earlier years was recognized as having had a chilling effect on negotiations and was eliminated from the model. By contrast, informal feedback from the arbitrator as to her "leanings" is seen as both clearing stumbling blocks to progress on occasion and encouraging movement in negotiation, in a manner not dissimilar to the proposed "consensus arbitration" model. And indeed the arbitrator has on occasion ordered the parties back to mediation—a "mediation window" so to speak—following the arbitration hearing as an additional feature of the model promoting settlement over arbitral determination wherever possible.

At times a party has been able to reasonably confidently predict its winning prospects in arbitration and has had little incentive to modify its position further in an effort to settle. This was the case for the NZPA in 2009. On the other hand, if one party can predict a win in arbitration, it can be argued that the other party should be equally able to predict a loss and modify its position accordingly. Also the ability of either party to modify its final position following the formal arbitration requires that the parties focus on how their own positions stack up against the statutory criteria, rather than focusing solely on a comparison between their own positions and those of the other party.

In 2012, for example, the NZPA was comfortable in predicting that its simple ATB proposal would win out in arbitration over the employer's complex proposal for change. However, there could have been no certainty that the NZ Police would not change tack to a similarly simple, but competing, ATB proposal following the arbitration hearing. Police management attempted something like that in 2009, on the basis of feedback about the neutral's inclinations stemming from discussions within the tripartite arbitration panel, itself another feature of the model that encourages settlement.

In the New Zealand model, the arbitrator witnesses only "formal negotiations" and is not privy to the parties' private negotiations or their interaction with the mediator in caucus. Efforts at actual deal making, including with the involvement of the mediator, occur outside the view of the arbitrator, so that proposals aimed at settlement through compromise do not run the risk of undermining a party's position in arbitration, a commonly recognized flaw in a conventional med-arb model, and addressed somewhat awkwardly in the arb-med model.

Limitations of the Model

While the New Zealand police med+arb model can be considered successful in encouraging negotiated agreements most of the time, guaranteeing a resolution the rest of the time, and avoiding any disruption to law enforcement all of the time, it does have its limitations.

It is a very resource-intensive model in terms of neutrals' time and energy and expense. In New Zealand, the mediator and arbitrator are funded from the public purse, but of course there is only a single police force. To provide a similar level of neutral service in a system involving many state, provincial, and local law enforcement agencies involved in collective bargaining could be quite a financial burden.

Second and more fundamentally, it is—for better or worse—an inherently conservative model. It is probably reasonable to say that arbitrators themselves are not a reckless breed by nature; they tend to be pretty conservative. And FOA-by-package would be the most conservative model of arbitration in which they could operate. Most of the time parties might consider that to be a good thing. It produces moderation of ambition and outcomes. However, where a party wants, or believes that it needs to advance a programme of more fundamental change, an FOA-by-package process is unlikely to produce quick and radical results. It requires a strategic approach and "a long game."

Police management was conspicuously frustrated by its inability to achieve fundamental change in remuneration structures in 2012. Conventional arbitration or even FOA issue-by-issue would have offered better prospects for advancing parts, but probably not all, of the Commissioner's far-reaching remuneration agenda. The likelihood is that, if it is to be advanced by FOA-by-package awards, it will move much more slowly. Arguably it should move slowly, given that the parties acted together over some years to construct the arrangements that eventually came to be seen by police management as problematic.

Finally, one of the strengths of the New Zealand police med+arb system over time has been the value of proactive mediation conducted in the shadow of arbitration. Mediation, often with substantial doses of more directive conciliation in the New Zealand sense, assisted the parties through the remuneration review in the 1990s, through significant rancour at the bargaining table at various times, and in the refinement of the *PNF*, in addition to sorting through more routine bargaining bumps along the way. In the design of the *PNF* following the 1993–1994 negotiations, the parties recognized and promoted a central role for active mediation, and the review of the *PNF* after the 1997–1998 arbitration experience reaffirmed that mediation was to be central to the process that the parties were evolving.

In more recent times, the influence of mediation in the model is acknowledged to have retreated somewhat. That development clearly suited the purposes of the parties for a number of years during which an easy, "deal making" environment prevailed.

The value of proactive mediation or conciliation in a mixed method dispute resolution model is evident where mediation is given sufficient deference and import, as it is for example in the BC "mediation assisted arbitration" model. And there are many examples of parties negotiating fundamental change with the assistance of active mediation or conciliation (Moroni 2008).

It may be that a return to a proactive, directive style of conciliation and mediation assistance in the future could strengthen the med+arb model's capacity to manage calls for more fundamental, complex, and far-reaching change in remuneration structures as well as other issues. Experience to date would suggest that, if that be the case, the parties are likely to make the necessary adjustments to make it work, while preserving the integrity of the model.

References

Brenninkmeijer, A., Sprengers, L., de Roo, A., and Jagtenberg, R. 2006. *Effective Resolution of Collective Labour Disputes*. Groningen: Europa Law.

Dendorfer, R. and Lack, J. 2007. "The Interaction between Arbitration and Mediation: Vision v Reality." *Dispute Resolution International*, 1: 73–98.

Goldberg, S. B. 2003. "A Modest Proposal for Better Integrating Collective Bargaining and Interest Arbitration." *The Labor Lawyer*, 19(1): 97–106.

Hanany, E., Kilgour, D. M. and Gerchak, Y. 2007. "Final-Offer Arbitration and Risk Aversion in Bargaining." *Management Science*, 53(11): 1785–92.

International Labour Organization 2003. *Public Emergency Services: Social Dialogue in a Changing Environment*. Geneva: ILO.

Johnson, S. J. T. 2010. "First Contract Arbitration: Effects on Bargaining and Work Stoppages." *Industrial & Labor Relations Review*, 63(4): 585–605.

Kochan, T., Lipsky, D. B., Newhart, M. and Benson, A. 2010. "The Long-haul Effects of Interest Arbitration: The Case of New York State's Taylor Law." *Industrial & Labor Relations Review*, 63(4): 565–84.

McAndrew, I. 2003. "Final-offer Arbitration: A New Zealand Variation." *Industrial Relations*, 42(4): 736–44.

McAndrew, I. 2012. "Collective Bargaining Interventions: Contemporary New Zealand Experiments." *International Journal of Human Resource Management*, 23(3): 495–510.

Moroni, M. 2008. *Mediation and Strategic Change: Lessons from mediating a nationwide doctors' strike*. Lanham, MD: Hamilton Books.

Ross, W. H. and Conlon, D. E. 2000. "Hybrid Forms of Third-party Dispute Resolution: Theoretical Implications of Combining Mediation and Arbitration." *The Academy of Management Review*, 25(2): 416–27.

Slater, J. E. 2012. "Public-sector Labor in the Age of Obama." *Indiana Law Journal*, 87(1): 189–229.

Vipond, M. 2010. "First Contract Arbitration: Evidence from British Columbia, Canada, of the Significance of a Mediator's Non-binding Recommendations." <http://works.bepress.com/melanie_vipond/1> accessed 10 Dec. 2012.

Witkin, N. 2010. "Consensus Arbitration: A Negotiation-based Decision-making Process for Arbrbitrators." *Negotiation Journal*, 26(3): 309–25.

CHAPTER 16

....

EXPERIENCES OF JUDICIAL MEDIATION IN EMPLOYMENT TRIBUNALS

....

PETER URWIN AND PAUL L. LATREILLE

INTRODUCTION AND BACKGROUND

THE UK Employment Tribunal (ET) system exists to adjudicate in rights-based disputes between employers and actual or potential employees. As independent judicial bodies, ETs deal with a range of jurisdictions (or complaints) by workers, including unfair (unjust) dismissal, breach of contract, unlawful deductions from wages, redundancy payments, and various types of discrimination (Urwin et al., 2012). Successive governments, concerned at what had appeared an almost inexorable rise in the volume and complexity of claims in recent years (see Dix et al., 2009), have explored various measures aimed at reducing pressure on the system.

Although the number of ET claims has fallen back from its 2009–10 peak of 236,000, the "weed, concede, and speed" strategy documented by Latreille et al. (2007: 137) continues, with reforms seeking to deter weak or vexatious cases; to encourage and promote earlier resolution between the parties; to deal with claims more rapidly; and, in all of this, to reduce the perceived risks associated with employment expansion to businesses and the costs of the system to the taxpayer. Among the most significant recent changes are:

- increases in the amount of costs that may be awarded against losing parties and the introduction in 2013 of fees for using the ET system, including the bringing and hearing of claims, and for appeals to the Employment Appeal Tribunal (EAT);

- the introduction of "early conciliation" from 2014, with a mandatory period of conciliation by the Advisory, Conciliation and Arbitration Service (Acas) before claims can be accepted by the ET; and
- the addition from 2012 of unfair dismissal to the jurisdictions where decisions can be made by an Employment Judge sitting alone rather than with lay members, and in due course for this to become the default position at the EAT (see Corby and Latreille, 2012a, 2012b).

In relation to the second of these, successive governments have also been keen to encourage the greater use of various forms of alternative dispute resolution (ADR). This focus on ADR as a possible tool to achieve more timely resolution of disputes including ET cases, placing less financial and emotional burden on parties from such manifestations of conflict, has been a common theme of UK policy initiatives. The increased use of ADR was a specific policy objective for the Department for Constitutional Affairs (DCA; now Ministry of Justice) arising from the 2004 *Transforming Public Services: Complaints, Redress and Tribunals* White Paper. This expressed the desire to "promote the development of a range of tailored dispute resolution services, so that different types of dispute can be resolved fairly, quickly, efficiently and effectively, without recourse to the expense and formality of courts and tribunals where this is not necessary" (DCA 2004: 6). Focusing specifically on employment disputes, the Gibbons Review published in 2007 had the remit of identifying measures to simplify and improve dispute resolution in this context, both within the organization/workplace and in the ET process. Noting the positive experiences of employment dispute mediation in New Zealand and the US, as well as in UK civil and family disputes (Gibbons, 2007: 9), the wider adoption of such methods was accordingly listed among the report's recommendations (Gibbons, 2007: 55–6). A revised Acas *Code of Practice on Discipline and Grievance*, which included mediation in its Foreword and discussed the concept at length in its accompanying *Guidance*, was one corollary. A regional mediation pilot for small and medium-sized employers (SMEs) established by the Department for Business, Innovation and Skills (BIS) following its *Resolving Workplace Disputes* consultation in 2011, and currently in progress, reflects the ongoing drive to promote the use of ADR in this arena.

This chapter, however, focuses on an earlier ADR initiative that is in many ways unique, both in terms of its provisions and the accompanying DCA-commissioned evaluation of its impact. The initiative concerned a judicial mediation service piloted in three regions of the UK (Newcastle, Central London, and Birmingham) by the Employment Tribunal Service (ETS) for ET claims starting between June 2006 and March 2007. Judicial mediation in this context refers to mediation of a facilitative rather than evaluative variety undertaken by a judge. The aim was to gauge the extent to which such an intervention was able to resolve discrimination cases without the need for a full merits hearing;[1] to determine whether this resulted in a lower cost to the ETS; and to identify any benefits for claimants and employers,[2] both in terms of recorded satisfaction with "outcome" and also "process."

In this chapter we describe some of the key findings from our earlier published work in relation to this evaluation and augment this with further exploration of the data from a telephone survey carried out in 2007 as part of the evaluation. This secured responses from claimants and employers who were party to a claim and who had expressed an "in principle" interest in judicial mediation. Just under 50% of claimants and two-thirds of employers responding to the survey took part in judicial mediation in an attempt to resolve the dispute. These data therefore provide a unique insight into the experiences of those taking part in this form of ADR, permitting a comparison of their experiences with a sample of respondents who had voiced a similar desire to resolve the dispute but had not taken part in judicial mediation.

We pursue a number of avenues of investigation, including the extent to which experiences varied according to previous experience of ET claims, initial expectations of the case and a range of demographic characteristics. Such a detailed analysis was not included in the original evaluation, where the focus was on comparing mediated and unmediated cases in order to identify any statistically significant differences in rates of resolution that avoided costly ET Hearings.

The remainder of the chapter is set out as follows. In the following section we document how the literature on mediation specifically, and ADR in general, suggests a wider range of potential benefits arising from this less litigious form of dispute resolution (see also Chapter 9 in this volume). The aim of our analysis is, at least partly, to shed some light on the extent to which these potential additional benefits are observed in the responses to our survey of those experiencing judicial mediation. The small, existing literature on judicial mediation specifically is also described. The subsequent section sets out the information available in the survey, the methods we use to analyze the data and also describes in more detail the nature of the pilot. The *Analysis* section of our study then outlines the main findings of interest from our analysis of the 2007 survey and also from consideration of our published work to date. The *Conclusion* brings together our findings and considers their importance for existing theory and practice.

MEDIATION AND ITS BENEFITS

The commissioning of the judicial mediation pilot is an example of UK policy-makers seeing ADR as a means to achieve "earlier and more proportionate resolution of legal problems and disputes" (Urwin et al., 2010) The nature of the metrics used to evaluate impact were accordingly much more focused on early resolution that avoided a full merits ET Hearing and the associated reduction of cost (see Urwin et al., 2010). While there was some consideration of satisfaction levels amongst claimants and employers experiencing judicial mediation, the main criterion for success was value for money, as determined by the results of a cost–benefit analysis. In contrast, the existing literature sees the benefits of mediation as potentially more wide-ranging when compared to litigation (see Chapter 9). Using Genn's (1998: 1–2) wording, mediation is seen as:

- a flexible procedure applicable to a wide range of mediation disputes;
- capable of achieving creative solutions to disputes that would not be available in court adjudication;
- capable of reducing conflict;
- able to achieve a reconciliation between the parties;
- less stressful of parties than court procedures;
- able to save legal and other costs and lead to speedier settlements than would be achieved through litigation procedures.

As noted in Chapter 9, parties in mediation have greater control of both process and outcome, and as such it can be an empowering experience. Indeed, this is often identified as one of the main features that participants claim appeals to them. Parties also avoid the potential danger of an unfavorable ruling at adjudication. In contrast, "Litigation . . . frequently produces binary, win-lose outcomes. When it does not, both parties lose to some extent" (Seul, 2004: 893). Mediation is seen to have the potential to transform a dispute into one where each side can "win." From these hypothesized benefits, there is some potential for mediation to lead to more enduring outcomes; mediation is not simply "same outcome, lower cost," when compared to litigation.

In a number of publications, we have detailed the headline findings from evaluation of the judicial mediation pilot. These suggest that judicial mediation does not have a discernable, statistically significant impact on rates of early resolution or satisfaction when compared to a matched control group, while provision of the service also involves a large net cost to the taxpayer. However, as well as the quantitative analysis that focused on headline statistical metrics (Urwin et al., 2010, 2012) and the analysis of more qualitative data that came out of the judicial meditation events themselves (Boon et al., 2011), there remains an untapped wealth of information from the specially commissioned survey of judicial mediation administered by British Market Research Bureau Ltd (BMRB).

In the following section we describe the judicial mediation pilot design, the information collected and the methods used to analyze these data. However, it is first important to consider the nature of judicial mediation, since it has some unique characteristics that set it aside from other forms of ADR. As a result there is potential for claimant and employer responses and experiences to differ from those seen in other studies of ADR. One such dimension is neatly articulated by Grima and Trépo (2009: 1176) who, surveying the broader mediation literature, describe how status resources affect a mediator's ability to undertake their task. First, mediators' interventions are at least partially legitimized by the institutions they represent. Second, high social position is something of a double-edged sword, and can either augment the range of options available, or intimidate the parties. Such arguments are likely to apply a fortiori to judges, whose position implies impartiality, authority, and a knowledge of the law within which the dispute is framed, lending credibility to the process (Otis and Reiter, 2006). Existing evidence also suggests judges may use tactics unique to mediation (Wall and Rude, 1985) and that are more forceful (Wall and Rude, 1987), and that parties may anticipate a more evaluative approach.[3] The process also of course, requires a change of approach from judges more used to adjudication (Otis and Reiter, 2006: 367).

As the above suggests, although novel in the ET context, judicial mediation already operates in other contexts, primarily in the US and in China,[4] albeit with important variations on its practice. In the US context for example, where judicial mediation is most commonly used in civil cases, the impetus has at least partly emerged (as with ETs), as an attempt to reduce the backlog of cases (Rich, 1980; Resnik, 1985; Wall and Schiller, 1982; see Galanter, 1985–6 for a historical overview). Mediation typically takes place by the same judge who would hear the case were it to come to court, via a pre-trial conference (Galanter, 1985; Wall and Rude, 1987; although Brunet, 2002/3, suggests this position is changing). This raises issues concerning legally admissible and ethically appropriate behavior by the judge (see Wall and Schiller, 1982: 29–33; Galanter, 1985–6; Robinson, 2006). Importantly too, the meeting is generally with the parties' lawyers rather than the litigants, and in many cases (but by no means all) the approach is also evaluative rather than facilitative (Brunet, 2002/3) and interventionist (Galanter, 1985–6). The Canadian case, in contrast, is not evaluative (Otis and Reiter, 2006). Notwithstanding these differences in judicial mediation approaches, which are reflected in most of the literature, the US context does provide some interesting insights that are of value here.

For example, in a survey of US lawyers, Wall and Schiller (1982) establish the most commonly used judicial mediation techniques (see also Burns, 1998, 2001) and the extent to which these are perceived to be (un)ethical. Many of the frequently used methods are similar to those in more conventional mediation such as meeting lawyers, moving discussion to areas where settlement is most likely, and shuttle diplomacy (see also Galanter, 1985). Others, however, are not relevant in the context of judicial mediation as applied in the present study (e.g. delaying rulings/trial dates). Among the frequently cited methods that were most likely to be seen as unethical, pressuring lawyers to settle, discussing the strengths and weaknesses of a case, and emphasizing/de-emphasizing these to the benefit of one side are also pertinent in the present context. Not surprisingly, coercion is reported as the most frowned-upon of the frequently observed tactics.

One obvious question that is pertinent for judicial mediation, as with non-judicial mediation, is the effect on outcomes.[5] Citing the early work by Gillespie (1976), Church et al. (1978), and Flanders (1978), Galanter (1985: 8–9) concludes there to be "little evidence that judicial efforts bring about production gains…at least so far as production is measured by the number of cases disposed of" or speed of disposition, a finding echoed by Provine in her review of court settlement procedures. This Galanter surmises, is "not surprising…most cases would settle anyway." Resnik (1985: 686) goes further, suggesting that "judicial management techniques impose additional costs and pose the risk of abuse of judicial power in the quest for greater economies."

Finally, in a more recent study, Wall and Rude (1991) are more sanguine. Using an experimental survey approach, a representative product liability case was posted to a sample of state judges, who were informed of both the case and the techniques used by the judge. They were then asked to assess the probability of settlement, as well as the likely satisfaction of participating lawyers and plaintiffs. Among the 637 respondents, both the number and assertiveness of techniques (and their interaction) were positively related to the perceived likelihood of settlement, in conformity with results elsewhere in the mediation literature, and also to satisfaction. In the same paper, the findings with regard to settlement were corroborated by evidence from the outcomes of real, mediated cases recorded by one judge over the course of a year.

As suggested in Urwin et al. (2012) "Given the central role of the judiciary in both the process of litigation and judicial mediation, one may expect the parties in a case to view judicial mediation differently to other forms of ADR." It is quite possible that claimants and employers see judicial mediation as a process outside the official mainstream ET process, in the same way as other forms of ADR. Conversely, the presence of a judge (who in this context is not the same judge assigned to their claim) may alter this perception in some instances. It is not clear a priori whether this works to the benefit of the process, or against it, and is an issue to which we return.

In the judicial mediation pilot, employment judges (then known as Chairmen) were trained by Acas representatives to administer "facilitative," rather than "evaluative" mediation. As described in Chapter 9, facilitative mediation encourages the parties to communicate and understand the issues, and in doing so, attempts to empower them to arrive at their own solutions. In the pilot, parties were informed that a trained tribunal Chairman would "remain neutral and try to assist the parties in resolving their dispute," and would "not make a decision about the case, or give an opinion on the merits of the case." As we shall see from our analysis of the data, the comments from a number of claimants and employers suggest that they would have perhaps preferred a more evaluative or directive approach, something that formed an expectation among several of the participants in an earlier Acas small firms mediation pilot (Seargeant 2005).

Adopting a facilitative form of mediation, even when administered by members of the judiciary, leaves us with less of a clear distinction between judicial mediation and the services provided by Acas as part of their statutory duty to conciliate in ET cases. For instance, consider the definition put forward by Boulle and Nesic (2001) of mediation's "core" features as:

> a decision-making process in which the parties are assisted by a third party, the mediator; the mediator attempts to improve the process of decision-making and to assist the parties reach an outcome to which each of them can assent.

> (Boulle and Nesic 2001: 3)

As noted in Chapter 9, this describes mediation as facilitating superior decision-making rather than emphasizing its role in terms of dispute resolution, while Mackie et al. regard it as:

> a process of negotiation, but structured and influenced by the intervention of a neutral third party who seeks to assist the parties to reach an agreement that is acceptable to them.

> Mackie et al. (1995: 9)

These definitions could equally well be used to describe the process of "conciliation" undertaken by Acas. While the two processes are similar in many ways, Acas itself describes the difference between the two concepts in terms of whether there exists a statutory duty for them to intervene, as is the case for conciliation, which is also provided free to the users; its mediation offering in contrast, as with most providers in the workplace/employment context, is a "charged-for" service. In addition, conciliation is typically carried out over the phone in most cases and will often take place over a period of weeks or even months; most mediation (regardless of provider) takes place face-to-face and is usually completed within a day. In the judicial mediation pilot, besides the fact that the process was delivered by a member of the judiciary, it nominally shared more in common with conventional mediation and was provided without charge. The last is due to change under the Enterprise and Regulatory Reform Bill, with a fee of £600 to employers for using the service, possibly reflecting a belated recognition that the service is revenue-negative, albeit this figure does not recover the full, direct net cost of the service, estimated in the pilot evaluation at £908. How this will impact on demand for the service is unclear, but basic economics suggests it is likely to significantly curtail its uptake.

As the above might suggest, there is clearly some inter-dependency and overlap in the ET process when considering judicial mediation and Acas conciliation, and this is particularly apparent when we consider the extent to which mediation agreements are legally binding. If a member of the judiciary feels that judicial mediation has arrived at an agreement between both parties, a standard "COT3" form may be used to record the settlement (the same form is used for Acas-conciliated resolution). All COT3 agreements must involve an Acas conciliator and therefore any agreement made within the judicial mediation event is not legally binding unless either a COT3 can be drawn up at the end with the relevant Acas conciliator present or a so-called compromise agreement is signed, the latter requiring the employee to have received independent legal advice. Both protect parties' best interests in that neither side benefits from an agreement that starts to unravel afterwards or was entered without due care and subsequently regretted.

From Boon et al. (2011) and three direct observations of the project team, judicial mediation chairs tended to use shuttle diplomacy and followed a process similar to that described by Genn (1999). For cases that were not overly adversarial, mediations began with a joint meeting between the parties where the mediator explained the process and allowed each side an opportunity to set out their perspective without interruption. The parties proceeded to negotiate separately and in turn with the mediator (necessitating the use of three rooms), who then attempted to establish common ground, using the information gleaned in the series of meetings with the two parties. We now move on to describe the data used in the survey of cases expressing an interest in judicial mediation, and readers should refer to Boon et al. (2011) for more detail on the approaches used by members of the judiciary who served as mediation chairs.

Data, Method, and Pilot Design

The project team worked with the ETS to formulate guidance for pilot regions on the collection of information. When a claim or response form was received in a case involving discrimination, copies of the Claim (ET1) and Response (ET3) forms were retained and, as the case progressed, further relevant information was added as follows:

1. Following a Case Management Discussion (CMD), a *CMD Offer to Mediate Form* was completed by the Chair, recording the details of whether an explanation/offer of judicial mediation had been given and whether the parties had expressed an interest in principle (many cases were given seven days to consider the offer).
2. The aim was always to return the record of the CMD to the parties and Acas within two working days. If the parties expressed interest in judicial mediation, a two-week mandatory period was allowed for Acas to attempt further conciliation, before the Judicial Mediation was listed.
3. For cases where an offer of judicial mediation had been made to the parties, the Regional Chairman held a second CMD (usually by telephone) to make appropriate arrangements. Once a case had been "routed" to the mediation process all other case management actions and activities were suspended or deferred pending the outcome of the mediation. Figure 16.1 provides an overview of the specific cases targeted and the numbers of cases considered during the duration of the pilot.

The focus of the pilot was on cases involving at least one discrimination jurisdiction,[6] as there is often more of a personal, rather than purely business context to the conflict, allowing greater scope for the sort of (non-pecuniary) resolutions that are often considered more likely as outcomes of mediation (see for instance, Genn, 1998: 1–2; Seul, 2004: 893). In addition, there was a focus on discrimination cases perceived as harder to resolve. In the first CMD, a decision was made on whether a case was relatively complicated and could be expected to take up three or more days at a hearing. These cases, involving discrimination jurisdictions and perceived as more complicated, were offered judicial mediation.

Claimant and employer surveys were conducted during October and November 2007.[7] As the bottom of Figure 16.1 suggests, there were 116 mediated and 80 unmediated (but interested) cases considered for the initial target sample for the Judicial Mediation Survey Questionnaire. As a result of incomplete information on residence and other case details, a sample of 139 claimant contacts was issued and a total of 68 interviews achieved. Of the achieved interviews, 32 cases had undergone judicial mediation and 36 had not. The survey was carried out by telephone, with a letter alerting the potential respondent to the call by a member of the BMRB survey team. There were 32 questions

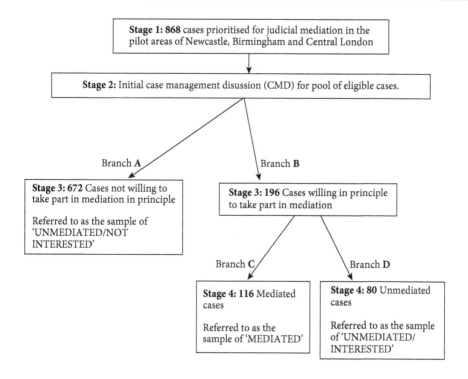

Stage 1: 868 cases prioritised for judicial mediation in the pilot areas of Newcastle, Birmingham and Central London

Stage 2: Initial case management disussion (CMD) for pool of eligible cases.

Branch **A**

Branch **B**

Stage 3: 672 Cases not willing to take part in mediation in principle

Referred to as the sample of 'UNMEDIATED/NOT INTERESTED'

Stage 3: 196 Cases willing in principle to take part in mediation

Branch **C**

Branch **D**

Stage 4: 116 Mediated cases

Referred to as the sample of 'MEDIATED'

Stage 4: 80 Unmediated cases

Referred to as the sample of 'UNMEDIATED/ INTERESTED'

FIGURE 16.1 Flow Diagram of Judicial Mediation Pilot

included in the claimant version of the questionnaire and the interviews lasted for, on average, 25 minutes.

For the survey of employers, a sample of 166 contacts was issued and a total of 75 interviews achieved. Of the achieved interviews, 47 cases had undergone judicial mediation and 28 had not. As with the claimant survey, interviews were carried out by telephone, with a letter alerting the potential respondent to the call by a member of the BMRB survey team. There were 34 questions included in the employer questionnaire and the interviews also lasted an average of 25 minutes. The following headings give an idea of the content of the two questionnaires, which tackled a similar range of issues:

- current status of the case;
- present employment;
- initial expectations of the claim;
- offer and uptake of mediation and conciliation (excluding judicial mediation);
- judicial mediation;
- previous ET claims;
- other issues relating to current claim;
- satisfaction with the ET system;
- demographics (asked only of claimants).

It is unfortunate that the high response rates (of close to 60%) experienced in the early stages of the fieldwork were not sustained. The final response rate for employers was 45% and clearly driven down by those who, whilst expressing an interest in principle, did not take part in mediation. For claimants, the response rate of 49% was closer to the 50% originally envisaged, but the inability to identify telephone numbers for nearly 30% of cases significantly reduced the issued sample.

When considering the number of questionnaire respondents, there are clearly limitations placed on the amount of quantitative analysis that can be carried out. However, in the following analysis it is possible to boost numbers by pooling claimant and employer responses where data permit. More specifically, it is possible to consider the following, different samples:

- A straightforward pooled sample, in which claimants and employers from the same case are counted twice. This is used primarily for analysis of satisfaction, where the purpose is to gauge differences between mediated and unmediated cases, whether claimant or employer.
- A "case-based" sample from the main survey including both claimants and employers, but where there are responses from parties to the same case, only one (the employer) response is used. This leads to the creation of a sample that can be used in the analysis of case characteristics, such as current status, that are factual and asked of both protagonists.
- Finally, one can consider the claimant and employer responses separately as two independent samples.[8]

The majority of questions asked in the questionnaire were closed, but there were three free text fields and these form part of the qualitative analysis. In addition to the questions under the above headings, the questionnaire also asked respondents if they would be willing to be contacted by staff from the University of Westminster to discuss further their experiences of the ET process.

These qualitative in-depth interviews were organized during February, after the initial results of the quantitative survey had been made available. The purpose of the interviews was mainly to explore some of the interesting quantitative findings further, as well as to resolve issues that had remained unclear (see Boon et al., 2011).

ANALYSIS

To date there have been a number of publications which have focused on different aspects of the judicial mediation pilot and the findings arising from the qualitative and quantitative aspects of investigation. In Urwin et al. (2012) we took a step back and considered the findings from our quantitative evaluation within a wider context and discussed the implications for ADR more generally. For instance, our multivariate analysis suggested that female claimants were more likely to take up the offer of mediation, when compared to men; as were employers without representation.

More generally, across all of our work on this issue, employers seem much more likely to view judicial mediation favorably. In Boon et al. (2011) we suggest that this may be because, "facilitative mediation is a lightly regulated negotiation which favors parties familiar with the processes" (2011: 80). Furthermore, our detailed analysis of the mediation reports suggest that "claimants typically settled for sums significantly less than those set out in their schedule of loss"—something that we may expect to impact on the satisfaction levels of employers.

However, whilst employers experiencing judicial mediation display higher levels of satisfaction with the ET process as a whole, when compared to both employers who do not take part in mediation and also claimants who did, it was still the case that we could find no significant difference in rates of resolution or satisfaction using our statistical matching techniques. This is an issue to which we return in the conclusions to this chapter, where we ask the question "what should be captured in ADR evaluations?"

More specifically, when considering the results of the judicial mediation evaluation, we are focused on consideration of the early resolution of cases that avoid a hearing, and this drives the findings of our cost–benefit analysis. However, when we compare this to our discussion of the literature, which can be characterized as suggesting that mediation (and ADR in general) does not simply represent "same outcome, lower cost," there seems to be something of a mismatch. Surely if we are to truly evaluate the impacts of judicial mediation, we need to compare the quality of outcomes, not just how quickly they were arrived at?

To some extent, this chapter and the Boon et al. (2011) paper do attempt to do this using a more qualitative approach—hence the discussion in our conclusion to this chapter. However, in the case of the specific UK judicial mediation pilot being considered, it is important to re-iterate our findings from previous papers. In Urwin et al. (2012) we note "that judicial mediation in this instance is being added to an environment where ADR is already provided, primarily through Acas conciliators' (2012: 585) and that "the ET system already had in place a process of ADR where take-up is voluntary; we have an official facilitating the process and any outcomes must be consensual" (2012: 586). In Boon et al. (2011) we make a similar point, arguing that, "Preventing judicial mediators from evaluation in any circumstances limits opportunities for satisfactory resolution" (2011: 81).

The range of data collected as part of the judicial mediation pilot provides us with a great insight into the process, the experience of claimants and employers. In the conclusion to this chapter we consider how this information could inform future evaluations. However, one of the main lessons for policy-makers that we have already underlined from analysis of this specific judicial mediation pilot is that, even if one were to use alternative measures, it is highly unlikely that one would identify a significant impact of judicial mediation (whatever the metric for evaluation) as it simply represents a rather expensive (see Urwin et al., 2010) duplication of ADR processes already in place.

Having provided a background to the analysis in this chapter, we now set out some of the main findings that can be gleaned from the 2007 survey of judicial mediation.

The sample used for analysis consists of 168 responses, 88 employers, and 80 claimants. Among these responses, 86 relate to mediated cases (35 claimants and 51 employers).

In the questionnaire survey carried out as part of the pilot, employers experiencing mediation reported higher levels of satisfaction with the ET process (73% either satisfied or very satisfied) than their unmediated counterparts (53%) and were more likely than claimants to say that they would use the process again. A pronounced differential also exists between satisfaction with mediation outcomes amongst mediated employers against their unmediated counterparts (66% compared to 50%).

Claimants as a whole were less positive about both aspects of the experience (54% with the ET process and 46% with the outcome), with no differences between mediated and unmediated cases.[9] This is a striking finding, and resonates with Colling's (2004) critique of ADR as "privatizing" dispute resolution; while the process remains operated by the state and its actors, it "raises questions about the quality of justice likely to be done... [and] limits... the extent to which justice is seen to be done" (2004: 573). Certainly these data suggest the process appears to offer more to employers, or at least, that their expectations are perhaps better fulfilled (something explored further below).

Among the 101 main sample "case based" responses where the case had been resolved, methods of resolution differ markedly according to whether the respondent reported experiencing judicial mediation,[10] as might be expected and shown in Table 16.1.

Two features of this table stand out. First, by definition, judicial mediation was not available for the unmediated sample. However, as can be seen, among this group a higher proportion of cases proceeded to a hearing. From the verbatim responses, almost all of the unclassified "Other" responses (9 out of 10) in fact appear to be forms of settlement via solicitors, private mediation or pre-hearings, with just one (unmediated) case reporting going to tribunal. Thus, when completed, 91% of mediated and 72% of unmediated cases resulted in some form of settlement.[11] As the data show, while the

Table 16.1 How the Case was Resolved (%)

Method	Mediated	Unmediated
Determined at ET Hearing	7.41	17.02
Acas settlement	7.41	29.79
Resolved privately	12.96	31.91
Resolved through judicial mediation	68.52	0.00
Withdrawn	1.85	8.51
Other	1.85	12.77
Base	*54*	*47*

Notes: Survey data using "case-based" sample (excludes pilot responses).

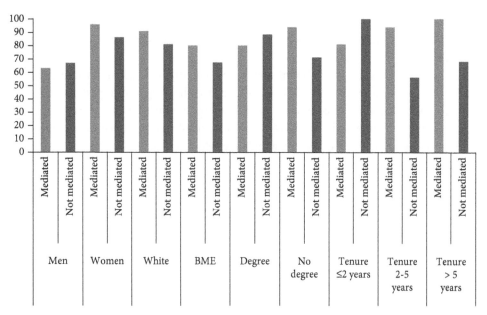

FIGURE 16.2 Tribunal Avoidance Rates by Demographics and Judicial Mediation—Claimant Characteristics

Notes: Samples vary. Gender and tenure comparisons use administrative data and "case-based" sample; white/BME and degree/no degree use claimant survey data and sample.

proportion of mediated cases requiring a hearing is lower than for unmediated cases, there is clearly some "displacement" of what would otherwise be Acas and private settlements, while judicial mediation also appears to result in some cases that would otherwise be withdrawn being resolved through this means. However, as the more formal propensity score matching approach in Urwin et al. (2012) reveals, such differences are not statistically significant when comparing outcomes from "matched" samples, a finding that is reminiscent of Galanter (1985).

Nonetheless, the survey data do allow some exploration of the correlates of success defined in terms of hearing avoidance (a definition that includes withdrawn cases, as these represent an administrative saving). While the sample sizes are small, and the data do not permit us to undertake the sort of matching undertaken in Urwin et al. (2010, 2012), they are still informative.

As Figures 16.2 and 16.3 show, tribunal avoidance rates are generally higher for mediated than for unmediated cases. However, when considering the relation with gender in Figure 16.2 (which uses data matched from administrative data and accordingly the "case-based" sample), it is evident that cases involving female claimants are more likely to be resolved prior to a hearing than those involving males. While acknowledging the very small cell sizes for the latter in particular, the data in Figure 16.2 suggest that ceteris paribus, mediation has a positive effect on hearing avoidance rates for women, but a small or even negative effect for men. To the extent that women are more likely to enter mediation in the first place (as noted above), this is a striking finding and resonates with evidence elsewhere that mediation may be a gendered activity (Latreille, 2011: 46; see also Relis, 2008).

In contrast, based on the claimant survey, cases involving Black and Minority Ethnic (BME) claimants appear more likely to proceed to a hearing than for whites. For both groups however, judicial mediation appears to increase hearing avoidance rates. A more complex pattern emerges by qualifications—specifically having a degree—with mediation only appearing to raise hearing avoidance rates for those without such a qualification, and if anything reducing it for those who do.

Returning to the case-based administrative data, a similarly complex pattern is evident in relation to employee tenure. For mediated cases, avoidance rates rise with length of service. For unmediated cases, however, employees with the shortest tenure appear least likely to proceed to a full hearing. When comparing mediated with unmediated cases therefore, the upshot is that mediation appears to raise avoidance rates only for employees with tenure in excess of two years.

Turning to organizational characteristics, the data show hearing avoidance rates are again higher in mediated than in unmediated claims (Figure 16.3). Using case-based administrative information, a relatively modest impact of mediation on avoidance rates is apparent when splitting by employer size (based on number of employees), and only for medium and large organizations (those employing 50 or more staff), for whom

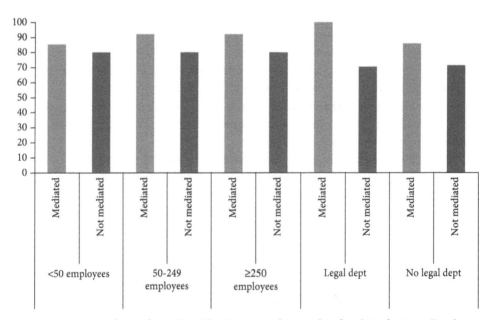

FIGURE 16.3 Tribunal Avoidance Rates by Demographics and Judicial Mediation—Employer Characteristics

Notes: Samples vary. Organizational size comparisons use administrative data and "case-based" sample; legal dept/no legal dept uses employer survey data and sample.

mediation appears more likely to result in resolution. As Figure 16.3 shows, however, the impact is much greater among organizations that have legal departments that deal with HR issues, although the 100% figure should, as with the precise numbers throughout this section, be treated with extreme caution, being based on very small numbers of observations (in this instance, 16). Even smaller sample sizes preclude a similar comparison according to whether the organization had previously been the subject of an ET claim, although it is interesting to note that, overall, hearing avoidance rates are higher among organizations with previous experience. This might be taken to suggest that with experience comes a recognition that the uncertainty of hearings is to be avoided where possible.

One question prompted by the above is the extent to which it is the judicial mediation process that is responsible for hearing avoidance, or some other factor. Survey respondents who had experienced judicial mediation were asked whether it had helped bring the case closer to a resolution. Around three-quarters of claimants agreed that it had. However, there are interesting variations across the earlier demographics, with female claimants being more likely to agree that mediation was very effective or of some help (79%) compared with men (67%), albeit on the basis of just six male respondents. Those with degrees were much less sanguine about the process than those without (61% and 85% respectively), as were those from BME groups (69% compared with 76%). As noted, employers were more positive as a group, with those organizations having legal departments being especially so (94%), together with those with prior ET experience. Smaller organizations also appear slightly more positive, which stands in contrast to the lower avoidance rates for this group discussed above.

Some interesting variations also emerge in relation to a series of questions about the judicial mediation process. Again, while the sample size for men is tiny, they appear more likely than women to report being able to contribute as much as they would have liked and that there was plenty of time allowed for mediation, but less inclined to consider the mediator was competent or that they would participate in the process again. All of these appear consistent with findings elsewhere that men are potentially more confident in contexts where there is some element of competition (see for instance, Booth and Nolen, 2012).

A similar pattern of responses also applies for those with degrees compared with those who do not possess such a qualification. An especially interesting finding is that those with degrees are far less likely to view the mediator as competent (71% compared with 93%), suggesting that they are less impressed by status. Those from BME groups also appear to find the judge's position as one that implies competence (91%, cf 71% among whites), but while finding the process one in which they feel able to participate fully, they are less likely to say that they would use it again (64% cf 70%), perhaps reflecting the lower efficacy noted above. In contrast, employees with longer tenure appear more positive across each measure, including that they would use it again (82% for those with more than five years of tenure compared with 44% for those with two years or less).

For employers, larger organizations typically appear less sanguine about the process, with just half of the largest organizations saying they would use it again, despite mediation apparently resulting in higher tribunal avoidance rates for this group. This divergence between process and outcome seems to reflect, in particular, a perception among larger organizations that insufficient time was allowed.

In relation to the free-text responses about the ET system among those who were mediated, some interesting responses are again revealed. Confirming the quantitative data, employers were typically more positive than claimants, with several comments along the lines that it "worked very well," was "prompt and fast," and "saved us a lot of time," with one arguing that it "is the way forward." Several employers, however, commented on biases in the ET system more generally that appeared to favor the employee and allowed weak/unfounded claims.

While several claimants were positive about the process and about staff at the ET, they were typically less so in relation to judicial mediation than employers, with some commenting on the legalistic nature of the ET process and the way this appeared to impart a bias to the processes. Strikingly, however, few mentioned (at least unprompted) the chance to have their day in court, with some mentioning the awkwardness involved in being in the same space as the employer.

CONCLUSIONS AND WIDER IMPLICATIONS FOR ADR

Judicial mediation was introduced in a context where conciliation already exists via Acas, where resolution rates without a hearing are already quite high and where no extra resource was provided for chair/mediator's time. The challenge set was to improve resolution rates. However, as the evaluation of the pilot revealed, it did not do so in a statistically significant fashion and was found to result in additional costs. We recognize in these discussions some potential for the relatively small numbers in the pilot to make the identification of a statistically significant impact more problematic. However, such impacts are likely be small and it is therefore highly unlikely that any impact would be of sufficient size to offset the high costs (see Urwin et al., 2010), which make judicial mediation a particularly expensive process to administer.

In a climate where resources are scarce, it is perhaps therefore surprising that the approach was subsequently rolled out nationwide in January 2009. This seems to reflect a change of emphasis/criterion at the Tribunals Service, with cost/hearing savings being replaced by satisfaction to assert that "Results from the pilot were very positive" (*Tribunals Service Annual Report and Accounts, 2008–2009*: 27). That judicial mediation did not deliver significantly higher resolution rates or cost savings is perhaps unsurprising with the benefit of hindsight. While the process combines "some of the legal and moral gravitas of adjudication with the flexibility and adaptability of ADR" (Otis and Reiter, 2006: 12), as the "mediation abacus" presented in Urwin et al. (2010) shows, judicial mediation is similar to conciliation on many dimensions. The implications for ADR are that something different is needed in order to generate significant impacts.

In policy terms, one is also struck by a potential conflict between the aims of policy-makers who wish to utilize ADR (and specifically mediation) as part of a strategy to reduce cost and bring about speedier resolution, and the potential for wider benefits arising from ADR. Settlement is, of course, not always preferable to adjudication: the quality of settlements also matters (Galanter and Cahill, 1994; see also Bush, 1989). Notwithstanding the various potential private and public benefits claimed for settlements (which may include those arrived at via mediation), Galanter and Cahill conclude that "the task for policy is not promoting settlements or discouraging them, but regulating them" (1994: 1388). Such an argument mirrors one that has in the past been leveled at Acas conciliation, namely that the pursuit of settlement is more important than its nature (e.g. fairness) (Gregory, 1986; Dickens, 2000).

All of this therefore raises the interesting question as to whether there are ways of making judicial mediation work more effectively, perhaps selecting cases where the gravitas of a judge truly makes a difference? Or should we commit to a more radical (but not too radical) alternative to what happens now? What would we design if we had a free hand?

Notes

1. This is to be distinguished from interlocutory hearings. These primarily deal with procedural matters, but a pre-hearing review may result in a claim or defence being "struck out."
2. In the ET system, employers are usually referred to as "respondents." For the avoidance of confusion, we use the term "employer" to denote the organization against whom the claim was brought, and "respondent" to indicate a survey participant.
3. Wall and Rude (1987) find evidence to suggest that lawyers prefer more forceful tactics than judges offer. Interestingly, Seargeant's study of a mediation pilot for small and medium-sized employers run by Acas suggests a preference among some parties for more evaluative styles. One tactic that has been described in an ethnographic study of the US judicial mediation of large civil cases is that of trying to get the parties to consider the worst case scenario—i.e. to think their "darkest thoughts" (Burns, 2001). This is reported to be a powerful tool in eliciting concessions.
4. For an introduction to the latter context, see Huang (2006) and Wang (2009). DeGaris (1994) describes the role of Australian judges in settlement.
5. See Tyler (1988/9) for a useful exploration of measurement issues in evaluating such interventions, including identifying objectives, cost, delay, and the climate between parties.
6. According to *Employment Tribunal and EAT Statistics* March 2008, of the total 189,303 ET cases dealt with in the preceding financial year, 41,110 (22%) included a discrimination jurisdiction.
7. Pilots were also carried out for both the Claimant and Employer surveys between 6 and 19 August. For the claimant survey, a sample of 24 contacts was issued and a total of 12 interviews were achieved and for the employer survey a sample of 24 contacts was issued and a total of 13 interviews were achieved. These responses are included in the analysis where

possible, although changes to some of the questions between pilot and main stage means this is not always feasible.

8. It would in principle be possible to examine only those cases where there are survey responses for both parties, but this sample is too small ($n = 25$) to allow meaningful analysis.

9. The numbers here differ from the published data due to the exclusion of pilot cases from the bases and the inclusion of "Don't know" responses, but the pattern is qualitatively unaffected.

10. There is a small number of cases where survey responses are at variance with the official data. We generally use the latter except where routing in the survey depends on the response provided to this question.

11. Of the full "case-based" sample, around 14% of both mediated and unmediated cases were ongoing at the time of the survey.

References

BIS 2011. *Resolving Workplace Disputes: A Consultation*. London: Department for Business, Innovation and Skills.

Boon, A., Urwin, P. J., and Karuk, V. 2011. "What Difference Does It Make? Facilitative Judicial Mediation of Discrimination Cases in Employment Tribunals." *Industrial Law Journal*, 40(1): 45–81.

Booth, A. and Nolen, P. 2012. "Choosing to Compete: How Different are Girls and Boys?" *Journal of Economic Behavior and Organization*, 81(2): 542–55.

Brunet, E. 2002/3. "Judicial Mediation and Signaling." *Nevada Law Journal*, 3: 232–58.

Burns, S. 1998. "The Name of the Game is Movement: Concession Seeking in Judicial Mediation of Large Money Damage Disputes." *Mediation Quarterly*, 15(4): 359–71.

Burns, S. 2001. " 'Think Your Blackest Thoughts and Darken Them': Judicial Mediation of Large Money Damage Disputes." *Human Studies*, 24: 227–49.

Bush, R. A. B. 1989. "Defining Quality in Dispute Resolution: Taxonomies and Anti-taxonomies of Quality Arguments." *Denver University Law Review*, 66(3): 335–80.

Church, T., Carlson, A., Lee, J., and Tan, T. 1978. *Justice Delayed: The Pace of Litigation in Urban Trial Courts*. Williamsburg, VA: National Center for State Courts.

Colling, T. 2004. "No Claim, No Pain? The Privatization of Dispute Resolution in Britain." *Economic and Industrial Democracy*, 25(4): 555–79.

Corby, S. and Latreille, P. 2012a. "Tripartite Adjudication—An Endangered Species." *Industrial Relations Journal*, 43(2): 94–109.

Corby, S. and Latreille, P. 2012b. "Employment and the Civil Courts: Isomorphism Exemplified." *Industrial Law Journal*, 41(4): 387–406.

DCA 2004. *Transforming Public Services: Complaints, Redress and Tribunals*. London: Department for Constitutional Affairs.

DeGaris, A. H. 1994. "The Role of Federal Court Judges in the Settlement of Disputes." *Tasmanian Law Review*, 13: 217–36.

Dickens, L. 2000. "Doing More with Less: ACAS and Individual Conciliation." In B. Towers and W. Brown (eds), *Employment Relations in Britain: 25 Years of the Advisory, Conciliation and Arbitration Service*. Oxford: Blackwell, 67–91.

Dix, G., Sisson, K., and Forth, J. 2009. "Conflict at Work: The Changing Pattern of Disputes." In W. Brown, A. Bryson, J. Forth, and K. Whitfield (eds), *The Evolution of the Modern Workplace*. Cambridge: Cambridge University Press, 176–200.

Flanders, S. 1978. "Case Management in Federal Courts: Some Controversies and Some Results." *Justice Systems Journal*, 4: 147–64.

Galanter, M. 1985. ". . . 'A Settlement Judge, Not a Trial Judge:' Judicial Mediation in the United States." *Journal of Law and Society*, 12(1): 1–18.

Galanter, M. 1985–6. "The Emergence of the Judge as a Mediator in Civil Cases." *Judicature*, 69: 257–62.

Galanter, M. and Cahill, M. 1994. "'Most Cases Settle': Judicial Promotion and Regulation of Settlements." *Stanford Law Review*, 46: 1339–91.

Genn, H. 1998. *The Central London County Court Pilot Mediation Scheme: Evaluation Report.* London: Department for Constitutional Affairs.

Genn, H. 1999. *Mediation in Action: Resolving Court Disputes Without Trial.* London: Calouste Gulbenkian Foundation.

Gibbons, M. 2007. *A Review of Employment Dispute Resolution in Great Britain.* London: DTI.

Gillespie, R. W. 1976. "The Production of Court Services: An Analysis of Scale Effects and Other Factors." *Journal of Legal Studies*, 5: 243–64.

Gregory, J. 1986. "Conciliating Individual Employment Disputes: A Shabby Compromise?" *Employee Relations*, 8(1): 27–31.

Grima, F. and Trépo, G. 2009. "Knowledge, Action and Public Concern: The Logic Underlying Mediators' Actions in French Labour Conflicts". *International Journal of Human Resource Management*, 20(5): 1172–90.

Huang, P. C. C. 2006. "Court Mediation in China, Past and Present." *Modern China*, 32(3): 275–314.

Latreille, P. L. 2011. "Mediation: A Thematic Review of the Acas/CIPD Evidence." Advisory, Conciliation and Arbitration Service Research Papers, No. 13/11.

Latreille, P. L., Latreille, J. A., and Knight, K. G. 2007. "Employment Tribunals and Acas: Evidence from a Survey of Representatives." *Industrial Relations Journal*, 38: 136–54.

Mackie, K., Miles, D. and Marsh, W. 1995. *Commercial Dispute Resolution: An ADR Practice Guide.* London: Butterworths.

Otis, L. and Reiter, E. H. 2006. "Mediation by Judges: A New Phenomenon in the Transformation of Justice." *Pepperdine Dispute Resolution Law Journal*, 6(3): 1–54.

Provine, D. M. 1987. "Managing Negotiated Justice: Settlement Procedures in the Courts." *The Justice System Journal*, 12(1): 91–112.

Relis, T. 2008. *Perceptions in Litigation and Mediation: Lawyers, Defendants, Plaintiffs, and Gendered Parties.* Cambridge: Cambridge University Press,

Resnik, J. 1985. "Managerial Judges: the Potential Costs." *Public Administration Review*, 45: 686–90.

Rich, E. M. 1980. "An Experiment with Judicial Mediation." *American Bar Association Journal*, 66: 530.

Robinson, P. 2006. "Adding Judicial Mediation to the Debate about Judges Attempting to Settle Cases Assigned to them for Trial." *Journal of Dispute Resolution*, 2006(2): 335–85.

Seargeant, J. 2005. "The Acas Small Firms Mediation Pilot: Research to Explore Parties' Experiences and Views on the Value of Mediation." Acas Research Paper, No. 04/05.

Seul, J. S. 2004. "Settling Significant Cases". *Washington Law Review*, 79: 881–968.

Tribunals Service. 2009. *Annual Report and Accounts, 2008–2009.* London: The Stationery Office.

Tyler, T. R. 1988/9. "The Quality of Dispute Resolution Procedures and Outcomes: Measurement Problems and Possibilities." *Denver University Law Review*, 66: 419–36.

Urwin, P., Karuk, V., Latreille, P., Michielsens, E., Page, L., Siara, B., Speckesser, S. with Chevalier, P.-A. and Boon, A. 2010. "Evaluating the Use of Judicial Mediation in Employment Tribunals." *Ministry of Justice Research Series*, 7/10.

Urwin, P., Latreille, P. L., and Karuk, V. 2012. "Quantitative Evidence in the Evaluation of ADR: The Case of Judicial Mediation in UK Employment Tribunals." *International Journal of Human Resource Management*, 23(3): 567–89.

Wall, J. A. and Rude, D. 1985. "Judicial Mediation: Techniques, Strategies and Situational Effects." *Journal of Social Issues*, 41: 47–64.

Wall, J. A. and Rude, D. E. 1987. "Judges' Mediation of Settlement Negotiations." *Journal of Applied Psychology*, 72: 234–39.

Jr.Wall, J. A. Jr. and Rude, D. 1991. "The Judge as a Mediator." *Journal of Applied Psychology*, 76(1): 54–9.

Wall, J. A. and Schiller, L. F. 1982. "Judicial Involvement in Pre-trial Settlement: A Judge is Not a Bump on a Log." *American Journal of Trial Advocacy*, 6: 27–45.

Wang, L. 2009. "Characteristics of China's Judicial Mediation System." *Asia Pacific Law Review*, 17: 67–74.

PART 4

INTERNATIONAL DEVELOPMENT

Introduction to Part 4

WILLIAM K. ROCHE, PAUL TEAGUE, AND ALEXANDER J. S. COLVIN

Introduction

An evergreen in the study of comparative employment relations is whether common patterns of employment and work exist simultaneously across countries or whether each national employment system is distinctive, made up of its own unique institutions and rules. Although both views have had their strong advocates over the years, a fair amount of consensus now exits that employment relations in different countries display both diverging and converging trends in one form or another: national employment systems may stand apart institutionally and culturally and at the same time experience broadly similar employment relations developments. Just as this is the case in relation to pay, trade union membership, performance management, and so on, so it is also true for workplace conflict management.

The chapters that make up Part 4 of the Handbook neatly highlight how different countries are encountering similar conflict management developments yet exhibit contrasting features with regard to how workplace conflict is governed.

The Divergences

Each chapter shows that workplace conflict and its management have important country-specific, idiosyncratic features. In his assessment of the German case, Behrens argues that the resolution of employment disputes and grievances is partly embedded in the country's complex set of labor market institutions, which, over the years, has helped produce high levels of economy-wide coordination. Thus, for example, the system of sector-level wage bargaining, which operates mostly at the national level, has kept the potentially divisive topic of pay setting outside the firm. As a result, management and employee representatives inside organizations have greater scope to develop more consensual relationships, with the effect of reducing the incidence of conflict. This situation is reinforced by the renowned system of firm-level works councils that provide an effective voice for employees to raise problems and complaints, thus operating as an effective mechanism for conflict prevention. However, work councils also have built-in procedures to address different forms of conflict should these arise.

At the same time, Germany has a highly "juridified" system of industrial relations that ensures the law and courts play an important role in the resolution of workplace conflict, mostly related to the exercise of employment rights. Recently, this aspect of conflict resolution has gained greater prominence as more and more employees are seeking vindication of their employment rights, mostly in the areas of discrimination and harassment. Behrens argues that market developments rather than institutional innovations have induced change to established methods of addressing workplace conflict. In particular, he suggests that the growth of the non-union sector as well as a big increase in the number of small and medium-sized firms have led to new procedures being introduced to address workplace conflict. Behrens concludes by suggesting that the current crisis has not had much impact on the manner in which workplace conflict has been resolved. However, he warns that if the current trend toward the decentralization of collective bargaining continues apace, then the implications for the nature and scale of workplace conflict could be significant.

Benson argues that fragmentation and experimentation are the bywords to describe conflict resolution in Japan. Traditionally, as in Germany, management of workplace conflict was tied to key features of the Japanese employment system, most notably enterprise unions and *shunto*, a system of joint consultation between enterprise management and workers. The functioning of these institutions ensured that as much emphasis was placed on conflict prevention (mostly by providing employees with a voice at the workplace) as on conflict resolution. Moreover, these institutions were invariably successful at resolving workplace problems in an orderly and efficient manner: with regard to collective disputes, for example, unpredictable, wild cat action was almost unknown. However, over the past decade the traditional pillars of the Japanese employment system have been under intense pressure. Depressed macroeconomic conditions, the eclipse of the once dominant manufacturing sector, and the rise of a non-union business sector have seriously weakened key industrial relations institutions such as the *shunto*. The result has been a fragmentation of traditional methods employed to resolve workplace problems.

In response to this fragmentation, governments have introduced a number of changes to the public dispute resolution system for employment conflict. In 2006, for example, a new employment tribunal system was established for the first time, which focuses mostly on addressing the growing tide of individual employment rights cases. However, Benson suggests that a number of other conflict resolution experiments have emerged alongside government-led institutional innovations. He points to the rise of community unionism in the country as well as to the growth of joint action by individual workers on workplace problems as examples of the search for new methods and procedures to resolve conflict at work. For the foreseeable future, conflict resolution in Japan is predicted to be a story of continuing fragmentation prompting more experimentation.

Just like so many other features of American life, workplace conflict resolution in the US is exceptional. Unlike most other advanced economies, the US does not possess public bodies, such as employment tribunals or labor courts, to address workplace conflict. In the absence of specialized semi-judicial bodies, employment-related disputes were mostly addressed by the formal court system. For the most part, the dominant story of workplace conflict resolution in the US over the past two decades has been efforts by firms to bypass the formal legal system by establishing alternative dispute resolution (ADR) procedures at the workplace to address disputes and grievances. Lipsky, Avgar, and Lamare tell this story. ADR practices cover a fairly wide range of procedures to address workplace conflict. Sometimes employers introduce ADR systems to oblige employees to use arbitration rather than legal processes to settle a grievance. Other times the intent is to widen the repertoire of practices used to solve problems by diffusing innovative procedures such as ombudsperson, peer view, or mediation.

Building on previous empirical work, Lipsky and his colleagues show that US firms have both deepened and widened their use of ADR practices during the past decade. They also argue that organizations are adopting a more strategic approach to workplace conflict as evidenced in a number of interesting developments. One is an increased incidence of ADR systems, which are seen to be sets of integrated ADR practices. The other is that human resource (HR) managers in union and non-union firms appear to be learning from each other with regard to the use of ADR practices. Lipsky, Avgar, and Lamare suggest that these developments should be regarded as significant as they amount to fairly marked changes to the manner in which workplace conflict is managed in the US.

In contrast to the US where public employment dispute resolution agencies are more or less absent, Australia has long established institutions, both at federal and state level, to help settle workplace conflict. A traditional feature of these institutions, mainly at federal level, is that in addition to supporting the resolution of employment disputes they also played an important wage setting role: their authority to make awards to settle certain types of collective bargaining disputes led to the creation of minimum levels of pay and conditions for important areas of the economy. Thus, these public agencies performed both a standard-setting and a conflict resolution role. Van Gramberg, Bamber, Teicher and Cooper set out the institutional contours of this conflict resolution system and show how it supported collective industrial relations by promoting fairness in the labor market.

They argue that the shift away from collective industrial relations alongside the growth of neoliberal ideas precipitated successive waves of reform to the public regime for employment conflict resolution during the past two decades. The intention of a first round of reform was to weaken the public conflict management system by encouraging more disputes to be settled by firms themselves, also by promoting the delivery of conflict management services by private firms or consultants—an attempt effectively at privatizing workplace conflict resolution. These efforts at market-led, deregulatory change were seen as being reined in by a second round of reform, introduced by a new Labour Government, designed to once again strengthen the role of public dispute resolution bodies. Van Gramberg and her co-authors suggest these recent reforms have led to important institutional innovations such as the creation of the Fair Work Ombudsman. Yet, they are skeptical whether the changes will be far reaching enough to halt the ongoing decline of collective industrial relations or provide employees in precarious forms of work with effective means to seek redress for employment grievances.

Even more or so than Australia, public employment resolution processes in New Zealand have oscillated from one policy change to another over the past twenty years. Rasmussen and Greenwood map out this roller coaster policy ride. Their analysis begins with a description of the public dispute resolution system that prevailed in the country for the best part of the 20th century. Resting on the twin pillars of conciliation and arbitration, this system operated mostly to support collective industrial relations. In addition, like the situation in Australia, the public dispute resolution bodies played an important role in establishing minimum standards in relations to pay and working conditions. If the system had a weakness, it was the relatively underdeveloped processes to address individual forms of workplace conflict, even though changes were made in the 1970s to improve this situation.

In the early 1990s this public system for workplace conflict resolution experienced what amounted to a policy shock. New legislation was introduced abolishing the ability of the public dispute resolution machinery to make awards, the mechanism through which it established minimum levels of pay and working conditions. Two institutions were created—an Employment Tribunal and an Employment Court—which shifted the focus of the system radically away from supporting collective bargaining to addressing the burgeoning number of individual employment rights cases. The main thrust of the legislation was to decentralize employment relations to the enterprise and to weaken, if not end, state support for collective industrial relations. In 2001, a new Labour Government sought to row back on these market oriented reforms by introducing legislation designed to promote "good faith" bargaining and stable employment relations. The policy intention was to shift the balance toward collective bargaining and away from individual employment rights. However, Rasmussen and Greenwood suggest these efforts at giving collective bargaining a shot in the arm have had limited success. At the same time, they point out that despite the various policy upheavals the dispute resolution agencies have been doing interesting work to innovate their conflict resolution processes, most notably in the area of mediation.

Like other chapters, Dix and Saundry, when assessing conflict resolution in the UK, chart the decline of collective industrial disputes and the rise in the number of individual employment rights cases being handled by the country's employment tribunal system. However, they caution against making broad assertions about the shift away from collective disputes toward the individualization of employment conflict. They argue that there are segments of the British economy, most notably the public sector, where the potential for collective disputes remains high. Moreover, they point to survey evidence which suggests that there has been no significant increase in the level of individual-based conflict at the workplace. For Dix and Saundry, patterns of conflict, and the capacity to resolve these, are fundamentally influenced by the nature of workplace and managerial relations and here they point to a worrying development. In particular, they argue that a "resolution gap" has emerged in many workplaces caused by the erosion of effective structures of employee representation on the one hand and the devolution of responsibility for conflict-handling from human resources practitioners to poorly trained operational line managers on the other hand.

Dix and Saundry also review the public debate that has continued for well over a decade about whether the rise in the number of individual employment disputes has rendered the employment tribunal system incapable of delivering a fast, reliable service. The prevailing official view seems to be that tribunals have betrayed their original mission by becoming too legalistic and cumbersome and as a result require reform. The authors chart the growing interest in the use of ADR-type practices, particularly mediation, to resolve workplace problems informally. However, they are less than sanguine about whether there will be sufficient commitment either by government or firms to build up the organizational capabilities necessary to resolve workplace problems with the use of ADR procedures.

China's full-hearted embrace of markets and free enterprise has had far reaching consequences for how the employment relationship is conceived, let alone managed, in the country. Inevitably, market liberalization has had an impact not only on the scale and nature of workplace conflict, but also on the procedures used to resolve it. Mingwei Liu argues that data limitations prevent a fully accurate assessment being made of the extent of employment disputes in the country. But he is firmly of the view that there has been a massive increase in workplace conflict during the past decade or so, although the incidence of conflict varies a great deal across regions and economic sectors (unsurprisingly, the heavily industrialized regions and manufacturing industries are identified as more prone to employment disputes). A painstaking effort is made to assemble together statistics from various official sources on employment conflict. The chapter also sets out the country's formal labor dispute resolution system, which has three stages: mediation, arbitration, and two court trials. However, the law also encourages various forms of informal dispute resolution—consultation, negotiation, or conciliation between aggrieved workers and employers.

Mingwei Liu identifies a number of shortcomings with the emerging system of conflict management. First of all, he suggests that the various voice mechanisms introduced by government to improve employee involvement in organizational decision-making—enterprise trade unions, consultative and mediation committees—tend to be dominated by management and thus lack credibility with employees. Second, the government, in line with Chinese culture and tradition, has placed a heavy emphasis on the role of mediation in the resolution of workplace conflicts. Yet too many institutions are used to deliver this service and some—such as enterprise mediation committees—are flawed in several important respects. Third, the political authorities are finding it difficult to deal with the increase in spontaneous industrial action by employees as it challenges the impulse of the Communist Party to seek order and to control. Mingwei Liu reaches the conclusion that the country will require more sophisticated conflict resolution institutions as economic and social modernization deepens.

THE CONVERGENCES

The various country case studies clearly show that the contingencies of domestic economic and political life have a strong influence on the nature of workplace conflict and how it is resolved. For example, the election of a new government with strong economic views can have an immediate and far reaching impact on established public bodies with the mission to support workplace conflict resolution. Yet the case studies also show that most of the countries are grappling with similar developments in relation to workplace conflict. One trend shared by most of the case studies has been the decline of collective industrial relations processes, including collective mechanisms to solve disputes. This is a pretty far-reaching development, for in the past collective industrial relations assigned trade unions a special public status and ensured that collective bargaining played an important role not only in establishing the rights and rules through which people were incorporated into the labor market, but also in shaping the expectations and obligations that employees, employers, and societies had for work and employment relationships.

In a sense, collective industrial relations gave rise to a particular form of economic citizenship that worked from a (quasi) collective contract toward the status of individuals: on the basis of a collective bargain between employers and workers, which balanced conflicting interests at the aggregate level; rights and obligations were ascribed to individual workers and enterprises in a way which tended, for the most part, to exclude serious conflict or ensured that it was addressed through agreed collective procedures. On occasions, however, collective industrial relations processes malfunctioned, leading to some form of conflict. Many governments considered it less than prudent to assume that collective industrial relations processes would in all circumstances self-correct—have the ability to resolve conflict on their own. As a result, almost everywhere (the USA being the most celebrated exception) collective industrial relations systems were buttressed in one way or another by public agencies with the mission to support the settlement of conflict at work.

In many of the case-study countries, the decline in collective indus-trial relations processes has been challenging for public employment dispute resolution agencies. Either at the behest of government policy or as a result of internal reflection, most of the agencies have experi-enced some degree of reform. For the most part, the motive behind the change agenda has been to renew their organizational identity so that they are seen as not simply being an institutional appendage to collec-tive industrial relations, but also well equipped to deal with more indi-vidualized and less organized forms of workplace conflict. In concrete terms, this has meant many agencies placing less emphasis on deliver-ing conciliation and arbitration services, though by no means aban-doning these processes entirely, and developing more comprehensive mediation capabilities. Almost everywhere during the past decade, public agencies charged with supporting workplace conflict resolution have upgraded their mediation programs or services.

Another development shared by most of the case-study countries has been an increase in individualized forms of workplace conflict. Most of the chapters identify the growth of legislation on individual employment rights in areas, such as equality and unfair dismissal, as the driver behind the growing individualization of conflict. The signif-icance of this development has yet to be fully assessed. Some downplay the shift from collective to individualized forms of conflict; others, like Benson in the chapter on Japan, suggest that it will precipitate fragmentation and experimentation; while others still argue that the consequences will be far reaching because the increase in individual employment law is encouraging employees to adopt new norms and expectations about employment and work. In particular, instead of possessing occupational or collective identities that once provided the socio-psychological foundations for collective industrial rela-tions, employees now engage with employers as legal subjects as much as anything else. As a result, they are quite prepared to use the law, even opportunistically at times, to defend or advance their interests at work. To some extent, it is these social processes that lie behind popu-lar arguments made almost everywhere about employees becoming far more litigious than ever before.

If the argument that the rise of individualized forms of conflict is far reaching holds true, then we can expect significant innovations in the manner in which HR managers approach workplace conflict. Just what form these innovations will take remains an open question. So far, as shown in the case studies, firms in advanced economies out-side the USA have shown no eagerness to adopt ADR-type procedures even though, as Lipsky, Avgar, and Lamarre show, these arrangements have become fairly well ensconced in the American workplace. It can be plausibly argued that HR managers may focus more on developing conflict prevention initiatives rather than on conflict resolution schemes. Whatever strategies employed in the end by firms, it is certain that the change and reform highlighted by the country case studies will continue unabated for some time to come.

CHAPTER 17

CONFLICT RESOLUTION IN GERMANY

MARTIN BEHRENS

Introduction

EMPLOYMENT relations in Germany have frequently been described in terms of "social partnership." In the German context, social partnership is normally taken to mean a collaborative relationship between strongly organized employers represented by national-level employers' associations on the one hand and employees, represented by national unions and establishment-level works councils, on the other (Turner, 1998). This perspective resonates with Nell-Breuning's influential account, published almost two decades after the end of the Second World War, which sees social partnership as rooted within the mutual interdependence of capital and labor, whereby neither group can exist without the other (Nell-Breuning, 1964).

However, by using the term "conflict partnership" several decades later, Müller-Jentsch reminds us that it would be inappropriate to view this system as free of conflict (Müller-Jentsch, 1999: 8; see also Weltz, 1977). Employment-related conflict occurs at various levels:

- first, as part of collective bargaining between employers and unions in the shape of strikes and lockouts
- second there are various forms of conflict at the workplace level between works councils and plant management—including the use of arbitration panels, but also the playing out of various types of resistance tactics (Heiden, 2011)
- finally, conflict also occurs at the individual level between co-workers as well as between individual employees and their superiors.

While conflict is omnipresent, it is striking that this subject is rarely addressed within the academic debate about German employment relations. This lack of academic attention is most notable in the field of Human Resource Management (HRM). Only one out of the four most recently published textbooks in the field of HRM (Berthel and Becker, 2010; Ridder, 2009; Scholz, 2011; Stock-Homburg, 2010) covers the subject of conflict at all (Berthel and Becker, 2010: 132).[1] Even in this exceptional case the discussion of conflict is limited to the context of team-based workplace practices. Moreover, none of the four textbooks examines particular dispute resolution procedures, let alone *alternative* dispute resolution procedures, and there is no detailed description of how individual or collective workplace-related conflict is resolved.

If conflict in German employment relations has not ceased to exist, why is there so little research on specific dispute resolution mechanisms? The explanation put forward in this chapter is that key institutions in different constituent parts of the German employment relations perform an important role in diffusing and limiting conflict. As a result, there is no overarching dispute resolution system that may have encouraged scholars to take conflict resolution for granted. The chapter shows that many of the key elements of German employment relations, which emerged not through deliberate political design but through practice, resulted in different aspects of employment-related conflict being assigned to well-defined spheres or "arenas" (Müller-Jentsch, 1982) within which they can be addressed or even resolved.

The chapter is organized as follows. In the next section, the key elements of the German employment system are described and their mutual dependence is analyzed. The following section then investigates more recent advances in this traditional system of conflict resolution. Three recent additions to the traditional German system of dispute resolution deserve particular attention: non-statutory forms of employee representation, the new Anti-Discrimination Law of 2006 and the Mediation Law of 2012. Moving from new institutions and procedures to outcomes, the following section analyzes how established dispute resolution practices are subject to change. This section first investigates how the traditional separation of conflict into different arenas (one inside establishments and the other outside establishments) has been eroded before analyzing the impact of the economic crisis in 2008 and 2009 on the resolution of conflict. It asks whether increasing economic pressure on companies in export-driven industries has undermined social partnership. The final section concludes by asking whether traditional institutions for conflict resolution are still adequate to address workplace-related conflict in the future.

TRADITIONAL KEY INSTITUTIONS OF DISPUTE RESOLUTION

For a long time, two key concepts captured the essence of German employment relations: "juridification" and the "dual system of interest representation." Juridification or *Verrechtlichung* refers to a dense web of statutory rules and procedures that restricts the behavior of key collective actors in an effort to reduce levels of conflict at work (Müller-Jentsch, 1997: 303; Keller, 2008: 66–7). After the Second World War, a system of labor and employment law developed based on a series of statutes regulating the individual employment relationship (the so-called "individual labor law"). A wide range of matters fall within the scope of the statutes, including dismissals, vacation time, maternity leave, maximum working hours, health and safety at the workplace, vocational training, and employment of under-age workers. Employees can seek vindication of employment rights in a labor court. In addition, a system of so-called "collective labor law" has evolved, covering issues such as collective bargaining (which stands out as a main exception to the rule, being almost exclusively subject to case law rather than a statute), plant-level employee representation through works councils, co-determination of employee delegates at the level of enterprise boards, and European Works Councils.

The German Court System

In addition to this dense web of rules, independent courts, presided over by judges, play an important role in the resolution of employment disputes. Compared with the American legal system, these courts are rather sheltered from the influence of organized interests (Rehder, 2011: 38). Labor courts are constructed as an independent court system along a three-tier structure with a local labor court in each major city, state-level courts of appeal, and a national labor court (*Bundesarbeitsgericht*) located in Erfurt. For the year 2004, it has been estimated that the entire labor court system employed 1,100 judges (Rehder, 2011: 245). In particular, at the local level, a chamber, constituted by a professional lawyer as the chair and two voluntary judges nominated respectively by the unions and employers' associations, is easily accessible to employees. At this lowest level, complainants do not need to be represented by an attorney. In addition, formal requirements as well as court fees are relatively moderate. Between 2000 and 2010, there were more than 400,000 new cases submitted to the labor court system annually; at its peak in 2003, the number of new cases reached more than 640,000 (Statistisches Bundesamt, Fachserie 10, Reihe 2.8, 2010). Major conflicts between employers and individual employees are resolved at this level—with the majority of these cases involving disputes over dismissals, followed by disputes about wages. Taken together these two issues represent the lion's share of all cases dealt with in the labor court system.

The "Dual System" of Interest Representation

The second key concept is the so-called "dual system" of interest representation,[2] which ensures that workers' interests are represented at the plant level through establishment-level works councils on the one hand, and through collective bargaining, conducted between trade unions and employers' associations (or single employers), above the company level on the other hand. Works councils which, according to the Works Constitution Act (WCA), can be formed in establishments with more than five employees are elected by the entire workforce (rather than just by union members). They represent workers' day-to-day interests in areas such as hiring, transfers, dismissals, company restructuring, discipline, working time regulation, overtime work, and the administration of company facilities such as cafeterias, childcare, or housing. Yet the WCA also imposes limits on the scope of works council activities. In particular, works councils are not allowed to bargain collectively (section 77 III WCA) or to call a strike (section 74 II WCA). In 2011, 44% of all west German employees in establishments with more than five employees were represented by a works council. In east Germany, only 36% of all employees were covered (Ellguth and Kohaut, 2012: 303).

In contrast, collective bargaining is the responsibility of unions and employers' associations. Agreements are mostly negotiated for an entire industry within a certain region (in most cases this is one of the 16 German states (*Länder*)), but a number of national-level agreements also exist, for example in banking and the public sector. However, the German Collective Bargaining Act (*Tarifvertragsgesetz*) also allows for company-level agreements to be negotiated between a union and a company's management. Today, most multi-employer agreements are negotiated between one of the approximately 700 employers' associations (most of them directly or indirectly affiliated with the Confederation of German Employers, BDA) and one of the eight affiliates of the German Trade Union Confederation, DGB. In 2011, 34% of establishments in west Germany and 21% in east Germany were covered by a collective agreement (both types: industry and plant level) (Ellguth and Kohaut, 2012: 299). Because collective bargaining coverage increases along with company size, this has led to 61% of all employees in west Germany and 49% in east Germany being covered by a collective agreement (Ellguth and Kohaut, 2012: 298).

In contrast to the first key area of dispute resolution, "juridification", which rests on a dense network of labor and employment law and an accessible court system and which is available to all employees, the "dual system" of employment relations covers a minority of employees, albeit a large minority. As shown in Figure 17.1, in 2011 only 35% of all German employees (working in the private sector in establishments with more than five employees) were fully covered by both key institutions within the dual system, collective bargaining and works council, while 30% were covered by only one of the two institutions. Importantly, 34% of employees were not covered by either a works council or collective bargaining, indicating a significant "representation gap."

Thus, in relation to the resolution of workplace conflict, whereas the law has almost universal reach, the voluntary institutions of employment relations (works councils and collective bargaining) have more limited coverage as a significant minority of employees are neither represented by a union nor a works council. About a third of German private sector employees, displayed in the upper left section of the circle in Figure 17.1, represent the German equivalent to what in the US is known as the non-union sector. Thus, it needs to be remembered that not all employees are covered by the conflict resolution instruments analyzed below.

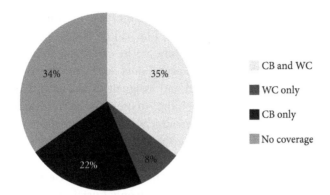

FIGURE 17.1 Works Councils and Collective Bargaining at German Workplaces, 2011 (due to rounding, shares do not add up to 100%).

Source: IAB Establishment Panel.

Table 17.1 The Dual System of German Employment Relations

Level	Establishment	Above Establishment
Key actors	Works councils, plant management	Labor unions, employers' associations, single employers
Major laws applicable	Works Constitution Act	Collective Bargaining Act, Section 9 III German Constitution
Major key tasks	Regulation at the workplace level, applying content of collective agreements	Negotiating collective agreements on wages, hours, and working conditions
Dominant expression of conflict	WC's withdrawal from cooperation, pressure tactics	Strike, warning-strike, lockouts, go-slow
Dominant mode of conflict resolution	Grievance rights, arbitration panels	Mediation (voluntary procedure)
General principles	*Integrative Bargaining*, "trustful collaboration" (Section 2 I WCA)	*Distributive Bargaining*

As shown in Table 17.1, in an admittedly stylized and simplified fashion, the two pillars of the dual system (establishment-level co-determination through works councils and company and multi-employer collective bargaining) are each based on a number of distinct core principles. The two arenas are dominated by different actors; both arenas are regulated by different laws that assign different tasks and responsibilities to each area. Most importantly, as already noted above, the WCA prohibits works councils from negotiating collective agreements, while section 2 of the Collective Bargaining Act assigns the sole responsibility for concluding agreements on wages, hours, and working conditions to unions, employers, and employers' associations.

This—de jure—rigid separation of responsibilities also has important consequences for potential employment-related conflict. (As will be shown below, the boundaries between the two pillars of the dual system are less clear-cut than intended by law.) As responsibility for matters such as wages, hours, and working conditions is mostly removed from the establishment level and assigned to collective bargaining parties, conflict arising from "distributive bargaining," to use the term introduced in Walton and McKersie's (1965) seminal work, has been largely removed from the plant level. And even within this rather "conflict prone" arena, the absolute level of conflict activity is rather moderate when compared to other OECD countries. In terms of average numbers of working days lost per 1000 employees for the years 2004–7, Germany's strike activity has been at the lower end of the distribution with only Austria, Sweden, Switzerland, the Netherlands, and Poland having less strike activity (Dribbusch, 2010: 159). In terms of the collective bargaining process, several German multi-employer agreements include voluntary mediation agreements (*Schlichtungsabkommen*), for example agreements for the construction industry and the public sector. While provision may vary between industries, most of these agreements stipulate that if negotiations reach a stalemate the issue is to be referred to a mediation committee. Mediation committees usually consist of an equal number of representatives from the union and employers' side with a neutral chair having the casting vote. The final decision of the mediation committee, however, is non-binding on the parties so that mediation mostly constitutes moral obligations and serves as a cooling-off mechanism in negotiations (WSI 2009: 259–60).

Being relieved of the task of having to negotiate over wages (at least to some degree), plant-level management and works councils are free to address other issues and problems. To use another of Walton and McKersie's (1965) concepts, "integrative bargaining" matters dominate their deliberations, with the focus very much on problem solving rather than on distributing a cake of a fixed size. Working together to solve problems strengthens a collaborative ethos between plant-level management and works councils. This does not mean, however, that no scope exists for establishment-level conflict. While plant-level conflict is to some extent "bounded," there is still nevertheless plenty of space for diverging interests at the establishment level. To mention just a few examples: while the length of the working week is to be regulated by collective bargaining, the distribution of these hours over the working week, rules determining the beginning and end of the working day, overtime work, the introduction of working time accounts (whereby hours could be banked to take time off at a later point in time), as well as procedures for the measurement and documentation of working time are all the responsibility of the works council. The same is true for a full range of other matters including the protection of jobs, procedures for granting vacation time, work restructuring and work organization.

The flipside of works councils being freed from collective bargaining is unions, as the sole bargaining agents for workers, being relieved from having to provide day-to-day services to their members at the plant level. Only in a small number of industries are there union representative bodies at the plant level. Such shop steward systems

(*Vertrauensleutekörper*) exist mostly in large establishments in metalworking or chemical engineering (Wassermann, 2003; Prott, 2006).

Although the law separates key actors, responsibilities, and conflict into different spheres, unions have consistently sought to create connections between each sphere. Ever since the Works Constitution Act (1952) was adopted, German unions have been eager to prevent works councils from establishing themselves as company unions competing with the DGB and its affiliates. Besides establishing shop steward bodies, unions have made great efforts to organize the members of works councils into their own ranks. Today, more than 60% of all works council members are a member of one of the DGB's eight affiliates (Behrens, 2009: 283), although this figure is lower than in the 1970s. Based on this high cross-membership, a mutual dependency has been established whereby unions provide works councils with training seminars and support when major conflict erupts with plant-level management, while, in turn, works councilors provide union members (as with other employees who do not belong to a union) with basic workplace-related services and significantly assist the recruitment of new members into the union (Behrens, 2009). At the establishment level, union representatives might serve as a welcomed adviser or even supporter of the works council (a function that is also acknowledged by the WCA by way of providing union representatives with the right to participate in works council meetings or works assemblies), but they play no active role in establishment-level dispute resolution.

The WCA provides for two major channels of dispute resolution:

- the right of each employee to voice grievances
- arbitration panels to be initiated by either the management or the works council.

Grievance Right

The right to voice a grievance is guaranteed by section 84 of the WCA. Complaints can be made in cases where employees consider themselves to be subject to unfair treatment either by their employer or by fellow workers. The law provides that such complaints are to be addressed to the "unit in charge" or to the works council and that it is illegal to discriminate against workers because they exercise their grievance right. If employees address their grievances to the works council, the works council is obliged to receive them, and if they consider them to be of substance urge the employer to remove the cause of the unfair treatment. It should be noted, however, that unlike in the US system, grievance rights under the WCA do not include a multi-step procedure, whereby grievances first have to be addressed orally with the supervisor before being pursued at higher levels (see Katz et al., 2008: 284). Data on how widely this procedure is used in German workplaces are not available.

Arbitration Panels

Arbitration panels constitute a second procedure for conflict resolution at the establishment level. In contrast to the grievance right, these panels are mostly used to resolve collective-level conflict between works councils and management. In cases of workplace conflict concerning "differences of opinion", an arbitration panel is required by the WCA to produce a legally binding decision (section 76 I WCA). There are two different ways such panels can be set up: a voluntary and a mandatory route. The choice of which route is used is related to which of the participation rights of a work council are involved in the conflict.

In general, the WCA grants three different types of participation rights. The weakest rights are pure "information rights" which require the employer to provide the works council with sufficient information in a timely manner. "Consultation rights" are more substantial: in addition to information rights (which are included in consultation rights), an employer has to provide the works council with the opportunity to voice its view on the matter and to listen to any suggestions it may put forward. Stronger still are "co-determination rights," which include all the features of information and consultation rights, but also require an employer to obtain the consent of the works council before acting on a particular matter. The employer cannot act unilaterally. Co-determination rights exist in areas such as the distribution and extension of working time, principles for workers taking vacation time, occupational health and safety, general principles for pay (performance-based pay), surveillance, company facilities (such as cafeterias), and group work.

In conflicts that involve matters where works councils enjoy statutory co-determination rights (not just information or consultation rights), the arbitration procedure can be activated by one side, either the WC or the employer. This is the "mandatory procedure." Although both parties have the right to initiate arbitration, it is the works council that does so in the majority of cases (Oechsler and Schönfeld, 1989: 35).

Arbitration panels are usually established as the need arises, but they can also be established as permanent bodies. They are composed of an equal number of works council and employer representatives, as well as a neutral chair. In practice, the chair is usually a professional judge from the local labor court. The decision taken by the arbitration panel has the character of a works agreement, which is an enforceable contract-like document. Because the panel decides according to a simple majority, the neutral chairperson has the casting vote. Conflicts involving issues where works councilors lack statutory co-determination rights—for example, the integration of foreign workers, or ecological issues—the arbitration panel can only be set up with the agreement of both parties. This is the "voluntary procedure."

Empirical research has established that the use of arbitration panels at German workplaces has been relatively stable over time (Knuth et al., 1984; Oechsler and Schönfeld, 1989; Behrens, 2007). The most recent study carried out by Behrens (2007: 180) found that about 11% of establishments (only private sector establishments with more than 20 employees possessing a works council) had used arbitration in the previous two years, with the figure for west Germany (12%) being somewhat higher than the level in east Germany (9%). While the likelihood of establishments making use of arbitration panels increases with company size (25% of works councilors in establishments with more than 2,000 employees have indicated that they had used arbitration), research also indicates that if used at all, the number of cases dealt with by this procedure is rather limited. In the same survey, respondents reported that arbitration panels had not been used more than three times in 86% of establishments during the previous two years. Further statistical work revealed that the likelihood of establishments using arbitration panels increases when works councilors indicate that management frequently interferes with their participation rights—as granted by the WCA—and when management provides works councils with insufficient relevant information. The respondents also reported that arbitration panels help to take the edge off plant-level conflict by formalizing its resolution.

As already indicated in Figure 17.1, arbitration panels are only available to a minority, albeit a sizeable one, of 44% of the workforce, who are employed in an establishment with a works council. But how is conflict to be resolved in all the other establishments— mostly small and medium-sized—that employ the remaining 56% of the workforce?

Advances in the Institutions of Dispute Resolution

Non-Statutory Representation Bodies

The existence of the German equivalent of a "non-union sector" has long been recognized. For the purposes of this chapter the "non-union sector" refers to the absence of works councils, which immediately raises questions about whether and how workers are able to resolve conflicts through alternative channels of interest representation. As studies of the small-firm sector have discovered (Kotthoff and Reindl, 1990), there are ways in which employee interests can be represented beyond those guaranteed by the Works Constitution Act. Hilbert and Sperling (1993: 185), for example, found in the early 1990s that some employers had established voluntary forms of employee participation. But it took almost another ten years before scholars—as part of a series of research projects studying labor relations in the rapidly growing information technology (IT) and media industries—began studying this phenomenon in greater detail (Boes and Baukrowitz, 2002; Artus et al., 2006; Ittermann, 2009).

Two studies in particular have sought to analyze in more detail the diffusion, function, and effectiveness of alternative forms of employee interest representation. The first study is the so-called BISS survey, which was conducted in 2005 as a computer-aided telephone survey. Respondents to the survey were representatives from management and (if available) works councils in 3,200 establishments in the private sector with more than ten employees (Hauser-Ditz et al., 2006, 2008). The second study, or perhaps more accurately data set, is derived from the annual IAB establishment panel, which—based on personal interviews—surveys about 16,000 establishments of all sizes (respondents are management representatives or owners of the company). The survey has been conducted every year since 1993. In 2003 the IAB began to include a question in the questionnaire which asked respondents to indicate whether there were "other establishments' specific forms of employee-interest representation such as a spokesperson, round table or similar bodies" (Ellguth, 2005: 152). As shown in Table 17.2, the share of establishments that has just an "other non-statutory form" of interest representation and no works council is between 8% (IAB panel) and 19% (BISS study), covering between 13% (IAB) and 11% (BISS) of all employees. In contrast to the case of works councils, which are more common in large establishments, the likelihood of finding a non-statutory form of interest representation is remarkably constant over the size categories (Ellguth, 2009: 113).

While the existence of voluntary interest representation bodies is widely recognized, there is only limited information on their structure and their effectiveness in representing employee interests and in resolving workplace-level disputes. The most detailed information on these matters is contained in the BISS survey. Hauser-Ditz et al. (2008: 76) interrogated the data in this survey to find out whether these bodies are elected by the workforce or appointed by management and if they are joint bodies of labor and management representatives or—as in the case of works councils—just employee representation bodies. This investigation revealed that the "appointed joint committee of management representatives and employees" was the most frequent incidence of non-statutory representative bodies (42%). The next most popular case was "elected

Table 17.2 Studies on Establishments with Other Forms of Interest Representation

	IAB Establishment Panel 2007 (establishments 5+ employees only)		BISS Study 2005 (establishment 10+ employees only)	
	All Cases	Only Cases Without Works Council	All Cases	Only Cases Without Works Council
Share of establishments with other forms of interest representation	8%	8%	29%	19%
Share of employees covered by other forms of interest representation	10%	13%	n/a	11%

Source: (Ellguth, 2009: 112–113; Hauser-Ditz et al., 2009: 142, 2008: 104).

employee representation," a body most similar to an elected works council, which represented 23% of all cases of non-statutory representation. Third in the ranking was the "elected joint committee of management representatives and employees," which made up 22% of total cases. Finally, 14% of cases were defined as "appointed employee representation" (Hauser-Ditz et al., 2009: 140).

Hertwig (2011b) examined more closely eight of those cases identified by Hauser-Ditz et al., using a qualitative case-study research design. He found that despite substantial variation in structures, resources and outcomes of representation, many of those bodies were first established in the context of company growth (Hertwig, 2011b: 203). Because the existing, mostly individualized, forms of employee relations were deemed insufficiently sophisticated to provide channels for communication to support business expansion, new representation bodies were created to fill the void. While many of those bodies are geared towards complementing the leadership role of management, Hertwig also identified several cases where the new bodies served as tools for conflict resolution (Hertwig, 2011b: 91). In a similar vein, Schlömmer et al. examined 809 small and medium-sized companies and found that in 17.5% of cases where companies had reported that a non-statutory representation body had been created (15.7% of all cases), the motivation behind the initiative was to address conflict between employees and management (Schlömmer et al., 2007: 55).

When comparing works councils with non-statutory representation bodies, Ellguth (2009:115) found remarkable differences in terms of their longevity. While there was little turnover within the population of works councils, 50% of the population of non-statutory representation bodies had disappeared after just one year (to be replaced by new bodies, often at different establishments). In contrast to arbitration panels under the WCA, which come and go depending on the concrete demand for dispute resolution, a logic of "mission accomplished" seems to prevail amongst non-statutory bodies, whereby a round table, task force, or similar body is abolished after having served its purpose.

Anti-Discrimination Law

A second major innovation in employment relations concerns individual-level rights at the workplace. When the new General Equal Treatment Act (Allgemeines Gleichbehandlungsgesetz, AGG) was established in August 2006, it echoed developments that were occurring at the European level. Before the introduction of the AGG, Germany had anti-discrimination laws, which mostly focused on prohibiting gender-based discrimination, but the system could only be considered patchy and in some cases even lacking strong enforcement mechanisms. This changed dramatically when Germany transposed four European Directives into national law.[3] The AGG expanded the grounds on which discrimination is prohibited to include gender, race, ethnic background, sexual orientation, age, and religion and relaxed the requirements for the burden of proof, making it much easier for employees to bring their case to court.

The AGG mostly establishes individual rights for employees on equal treatment, which can be vindicated in court by claiming compensation for damages but also for pain and suffering. In contrast to the US legal system, however, the German system does not award punitive damages. In addition to strengthening individual employment rights, the AGG also has important consequences for collective-interest representation through works councils. Based on Section 75 WCA, the works council has to monitor labor relationships to see that there is no discrimination against employees within an establishment based on gender, race ethnic background, sexual orientation, age, or religion. The works council is also required to contribute towards enforcing these principles in the situation of hiring, firing, job transfers, and promotions. In addition, employers are required to initiate pre-emptive measures to avoid discrimination, to take appropriate measures in the event of employees discriminating against their co-workers, to establish a unit to which employees can refer their grievances against alleged discrimination, and to educate their workforce on the rights and duties arising from the AGG (Leisten, 2007).

When EU anti-discrimination Directives were being transposed into national law, many observers, some of them maintaining close ties to the business community, voiced concerns that the new law would lead to a flood of court cases and an increase in the number of frivolous legal suits. Some of these initial concerns were raised because the AGG does not only apply to employment relationships, but also to other private-law contracts such as leases. However, previous experience with implementing the original law prohibiting discrimination against women suggested it would be unlikely that the new legislation would result in a substantial increase in the number of discrimination-related court cases: the introduction of section 611a into the German civil code in 1980, a provision that allows employees to claim compensation when they are discriminated against on grounds of their gender, led to only 112 cases in court (1982–2004), an average of about five cases a year (Pfarr, 2005).

Mediation Law

As already indicated above, in Germany there is a tradition of voluntary mediation agreements, which are applied in the context of industry-wide collective bargaining. In 2012 a new law took effect, providing for mediation in the case of labor and welfare state law. As with the case of the Anti-Discrimination Law, the new Mediation Law (*Mediationsgesetz*) is based on a European Directive. Mediation is a voluntary procedure but can, with the agreement of the involved parties, result in a written agreement. While the law provides for detailed standards applying to neutral mediators, their qualification, neutrality, and requirements for confidentiality, little is said about procedures for the enforcement of mediation agreements. While it remains to be seen whether this new procedure will be used in practice, some critics have already considered it to be at best superfluous, because employees' right to complain and arbitration are already procedures well established by the Works Constitution Act (Stiel and Soppkotte, 2012).

Evolution of Established Practices

The previous section has shown how new laws and institutions contribute towards adding new tools and subjects to the traditional repertoire of plant-level dispute resolution. This section focuses on processes through which well-established institutions and procedures for dispute resolution might change.

Is the Dual System Still Dual?

As highlighted above, one of the key characteristics of the dual system of interest representation is to separate and isolate different conflict arenas: conflict on wages, hours, and working conditions is addressed by unions and employers associations in the arena above the establishment level whereas workplace-related conflict falls within the jurisdiction of works councils and establishment-level management. This system functions much better when the different conflict arenas are kept apart from each other. However, in practice, this division has never been without tensions. On the one hand, "wildcat militancy," which normally involved ambitious wage increases being demanded of prosperous firms, has occasionally called into question the ability of unions to police effectively the collective bargaining process (Rogers and Streeck, 1995: 12). On the other hand, there has been "wildcat cooperation," in which concessionary agreements at the workplace level undermines the ability of unions to establish and implement industry-wide collectively bargained minimum norms (Seifert and Massa-Wirth, 2005; Bispinck, 2006). Concerns about the stability of the dual system mostly focus on wildcat cooperation, the incidence of which has become more frequent due to the decentralization of collective bargaining. Increasingly, decisions relating to pay, hours, and working conditions are being decentralized from the national collective bargaining arena to the firm level, leading to works councils and plant-level management gaining greater responsibility for these matters. Focusing on the way decentralization emerges, scholars often differentiate between "organized" and "disorganized" decentralization (Traxler, 1995) or "controlled" and "wildcat" decentralization (Bispinck and Schulten, 1999). Organized decentralization leads to bargaining tasks being delegated to the establishment level in an orderly manner. In contrast, disorganized decentralization frequently involves outright labor-market deregulation or key actors, such as employers, refraining from engaging fully with the established, more centralized system (Traxler, 1995:6–7). Organized decentralization has progressed significantly since its beginnings in the mid-1980s, when the IG Metall included an "opening" clause in its famous multi-employer collective agreement on the introduction of the 35-hour working week. This opening clause allowed works councils and management at the company level to adjust flexibly the working-time provisions set out in the collective agreement (Schmidt and Trinczek, 1986; Thelen, 1991). Today, opening clauses are widely used, which results in collective bargaining powers being transferred to establishment-level actors (Bispinck and Schulten, 2011). In part, such clauses have been used to customize collectively agreed standards to the specific conditions of a company. However, they have also been used to introduce new types of plant-level agreements, many of them known as "Pacts for Employment and Competitiveness." Such pacts usually involve works councils making concessions on matters such as increased working-time flexibility, reduced bonuses and in some cases even pay cuts in exchange for job security or investment guarantees by an employer. In the case of the IG Metall, such establishment-level negotiations were combined with a strategy to mobilize union members at the plant level and to recruit directly new members into the union (Turner, 2009).

While the decentralization of collective bargaining and corresponding mobilization strategies such as those pursued by the IG Metall have helped to generate new sources of power for the union, they have also raised the level of conflict at the establishment level. As Haipeter has emphasized (2011: 192), actors become increasingly conflict orientated simply because issues of distributional bargaining, initially kept away from the shop floor, have found their way back into the plant or company. The second issue, in addition to the increased propensity for conflict at plant level, concerns the negative impact of decentralization on works councils' legitimacy. In cases where establishment-level agreements fail to live up to original expectations, or are even ended by way of unilateral withdrawal by the employer (which according to Bogedan et al., 2011, happened in about 5% of the cases they studied), the blame is frequently borne by the works council (Haipeter, 2011: 190, see also Rehder, 2006).

Dispute Resolution and Economic Shocks

The slow erosion of the boundaries between the two main pillars of the dual system can be understood as an incremental process, commencing about 30 years ago. So far it is an open question as to how these traditional structures and institutions of dispute resolution will react to the more punctuated shock triggered by the recent world financial crisis. Such a severe economic crisis holds increased potential for workplace conflict: jobs are at stake and disputes about the distribution of shrinking resources might intensify. But as classic accounts, such as the seminal Marienthal study by Jahoda et al. (1975, first published 1933) remind us, frustration and paralysis are as likely an outcome of crisis as worker resistance and contention. Thus, the potential impact of an economic crisis on the level of workplace conflict cannot be predetermined. The same might also hold true for the capacity of established conflict- resolution practices to deal with conflict.

To analyze whether works councils and established conflict resolution mechanisms such as arbitration panels are capable of sustaining severe economic shocks, this section now focuses on the years 2007–10. Between the arrival of the global recession in Germany in early 2008 and the first shoots of economic recovery in 2010, GDP declined by 5%—the most severe recession in German post-war history (Herzog-Stein et al., 2010).[4] To estimate the effects of the crisis on the level of disputes and on the use of dispute resolution practices, the following analysis uses data from the annual WSI works council survey 2007–10. This is a panel survey of works council members from private sector establishments with more than twenty employees. Interviews were conducted by Infas, one of Germany's major polling institutes, mostly with presidents of local works councils. Because the aim is to compare respondents' perceptions prior to the crisis (fall 2007) with their views after two years of recession (spring 2010), the analysis includes only those cases ($n = 1008$) where the survey has generated interviews from the same establishments and where possible with the very same individual respondents at both points in time.

As far as the usage of arbitration panels is concerned, there is remarkably little change during the two years of crisis. In fall 2007, at a time when the crisis had yet to impact fully on the German economy, 11% of responding works councilors indicated that in the previous two years they had made use of at least one arbitration panel. More than two years later, in spring 2010, this share had declined to 9.6%. No notable change was evident with regard to how frequently arbitration panels were used: of those that used arbitration panels in 2007, respondents indicated that they had on average 2.7, while this number declined to 2.1 panels in 2010. But how should the slightly declining incidence of the use of dispute-resolution practices be read? One possible interpretation might be that the crisis had a chilling effect on conflict at the establishment level. In this case, works councils are reluctant to process conflict through the normal dispute resolution system because they fear that at times of declining company profits the neutral chair could be inclined to vote in favor of management. Low utilization of arbitration panels could be the result of such a calculation, which reflects the "Marienthal effect." A second interpretation might refer to the generally reduced level of establishment-level conflict, which would weaken the demand for arbitration. In this case, crisis may well lead key actors at establishment level to increase collaboration to safeguard jobs and to help the company survive the times of crisis.

To test the "chilling effect" hypothesis, first separate analysis is provided for those establishments for which works councilors have indicated that they were negatively affected by the crisis and those which were not. In total, 52% of respondents indicated that their establishment was affected by the crisis, correspondingly another 48% observed little or no impact of the crisis (for obvious reasons this question has been included in the 2010 questionnaire only). Table 17.3 reports the results. First, those establishments that did not feel an immediate impact of the crisis are considered. While 13.5% of those establishments reported the use of at least one arbitration panel in 2007 (covering the time period from September 2005 to September 2007) this share had declined to 10% by 2008 (covering panels that occurred in the time period from February/March 2008 to February/March 2010). In contrast, works councilors from establishments affected by the crisis reported a slight increase in the use of arbitration panels, from 8.6% in the 2007 survey to 9.2% in 2010.

If being negatively affected by the crisis would lead works councils to refrain from using arbitration panels, as has been suggested by the "chilling effect" hypothesis, the expectation would be that the share of establishments using arbitration panels in 2008–10

Table 17.3 Use of Arbitration Panels Dependent on Impact of Crisis

	Establishment Affected by the Crisis (2010)	Establishment *not* Affected by the Crisis (2010)	All Establishments (2010)
Arbitration panels used 2005–07	8.6%	13.5%	11.0%
Arbitration panels used 2008–10	9.2%	10.0%	9.6%

Source: WSI Works Council Survey, Panel 2007/2010.

would be lower than in 2005–7. Apparently the opposite is the case as the use of arbitration panels increased in establishments affected by the crisis (column 2 of Table 17.3). If there is any chilling effect at all, somewhat surprisingly it materializes within the group of establishments that were not directly feeling the impact of crisis (column 3 of Table 17.3).

One possible explanation for this finding is that changes might have occurred to the general level of conflict during the period. To follow up on this interpretation it is necessary to look at a question in the WSI works council survey that is used as a proxy for establishment-level conflict. The question is: "Does management interfere with the legal participation rights of works councils?" Respondents could choose from the categories "never," "sometimes," "often," with the latter category used as a proxy for a high level of establishment-level collective conflict. While in the 2007 survey 13.9% of respondents indicated that their employer "often" interfered with the works council's participation rights, this share had declined to 10.2% by the time the crisis was drawing to an end. This remarkable reduction in conflict between management and works councils reflects, to some degree, the observations made by other scholars based on qualitative research. As a result of group conversations and interviews held with union shop stewards, Detje et al. (2011) concluded that at first glance the crisis had proceeded—in a somewhat odd way—without friction. Unlike other neighboring European countries, Detje et al. pointed out that there was no general strike, occupation of plants, or "Boss napping" (Detje et al., 2011: 8) in Germany.

However, a closer look into the data reveals that the impact of the crisis is more mediated by other factors than commonly assumed. As shown in Table 17.4, incidents of frequent interference with works council's participation rights are again analyzed separately for those establishments that were affected by the crisis and those that were not. The results are somewhat surprising.

While there is a reduction in workplace-level conflict between works council and management in both groups (establishments affected by the crisis and those not affected), the decline is larger in the group of establishments that watch the crisis from the sidelines (1.9% reduction in the case of establishments affected and 5.5% in the case of establishments not affected by crisis). One possible reading of this data might be that

Table 17.4 Interference with Works Councils' Participation Rights Depending on Impact of Crisis

	Establishment Affected by the Crisis (2010)	Establishment *not* Affected by the Crisis (2010)	All Establishments
2007, management has "often" interfered with works councils' rights	14.1%	13.7%	13.9%
2010, management has "often" interfered with works councils' rights	12.2%	8.2%	10.2%

Source: WSI Works Council Survey, Panel 2007/2010.

workplaces with more collaborative labor relations (and thus a lower level of plant-level conflict) are better positioned to master the effects of the crisis and thus consider themselves—when asked in the survey—not to be affected by the economic downturn. Put in a nutshell: collaboration pays for labor and business during times of crisis. An observation that would support this claim refers to working time accounts, which is considered to be one of the most important instruments associated with Germany's excellent labor market performance during the crisis (Zapf and Herzog-Stein, 2011). Working time accounts were much more common in establishments with collaborative labor relations when compared with those with a higher incidence of conflict. In 2007, 73% of all establishments in the sample indicated using working time accounts while this share was only 66% for the group of establishments where respondents indicated that management often interferes with works councils' rights.

Some studies suggest that the crisis impacted on collaborative labor relations in an unexpected way. In Germany, the economic crisis has been debated within the whole of society so that key actors at establishment-level increasingly switched into cooperation mode, which is perceived as appropriate behavior to safeguard jobs. According to Detje et al. the reason for this mode of "crisis cooperation" is not just rooted within the dual system, which prescribes cooperative behavior as the major mode of social behavior within the arena of plant-level cooperation, but also in a bundle of other societal factors that make radicalization and mass mobilization highly unlikely, at least for the moment. Following Offe (2010) they argue that the crisis has led to a splitting of the workforce in two different fractions, each with their own orientation. There are, first, those workers in precarious employment who react to the crisis with frustration. In contrast, large parts of the core workforce (most of them with permanent work contracts) feel that the crisis might even work to their personal advantage and thus refuse to be part of an adversarial collective identity.

The data available does not allow a definitive answer as to whether collaboration helps to buffer the effects of crisis or whether the crisis influences works councilors' perceptions of collaboration. But whatever the interpretation is, the evidence strongly suggests that even under the condition of severe shocks the dual system of interest representation maintains much of its capacity to keep conflict within bounds.

Conclusion

Conflict related to the governance of the employment relationship might occur at different levels: at the macro level between national unions and powerful employers' associations, at the meso or establishment level between works council and plant management, and finally at the micro level between individual employees and their supervisors or even among co-workers (Hocke, 2012: 58). As the preceding analysis of conflict management in Germany shows, different systems of dispute resolution dominate at different levels of conflict: disputes occurring at the macro level (such as strikes) might be made subject to mediation (in rare cases also to litigation), while conflict between collective actors at the establishment level might be submitted to the arbitration procedure. Micro-level conflict in turn, might either be resolved by the public labor-court system or addressed by establishment-level grievance bodies. Arguably, this system, which assigns particular types of conflict to different arenas and processes for conflict resolution, has contributed towards creating strong and enduring foundations for "social partnership." Importantly, this system has never been static, as the more recent changes have proved: European standards targeted to fight discrimination have made their way into national law and have helped make German anti-discrimination law more comprehensive. Also, it has been shown that new types of non-statutory interest representation bodies can be found throughout the country, in establishments that already have a works council and in those that do not.

While these developments help to stabilize the employment system, other processes of change give reason for concern. With the two "pillars" of the dual system "crumbling" (Hassel and Streeck, 2003), certain types of conflict may get diffused into new areas where procedures may not be immediately available to find a resolution. Although it can be plausibly be argued that collaborative employment relations are intensified on the arrival of an economic shock, the prospects of partnership-type relations appear to be fairly bleak in the long run. So far, decentralization has had a greater impact than the economic crisis on the nature of dispute resolution practices in German employment relations. With bargaining responsibilities increasingly being transferred to establishment-level works councils, the danger is that conflict arising from distributive bargaining may negatively affect other features of employee-management relations at the workplace. It remains to be seen whether the German labor relations system will be able to adjust to distributional conflict being more or less a permanent feature of organizational life.

NOTES

1. Apparently, little has changed since Krüger (1972: 16) complained that within the discipline of business administration little effort has been made to study conflict.
2. Not to be confused with the "dual system" of vocational education (a combination of classroom education in public apprenticeship schools and on-the-job training in mostly private companies), the "dual system" of broadcasting (private and public broadcasting), or the "dual system" of waste management (collection and recycling of packaging material). In Germany, observers might believe that almost everything is "dual."
3. Directive 2000/43/EG implementing the principle of equal treatment between persons irrespective of racial or ethnic origin, Directive 2000/78/EG establishing a general framework for equal treatment in employment and occupation, Directive 2002/73/EG clarifying the Equal Treatment Directive, and Directive 2004/113/EG implementing the principle of equal treatment between men and women in the access to and supply of goods and services.
4. Compared to the peak of the crisis (first quarter 2009) GDP decline had been 6.5%.

REFERENCES

Artus, I., Böhm, S., Lücking, S., and Trinczek, R. (eds), 2006. *Betriebe ohne Betriebsrat. Informelle Interessenvertretung in Unternehmen*. Frankfurt/New York: Campus.

Behrens, M. 2007. "Conflict, Arbitration, and Dispute Resolution in the German Workplace." *International Journal of Conflict Management*, 18(2): 175–92.

Behrens, M. 2009. "Still Married after All These Years? Union Organizing and the Role of Works Councils in German Industrial Relations." *Industrial and Labor Relations Review*, 63(3): 275–93.

Berthel. J. and Becker, F. G. 2010. *Personalmanagement. Grundzüge für Konzeptionen betrieblicher Personalarbeit*. 9th edn. Stuttgart: Schäffer-Poeschel.

Bispinck, R. 2006., "Abschied vom Flächentarifvertrag? Der Umbruch in der deutschen Tariflandschaft." In WSI (ed.), *Tarifhandbuch 2006*. Frankfurt. Bund Verlag, 41–66.

Bispinck, R. and Schulten, T. 1999., "Flächentarifvertrag und betriebliche Interessenvertretung." In W. Müller-Jentsch (ed.), *Konfliktpartnerschaft. Akteure und Institutionen der industriellen Beziehungen*. 3rd edn. Munich and Mehring: Rainer Hampp Verlag, 185–212.

Bispinck, R. and Schulten, T. 2011. *Sector-level Bargaining and Possibilities for Deviations at Company Level: Germany*. Dublin: European Foundation for the Improvement of Living and Working Conditions.

Boes, A. and Baukrowitz, A. 2002. *Arbeitsbeziehungen der der IT-Industrie. Erosion oder Innovation der Mitbestimmung?* Berlin: Edition Sigma.

Bogedan, C., Brehmer, W., and Seifert, H. 2011., "Wie krisenfest sind betriebliche Bündnisse zur Beschäftigungssicherung?" *WSI-Mitteilungen*, 64(2): 51–9.

Detje, R., Menz, W., Nies, S., and Sauer, D. 2011. *Krise ohne Konflikt? Interessen- und Handlungsorientierungen im Betrieb—Die Sicht der Betroffenen*. Hamburg: VSA.

Dribbusch, H. 2010. "60 Jahre Arbeitskampf in der Bundesrepublik." In R. Bispinck and T. Schulten (eds), *Zukunft der Tarifautonomie. 60 Jahre Tarifvertragsgesetz: Bilanz und Ausblick*. Hamburg. VSA, 145–68.

Ellguth, P. 2009., "Betriebsspezifische Formen der Mitarbeitervertretung—welche Betriebe, welche personalpolitischen Wirkungen?" *Industrielle Beziehungen*, 16(2): 109–35.

Ellguth, P. 2005., "Betriebe ohne Betriebsräte—welche Rolle spielen betriebsspezifische Formen der Mitarbeitervertretung?" *Industrielle Beziehungen*, 12(2): 149–76.

Ellguth, P. and Kohaut, S. 2012., "Tarifbindung und betriebliche Interessenvertretung: Aktuelle Ergebnisse ais dem IAB-Betriebspanel 2011." *WSI-Mitteilungen*, 65(4): 297–305.

Hassel, A. and Streeck, W. 2003. "The Crumbling Pillars of Social Partnership." In H. Kitschelt and W. Streeck (eds), *Germany: Beyond a Stable State*. London: Frank Cass, 101–24.

Hauser-Ditz, A., Hertwig, M., and Pries, L. 2006., "Betriebsräte und andere Vertretungsorgane im Vergleich–Strukturen, Arbeitsweisen und Beteiligungsmöglichkeiten." *WSI-Mitteilungen*, 59(9): 500–6.

Hauser-Ditz, A., Hertwig, M., and Pries, L. 2008. *Betriebliche Interessenregulierung in Deutschland. Arbeitnehmervertretung zwischen demokratischer Teilhabe und ökonomischer Effizienz*. Frankfurt/New York: Campus.

Hauser-Ditz, A., Hertwig, M., and Pries, L. 2009. "Kollektive Interessenregulierung in der 'betriebsratsfreien Zone', Typischer Formen 'Anderer Vertretungsorgane,'" *Industrielle Beziehungen*, 16(2): 136–53.

Heiden, M. 2011. "Der arbeits- und industriesoziologische Konfliktbegriff und die Notwendigkeit seiner Erweiterung." *Arbeits- und Industriesoziologische Studien*, 4(2): 27–44.

Hertwig, M. 2011a. "Patterns, Ideologies and Strategies of Non-statutory Employee Representation in German Private Sector Companies." *Industrial Relations Journal*, 42(6): 530–46.

Hertwig, M. 2011b. *Die Praxis "Anderer Vertretungsorgane". Formen, Funktionen und Wirksamkeit*. Berlin: Edition Sigma.

Herzog-Stein, A., Lindner, F., Sturn, S., and van Treeck, T. 2010. "From a Source of Weakness to a Tower of Strength? The Changing German Labor Market." IMK-Report No. 56, Nov.

Hilbert, J. and Sperling, H.J. 1993. *Die kleine Fabrik. Beschäftigung, Technik und Arbeitsbeziehungen*. Munich and Mehring: Rainer Hampp Verlag.

Hocke, S. 2012. *Konflikte im Betriebsrat als Lernanlass*. Wiesbaden: Springer VS.

Ittermann, P. 2009. *Betriebliche Partizipation in den Unternehmen der neuen Medien. Innovative Formen der Beteiligung auf dem Prüfstand*. Frankfurt/New York: Campus.

Katz, H. C., Kochan, T. A., and Colvin, A. J. S. 2008. *An Introduction to Collective Bargaining & Industrial Relations*. 4th edn. Boston: McGraw-Hill.

Keller, B. K. 2008. *Einführung in die Arbeitspolitik. Arbeitsbeziehungen und Arbeitsmarkt in sozialwissenschaftlicher Perspektive*. 7th edn. Munich: Oldenbourg.

Knuth, M., Büttner, R., and Schank, G. 1984. *Zustandekommen und Analyse von Betriebsvereinbarungen und praktische Erfahrungen mit Einigungsstellen*. Bonn: Institut für Sozialforschung und Sozialwirtschaft e.V., Forschungsbericht im Auftrag des Bundesministers für Arbeit und Sozialordnung, 1(107).

Kotthoff, H. and Reindl, J. 1990. *Die soziale Welt kleiner Betriebe. Wirtschaften, Arbeiten und Leben im mittelständischen Industriebetrieb*. Göttingen: Otto Schwartz & Co.

Krüger, W. 1972. *Grundlagen, Probleme und Instrumente der Konflikthandhabung in der Unternehmung*. Berlin: Duncker & Humblot.

Leisten, C. 2007. *Das Allgemeine Gliechbehandlungsgesetz—Leitfaden für Betriebsräte*. Düsseldorf: Edition der Hans-Böckler-Stiftung.

Müller-Jentsch, W. 1982. "Gewerkschaften als intermediäre Organisation." *Kölner Zeitschrift für Soziologie und Sozialpsychologie*. Special Issue 24: 408–32.

Müller-Jentsch, W. 1997. *Soziologie der industriellen Beziehungen. Eine Einführung.* 2nd edn. Frankfurt/New York: Campus.

Müller-Jentsch, W. 1999. "Vorwort des Herausgebers." in W. Müller-Jentsch (ed), *Konfliktpartnerschaft. Akteure und Institutionen der industriellen Beziehungen.* 3rd edn. Munich and Mehring: Rainer Hampp, 7–11.

Nell-Breuning, O. von, 1964. "Partnerschaft." In E. Beckerath et al. (eds), *Handwörterbuch der Sozialwissenschaften.* Stuttgart: Fischen, Tübingen: J.C.B. Mohr, and Göttingen: Vandehoeck & Ruprecht, vol. 8.

Oechsler, W. and Kerzel, M. 1984. *Die Bedeutung von Einigungsstellen im Rahmen der Betriebsverfassung—Empirische Analysen der Wirkungsweise und Funktionsfähigkeit von Einigungsstellenverfahren—Teil I. Theoretische Grundlagen.* Stuttgart: Poeschel Verlag.

Offe, C. 2010. "Keine Aussicht auf eine Repolitisierung in Zeiten der Krise." Interview, in W. Heitmeyer (ed.), *Deutsche Zustände, Folge 8.* Berlin: Edition Suhrkamp, 283–95.

Pfarr, H. 2005. "Sorgen vor der Klageflut unbegründet." In *Böckler-Impuls,* 02/2005, 3.

Prott, J. 2006. *Vertrauensleute. Ehrenamtliche Gewerkschaftsfunktionäre zwischen Beruf und sozialer Rolle.* Münster: Westfälisches Dampfboot.

Rehder, B. 2006. "Legitimitätsdefizite des Co-Managements. Betriebliche Bündnisse für Arbeit als Konfliktfeld zwischen Arbeitnehmern und betrieblicher Interessenvertretung." *Zeitschrift für Soziologie,* 35(3): 227–42.

Rehder, B. 2011. *Rechtsprechung als Politik. Der Beitrag des Bundesarbeitsgerichts zur Entwicklung der Arbeitsbeziehungen in Deutschland.* Frankfurt/New York. Campus.

Ridder, H.-G. 2009. *Personalwirtschaftslehre.* 3rd edn. Stuttgart. Kohlhammer.

Rogers, J. and Streeck, W. 1995. "The Study of Works Councils: Concepts and Problems." In J. Rogers and W. Streeck (eds), *Works Councils. Consultation, Representation, and Cooperation in Industrial Relations.* Chicago: University of Chicago Press, 3–26.

Schlömmer, N., Kay, R., Backes-Gellner, U., Rudolph, W., and Wassermann, W. 2007. *Mittelstand und Mitbestimmung. Unternehmensführung, Mitbestimmung und Beteiligung in mittelständischen Unternehmen.* Münster: Westfälisches Dampfboot.

Schmidt, R. and Trinczek, R. 1986. "Erfahrungen und Perspektiven gewerkschaftlicher Arbeitszeitpolitik." *Prokla,* 64: 85–108.

Scholz, C. 2011. *Grundzüge des Personalmanagements.* Munich: Vahlen.

Stock-Homburg, R. 2010. *Personalmanagement. Theorien—Konzepte—Instrumente.* 2nd edn. Wiesbaden: Gabler.

Seifert, H. and Massa-Wirth, H. 2005. "Pacts for Employment and Competitiveness in Germany." *Industrial Relations Journal,* 36(3): 217–40.

Stiel, C. and Stoppkotte, E.-M. 2012. "Kooperation statt Konfrontation. Mediationsgesetz in Kraft." *Arbeitsrecht im Betrieb,* 11/2012: 631–5.

Thelen, K. 1991. *Union of Parts. Labor Politics in Postwar Germany.* Ithaca/London: Cornell University Press.

Traxler, F. 1995. "Farewell to Labor Market Associations? Organized versus Disorganized Decentralization as a Map for Industrial Relations." In C. Crouch and F. Traxler (eds), *Organized Industrial Relations in Europe: What Future?* Avebury: Ashgate Publishing, 3–19.

Turner, L. 1998. *Fighting for Partnership: Labor and Politics in Unified Germany.* Ithaca/London: Cornell University Press.

Turner, L. 2009. "Institutions and Activism: Crisis and Opportunity for a German Labor Movement in Decline." *Industrial and Labor Relations Review,* 62(3): 294–312.

Walton, R. and McKersie, R. 1965. *A Behavioural Theory of Labor Negotiations: An Analysis of a Social Interaction System*. New York: McGraw-Hill.

Wassermann, W. 2003. "Gewerkschaftliche Betriebspolitik." In W. Schroeder and W. Weßels (eds), *Die Gewerkschaften in Politik und Gesellschaft der Bundesrepublik Deutschland. Ein Handbuch*. Wiesbaden: Westdeutscher Verlag, 405–28.

Weltz, F. 1977. "Kooperative Konfliktverarbeitung. Ein Stil industrieller Beziehungen in deutschen Unternehmen." *Gewerkschaftliche Monatshefte*, 28(5): 291–301.

WSI 2009. *WSI-Tarifhandbuch 2009*. Frankfurt: Bund Verlag.

Zapf, I. and Herzog-Stein, A. 2011. "Betriebliche Einsatzmuster von Arbeitszeitkonten während der Großen Rezession." *WSI-Mitteilungen*, 64(2): 60–8.

CHAPTER 18

CONFLICT RESOLUTION IN JAPAN

JOHN BENSON

INTRODUCTION

THE success of the post-war Japanese economy and the growing dominance of its manufacturing companies on global markets led many to attribute this success, at least in part, to the Japanese form of industrial relations and dispute resolution practices (Christopher, 1987; Dore, 1990). This view, however, came under increased scrutiny with the collapse of the so-called "bubble" economy in the late 1980s and the commencement of a sustained period of low economic growth in the early 1990s. These events, coupled with the increasing global competition from Korea and China, gave rise to important sectoral shifts in the Japanese economy and changes in the forms of employment. Union membership declined (JILPT, 2011: 70), which in turn led to a decline in collective industrial disputes. Nevertheless, workplace conflict can, however, manifest itself in various ways (Roche and Teague, 2011) and in Japan the fragmentation of collective industrial relations allowed for experimentation with, and the development of, a range of alternative dispute resolution (ADR) practices (Nakakubo, 2006: 2).

This chapter will examine the shift to a variety of ADR practices used to resolve workplace conflict, why such changes are occurring, and whether this is part of a longer term trend in Japanese industrial relations. The chapter commences with an outline of the development and operation of the "traditional" Japanese system of industrial relations and dispute resolution. This is followed by a commentary and analysis of the economic and industrial relations developments since 1990 that have impacted on the nature of industrial disputes in Japan. The next section then explores the recent fragmentation of dispute resolution, noting the significant shift to external, individually-focused, statutory mechanisms. This is then followed by an analysis of these changes and why such changes have occurred. The penultimate section discusses some recent experimentation in dispute resolution that is emerging in Japan and which I have labelled "collective individualism." The chapter concludes by suggesting that the growth in ADRs represents management abandonment of the "social contract" and a critique of enterprise unionism.

The "Traditional" System of Industrial Relations and Dispute Resolution

From the mid-1950s Japanese companies advocated and supported the formation and development of enterprise unions and generally sought to resolve industrial disputes internally through a combination of collective bargaining with these unions and a range of management-sponsored, consultative practices (Benson, 2012). Where these practices failed to resolve a dispute then companies and/or unions could utilize an external, statutory system. This section provides a brief outline and assessment of this "traditional" system of dispute resolution in Japan and starts with a discussion of enterprise unionism.

Enterprise Unions

By the early 1930s Japanese unionism had developed significantly, with unions generally organized along industrial or craft lines, although about one-third of unions were enterprise based (Benson, 2008). By the mid-1930s and with the onset of war, this fledgling union movement suffered a severe setback as the government sought to dismantle unionism to gain control over industrial production. With the end of World War Two, and under US occupation and a new constitution, unionism grew rapidly. As the economy began to prosper, workers sought to gain some of the economic benefits through strikes and other industrial action. These activities were led by industrial unions, and employers responded by dismissing militant industrial union activists and supporting the more cooperative, enterprise-based union structure. Workers generally accepted this form of unionism as they were excluded from the emerging social partnership arrangements and so had few alternative avenues available to improve wages and working conditions (Benson, 2008).

Enterprise unions generally recruited only full-time, regular employees (Benson, 2008). This strategy was underpinned by the development of an internal labor market, where recruitment to the company was usually into entry-level jobs, and where there existed de facto, if not de jure, lifetime employment. As a consequence, promotion was based on seniority and skill acquisition, continuous on-the-job training took place, and employees were incorporated into decision-making processes. In this environment, union membership grew steadily, with membership reaching a peak of 12.7 million in 1994, although by this time union density had fallen to 24.1%; well below the 55.8% density figure of 1949 (Fujimura, 1997: 299). The overwhelming majority of unionists were to be found in large companies where a critical mass of potential members existed and working relationships formalised. As such workers in small and medium-sized companies were often denied union representation. For example, in 1990 the unionization rate for large companies (1,000 or more employees) was 61.0% while for small companies (fewer than one hundred employees) the rate was 2.0%. Similarly, in 2010 the respective figures were 46.6% and 1.1% (JILPT, 2011: 71).

The events of the 1930s and the 1940s, coupled with a strong focus on economic goals and exclusive representation, meant that enterprise unions were prepared, as will be discussed later, to engage in cooperative arrangements with employers in exchange for guarantees of employment security. This led to the terms and conditions of employment being almost entirely determined by enterprise-based activities such as workplace bargaining between management and unions, albeit with some degree of coordination at the industry and national levels (Benson, 2008). As a consequence, industrial action was rare and typically designed as a protest or an attempt to embarrass the company rather than to inflict significant economic pain. This led to industrial action being low by international standards (see Bamber and Lansbury, 1987: 261; Keizai Koho, 1990: 71, 1997: 91; Bamber, Lansbury, and Wailes, 2004: 387).

Wage Bargaining and Dispute Settling Procedures

The development and consolidation of enterprise unionism meant that in Japan enterprise-level collective bargaining became from the mid-1950s the mainstay of the wage determination process. At this time there emerged a united campaign led by the peak union bodies and industrial unions that became known as the Spring Wage Offensive or *shunto*. Under this arrangement claims would be formulated by peak and industry unions and openly debated at the national or industry level with employers. This process served to narrow the gap between enterprise unions and companies, who then continued the negotiations within these parameters. Industrial action, if undertaken, was short and often symbolic in nature. This process led to a system of coordinated enterprise wages settlements at the industry and national levels (Sako, 1997; Suzuki, 1997: 78); an approach which employers considered important in preventing the loss of market share to competitors when industrial action took place (Nimura, 1994: 81). While it was generally the large companies that participated in this process, *shunto* also served as a pattern-setting mechanism for unions in small companies and in the public sector (Sano, 1980; Hart and Kawasaki, 1999: 44–5).

Paralleling the development of *shunto* was a system of joint consultation between enterprise management and workers (Morishima, 1992) which gained impetus with the increased competitive pressures of the "oil shock" of 1973 (Shimada, 1982). This system was promoted among unionized companies and by 1974 over 60% of unionized companies had established a joint consultation committee (JCC) (Hart and Kawasaki, 1999: 50). Non-unionized companies also adopted joint consultation mechanisms, although the percentage of companies doing so was lower (Hart and Kawasaki, 1999: 50). The JCCs served a variety of purposes ranging from providing information to acting as a pre-*shunto* wage discussion exercise (Morishima, 1992) and operated independently of, or were integrated into, collective bargaining (Inagami, 1988). When used as a pre-*shunto* mechanism JCCs generally reduced the probability of "prolonged and difficult negotiations" and led to "smaller differences between the union's initial demand and final settlement" (Morishima, 1991: 481). Employers were generally supportive of using JCCs in this way as while matters were being discussed unions could not "exercise their right to strike" (Shirai, 1983: 120). The JCCs also provided increased flexibility to union leaders as they were not subjected to the same level of member scrutiny that formal bargaining placed on them (Nitta, 1984).

Some workers also had the opportunity to process issues through a formal grievance procedure. The National Enterprise Labour Relations Law requires companies to establish mechanisms to handle individual grievances (Koshiro, 2000). These procedures were first introduced into Japan in 1946 (Labour Adjustment Law) by the occupying American forces as a way to democratize the workplace (Kagawa, 1993). A survey conducted by the Ministry of Labour in 1999 found, however, only 25.2% of enterprises had a functioning grievance procedure (MOL, 2000). Part of the reason for this low establishment rate is that small companies tended to focus on informal mechanisms such as "employees' consultations with managerial officers," and only large enterprises developed more formal mechanisms, such as grievance committees (JILPT, 2008: 4). The same survey found only 37.4% of employees had presented grievances or complaints to their supervisors (MOL, 2000). While this finding may demonstrate the success of other mechanisms it may also be the case, as research by Elbo (2004: 8) found, that only a small percentage of those seeking assistance (20.3%) "had been helped by the system."

Japanese companies also have a variety of management-sponsored, consultative practices that, to some extent, contribute to the resolution of industrial disputes. While these practices are aimed at improving productivity and enterprise performance they also serve as voice mechanisms for workers and so may have prevented disputes by resolving work-related problems early. Suggestions schemes, team meetings, and quality circles are examples of these practices. Suggestions schemes have been popular in Japanese manufacturing companies, with around four-fifths of enterprises having such a scheme in 1991 (Benson, 1996: 48). Workers are generally not restricted as to the issues they can raise, although most suggestions relate to work matters. According to Ballon (1992: 131), about two-thirds of workers participate in these schemes and about four-fifths of the suggestions are ultimately adopted. By accepting worker's suggestions, discontent with work processes and other matters can be addressed quickly. As a result, workers gain a degree of ownership of the production process.

Team meetings in Japanese companies generally focus on work operations, health and safety, welfare matters, management plans, and education and training (Inagami,

1988: 26) and, as with suggestion schemes, provide workers the opportunity to raise their concerns directly with their supervisors and management. Such practices are quite widespread, with team meetings occurring regularly in about three out of every five manufacturing workplaces (Benson, 1996: 48) and allow a collective view to be presented in a collaborative manner. This approach is preferred by Japanese workers as they generally do not like direct confrontation (Christopher, 1987: 172) and feel uncomfortable raising issues that could cause themselves or others to lose face (Maeda, 1999: 1). Importantly, employment options for disgruntled workers within an internal labor market are limited and if such meetings are not held then workers may prefer to remain silent or to air their grievances in informal ways, such as when socializing with their supervisor and colleagues after work (Clark, 1987: 200; Tada, 2012: 24–25).

Quality circles, although a less direct mechanism than team meetings, normally involve workers meeting in their own time to discuss ways to improve productivity and quality. As with suggestion schemes and team meetings, quality circles are quite widespread, with Benson (1996: 48) finding 65.5% of manufacturing companies had such a system in place. While quality circles have the potential to "foster consensus building and company orientation" (Porter, Takeuchi, and Sakakibara, 2000: 73) there has been considerable debate as to what participation in quality circles really means (Abegglen and Stalk, 1987; Briggs, 1988). Nevertheless, quality circles do require "management to provide information on business operations" and share "some decision-making with workers" (Hart and Kawasaki, 1999: 54) and so, notwithstanding their strong underpinning managerial prerogative, quality circles have provided workers with an additional channel of communication within the workplace and an opportunity to participate in decision-making (Tachibanaki and Noda, 1996: 477, 2000: 140).

External Dispute Resolution Mechanisms

If disputes cannot be resolved through the internal, enterprise-level dispute mechanisms then the company and/or its union can seek resolution through statutory provisions and, in limited circumstances, the civil courts. These statutory provisions aim to ensure a fair internal system as well as a final court of appeal. A key external provision is the Trade Union Law which protects the right of employees to organize, makes it illegal for employers to engage in unfair labor practices, and provides a tribunal system to resolve disputes (Doko, 2006: 32–44; JILPT, 2009b: 99). These tribunals, known as labor relations commissions, function at the prefectural and central levels and have the power to investigate and settle cases involving unfair labor practices (refusal to engage in collective bargaining, interference in the affairs of trade unions, and prejudicial treatment of union members) and to coordinate the processes of industrial dispute settlement arising from collective bargaining (Maeda, 1999: 3; JITPT, 2009c: 222). The various commissions are tripartite bodies made up of representatives of the government, employees, and employers.

In instances of suspected unfair labor practices a union can file a complaint which will lead to an investigation being carried out, meetings of the tribunal, and the issuance of an order (JILPT, 2009b: 99). The decision of a prefectural labor relations commission can be appealed to the Central Labour Relations Commission, the national overseer of the prefectural commissions. In the case of collective bargaining, failing to resolve a union demand, and where there is a risk that industrial action may occur, a labor relations commission, under what is known as the "Dispute Adjustment System," can undertake conciliation, mediation, and arbitration. In these cases, conciliators are appointed from a register and, following meetings to determine the issues, a conciliation proposal is produced. The parties are free to accept or reject this proposal. If conciliation is unsuccessful, and following an application from both parties, a tripartite mediation committee will be formed and a mediation proposal developed. Again, the parties are free to accept or reject this proposal. If the proposal is again rejected arbitration may be undertaken should an application be received from one or both parties and will be conducted by a three-member committee drawn from the government representatives of the commission and approved by the parties. A final arbitrated decision will then be handed down which will have equal force to that of a collective agreement (JILPT, 2009a: 100).

Performance of the "Traditional" System

The reliance on internal labor markets, and the development of enterprise unionism with a strong economic focus, meant that enterprise-level activities were considered the appropriate mechanisms for resolving industrial disputes. While collective bargaining and joint consultation were the most publicized dispute settling mechanisms, other less direct mechanisms such as suggestion schemes, team meetings, and quality circles were also important. This proved to be an effective approach and was underpinned by a wider, unwritten "social contract" where the unions' challenge to managerial prerogative over control of work and production practices was traded off for employment security (Benson and Debroux, 2004: 45). In those cases where unfair labor practices existed or disputes remained unresolved, statutory tribunals and civil courts could become involved, although such mechanisms were not widely used.

The nature and structure of enterprise unions meant, however, that this system was generally limited to large enterprises. This meant that as large Japanese companies became global brands many of the workers in the myriad of subcontracting and supplier companies that supported this success, as well as workers in sectors outside of manufacturing, were denied the benefits that accrued to Japan in these growth decades. Similarly, many of the collaborative management and industrial relations practices attributed to Japanese companies were more common in large enterprises. Nevertheless, while workers in small companies had little direct union representation, the high economic growth up to the early 1990s created labor shortages which led to many of these small companies following, at least in part, the practices of large companies (Morishima, 1995: 122).

ECONOMIC AND INDUSTRIAL RELATIONS DEVELOPMENTS SINCE 1990

From the early 1990s the traditional industrial relations system came under increasing pressure due to the decline in the Japanese economy and increased global competition. Real GDP growth has averaged less than 1% per year since 1991 (IMF, 2011) which is in sharp contrast to the 10% average growth rates of the 1950s and 1960s and the 5% average growth rates of the 1970s and 1980s (Benson, 2011). Much of this decline in economic activity has resulted from poor domestic consumer demand and improved competitiveness of other countries, which led many Japanese manufacturers to relocate parts of their operations overseas, particularly to low wage Asian countries. This "hollowing out" of manufacturing saw employment in this sector fall from 13.1 million in 1990 to 10.5 million in 2010, a reduction of 2.6 million employees, or 19.8% of the manufacturing workforce (JILPT, 2004: 24, 2011: 23).

While the loss of jobs during this period was more than compensated for by an increase in employment in the services sector, many of the new jobs were temporary or part time. This shift away from full-time work partly accounts for the rapid increase in non-regular employment in Japan; from 24.5% of the workforce in 1990 to 34.3% in 2010 (JIL, 1990: 25; JILPT, 2011: 33). The uncertain nature of this form of employment and the lower wages paid to these workers have raised concerns as to "whether such employment can support career development and family aspirations" (Whittaker, 2004: 30). These events have led to a more than doubling of the unemployment rate since 1990, which in 2010 stood at 5.1% of the labor force (JILPT, 2011: 42). In addition, the national savings rate has fallen substantially since 1995 (JILPT, 2011: 77) and cuts in company pensions has made it necessary for many workers to continue working beyond their "planned" retirement age. Income distribution, which had been quite even in Japan when compared with most industrialized nations, has now become more concentrated, with 25% of households earning 75% of total income (Benson, 2011).

This sustained period of economic decline has significantly impacted on industrial relations. The number of unions declined by 22.6% in the period 1990–2010 as did the number of union members and union density (18.0% and 26.8%, respectively). The reduced consumer demand placed pressure on Japanese companies whose structure was based on product market growth. This was especially the case for small companies who were increasingly struggling to meet the wage flow-on demands arising from the annual wage bargaining exercise between the large companies and their unions. After a number of years of little or no wage increases, *shunto* was discontinued in 2002. By this time JCCs had, with the exception of wages, become the main mechanism for determining working conditions (JILPT, 2006: 75). Any possibility of improvement in wages and working conditions would now depend solely on enterprise negotiations and discussions (Weathers, 2003; Benson and Gospel, 2008) while the notion of a socially accepted wage had essentially disappeared from the Japanese system of wage determination (Nakamura, 2007).

These factors impacted significantly on the level of collective labor disputes. Notified disputes fell from 2071 in 1990 to 780 in 2009; down from an average yearly rate of 4500 in the period 1970–90 (JILPT, 2011: 75). Similarly, the average working days lost per worker halved from around two working days per 1,000 workers in the period 1993–7 to one working day per 1000 workers in the period 1998–2002 (EuroFound, 2005: 22). The reasons for disputes also changed and reflected the increasing abandonment of "lifetime" employment by management. For example, in 1990, 46.1% of all disputes involved wage increases; by 2009 this figure had fallen to 14.0%. In contrast, in the same period disputes involving discharge and reinstatement issues rose from 1.9% to 27.3% of all disputes (JILPT, 2011: 75). In short, by 2009 the traditional issues underpinning labor disputes such as wages and working conditions had been displaced by concerns over job security.

Companies also appeared to reduce their support for joint consultative arrangements. A Ministry of Labour survey conducted in 1994 found joint consultation existed in 55.7% of companies, down from 62.8% of companies in 1974 (Hart and Kawasaki, 1999: 50). There was also a decline in consultative management practices that may have prevented at least some disputes arising. A study by Benson, (2005: 67) found the percentage of manufacturing companies using suggestions schemes, team meetings, and quality circles fell by 6.7%, 19.2%, and 24.6% respectively in the period 1991–2001. Thus, with the exception of suggestion schemes, fewer than half of the companies surveyed had these potential voice mechanisms in place in 2001 (Benson, 2005: 67).

These changes to industrial relations and management practices have led to a partial breakdown of the traditional system of resolving disputes through enterprise bargaining and consultative management practices. This system worked well during periods of high economic growth when Japanese companies were focused on increasing their global market share which resulted in significant wage increases, "guaranteed" employment and union growth. With the economic downturn of the early 1990s, this system was increasingly unable to cope with worker concerns over job security, the accompanying increase in unemployment, and the shift to peripheral forms of employment. Workers were left with fewer enterprise-based opportunities to resolve disputes and so placed pressure on the state to expand existing statutory provisions and to also introduce new alternative, societal-based approaches to dispute resolution. The decline and structural deficiencies of enterprise unionism meant that any extended statutory system would need to allow access to individual workers.

FRAGMENTATION OF DISPUTE RESOLUTION MECHANISMS

Unfair Labor Practices

As union influence declined employers became more willing to challenge union agreements and bargaining rights. This can be seen in an increase of 8.8% in the number of unfair labor practices cases lodged with prefectural labor relations commissions in the period 2003–9. Although claims relating to unfair labor practices fluctuate from year to year the 2009 figure of 395 new cases represents an increase of 34.4% on the 2005 figure of 294 new cases. Moreover, changes have occurred as to how these types of disputes are settled. In particular, in the period 2003–9 there has been a 2.5% decline in the number of cases settled by withdrawal or agreement and an 11.2% decline in the number of cases settled by an order or decision. This has led to fewer cases being concluded, which sug- gests a more intransigent stance by management to such claims and a further weakening of union rights.

Terms and Conditions of Employment

If enterprise bargaining over the terms and conditions of employment break down, a prefectural labor relations commission or the Central Labour Relations Commission can take charge of the matter, particularly if industrial action is threatened. Generally, the number of these "dispute adjustment" cases fell in the period 2004–8, with con- ciliation being the overwhelming method used to resolve such cases. The number of cases being withdrawn has also significantly declined and this, coupled with a slight decline in the number of cases settled, has led to a fall in the resolution rate. In contrast, the number of cases being abandoned increased in 2008 by 36.1% on the 2004 figure (JILPT, 2009b: 105–7). The causes of these disputes have remained reasonably stable over the period 2003–7: financial reasons—wages, lump sum payments, working hours, and holiday leave—accounted for nearly 40% of cases, while non-financial reasons— management, pursuit of collective bargaining, and union approval or activities—were responsible for slightly over 60%. Over 90% of unions surveyed in 2007 by the Ministry of Health, Labour and Welfare reported, however, they had not been involved in a labor dispute, and where they had nearly half (49.7%) were able to resolve it through discus- sion (MHLW, 2008). The decline in the number of cases, the fall in the resolution rate, and the resolution of matters through discussion, demonstrate that unions were finding it increasingly difficult to achieve positive outcomes for their members.

Individual Labor Disputes

With the declining influence of trade unions and collective dispute resolution Japanese workers increasingly looked for other ways to resolve their disputes with manage- ment. This proved difficult, as in Japan there is no specialized court that hears indi- vidual labor disputes (JILPT, 2009c: 222), although there are now administrative and judicial mechanisms that handle such cases. The administrative system is based on the Law for Promoting the Resolution of Individual Labor Disputes, enacted in 2001 in response to the increasing trend towards individual workers' grievances (Sugeno, 2006: 8). The law sets out three steps for those disputes that cannot be resolved within the enterprise: information provision and consultation; advice and guidance; and conciliation (JILPT, 2008: 3, 2009b: 104). The first step provides workers with an opportunity to receive current information on their rights and the chance to talk to someone about their particular issue. In 2010 there were 246,907 individual civil labor dispute consultations which represents a 139.3% increase on its first full year of operations in 2002 (103,194). The major source of grievances considered in these consultations were dismissal (37.5%), bullying and harassment (13.9%), working conditions (17.8%), termination of employment (8.0%), and pressure to retire (7.6%) (JILPT, 2012a: 118). This rise in individual labor disputes clearly reflects the increasing inability of enterprise unions to protect union members and workers more generally.

Little is known about the outcomes of these "consultations." Some workers would take the information back to management, and reach a settlement. Other workers may decide not to take the matter further because the information received provided little support for their claim, or because it suggested the chances of success were remote. Still other workers may wish to take matters further through either seeking advice and guidance or requesting conciliation of their grievance. In 2010 some 7,692 cases proceeded to the advice and guidance stage, an increase of 20.8% over 2005. In this stage workers are provided with detailed advice of the various options open to them. Of the 6,662 cases dealt with in 2007, 48.2% of these workers were employed on a part-time basis, with over half coming from companies with fewer than fifty employees, and 68% coming from non-union enterprises (JILPT, 2009b: 105–7). These findings suggest that this more individual statutory system is providing a mechanism for non-union workers to gain some resolution of their grievances.

After receiving advice, workers can either drop the matter or enter into discussions about the problem with their employer, or proceed to conciliation. At the conciliation stage an attempt is made to resolve the issue using the services of tribunal appointed conciliators. The number of cases proceeding to conciliation directly, or following the advice and guidance stage, in 2010 was 6,390, a fall of 7.2% on the 2005 figure. While this figure suggests a slightly diminished use of conciliation it may reflect the lessening chances of success. For example in 2007, of the 7,844 conciliation cases only 38.4% or 2,976 resulted in an agreement between the parties. The most likely outcome was that discussions were broken off, as occurred in 4,166 cases, or 53.8% of the total. The remaining cases were withdrawn (JILPT, 2009b: 105–7). Like consultation cases, workers who have elected to use conciliation tended to come from small, non-unionized companies. These figures suggest that in the vast majority of more difficult cases little redress is being offered to workers via such avenues.

Individual disputes can, however, also be processed through the judicial system. Two avenues are open to workers: civil litigation and the labor tribunal system. Civil litigation over labor matters proceeds in much the same way as other matters taken through the civil litigation process. Claims are lodged and after hearing evidence the court hands down a decision. In 2009, 3,218 cases of civil litigation came before the various district courts, an increase of 32.3% on the number of cases in 2003. Of the cases heard 95.7% (3,080 cases) involved the employer as the defendant (JILPT, 2012a: 123). While a variety of issues underpinned these claims, the most common matters in 2007 were wages (59.2%) and employment contracts (25.5%). A particular problem with this approach has been that the process is cumbersome, with disputes taking an average of 11.7 months to resolve (JILPT, 2009b: 109).

To streamline and speed up the approach to dispute resolution the labor tribunal system was introduced in April 2006 (Sugeno, 2006: 10). This system focuses on the rights and obligations of individuals; the overall aim being to resolve issues quickly by utilizing experts in the field (Kezuka, 2006: 13–15). Matters are heard by a tribunal made up of a judge and two lay members, who are labor relations specialists (JILPT, 2009c: 226). Once a claim has been lodged, the tribunal will seek a response from the employer before attempting to mediate the dispute. If mediation fails to resolve the dispute, the tribunal will deliberate on the matter, and then hand down a decision. This decision is not, however, legally binding and if either party objects within two weeks to the ruling, the matter becomes a civil litigation issue and is transferred to a civil proceeding (Sugeno, 2006: 11). In 2009, 3,468 new cases came before labor tribunals, an increase of 295.4% on the number of cases in 2006. Disputes were roughly split between pecuniary issues, such as wages and retirement allowances, and non-pecuniary issues, such as declarations of employment status (1,793 cases and 1,675 cases, respectively). Over two-thirds (68.2%) of these disputes were settled by mediation, while about a fifth (18.6%) involved a decision by the tribunal—although in nearly two-thirds of these cases (64.7%) an objection was filed. The remaining disputes were withdrawn, rejected, or transferred to another body (JILPT, 2009b: 111).

The introduction of this "fast track" system was expected to reduce the number of civil litigation cases; this does not appear to have been the case. Both dispute resolution avenues have seen a substantial increase in the number of cases since 2006 (JILPT, 2012a: 123). The figures do suggest, however, that some workers now choose to process their dispute through the new system rather than go through the slow and cumbersome civil litigation process. Moreover, by doing so, workers are not precluded from taking subsequent action in the civil courts. In the course of hearing a dispute a labor tribunal can refer the matter to other jurisdictions, including civil courts, although this does not often occur (JILPT, 2012a: 125–6). Overall, the increase in both civil and labor tribunal cases illustrates the ongoing fragmentation of the traditional system of dispute resolution and the rise of a new legal mentality among workers as they seek to resolve their grievances.

THE CHANGING NATURE OF DISPUTE RESOLUTION IN JAPAN

The adoption of an internal labor market model by Japanese companies, coupled with enterprise unionism, meant that internal mechanisms such as collective bargaining and joint consultation, coupled with a variety of management practices that incorporated workers into the decision-making mechanisms of the enterprise, were the major ways in which employment disputes were resolved during much of the last half of the twentieth century. Strong economic conditions in Japan over this period also meant that outcomes negotiated by unions tended to spill over, at least in part, to non-union enterprises. Underpinning this system was a strong informal "social contract" that placed considerable pressure on companies to resolve disputes internally. This social contract was promoted by groups such as the Japan Productivity Centre, who argued that the "fruits of productivity should be distributed fairly among labor, management, and consumers" (JPC, 2010). This led to shared expectations on the part of employers and workers and meant that workers would share in the benefits of economic success (Debroux, 2003). While a legal framework underpinned Japanese industrial relations, there was minimal use of the law during this period to resolve employment disputes, including those of an individual nature. This model worked particularly well, but not exclusively, for large companies, and resulted in productivity improvements for Japanese companies and high levels of economic growth for Japan.

With the collapse of the bubble economy in the late 1980s and early 1990s Japan entered a period of low economic growth. This period saw the rise of globalization, particularly the growth of China as a manufacturing centre, and was accompanied by higher levels of unemployment, a decline in trade union density and coverage, a fall in real wages, and substantial reductions to pension schemes. Japanese companies found it more difficult to compete with their global competitors, especially the fast growing Asian economies, and so experienced a significant loss of their global market share. This is well illustrated by the dramatic decline in employment in the manufacturing sector (see Economics and Industrial Relations Developments since 1990), a sector where union coverage was high and collective bargaining the preferred method to resolve disputes. Japanese companies responded by introducing their own reforms which enterprise unions, given their declining influence and the state of the economy, had little power to resist. Indeed, by this time enterprise unions had less than a "fifty-fifty" chance of resolving workers' grievances (Hisamoto, 2012: 54). These reforms resulted in a harder and more management-dominated approach and a decline in the internal mechanisms for workers to participate in company decision-making. As a result workers, in the face of management intransigence, increasingly resorted to the legislative provisions to resolve grievances and local disputes.

The inadequacy of the legal provisions and processes led to legislative amendments that aimed to simplify and shorten legal proceedings and this, coupled with a growing realization among the Japanese that the previous social and psychological contracts with employers had weakened considerably, resulted in further increases in the use of legislative provisions by unions and individual employees. As a result, collective bargaining further declined in importance and only wage disputes in large companies are likely to be settled by this process; typically, all other matters are settled by joint consultation mechanisms or, in small companies, by management decree. As the traditional collaborative managerial approach gave way to a more "hard-edged" approach that included

redundancies, forced retirements, and unilateral action by management on such matters as wages and pensions, individualism through legislative provisions began to con-
solidate itself as a legitimate means to resolve disputes with employers.

EXPERIMENTATION IN DISPUTE RESOLUTION

The decline in the strength and influence of enterprise unionism and the shift toward a
more legalistic and individualistic dispute resolution process has prompted the emergence of a "nationwide network of ADRs for individual labor disputes" (Sugino and
Murayama, 2006: 53). These ADRs have provided all employees, irrespective of whether
they belong to an enterprise union or are in regular, full-time employment, with possible redress and compensation in the event of a grievance with management. This move
towards a more individualistic system of dispute resolution demonstrates a breakdown
and fragmentation of the traditional methods of collective dispute resolution based on
enterprise unions. At the same time, some workers have responded to these changes by
utilizing some form of statutory individual ADR in a collective way to improve their
chances of success. In this section two emerging, experimental approaches, where
workers collectively seek to use individual mechanisms, will be discussed. Both these
practices are examples of collective individualism.

Community Unionism

A number of alternative forms of unionism have developed in recent times in Japan,
including general (nationwide or local) unions, community unions, local unions of
regional federations, and local unions established by peak union bodies (JILPT, 2005: 21).
The one common feature of these unions is that they are not enterprise based and their
membership includes part-time, temporary agency, and foreign workers who have traditionally been excluded from enterprise unions. The formation of such unions has been
significant in raising the proportion of non-regular workers in total union membership
from 3.6% in 2004 to 7.3% in 2010 (JILPT, 2011: 73). These workers have long been mar-
ginalised in the Japanese workplace and only now have the opportunity to join a union
when faced with a work-related problem and when they need some assistance to process
their claim. This instrumental approach to unionism can be seen by the high number of
cases general unions handle each year given their overall size (Oh, 2012: 81) This recon-
figuration of interest representation to the wider labor market and away from enterprise
unions where some common bond between members existed runs contrary to strategies
adopted by unions in many other industrialized countries which have sought in one way
or another to adapt to greater individualism in dispute settlement.

   One example of these "new" Japanese unions is community unions, which are open
to all workers irrespective of their employment status. By 2008 community unions had

developed into a network of seventy-four unions with 15,000 members and had achieved a high rate of dispute settlement, provided some dignity to the workers affected, and highlighted problems with enterprise management practices (Oh, 2010: 84). This was illustrated by Oh (2010) in his study of the *Rengo* Fukuoka Union. This union was established in 1996 and by mid-2007 had 411 members. The union has averaged about two labor consultations a day, with about half of these consultations (53.7%) involving regular employees. Since its establishment, the union has handled 693 individual labor dispute cases involving 1374 different workers. The key issues involved in these disputes were employment (70.0%), wages (16.7%), and labor contracts (6.1%). The majority of cases were settled by voluntary dispute resolution procedures (79.9%), although 11.6% of cases were referred to a labour relations commission, and 8.5% of cases resulted in a court hearing.

The low number of members and high number of cases handled by these unions suggest that workers join a community union when a problem arises and once resolved move onto other jobs or regions and cease to be a member of that union. This fee-for-service or union-on-demand approach can be criticized for promoting short-term unionism which, in turn, does little to engender a degree of solidarity among the membership. On the other hand, these unions do provide a collective response to managerial prerogative and a level of protection that has been long denied to workers employed under peripheral work arrangements. While community unions are not typical of the majority of unions in Japan they appear to be at the forefront of the move towards the adoption of ADR practices and a union-on-demand model.

Joint Action by Individual Workers

Where there is little or no union presence in a company, or where workers are excluded from union membership due to their employment status, then apart from the alternative forms of unionism outlined above the only other recourse available to workers is through the individual statutory mechanisms. In these circumstances, if the matter is to be considered and appropriate compensation awarded, individual workers are required to lodge an application. A recent study on employment termination in Japan (JILPT, 2012b) sheds some light on how these individual processes have attracted collective action. In that study a sample of 1,144 or 13.5% of the 8,457 conciliation cases involving individual labor disputes throughout Japan in 2008 were analyzed. Nearly half the cases involved non-regular workers (49%) and occurred in companies with fewer than one hundred employees (58.2%). Of these cases 756 (66.1%) involved termination of employment (Hamaguchi, 2011: 119; JILPT, 2012b: 26–27).

Surprisingly, cases were found where groups of workers from the same company had banded together and lodged their applications over the same issue and at the same time. While each worker was given a unique case number as administratively required, the information provided by each worker from the company was identical and their case numbers were consecutive. Analysing the detailed data provided in the report, thirty-one such cases were identified, covering 145 workers. This represented 12.7% of all respondents in the sample. The cases included the dismissal of seven childcare workers due to the bankruptcy of the parent company and, in another case, three workers being asked to quit due to the company's poor performance. In both cases the dismissed employees were female and regular workers. The companies were not unionized and while the size of the workforce was not stated in the application the profile would suggest relatively small companies (JILPT, 2012b: 229).

Unionized companies were not excluded from such action. One was a company that employed 400 workers and who dismissed sixteen non-regular workers. All of the dismissed workers had been employed continuously for over 13 years under various forms of employment, including continuing, fixed-term, and casual contracts. At the conciliation stage the mediator suggested that the unfair dismissal law may apply as the company had automatically renewed their contracts in the past. The company was not prepared to negotiate, citing lack of demand and company restructuring. The report pointed out that all workers were foreigners and suggested that requests to join the Japanese social security system may be at the core of the dismissals. Irrespective of this speculation the report concluded this was a case of collective action, but as the workers were foreigners and not union members they had no other option but to seek individual redress (JILPT, 2012b: 223–4).

The second unionized company case involved thirty-nine male taxi drivers employed as regular workers who were dismissed due to company restructuring. The company was quite small, employing only seventy-three workers and again the dismissed workers had not joined the union. Despite a union "presence" and the fact that the actions of the company involved over half of the workforce, the company was not prepared to resolve this matter through discussion or conciliation. The report concluded this was a case where collective action could have been taken; but as they were not union members they had little alternative but to seek individual recourse to their grievances (JILPT, 2012b: 234). Importantly, the case raises questions concerning how the union was structured and how it operated in this company.

While the cases referred to above represent only a small percentage of the claims for unfair dismissal, they point to the emergence of some form of collectivism, albeit without traditional union support, in the use of mechanisms designed to resolve disputes between an individual worker and their employer. This collective individualism raises important questions in Japan concerning disputes and their resolution. Clearly, the decline in union density in Japan suggests many workers may need to resort to this form of action in the future. These cases also point to the weakness of enterprise unions and the structural deficiencies in this form of unionism, a point made by the author of the report (JILPT, 2012b: 326). The cases also suggest that those often on the periphery of employment in Japan, such as women and foreign workers, may have found a way to express collective voice, albeit through a more legalistic process. Finally, as most of the dismissals were seemingly prompted by economic considerations (poor company performance, company restructuring) another "collective" avenue by which to redress workers' powerlessness in these circumstances has emerged.

CONCLUSION

This chapter has examined the shift to ADR practices in Japan, why this might be so, and whether it forms part of a longer term trend in dispute resolution. Overall, the conventional system involving collective bargaining and collaborative management practices was found to be in decline and was being replaced by a more legalistic process coupled with a harder and more economic-focused management approach. This has forced workers to seek individual legal redress in an attempt to resolve disputes. The government has responded by introducing new, more individually focused, legal dispute resolution processes. This has, in turn, contributed to the development of other forms of unionism and collective action, such as union-on-demand and collective individualism.

The shift from collectivism to individualism and internal enterprise mechanisms to societally based mechanisms, particularly the increased use of ADR and statutory individual dispute resolution mechanisms, can be linked to the poor state of the economy, sectoral shifts that have occurred in Japan, and the decline in enterprise trade union membership. Underpinning this shift has been the breakdown of the "social contract," where many workers who had traded off shorter hours of work, job control, and wages for employment security were retrenched or transferred to less secure forms of employment. This has led many young workers to take more individualistic attitudes to work, employment, unions, and dispute resolution. Japanese workers now, regardless of union membership or type of employment, have access to some form of legal means to resolve employment disputes, particularly workplace grievances. On the other hand, workers now have fewer internal enterprise avenues to resolve issues over wages and the conditions of employment, and the poor state of the economy means that with the exception of large companies these terms of employment will be set unilaterally by management.

The growth in ADR provides a strong critique of enterprise unionism. In good economic times, when product markets were expanding and skilled labor was in demand, enterprise unions were able to protect the interests of their members while not threatening the commercial interests of companies. This worked well for four decades, and the wider "social contract" was generally honoured by all parties. With the onset of economic decline in the early 1990s these competing interests could no longer be met, and companies, often with the support of their unions, avoided bargaining over the key conditions of employment and instituted large structural adjustments to the company. This left workers with little choice but to seek out alternative means for resolving disputes, which by this time generally centred on job security. Unions, while attempting to widen their membership bases through the recruitment of part-time and temporary workers, and by recruiting members from related companies, have not been able to halt the decline in membership. Enterprise unionism in Japan remains the stronghold of full-time male workers. If this situation continues, and the vast majority of workers continue to be left with little workplace representation, Japanese legislators may be forced to extend the legal dispute-settling provisions to accommodate the setting of wages and the terms of employment through such processes as mediation, conciliation, and arbitration.

References

Abegglen, J. and Stalk, G. 1987. *Kaisha: The Japanese Corporation*. Tokyo: Tuttle.

Ballon, R. (1992). *Foreign Competition in Japan: Human Resource Strategies*. London: Routledge.

Bamber, G. and Lansbury, R. 1987. *International and Comparative Industrial Relations*. Sydney: Industrial Relations Research Centre, University of New South Wales.

Bamber, G., Lansbury, R., and Wailes, N. 2004. *International and Comparative Employment Relations: Globalization and the Developed Market Economies*. Sydney: Allen and Unwin.

Benson, J. 1996. "Management Strategy and Labour Flexibility in Japanese Manufacturing Enterprises." *Human Resource Management Journal*, 6(2): 44–57.

Benson, J. 2005. "Employment and Human Resource Developments in Japan." *Journal of Comparative Asian Development*, 4(1): 55–76.

Benson, J. 2008. "Trade Unions in Japan: Collective Justice or Managerial Compliance." In J. Benson and Y. Zhu (eds), *Trade Unions in Asia*. London: Routledge, 24–42.

Benson, J. 2011. "Labour Markets in Japan: Change and Continuity." In J. Benson and Y. Zhu (eds), *Labour Markets in Asia*. London: Routledge, 31–60.

Benson, J. 2012. "Alternative Dispute Resolution in Japan: The Rise of Individualism." *International Journal of Human Resource Management*, 23(3): 511–527.

Benson, J. and Debroux, P. 2004. "The Changing Nature of Japanese HRM: The Impact of the Recession and the Asian Financial Crisis." *International Studies of Management and Organization*, 34(1): 32–51.

Benson, J. and Gospel, H. 2008. "The Emergent Enterprise Union: A Conceptual and Comparative Analysis." *International Journal of Human Resource Management*, 19(7): 1367–1384.

Briggs, P. 1988. "The Japanese at Work: Illusions of the Ideal." *Industrial Relations Journal*, 19(3): 24–30.

Christopher, R. 1987. *The Japanese Mind*. Tokyo: Charles E. Tuttle.

Clark, R. 1987. *The Japanese Company*. Tokyo: Charles E. Tuttle.

Debroux, P. 2003. *Human Resource Management in Japan: Changes and Uncertainties*. Aldershot, UK: Ashgate.

Doko, T. 2006. "The Labor Relations Commission as an Organization to Resolve Collective Labor Disputes." *Japan Labor Review*, 3(1): 32–50.

Dore, R. 1990. *British Factory—Japanese Factory: The Origins of National Diversity in Industrial Relations*. Berkeley, CA: University of California Press.

Elbo, R. 2004. "Labor Tribunal System: Prospects of Japan's New Approach Toward the Efficient Settlement of Individual Labour Disputes." Visiting Researchers' Report No. 2004.04.25-06.02. Tokyo: Japan Institute for Labour Policy and Training.

EuroFound 2005. *Industrial Relations in the EU, Japan and the USA, 2003-2004*. Dublin: European Foundation for the Improvement of Living and Working Conditions.

Fujimura, H. 1997. "New Unionism: Beyond Enterprise Unionism?" In M. Sako and H. Sato (eds), *Japanese Labour and Management in Transition: Diversity, Flexibility and Participation*. London: Routledge, 296–314.

Hamaguchi, K. 2011. "Analysis of the Content of Individual Labor Dispute Resolution Cases: Termination, Bullying/Harassment, Reduction in Working Conditions, and Tripartite Labor Relationships." *Japan Labor Review*, 8(3): 118–37.

Hart, R. and Kawasaki, S. 1999. *Work and Pay in Japan*. Cambridge: Cambridge University Press.

Hisamoto, N. 2012. "The Functions and Limits of Enterprise Unions in Individual Labour Disputes." *Japan Labor Review*, 9(1): 44–62.

Inagami, T. 1988. *Japanese Workplace Industrial Relations*. Report No. 14, Japanese Industrial Relations Series. Tokyo: Japan Institute for Labour.

International Monetary Fund (IMF) 2011. *World Economic Outlook*, Apr. <www.imf.org/external/data.htm> accessed 19 May 2011.

Japanese Institute for Labour (JIL) 1990. *Japanese Working Life Profile 1990—Statistical Aspects*. Tokyo: JIL.

Japan Institute for Labour Policy and Training (JILPT) 2004. *Japanese Working Life Profile 2004/2005: Labour Statistics*. Tokyo: JILPT.

Japan Institute for Labour Policy and Training (JILPT) 2005. *Labor Situation in Japan and Analysis: Detailed Exposition 2005/2006: Labour Statistics*. Tokyo: JILPT.

Japan Institute for Labour Policy and Training (JILPT) 2006. *Japanese Working Life Profile 2005/2006: Labour Statistics*. Tokyo: JILPT.

Japan Institute for Labour Policy and Training (JILPT) 2008. "Research on Support for Development of In-house Dispute Settlement Systems—Summary." *Research Report No. 98*. Tokyo: JILPT.

Japan Institute for Labour Policy and Training (JILPT) 2009a. *Labor Situation in Japan and Analysis: Detailed Exposition*. Tokyo: JILPT.

Japan Institute for Labour Policy and Training (JILPT) 2009b. *Labor Situation in Japan and Analysis: General Overview 2009/2010*. Tokyo: JILPT.

Japan Institute for Labour Policy and Training (JILPT) 2009c. *Databook of International Labour Statistics*. Tokyo: JILPT [in Japanese].

Japan Institute for Labour Policy and Training (JILPT) 2011. *Japan Working Life Profile, 2011/2012*. Tokyo: JILPT.

Japan Institute for Labour Policy and Training (JILPT) 2012a. *Labor Situation in Japan and Its Analysis: General Overview 2011/2012*. Tokyo: JILPT.

Japan Institute for Labour Policy and Training (JILPT) 2012b. *Employment Termination in Japan*. Tokyo: JILPT [in Japanese].

Japan Productivity Centre (JPC) 2010. *Three Guiding Principles 1955*. Tokyo: JPC <http://www.jpc-net.jp/eng/mission/principle.html> accessed 31 May 2010.

Kagawa, K. 1993. "Comparative Study on Grievance Procedure and Voluntary Arbitration in Collective Agreements among American Companies, America-Japan Joint Companies and Japanese Companies." *Doshisha American Studies*, 29: 25–35 [in Japanese].

Keizai Koho 1990. *Japan 1991: An International Comparison*. Tokyo: Japan Institute for Social and Economic Affairs.

Keizai Koho 1997. *Japan 1998: An International Comparison*. Tokyo: Japan Institute for Social and Economic Affairs.

Kezuka, K. 2006. "Significance and Tasks Involved in Establishment of a Labor Tribunal System." *Japan Labor Review*, 3(1): 13–31.

Koshiro, K. 2000. "Formal and Informal Aspects of Labour Dispute Resolution in Japan." *Law and Policy*, 22(3–4): 353–67.

Maeda, N. 1999. *ADR in Japan*. Tokyo: Japan Commercial Arbitration Association <http://www.jcaa.or.jp/jcaa-j/jigyou/textadrinjapan.html> accessed 18 Dec. 2009.

Ministry of Health, Labour and Welfare (MHLW) 2008. *Survey of Collective Bargaining and Labour Disputes*. Tokyo: MHLW.

Ministry of Labour (MOL) 2000. *Survey on Labor Management Relations.* Tokyo: MOL.

Morishima, M. 1991. "Information Sharing and Collective Bargaining in Japan: Effects on Wage Negotiations." *Industrial and Labor Relations Review,* 44(3): 469–85.

Morishima, M. 1992. "Use of Joint Consultation Committees by Large Japanese Firms." *British Journal of Industrial Relations,* 30(3): 405–23.

Morishima, M. 1995. "The Japanese Human Resource Management System: A Learning Bureaucracy." In L. Moore and P. Jennings (eds), *Human Resource Management on the Pacific Rim: Institutions, Practices, and Attitudes.* Berlin: Walter de Gruyer, 119–50.

Nakakubo, H. 2006. "Introduction-Feature Articles: Labor Dispute Resolution System." *Japan Labor Review,* 3(1): 2–3.

Nakamura, K. 2007. "Decline or Revival? Japanese Labor Unions." *Japan Labor Review,* 4(1): 7–22.

Nimura, K. 1994. "Post-second World War Labour Relations in Japan." In J. Hagan and A. Wells (eds), *Industrial Relations in Australia and Japan.* St. Leonards, NSW: Allen and Unwin, 64–91.

Nitta, M. 1984. "Conflict Resolution in the Steel Industry: Collective Bargaining and Workers' Consultation in a Steel Plant." In T. Hanami and R. Blanpain (eds), *Industrial Conflict Resolution in Market Economies.* Antwerp: Kluwer, 233–47.

Oh, H. 2010. "Occurrence Mechanisms and Resolution Process of Labor Disputes: Cases of Community Unions (Kyushu Area)." *Japan Labor Review,* 7(1): 83–101.

Oh, H. 2012. "The Current Status and Significance of General Unions: Concerning the Resolution of Individual Labor Disputes." *Japan Labor Review,* 9(1): 63–85.

Porter, M., Takeuchi, H., and Sakakibara, M. 2000. *Can Japan Compete?* London: Macmillan.

Roche, W. and Teague, P. 2011. "Firms and Innovative Conflict Management Systems in Ireland." *British Journal of Industrial Relations,* 49(3): 436–59.

Sako, M. 1997. "Shunto: The Role of Employer and Union Coordination at the Industry and Inter-sectoral Levels." In M. Sako and H. Sato (eds), *Japanese Labour and Management in Transition: Diversity, Flexibility and Participation.* London: Routledge, 236–64.

Sano, Y. 1980. "A Quantitative Analysis of Factors Determining the Rate of Increase in Wage Levels during the Spring Wage Offensive." In S. Nishikawa (ed.), *The Labor Market in Japan.* Tokyo: Japan Foundation, 216–235.

Shimada, H. 1982. "Perceptions and the Realities of Japanese Industrial Relations: Role in Japan's Postwar Success," *Keio Economic Studies,* 19(2): 1–21.

Shirai, T. 1983. "A Theory of Enterprise Unionism." In T. Shirai (ed.), *Contemporary Industrial Relations in Japan.* Madison, WI: University of Wisconsin Press, 117–43.

Sugeno, K. 2006. "Judicial Reform and the Reform of the Labor Dispute Resolution System." *Japan Labor Review,* 3(1): 4–12.

Sugino, I. and Murayama, M. 2006. "Employment Problems and Disputing Behavior in Japan." *Japan Labor Review,* 3(1): 51–67.

Suzuki, F. 1997. "Labour Relations, Trade Union Organizations, Collective Bargaining, and Labour Management Consultation." In DGB-JTUC *Future of Work, Future of Social Welfare State, Future of Trade Unions.* Tokyo: Japanese Trade Union Confederation.

Tachibanaki, T. and Noda, T. 1996. "Enterprise Unionism: The Japanese System at Work." *Economic Policy,* 11(23): 469–85.

Tachibanaki, T. and Noda, T. 2000. *The Economic Effects of Trade Unions in Japan.* London: Macmillan.

Tada, N. 2012. "Informality for an Organizational Ombudsman in Japan." *Journal of the International Ombudsman Association,* 5(2): 23–6.

Weathers, C. 2003. "The Decentralization of Japan's Wage Setting System in Comparative Perspective." *Industrial Relations Journal,* 34(2): 119–34.

Whittaker, D. 2004. "Unemployment, Underemployment and Overemployment: Re-establishing Social Sustainability." *Japan Labor Review,* 1(1): 29–38.

CHAPTER 19

CONFLICT RESOLUTION IN THE UNITED STATES

DAVID B. LIPSKY, ARIEL C. AVGAR, AND
J. RYAN LAMARE

Introduction

THE handling of workplace conflict in the United States has changed dramatically over the last four decades. Non-union employers began to use mediation, arbitration, and other third-party dispute resolution techniques to resolve these conflicts in the 1970s, and the term "alternative dispute resolution" (ADR) was coined to describe this phenomenon. Using mediators, arbitrators, and other private parties to resolve disputes seemed a better alternative to using the court system and regulatory agencies. Both practitioners and scholars agree that the shift from litigation to ADR was principally motivated by the desire of employers to avoid what they perceived to be the growing time and costs associated with litigation. As the use of ADR continued to grow in the 1980s and 1990s, there was increasing awareness that a so-called ADR revolution was underway in the United States, in the handling not only of workplace disputes but also of consumer, environmental, and a wide array of other disputes as well. Some scholars noted that the ADR revolution represented the virtual privatization of the system of justice in the United States.

In this chapter, we examine the state of conflict resolution in the United States through the lens of two underlying tensions, one between individualism and collectivism and the other between reactive and strategic organizational approaches to conflict management. The first section examines how these key tensions have played out in recent years by analyzing data on corporate ADR practices and policies recently obtained from a survey of the Fortune 1000 (the 1000 largest US-based corporations). Then the tension between individualism and collectivism is assessed by examining the relation-ship between the extent of unionism in these large corporations and their use of ADR. Conventional wisdom in our field suggests that employers often use ADR practices and systems as a means of avoiding the unionization of their facilities, that is, ADR is viewed as a union-avoidance or union-substitution strategy. Our empirical evidence suggests that union avoidance may be a motive for some employers to use ADR, but that the rela-tionship between unionism and ADR is a more nuanced one than conventional wisdom recognizes.

In the third section we use our Fortune 1000 data to consider the tension between strategic and reactive approaches to conflict management. Most scholars and commen-tators have viewed the use of ADR in the United States as a means for employers to avoid the costs of litigation, which we consider to be principally a reactive (or tactical) use. There are at least two levels of analysis pertinent to an assessment of the tension between strategic and reactive approaches to conflict management. One revolves around the question of whether organizations use ADR policies in a truly strategic fashion or prin-cipally as a reaction to periodic events (such as lawsuits). That is, do they develop such policies in a proactive, anticipatory fashion and hope that such policies will help their organizations achieve central strategic goals and objectives? Or do they employ ADR practices on an *ad hoc* basis, merely as a reaction to critical incidents or crises that have interrupted their ordinary course of operations? The other level of analysis deals with the nature of the conflict management strategies organizations pursue. Is it the case that corporations adopt conflict management strategies mainly as a means of avoiding litiga-tion, as conventional wisdom holds? Or are corporations motivated by other factors, including but not limited to litigation avoidance?

The Use of ADR by Fortune 1000 Corporations: An Overview of Our Findings

In 1997 Cornell University conducted the first comprehensive survey of the use of ADR by Fortune 1000 corporations. In brief, the 1997 survey documented: (1) the growing use of ADR (especially arbitration and mediation) to resolve workplace disputes; (2) the corporate preference for interest-based (rather than rights-based) methods of resolving disputes; and (3) the emergence of a new phenomenon, namely, integrated conflict man-agement systems (see, especially, Lipsky et al., 2003). Although there is no standard defi-nition of a conflict management system in the literature or in practice, there is a growing consensus that a system differs from a practice or technique in four ways: (1) a system entails a comprehensive, proactive approach to managing and resolving conflict in an organization; (2) it has a broad scope, allowing many different types of disputes (statu-tory and non-statutory, for example) to be handled within the system; (3) it provides multiple access points for employees (an employee can file a complaint with his super-visor, the counsel's office, the human resource function, or the office that manages the system, for example); and (4) it provides multiple options for resolving disputes (such as both interest-based and rights-based methods) (Lipsky et al., 2003: 3–22).

About five years ago, the Scheinman Institute on Conflict Resolution at Cornell, the International Institute for Conflict Prevention and Resolution (CPR), and the Straus Institute for Dispute Resolution at Pepperdine University decided that a new survey of the use of ADR practices by Fortune 1000 firms would be a worthwhile undertaking. The faculty and staff of the three co-sponsors developed a new survey instrument that in part replicated the 1997 instrument and in part included new items designed to capture ADR developments that had occurred since the first survey was conducted.

Our objective, as it was in the 1997 survey, was to interview the general counsel (GC) in each of the Fortune 1000 corporations. If we were unable to interview the GC, we interviewed one of the GC's top deputies. We succeeded in conducting interviews with top attorneys in 368 of the Fortune 1000 companies. In 1997, we had succeeded in con-ducting interviews in 606 corporations. (The survey experts at SRI attributed the decline in the response rate principally to "survey fatigue," which had affected most of the sur-veys SRI had administered in recent years.) About 46% of the respondents were GCs and the remainder consisted of other top attorneys (such as deputy counsel or employment counsel) in the GC's office. The 368 corporations in our sample are a good cross-section (in terms of number of employees, revenue, industry, and so forth) of all of the corpora-tions included in the Fortune 1000 list.

The results of the new survey provide a rich tapestry of data on the use of ADR and conflict management systems by the corporations in our sample. They also provide a basis for comparing the ADR policies and practices pursued by major corporations in 2011 with those pursued by major corporations in 1997. A comparison of various types of ADR practices used by major US corporations in 1997 and 2011 appears in Figure 19.1. It is important to note that this comparison includes not only employment disputes but also consumer, commercial, and other types of corporate disputes. In addition, some caution must be used in interpreting the results because the companies included in the Fortune 1000 in 1997 differed from the companies included in 2011. There was a marked decline in the number of manufacturing companies included in the newer list, for exam-ple, and a marked increase in the number of retail and wholesale trade, finance, and insurance companies. It is also important to note that Figure 19.1 shows the proportion of corporations that used a particular technique at least once in the previous three years. This particular metric, of course, is only one of several that might have been used to gauge the frequency of ADR usage. In fact, we know that the majority of corporations in our sample used some of the techniques (primarily arbitration and mediation) a num-ber of times within the previous three years.

Figure 19.1 shows that the vast majority of corporations in both 1997 and 2011 relied on mediation and arbitration as techniques to resolve workplace and other disputes. The figure shows, in fact, that the proportion of companies using mediation increased from 87% to 98% over the course of fourteen years. There was also a discernible

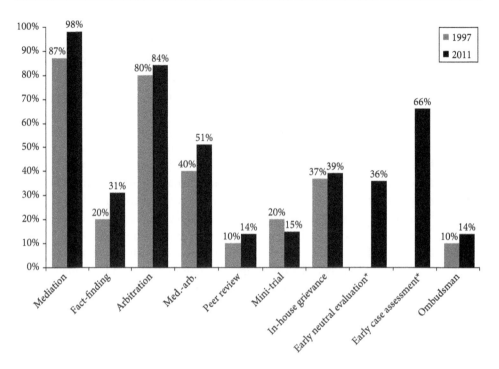

* These options were include only in the 2011 study

FIGURE 19.1 Experience with Types of ADR among Fortune 1000 Companies, 1997 and 2011

increase in the proportion of companies using fact-finding and mediation-arbitration (med-arb). Of special note is the finding that the proportion of corporations having an ombuds function increased from 10% to 14%—in relative terms, a 40% increase. In the contemporary organization, the ombuds office is frequently the hub of a conflict management system. Figure 19.1 also includes two techniques (early neutral evaluation and early case assessment) that were not a part of our 1997 survey. These techniques were novel in 1997, but the figure shows that by 2011 they had become prominent in the ADR portfolio.

Our 2011 results revealed that the use of *mediation* had remained relatively stable across a variety of disputes (employment, commercial, and consumer, for example) over the fourteen-year period but that there was a noteworthy decline in the use of *arbitration* across a variety of disputes. We do not show a figure depicting the results for mediation here, but Figure 19.2 shows that the proportion of corporations that reported using employment arbitration at least once in the previous three years declined from 62% to 38%—in relative terms, about a 40% decline. Note also that Figure 19.2 shows that the use of arbitration in construction disputes declined from 40% to 22%, and the use of arbitration in commercial disputes declined from 85% to 62%.

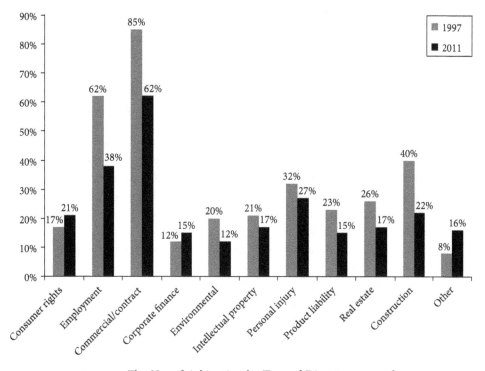

FIGURE 19.2 The Use of Arbitration by Type of Dispute, 1997 and 2011

It is possible that a major reason for the decline in the use of arbitration was the recession that began in 2008. Professor Stipanowich, the Director of the Straus Institute, points out that the dramatic decline in new construction caused by the recession probably means that there was not enough activity in the industry to generate disputes that might have been settled by arbitration. We lack the data to test this proposition. The respondents in our survey provided other reasons for the decline in the use of arbitration. Many of them believe that arbitration has increasingly become similar to litigation, and they suggest that "external law" (relevant statutes and court cases) has made arbitration more costly, complex, and time consuming. Our new survey confirms the finding of our 1997 survey that corporate attorneys prefer to use mediation and other interest-based options rather than arbitration and other rights-based options to resolve employment and other types of disputes.

Another possible reason for the decline in the use of employment arbitration is the rise in the use of conflict management systems in US corporations. Among the hallmarks of a conflict management system is their emphasis on resolving employment disputes within the organization, using internal dispute resolution mechanisms rather than resorting to outside arbitrators or mediators. On the basis of our 1997 survey, we estimated that about 17% of the Fortune 1000 corporations used a conflict management system (Lipsky et al., 2003: 126). A major objective of our 2011 survey was to discover how many corporations had adopted and were currently using a conflict management system. We included several questions in our survey instrument designed to provide an estimate of the use of such systems by major corporations. The metrics needed to make such an estimate, however, have proven to be laden with ambiguities and definitional difficulties that make arriving at a precise estimate challenging. In part, as noted earlier, this is because there is no standard definition of a conflict management system and many corporate attorneys and other practitioners view the use of ADR techniques (such as arbitration and mediation) as synonymous with the use of a system. Thus, when we asked our respondents, "Do you believe your company has a conflict management system?" about 67% answered "yes." Fortunately, the inclusion of other items in our survey instrument that covered core characteristics of an authentic conflict management system allowed us to develop more valid estimates of the proportion of our respondents that actually had such a system.

For example, we asked each respondent whether his or her company had "an office or function dedicated to managing your dispute resolution program." About 38% responded "yes" to this question. Although some systems are managed directly by the corporate counsel's office or by the human resource function, past research suggests that the most fully developed systems are managed by independent or semi-autonomous offices within the organization (Lipsky et al., 2003). These offices are often given names intended to suggest their central function: Prudential's conflict management system, for example, was managed under the rubric "Roads to Resolution" and was headed by a vice president who was also the corporation's chief ethics officer (for discussion of the Prudential conflict management system, see Lipsky et al., 2003: 147–152). The US Postal Service has "REDRESS," General Electric has "Resolve," Alcoa has "Resolve It," PECO Energy has "PEOPLE*SOLVE," and other organizations use their own unique names.[1]

By using other data in our survey, we were able to refine further our estimate of the number of corporations in our sample that have either all or most of the characteristics of an authentic conflict management system. Our best estimate is that roughly one-third of the corporations do. Our confidence in this estimate is buttressed by the identity of the corporations that met the criteria we used to define a system. That list includes corporations that are well known among scholars and practitioners for having sophisticated ADR programs: Coca Cola, General Electric, Eaton, Macy's, Harman International, Prudential, and Werner Enterprises, among others.

Our results disclose considerable variation in the use of a combination of ADR and conflict management systems in Fortune 1000 corporations. Although as many as one-third of these companies use a form of a conflict management system, our data suggest that as many as 40% rarely use any ADR techniques; instead they continue to rely largely on traditional methods, including litigation, to resolve disputes. Our findings also show that major US corporations that rely on ADR have adopted a wider array of ADR techniques over the past fourteen years, including so called hotlines, open-door policies, early neutral evaluation, early case assessment, and conflict coaching. In sum, there appears to be a growing diversity in the conflict management strategies used by US corporations.

Unions and ADR: The Contemporary Tension between Individualism and Collectivism

In this section we examine the tension between individualism and collectivism in US industrial relations, analyzing the relationship between collective bargaining and ADR practices—practices that operate at the level of individual employees and their supervisors—in major corporations.

Conceptual Overview

Researchers have long recognized that culture has a significant effect on conflict resolution (Gabrielidis et al., 1997; Avruch, 1998; Xie et al., 1998). Lewicki and his coauthors (2010: 441) defined the term culture as follows: "Although the term culture has many possible definitions, we use it to refer to the shared values, beliefs, and behaviors of a group of people." Perhaps the best-known researcher on cross-culture comparisons is Geert Hofstede, who conducted an in-depth analysis of the role of culture in business decisions (1980; see also Hofstede, 1991). Based on data he collected from more than 100,000 IBM employees around the world, Hofstede identified five dimensions of culture; one of the dimensions, individualism/collectivism, is a tension we use to frame this chapter. The individualism/collectivism dimension refers to the degree to which a society is organized either around individuals or the group (Hofstede, 1980; see also Hofstede, 1994).[2] Other researchers have found significant variation in the individualism/collectivism dimension, not only across societies but also across ethnic groups and regions within societies (Oyserman et al., 2002).[3]

The culture of the United States, according to Hofstede's findings, ranks at the top of the list of seventy nations on valuing individualism, but near the bottom of the list on accepting unequal power distributions, valuing the quality of life (according to Hofstede, a so-called feminine characteristic), avoiding uncertainty, and having a long-term orientation (Hofstede, 1991, 1994: 11). In other words, Hofstede views Americans as being rugged individualists, willing to challenge authority, tolerate ambiguity, and focus on short-term gains. These characteristics have been linked to the approach that Americans take in conflict situations. For example, in a study of managers in Japan, Hong Kong, Great Britain, and the United States, Xie and her coauthors (1998: 203–4) found that American managers' emphasis on individualism and short-term gains made them *more* likely to seek compromise deals than their counterparts in the other countries.[4] In a study of managers in the United States and Hong Kong, Leung (1987) found that collectivistic Chinese managers favored negotiation and mediation to a much greater extent than individualistic American managers. Chinese managers, to a much greater degree than American managers, valued procedures that reduced animosity between the disputants. In what follows we examine this tension in the context of American workplace conflict management.

Individualism and Collectivism in US Conflict Management: Empirical Evidence

In this section we explore the tension between collectivism and individualism in conflict resolution by analyzing the extent to which ADR practices complement or substitute for collective bargaining. We have not been able to uncover empirical research that directly tests the role that either union avoidance or union complementarity plays in serving as a catalyst for a firm's adoption of conflict management procedures for its non-union employees. Our 2011 survey of the ADR practices at the Fortune 1000 has provided evidence, however, that allows for key inferences to be made that shed empirical light on this tension.

The data indicate that just over half the firms surveyed had at least some level of union presence within the company. However, statistical analysis of the survey responses reveals that unionized firms were no more likely to offer larger aggregate numbers of ADR practices to their workforce than were non-union firms. These individual practices ranged from basic elements of ADR like mediation and arbitration to more recent developments like early case assessment and early neutral evaluation. In exploring the extent to which the Fortune 1000 survey helps resolve the tension between collectivism and individualism, these results are useful, in that when looking at the sheer number of conflict resolution options available to employees, firms tend to view unions in neither complementary nor competing terms. In other words, the debate over individualism versus collectivism (if this debate can be manifested in terms of the influence of union presence on ADR) does not appear to affect the absolute number of ADR options firms provide to their workers.

However, the collectivism/individualism tension is shown to be more strongly affected when one considers the influence of union presence at a corporation on the firm's usage of individual ADR practices. Survey responses indicate that unionized companies are significantly *more* likely to provide arbitration for their non-union workforce than are non-union companies. This result remains after controlling for such other effects on arbitration usage as industry, size, quality of workforce, and overall commitment to ADR. On the whole, after accounting for several influences on the Fortune 1000's usage of arbitration, the survey results demonstrate that unionized firms provide arbitration to non-union workers at rates 6.8% higher than do firms with no union presence. This finding supports the notion that unions serve as complements to the arbitration practices of corporations, and that arbitration is not a union-avoidance technique. Indeed, the finding of a positive relationship between unionism and non-union arbitration suggests, beyond simple complementarity, that there may be diffusion from the union sphere of activity into the non-union conflict resolution environment. Unionized firms, by their nature, are experienced in grievance arbitration, often highly so. It is plausible that this experience with grievance arbitration in the unionized sector provides the conduit through which corporations are comfortable introducing arbitration for the non-union workforce.

Companies were asked more detailed questions regarding their use (and non-use) of arbitration. Specifically, firms were queried to explain their rationale for not using arbitration in cases where they chose to employ a different means of dispute resolution (either litigation or an alternate ADR practice). These responses were tested against the unionization status of each company, in order to better garner whether there was a nuanced connection between collective voice, on the one hand, and individual employment arbitration, on the other. This nuance showed through in two ways: first, respondents indicating that their firms chose not to use employment arbitration because it resulted in compromise outcomes were also substantially more likely to have a union presence. In fact, the proportion of respondents from unionized firms that suggested that the occurrence of compromise outcomes was a major reason they declined to use arbitration was 35.6% more than the proportion of respondents from non-union companies. This distinction was also revealed in a second relationship: companies indicating that they use other alternatives to arbitration due to its being difficult to appeal were substantially more likely to be unionized; companies with a union presence indicated that appeal difficulties were a primary concern in arbitration at rates 41% higher than non-union corporations.

These results fit with the debate regarding individualism and collectivism in ADR in several ways. First, if the previous results imply that ADR and unionism are complementary rather than conflicting, these outcomes indicate that unionism also diffuses a considerable level of understanding regarding both the benefits and drawbacks of arbitration. Although unionized firms tend to provide non-union workers with higher levels of arbitration, they also show a clear awareness of the procedural and outcome limitations of the practice—it cannot be appealed, and it requires compromise. These two facets of arbitration are likely learned within the unionized grievance environment, and this knowledge is applied to non-union realms within the company.

Finally, survey respondents were asked the extent to which non-union employees were covered by ADR. This measure, which can be used to proxy a company's commitment to ADR amongst its non-union workforce, was compared against the union status of each corporation. In so doing, a measure of direct diffusion of ADR could be determined—did a firm's unionization status influence its likelihood of providing coverage to non-union workers? The answer, again controlling for a variety of other factors influencing commitment to ADR, was a robust yes. Non-union companies refused to provide ADR coverage to any portion of their workforce at rates 45.3% higher than unionized companies. On the other hand, firms with a union presence offered ADR coverage to high numbers of their non-union workforce at a rate 15% greater than firms without a union presence. These results held up under rigorous empirical testing. The implication of these findings is that unionization, which can arise from either internal strategic attitudes or external forces, leads to substantially larger internal commitment to non-union ADR across the Fortune 1000, irrespective of the genesis of the collective voice mechanism.

Taken together, the Fortune 1000 evidence contributes to two intersecting debates in the ADR literature. On the first, regarding complementarity versus competition in terms of the role unions play alongside non-union ADR mechanisms, the outcomes of the survey strongly favor the complementarity thesis (notwithstanding the possibility of outlier cases, where some firms may indeed view ADR as a union-substitution tool). On the second, regarding the broader tension between individualism and collectivism, these results support the notion that framing the two concepts around mutual exclusivity, with individualism and collectivism waging constant battle against each other in any society's writing of its social contract, may be a mistake, or at least an oversimplification. Having considered empirically the experience of Fortune 1000 firms (a group of corporations with enough economic and political muscle to have considerable influence on the revision of any social contract in the United States), the findings suggest that these concepts might instead be framed around mutual gains. A nuanced interpretation of the relationship between ADR and individualism/collectivism should consider the possibility that many aspects of collective voice are capable of informing and existing comfortably alongside individual voice arrangements.

The Strategic Underpinnings of Organizational Deployment of Conflict Management Practices in the United States

Workplace Conflict Management in the United States: From Reactive to Strategic

The reactive tendencies toward organizational conflict management are clearly evident in the shift from litigation management to dispute management that emerged in full force in the United States in the mid-1970s. Volumes of research on the rise of ADR have documented the dominant external pressures that pushed organizations to reconsider their predominately litigation-based approach to dealing with workplace conflict (see, for example, Lewin, 2008; Bingham et al., 2009; Roche and Teague, 2012). First, dispute resolution scholars pointed to the rising costs of litigation (Singer, 1994; Estreicher, 2001; Lipsky et al., 2003; Sherwyn et al., 2005). In the early 1970s and 1980s, the monetary costs, alongside the time and energy associated with adjudicating workplace conflict, created a substantial burden on a growing number of organizations, which, in turn, provided a real push to seek out and adopt new methods for dealing with conflict.

The potency of this litigation threat as a driver for the rise of ADR was strengthened by the dramatic growth in the legal regulations of the workplace, beginning with the Civil Rights Act of 1964 and the myriad of laws, such as the Age Discrimination in Employment Act of 1967 and the Occupational Safety and Health Act of 1970, intended to provide employees with individualized protections (for a more detailed discussion, see Lipsky and Avgar 2008). Organizations seeking to buffer themselves from this imposing external threat turned to internal mechanisms that, in many cases, alleviated a lot of the costs and risks associated with litigation (Edelman et al., 1993).

Alongside the threat of litigation, the adoption of dispute resolution practices has also been driven by efforts either to avoid unions altogether or to substitute their core voice-related function (for a fuller discussion, see Avgar, 2011). Union density in the United States has been in decline since the 1950s, but the fierce attempts by many organizations and their managers to limit unionization totally escalated in the 1980s and beyond (Kochan et al., 1994; Lewin, 2008). The rise of ADR has therefore also been attributed to a growing resistance to unions on the part of American firms. Although our own research, reported in the previous section, suggests that the relationship between unionism and ADR is more complicated than many scholars believe, to the extent that firms have turned to ADR as a means of avoiding or substituting for the role of unions, the shift to conflict management can also be seen as a firm's reactive response to an external pressure, as opposed to a strategic choice based on an effort to advance broader organizational goals and objectives (Avgar et al., 2013).

Finally, evidence of the reactive roots of the shift from litigation management to dispute management in the United States can be found in the tremendous competitive pressures placed on firms in the 1970s and 1980s, which were likely to place a higher premium on the ability to address costly workplace disputes. This increased market competition pushed many United States firms to reexamine organizational design and structure (Appelbaum and Batt, 1994; Kochan et al., 1994; Appelbaum et al., 2000). Although much of the scholarly attention regarding this organizational restructuring focused on the design of work and human resource management practices, this external pressure is likely to have resulted in a restructuring of conflict management practices as well (for a similar argument, see Lipsky et al., 2012).

Taken together, ADR scholarship supports the argument that the first major conflict management transformation in the United States, which began to take hold in the mid-1970s, was born, in large part, out of a reactive approach to workplace conflict and its management. This is not to say that strategic choice was completely absent from this dramatic conflict management transformation (for a similar claim, see Lipsky and Avgar, 2008). It does, however, suggest that, in moving away from their traditional litigation-centered approach to conflict management, organizations were primarily responding to a powerful set of external pressures that provided extremely strong incentives for this important departure.

If the first dominant shift away from a litigation-centered approach to conflict management was the product of the reactive conflict management tendencies of many US firms, the second shift toward a broader systematic approach was, according to our argument, the result of a growing link between the management of conflict and strategic choices made by firms and their managers (Lipsky et al., 2003; Avgar, 2008; Lipsky and Avgar, 2008). Beginning in the 1990s, a second phase in the transformation of American workplace conflict management was underway. This shift entailed a movement away from the adoption of single ad hoc practices designed to deal with formalized disputes (Lipsky et al., 2003). Instead, a growing proportion of large United States firms began to employ a broader set of practices designed to deal with less formal everyday forms of conflict, among other things (Costantino and Merchant, 1996; Rowe, 1997; Lipsky et al., 2003). As noted above, a survey of the Fortune 1000 conducted in 1997 found that approximately 17% of firms had implemented key elements of a conflict management system (Lipsky et al., 2003). Our more recent survey finds a substantial growth in the adoption of conflict management systems, with approximately 33% of respondents indicating that they had key elements in place (Lipsky et al., 2012).

Organizations pursuing this approach designed and adopted what are referred to as integrated conflict management systems, which include a mixture of different types of conflict management practices (Costantino and Merchant, 1996; Rowe, 1997; Bingham and Chachere, 1999; Lipsky et al., 2003; Rowe and Bendersky, 2003; Seeber and Lipsky, 2006). In contrast to ADR, conflict management systems provide a much broader array of decision points for organizations. One of the hallmarks of these systems, for example, is the integration of both rights-based dispute resolution options, like arbitration, and interest-based options, like mediation. Similarly, conflict management systems include different access points allowing employees to bring forth a conflict or dispute by activating different components of the system. Finally, conflict management systems allow employers to include a broad spectrum of conflict and dispute categories (Lipsky et al., 2003). The growth of conflict management systems in US firms meant, therefore, that these organizations had a more flexible and varied arsenal of tools to deal with workplace conflict and disputes. The availability of a more varied bundle of practices provided employers with greater choice in terms of what practices they adopted. We maintain, therefore, that the adoption of conflict management practices over the past two decades has been increasingly driven by strategic considerations.

Fundamental to this shift away from the dispute management focus associated with ADR to a conflict management focus is the notion that different organizations can adopt different configurations of practices. Furthermore, these different configurations of practices are likely to advance different organizational objectives. According to Lipsky and Avgar (2008, 2010), there are three central organizational objectives that conflict management systems can be leveraged to advance: (1) the resolution of specific ad hoc conflicts; (2) enhancing employee voice; and (3) advancing organizational coordination. Accordingly, organizations vary in terms of the outcomes they seek to promote when adopting conflict management systems; this variation calls for clear choices about which configuration of practices should be put into place. This is important because it creates the foundation for the strategic potential associated with organizational conflict management decisions (for a similar argument pertaining to work practices, see Osterman, 1987). Firms working toward the adoption of such a system must make increasingly strategic decisions about which outcomes they are interested in advancing. They thus accrue more degrees of freedom in advancing specific goals and objectives, using different configurations of practices.

In addition to these inherently strategic elements associated with conflict management systems, their growth has also coincided with the rise of a more strategic approach to the deployment of work arrangements and human resource management practices (see, for example, Colvin, 2003, 2004; Avgar, 2008). One of the most well-established elements of this industrial relations shift is the increased prevalence of work practices designed to increase employee participation, input, and discretion (Appelbaum et al., 2000). Prominent among these innovations is the high-performance work system, which includes, among other things, a shift toward teamwork, individual and team-based performance compensation, increased employee discretion, and a focus on employee skills and training (Huselid, 1995; Osterman, 2000). This restructuring of work organizations is important to the aforementioned conflict management shift since it represents a parallel structural shift inside organizations that both influenced and was influenced by conflict and its management. Specifically, this prevalent workplace restructuring alters the internal relational dynamics by increasing the importance of horizontal or peer-based interactions, which changes the stakes associated with everyday conflict inside organizations (see, for example, Barker, 1993).

It has been argued that the emergence of conflict management systems was, among other things, a response to the restructuring taking place in many US firms and the implications the restructuring had for the relational dynamics among organizational members. Nevertheless, in contrast to the reactive responses associated with the external pressures reviewed earlier, firms' conflict management responses to work restructuring (such as high-performance work systems) had a strategic orientation since they needed to be aligned with a complex array of internal changes. Building on the argument that different conflict management system configurations are likely to advance different workplace outcomes, it is also likely that different organizational structures and designs will affect the centrality of certain outcomes. Thus, our argument regarding the increasingly strategic nature of conflict management decision-making in American firms over the past two decades is also based on an analysis of parallel changes in the internal structures of many US companies—changes that we believe call for strategic complementarities between work organization and conflict management patterns.

Strategic Choice and Conflict Management: Empirical Evidence

The argument outlined above proposes an increasingly strategic orientation driving the adoption of conflict management in American firms. We believe that, while the early rise of ADR was likely to have been a reactive response to external pressures and threats, more recent conflict management trends in the United States are the product of growing levels of strategic choice in this domain. Support for this proposition would require the establishment of a significant statistical relationship between different strategic orientations and the adoption of specific ADR practices and conflict management systems. In a recent paper analyzing data from our Fortune 1000 survey, we tested the link between firms' strategic orientation and their use of ADR and conflict management systems (Lipsky et al., 2012). Specifically, building on the existing conflict management literature, we explored the relationship between each of three dominant benefits associated with alternative conflict management approaches—legal, managerial, and efficiency— and the likelihood of adopting a specific set of practices.

We included an assessment of a firm's emphasis on anticipated *legal benefits* and the adoption of conflict management practices, since as noted, many organizations that use ADR and conflict management systems do so as a means of avoiding litigation and reducing associated costs (for a summary of the research on this motive, see Seeber and Lipsky, 2006). But companies use ADR not only to save the time and money associated with litigation but also because doing so has other benefits. One of the other "legal" benefits of using ADR, for example, is the organization's desire to ensure that confidentiality is maintained in employee disputes. This strategic objective is consistent with early ADR research that focused on the role that external threats like litigation played in motivating the adoption of ADR practices.

Nevertheless, as just discussed, organizational adoption of different conflict management patterns is also likely to be influenced by *managerial benefits* that go beyond the advancement of legal benefits. A growing proportion of organizations, we believe, adopt a conflict management system as a means of addressing internal problems and inadequacies. Thus, organizations adopting a conflict management system may view this approach as a means of improving internal relationships (between supervisors and employees or employees and employees, for example) and enhancing employee access to voice. This strategic orientation is consistent with research reviewed earlier that is focused on the relationship between ADR and conflict management systems, on the one hand, and internal organizational needs and restructuring, on the other. Finally, conflict management practices can also be adopted as a means of advancing organizations' *efficiency gains* through the use of ADR and conflict management systems. This strategic orientation views conflict management as a tool for reducing the costs of conflict and disputes.

We maintain that each of these strategic orientations to conflict management will lead to a different level of adoption of ADR and conflict management systems. By focusing on the actual conflict management motivations of firms in our research, we were able to address fundamental questions regarding the drivers of this dramatic organizational shift. One such question was, do organizations that emphasize the legal benefits of ADR and conflict management systems have higher levels of adoption than organizations that emphasize ADR's managerial or efficiency benefits?

Analysis of data from the Fortune 1000 survey provides strong support for our argument that the adoption patterns of conflict management practices are influenced by specific organizational strategies. More specifically, we documented a significant relationship between two conflict management strategic orientations and the adoption of

ADR practices. Organizations seeking to address managerial challenges and shortcomings (a managerial benefit orientation) were significantly more likely to adopt a broader array of ADR practices. Similarly, a legally centered strategic approach to conflict management (legal benefit orientation) was also significantly related to the adoption of a broader ADR portfolio. A conflict management strategy emphasizing efficiency gains, on the other hand, was not significantly related to ADR adoption rates.

Interestingly, strategic conflict management orientations also explain the adoption of conflict management systems (beyond specific practices), but with different effects than those reported for ADR practices. More specifically, managerial- and efficiency-focused strategies were shown significantly to increase the likelihood of adopting a conflict management system. Thus, unlike the documented drivers of ADR practice adoption, legally centered conflict management objectives were not shown significantly to predict organizational adoption of a conflict management system. This finding is consistent with the existing literature on conflict management systems, which emphasizes the potential vested in these systems to address internal organizational issues (Lipsky et al., 2003; Lipsky and Avgar, 2008). On the other hand, an efficiency focused conflict management strategy, which did not have a significant effect on the adoption of ADR practices, was significantly related to the establishment of a conflict management office. This suggests that while ADR and conflict management systems each represent an alternative method for dealing with workplace conflicts and disputes, the decision to pursue them is motivated by both overlapping and distinct strategic objectives. Taken together, our empirical results demonstrate a clear relationship between organizations' strategic conflict management posture and the decision to adopt ADR practices and conflict management systems. Thus, this evidence supports the proposition that organizational conflict management decisions are a product of managerial strategic choice, in addition to other factors.

CONCLUSIONS

Workplace conflict and its management in the United States have undergone dramatic transformations over the course of the past century, especially over the past forty years. Overarching changes in societal and organizational approaches to the resolution and management of workplace conflict have, among other things, affected the types of conflict management practices adopted by organizations and, more importantly, the principles that govern the adoption, implementation, and use of these different practices. In this chapter, we have argued that a comprehensive understanding of the current state of workplace conflict management in the United States requires an examination of the forces and pressures that have shaped the ways in which organizations, employees, and their representatives deal with tensions, disagreements, and conflict.

Our chapter has set forth the argument that the conflict management landscape in the United States has been shaped in part by the persistent tensions between individualism and collectivism and between reactive and strategic organizational tendencies. Regarding the first tension, our review of the evolution of conflict management in the United States documents the oscillation between general individualistic and collectivistic approaches and the implications of this oscillation for the manner in which workplace conflict has been dealt. The contours of the regimes governing US conflict management have been strongly influenced by the extent to which the overarching logic was collective or individualistic in nature. Thus, during the New Deal era, which was characterized by the promotion of and support for a collectivist-centered industrial relations logic, for example, the management of conflict in organizations was largely addressed through the collective bargaining relationship between labor and management. The erosion of this industrial relations approach led to the rise of ADR in the 1970s and, more recently, to conflict management systems, both representing approaches that are fundamentally anchored around the individual resolution of disputes and conflict.

Our chapter has also presented the argument that the current state of conflict management in the United States is the product of broader tension between reactive and strategic approaches to organizational management. We maintain that, like the evolution of other workplace and human resource management practices, conflict management has evolved over the past four decades from a set of primarily reactive approaches to an increasingly strategic and systemic configuration of practices. We believe that this is one of the most important characteristics of emerging organizational approaches to conflict management in the United States and one that requires additional research.

In addition to outlining these two central tensions and the manner in which they have shaped organizational conflict management, we also presented evidence from our research of Fortune 1000 firms. Our analysis of survey data from Fortune 1000 firms points to a number of important insights regarding the current state of conflict management in the United States. First, a comparison of surveys conducted in 1997 and 2011 highlights the prevalence of alternative approaches to conflict management. For the most part, organizational use of different conflict management techniques has either increased or remained consistent since 1997. Both surveys provide support for the argument that conflict management in the United States has undergone a dramatic transformation, with a majority of large firms making use of a wide array of conflict management practices. In addition, our 2011 survey suggests a relatively large increase in the use of conflict management systems in large firms. Specifically, we document such an increase from 17% of the Fortune 1000 firms surveyed in 1997 to 33% of the Fortune 1000 firms surveyed in 2011. This evidence supports the claim that the use of conflict management systems in large American firms is becoming increasingly institutionalized and that this phenomenon may be reaching a tipping point in terms of its prevalence. It further suggests that the use of conflict management systems is likely to be more than a temporary management fad and should be viewed as a more permanent and stable component of organizational conflict management in the United States.

Second, analysis of our Fortune 1000 survey data also informs our discussion regarding the tension between individualistic and collectivistic pressures shaping the state of US workplace conflict management. Specifically, we provide evidence for the complementarity between unionization and the adoption of ADR practices for non-union employees. Thus, although the emerging conflict management era in the United States appears to be one that is characterized by a predominately individualistic approach, there are still important linkages and synergies between the manner in which conflict is resolved in the collective bargaining arena and the diffusion and use of those practices put in place for non-union employees.

Finally, we reported on findings from our Fortune 1000 survey that support our general argument that the use of conflict management practices in large firms appears to be influenced by the strategic posture of the organization. Much of the literature on ADR has treated the rise of new workplace conflict management practices as a reactive response to a variety of external and internal pressures. In shifting toward a broader and more systemic approach to conflict management, organizations have also created the foundation for a more strategic approach. Given the wider array of configuration of practices that can be adopted by organizations, strategic choices have become an increasingly important source of variation in adoption patterns.

We believe that the portrait that emerges from these findings indicates that these are extremely interesting times for the study and practice of conflict management in the United States. The combination of new and traditional practices being adopted by organizations, the dramatic changes in the overarching logic governing these practices, and their increasingly strategic deployment all create the conditions under which existing assumptions about the practice of conflict resolution are challenged and new institutional patterns emerge. Despite the many changes that lay ahead, one element remains stable: the conflict management landscape in the United States will continue to reflect evolving societal and organizational approaches to persisting tensions.

One might say that these tensions are conflicts over the most effective approach to conflict resolution. Other scholars have noted that the lack of an underlying consensus on values and politics in the United States has resulted in an instability in the handling of employment and labor relations (and quite likely other realms as well)—an instability likened to a pendulum that swings over time in one direction and then in another, resulting in risk and uncertainty.

ACKNOWLEDGMENTS

Some parts of this chapter use data drawn from a 2011 survey of the Fortune 1000, jointly sponsored by the International Institute for Conflict Prevention and Resolution (CPR), the Straus Institute for Dispute Resolution at Pepperdine University, and the Scheinman Institute on Conflict Resolution at Cornell University. We are indebted to Kathy Bryan, President of CPR, and Thomas Stipanowich, Director of the Straus Institute, for their support of this survey. We express our sincerest thanks to Sally Klingel for her invaluable assistance in developing the instrument used in the Fortune 1000 survey. Several graduate students assisted us in collecting the data used here and preparing this chapter: we are especially grateful to Abhishek Gupta and Michael Maffie for their able assistance. As always, we are also grateful to Missy Harrington for her excellent assistance at every stage of this undertaking.

Notes

1. For discussion of the dispute resolution program, called REDRESS, at the U.S. Postal Service, see Bingham 2001; for discussion of the program at General Electric, see Nordstrom, 2004; for discussion of the program at Alcoa, see Perdue, 2004; and for discussion of the program at PECO Energy, see Lipsky et al., 2003: 148–50.
2. The other dimensions identified by Hofstede are power-distance, career success/quality of life, uncertainty avoidance, and long-term orientation (Hofstede, 1980; see also 1994). A fifth dimension, long-term orientation, was added by Hofstede in his 1994 article.
3. Oyserman et al. provide a meta-analysis of all the English-language research published on individualism and collectivism since 1980—over 250 studies.
4. In the case of the Chinese and Japanese managers, face saving was an important value and helped to explain why they were less willing to compromise than American managers (Xie et al., 1998: 203–4).

References

Appelbaum, E. and Batt, R. 1994. *The New American Workplace: Transforming Work Systems in the United States*. Ithaca, NY: Cornell University Press.

Appelbaum, E., Bailey, T., Berg, P., and Kalleberg, A.L. 2000. *Manufacturing Advantage: Why High-Performance Systems Pay Off*. Ithaca, NY: Cornell University Press.

Avgar, A. C. 2008. *Treating Conflict: Conflict and Its Resolution in Healthcare*. Ph.D. Dissertation. Ithaca, NY: Cornell University.

Avgar, A. C. 2011. "The Ombudsman's Ability to Influence Perceptions of Organizational Fairness: Toward a Multi-Stakeholder Framework." *Journal of the International Ombudsman Association*, 4(1): 5–15.

Avgar, A. C., Lamare, J. R., Lipsky, D. B., and Gupta, A. 2013. "Unions and ADR: The Relationship between Labor Unions and Workplace Dispute Resolution in U.S. Corporations." *Ohio State Journal on Dispute Resolution*, 28(1): 63.

Avruch, K. 1998. *Culture and Conflict Resolution*. Washington, DC: United States Institute of Peace Press, 31.

Barker, J. R. 1993. "Tightening the Iron Cage: Concertive Control in Self-Managing Teams." *Administrative Science Quarterly*, 38(3): 408–37.

Bingham, L. B. 2001. "Addressing the 'Redress': A Discussion of the Status of the United States Postal Service's Transformative Mediation Program," *Cardozo On-Line Journal of Conflict Resolution*, 2. Accessed at <http://www.cardozo.yu.edu/cojcr/final_site/symposia/vol_2_symposia/postal_trans.htm>.

Bingham, L. B., and Chachere, D. R. 1999. "Dispute Resolution in Employment: The Need for Research." In A. E. Eaton and J. H. Keefe (eds), *Employment Dispute Resolution and Worker Rights in the Changing Workplace*. Champaign, IL: Industrial Relations Research Association, 95–135.

Bingham, L., Hallberlin, C. J. Walker, D. A., and Chung, W. 2009. "Dispute System Design and Justice in Employment Dispute Resolution: Mediation at the Workplace." *Harvard Negotiation Law Review*, 14(1): 1–50.

Colvin, J. S. 2003. "The Dual Transformation Workplace Dispute Resolution." *Industrial Relations: A Journal of Economy and Society*, 42(4): 712–35.

Colvin, J. S. 2004. "Adoption and Use of Dispute Resolution Procedures in the Nonunion Workplace." In David Lewin and Bruce E. Kaufman (eds), *Advances in Industrial and Labor Relations*. Greenwich, CT: JAI Press, 13: 69–95.

Costantino, C. A. and Merchant, C. S. 1996. *Designing Conflict Management Systems*. San Francisco, CA: Jossey-Bass.

Edelman, L. B., Erlanger, H. S., and Lande, J. 1993. "Employers' Handling of Discrimination Complaints: The Transformation of Rights in the Workplace." *Law and Society Review*, 27(3): 497–534.

Estreicher, S. 2001. "Saturns for Rickshaws: The Stakes in the Debate over Predispute Employment Arbitration Agreements." *Ohio State Journal on Dispute Resolution*, 16(3): 559–70.

Gabrielidis, C., Stephan, W. G., Ybarra, O., Dos Santos Pearson, V. M., and Villareal, L. 1997. "Preferred Styles of Conflict Resolution? Mexico and the United States." *Journal of Cross-Cultural Psychology*, 28(6): 661–77.

Hofstede, G. 1980. *Culture's Consequences: International Differences in Work Related Values*. Beverly Hills, CA: Sage.

Hofstede, G. 1991. *Culture and Organizations: Software of the Mind*. London: McGraw-Hill.

Hofstede, G. 1994. *Values Survey Module 1994 Manual*. Maastrict, the Netherlands: Institute for Research on Intercultural Cooperation.

Huselid, M. A. 1995. "The Impact of Human Resource Management Practices on Turnover, Productivity, and Corporate Financial Performance." *Academy of Management Journal*, 38(3): 635–72.

Kochan, T. A., Katz, H. C., and McKersie, R. B. 1994. *The Transformation of American Industrial Relations*. (2nd ed.). Ithaca, NY: ILR Press.

Leung, K. 1987. "Some Determinants of Reactions to Procedural Models for Conflict Resolution: A Cross-National Study." *Journal of Personality and Social Psychology*, 53(5): 898–908.

Lewicki, R. J., Barry, B., and Saunders, D. M. 2010. *Negotiation*. 6th edn. New York, NY: McGraw-Hill Irwin.

Lewin, D. 2008. "Workplace ADR: What's New and What Matters?," In S. E. Befort, and P. Halter (eds), *Workplace Justice for a Changing Environment, Proceedings of the 60th Annual Meeting, National Academy of Arbitrators*. Washington, DC: Bureau of National Affairs, 23–39.

Lipsky, D. B., and Avgar, A. C. 2008. "Toward a Strategic Theory of Workplace Conflict Management." *Ohio State Journal on Dispute Resolution*, 24(1): 143–90.

Lipsky, D. B., and Avgar, A. C. 2010. "The Conflict over Conflict Management." *Dispute Resolution Journal*, 65(2–3): 11, 38–43.

Lipsky, D. B., Seeber, R. L., and Fincher, R. D. 2003. *Emerging Systems for Managing Workplace Conflict: Lessons from American Corporations for Managers and Dispute Resolution Professionals*. San Francisco, CA: Jossey-Bass.

Lipsky, D. B., Avgar, A. C., Lamare, J. R., and Gupta, A. 2012. "The Antecedents of Workplace Conflict Management Systems in U.S. Corporations: Evidence from a New Survey of Fortune 1000 Companies." Paper presented at the 16th World Congress of the International Labor and Employment Relations Association. Philadelphia, PA.

Nordstrom, M. 2004. "General Electric's Experience with ADR." In S. Estreicher and D. Sherwyn (eds), *Alternative Dispute Resolution in the Employment Arena: Proceedings of New York University 53rd Annual Conference on Labor*. New York, NY: Kluwer Law International, 197–226.

Osterman, P. 1987. "Choice of Employment Systems in Internal Labor Markets." *Industrial Relations: A Journal of Economy and Society*, 26(1): 46–67.

Osterman, P. 2000. "Work Reorganization in an Era of Restructuring: Trends in Diffusion and Effects on Employee Welfare." *Industrial and Labor Relations Review*, 53(2): 179–96.

Oyserman, D., Coon, H. M., and Kemmelmeier, M. 2002. "Rethinking Individualism and Collectivism: Evaluation of Theoretical Assumptions and Meta-Analyses." *Psychological Bulletin*, 128(1): 3–72.

Perdue, D. C. 2004. "Employment Dispute: Resolve It! Alcoa at the Forefront of Alternative Dispute Resolution." In S. Estreicher and D. Sherwyn (eds), *Alternative Dispute Resolution in the Employment Arena: Proceedings of New York University 53rd Annual Conference on Labor*. New York, NY: Kluwer Law International, 233–4.

Roche, W. and Teague, P. 2012. "Do Conflict Management Systems Matter?." *Human Resource Management*, 51(20: 231–58.

Rowe, M. P. 1997. "Dispute Resolution in the Non-Union Environment: An Evolution toward Integrated Systems for Conflict Management." In S. E. Gleason (ed.), *Workplace Dispute Resolution: Directions for the Twenty-First Century*. East Lansing, MI: Michigan State University Press, 79–106.

Rowe, M. and Bendersky, C. 2003. "Workplace Justice, Zero Tolerance, and Zero Barriers." In T. A. Kochan and D. B. Lipsky (eds), *Negotiations and Change: From the Workplace to Society*. Ithaca, NY: ILR Press, 117–37.

Seeber, R. L. and Lipsky, D. B. 2006. "The Ascendancy of Employment Arbitrators in U.S. Employment Relations: A New Actor in the American System?" *British Journal of Industrial Relations*, 44(4): 719–56.

Sherwyn, D. S., Estreicher S., and Heiss, M. 2005. "Assessing the Case for Employment Arbitration: A New Path for Empirical Research." *Stanford Law Review*, 57(5): 1557–91.

Singer, L. R. 1994. *Settling Disputes: Conflict Resolution in Business, Families, and the Legal System*. 2nd edn. Boulder, CO: Westview Press.

Xie, J., Song, X. M., and Stringfellow, A. 1998. "Interfunctional Conflict, Conflict Resolution Styles, and New Product Success: A Four-Culture Comparison." *Management Science*, 44(12): 192–206.

CHAPTER 20

....

CONFLICT MANAGEMENT IN AUSTRALIA

....

BERNADINE VAN GRAMBERG, GREG J. BAMBER, JULIAN TEICHER, AND BRIAN COOPER

INTRODUCTION

THIS chapter reviews the Australian system of workplace conflict management, with an emphasis on recent developments. While industrial relations tribunals have been central to the system for settling workplace disputes, until the 1990s the tribunals dealt mainly with collective disputes. Two developments have induced a major shift in emphasis: first, under the influence of neoliberal ideas successive governments have attempted to "deregulate" the labor market, in effect a form of re-regulation designed to undermine the capacity of organized labor and to weaken collective bargaining. These measures have fostered greater individualization of the employment relationship and have contributed to transforming the nature and incidence of workplace conflict. Second, governments and tribunals have decentralized industrial relations to the workplace, leaving much of the setting of terms and conditions of employment as well as conflict resolution to workplace parties (Bamber et al., 2010; Lansbury and Wailes, 2011).

Since the institutional context is distinctive, we first provide an overview of the Australian industrial relations system, tracing its development from the federation of the nation through to its current form. In particular, we note two important trends: first, there has been an increase in the jurisdiction of the federal industrial relations tribunal at the expense of state tribunals; and second, a shift in the role of the federal tribunal from one focusing on collective industrial matters to having a more flexible approach to dealing with collective and individual issues. We then address contemporary trends in workplace conflict, including the scale, pattern, and duration of industrial disputes. We show how these trends are changing in relation to a shift from collective to individual disputes.

INDUSTRIAL RELATIONS CONTEXT: CENTRALIZATION AND DECENTRALIZATION

Australia is a large island continent. It is sparsely populated and relatively remote from Europe and the Americas. Australia comprises a federation of states[1] and territories. The six states were each separate colonies of Britain until they federated in 1901.[2] In terms of the varieties of capitalism literature, Australia is a liberal market economy (LME), with similarities to other English-speaking LMEs including the US, the UK, Canada, Ireland, and New Zealand (Hall and Soskice, 2001). In contrast to coordinated market economies such as Germany, Austria, and the Scandinavian countries, and like other LMEs, Australia has a tradition of adversarialism in industrial relations, although historically the majority of disputes have been settled by conciliation. To a greater extent than the US, however, Australia has long had an extensive degree of government intervention in labor-market arrangements, including dispute resolution.

During the nineteenth century, different systems of industrial relations regulation were developed in the separate colonies. Some aspects of dispute resolution were innovative and diverged significantly from the British legacy, notably the development of forms of compulsory conciliation and arbitration in four of the six colonies. The others developed tripartite "wages boards" for settling industrial disputes. In general, industrial relations regulation reflected a perceived need to manage industrial relations *conflict*, rather than to regulate workplace *peace*. This focus on regulating conflict has continued to be a characteristic of labor-market policy, though the details of the regulation have been subject to frequent change reflecting the changing power dynamics of state (and later, federal) governments.

The federal industrial relations system was developed in the aftermath of the "Great Strikes" of the 1890s which centered on three key sectors: the maritime, wool, and mining sectors across several of the colonies (Svensen, 1995). In most cases the strikes were prompted by employers trying to avoid collective bargaining and demanding freedom from association (Creighton, 2000). The union response to employer demands for freedom of contract was rapid, organized, and widespread with hundreds of thousands of workers striking. The employers retaliated strongly, with colonial government support, including the use of armed escorts at workplaces for strike breakers or "scabs"—many of them unemployed or striking workers from elsewhere (Baker, 2001).

Coinciding with a major economic depression, these industrial disputes were widely seen as damaging to the economy, particularly on the main export industries and there was also concern about the effect on the fabric of Australian society. Consequently, the politicians who drafted the Australian Constitution included a clause (s.51(xxxv)), enabling the Parliament to legislate to provide for compulsory conciliation and arbitration of industrial disputes which crossed state borders. In principle this left the federal government with a "residual" power over industrial disputes and the states with primary responsibility for regulating industrial relations, particularly for state- and local-government employment and those industries that were deemed as being of an intra-state character. From then until the 1980s, it was widely assumed that the Constitution did not enable the government to regulate certain other industrial relations matters directly.

At the same time, a federal system of conciliation and arbitration was created and in effect overarching the industrial relations systems existing at state level. The *Conciliation and Arbitration Act 1904* (C&A Act) established the Commonwealth Court of Conciliation and Arbitration with powers of compulsory conciliation and arbitration over industrial disputes between parties who were registered under the Act (Harbridge et al., 2006). Partly for the administrative convenience of not having to deal with large numbers of individual employees, access to the system via registration was limited to employers, employers' associations and unions, which registered under the Act. An early president of the Court, Justice Henry Bournes Higgins (1915) provided a colorful description of the rationale for the new law:

> The process of conciliation, with arbitration in the background, is substituted for the rude and barbarous processes of strike and lockout. Reason is to displace force; the might of the State is to enforce peace between industrial combatants as well as between other combatants...
>
> (Higgins, 1915: 2)

The Court of Conciliation and Arbitration was the first federal court concerned with workplace dispute resolution, which was empowered to make a legally binding "award."[3] Originally, an award was the legal embodiment of a decision of the Court, though over time awards became more complex instruments regulating many aspects of the wages and conditions of workers in a diverse range of industries and occupations. Under the Constitution, technically an award was the outcome of an industrial dispute, though in practice its terms could be determined by a range of processes including collective bargaining or following conciliation or arbitration, or a mixture of these processes. Awards specifying wages and conditions were determined by the Court (as it was known until 1956) and contained legally enforceable minimum terms and conditions of employment. Awards were a form of quasi-legislation that left scope for the parties to negotiate agreements above this minimum level.

In a key case (*R v Kirby; Ex parte Boilermakers' Society of Australia* HCA 10; 94 CLR 254) in 1956, the High Court ruled that it was unconstitutional for the Court of Conciliation and Arbitration to exercise arbitral as well as judicial powers. The government responded by establishing the Commonwealth Conciliation and Arbitration Commission to conciliate and arbitrate industrial disputes, leaving the Commonwealth

Industrial Court and its successors to interpret and enforce decisions of the Commission (Stewart, 2009). In 1972, the Commission became the Australian Conciliation and Arbitration Commission. In 1977, the Industrial Court was subsumed into a newly created Federal Court.

From its early days, Australian labor market regulation was infused with notions of fairness and was collectivist in character. There were pervasive egalitarian ideas of equity and comparative wage justice. However, the collectivist character began to change in the 1980s as neoliberal ideas became increasingly fashionable. For more than a century, the system consisted of a federal tribunal and six independent state tribunals, with the latter generally exercising jurisdiction over state and local government employees and those in industries that were seen as intra-state in character (e.g. most small and medium sized enterprises). In practice the extent of the federal jurisdiction over dispute settlement varied from state to state. However, the growing role of the federal government alongside the increasing integration of the Australian economy and society were catalysts for the increasing dominance of the federal tribunal. Over time, the federal tribunal became increasingly dominant over the state tribunals with its decisions on key issues being followed to varying degrees by the state tribunals (even though they were legally independent of each other and the federal tribunal). Until the 1980s, industrial relations legislation was silent on the relationships between federal and state tribunals, though informally they developed loose coordination mechanisms (Romeyn and Teicher, 1987).

With the ascendancy of neoliberal ideas, the system of conciliation and arbitration faced increasing criticism, especially from some business interests, employers' organizations and right-wing lobbyists. They argued that the system was too centralized; imposing costs on employers regardless of their capacity to pay. For instance, by 1980 state or federal awards determined pay and conditions for more than 90% of Australian employees (Ellem and Franks, 2008: 51).

In a forlorn effort to defuse this criticism, in 1983 the incoming Labour government commissioned a review of the industrial relations system. The Report of the Committee of Inquiry into Australian Industrial Relations Law and Systems concluded that it would be unwise to abandon the centralized conciliation and arbitration system and undesirable to move away from a collective industrial relations framework (Hancock, 1985). The Report commented approvingly on the centralized system for its ability to: manage Australia's macroeconomic objectives; curb inflation; avoid unemployment; and make decisions in the public interest. It also maintained that those in favor of labor market deregulation ignored the power differentials in the employment relationship.

The Report precipitated a range of criticisms (Fane, 1988; O'Brien, 1994: 449). The government's response was to implement a modest set of reforms in the *Industrial Relations Act 1988* (IR Act), which replaced the C&A Act and renamed the federal tribunal: the Australian Industrial Relations Commission (AIRC). In terms of developing approaches to dispute settlement, the IR Act mandated the inclusion of dispute resolution procedures in "consent awards" and collective agreements (Van Gramberg, 2006). This provision foreshadowed an attempt to encourage dispute resolution at the level of the workplace without tribunal involvement.

Two lobby groups had particular influence in the subsequent transformation of Australian industrial relations. First, the HR Nicholls Society influenced the policies of the right-wing political parties. The Society was strident in its attacks on the Commission, calling for its abolition (e.g. Moore, 2004). Des Moore was influential in the HR Nicholls Society and another conservative lobby group, the Institute for Public Affairs. He denied that there was unequal bargaining power between workers and their employees:

> The labour market is subject to the same economic forces of demand and supply that operate in other markets and the natural distribution of bargaining power does not necessarily favour employers

> (Moore, 1998: 4).

Second, a new employers' organization was formed to represent the largest corporations: the Business Council of Australia (BCA). Its report, *Towards an Enterprise Based Industrial Relations System* (BCA, 1987), emphasized its aim to remove "third parties" (especially unions) and focus on the direct employee–employer relationship. The BCA argued that the pluralist industrial relations system in Australia was outmoded because of its assumption of conflict in the employment relationship:

> We need to jettison the "industrial relations" mindset within our enterprises where it still rests on the outmoded assumption of conflict, and move to "employee relations" in which industrial relations becomes a subsidiary part of relationships at work.

> (BCA, 1989: 5)

The BCA argument was that a move away from a (pluralist) "industrial relations" paradigm to a more unitarist notion would largely avoid workplace conflict, perhaps because the focus would be more about "relationships at work" and the shared goal would be a "competitive advantage" of the enterprise. Under the BCA model, the role of tribunals in dispute settlement would be only marginal, particularly in providing conciliation and arbitration of industrial disputes.

Elements of these arguments were enthusiastically embraced by the federal Treasury and the Labor governments, which held office from 1983 until 1996, on the grounds that a more decentralized model of industrial relations was key to increasing international competitiveness. A Labor government implemented a more profound set of changes, the *Industrial Relations Reform Act 1993* which, among other things, facilitated "enterprise" bargaining, re-cast awards as safety nets, and initiated a federal-level unfair dismissals jurisdiction. The 1993 Act was an important step in shifting the locus of industrial relations regulation and dispute settlement to workplaces, providing, for the first time, for a legislated form of collective bargaining including the right to take lawful industrial action in certain circumstances. The result was a major shift away from the provision of conciliation and arbitration by the Commission, leading to a decline in the proportion of employees covered by awards.

The 1996 election of a coalition of two right-wing parties, the Liberal and National Parties, precipitated a dramatic reshaping of Australian industrial relations and workplace conflict management. This occurred in two stages: first, the *Workplace Relations Act 1996* (WRA) and, second, the *WorkChoices* amendments in 2005. The 1996 Act accelerated the individualization of industrial relations regulation. It provided for a new statutory form of individual "agreement": an Australian Workplace Agreement (AWA) between employers and individual employees (without unions). In practice, AWAs were usually a form of employer-imposed contract with employees as there was no requirement for negotiation to precede the making of an "agreement." Despite the rhetoric about these being individually based agreements, tailored to the needs of the employer and employees, employees performing similar work in an enterprise were usually employed under identical agreements.

The 1996 Act defined the Commission's role as conducting *conciliation*, and, for most practical purposes, it removed the scope for compulsory arbitration from the federal jurisdiction. The underlying policy was that the parties should settle their disputes at workplaces to a much greater extent than previously (Van Gramberg, 2006). For individual disputes arising under AWAs, the 1996 Act provided a model dispute resolution process culminating in private mediation, rather than referral to the Commission (Schedule 9, sub-reg. 30ZI (2)). The Commission retained the power to undertake compulsory arbitration only in the areas of unfair dismissals and actual or threatened stoppages that endangered the economy or public safety. The Liberal–National government not only sought to reduce the role of the Commission, but at least partially to privatize workplace dispute resolution. This was demonstrated by reports which advocated the opportunities for private mediators in Australian workplaces (e.g. Reith, 1999). The government later amended the WRA 1996 to include a model dispute settlement procedure for parties to collective agreements, which also promoted the use of private mediators. These model procedures applied where parties to workplace agreements did not specify a procedure for resolving disputes at the workplace (Stewart, 2009). These changes created the possibility for employers to develop their own dispute resolution procedures without the involvement of the Commission and with little supervision of the practicality of the procedure.

Unexpectedly in the 2004 federal election, the Liberal- National coalition won a majority in both Houses of Parliament. This emboldened that government to enact the *Workplace Relations Amendment Act 2005 (WorkChoices)*. WorkChoices was arguably the most fundamental reshaping of industrial relations regulation in Australia since the early twentieth century, not least as it embodied an attempt to implement a single national system (Teicher et al., 2006). *WorkChoices* relied on the Constitution's "corporations power," which enabled the government to make laws regulating trading and financial corporations, rather than using the more limited "industrial relations power." This wide interpretation of the Constitution was challenged unsuccessfully by the states, with the High Court upholding the validity of laws relating to corporations, regardless of whether the law related to the "foreign, financial or trading" nature of the corporation (Roth and Griffith, 2006). As a result, the path was clear for the federal government to establish a national system of labor market regulation: the states were left with responsibility for employees only in unincorporated organizations, as well as state and local government employees. Further, *WorkChoices* brought into the new national system government employees of state-owned corporations, which were primarily engaged in financial or trading activities.

WorkChoices had specific implications for the management of workplace conflict. Enterprises employing up to 100 employees, the majority of employers, were exempt from the unfair dismissal jurisdiction. *WorkChoices* also exempted employers that undertook genuine redundancies (Stewart, 2009). Hence unfair dismissal claims began to diminish, even though earlier such claims had become a mainstay of the Commission's dispute-settlement work.

Those who designed *WorkChoices* tried to deliver the government's policy of partly privatizing dispute settlement by restricting access to the Commission. The Act also restricted the Commission's scope to offer a range of dispute resolution techniques (particularly compulsory arbitration), but did not impose the same restrictions on private dispute resolution providers. Furthermore, *WorkChoices* limited the range of disputes that the Commission could address. The government's preference for private mediation was explicit in the Explanatory Memorandum) to *WorkChoices*, which promised to:

> establish a system of registered private alternative dispute resolution (ADR) providers that will support genuine choice between the Australian IR Commission's dispute settling expertise and other dispute resolution specialists.

> (House of Representatives, 2005: 21)

Later, in 2006 the government announced financial subsidies for those who wished to use a private mediator under the Alternative Dispute Resolution Assistance Scheme (ADRAS). *WorkChoices* made the process of referring a dispute to the Commission more onerous than opting for a private provider. This bias had the potential to create a boom for private mediators, including law firms, but this did not eventuate, in part because the Liberal–National coalition government lost office in the following year.

The incoming Labor government replaced the *Workplace Relations Act* with the *Fair Work Act 2009* (FWA, 2009). Labor maintained many aspects of the national system implemented by its predecessor. It also tried to operationalize its campaign slogan "Forward with Fairness" to show that it was keeping its pre-election promise to remove some of the "harshest" aspects of *WorkChoices* (Gillard, 2008). The re-naming of the federal tribunal as Fair Work Australia (FWA; later changed to the Fair Work Commission (FWC)) was also emblematic of the Government's fairness agenda.

Under the 2009 Act the Commission gained powers to carry out a wide range of functions including: providing a safety net of minimum conditions among other things providing for minimum wages in awards; facilitating "good faith bargaining" and the making of enterprise agreements; granting remedies for unfair dismissal; regulating industrial action; resolving a range of collective and individual workplace disputes through conciliation, mediation, and in some cases arbitration; other roles in connection with workplace determinations, equal remuneration, transfer of business, general workplace protections, right of entry and stand down.[4]

When making decisions, the Commission has to have regard to "equity, good conscience and the merits of the matter."[5] The 2009 Act removed the provision for individual contracts (AWAs), which had been controversial as their object was to displace collective bargaining and marginalize trade unions. Nevertheless, the Act provided for a diluted form of individual agreements known as Individual Flexibility Agreements (IFAs). An IFA can vary certain award terms to "meet the genuine individual needs of the employer and the individual employee," but only if the employee is "better off overall" compared to the award conditions. This approach built upon the safety-net concept of awards, which employees in certain classification or industries were entitled to receive, unless they genuinely agreed to change them to reflect their personal circumstances. There are restrictions on the use of IFAs (compared to AWAs) as they can be offered only to existing employees and they can vary award terms only in relation to working hours, overtime and penalty rates, allowances and leave loadings. In keeping with the goal of increasing flexibility, there is no requirement for IFAs to be registered with the Commission.[6]

The 2009 Act also made significant changes to unfair dismissal laws, enabling employees to claim for unfair dismissal, provided they met a minimum period of employment criterion and were not excluded for other reasons, for instance, being high-earning employees or employed on short-term employment contracts. In practice, the Commission seeks to settle all such claims by conciliation, but where this fails, it invokes arbitration. Under the Act, the process commences with an attempted conciliation (usually by telephone) conducted by civil servants appointed as conciliators.[7] The Commission becomes involved only if conciliation has failed. When arbitrating, it can reject applications, reinstate dismissed employees or award compensation to a maximum of what the employee would have earned in six months. In one year, 81% of unfair dismissal applications were categorized as resolved at or before conciliation, compared to only 4% that were determined by a Commission decision.[8]

Another feature of the 2009 legislation is that the Commission was required to merge a large number of diverse awards into a smaller and simpler range of "modern awards" and to reinforce the role of awards as a "safety net" mechanism to underpin workplace bargaining. Award modernization strengthened the development of the national system by rationalizing the large number of federal and state awards into fewer "industry" or occupational awards.

During the award modernization process the Commission inserted into all awards a standard dispute resolution clause, which provided for the Commission to conduct mediation or conciliation if the parties are unable to resolve their dispute at the workplace. Unlike the *WorkChoices* regime, the standard procedure enables the Commission to arbitrate with the consent of all the parties.

With regard to enterprise bargaining agreements, the 2009 Act also provides a model procedure for dealing with disputes. Alternatively, the parties may negotiate their own procedure, provided it is consistent with the Act (s.186(6)). Stewart (2009) notes that although less prescriptive than the 1996 Act, the 2009 Act still prescribes how workplace disputes must be handled. The model provides for unresolved workplace disputes to be referred to the Commission for mediation, conciliation, or arbitration where agreed between the parties.

Of course industrial relations tribunals are not the only vehicles for resolving workplace disputes. Employing organizations have informal ways of settling disputes. As already observed, all awards and agreement must include a dispute resolution procedure. Moreover, laws covering occupational health and safety and equal employment opportunity also oblige employers to establish dispute resolution procedures. This situation is further complicated because many enterprises with a well-developed human resources function, establish their own in-house dispute resolution procedures to address a range of rights and interest disputes. Consequently, some enterprises use a variety of dispute procedures and there is not necessarily a clear logic in the choice between these.

The parties and individuals use such procedures to settle most disputes in-house. Those that are referred to tribunals probably represent only the "tip of the iceberg," that is, they are only a small proportion of all the disputes that arise in workplaces. Nonetheless the Commission is still much involved in workplace dispute resolution; for example, Hamberger (2012) reports that approximately 1,600 disputes were referred to the Commission under the terms of a dispute resolution procedure in the year to June 2011.

Two other features of dispute resolution procedures warrant comment. First, the *Fair Work Act* continues to allow independent "third parties" such as private ADR practitioners to resolve disputes (including by arbitration) with the consent of the parties (FWA, 2009: s.740). However, unlike the *WorkChoices* regime, the Commission is no longer marginalized from dispute resolution processes. In practice, the Commission (and the state-based tribunals) are still the prime institutions involved in trying to settle intractable workplace-based conflicts. Second, if the dispute involves an alleged breach of a term of an agreement, an employer, employee, or union involved in the agreement can invoke the dispute settlement process or seek to enforce the agreement in a court. This is in contrast to the widespread practice in the USA of requiring employees in non-union workplaces to sign compulsory employment arbitration clauses; these may remove employees' rights to sue their employer (Seeber and Lipsky, 2006: 724–5; Bingham and Good, 2009; Forsyth, 2012). In practice, relatively few people in Australia seek recourse in the courts. The advantage of utilizing the Commission is that it is a public service, which does not charge fees. Moreover, it is able to settle cases more quickly and less formally than the courts.

Under the 2009 Act there is also provision for compulsory arbitration (known as a "workplace determination") in relation to *interest* disputes, but only under limited circumstances (FWA, 2009: ss. 258–281A). These circumstances are: in relation to low-paid workers where bargaining is unlikely to result in an agreement; where the Commission has issued bargaining orders to facilitate the making of an agreement and it has determined that a serious breach of those orders has occurred; or where the Commission has issued orders terminating protected industrial action and subsequent bargaining has not resolved the issues in dispute. The latter provision was invoked in a major dispute involving the national airline Qantas that threatened major disruption to the economy and society and which was precipitated by the airline's decision to ground its worldwide fleet (Bamber, 2011).[9] Further, the Commission can eventually arbitrate in response to a party failing to obey orders made by the Commission in relation to good faith bargaining. However, by mid-2013, this power had not been used (Smith, 2013).

Commission Members are statutory appointees and hold office until aged 65. Members of the Commission cannot be removed from office by executive government (Smith, 2013). Most are full-time and are appointed from among practitioners with unions, employer organizations, large enterprises, legal practitioners, government officials, or academics in the field of industrial relations or labor economics. In recent years there has been a tendency for Labour governments to appoint more Commission Members from unions, while non-Labour governments have tended to appoint more Commission Members from employers' associations or other sources related to employers. In spite of their previous background, Members are widely regarded as impartial umpires, and this can be ascribed to several factors including their: understanding of the relevant legal and practical issues; scope for the exercise of discretion under the Act is limited; and because decisions are subject to appeal. Disputing parties can appeal Commission decisions to a "full bench" of the Commission and these decisions can be reviewed only by the Federal Court on questions of law and by the High Court on matters relating to an interpretation of the Constitution.

Commission Members are trained in a wide range of ADR techniques including conciliation, mediation, and arbitration. They are skilled in helping employers and employees resolve workplace disputes and can suggest means of resolving differences that may not have been immediately apparent to those directly involved. Nevertheless, the changing nature of workplace disputes has placed increasing pressure on the Members to develop skills and techniques to deal with individual disputes, particularly those raised by unrepresented individuals.

Before the 1990s, nearly all cases submitted to the Commission involved union representation. In the twenty-first century, relatively few cases involve union representation. This change reflects the decline in union density (discussed below) and the growth in the individual rights jurisdiction. The individualization of disputes presents new challenges for the Commission, since many cases involve employees who are "one-time users" and have no experience in presenting cases. In response, the Commission has introduced a pilot program to provide *pro bono* legal advice for unrepresented parties in unfair dismissal matters. This is part of the Commission's *Future Directions* strategy initiated by the current Commission President, Justice Iain Ross.[10]

Future Directions has foreshadowed, appropriately in our view, that by focusing on an agenda to assist workplaces in the prevention and settlement of disputes, as well as promoting harmonious and cooperative workplace relations, the Commission will contribute to more productive and higher performing workplaces. These goals have been central to the federal industrial relations tribunal since its inception and their application to more individualized employment relationships potentially opens a new phase in the Commission's role. Moreover, following the recommendations of a House of Representatives Committee, amendments to the *Fair Work Act* conferred on the Commission the function of "promoting more co-operative and productive workplace relations and the prevention of disputes."[11] As the Commission has long utilized a "panel" system where Members specialize in particular enterprises and industries, this structure is likely to become more important as a vehicle to maintain contact with the industrial relations parties in order to exchange information and to advise on dispute prevention and the promotion of harmonious relations.

THE FAIR WORK OMBUDSMAN

Besides paving the way for the Fair Work Commission, the 2009 Act created another new institution: the Fair Work Ombudsman (FWO). In effect this was a revamping and expansion of the compliance regime that had been established under *WorkChoices*. The FWO's role is "to promote harmonious, productive and cooperative workplace relations and ensure compliance with Australian workplace laws." The FWO provides assistance and advice in relation to compliance with rights and obligations and claims to have particular expertise in relation to small and medium sized enterprises. In exercising its functions, the FWO: offers people a single point of contact for accurate and timely information about Australia's workplace relations system; educating people about fair work practices, rights and obligations; investigating complaints or suspected contraventions of workplace laws, awards, and agreements; litigates to enforce workplace laws; and building strong and effective relationships with industry, unions, and other stakeholders.[12]

As we have observed elsewhere, individual rights have achieved greater prominence under the 2009 Act and this is reflected in the compliance roles of the FWO which relate to adverse action (e.g. dismissal on the grounds of union membership or non-membership); coercion (e.g. demoting a worker for refusing to vote for an enterprise agreement); undue influence (e.g. an employee is forced to cash out his or her annual leave due to an employer threat to close the business to cover the person's absence); or misrepresentation (e.g. knowingly or recklessly misrepresenting to an employee in relation to an entitlement to maternity leave).[13]

In its compliance role, the FWO appoints inspectors to investigate possible breaches of the 2009 Act, awards and agreements, and to undertake litigation as necessary. An under-researched development is the use of trained mediators as part of the enforcement process. Mediation occurs on the recommendation of an inspector and at any time after a complaint is lodged, during an investigation or prior to the taking of legal action. The scope of mediation is prescribed under the FWO Mediation Charter. Complaints that are suitable for mediation may involve: complaints where the facts are in dispute (e.g. hours of work performed or an employee's classification level); or when the amount of alleged underpayment is in dispute; or workplace discrimination.

The mediation unit is separate from the inspectorate and mediators take no part in the subsequent investigation or enforcement. Similarly, inspectors have no access to information disclosed during mediation and mediators are bound to confidentiality. In this way the FWO seeks to ensure that parties are willing to participate in the mediation process and fully cooperate in the discussions that ensue. A mediator has to terminate mediation in certain circumstances, including where an agreement would be illegal or unconscionable. Agreements reached in mediation are not enforceable by the FWO.

Dispute-prone Industries and Occupations

Periodically, governments have seen certain occupations and industries as deserving special treatment in terms of dispute resolution, for instance: if they were particularly prone to disputes; were strategically important to the national economy; or were prone to the exercise of coercion or possibly engaged in criminal conduct. For example, at various times there have been special tribunals with exclusive jurisdiction over airline pilots, waterside workers, coal miners, and building and construction workers. At present special regulations apply only to the building industry.

In 2012, the Labor government created an independent agency, Fair Work Building and Construction to implement another of an election promise to abolish the former Australian Building and Construction Commission (ABCC). The former Liberal–National government had initiated that Commission following a Royal Commission investigating unlawful industrial conduct in the building industry and had given the ABCC coercive powers over unions and industrial action. Unlike earlier special tribunals, Fair Work Building and Construction has not been involved in setting pay and conditions in the industry. As an example of how public policy in this field reflects changing governments, a coalition of the Liberal Party and the National Party elected in September 2013 has promised to abolish Fair Work Building and Construction, and to re-establish the ABCC. It saw a revived ABCC as a regulator with significantly increased powers and funding as necessary to suppress union 'lawlessness' in the sector.[14]

Changing Patterns of Workplace Conflict

In Australia data are collected on a range of overt forms of industrial conflict including unauthorized stop-work meetings; general strikes; sympathy strikes; political or protest strikes; rotating or revolving strikes (i.e. strikes which occur when workers at different locations take turns to stop work); unofficial strikes; and work stoppages initiated by employers. The Australian Bureau of Statistics (ABS) records industrial disputes only if the number of working days lost by an employer is at least ten in a particular enterprise. This approach is in accord with international guidelines adopted by the 1993 International Conference of Labour Statisticians.

Figure 20.1 shows that the number of working days lost due to industrial disputes per year has declined from a peak of about 6 million in 1974 to a low of 50,000 in 2007. In recent years there has been a small increase in working days lost. For example, working days lost due to industrial disputes rose from 50,000 days in 2007 to 241,000 in 2011 (see Figure 20.1).

Figure 20.2 shows that the decline in working days lost due to industrial disputes has taken place almost simultaneously in different sectors of the economy, though these data are not available for all sectors. Figure 20.2 also shows that the recent increase in working days lost to industrial disputes is most dramatic in the mining sector due to a combination of factors including a return to collective industrial relations under the 2009 Act and strong export demand for Australian minerals.

It could be concluded that the decline in strikes after the 1970s presages the end of workplace conflict; however, there is much evidence that there is still widespread, but less visible conflict in the form of individual and small group disputes. This phenomenon is not confined to Australia, but is evident in other liberal market economies. Bingham (2003) finds a decline in collective disputes in the US, but a concurrent rise in individual conflicts. Walker and Hamilton (2011: 40) observe similar trends in the UK

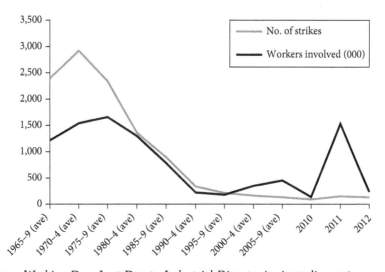

FIGURE 20.1 Working Days Lost Due to Industrial Disputes in Australia, 1969–2011

Source: Industrial Disputes, Australia (ABS cat. no. 6321.0.55.001).

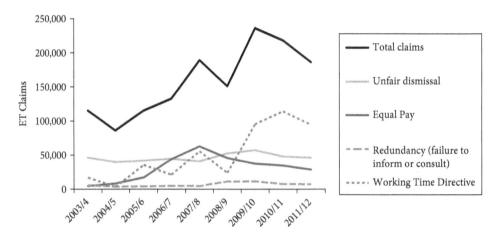

FIGURE 20.2 Working Days Lost Due to Industrial Disputes by Industry

Source: Industrial Disputes, Australia (ABS cat. no. 6321.0.55.001).

where individual employees have filed claims and lawsuits to a greater extent than in the past, leading them to conclude that "individual disputes may now be the most relevant indicator of conflict." Similarly Godard (2011: 283) asks: "if conflict is fundamental to the employment relation, has it simply been diverted into alternative, these less organized and less overt forms since the 1970s?"

In the Australian context too there has been a growth in reports of individualized workplace conflict. As shown in Figure 20.3, since 2000 there has been an increasing number of complaints that involve employment discrimination to the Australian Human Rights Commission (AHRC) and its predecessor, the Human Rights and Equal Opportunity Commission (HREOC). The 84% increase observed in the areas of disability, sex, race, and age between 2004–5 and 2010–11 is unlikely to be entirely a result of growing public awareness of these avenues for resolving complaints. These employment-related complaints constitute the largest proportion of matters dealt with in the areas of disability, sex, race, and age discrimination; for example, in the last decade, employment-related complaints constituted 86% of all areas of complaint under the *Sex Discrimination Act 1984*, 44% of areas under the *Racial Discrimination Act 1975*, 44% of areas under the *Disability Discrimination Act 1992*, and 62% of areas under the *Age Discrimination Act 2004* (HREOC, 2010). In interpreting these data it should be noted that one complaint may involve multiple areas in which discrimination is reported to have occurred. Despite the general growth in the number of complaints, there was been a slight reduction in the total number of complaints to the AHRC in 2010–11, but it is too soon to judge whether this is a trend or an outlier.

The increased number of "informal enquiries" to the AHRC concerning employment-related matters provides another indicator of the continuing incidence

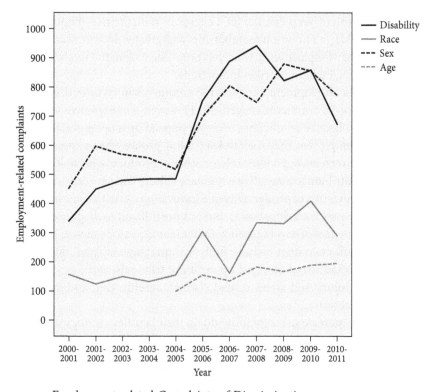

FIGURE 20.3 Employment-related Complaints of Discrimination

Note: The Age Discrimination Act has only been in existence since 2004–5.

Source: HREOC/AHRC Annual Reports.

of workplace conflict. These are enquiries made by employees seeking advice and information, often at an early stage of their conflict, and may herald future claims. The number of informal enquiries grew by 178% to 3,787 between 2000–1 and 2010–11.[15] In another area of individual dispute notifications, the Fair Work Commission's predecessors recorded an increase in the number of disputes referred from failed workplace dispute settling procedures from 851 in 2004–5 to 1,243 in 2009 (AIRC, 2009). This type of data is no longer collected but, unofficially, Hamberger (2012) notes that as many as 1,600 disputes were referred to the Commission in 2010/11 as a result of a failed workplace dispute procedure. Thus, while strikes have subsided, workplace conflict as a whole has not.

As explained above, since the 1980s, a series of Australian industrial relations reforms have contributed to decentralizing the locus of industrial relations regulation. The increasing enterprise focus has tended to reflect unitarist assumptions, for example, the assumption that individual employment relationships are less likely than collective relationships to result in overt conflict (cf. Fox, 1974). With the rise of human resources management (HRM), fall in union membership, and greater decentralization of industrial relations to the workplace level, there has been a decline in the level of overt collective industrial action, including strikes in Australia.

Superficially, this development supports the arguments in favor of the deregulation and decentralization of conflict management. However, an alternative view is that in some cases overt collective conflict has been suppressed or is not a practicable option. As a result, some employees may seek to keep a low profile when expressing negative feelings through absenteeism, poor morale, or other unproductive behaviors. Aggrieved employees may contribute to a negative workplace culture and generally do not work to their full potential in terms of productivity and innovation. As with overt industrial conflict, such behavior may have direct costs, but is more difficult to diagnose and respond to than the consequences of covert conflict. Other manifestations such as less organized and individual forms of conflict include: bullying, interpersonal, and individual grievances submitted to industrial or equal opportunity tribunals, workers' compensation claims (including injury and stress-related claims), absenteeism, and labor turnover (e.g. Shulruf et al., 2009).

Such conflicts may create stress for individuals, their families, communities, and society and they place high costs on employers. Fox and Stallworth (2008), for instance, have noted that workplace bullying alone results in loss of productivity, increased accidents, diminished corporate reputation, high turnover, absenteeism, strained loyalty, distrust, sabotage, resentment, uncivil climate, decreased communication, potential escalation to workplace aggression or violence as well as the direct costs of legal liability and higher workers' compensation. Further, much damage in workplaces is caused by the adverse behaviors of those who feel aggrieved (Goldman et al., 2008). Disputes impact not only on employers, but also on the health of workers (Kieseker and Marchant, 1999). Increasingly it is recognized that illnesses may be induced or exacerbated by workplace conflict (Bowles and Cooper, 2010). The Australian Productivity Commission (2010: 287) reports the annual costs to the economy could be as high as AU$36 billion. We conclude that if we adopt a broad definition, workplace conflict is not disappearing. Against this background, the role of unions in workplaces and their relationship to conflict is worth considering.

AUSTRALIAN UNIONS AND DECLINING COLLECTIVISM

The first unions in Australia were formed in the nineteenth century and for the most part they were independent of British unions. Nevertheless, they displayed similar characteristics to the range of unions that were in Ireland and the UK, reflecting the predominant source of Australian immigration. There is a comprehensive regulation and reporting regime for unions, which is contained in the *Fair Work (Registered Organisations) Act 2009* (ROA). Under this legislation, unions have a range of rights and responsibilities in relation to their members' industrial relations interests. Unions have the right to enter employers' premises to investigate suspected breaches of the 2009 Act and of awards or enterprise agreements that relate to employees. This role has been longstanding and complements the enforcement of rights of the FWO, but the right of entry was greatly restricted under the *Workplace Relations Act 1996* and the incoming Liberal-National coalition government has promised a return to a restrictive regime.

Union density peaked at about 61% in 1954; it remained at a relatively high level until the mid-1970s after which it went into a long-term decline (Ellem and Franks, 2008: 46). By 2011 union density had fallen to 18% (20% for full-time employees and 14% for part-time employees). Union membership is higher in the public sector (43%) compared to only 13% of private-sector employees (ABS 2011). Union density is still relatively high in the utilities, transport, public administration, health care, and education.

Some commentators seem to assume that, in general, the decline of industrial action (including strikes) is associated with the decline of union density (e.g. Shalev, 1992). There may be an association, in that industrial action requires a level of organization, planning, and consultation that unions have generally provided for their members. Also unions are registered under Australian law for the purposes of representing their members, for instance, in industrial tribunals and making enterprise agreements. In the process of making agreements, unions may also organize legal forms of industrial action (protected action). Without this facilitation of legal industrial action, unions and individuals may be subject to heavy penalties under State and federal laws. In particular, the 2009 Act contains strict procedures that must be followed in order for industrial action to be "protected." With the decline of union density in many industries, there are fewer opportunities for employees to organize strikes or other types of collective action. Declining industrial action, then, may more accurately reflect the decline in a potential voice mechanism than a decline in workplace conflict (Pyman et al., 2010).

In the absence of a union to represent them, employees perceiving an injustice at work do not have a union avenue for dealing with their disputes either individually or collectively. However, as we have shown, increasingly disputes are settled in an individualized way through machinery that includes dispute-settlement procedures, and tribunals that deal with discrimination or occupational health and safety and workers' compensation.

Conclusions

From the early days of the Australian Federation, the regulation and management of workplace conflict was premised upon forms of publicly provided dispute resolution in which registered organizations (trade unions, employers, and employers' organizations) were the participants. Legislation providing for a national system of workplace dispute resolution was enacted in 1904 (but the development of a truly national system took much longer), and while the legislation has been much amended and renamed over the years, there has been a surprising degree of continuity, particularly in relation to the federal tribunal.

The history of Australian industrial relations regulation demonstrated the early growth in the role and significance of the federal tribunal. This continued until the late 1980s, when a mixture of economic and political forces initiated the trend to decentralize dispute resolution and in some ways to re-regulate the industrial relations system, especially in relation to union behavior and industrial action. While the major political parties broadly agreed on the notion of decentralization, they differed fundamentally on the role of institutions, particularly unions and industrial tribunals in the conflict management machinery. Consequently, changes of government have precipitated major changes to the legislation as is illustrated by the introduction of the *Workplace Relations Act 1996*, the subsequent *WorkChoices* laws and then the *Fair Work* Act 2009. With the election of a coalition of Liberal and National parties in 2013 further changes have been foreshadowed, but lacking a Senate majority such changes are not imminent.

We draw three broad conclusions: the decline of unions, the longevity of the Commission, and the impact of the changing nature of workplace disputes. First, the decline in union membership in Australia has had ramifications both for the manifestation of workplace conflict and its consequences. Strikes are at relatively low levels, but the growth of individual disputes raised under employment rights legislation has led to a phenomenon of unrepresented employees attempting to argue their cases before the federal and other tribunals. As noted, the Commission is developing support mechanisms such as *pro bono* advice to assist these litigants.

Second, the Commission has remained a relevant and crucial part of workplace conflict resolution. *WorkChoices* significantly weakened the national tribunal and attempted unsuccessfully to induce a shift to private dispute resolution through measures including mandatory dispute-resolution procedures in enterprise bargaining and individual agreements, which provided for private mediators rather than the Commission. There is still relatively little private workplace dispute resolution in Australia. Under the 2009 Act the Fair Work Commission has a bigger role than under *WorkChoices* in dispute resolution, in terms of interest and rights disputes. Some of its powers to conduct voluntary and compulsory arbitration have been restored if not enhanced. One development has been to partially reinstate the Commission's role in workplace dispute resolution, including through the model dispute resolution procedures.

The Commission has demonstrated its ability to respond flexibly to the shift from collective to more individualized disputes and through its current change strategy, *Future*

Directions, it will engage more directly with workplaces and industries to promote a more proactive approach to harmonious workplace relations. The Commission's longevity contrasts with the situation of public dispute settlement agencies in some countries, which have struggled to maintain their role in the face of fewer strikes, declining union density, less collective bargaining, and budget cuts.

The third conclusion relates to the nature and manifestation of workplace conflict in Australia. The shift to a re-regulated system of industrial relations, which has been associated with declining union membership and workplace-based agreement making, has not seen industrial conflict disappear. Rather there has been a change in the form of industrial conflict and in particular an increase in the number of individual disputes, as indicated by the growing streams of court and tribunal cases for unfair or unlawful dismissal, harassment, bullying, workplace stress, and similar issues. Consequently, Australian tribunals continue to be busy, though they are dealing with rights-based disputes, to a greater extent than interest-based disputes.

The post-2009 regime is the latest episode of independent, government-sponsored management of workplace conflict in Australia. In general, the 2009 Act meets international standards of best practice for the resolution of disputes about individual employment rights as well as disputes about interests (Forsyth, 2012). The prevention and settlement of disputes has been an historical objective of the governing legislation, but has recently become an explicit function of the Commission and will constitute much of its new advisory role to workplaces. In this way, the Australian system may move closer to its roots and to its counterparts such as the Advisory Conciliation and Arbitration Service (ACAS) in the UK.

Policy-makers in several other countries have been keen to learn from the Commission's long experience of conflict management in Australia. In view of the history of frequent changes to the legislative framework, it is uncertain how the Commission's role and the regulatory regime will change in the years ahead. As in the past, much will depend on the prevailing national political and economic priorities and ideologies.

ACKNOWLEDGMENTS

We acknowledge that the research on which this chapter draws was made possible by an Australian Research Council (ARC) Discovery Project grant to the authors. We are grateful to current and former members of the Fair Work Commission (or its predecessors) whom we interviewed including those who commented helpfully on a draft of this chapter: Jonathan Hamberger, Joe Isaac, and Greg Smith. We also thank Dr Youqing Fan who helped to compile the data included in this chapter.

NOTES

1. When we discuss the government, tribunals, and the Commission, unless otherwise specified, this means the federal Government of the Commonwealth of Australia and the federal tribunals or the Fair Work Commission and its national level predecessors. The Commission has full jurisdiction over all employers and employees in the territories and the State of Victoria. There are state-based tribunals in the other five states. Their policies and practices may differ from those of the Commission. However, the latter exerts a national leadership role and the majority of employees are in the jurisdiction of the Fair Work Commission. State governments' policies and practices may differ from those of the federal Government, especially if competing political parties lead these governments. There is insufficient space here to consider variations in the states or the role of the courts, which may exercise judicial power in relation to conflict management in organizations especially in difficult cases.
2. <http://australia.gov.au/about-australia/australian-stories/history-colonial-conflict-and-modern>.
3. For a short glossary of Australian industrial-relations terms, see: <www.fwc.gov.au/index.cfm?pagename=assistglossary> accessed 1 Apr. 2013.
4. <www.fwa.gov.au/index.cfm?pagename=aboutrole> accessed 25 Feb. 2013.
5. Section 578(b) of the *Fair Work Act 2009* (Cth).
6. <www.findlaw.com.au/articles/4622/how-flexible-are-individual-flexibility-agreements.aspx> accessed 4 Dec. 2012.
7. <www.fwa.gov.au/index.cfm?pagename=dismissalsprocess> accessed 26 Dec. 2012.
8. Fair Work Australia, *Annual Report 2011–12, Melbourne*: 28, available at: <www.fwc.gov.au/documents/annual_reports/ar2012/FWA_Annual_Report_2011-12.pdf>.
9. Also see: <www.aph.gov.au/About_Parliament/Parliamentary_Departments/Parliamentary_Library/pubs/BN/2011-2012/ChronQantas> accessed 27 Feb. 2013.
10. <www.fwc.gov.au/documents/media/releases/29-Oct-2012.pdf>   <www.fwc.gov.au/documents/media/releases/15-Mar-2013.pdf> accessed 31 Mar. 2013.
11. <www.aph.gov.au/Parliamentary_Business/Bills_Legislation/Bills_Search_Results/Result?bId=r5028> accessed 13 May 2013.
12. <www.fairwork.gov.au/about-us/our-role/pages/default.aspx> accessed 27 Dec. 2012 and www.comlaw.gov.au/Details/C2013A00073 accessed 18 Dec. 2013.
13. <www.fairwork.gov.au/employment/general-protections/pages/what-are-workers-protected-from.aspx> accessed 27 Feb. 2013.
14. <http://ministers.employment.gov.au/abetz/strong-and-effective-watchdog-building-industry>.
15. These are the enquiries that are explicitly work-based and use employment enquiries to the former Human Rights and Equal Opportunity Commission (HREOC) as well as to its successor: the Australian Human Rights Commission (AHRC).

REFERENCES

ABS 2011. Catalogue number 6321.0.55.001—Industrial Disputes, Australia, Sept. available at <http://www.abs.gov.au/AUSSTATS/abs@.nsf/Lookup/6321.0.55.001Explanatory%20Notes1Sep%202011?OpenDocument>.

AIRC 2009. *Annual Report of the President of the Australian Industrial Relations Commission 2008–2009.* Canberra: AGPS.

Australian Productivity Commission 2010. *Performance Benchmarking of Australian Business Regulation: Occupational Health & Safety.* Research Report, Canberra.

Baker, D. 2001. "Barricades and Batons: A Historical Perspective of the Policing of Major Industrial Disorder in Australia." In M. Enders and B. Dupont (eds.), *Policing the Lucky Country.* Annandale, NSW: Hawkins Press.

Bamber, G. J. 2011. "The Qantas Dispute: What Next and a Recap." *The Conversation,* published online 23 Nov. 2011 <http://theconversation.edu.au/the-qantas-dispute-what-next-and-a-recap-4411> accessed 28 Oct. 2012.

Bamber G. J., Pochet, P., Allan, C., Block, R., Burchill, F., Cuillerier, J., Fitzner, G., French, B., Hickox, S., Keller, B., Moore, M. L., Murhem, S., Murray, G., Nakamichi, A., Nienhauser, W., and Rasmussen, E. 2010. "Regulating Employment Relations, Work and Labour Laws: International Comparisons between Key Countries." Special Issue, *Bulletin of Comparative Labour Relations,* 74.

Bingham, L. B. 2003. *Mediation at Work: Transforming Workplace Conflict at the United States Postal Service.* Arlington, VA: IBM Center for The Business of Government.

Bingham, L. B. and Good, D. H. 2009. "A Better Solution to Moral Hazard in Employment Arbitration: It is Time to Ban Predispute Binding Arbitration Clauses." *Minnesota Law Review* Headnotes, 93(1): 1–13.

Bowles, D. and Cooper, C. 2010. *Employee Morale: Driving Performance in Challenging Times.* New York: Palgrave Macmillan.

Business Council of Australia (BCA) 1987. "Towards an Enterprise Based Industrial Relations System." *Business Council Bulletin,* 32.

Business Council of Australia (BCA) 1989. *Enterprise-based Bargaining Units: A Better Way of Working.* Business Council of Australia, Melbourne.

Creighton, B. 2000. "One Hundred Years of the Conciliation and Arbitration Power: A Province Lost?" *Melbourne University Law Review,* 33.

Ellem, B. and Franks, P. 2008. "Trade Union Structure and Politics in Australia and New Zealand." *Labour History,* 95(1): 43–67.

Fane, G. 1988. "Reforming Australian Industrial Relations Law: A Review of the Hancock Report." *Australian Journal of Management,* 13(2): 223–252.

Forsyth, A. 2012. "Workplace Conflict Resolution in Australia: The Dominance of the Public Dispute Resolution Framework and the Limited Role of ADR." *International Journal of Human Resource Management,* 23(3): 476–494.

Fox, A. 1974. *Beyond Contract: Work, Power and Trust Relations.* London: Faber and Faber Limited.

Fox, S. and Stallworth, L. E. 2008. "Bullying and Mobbing in the Workplace and the Potential Role of Mediation and Arbitration Pursuant to the Proposed National Employment Dispute Resolution Act," in S. F. Befort, P. Halter, and P. Staudohar (eds.), *Arbitration 2007: Workplace Justice for a Changing Environment: Proceedings of the Sixtieth Annual Meeting National Academy of Arbitrators.* Arlington, VA: BNA, 161–225.

Gillard, The Hon. J. 2008. "Introducing Australia's New Workplace Relations System." Speech delivered to The National Press Club, Canberra, 17 Sept. available at: <http://ministers.deewr.gov.au/gillard/introducing-australias-new-workplace-relations-system>.

Godard, J. 2011. "What has Happened to Strikes?" *British Journal of Industrial Relations*, 49(2): 282–305.

Goldman, B. M., Cropanzano, R., Stein, J. H., Shapiro, D. L., Thatcher, S. and Ko, J. 2008. "The Role of Ideology in Mediated Disputes at Work: a Justice Perspective." *International Journal of Conflict Management*, 19(3): 210–233.

Hall, P. A. and Soskice, D. (eds.) 2001. *Varieties of Capitalism: The Institutional Foundations of Comparative Advantage*. Oxford: Oxford University Press.

Hamberger, J. 2012. "The Development of a Dual System of Workplace Dispute Resolution in Large Australian Organisations." *Advances in Industrial and Labour Relations*, 20: 139–59.

Hancock, K. 1985. *Report of the Committee of Review into Australian Industrial Relations Law and Systems*. Canberra: AGPS.

Harbridge, R., Fraser, B., and Walsh, P. 2006. "Industrial Relations in Australia and New Zealand: The Path from Conciliation and Arbitration." In M. Morley, P. Gunnigle, and D. Collings (eds), *Global Industrial Relations*. Oxford: Routledge.

Higgins, H. B. 1915. "A New Province for Law and Order." *Harvard Law Review*, 29: 13–39.

HREOC 2010. "Australian Human Rights Commission Annual Report 2009–2010." Australian Human Rights Commission, Canberra, available at: <www.humanrights.gov.au/about/publications/annual_reports/200809-10/>.

HR Nicholls Society 2012. "The Aims of the Society." Available at: <http://www.hrnicholls.com.au/aims.php>.

Kieseker, R. and Marchant, T. 1999. "Workplace Bullying in Australia: A Review of Current Conceptualisations and Existing Research." *Australian Journal of Management and Organisational Behaviour*, 2(5): 61–75.

Lansbury, R. D. and Wailes, N. 2011. "Employment Relations in Australia." In G. J. Bamber, R. D. Lansbury, and N. Wailes (eds.), *International and Comparative Employment Relations: Globalisation and Change*, 5th edn. London: Sage; Sydney: Allen & Unwin, 117–37.

Moore, D. 1998. "The Case for Further Deregulation of the Labour Market." Research Paper prepared on Behalf of Contributing Members of the Labour Ministers Council. Canberra: Department of Employment, Workplace Relations and Small Business (DEEWR), available at: <http://foi.deewr.gov.au/system/files/doc/other/the_case_for_further_deregulation_of_the_labour_market.pdf>.

Moore, D. 2004. "Overmighty Judges: 100 Years of Holy Grail is Enough." Paper presented to the HR Nicholls Society's XXVth Conference, 6–8 Aug. Melbourne: HR Nicholls, available at: <www.hrnicholls.com.au/archives/vol25/moore2004.pdf>.

O'Brien, J. 1994. "McKinsey, Hilmer and the BCA: The 'New Management' Model of Labour Market Reform." *Journal of Industrial Relations*, 34(2): 468–91.

Pyman, A., Holland, P., Teicher, J., and Cooper, B. 2010. "Industrial Relations Climate, Employee Voice and Managerial Attitudes to Unions: An Australian Study." *British Journal of Industrial Relations*, 48(2): 460–80.

Reith, P. 1999. "The Continuing Reform of Workplace Relations: Implementation of 'More Jobs, Better Pay'," *Implementation Discussion Paper*, 6 May, Canberra: AGPS.

Romeyn, J. and Teicher, J. 1987. "The Role of State and Special Tribunals." In G. W. Ford, J. M. Hearn, and R. D. Lansbury (eds.), *Australian Labour Relations Readings*. 4th edn. Melbourne: Macmillan, 147–78.

Roth, L. and Griffith, G. 2006. "The Workplace Relations Case: Implications for the States." NSW Parliamentary Library Research Service Briefing Paper No. 18/06, Nov. Sydney.

Seeber, R. L. and Lipsky, D. B. 2006. "The Ascendancy of Employment Arbitrators in US Employment Relations: A New Actor in the American System?" *British Journal of Industrial Relations*, 44(4): 719–56.

Shalev, M. 1992. "The Resurgence of Labour Quiescence." In M. Regini (ed.), *The Future of Labour Movements*. London: Sage, 102–32.

Shulruf, B., Woodhams, B., Howard, C., Johri, R., and Yee, B. (2009). "Grievance Gravy Train Picking up Speed: Myths and Reality around Employment Disputes in New Zealand." *Journal of Industrial Relations*, 51(2): 245–61.

Smith, G. R. 2013. "ASEAN Workshop on Resolving Employment Disputes." Unpublished Paper. Melbourne: Fair Work Commission.

Stewart, A. 2009. "Fair Work Australia: The Commission Re-born?" Sir Richard Kirby Lecture, Industrial Relations Society of Victoria, Melbourne, 21 May.

Svensen, S. 1995. *Industrial War: The Great Strikes 1890–1894*. Wollongong, NSW: Ram Press.

Teicher, J., Lambert, R., and O'Rourke, A. (eds.) 2006. *Workchoices: The New Industrial Relations Agenda*. Frenchs Forest, NSW: Pearson.

Van Gramberg, B. 2006. *Managing Workplace Conflict: Alternative Dispute Resolution in Australia*. Sydney: Federation Press.

Walker, B. and Hamilton, R. T. 2011. "Employee–employer Grievances: A Review." *International Journal of Management Reviews* 13(1): 40–50.

Workplace Relations Amendment (Work Choices) Bill 2005 Explanatory Memorandum, available at: <www.austlii.edu.au/au/legis/cth/bill_em/wracb2005428/memo_0.html>.

Websites

Australia   <http://australia.gov.au/about-australia/australian-stories/history-colonial-conflict-and-modern> accessed 14 Oct. 2012.

<www.fairwork.gov.au/about-us/our-role/pages/default.aspx> accessed 22 Oct. 2012.

<www.findlaw.com.au/articles> accessed 4 Dec. 2012.

<www.fwa.gov.au/index.cfm?pagename=aboutrole> accessed 23 Oct. 2012.

<www.fwc.gov.au/documents/media/releases/15-Mar-2013.pdf> accessed 31 Mar. 2013.

<www.fwc.gov.au/index.cfm?pagename=assistglossary> accessed 1 Apr. 2013.

Legislation and Legal Cases Cited*

Commonwealth of Australia Explanatory Memoranda Fair Work Act 2009 <http://www.austlii.edu.au/au/legis/cth/bill_em/fwb2009124/memo_0.html> accessed 13 May 2013>.

* All are in the Commonwealth jurisdiction.

Conciliation and Arbitration Act 1904 Industrial Relations Act 1988 (IR Act) *Workplace Relations Act 1996* (WRA).

Workplace Relations Amendment Act 2005 (*WorkChoices*) *Fair Work Act 2009* (FWA 2009).

R v Kirby; Ex parte Boilermakers' Society of Australia HCA 10; 94 CLR 254

CHAPTER 21

CONFLICT RESOLUTION IN NEW ZEALAND

ERLING RASMUSSEN AND GAYE GREENWOOD

INTRODUCTION

LEGISLATIVE structures and state-sponsored employment institutions (see Table 21.1) have had an enduring influence on employment relations conflict and dispute resolution in Aotearoa[1] New Zealand. The country has possessed highly regulated, state-funded conflict and dispute resolution institutions since setting up the world's first national conciliation and arbitration system in 1894. While state-sponsored dispute resolution processes remain dominant, several far-reaching changes have taken place to public policy and the dispute resolution system in recent decades. These changes have both reflected and accelerated a shift from collective conflict to individual employment disputes. In terms of public policy interventions, the changes have heralded a move away from formal legalism and precedent in employment relationship dispute resolution and the instalment of a wide range of process options on the dispute resolution continuum from informal negotiation, mediation, and facilitation to inquisitorial determination. The main argument of this chapter is that while state provision of conflict resolution mechanisms remain embedded, these arrangements have been subject to almost continuous reform to the extent that a strong preference has emerged for individual employment disputes and workplace bargaining being settled through informal processes rather than judicial intervention.

The chapter is organized as follows. The first section provides a historical overview of the pre-1991 conciliation and arbitration system. The next section discusses the radical reform of the public dispute resolution system for employment introduced by the Employment Contracts Act 1991 (ECA). The third section highlights the tensions

Table 21.1 New Zealand Employment Institutions: Processes and Outcomes

Legislation	Employment Institutions	Purpose	Process	Outcomes
Industrial Conciliation and Arbitration Act 1894	Conciliation Boards elected employer & employee representatives chaired by Government appointed commissioners	Intended to create informal state sponsored dispute resolution conciliation service. Intervention in labor disputes, impose settlement if parties were unable to resolve differences in collective disputes.	Conciliation Boards investigated and conciliators made decisions. Positional distributive bargaining Lack of preliminary processes Political appointments	Prohibited strikes and lockouts during conciliation and arbitration. No process for resolution of individual personal grievances some unions deregistered to enable individual employer–union negotiations.
	The Arbitration Court	Heard appeals on conciliation decisions, made binding judgments, awards, and set wages and conditions for registered union labor.	Judges from the Supreme Court elected assessors from employer associations and union representatives to inform binding judgments, awards, and set wages and conditions.	Strengthened weak unions' bargaining position with employers through wage fixing across industry sectors
The Industrial Conciliation and Arbitration Amendment 1970	Industrial mediation service	Mediation in the workplace	Government representatives provided mediation services for collective bargaining Introduction of mediation of personal grievances for union members	Perceived lack of neutrality of government appointed mediators, power bargaining, lack of preliminary processes, lack of understanding about the role of the mediator lack of power for mediator intervention, resistance to option generation and eagerness for strike and lockout

The Industrial Relations Act 1973	Industrial Mediation Service Industrial Conciliation Service The Arbitration Court	To improve industrial relations by differentiating between disputes of 'rights' and interests. Disputes of 'interests' were created to procure a collective agreement or an award setting terms and conditions. Initiation of collective bargaining required identification of disputes of 'interests'. Disputes of 'rights' concerned the interpretation, application or operation of a collective agreement or award or a personal grievance.	Mediators' aimed to prevent industrial disputes by maintaining close liaison with industry offering facilitation to assist settlement make suggestions and recommendations and, where the parties agreed, make decisions. Mediators were prohibited from intervention in disputes of interest where conciliation or arbitration proceedings had begun. Disputes of interest were facilitated by Conciliation service conciliators who conducted processes for preliminary exchange of information and mediation but did not make decisions. Conciliators chaired industrial disputes committees for disputes of rights where decisions were made and appealable in the Arbitration Court. Personal grievances involved hierarchical process: (1) self-help submission to supervisor, (2) union branch secretary acted as advocate, (3) submission of the case to a grievance committee with representatives from the union and the employer in attendance, if there was no settlement nor agreement reached dispute was referred to the Arbitration Court	Introduction of the right to take a personal grievance for union members The Mediation service concentrated on rights and grievances while the conciliation service focused on collective bargaining. Mediator focus was on prevention and education of parties in dispute. Public confusion about procedural differences between mediation and conciliation. Mediators often arbitrated.
The Employment Contracts Act 1991	The Employment Tribunal The Employment Court	Abolition of the mediation service. Individual employees permitted to take their own personal grievance to the Employment Tribunal irrespective of union membership. Dual emphasis on mediation and adjudication.	Provide mediation and adjudication, however the same person did not provide both processes. No longer med/arb hybrid approach. Increased focus on case law and precedent in the Tribunal.	Rise in the number of personal grievances and individual disputes. Rise in legal representation at mediation and increased lay advocacy. Widespread critique of overzealous legal advocacy, increased costs for parties in dispute and long delays for mediation in the Tribunal.

(Continued)

Table 21.1 Continued

Legislation	Employment Institutions	Purpose	Process	Outcomes
The Employment Relations Act 2000	Call centre 0800 number and Website fact sheets Employment Relations Service	Provision of self-help information for negotiation of employment relationship problems. Aimed for provision of 'free, fast, fair' (Wilson, 2000) confidential mediation service, which was formerly provided through the Department of Labour and currently by the Ministry of Business Innovation and Employment.	Provision of materials to guide parties to resolve workplace conflict themselves. Direction to fact sheets employment rights, agreement writing, and employment law. Referrals to union employer associations, lawyers, community law centres and citizens advice bureaus and the mediation service. Mediated settlements whether settled privately outside mediation and forwarded for recording or settled in the state sponsored mediation service are signed off by mediators under s149 ERA 2000. Settlement agreements are confidential to the parties and the mediation service; do not go to the Employment Relations Authority except in circumstances involving enforcement and compliance. There is wide statutory protection of confidentiality during mediation. Any oral or written statements, admissions made, documents produced or created are all protected specifically at s148. In addition, to no evidence being admissible in any court or judicial body nothing in the Official information Act 1982 can apply to any part of the mediation s149 (3). Mediators can provide written recommendations by s149 (1) at the parties written request. Recommendation/s can become final binding and enforceable by s 149(1) (b) ERA unless one or both of the parties do not accept the recommendation/s149 (3). ERA. A party may not seek to challenge an accepted recommendation in the Authority or the Court BY s149(5)(b) ERA.	The primary work of mediators continues to be personal grievances following employees' termination of employment. Around 95% of employment relationship problems were referred to the Mediation Service and were settled without referral onto the Employment Relations Authority (see Department of Labour, 2012a). Mediators and Employment Relations Authority members have been involved in high profile collective bargaining cases in the New Zealand police and fire services and other sectors including health, meat industry, rest home, manufacturing, energy, and transport and stevedore sectors.

Institution	Role	Description	Commentary
Employment Relations Authority	Facilitation of collective bargaining Determination in the Employment Relations Authority	ERA 2000 was amended in 2010 to include early assistance mediation which may include processes such as conflict mapping, conflict coaching, and interactive workshops. If parties cannot reach agreement during mediation then they can pursuant to s150 of the ERA 2000 request the mediator make a final binding decision that cannot be challenged in the Employment Relations Authority thus mediators make decisions at the parties' request. An inquisitorial process led by an Authority Member who has the power to explore the facts of the case in an informal manner by: holding interviews, calling meetings, requesting evidence, conducting investigations and reaching decisions on the merits of the case rather than legal technicalities.	While the ERA 2000 has enhanced the existing Employment Institutions with the purpose of prevention and resolution of employment relationship problems rather than adherence to rigid formal procedures (McAndrew et al. 2004) those aims are less likely to be realized in the Employment Relations Authority since the 2010 amendments at s160 (2) (2A) allow cross-examination.
The Employment Court	Litigation: judicial hearing seeking of damages, injunction compliance, or challenge determination of the Employment Relations Authority.	Challenges to a determination of the Employment Relations Authority involve a full judicial hearing de novo—the case is heard afresh. The Court and the Authority must determine whether mediation would be of no further use. If the Authority member or Judge deems the dispute resolvable by mediation refer the parties back to mediation by s159 (1)(a) (b) ERA2000.	

encountered by public dispute resolution bodies when trying to balance the right to collective action with the rise of individual employment disputes. The following section takes a closer look at the significant growth in the number of individual and personal grievances that have occurred since the passing of the ECA 1991. The penultimate section examines the changing character of collective disputes highlighted by recent industrial action in the film and waterfront industries. The conclusion brings together the arguments of the chapter.

HISTORICAL CONTEXT

Prior to the Industrial Conciliation and Arbitration Act 1894, New Zealand employment relations were heavily influenced by the British "voluntarist" tradition, which discourages government intervention in industrial relations, with free collective bargaining seen as the primary means to set terms and conditions of employment. This regime changed dramatically with the Industrial Conciliation and Arbitration Act (IC&A Act) in 1894 which brought dispute settlement to the forefront of New Zealand employment relations.[2] The main objective of this Act was to protect unions and workers in the private sector by providing institutional structures and interventions that helped to resolve collective conflict at work in a manner that balanced the interests of employers and employees.

It created for the first time a conciliation and arbitration system to address workplace conflict that was proving hard to resolve. This system was given backbone by the Act prohibiting strikes and lockouts when disputes were being conciliated or arbitrated. The institutional contours of the system only fully crystallized after an amendment to the Act in 1908. A series of Conciliation Boards made up of elected employer and employee representatives and with a strong regional focus were established, charged with investigating disputes, and reaching decisions. The Boards were chaired by government-appointed Commissioners who were "forerunners of employment mediators" (Franks and Dell, 2007: 2). If parties disagreed with the outcome of a Conciliation Board, they had the right to appeal to a newly created Arbitration Court, which was presided over by a Supreme Court Judge flanked by elected assessors from employer associations and trade unions. The Court's sole remit was to deal with collective industrial relations matters and it had the authority to make binding judgments on pay and working conditions in disputes involving registered unions. However, the Court had no jurisdiction to hear individual employment cases.

The creation of this conciliation and arbitration system had a number of unintended consequences. First of all, the union registration procedure established as part of the system, not only strengthened the collective bargaining hand of registered unions vis-à-vis employers, but also gave them an advantage against non-registered unions when recruiting new members. Secondly, and perhaps more importantly, the ability to make binding awards had the effect of setting minimum wages. As a result, wage-fixing became a core function of the conciliation and arbitration system as binding awards quickly became the core (minimum) employment conditions for most employees. This procedure clearly advantaged the relatively weak unions at the time as a binding award effectively amounted to "blanket coverage" regulation; collective agreements for an entire industry sector or occupational group were established by proxy.

However, the wage-fixing role of the conciliation and arbitration role had a downside. The original intention of the 1894 Act was to provide an informal dispute resolution service that would largely involve the use of conciliation to help settle collective bargaining disputes. But when binding awards with industry or occupation-wide effect started to be made, the system became heavily formalized and legalized. It encouraged "ritual bargaining" between unions and employers, as unions calculated that it may be in their interests not to reach a settlement, but to get the Court to make a binding award. Of course, this exacerbated employer–union conflicts, fermenting an adversarial ideology in New Zealand industrial relations. A further problem was that at times the Arbitration Court, when making binding awards, put the interests of a government's wider economic and social welfare program before those of the involved parties: binding awards occasionally were surrogate income policies. Yet a further shortcoming was that the system provided no institutional support for individual employment grievances. For example, no avenue was created for the aggrieved employee who had been dismissed or disciplined to seek redress. The institutional focus of the system was very much on the tripartite relationship between government, unions, and employer associations.

Over time, through a rather fragmented process and with a lot of influence from individual conciliators and arbitrators, an adversarial dispute resolution style emerged. In the independent government appointed conciliation boards, the bargaining and conciliation process was strongly directed by conciliation commissioners (Dell and Franks, 2009: 45). As a result, the process often became a ritualized "dance" ending in arbitration awards made by the conciliation commissioners. According to Foster and McAndrew (2003), there was limited negotiation involved in the process.

For most of the 20th century, the conciliation and arbitration system faced two major issues. One was to establish an orderly, predictable pattern of collective bargaining between employers and unions. The other was the absence from the system of any developed procedure to address individual employer–employee disputes: a handful of these individual disputes may have been addressed through the collective bargaining machinery, but most fell by the way side. Putting right these two shortcomings was a key motivation behind the Industrial Relations Act 1973. It sought to do so by: (1) permitting more direct bargaining outside the conciliation and arbitration system; (2) making an explicit distinction between disputes of rights and interests; (3) introducing the notion of a personal/individual grievance; and (4) creating a number of new institutions, which are set out in Table 21.1. These were far reaching changes, which continue to influence the dispute resolution system today. Consider the distinction introduced between disputes of rights and disputes of interest. Whereas disputes of interest concerned disagreements over bargaining, and allowed for strikes and lockouts, disputes of rights related to disagreements over terms in an existing agreement. Disputes of rights needed to be resolved within the conciliation and arbitration system, with strikes and lockouts being deemed unlawful during the process (Williams, 1981: 9–17).[3] It was hoped that making the distinction between interest and rights-based disputes would prevent strikes and lockouts. It was also hoped that the distinction would allow more focused efforts on the early resolution of conflict through the use of mediation and conciliation. Actually, in 1970, an Industrial Mediation Service, modelled on the US Federal Mediation and Conciliation Service, had already been introduced to address disputes of rights which freed up the Conciliation Service to concentrate on collective bargaining (Dell and Franks, 2009: 46).

The 1973 Act also made provision for the taking of a personal grievance to mediation where a settlement agreement could be facilitated. The aim of this change was to further reduce the possibility of strikes and lockouts by taking personal grievances outside the realm of collective disputes. Although the Act placed the emphasis on mediation in solving personal grievances, over time, largely as a result of the actions of individual conciliators, a hybrid process emerged which coupled together mediation and arbitration (med/arb): if parties could not agree a settlement through mediation then individual conciliators would arbitrate the case.

THE EMPLOYMENT CONTRACTS ACT 1991

Whereas the 1973 Act only modified the conciliation and arbitration arrangements established by the original IC&A Act, the Industrial Relations Amendment Act 1984 abolished compulsory arbitration and the Employment Contracts Act 1991 (ECA) abolished the award system and ended the registration and regulation of trade unions. Thus, the ECA 1991 must be viewed as introducing a root and branch transformation to the system, which still casts a long shadow over the current legislative framework and workplace practices.

Based on neoclassical economics and libertarian philosophy, the ECA had no empathy with established thinking about the need for public institutional support to help solve collective employment relations problems (Grills, 1994; Deeks and Rasmussen, 2002: 67–72). The abolition of the award system and union monopoly rights facilitated an enterprise-bargaining model in both the private and public sectors. These changes prompted a sharp fall in union density and in collective bargaining coverage: union density was halved to around 20% in 5 years, collective bargaining was decentralized to workplace level and most employees were covered by individualized employment agreements (see Figure 21.1).[4]

While the award system was broken up, the conciliation and arbitration services remained more or less intact, although two new institutions were created, the Employment Tribunal and the Employment Court (see Table 21.1). These bodies assumed a key role in the dispute resolution system during the 1990s when the number of personal grievances cases soared dramatically (see Table 21.2). All individual employees irrespective of union membership were permitted to take their personal grievance

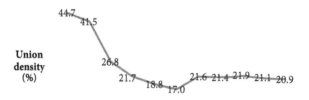

Years: 1989–2010 (every second year shown)

FIGURE 21.1 Trade Union Density, 1989–2010

Source: Crawford et al., 2000; Blumenfeld and Ryall, 2010; New Zealand Department of Labour's database.

Table 21.2 Personal Grievance Claims before the Employment Tribunal, 1992–9

Year to June	Outstanding Applications at Start	Applications Received	Applications Withdrawn	Applications Disposed	Outstanding Applications at End
1992	17	2,332	459	743	1,079
1993	1,079	3,207	743	1,568	1,919
1994	1,919	3,592	1,046	2,447	1,954
1995	1,954	4,248	976	3,040	2,184
1996	2,184	5,144	1,121	3,218	2,985
1997	2,985	5,424	1,190	3,787	3,432
1998	3,432	5,332	1,299	3,768	3,787
1999	3,787	4,466	1,490	3,501	3,364

Source: Rasmussen, 2009: 98.

to the Employment Tribunal. For mediation and, if necessary, adjudication, unions were no longer "gatekeepers." While the dispute resolution processes could provide the med/arb approach that had emerged incrementally after the 1973 Act, the Employment Tribunal ensured that the same person did not both mediate and adjudicate on the same dispute, which had the positive side effect of ensuring that the mediation process was based on the principles of neutrality, without prejudice, privilege, and confidentiality.

The rise of personal grievances and individual disputes are discussed more fully in the fourth section of the chapter. At this stage, it is sufficient to say that from 1991 onwards the extension of the personal grievance to all employees coincided with a rise in work-place and individual bargaining and a more volatile labor market. It was also influenced by a major extension of individual employee rights in the areas of anti-discrimination, privacy, and equality. The combination of these factors—as well as some confusion amongst employers regarding legal precedent and proper procedures—resulted in a strong rise in personal grievance cases and the consequential delays prompted on-going criticism of the Employment Tribunal. Overall, the ECA fundamentally transformed the New Zealand employment relations. It brought to an end the award system and it provided the legal framework for the individualization of the employment relationship (Deeks and Rasmussen, 2002).

THE EMPLOYMENT RELATIONS ACT 2000

The employment dispute resolution system went through even further change with the introduction of the Employment Relations Act 2000. The main thrust of this piece of legislation was to row back on the strong market orientation of the 1991 Act by emphasizing the importance of good faith bargaining for stable employment relations (Rasmussen, 2009). In so doing, it sought to shift the balance towards collective bargaining and away from individual employment rights. However, these efforts to give collective bargaining and trade unionism a shot in the arm have had limited success (Waldegrave et al., 2003). In the private sector, for example, trade union density has declined further to less than 10% of the workforce (Blumenfeld and Ryall, 2010). Many reasons have been put forward for why the legal promotion of collectivism has borne little fruit (see Rasmussen et al., 2012), but the bottom line is clear: collective bargaining has diminished in importance and unions have limited influence on personal grievance, resolution, settlement, or remedies.

While the ERA endorsed collective employment relations, it did not modify the emphasis on individual choice and on individual employment rights introduced under the ECA in 1991. In a sense, the ERA created legal frameworks for both collective employment relations and individual employment rights. Trying to do these two things at the same time came in for criticism. On the one hand, giving legal sanction to the individualization of the employment relationship was seen as undermining the objective of promoting collective bargaining and it has even been argued it is one of the reasons why collective bargaining did not take off in the post-2000 period (Rasmussen et al., 2006a). On the other hand, it has been suggested that the Act did not do enough to ensure individual choice was a viable option for all employees. Vindicating employment rights was seen as being effectively closed off for many employees due to power imbalances at some workplaces, with some employees not having sufficient resources, and others having their employment status changed to contractors and new employees on probation being denied the personal grievance right. As a result, seeking redress to an employment grievance was seen as very much favoring well-educated, highly paid employees.

In terms of dispute resolution, the institutions established by the ERA—the Mediation Service, Employment Relations Authority, and Employment Court—clearly had links with the institutional framework under the ECA (see Table 21.1) but there were also differences. Thus, the ERA promotes mediation as a low-cost, flexible, first stop service to

Personal grievance claims, 2003–6

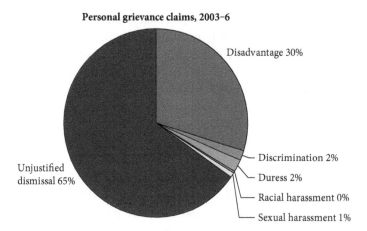

Disadvantage 30%

Unjustified
dismissal 65%

Discrimination 2%

Duress 2%

Racial harassment 0%

Sexual harassment 1%

FIGURE **21.2** Types of Personal Grievance Claims, 2003–6

Source: Rasmussen, 2009: 155.

solve disputes—the entire emphasis of the institutional reforms made by the ERA was to ensure speedy, informal, and practical justice (Rasmussen, 2009: 119). In that respect, the ERA was responding to criticisms of the Employment Tribunal in the 1990s for having long delays, being too legalistic—dominated by lawyers and possessing overly judicial processes—and being too expensive relative to compensation and awards. The new focus on mediation was seen as a way of dealing with delays and avoiding overly legalistic processes.

The institutional changes made in 2000 had several significant impacts. Unsurprisingly, the caseload of the Mediation Service grew rapidly, breaching 9,000 cases a year by 2003 (Rasmussen, 2009: 155). Encouraging those involved in a dispute to try mediation first before entering into more formal processes brought to an end the traditional med/arb approach and ensured the separation of consensual and determination processes. Increasing the use of mediation may have contributed to not only a faster turnaround of cases, but also to high settlement rates (McAndrew et al., 2004). The reduction in waiting times has been noted as a major success and various "client" satisfaction surveys have also recorded high levels of satisfaction (McDermott Miller, 2007; Woodhams, 2007). Still, it is noticeable that the *types* of cases have been rather stable in the last two decades with unjustified dismissals and disadvantaged grievances constituting over 90% of cases. Figure 21.2 shows that unjustified dismissals constituted 65% of all cases during 2003–6.

Amendments to the Employment Relations Act

While the ERA is the current legislative framework, three important changes along with other more minor adjustments have been made to the Act, with some unintended outcomes.[5] The major legislative adjustments have been: the Employment Relations

Amendment Act 2004, the adjustment to personal grievance rights in 2008 and 2010, and the Employment Relations Amendment Act 2010. The ER Amendment Act 2004 sought to address the concern that the existing Act had insufficiently advanced good faith and collective bargaining. It provided further guidelines on how to conclude collective agreements. There was also clarification about "justification" in respect of unjustified dismissals, a core part of personal grievance cases (see Figure 21.2). Finally, the Act encouraged mediators to be more active and flexible by extending their powers to enable them to deal with contractor/principal relationships (Rasmussen and Walker, 2009: 163).

While the 2004 changes were mainly attempting to strengthen the ERA, the post 2008 changes—associated with a shift to neoliberal National Party-led governments—were more focused on introducing greater flexibility into employment relationships, which, on the surface at least, seemed to sit uneasily with the ERA's attempts at promoting collective bargaining and unionism. Some of these changes had considerable impact on the rights of new employees in terms of their ability to pursue personal grievances. From March 2009, employers with less than 20 employees could include—with the employee's acceptance—a 90-calendar-day "trial and probationary" period. After the ER Amendment Act 2010, this was extended to include all employers. Thus, all new employees can potentially be asked to sign an employment agreement which suspends personal grievance rights during probation. While the 90-day probationary period needs the acceptance of the employee, it is difficult in practice for young people and low paid employees starting a new job to turn down such a request.

Overall, it is difficult to make an authoritative evaluation of the ERA. The measures introduced to promote collective action clearly did not have the desired effect as private sector collective bargaining and union density are now lower than ever. However, it is still too early to assess properly the effectiveness of the new dispute resolution processes instituted under the ERA. A worry would be that the ongoing amendments being made to the ERA and its supporting legislation could result in the public dispute resolution institutions being straddled with too many objectives, causing a lack of coherence in the system.

THE RISE OF PERSONAL GRIEVANCES AND INDIVIDUAL DISPUTES

At this stage, it is appropriate to examine more closely the rise of personal grievances as these have become a key feature of dispute resolution in New Zealand. The personal grievance right was first introduced in New Zealand by the Industrial Conciliation and Arbitration Amendment Act 1970 but, according to Anderson (1988: 261), the first *effective* grievance procedure was launched by the Industrial Relations Act 1973. That Act required all awards and collective agreements to have a settlement procedure for personal grievance. While this was a personal (individual) grievance entitlement, it was very much part of the collective legislative framework since it only pertained to union members covered by awards or agreements and it was only effective when the unions decided to support the employee's personal grievance claim (Anderson, 1988: 262). Thus, unions were effectively the "gatekeepers" of individual grievance claims and union advocates conducted these grievance cases.

The Employment Contracts Act 1991 brought personal grievance rights to the fore of New Zealand employment relations. By making a personal grievance claim something that all employees could invoke, the Act extended the right beyond union members— around a third of all employees had not been covered before—and it effectively brought to end the gate keeping role unions had performed in relation to personal grievances. As union membership continued to fall, triggering a decline in collective bargaining, individual employer–employee disputes started to dominate media reports and employment dispute statistics (see Table 21.2).

The sharp shift from collective towards individual disputes was influenced by a number of factors. Legislative changes increased the number of employees able, not least in terms of skills and financial power, to take personal grievances against an employer. Furthermore, the lodging of an unjustifiable dismissal claim negated the "stand-down period" (before the unemployment benefit could be received) and, according to Cullinane and MacDonald (2000: 57), contributed to an increase in the number of grievances filed. Finally, the range of individual employee rights was extended by the Human Rights Act 1993 and Privacy Act 1993, prompting talk about employees adopting an "American litigation" mindset (Rasmussen, 2009: 99).

The high level of personal grievance cases has continued throughout the ERA period, from a low of 4,000 applications a year to a high of more than 9,000 applications. While some applications are withdrawn before mediation, it still leaves a considerable number of mediations every year. For example, there were 5,850 completed mediations in 2011– 2012, of which 81% were settled (Department of Labour, 2012a). Likewise, the dominant types of personal grievances have not changed much over the last 20 years (see Figure 21.2). The Employment Relations Act gives all employees the right to pursue a personal grievance if they have experienced any of the following: unjustifiable dismissal; unjustifiable action which disadvantages the employee; discrimination; sexual harassment (by someone in authority or by co-workers); racial harassment; duress over membership of a union or other employee organization.

The manner in which personal grievances are handled is the subject of on-going debate, relating to such matters as delays, procedural fairness, employer complaints about non-meritorious cases, the risk of a return to the hybrid style of mediation and arbitration (med/arb), different types of mediation approaches, the over-use of lawyers and excessive legalism, cost issues and the size of awards. In relation to delays, a 1993 official report argued that some cases took a year to settle, leading to "disillusionment with the Government's ability to provide equity in the labour market" (NZHR, 1993: 39.11). The use of lawyers was seen as a cause of delay since "the legalistic nature of many cases has drawn out hearing times…" (NZHR, 1993: 42). By 2000, the need for less legalistic and fast access to early informal mediation was a consistent theme of submissions to the Employment Relations Bill. While the ERA did a valiant attempt to reduce legalism and formality, particularly through more use of mediation, it is not at all certain that it has succeeded as there are still regular complaints of "creeping legalism and formality" (McAndrew et al., 2004). There is even concern that legalism and formality have become embedded (Department of Labour, 2010). Finally, the 2010 amendments to the ERA 2000 allowed cross-examination and this appears to have further embedded formal legal processes (see Table 21.1). Table 21.3 is an illustration of these concerns as the level of applications at the Employment Relations Authority has stayed at a constantly high level in recent years, despite on-going attempts at encouraging dispute resolution through mediation.

Part of the wider debate about legalism and formality was the discussion about the alignment of costs and awards. While media stories highlighted large awards and employers talked about a "gravy train" (Canterbury Manufacturers Association, 2006; EMA Northern, 2006) this was *not* the reality in most personal grievance cases (McAndrew, 2010). In fact, there were complaints that the level of payouts—remedies— had eroded the effectiveness of the personal grievance protection (Caisley, 2004). With most employees obtaining rather minor awards of less than NZ$10,000—even in the majority of personal grievance cases pertaining to unjustified dismissal—the case is further strengthened for speedy and low-cost mediation (Rasmussen and Walker, 2009: 157–158).

Over the years, employers have complained that dispute resolution agencies have applied procedural fairness criteria too rigidly and formally. Procedural fairness relates to the extent managers have followed good employment practices when handling grievances and disputes: for example whether employers follow agreed procedures, whether

Table 21.3 Applications to the Employment Relations Authority, 2007–12.

	Applications to the Employment Relations Authority by year				
	Outstanding Applications at Start	Applications Received	Disposed-off	Withdrawn	Outstanding Applications at End
2007	919	2,321	596	1,550	1,094
2008	1,094	2,393	680	1,565	1,242
2009	1,242	2,587	818	1,621	1,390
2010	1,390	2,438	842	1,693	1,293
2011	1,293	2,243	687	1,467	1,382
2012	1,382	1,989	667	1,749	955

Source: Statistics provided by the Ministry of Business, Innovation and Employment.

employees were provided the opportunity to be heard before a dismissal and whether employees received a warning for conduct that may justify dismissal. The employer case is that the dispute resolution agencies are too quick to rule against the employer where it is found that fair procedures are not in place. As mentioned earlier, the hybrid med/arb approach that had become engrained in the dispute resolution system throughout the 20th century was uprooted by ERA. Instead, a distinct Mediation Service was established and the Act directs that the Employment Relations Authority and Employment Court send parties back to mediation in most cases.[6] McAndrew (2010: 91) has argued that the state provision of employment relations mediation is a success story, studied and copied by other countries. Walker (2009) on the other hand, claimed there was a propensity for mediation to be more akin to the exit settlement negotiation of a personal grievance when the employment relationship had ended. But as explained in the next section there are a range of mediation approaches that can provide early assistance to resolve conflict before escalation to dispute and prevent the breakdown of the employment relationship in individual and collective employment relationship problems.

RECENT CHANGES AND ISSUES

While the move towards individualism has been the major story of the last two decades, there are still interesting developments in collective bargaining and dispute resolution. In this section we detail some of the recent collective bargaining developments where the use of mediation, facilitation, and Maori-inspired dialogue are interesting approaches. There have also been some tentative shifts, strengthening the options of early assistance and reinforcing the wide range of structured and unstructured mediation procedures available under the ERA 2000. The following subsection explores some of the experimentation that is occurring.

Bargaining and Negotiating the Employment Relationship

Recently, bargaining and dispute resolution processes in three high profile disputes—known as the Hobbit/Actors Equity, Ports of Auckland/Stevedores, and Talley AFFCO/Meat workers—have caused considerable debate. The disputes had ambiguous effects. On the one hand, the three disputes signaled a further shift away from collectivism by strengthening individualistic contractual relationships, but on the other hand, they heralded a return to high profile state interventions in disputes. Similarly, they resulted in the government adjusting good faith bargaining obligations in favor of employers and reducing the country's plinth of employment protection by categorizing workers as contractors. Yet, at the same time, positive dispute resolution developments emerged from the disputes, particularly in the Talley AFFCO/Meat workers case where Maori-leaders facilitated a settlement. The dispute had put employment in Maori communities at risk, but this danger was averted when highly respected Maori community leaders initiated and facilitated a mutual interest-based negotiation which settled the dispute. The case highlights how the use of collaborative mutual interest-based negotiation can effectively break a deadlock.

(1) *The Hobbit/Actors Equity dispute* in 2010 was arguably one of the highest pro-file disputes in recent times.[7] It involved the Prime Minister and other Cabinet Ministers, world famous film director Peter Jackson and his associated busi-ness interests, one of the world's largest film companies, Warner Brothers, and international and national unions. The dispute had its origins in negotiations about standard employment terms and conditions and adherence to the volun-tary code for the film industry—the "Pink Book." An important antecedent was previous court decisions that had determined that a worker labeled a contrac-tor in an employment agreement was in fact an employee (see Nuttall, 2011). According to Jackson and Warner Brothers, this legal ruling had created a great deal of "uncertainty" in the film industry to the point that they threatened to transfer production of the Hobbit out of the country. Following direct negotia-tions between the New Zealand Prime Minister and Warner Brothers, a package of tax incentives, tourist marketing, and employment law changes was agreed (Tyson, 2011). The legislative change passed into law at 29 October 2010 and weakened the employment status and rights of all film production workers. The legislation also changed the dispute resolution options for film workers as they will have, as contractors, limited access to personal grievances. It may also have spill-over effects in terms of employer strategies and practices in other sectors. As such, it constitutes a major adjustment of the ERA.

(2) The *Ports of Auckland/Stevedores dispute* in 2011–12 again centered on the issues of flexibility, contracting, and collective bargaining. During collective bargain-ing between the Ports of Auckland Ltd (PoAL) and the Maritime Union New Zealand (MUNZ), the PoAL informed the union that it intended to contract out the port's stevedoring jobs. It was subsequently revealed that the contracting out proposal was driven by the port owner's new target of improving the return of equity from 6% to 12% by June 2016. It was also influenced by increased com-petition from Ports of Tauranga and international shipping companies seeking lower shipping rates.

Following nine strikes, two lockouts, and 22 meetings (10 with Department of Labour mediators) between September 2011 and March 2012, and an Employment Court injunction preventing restructuring or contracting out of work until collective bargaining had been concluded, the dispute went to facilita-tion in May 2012. The confidential facilitation aimed to break the deadlock and negotiate a new collective agreement. At the time of writing, facilitation through the Employment Relations Authority was heralded as an effective approach to resolving the dispute. However, the recommendations made by the Authority are yet to be agreed by the Ports of Auckland Ltd and the Maritime Union New Zealand.

(3) The *Talley/AFCCO/Meat workers dispute* involved a twelve week impasse in the negotiations for new pay and conditions for around 1,200 union workers. Disagreements over pay rises, seniority rules, and drug testing had prompted weeks of protests, negotiations, and lockouts and a raft of threats and accusations. The dispute was fuelled by the longstanding adversarial nature of employment relations in the meat industry and by the anti-union approach followed by the Talley family in other industries. Following an Employment Court hearing into the legality of the lockout, negotiations with the Talley family and the meat workers' union were facilitated by Iwi leaders—leaders of the local Maori tribes—that focused on building trust and confidence in open and regular dialogue. The involvement of Iwi leaders led to the respective parties committing for the first time to a form of interest-based bargaining, with considerable success. A settlement was reached, which included a two-year agreement with pay rises backdated, the seniority rule maintained, and urine drug testing being allowed. The case highlighted the gains that could be potentially accrued by diffusing interest-based bargaining more widely in the country.

Mediation Approaches and Early Assistance

The Department of Labour Mediation Service is empowered to implement a wide range of different mediation procedures whether "structured or unstructured, or do such things as he or she considers appropriate to resolve the problem or dispute promptly and effectively" (ERA 2000 section 146 2(a)). Cotter and Dell (2009), Department of Labour mediators, reported that basic principles of confidentiality,[8] impartiality, and empowerment of parties applied to all mediation interventions, although these were delivered in a range of flexible styles and models, *contingent* on the requirements of the parties. They claimed that one of five different mediation approaches could be used depending on the situation: settlement; facilitative; tradition-based; transformative; narrative. Of these, the settlement and facilitation approaches have been prevalent, but recently there has been growing interest in the use of the three last mediation approaches.

Cotter and Dell (2010) claimed the traditional forms of mediation—settlement and facilitative mediation—were still dominating. A *settlement mediation process* was normally implemented where "the objective was service delivery and access to justice" and if "the outcome was more important than the relationship and the parties wanted no future relationship" (Cotter and Dell 2010: 7). The latter was common because by the time many parties sought mediation, the relationship was already over. Thus, so-called "exit mediation," which sought a suitable "settlement," became a preferred option for the parties in many mediation cases (McAndrew et al., 2004; Walker and Hamilton, 2009).

Facilitative mediation is strongly promoted by the ERA. This approach is underpinned by the principles of integrative, interest-based negotiations (Walton and McKersie, 1965; Fisher and Ury, 1981; Mayer, 2000) and is sometimes referred to as the problem solving model (Moore, 1996). It is often used, according to Cotter and Dell (2010), when there are "on-going relationships and collective bargaining disputes."[9]

Recently, there has been more application of the three other mediation approaches. The *tradition-based approach*, reflects the consensual decision-making processes of the indigenous Maori based on community participation and restorative justice on the Marae.[10] The community aspect of this model values transparency and consultation over the confidentiality principle of mainstream mediation as it involves what Metge (2001: 33–9) referred to as Korero Tahi (participatory talking together in a circle, the passing of the stick, and facilitated criss-cross exchange). *Transformative mediation* (Bush and Foger, 1994, 2004) and *narrative mediation* (Winslade and Monk, 2000) were found to be most suited to workplace mediation where there was an on-going relationship that involved relational conflict and/or behavioral issues (Cotter and Dell, 2010: 8). Drawn from therapeutic principles focused on dialogue, in practice these theoretical constructs were "fluid in application" as mediators adapted models to fit the requirement of parties (Hurley, 2009; Cotter and Dell, 2010: 6–8).

Finally, an interesting development has been the growing number of so-called "recorded settlements" (Greenwood, 2012). When individuals reach a settlement to an employment relationship problem or grievance outside of the state provided mediation service, whether this involves them negotiating their own agreement or using lawyers or a private mediator, they can send in their written agreement to the Labour Department to be signed off by a mediator as a "recorded settlement."

Bullying and Harassment in the Workplace

Bullying and harassment in the workplace have had a high profile in recent years, including a couple of books being top of the "best-selling charts." There has been some confusion about the exact meaning of these two concepts (see Bentley et al., 2012), which was compounded by bullying and harassment being covered by two different legislative frameworks. Bentley et. al. (2010) adopted the dominant international approach that defined bullying as sustained, targeted unreasonable behavior causing harm, going beyond a one-off incident. This may be seen as different from harassment which may involve specific elements of diversity such as ethnicity, gender, sexual orientation, or any of the thirteen categories of discrimination under the Human Rights Act 1993. While the two may or may not co-exist, bullying in the workplace is considered a health and safety "hazard" under the Health and Safety in Employment Act 1992 and it can be pursued as a personal grievance under the ERA. This has prompted New Zealand practitioners, Takitimu and Freeman Greene (2009) to develop a cross-agency mediation approach, integrating the legislative directives of the Human Rights Commission under the Human Rights Act 1993 with the Employment Relations Mediation Service under the Employment Relations Act 2000.

In the last decade, a number of court decisions have built a solid legal precedent which has covered areas such as workplace stress, breach of an employer's duty to act fairly and reasonably, and breach of implied terms of trust and confidence in the employment relationship. Bullying has often appeared in personal grievance claims for unjustified disadvantage and constructive dismissal and McLay (2009: 19) has categorized workplace bullying cases dealt with by the Mediation Service as: parties either seeking redress following resignation, pre-resignation exit package negotiation or, in an on-going employment relationship, seeking assurances that bullying behavior would stop. Furthermore, bullying and harassment often appear in certain jobs and industries. They are, according to research by Bentley et al. (2009: i), "... relatively widespread across the health and education sectors.... and most evident in certain hotspots within hospitality." Thus, there are clear indications of what the legal situation is, what the standard "solutions" are, and where there is a strong need for preventive action. This is no sign, however, of a lull in the number of bullying and harassment cases taken.

Bullying and harassment cases have raised questions regarding the appropriateness of mediation. For example, McLay (2009: 19) has warned that "Rather than both parties being empowered by a mediation process, a more likely outcome is that process will reinforce the existing power dynamic where there is a significant imbalance." The New Zealand Chief High Court Judge, Justice Winklemann (2011: 7) has raised similar concerns: "mediation can increase the power of the strong over the weak, magnifying power imbalances and opening the door to coercion and manipulation by the stronger party." As bullying and harassment cases often involve employers (rather than middle managers) because of the prevalence of small and medium size enterprises in New Zealand, power imbalance issues are prevalent in many cases.

Finally, the high profile of bullying and harassment has prompted the search for appropriate prevention policies, training, peer mediation, conflict coaching, negotiation and communication training. This has become more prevalent in the last decade where, amongst others, the Department of Labour, the Human Rights Commission, Human Resource Institute New Zealand, employer organizations and unions have been very active. There have also been insights from practitioners who have suggested new policies and have developed training and coaching modules. For example, McCulloch (2010) has applied principles from the narrative and transformative models of mediation in her work as a mediator in the tertiary education sector and has developed new conflict coaching, peer mediation, and conflict resolution training techniques.

From Collective Bargaining and Individual Grievances to Solving Employment Relationship Problems?

Since 1991, there has been a considerable shift in the issues, workload, and processes associated with dispute resolution. The traditional role of state sponsored employment institutions in determining wage outcomes was abandoned by the ECA 1991 (Walsh, 1993). Instead personal grievances and their settlement became a major feature of dispute resolution in the 1990s. This also prompted a number of concerns which are still relevant: case backlog and delays, non-meritorious claims, procedural requirements, legalism and costs, and whether awards were too high or too low. These are concerns that the current legislative framework—ERA 2000—has tried to deal with in various ways.

However, the overall "score card" for the ERA has been pretty mixed with several unintended outcomes. The ERA has probably scored better in terms of dispute resolution than its predecessor the ECA. The promotion of mediation has gone some way to achieving the aim of providing "fast, free and fair" dispute resolution (Wilson, 2000). The problem-solving approach to employment conflict resolution was also embedded in the ERA and, 12 years on, there has been a discernible shift in focus to conflict prevention, conflict coaching, conflict mapping, conflict management, and a range of mediation approaches. The Employment Relations Amendment Act 2010 has reinforced the existing role of the state sponsored Employment Relations Service in the provision of options for early assistance. There is a growing awareness of the potential for and practice of, narrative and transformative models for workplace relationship conflict resolution. However, it is also debated whether mediation and early assistance in problem resolution is appropriate in circumstances that involve workplace harassment and bullying.

Despite the rise of individual disputes, facilitating the resolution of conflict during collective bargaining is still an important area for the state's dispute resolution machinery, although its failure to broker settlements in high profile disputes has been most visible to the New Zealand public. Unfortunately, resolving workplace conflict through mediation is not likely to be highlighted in the media due in part to the confidential nature of the process, but also because unresolved conflict and dispute impasses, particularly when they are high profile, are much better copy (Rasmussen and Ross, 2004; Greenwood, 2012). When mediation is unsuccessful during collective bargaining disputes, the public is informed through high profile media coverage of lockouts and strikes. The Department of Labour's statistics from its Annual Report for 2011/12 recorded that there were 267 mediation events related to collective bargaining matters and yet only three high profile cases dominated the media during the last year (Department of Labour, 2012b). For example, mediators worked on high profile collective bargaining disputes that included the New Zealand Police and Fire Services as well as cases in the health sector, meat industry, rest homes, major manufacturing firms, energy sector, and transport sectors. Some involved mediation assistance after strike or lockout notices were received. A particular area of endeavour was the Rugby World Cup where unions worked with mediators before the Rugby World Cup to prevent the potential of industrial action and there was no industrial action.

Under the ERA, it has become standard to conduct satisfaction surveys of "clients" of the employment institutions. These surveys tend to paint a positive picture of processes and outcomes since satisfaction scores tends to be high (e.g. Martin and Woodhams, 2007). The Labour Group Service Excellence Survey (carried out by independent researchers) found in 2012 that 82% of respondents were satisfied or very satisfied with their most recent contact with the employment institutions. This was a significant improvement over the previous year's level of 75%. Importantly, 88% felt that they were treated fairly.

Thus, there is a considerable amount of change, innovation, and experimentation in recent New Zealand dispute resolution. The limited available research has probably understated the extent of informal alternative dispute resolution. However, the issues about legalism, costs, and influence of the legal fraternity also suggest that the ERA's intention of speedy and low cost dispute resolution may need to be revisited.

CONCLUSIONS

This chapter illustrates how there have been radical and comprehensive changes in dispute resolution and conflict management in Aotearora New Zealand in the last two decades. There has been a sharp shift towards individual and workplace-based conflict resolution. Although there have been high profile collective bargaining disputes recently, these have occurred against a background of low collective bargaining coverage in the private sector. Instead the political debate over personal grievance rights continue unabated and, with employer-driven flexibility being facilitated by legislative and labor market changes, the protection of vulnerable workers has become a major media focus.

The ERA reflected the growing international trend to view mediation as more timely, less expensive, procedurally fair and achieving better settlement rates than adjudicatory processes such as arbitration or litigation. This has been supported by high settlement rates and positive survey feedback from "clients" of the Mediation Service and, as a fall-back option, determination in the Employment Authority. The aim of having either self-resolution or fast and low cost assistance has also been supported by a more comprehensive menu of services delivered via the Department of Labour's Mediation Service. While conflict management, recorded settlements and private provision of conflict resolution services outside of the Employment Institutions are emerging, these are still less visible than state-sponsored interventions.

While there is an increased emphasis on having suitable conflict management training, improved information and early and low-cost dispute resolution, there also appears to be an ingrained problem with some workplaces "missing out" on quality employment relationships and suitable dispute resolution processes. This seems most acute in that (growing) segment of the economy where atypical employment arrangements and low pay have become more embedded (Walker, 2011). Thus, managing workplace conflict is far from problem free, and it continues to be something of a "political football." Yet, it is remarkable how dynamic have been the models, processes, and practices associated with managing employment conflict. There has also been a consistently high level of "client" satisfaction. Thus, McAndrew (2010: 91) may have a valid point when he suggests that New Zealand has "a splendid set of institutions" which "are increasingly attracting the attention of governments and scholars overseas."

Notes

1. Aotearoa is one name for New Zealand in the Maori language, its meaning is "*long white cloud*". The use of the term honours the bicultural heritage of a nation where the founding constitutional document the *Treaty of Waitangi* directs the Crown to act in partnership, protection, participation with, and preservation of, "Tikanga" Maori (that is, the processes, practices, beliefs, social, and economic systems of the indigenous Maori people). As highlighted below, this has influenced dispute resolution processes.
2. As described in Holt (1986), the conciliation and arbitration system was changed continuously and thus, some of its characteristics were developed over time. For example, national coverage of awards only started in earnest after 1911, compulsory arbitration was repealed between 1932 and 1936 and compulsory union membership came and went several times. A brief overview of the conciliation and arbitration system, its changes, and its legacies can be found in Deeks et al. (1994: 45–64).
3. While the terms of disputes of interest and disputes of rights are no longer used in current legislation the distinction is still enshrined in the formulations of when strikes and lockouts are considered lawful.
4. While the terminology has shifted from employment contracts under the ECA 1991 to employment agreements under the ERA 2000 the same terminology—employment agreements—will be used throughout this chapter.
5. There have also been some significant changes in other Acts. In particular, the changes implemented to the occupational health and safety legislation in 2003 have introduced for the first time legally based employee participation structures in New Zealand firms (see Lamm, 2009, 2010). Similarly, there has been a major push to enhance workplace partnerships prior to 2008 which promoted stronger employer, union, and employee collaborations (Rasmussen et al., 2006a; Haworth, 2010). These and other initiatives are examples of conflict management in the workplace but whether they will have a wider influence on conflict resolution processes is still unclear.
6. The ERA states that the Authority and Court must send parties back to mediation unless "it would not contribute constructively to resolving the issue; it will not, in all the circumstances, be in the public interest or; will undermine the urgent or interim nature of the proceedings "(ERA ss 159, 188). Whether this directive borders on quasi mandatory mediation is debated by Boulle et al. (2008) and it may also undermine the core principle of mediation of having a voluntary consensual process of facilitated negotiation.

7. The Hobbit dispute has been a hot topic amongst the legal fraternity and it was the subject of a Special Issue of the *New Zealand Journal of Employment Relations*. That issue—33(3)— covers a range of angles beyond the legal issues and their impact on employee access to dispute resolution processes.

8. This excludes collective bargaining as a sixth model which, as a consensual process, is unable to retain confidentiality given the participatory democratic process of decision-making.

9. Facilitative mediation is a process that sits apart from the more complex facilitation of collective bargaining disputes under the determinative processes of the Employment Relations Authority.

10. Marae can be understood in English as the "village common" (Maori Language Commission, 1996: 245). However Marae communicates more than a common area: it is a place where community and collaboration are valued. There are specific behavioral protocols, sacred areas, and rules on the Marae with regard to respect during speaking and meetings based on traditional Maori systems and polices or "Tikanga."

References

Anderson, G. 1988. "The Origins and Development of the Personal Grievance Jurisdiction in New Zealand." *New Zealand Journal of Industrial Relations*, 13(3): 257–75.

Bentley, T. A., Catley, B., Cooper-Thomas, H., Gardener, D., O'Driscoll, M., Dale, A., and Trenberth, L. 2009. *Understanding Stress and Bullying In New Zealand*. Final report to OH&S Steering Committee, Massey University, Auckland.

Bentley, T. A., Catley, B., Cooper-Thomas, H., Gardener, D., O'Driscoll, M., Dale, A., and Trenberth, L. 2012. "Perceptions of Workplace Bullying in the New Zealand Travel Industry: Prevalence and Management Strategies." *Tourism Management*, 33: 351–60.

Blumenfeld, S. and Ryall, S. 2010. "Unions and Union Membership in New Zealand: Annual Review 2008." *New Zealand Journal of Employment Relations*, 35(3): 84–96.

Boulle, L., Goldblatt, V., and Green, P. 2008. *Mediation: Principles, Process, Practice*. Wellington: LexisNexis NZ.

Bush, R. A. B. and Folger, J. P. 1994. *The Promise of Mediation: Responding to Conflict through Empowerment and Recognition*. San Francisco: Jossey-Bass.

Bush, R. A. B. and Folger, J. P. 2004. *The Promise of Mediation: The Transformative Approach to Conflict*. San Francisco: Jossey-Bass.

Caisley, A. 2004. "The Law Moves in Mysterious Ways." In E. Rasmussen (ed.), *Employment Relationships: New Zealand's Employment Relations Act*. Auckland: Auckland University Press, 59–76.

Canterbury Manufacturers Association 2006. "The Hidden Costs of the Personal Grievance 'Gravy Train.'" *Media Release*, 14 Jun.

Cotter, A. and Dell, J. 2010. *Strengthening Mediation Practice: Developing Frameworks for Reflective Practice and Assessment*. Wellington: Department of Labour.

Crawford, A., Harbridge, R., and Walsh, P. 2000. "Unions and Union Membership in New Zealand: Annual Review for 1999." *New Zealand Journal of Industrial Relations*, 25(3): 191–8.

Cullinane, J. and MacDonald, D. 2000. "Personal Grievances in New Zealand." In J. Burgess and G. Strachan (eds), *Research on Work, Employment and Industrial Relations 2000*. Proceedings of the 14th AIRRANZ Conference Newcastle, 2–4 Feb.: 52–60.

Deeks, J. and Rasmussen, E. 2002. *Employment Relations in New Zealand*. Auckland: Pearson Education.

Deeks, J., Parker, J., and Ryan, R. 1994. *Labour and Employment Relations in New Zealand*. Auckland: Longman Paul.

Dell, J. and Franks, P. 2009. "Mediation and Collective Bargaining: Department of Labour." In C. Smith and P. Franks (eds), *Contemporary Mediation Practice: Celebrating 100 Years of Employment Mediation*. Wellington: Department of Labour.

Department of Labour 2010. *Views of the Personal Grievance Process: A Qualitative Study*. Wellington: Department of Labour.

Department of Labour 2012a. *Annual Report*. Wellington: Ministry of Business Innovation and Employment.

Department of Labour 2012b. *Performance Report, Labour Group*. Wellington: Business Process and Innovation of the Ministry of Business Innovation and Employment.

Employers and Manufacturers Association (EMA) Northern 2006. "Grievance Gravy Train Picking up Speed." *Media Release*, 15 Dec.

Franks, P. and Dell, J. 2007. *Mediation in the Statutory Context: Employment mediation in New Zealand*. Wellington: LEADR 9th International Alternative Dispute Resolution Conference. 21 Sept.

Fisher, R and Ury, W. 1981. *Getting to Yes: Negotiating Agreement without Giving In*. Boston: Houghton Mifflin.

Foster, A. B. and McAndrew, I. 2003. "Growth and Innovation through Good Faith Collective Bargaining: An Introduction." *New Zealand Journal of Industrial Relations*, 28(2): 118–20.

Greenwood, G. 2012. "Employment Conflict Transformation: A Multi Method Study of Policies Processes and Practices for Early Resolution of Workplace Relationship Problems in Primary Schools." Unpublished PhD Thesis, Auckland: Auckland University of Technology.

Grills, W. 1994. "The Impact of the Employment Contracts Act on Labour Law: Implications for unions." *New Zealand Journal of Industrial Relations*, 19(1): 85–101.

Haworth, N. 2010. "Economic Transformation, Productivity and Employment Relations in New Zealand 1999–2008." In E. Rasmussen (ed.), *Employment Relationships. Workers, Unions and Employers in New Zealand*. Auckland: Auckland University Press, 149–67.

Holt, J. 1986. *Compulsory Arbitration in New Zealand, The First Forty Years*. Auckland: Auckland University Press.

Howells, J. M. and Cathro, S. H. 1986. *Mediation in New Zealand: The Attitudes of the Mediated*. Palmerston North: The Dunmore Press, 171–8.

Hurley, D. 2009. "Employment Mediation: Opportunities and Outcomes." In C. Smith and P. Franks (eds), *Contemporary Mediation Practice: Celebrating 100 Years of Employment Mediation*. Wellington: Department of Labour.

Kelly, H. 2010. "Challenges and Opportunities in New Zealand Employment Relations: A CTU Perspective." In E. Rasmussen (ed.), *Employment Relationships. Workers, Unions and Employers in New Zealand*. Auckland: Auckland University Press, 133–48.

Lamm, F. 2009. "Occupational Health and Safety." In E. Rasmussen (ed.), *Employment Relations in New Zealand*. Auckland: Pearson Education.

Lamm, F. 2010. "Participative and Productive Employment Relations: The Role of Health and Safety Committees and Worker Representation." In E. Rasmussen (ed.), *Employment Relationships: Workers, Unions and Employers in New Zealand*. Auckland: Auckland University Press.

McAndrew, I. 2010. "The employment institutions." In E. Rasmussen (ed.), *Employment Relationships. Workers, Unions and Employers in New Zealand*. Auckland: Auckland University Press, 74–93.

McAndrew, I., Morton, J., and Geare, A. 2004. "The Employment Institutions." In E. Rasmussen (ed), *Employment Relationships: New Zealand's Employment Relations Act*. Auckland: Auckland University Press, 98–118.

McCulloch. B. 2010. "Dealing with Bullying Behaviours in the Workplace: What Works—A Practitioner's View." *Journal of the International Ombudsman Association*, 3(2): 39–51.

McDermott Miller Ltd. 2007. *Social and Economic Costs and Benefits of Employment Relationship Problems: Technical Report*. Wellington: Department of Labour.

McLay, L. 2009. "Workplace Bullying: To Mediate or Not." In Department of Labour (ed.), *Contemporary Mediation Practice: Celebrating 100 Years of Employment Mediation*. Wellington: New Zealand Government, Crown Copyright.

Maori Language Commission 1996. *Te Matataki: Contemporary Maori Words*. New Zealand: Oxford University Press.

Martin, M. and Woodhams, B. 2007. *Personal Grievance Mediations Conducted at the Department of Labour: A Snapshot*. Wellington: Department of Labour.

Mayer, B. S. 2000. *The Dynamics of Conflict Resolution: A Practitioner's Guide*. San Francisco: Jossey-Bass.

Metge, J. 2001. *Korero Tahi: Talking Together*. Auckland: Auckland University Press.

Moore, C. M. 1996. *The Mediation Process: Practical Strategies for Resolving Conflict*. San Francisco: Jossey-Bass.

New Zealand House of Representatives 1993. *The Report of the Labour Committee on the Inquiry into the effects of the Employment Contracts Act 1991 on the New Zealand Labour Market*. Wellington: New Zealand Government.

Nuttall, P. 2011. "...Where the Shadows lie": Confusions, Misunderstanding, and Misinformation about Workplace Status. *New Zealand Journal of Employment Relations*, 36(3): 71–88.

Rasmussen, E. 2009. *Employment Relations in New Zealand*. Auckland: Pearson.

Rasmussen, E. and Ross, C. 2004. "The Employment Relations Act through the Eyes of the Media." In E. Rasmussen (ed.), *Employment Relationships: New Zealand's Employment Relations Act*. Auckland: Auckland University Press, 21–38.

Rasmussen, E. and Walker, B. 2009. "Employment Relations in the Millennium." In E. Rasmussen (ed.), *Employment Relations in New Zealand*. Pearson Education, Auckland, ch. 6.

Rasmussen, E., Hunt, V., and Lamm, F. 2006a. "Between Individualism and Social Democracy." *Labour & Industry*, 17(1): 19–40.

Rasmussen, E., O'Neil, P., and Chalmers, P. 2006b. "International Experiences of Partnership." *Research Report*, Partnership Resource Centre, NZ Department of Labour, Wellington, 148 pages. See: <www.dol.govt.nz/PDFs/int_full.pdf> (There is also a 22 page Summary Report).

Rasmussen, E., Foster, B., and Murrie, J. 2012. "The Decline in Collectivism and Employer Attitudes and Behaviours: Facilitating a High-skill, Knowledge Economy?" ILERA World Congress, 2–5 Jul., Philadelphia, USA.

Takitamu, C. and Freeman-Greene, S. 2009. "Breaking Down the Barriers: Cross Agency Co-mediation." *Contemporary Mediation Practice: Celebrating 100 Years of Employment Mediation*. Wellington: New Zealand Government, Crown Copyright.

Tyson, A. F. 2011. "A Synopsis of the 'Hobbit Dispute.'" *New Zealand Journal of Employment Relations*, 36(3): 5–14.

Waldegrave, T., Anderson, D., and Wong, K. 2003. *Evaluation of the Short Term Impacts of the Employment Relations Act 2000*. Wellington: Department of Labour.

Walker, B. 2009. "For Better or for Worse: Employment Relationship Problems under the Employment Relations Act 2000." Unpublished PhD Thesis. Christchurch: Canterbury University, Jun.

Walker, B. 2011. "How Does Non-standard Employment Affect Workers? A Consideration of the Evidence." *New Zealand Journal of Employment Relations*, 36(3): 15–30.

Walker, B. and Hamilton, R. T. 2009. "Grievance Processes: Research, Rhetoric and Directions for New Zealand." *New Zealand Journal of Employment Relations*, 34(3): 43–64.

Walsh, P. 1993. "The State and Industrial Relations in New Zealand." In B. Roper and C. Rudd (eds), *State and Economy in New Zealand*. Auckland: Oxford University Press.

Walton, R. E. and McKersie, R. B. 1965. *A Behavioral Analysis of Labour Negotations*. New York: McGraw-Hill.

Williams, A. 1981. *Studies in Conflict: Cases in New Zealand Industrial Relations*. Palmerston North: Dunmore Press.

Wilson, Hon M. 2000. "Free, Fast and Fair—A New Mediation Service for New Zealand Businesses and Employees." *Media Release*, 13 Jul.

Winkelmann, Hon J. (2011). ADR and the Civil Justice System, Paper presented Arbitrators' and Mediators' (AMINZ) Conference: Taking Charge of the Future, Auckland, New Zealand, Aug. <http://www.courtsofnz.govt.nz/speechpapers/ADR%20and%20the%20Civil%20Justice%20System.pdf>.

Winslade, J. and Monk, G. 2000. *Narrative Mediation: A New Approach to Conflict Resolution*. San Francisco: Jossey-Bass.

Woodhams, B. 2007. *Employment Relationship Problems: Costs, Benefits and Choices*. Wellington: Department of Labour.

CHAPTER 22

CONFLICT RESOLUTION IN THE UNITED KINGDOM

RICHARD SAUNDRY AND GILL DIX

INTRODUCTION

RECENT decades have seen a significant shift in the pattern of workplace conflict in the UK. The most conspicuous symptom of this has been a sustained reduction in the scale and scope of collective industrial action and a rapid increase in litigation over individual employment disputes. However, while workplace conflict may have been re-shaped, there is little convincing evidence of any overall growth. Superficially, these changes would appear to reflect the individualization and juridification of employment relations. As the ability of trade unions to take effective collective action has been restricted, so the scope for legal enforcement of individual employment rights has widened. Against this backdrop, the policy focus in recent years has sharpened around easing the load on employers by reducing access to employment tribunals and lowering barriers to dismissal.

Less noticeable, but arguably more fundamental, has been the progressive decline in organizational conflict resolution capacity and in particular the social (and collective) processes through which competing interests have been traditionally accommodated in UK workplaces. The erosion of collective regulation and union organization has seen the disappearance of employee representation from many workplaces. At the same time, devolution of responsibility for conflict handling to line managers has arguably created a "resolution gap" which has been plugged by the prioritization of rigid procedural adherence and legal compliance.

This chapter is structured in four sections. First, we chart the changing pattern of workplace conflict in the UK and explore the key explanations for this. Second, we examine the development of the legal and institutional framework of dispute resolution in the UK. Successive governmental responses to perceived rigidities in the system and attempts to provide employers with greater flexibility and minimize use of employment litigation are then considered. Finally, we provide a brief analysis of key developments in the management of conflict.

From Collectivism to Individualism? The Pattern of Workplace Conflict in the UK

A rapid contraction in strike activity and a parallel increase in the volume of employment tribunal applications since 1980 has been widely interpreted as evidence of a fundamental transfer of the locus of conflict from the collective to the individual arena. The evidence suggests a much more complex picture that reflects more nuanced changes in both workplace relations and also in the legal, institutional, and policy context of conflict resolution.

Strike Action in the UK—a Disappearing Act?

Official assessments of the scale of collective conflict in UK workplaces are limited to three measures of strike action—numbers of strikes, workers involved in strike action, and the number of work days lost. This inevitably provides a partial account, as other types of industrial action, such as overtime bans, are not included. Nonetheless, it is clear that there has been a substantial reduction in strike activity with the annual average number of stoppages falling from 2,854 between 1968 and 1972, to just 123 between 2008 and 2012 (see Figure 22.1). There have been similar reductions in the number of days lost to strike action. Furthermore, there has been a change in the balance of strike activity across the period from manufacturing and extractive industries to public services. Between 2003 and 2012, the public sector accounted for 52% of stoppages and 87% of working days lost due to strike action (Hale, 2012).

The factors underpinning these changes have been widely discussed. There is little evidence that reduced strike activity reflects a broader diminution of discontent, for instance flowing from the development of more enlightened high involvement work practices. In fact, the decline in strike action during the 1990s coincided with a general deterioration in perceptions of employee relations and attitudes to work (Dix et al., 2009), attributed by some to work intensification (Green and Tsitsianis, 2005) more redolent of "hard" approaches to human resource management (HRM).

Macroeconomic factors have potentially been more influential. High unemployment and falling inflation in the 1980s and 1990s meant that those in work had less incentive to strike and faced a greater threat of joblessness (Edwards, 1995). While this fails to explain

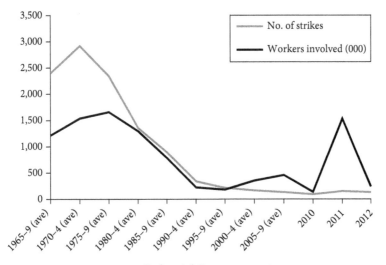

FIGURE 22.1 Industrial Stoppages, 1965–2011

Source: Office for National Statistics.

the sustained fall in strike activity in the face of rising employment after 1997, industrial restructuring and the globalization of production and competition (see Brown et al., 1997) contributed to the decline of heavily unionized and what were perceived as "strike-prone" industries (including coalmining, shipbuilding, and motor manufacturing).

This in turn led to a fundamental shift in the balance of workplace relations as trade union density, organization, and bargaining power eroded. The ability of unions to resist these changes was also stunted by the legislative restrictions on industrial action introduced by successive Conservative governments between 1980 and 1996. Accordingly, the changing distribution of strike activity arguably reflects the contraction of institutional industrial relations within private industry (Arrowsmith 2010) and the relative resilience of collective regulation and union organization in the public sector.

Individual Employment Disputes—a Growing Problem?

It could be argued that as collective avenues have weakened or disappeared, workplace conflict has been expressed through individual channels. Certainly, the numbers of registered employment tribunal applications grew rapidly during the 1990s and 2000s from 34,697 in 1989/90 to 236,100 two decades later (Dix et al., 2009; Ministry of Justice, 2011). Although there are signs that tribunal volumes are beginning to fall from this high point, they remain at a historically high level.

A number of explanations have been given for this. Falling union density has been associated with greater use of litigation (Burgess et al., 2000). As union influence and presence have eroded, collective processes of negotiation and resolution have disappeared from many workplaces (Charlwood and Terry, 2007; Saundry et al., 2011).

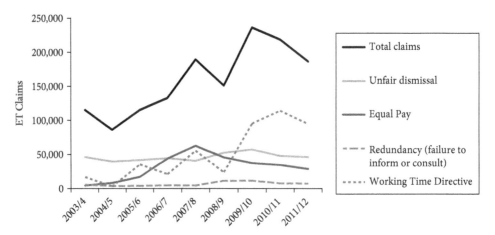

FIGURE 22.2 Employment Tribunal Applications, 2003–12

Source: Acas.

Instead, trade unions have placed greater emphasis on the legal enforcement of individual rights (Colling, 2012) while non-unionized workers often have little alternative but to turn to the law to defend their interests. Furthemore, the extension of employment protection, particularly following the election of the Labour government in 1997 and the growing influence of European law, extended the authority of employment tribunals to more than 60 separate jurisdictions (Ministry of Justice, 2012b). Consequently, some argue that the complexity of the legislative framework has made compliance more difficult, particularly for smaller organizations with limited HR expertise (Peters et al., 2010). At the same time, it might be suggested that increased awareness of employment rights among some groups of workers, easier access to legal advice and high expectations of monetary reward may have fueled tribunal claims.

The scale of individual employment disputes is often portrayed as a significant and growing problem, increasing costs to the state and business, and hampering economic growth (BIS 2011). However, the evidence for this is not clear. In recent years, much of the growth in tribunal application volumes can be explained by large-scale multiple claims relating to specific issues such as equal pay, redundancy, and working time (see Figure 22.2).

In fact, unfair dismissal claims have remained relatively stable while the number of single claims shows a small downward trajectory (Ministry of Justice, 2012a).

As far as other indicators of conflict are concerned, the 2011 Workplace Employment Relations Study (WERS) (van Wanrooy et al., 2013) found little sign of an upward trend in individualized conflict. The proportion of workplaces that reported any formal employee grievances in the previous 12 months fell from 38% in 2004 to 30% in 2011. There was also a small reduction in the incidence of disciplinary action—17% of managers dismissed at least one employee in 2011, compared to 19% in 2004 and 39% of managers used sanctions other than dismissal in 2011 compared with 43% in 2004. Moreover, there is little consistent evidence of any marked change in labor turnover or levels of sickness absence (Barmby et al., 2004; Kersley et al., 2006; van Wanrooy et al., 2013).

Of course, conflict may be suppressed due to employee concerns over recriminations or job security, particularly in times of recession. The 2012 Skills and Employment Survey (SES) (Gallie et al., 2013) found that fear of dismissal, discrimination and victimisation had increased since 2000 with a rise in anxiety levels among public sector workers in particular. Nonetheless, Dix et al.'s (2009) evaluation of evidence from the British Social Attitudes Survey, British Household Panel Survey, and WERS series suggests that although perceptions of employee relations and job satisfaction dipped during the early to mid-1990s, subsequent years saw a steady improvement. Notably, this trend appears to have been sustained, despite evidence of work intensification and the impact of the recession (van Wanrooy et al., 2013).

Explaining the Shape of Individual Conflict

While movements in the levels of individual employment disputes may be increasingly difficult to untangle, data from the WERS series has allowed us to build a more accurate picture of the shape of individual conflict inside British workplaces (Millward et al., 1992; Knight and Latreille, 2000; Kersley et al., 2006; Antcliff and Saundry, 2009). Workplace demographics are crucial, reflecting the extent to which different groups of workers experience problems at work and also the likelihood that they will seek to challenge managerial decisions. For example, WERS data consistently links the employment of women, older workers, and those in more skilled occupations with a lower incidence of disciplinary disputes (Knight and Latreille, 2000; Antcliff and Saundry, 2009). In contrast, workplaces with high proportions of non-white employees experience higher rates of disciplinary sanctions, dismissals, and employment tribunal applications. Younger workers also appear more likely to experience disciplinary action but are less likely to challenge this through litigation, possibly reflecting their relatively low level of awareness of employment rights (Casebourne et al., 2006).

Looking more broadly at workplace characteristics, it can be seen that employee grievances and disciplinary sanctions and dismissals are more likely as workplace size increases. Furthermore, smaller businesses are less prone to levy serious sanctions such as dismissal than larger organizations (Forth et al., 2006). This may point to a greater willingness to resolve issues informally, reflecting the personal nature of employment relations in such settings (Harris et al., 2008). The management of conduct and performance and the state of workplace relations will also shape the incidence of individual employment disputes. For example, a strong union presence is linked to lower levels of disciplinary action, as a result of unions either restraining managerial prerogative or facilitating informal paths of resolution (Edwards, 2000; Saundry et al., 2011). In contrast, employee grievances are more likely where employees can draw on union support.

These factors, and the context within which employment relations are conducted are echoed in sectoral patterns of individual conflict (Kersley et al., 2006). Public sector workplaces tend to be characterized by high levels of grievances and relatively high rates of absence but disciplinary sanctions and quits are less common. In short, conflict is more likely to manifest through avenues that challenge managerial authority, a process which may be bolstered by relatively well-organized trade unions, and, until recently, job security. Turning to the private sector, within manufacturing, rates of grievances and employment tribunal applications are again relatively high, possibly reflecting union presence, but low levels of absenteeism perhaps illustrate a more proactive approach to the management of such issues. In contrast, private services, and particularly industries such as retail, hotels, and restaurants, are characterized by frequent disciplinary action and high staff turnover. This may be explained by close control of the work process and robust application of managerial prerogative (Arrowsmith, 2010). At the same time, relatively low levels of grievances in these sectors point to a lack of access to employee voice and representation.

Therefore, while the UK has seen a decline in collective industrial action and British[1] employment tribunals have experienced an upsurge in applications, broad assertions that this merely represents the individualization of workplace conflict are too simplistic. Instead, it would appear that the pattern of conflict, and the capacity to resolve it, is fundamentally influenced by the nature of workplace and managerial relations. These features in turn are shaped by the economic and legal context within which organizations operate.

The Legal Framework of Conflict Resolution—Juridification and Formalization

There is little doubt that government intervention has had a significant impact on the nature and pattern of workplace conflict. The defining motif of UK state policy has been the rejection of a "voluntaristic" approach which relied on resolution through collective negotiation, as successive administrations have attempted to limit industrial action and "institutionalize" the management of individual disputes through legal and procedural arrangements inside and outside the workplace. However, it is argued that this approach has resulted in a system that has become unnecessarily complex, crowding-out informal "common-sense" approaches to dispute resolution, and encouraged litigation (Gibbons, 2007; BIS, 2011).

Regulating Industrial action—Consensus and Decline

Under the "voluntaristic" system that dominated post-war employment relations, the government largely relied on workplace systems of collective bargaining to manage and resolve conflict. Industrial action was protected by a system of legal immunities, with statutory intervention limited to plugging "gaps" where bargaining did not exist or jointly agreed resolutions had failed (Dickens and Hall, 2010). A prime example of this was the establishment of the Advisory, Conciliation and Arbitration Service (Acas) in 1975 to promote the improvement of industrial relations and encourage the extension and development of collective bargaining.

The Conservative government's program of employment legislation, introduced between 1980 and 1996, represented a radical break with this approach. It weakened union immunities by introducing requirements for postal ballots prior to industrial action and restrictions on the conduct of any consequent activity, particularly in regard to the deployment of pickets and the outlawing of secondary industrial action. In 1993, it also removed Acas' statutory duty to promote collective bargaining. While these measures drew criticisms that the UK had breached minimum international standards (Ewing, 1989), a political consensus developed around what some consider to be a neoliberal agenda (Smith and Morton, 2006), with the Labour government elected in 1997 leaving the key elements intact.

These reforms undoubtedly shaped the conduct of unions and reduced the impact of strike action in major industrial disputes, but there is less evidence that they had a direct role in reducing strike incidence (Wallace and O'Sullivan, 2006). Morever, while legislative reform may have forced unions to adopt a more selective approach to industrial action (Dickens and Hall, 2010), there is little indication that the use of postal ballots moderated outcomes of strike votes. In fact, ballots became an effective bargaining tool, with unions using positive results to win concessions from employers (Elgar and Simpson, 1993).

The rapid decline in strike action has been mirrored in the reduced use of Acas collective conciliation (Dawe and Neathey, 2008). On average, between 1973 and 1976, Acas dealt with more than 3,000 requests for collective conciliation per year compared to 974 between 2010 and 2013 (Podro and Suff, 2009; Acas, 2013). This not only reflects the changing scale of industrial action but also increased resistance to third-party intervention. Employers with greater bargaining power may be reluctant to conciliate, while union negotiators and leaders increasingly draw on a range of strategies to resolve collective disputes including balloting, legal action, and media campaigns (Heery and Nash, 2011).

Individual Employment Disputes—Institutionalizing Workplace Conflict

The legal framework governing individual employment disputes was also designed to reduce the incidence of industrial action by removing disciplinary and grievance issues from the ambit of collective bargaining (Deakin and Njoya, 2008). The introduction of a statutory right to claim unfair dismissal (in 1971) and the development of the employment tribunal system triggered the rapid formalization of disciplinary and grievance handling as employers adopted written procedures as protection against litigation (Edwards, 2000). This was bolstered by the introduction, in 1977, of the first Acas Code of Practice on "Disciplinary Practice and Procedures in Employment" which established a clear benchmark for organizational processes. Furthermore, faced with a dramatic reduction in collective influence and workplace organization, trade unions were forced to rely on the enforcement of written procedures in order to defend their members' interests. As a consequence, the application of procedure became the default setting for conflict handling in most UK workplaces.

Prior to 1971, as few as 8% of establishments used formal procedures for dealing with discipline and dismissals. By 1990, they were present in approximately 90% of workplaces employing 25 employees (Millward et al., 1992) and in 2011, 89% of workplaces, with five or more employees, reported having such a procedure in place (van Wanrooy et al., 2013). In some respects, the emphasis on written procedures could be seen as offering some degree of protection and regulation in the growing number of workplaces in which there were no structures of employee representation. However, it also represented a transition from the joint regulation of conflict towards unilateral managerial prerogative. According to data from WERS2011, disciplinary and grievance procedures were subject to negotiation in just 5% of workplaces, with five or more employees, and less than a quarter of workplaces in which unions were recognized.

Between 1996 and 2007, this formalization of workplace conflict resolution was extended by the Labour government's emphasis on promoting "good employment practices" (DTI, 2001: 14). Two key measures were introduced: a right for workers to be accompanied at disciplinary and grievance hearings, and statutory three-step procedures (in 2008) for dealing with disciplinary and employee grievances. In addition, access to claim unfair dismissal was extended to all those with 12 months' continuous employment (from two years) and the maximum limit on compensation was increased. These changes were promoted as providing a minimum "infrastructure of decency and fairness", seen as crucial in securing employee commitment and improved productivity (DTI, 1998: 2).

However, while some commentators suggested that the three-step procedures undermined protection for employees (Hepple and Morris, 2002; Sanders, 2009), the debate was dominated by concerns over their impact on the ability of employers to effectively manage disciplinary and grievance issues. The Gibbons Review, which was commissioned to "identify options for simplifying and improving all aspects of employment dispute resolution" (Gibbons, 2007: 7) argued that the procedures encouraged formal approaches and defensive attitudes, making litigation more likely. The subsequent abolition of the statutory three-step procedures and the adoption of Gibbons' suggestion for a shorter and less prescriptive statutory Acas Code of Practice underlined the government's acceptance of employers' demands for greater discretion over the management of workplace disputes.

A Break with the Past? De-regulation, Flexibility, and Managerial Discretion

Since 2010, the UK Coalition government has sought to increase and extend the flexibility afforded to employers in managing conflict, reduce the volume of employment tribunals, and promote the settlement of disputes. However, in seeking strategies to bring clarity to mechanisms to end the employment relationship (BIS, 2013), some have argued that the incentives for employers to work to resolve disputes in the workplace at an early stage have been blunted.

Employment Tribunal Reform—Balancing Efficiency and Justice?

The perceived cost of defending employment litigation has become a touchstone for the Coalition government and employers who feel that employment tribunals are weighted unfairly against them (BIS, 2011; British Chambers of Commerce, 2011; CBI, 2011). Originally conceived as an "accessible, speedy, informal and inexpensive" means of dispute resolution and source of workplace justice, tribunals have become increasingly "legalistic and adversarial" (Gibbons, 2007: 21). In particular, employers argue that the time and money needed to defend a claim can be significant and that organizations are forced to limit exposure by settling claims that have little chance of success. Moreover, it has been suggested that the costs regime—whereby costs are not normally awarded to the successful party—encourages claimants to lodge weak claims in the hope and expectation of settlement (BIS, 2011).

Thus, reforms have sought to provide employers with greater room for manoeuvre by, among other strategies, reducing the risk they face when seeking to dismiss staff. Only those employed continuously for two years now have the right to claim unfair dismissal. In addition, claimants will have to pay a fee to have their case heard by a tribunal. Finally, new provisions relating to "settlement agreements" mean that discussion around termination of employment may be inadmissible should an employee bring a subsequent employment tribunal claim. While these changes have generally been welcomed by employers' organizations, trade unions have argued that they erode workplace justice and reduce employer incentives to resolve disputes in the workplace and maintain employment relationships.

There is little doubt that the increased jurisdictional reach of tribunals and the development of case law in both domestic and European courts have increased the complexity of procedures and made legal representation increasingly important (Hudson et al., 2007; Buscha et al., 2012). The growth of no-win, no-fee legal representation has also arguably widened access to litigation (Gibbons, 2007). Nonetheless, it could be argued that the picture of a system weighted in favor of claimants is not supported by the evidence. For example, some commentators have suggested that the increasing juridification of the employment tribunal system poses a threat to equality as parties able to access legal representation are placed in a powerful position (Colling, 2010). According to data from the Survey of Employment Tribunal Applications (SETA), employers are much more likely to be represented at tribunal hearings by a legal specialist compared to claimants (Hayward et al., 2004; Peters et al., 2010). Moreover, there is some evidence to suggest that where respondents are legally represented, claimants are less likely to be successful (Buscha et al., 2012).

The assertion that the existing system encourages speculative claims is also questionable. Since 2001, tribunals have had the authority to award costs against claimants whose application has been "misconceived" but this power is rarely exercised (Morris, 2012). Furthermore, there is relatively little firm evidence of large numbers of weak claims. Although tribunals have increased powers to strike out claims with "no reasonable prospect of success," the proportion of claims struck out prior to hearing has remained relatively static in recent years. There has also been little change in the proportion of cases that fail at the preliminary stage. This could be illustrative of employers settling claims at a very early point or that tribunals are reluctant to use their authority to weed out weak claims. But, it might also suggest that the extent of baseless applications has been exaggerated.

Crucially, the employment tribunal system is reactive, mainly focused on compensating loss, rather than addressing deficiencies in the management of employment relations or, at the individual level, rebuilding relations (Dickens and Hall, 2010). It is important to remember that most claims that reach the tribunals are not successful. In addition, reinstatement or re-engagement in cases of unfair dismissal is extremely rare (see Morris, 2012). Thus, while defending employment tribunal claims inevitably imposes burdens on business, it is also important to examine the extent to which the system provides workers with a realistic opportunity to enforce their rights (Dickens, 2012).

Conciliation in Individual Employment Disputes

The other notable strand of public policy has been the promotion of alternative methods of dispute resolution. While the government has promoted the use of workplace mediation (which is discussed in greater detail in the section "Searching for innovation—the promise of mediation" below), concrete measures have been focused on the extension of Acas' conciliation services. Acas has a long-standing statutory duty to conciliate between employment tribunal claimants and respondents after a claim has been lodged. Around four out of every ten cases are resolved in this way (Peters et al., 2010). Following the Gibbons review, Acas received government investment to offer a pre-claim conciliation (PCC) service, to callers to the Acas Helpline who were involved in *potential* employment tribunal claims. This was designed to resolve disputes before litigation thus reducing costs to parties and the state (Davey and Dix, 2011). Crucially, this service was voluntary, confidential, and (unlike mediation) free of charge.

Between 2009 and 2013, more than 70,000 cases were subject to PCC. In 2012/13, 52% were resolved and only 23% progressed to tribunal (Acas, 2013). Users found PCC to be quicker, cheaper, and less stressful than litigation and there was evidence of consequent improvements to organizational practice. The service was also more widely accessed by small firms without HR expertise than was the case for employment tribunals, although the vast majority of cases were initiatied by employees. There was, however, less evidence that PCC had been successful in resolving disputes inside the workplace and preserving the employment relationship. In fact, most employees were no longer working

at the same establishment by the time they used the service and only a small proportion of cases resulted in employment being maintained (Acas and Infogroup/ORC
International, 2010; TNS BMRB, 2013).

The perceived success of PCC led to the development of a scheme for "Early
Conciliation" (EC) (to be introduced in April 2014) under which all prospective claimants will have to submit their details to Acas, and will be offered conciliation. Where this
fails or is rejected by either party, the claimant will be able to submit an application to the
employment tribunal. While EC provides an opportunity to all employment tribunal
claimants for an early resolution, its objective is focused more on avoiding litigation as
opposed to PCC which offers at least the possibility of earlier intervention within the
workplace. Furthermore, the fact that the introduction of charging for tribunal applications precedes the introduction of EC will almost certainly cast a veil over the precise
impact of this initiative.

The Management of Conflict in UK Workplaces—Bridging the Resolution Gap?

As the preceding discussion makes clear, the current direction of government policy
accepts that the ability of organizations to address and resolve individual employment
disputes has been hamstrung by legal regulation and the consequent development of
rigid and restrictive procedure. This assumes that, if freed from this burden, employers
have both the ability and motivation to manage conflict more proactively and effectively.
Unfortunately, this neglects fundamental changes to the network of management–union
relationships. Critically, it has been argued that the disappearance of effective structures
of employee representation, combined with an increasingly remote HR function have
weakened organizational conflict management capacity, creating a resolution gap.

Devolving Conflict Management to the Line—a Confidence Crisis?

Traditionally in the UK, responsibility for the day-to-day management of conflict rested
in the hands of personnel and HR practitioners who played an interventionist role
in dealing with both collective and individual issues. While this was often derided as
"fire-fighting," it was nonetheless central to attempts to avoid the escalation of disputes,
through social processes of negotiation and bargaining.

As the importance of collective employee relations diminished in many workplaces,
HR practitioners became increasingly responsible for the management of individual conflict, for instance through the design and oversight of workplace procedures.

Although operational managers may have had decision-making power, they were largely dependent on "personnel" or "HR" to deal with disciplinary, grievance, and other individual issues. However, the development of a more "strategic" focus in HR (Caldwell, 2003) has seen practitioners increasingly withdraw from day-to-day conflict management to one in which they provide expert advice to line managers who have been given the responsibility for handling employee conduct, capability, and performance. Thus, the changing role of HR places line and operational managers at the centre of organizational efforts to resolve conflict.

Line managers might be expected to welcome the greater freedom offered by current government policy. It has been suggested that they not only dislike the time and effort associated with due process, but favor informal approaches which allow them to respond to issues based on "gut feeling" (Rollinson et al., 1996: 51) and balance decisions against broader operational goals. For example, they may place greater weight on mitigating circumstances or chose not to tackle misbehavior or misconduct if it involves otherwise productive members of staff (Dunn and Wilkinson, 2002). However, the CIPD has argued that "managers are neither willing nor capable of taking this on effectively" (CIPD, 2008: 8) while the government claims that, "many more problems could be prevented from escalating into disputes if line managers were better able to manage conflict" (BIS, 2011: 17).

In fact, line and operational managers appear to be hamstrung by a lack of confidence and experience in dealing with conflict (Jones and Saundry, 2012). Difficult issues are often avoided or handled in a rigid and prescriptive manner as the threat of litigation and consequent ramifications for career progression encourage a risk-averse approach to disciplinary and grievance issues. This is arguably exacerbated by a shortfall in training and a lack of support from senior management, who may not see conflict management as a priority (Teague and Roche, 2011).

Mediating Workplace Relations? The Changing Role of HR Practitioners and Employee Representation

There is some evidence that the presence of HR practitioners in the workplace can underpin the development of line manager capability—building confidence and skills by working alongside inexperienced staff. Furthermore, where practitioners have a clear understanding of, and familiarity with, the organizational context, their advice is more likely to reflect the nuances and complexities faced by their operational colleagues (Saundry and Wibberley, 2012). However, this is threatened by moves towards centralized "business partner" and outsourced models of HR management, which can lead to a more distanced relationship between HR and the line. Jones and Saundry (2012) argue that this threatens to embed a culture of formality for two reasons. First, strong relationships between line managers and HR practitioners which underpin informal processes of dispute resolution may be more difficult to sustain. Second, HR advice will be reduced to an exercise in standardization and uniformity if HR practitioners have little contextual knowledge of the workplace or emotional stake in the outcome of a disciplinary decision.

In addition, within unionized workplaces, an increasingly detached HR function weakens the ability of practitioners to forge constructive relationships with union representatives. Indeed, the impact of employee representation is an issue that has been curiously overlooked within the policy debates rehearsed above. Trade unions can play a key role in "self-discipline" (Edwards, 2000), managing the expectations of members and negotiating with managers to resolve issues or minimize sanctions. However, the mere involvement of trade unions is not enough—if they are to be effective in averting and resolving disputes, high-trust workplace relations are needed to sustain more nuanced, social processes of dispute resolution (Oxenbridge and Brown, 2004; Saundry et al., 2011). In contrast, where this is not the case, representatives may be more likely to adopt adversarial approaches in defending members.

This suggests that reduced union presence in UK workplaces has important and worrying consequences for conflict resolution. In 2011, unions were recognized in only one-fifth of workplaces (21%) and only 27% of these had a union representative on-site (van Wanrooy et al., 2013).

Moreover, there is little evidence of any significant growth in stand alone non-union representation, which is found in just 7% of workplaces. It is rarer still for such representatives to play a substantive role within grievance and disciplinary processes (van Wanrooy et al., 2013). In the growing number of workplaces with no representational structures, workplace conflict is in danger of becoming an exercise in managerial authority—with resolution dependent on the ability of line managers who often lack the experience and confidence to address and resolve conflict at an early stage.

Searching for Innovation—the Promise of Mediation

In light of these difficulties, attention has turned to finding more innovative ways to manage workplace conflict. Within the UK, this has primarily focused on the promotion of mediation, hailed by the Gibbons Review as "a pragmatic, flexible and informal way of providing both parties with positive outcomes" (Gibbons, 2007). Certainly, mediation is generally found to be an effective way of resolving certain types of disputes that might otherwise escalate into complex, costly, and damaging litigation. In this respect it is seen as having clear advantages over traditional procedures. It is also seen as more likely to resolve underlying issues and restore the employment relationship (Latreille, 2011). Perhaps more importantly, it has been argued that in particular the introduction of in-house mediation schemes may have a positive impact on broader processes of conflict management. Indeed, in 2011, the government claimed that a growth in the use of mediation "has the potential to lead to a major and dramatic shift in the culture of employment relations" (BIS, 2011: 13).

Nonetheless, whether it can stimulate a more proactive approach to conflict management is more questionable. Certainly, recent research has suggested that involvement in mediation can have a transformative impact on the attitudes of key organizational actors and underpin the rebuilding of damaged social processes of resolution (Saundry et al., 2013). A key question, however, is whether organizations can establish and extend their use of mediation, particularly in light of the shortfall in HR support outlined above.

Very large organizations may face problems in promoting mediation across a large number of geographically dispersed workplaces. There is also likely to be resistance from organizational actors, particularly line managers who see the need for mediation as an admittance of failure (Saundry and Wibberley, 2012). Moreover, the sustainability of in-house mediation schemes is dependent on securing the support of senior management and the ability of mediators to carve out time for the role, given competing work pressures.

There are signs that awareness and use of workplace mediation is growing. Acas received 85 requests for mediation on individual issues in 2005/6 but by 2012/13, this had risen to 235 (Acas, 2013) and there is evidence that the introduction of the revised Acas Code of Practice on "Disciplinary and Grievance Procedures" in 2009 prompted the increased integration of mediation into policy and procedure (Latreille, 2011; Rahim et al., 2011). Nonetheless, its use is generally limited to larger organizations and those in the public sector. Research undertaken by Acas found that just 5% of private sector businesses had used mediation, falling to just 4% in SMEs (Williams, 2011). In addition, data from WERS2011 found that just 7% of all workplaces with five or more employees had used mediation to resolve a dispute in the 12 months prior to the survey. Therefore, as yet, there is little suggestion that mediation is "embedded in the culture of conflict handling" (van Wanrooy et al., 2013: 27).

Conflict Resolution in the UK—Future Prospects and Considerations

Many of the conditions that trigger workplace conflict in the UK are likely to remain and even intensify in the coming years. Continuing competition from emerging economies against a backdrop of stagnation and recession within Europe can be expected to lead to further private sector restructuring and a drive for increased efficiency. In the public sector, cuts in government spending have already led to downward pressure on terms and conditions, rationalization, and a growth in outsourcing. There is also evidence of a more robust approach to the management of performance and sickness absence (Taylor et al., 2010).

These factors may lead to growing discontent as workers attempt to cope with uncertainty and also adjust to new environments and expectations. However, the extent to which this will become manifest in industrial action or individual employment disputes is less clear. Although there has been widespread strike activity within the public sector in response to the effects of austerity, and in particular to changes to pension provision, trade unions in the public sector are not immune to the relative weakness of organized labor in the UK (Bach, 2011). At both a collective and individual level, workers facing substantial and rapid organizational change may also be reluctant to risk the consequences of contesting managerial authority against a background of high levels of unemployment and employment insecurity. Furthermore, public policy designed to deter litigation and encourage conciliated settlements may well lead to a reduction in employment tribunal volumes.

However, whether the emerging regulatory framework will provide a conducive environment for the resolution of issues *in the workplace* is not clear. Moves to extend the reach of conciliation are welcome. The concern is that this may well result in a focus on settling disputes in which the employment relationship has already been broken at the expense of seeking to repair relations at an earlier stage. There is also a danger that if employers percieve that the risks of litigation have been reduced, they may be less inclined to devote the necessary time, effort, and resources to those workers who have fallen below expected standards norms of conduct, capability, and performance.

This is perhaps less likely where there are high-trust relationships between employee representatives, managers, and HR practitioners. In such situations, organizations will be better placed to resolve such problems at an early stage through informal discussion. However, there is growing evidence that workplace structures that have traditionally supported the resolution of disputes have been progressively hollowed out. Social processes of negotiation have disappeared as trade union decline has left a void that has not been filled by new forms of representation. In addition, a resolution gap has appeared as the HR function in many organizations has adopted a more "strategic," centralized and some would argue, remote role. Accordingly, conflict management has been devolved to a community of line managers with little experience of, and confidence in, managing people issues, just as demands for increased efficiency have placed them under greater operational pressure.

At a broader level, it is important to note that there is limited evidence of organizations in the UK adopting innovative approaches to managing conflict. There are signs of increasing organizational interest in mediation and mounting evidence of its effectiveness in resolving inter-personal disputes and maintaining employment relationships. Moreover, there are indications that, in certain contexts, the use of mediation can replace adversarial approaches to individual conflict with a culture of resolution. Despite this, for the most part, mediation remains limited to larger organizations and even here appears to be used as an additional tool for dealing with intractable disputes rather than as part of more coordinated conflict management strategies.

Critically, the bedrock for innovation in this area is weak—it would seem that for most organizations in the UK, managing conflict is seen as a transactional function rather than a strategic priority that is central to meeting the challenges of intensified competition and increased pressure to reduce costs. Furthermore, it could be suggested that the business case for increasing the capacity of organizations to address and resolve workplace disputes, through investment in enhanced skills for line managers and the development of new, creative, and integrated approaches to the management of conflict, may be weakened if avoidance of litigation is given greater credence than the benefits of early resolution.

Note

1. Strike data are collected by ONS in respect of the United Kingdom (including Northern Ireland), while ET and WERS data refer only to Great Britain (England, Scotland, and Wales).

References

Acas 2013. *Annual Report and Accounts, 2012–2013*. London: Acas.

Acas and Infogroup/ORC International 2010. "Evaluation of the First Year of Acas' Pre-Claim Conciliation Service." Acas Research Paper, 08/10.

Antcliff, V. and Saundry, R. 2009. "Accompaniment, Workplace Representation and Disciplinary Outcomes in British Workplaces—Just a Formality?" *British Journal of Industrial Relations*, 47(1): 100–21.

Arrowsmith, J. 2010. "Industrial Relations in the Private Sector," in D. Colling and M. Terry (eds), *Industrial Relations: theory and practice*. Oxford: Wiley-Blackwell, 178–206.

Bach, S. 2011. "A New Era of Public Service Employment Relations? The Challenges Ahead." Acas Future of Workplace Relations discussion paper series, Aug.

Barmby, T., Ercolani, M. and Treble, J. 2004. "Sickness Absence in the UK 1984–2002." *Swedish Economic Policy Review*, 11(1): 65–88.

BIS (Department of Business, Innovation and Skills) 2011. *Resolving Workplace Disputes: A Consultation*. London: BIS.

BIS (Department of Business, Innovation and Skills) 2013. *Ending the Employment Relationship: Government Response to Consultation*. London: BIS.

British Chambers of Commerce 2011. *The Workforce Survey—Small Businesses, October 2011*. London: British Chambers of Commerce.

Brown, W., Deakin, S., and Ryan, P. 1997. "The Effects of British Industrial Relations Legislation 1979–1997." *National Institute Economic Review*, 161: 69–83.

Burgess, S. Propper, C., and Wilson, D. 2000. "Explaining the Growth in the Number of Applications to Industrial Tribunals 1972–1997." *Employment Relations Research Series, No. 10*. London: Department of Trade and Industry.

Buscha, F., Urwin, P., and Latreille, P. 2012. "Representation in Employment Tribunals: Analysis of 2003 and 2008 SETA." Acas Research Paper, 06/12.

Caldwell, R. 2003. "The Changing Roles of Personnel Managers: Old Ambiguities, New Uncertainties." *Journal of Management Studies*, 40(4): 983–1004.

Casebourne, J., Regan, J., Neathey, F., and Tuohy, S. 2006. "Employment Rights at Work—Survey of Employees." *Employment Relations Research Series, No. 51*. London: DTI.

CBI 2011. *Settling the Matter—Building a More Effective and Efficient Tribunal System*. London: Confederation of British Industry.

Charlwood, A. and Terry, M. 2007. "21st-Century Models of Employee Representation: Structures, Processes and Outcomes." *Industrial Relations Journal*, 38(4): 320–37.

CIPD 2008. *Leadership and the Management of Conflict at Work*. London: CIPD.

Colling, T. 2010. "Legal Institutions and the Regulation of Workplaces." In D. Colling and M. Terry (eds), *Industrial Relations: Theory and Practice*. Oxford: Wiley-Blackwell, 323–46.

Colling, T. 2012. "Trade Union Roles in Making Employment Rights Effective." In L. Dickens (ed.), *Making Employment Rights Effective: Issues of Enforcement and Compliance*. Oxford: Hart Publishing, 183–204.

Davey, B. and Dix, G. 2011. "The Dispute Resolution Regulations two years on: the Acas experience." Acas Research Paper, 07/11.

Dawe, A. and Neathey, F. 2008. "Acas Conciliation in Collective Employment Disputes." Acas Research Paper, 05/08.

Deakin, S. and Njoya, W. 2008. "The Legal Framework of Employment Relations." In P. Blyton, E. Heery, N. Bacon, and J. Fiorito (eds), *The Sage Handbook of Industrial Relations*. Los Angeles and London: Sage Publications, 284–304.

Dickens, L. 2012. "Fairer Workplaces: Making Employment Rights Effective" In L. Dickens (ed.), *Making Employment Rights Effective: Issues of Enforcement and Compliance*. Oxford: Hart Publishing, 204–28.

Dickens, L. and Hall, M. 2010. "The Changing Legal Framework of Employment Relations," in D. Colling and M. Terry (eds), *Industrial Relations: Theory and Practice*. Oxford: Wiley-Blackwell, 298–322.

Dix, G., Forth, J., and Sisson, K. 2009. "Conflict at Work: The Changing Pattern of Disputes." In W. Brown, A. Bryson, J. Forth, and K. Whitfield (eds), *The Evolution of the Modern Workplace*. Cambridge: Cambridge University Press, 176–200.

DTI (Department of Trade and Industry) 1998. "Fairness at Work." Cm3968. Norwich: The Stationary Office.

DTI (Department of Trade and Industry) 2001. *Routes to Resolution—Consultation Document on Dispute Resolution and Tribunal reform*. London: DTI.

Dunn, C. and Wilkinson, A. 2002. "Wish You Were Here: Managing Absence." *Personnel Review*, 31(2): 228–46.

Edwards, P. 1995. "Strikes and Industrial Conflict." In P. Edwards (ed.), *Industrial Relatons: Theory and Practice in Britain*. Oxford: Blackwell, 434–60.

Edwards, P. 2000. "Discipline: Towards Trust and Self-discipline?" In S. Bach and K. Sisson (eds), *Personnel Management: A Comprehensive Guide to Theory and Practice in Britain*. 3rd edn. Oxford: Blackwell, 317–39.

Elgar, J. and Simpson, B. 1993. "The Impact of the Law on Industrial Disputes in the 1980s." In D. Metcalfand S. Milner (eds), *New Perspectives on Industrial Disputes*. London: Routledge, 70–114.

Ewing, K. 1989. *Britain and the ILO*. London: Institute of Employment Rights.

Forth, J., Bewley, H., and Bryson, A. 2006. *Small and Medium-sized Enterprises: Findings from the 2004 Workplace Employment Relations Survey*. London: Routledge.

Gallie, D., Felstead, A., Green, F. and Inanc, H. (2013). *Fear at Work in Britain: First Findings from the Skills and Employment Survey, 2012*. <http://www.cardiff.ac.uk/socsi/ses2012/ [hidden]resources/4.%20Fear%20at%20Work%20Minireport.pdf>.

Gibbons, M. 2007. *A Review of Employment Dispute Resolution in Great Britain*. London: DTI.

Green, F. and Tsitsianis, N. 2005. "An Investigation of National Trends in Job Satisfaction in Britain and Germany." *British Journal of Industrial Relations*, 43(3): 401–29.

Hale, D. 2012. *Labour Disputes, Annual Article 2012*. London: Office for National Statistics.

Harris, L., Tuckman, A., Snook, J., Tailby, S., Hutchinson, S., and Winters, J. 2008. "Small Firms and Workplace Disputes Resolution." Acas Research Paper, 01/08.

Hayward, B., Peters, M., Rousseau, N. and Seeds, K. 2004. "Findings from the Survey of Employment Tribunal Applications 2003." *Employment Relations Research Series*. No. 33, London: Department of Trade and Industry.

Heery, E. and Nash, D. 2011. "Trade Union Officers and Collective Conciliation—A Secondary Analysis." Acas Research Paper, 10/11.

Hepple, B. and Morris, G. 2002. "The Employment Act 2002 and The Crisis of Individual Employment Rights." *Industrial Law Journal*, 31(30): 245–69.

Hudson, M., Barnes, H., Brooks, S., and Taylor, R. 2007. "Race Discrimination Claims: Unrepresented Claimants' and Employers' Views on Acas' Conciliation in Employment Tribunal Cases." Acas Research Paper, 04/07.

Jones, C. and Saundry, R. 2012. "The Practice of Discipline: Evaluating the Roles and Relationship between Managers and HR Professionals." *Human Resource Management Journal*, 22(3): 252–66.

Kersley, B., Alpin, C., Forth, J., Bryson, A., Bewley, H., Dix, G., and Oxenbridge, S. 2006. *Inside the Workplace: Findings from the 2004 Workplace Employment Relations Survey*. London: Routledge.

Knight, K. and Latreille, P. 2000. "Discipline, Dismissals and Complaints to Employment Tribunals." *British Journal of Industrial Relations*, 38(4), 533–55.

Latreille, P. 2011. "Workplace Mediation: A Thematic Review of the Acas/CIPD Evidence." Acas Research Paper, 13/11.

Millward, N., Stevens, M., Smart, D., and Hawes, W. 1992. *Workplace Industrial Relations in Transition*. Aldershot: Dartmouth.

Ministry of Justice 2011. *Employment Tribunals and EAT Statistics, 2010–11*. London: Ministry of Justice.

Ministry of Justice 2012a. *Employment Tribunals and EAT Statistics, 2011–12*. London: Ministry of Justice.

Ministry of Justice 2012b. <http://www.justice.gov.uk/tribunals/employment/claims/jurisdiction> accessed 20 Sept. 2012.

Morris, G. 2012. "The Develeopment of Stautory Employment Rights in Britain and Enforcement Mechansims" In L. Dickens (ed.), *Making Employment Rights Effective: Issues of Enforcement and Compliance*. Oxford: Hart Publishing, 7–28.

Oxenbridge, S. and Brown, W. 2004. "Achieving a New Equilibrium? The Stability of Co-operative Employer–union Relationships." *Industrial Relations Journal*, 35(5): 388–402.

Peters, M., Seeds, K., Harding, C., and Garnett, E. 2010. "Findings from the Survey of Employment Tribunal Applications 2008." *Employment Relations Research Series*, 107, Department of Business, Innovation and Skills.

Podro, S. and Suff, R. 2009. "The Alchemy of Dispute Resolution—the Role of Collective Conciliation." *Acas Policy Discussion Papers*. London: Acas.

Rahim, N., Brown, A., and Graham, J. 2011. "Evaluation of the Acas Code of Practice on Disciplinary and Grievance Procedures." Acas Research Paper, 06/11.

Rollinson, D., Hook, C., and Foot, M. 1996. "Supervisor and Manager Styles in Handling Discipline and Grievance. Part two—approaches to handling discipline and grievance." *Personnel Review*, 25(4): 38–55.

Sanders, A. 2009. "Part One of the Employment Act 2008: 'Better' Dispute Resolution." *Industrial Law Journal*, 38(1): 30–49.

Saundry, R. and Wibberley, G. 2012. "Managing Individual Conflict in the Private Sector—A Case Study." Acas Research Papers, 05/12.

Saundry, R., Jones, C., and Antcliff, V. 2011. "Discipline, Representation and Dispute Resolution—Exploring the Role of Trade Unions and Employee Companions in Workplace Discipline." *Industrial Relations Journal*, 42(2): 195–211.

Saundry, R., McArdle, L., and Thomas, P. (2013). "Reframing Workplace Relations? Conflict Resolution and Mediation in a Primary Care Trust," *Work, Employment and Society*, 27(2): 213–31.

Smith, P. and Morton, G. 2006. "Nine Years of New Labour: Neoliberalism and Workers' Rights." *British Journal of Industrial Relations*, 44(3): 401–20.

Taylor, P., Cunningham, I., Newsome, K., and Scholarios D. 2010. "'Too Scared to go Sick'—Reformulating the Research Agenda on Sickness Absence." *Industrial Relations Journal*, 41(4): 270–88.

Teague, P. and Roche, W. 2011. "Line Managers and the Management of Workplace Conflict: Evidence from Ireland." *Human Resource Management Journal*, 22(3): 235–51.

TNS-BMRB 2013. "Evaluation of Acas' Pre-Claim Conciliation Service 2012." Acas Research Papers, 06/13.

Van Wanrooy, B., Bewley, H., Bryson, A., Forth, J., Freeth, S., Stokes, L., and Wood S. 2013. *The 2011 Workplace Employment Relations Study—First Findings*. London: BIS.

Wallace, J. and O'Sullivan, M. 2006. "Contemporary Strike Trends Since 1980: Peering through the Wrong End of a Telescope." In M. Morley, P. Gunnigle, and D. Collings (eds), *Global Industrial Relations*. London: Routledge, 273–91.

Williams, M. 2011. "Workplace Conflict Management: Awareness and Use of Acas Code of Practice and Workplace Meditation—A Poll of Business." Acas Research Papers, 08/11.

....

CHAPTER 23

CONFLICT RESOLUTION IN CHINA

....

MINGWEI LIU

INTRODUCTION

CHINA's market-oriented reforms in the past decades have gradually transformed the nation's economy and employment system. Although the transformation has been largely smooth since the early 1990s, labor disputes have soared in the former "workers' paradise." To maintain industrial peace, a system of workplace dispute resolution that features various internal and external, formal and informal mechanisms has been instituted and continues to evolve. While this system clearly moves away from the traditional, strictly administrative approach, significant deficits exist in every mechanism of dispute resolution. It is therefore argued here that as the Chinese economy develops, more sophisticated mechanisms of conflict management will be required to address both collective and individual workplace disputes. To flesh out this argument, this chapter first examines the scale, pattern, nature, and causes of rising labor disputes, followed by a review of various internal and external labor dispute resolution institutions and mechanisms with a focus on their recent changes and problems. The chapter concludes by discussing possible future development of labor dispute resolution in China.

RISING LABOR DISPUTES

When the Chinese state was the single employer, committed to centralized planning, detailed plans were passed from the national level down to individual workplaces on production, allocation of resources and workers, and even wage and welfare levels. Managers, under the leadership of enterprise Communist Party committees, were simply agents of the state lacking autonomy on production and employment issues. Moreover, because they were not considered to be separate parties, fundamental conflicts of interest between workers and management were not supposed to exist. As a result, labor disputes between management and workers in the Chinese workplace were rare or concealed by the state-centered political and economic arrangements that aligned the interests of workers and managers with those of the state. Where labor disputes did occur, they were usually resolved quickly by the Party-state apparatus at the workplace.

China's market-oriented economic reforms have gradually transformed the Chinese workplace, replacing the old employment system of "iron rice bowl" (i.e. lifetime employment, stable and egalitarian wages, and guaranteed generous welfare) with a contract-based regime that emphasizes flexibility and efficiency. Managers in all types of enterprises, particularly in the booming private and foreign enterprises, have gained high or full autonomy on operational and employment decisions. As a result, labor relations at the workplace have changed from the former stable, administrative relationships between workers and the Party-state to more adversarial relationships that have led to a sharp increase in labor disputes. Here it should be noted that the concept of labor disputes is broad in the Chinese context, usually taken to mean any work-related issue raised by one party against another party or presented to a third party for mediation, arbitration, or trials (Taylor, Chang, and Li, 2003). For the most part, this chapter focuses on labor dispute resolution: it does not address workplace disputes in government departments and agencies, which are referred to as personnel disputes and resolved through a personnel dispute resolution system.

The exact number of labor disputes in China is unknown as they are numerous and often resolved informally. However, we can get a sense of their scale, distribution, and development through some official statistics. As Table 23.1 indicates, the number of labor dispute cases accepted by labor dispute arbitration committees (LDACs), along with the number of employees involved increased dramatically from 12,358 and 34,794 in 1993 to 589,244 and 779,490 in 2011: the number of labor disputes accepted by LDACs nearly doubled during 2008 when the Labor Contract Law and Labor Dispute Mediation and Arbitration Law (LDMAL) came into effect. However, since this spike there have been slight but steady decreases in recorded disputes in subsequent years. This decline does not necessarily mean that fewer actual labor disputes are occurring, as a large and increasing number of these are being settled by various mediation institutions rather than being filed with LDACs. According to the Ministry of Human Resources and Social Security (MHRSS), the number of labor dispute cases (including personnel dispute cases) handled by both LDACs and various mediation institutions in 2009 remained largely the same as in 2008 (about 1.24 million), but increased thereafter, reaching 1.32 million in 2011.

Moreover, due to the sharp fall in arbitrated cases won by employees after 2008 (which will be examined in the subsection of "Arbitration and Litigation", many workers

Table 23.1 Labor Disputes Accepted by LDACs

Year	Cases Accepted	Collective Labor Dispute Cases				Employees Involved in Collective Labor Dispute Cases	
		Total	% of Accepted Cases	Employees Involved, Total	Total	% of Total Employees	
1993	12358	684	5.53	34794	19468	55.95	
1994	19098	1482	7.76	77794	52637	67.66	
1995	33030	2588	7.84	122512	77340	63.13	
1996	48121	3150	6.55	189120	92203	48.75	
1997	71524	4109	5.74	221115	132647	59.99	
1998	93469	6767	7.24	358531	251268	70.08	
1999	120191	9043	7.52	473957	319241	67.36	
2000	135206	8247	6.10	422617	259445	61.39	
2001	154621	9847	6.37	467150	286680	61.37	
2002	184116	11024	5.99	608396	374956	61.63	
2003	226391	10823	4.78	801042	514573	64.24	
2004	260471	19241	7.39	764981	477992	62.48	
2005	313773	16217	5.17	744195	409819	55.07	
2006	317162	13977	4.41	679312	348714	51.33	
2007	350182	12784	3.65	653472	271777	41.59	
2008	693465	21880	3.16	1214328	502713	41.40	
2009	684379	13779	2.01	1016922	299601	29.46	
2010	600865	9314	1.55	815121	211755	25.98	
2011	589244	6592	1.12	779490	174785	22.42	

Source: *China Statistics Yearbook* (various years).

may have simply bypassed the formal labor dispute resolution system and engaged in spontaneous collective action. As to the geographical distribution of the labor disputes handled by LDACs, the majority are in economically developed coastal provinces, particularly Guangdong, Jiangsu, Shanghai, Beijing, and Zhejiang. Until 1996, 54% of the labor dispute cases handled by LDACs were in state-owned enterprises (SOEs) and collective-owned enterprises (COEs), but the share gradually declined to 12.86% by 2010. In contrast, the percentage of labor dispute cases in domestic private enterprises rose rapidly from 10% in 1996 to 52.44% in 2010 (MHRSS statistics).

Yet it needs emphasizing that only a very small percentage of labor disputes are filed with LDACs. According to a national survey by the All-China Federation of Trade

Unions (ACFTU) in 2007, 11.9% of the surveyed workers (which could be transformed to tens of millions of workers given the huge size of the national workforce) had been involved in labor disputes with their employers (ACFTU 2010). Statistics on collective industrial action by workers are difficult to come by due to the political sensitivity of labor strikes and protests in China. However, the LDACs do release annually the number of collective labor disputes they handle, which may provide some insight into the growing scale of this form of industrial conflict. As can be seen from Table 23.1, despite the still relatively overall small number, collective labor disputes increased twenty-seven times between 1993 and 2004; and the number of employees involved in collective labor disputes accounted for more than half of the employees involved in all of the accepted labor dispute cases up until 2006.

The number of collective labor dispute cases accepted by LDACs declined in the mid-2000s, but this was probably due to a fall-off in the large scale restructuring that had been occurring previously to SOEs and COEs. But this decline was dramatically reversed in 2008 when the number of collective labor disputes reached historically high levels, largely as a result of new labor laws taking effect. Interestingly, however, almost immediately the number of disputes dropped off sharply between 2009 and 2011 due mainly to three factors. First, in 2009, the official standard of defining collective labor disputes was revised upwards from involving at least three employees to at least ten employees. Second, LDACs started to disaggregate collective labor dispute cases into a number of individual cases to ease settlement. Third, collective labor disputes involving a large number of workers have been increasingly settled directly by government without going through mediation and arbitration procedures.

Collective labor disputes filed with LDACs are different from workers' spontaneous industrial actions such as work stoppages, strikes, and public demonstrations and protests. The MHRSS reported statistics on work stoppages and strikes in only a few selected provinces between 1993 and 1998. For instance, 1041 work stoppages and strikes in nine provinces were reported in 1995. With only patchy statistics available, the scale of worker industrial action can only be estimated. Based on news reports, *China Labor Bulletin* (2012) counted 553 strikes and protests between 2000 and 2010, an average of 55.3 per year. According to data released from the Ministry of Public Security, mass incidents (i.e. strikes, protests, and riots involving more than three people) increased from 8700 in 1993 to 87,000 in 2005, and it has been estimated that the number climbed to 127,000 in 2008, with about one-third of the mass incidents being labor protests (Jiang 2007; *China Labor Bulletin,* 2009). Another estimate by Jianrong Yu of the Chinese Academy of Social Sciences suggests that roughly 30,000 labor strikes and protests occurred in 2009 alone (*China Labor Bulletin,* 2011).

Although these disputes are only estimates, it is evident that there has been a rising trend of spontaneous industrial action by workers. It is also worth noting that while most of the strikes and protests are defensive, motivated usually to protect workers' legal rights, there has been an increasing number of offensive protests that demand wage increases or improvements in other working conditions above those stipulated by the law (Elfstrom and Kuruvilla, 2012).

Why has the number of labor disputes exponentially increased since the early 1990s? Fundamentally, this is caused by China's reform program changing the status of workers from "masters" of the country to commodities in labor markets. More specifically, market reform has generated a huge number of grievances from both state workers, who increasingly felt abandoned by the state, and the newly emerging labor force in the booming private sector, some of whom considered themselves to be suffering from capitalist exploitation in production. Whereas the main grievances of workers in the dwindling number of state enterprises, as well as laid-off workers and retirees, relate to the termination of the employment relationship, unpaid wages and pensions, defaults on medical subsidies, and inadequate collective consumption, workers in the private sector tend to get involved in disputes about wages, mandatory social insurance arrangements, and other working conditions (Lee, 2007; Liu, 2013a).

Several factors account for why the scale of labor disputes (particularly workers' spontaneous strikes and protests) is much larger in China than in many other transition economies, especially those in eastern Europe. First, China has become the workshop of the world and a top destination for foreign direct investment. Assuming the premise "where capital goes, conflict goes" (Silver, 2003: 41), Chinese workers may be subject to more capitalist exploitation than hitherto and therefore may have more grievances. Second, despite fairly good labor laws on paper, they are often ignored by employers due to the lack of a legal tradition as well as to the primitive development stage of many Chinese enterprises. Third, due to economic and fiscal decentralization, the Chinese state is no longer monolithic. While the central state remains concerned about regime legitimacy and social stability, local states are very obsessed with economic growth, given the incentives provided by economic decentralization (Lee, 2007). As a result, while the central state has enacted various laws providing basic labor and social protection to workers, local states enforce these laws weakly as they seek to attract capital and capture the benefits of market liberalization. Thus, the competing interests of the local and central state are the source of rising grievances of workers.

VARIETIES OF LABOR DISPUTE RESOLUTION

China established a labor dispute resolution system soon after the Communist Party took power. However, this system was suspended in 1956 after the socialist transformation of private ownership and the responsibility for settling labor disputes was transferred to the Letters and Visits Offices in various government agencies (Taylor et al., 2003). Until 1987, standard practice was for most labor disputes to be settled informally between aggrieved workers and management, while a few were mediated by Party organs or government supervisory agencies, or handled by the government Letters and Visits Offices (Ho, 2003). Whatever the settlement method, the political criterion of serving the interest of the state had to be followed first and foremost, and this at times resulted in rather arbitrary administrative decision-making influencing the outcomes of disputes.

Since initiating the economic reform program, the Chinese state has enacted various laws and administrative policies to regulate labor standards at the workplace. Given the authoritarian nature of the political regime, it is unsurprising that the labor legal system is centered on individual employment rights, while collective labor rights such as freedom of association and strikes have next to no place in the law. Nonetheless, as will be examined in the following two sections this legal system does provide standards or reference points for settling most labor disputes, either formally or informally.

Faced with rising labor disputes, the state revived the labor dispute resolution system in 1987 and further codified it in successive pieces of legislation: the Regulations for the Handling of Enterprise Labor Disputes, 1993; the Labor Law, 1994; LDMAL, 2007; and the Regulations on Enterprise Labor Dispute Negotiation and Mediation (ELDNMR), 2011. The core goal of this (revised and updated) system is to settle labor disputes through channels defined and controlled by government. At the moment, the formal labor dispute resolution system has three stages: mediation, arbitration, and two court trials. However, various forms of informal dispute resolution—consultation, negotiation, or conciliation between aggrieved workers and employers—are encouraged by the laws, particularly the 2011 ELDNMR. In addition, informal workplace dispute resolution institutions such as trade unions, collective consultation, and staff and workers representative congresses (SWRCs) have been either revived or introduced by the state.

Employers too have initiated informal dispute resolution methods, including employee hotlines, suggestion/grievance boxes, manager–employee meetings, and employee committees. Finally, administrative procedures including petitioning to Party organs, government agencies, or Letters and Visits Offices and complaining to labor inspection agencies remain important ways of resolving labor disputes. Statistics on the share of labor disputes handled by each of the settlement methods are not available. However, according to a national survey in 2007 the final settlement method was as follows: consultation (40.7%); conciliation and mediation (28.1%); arbitration (3.7%); litigation (3.8%); and others (23.7%) (ACFTU, 2010). Clearly, labor disputes in China are most likely to be settled informally through consultation or other similar practices. Whether these formal and informal dispute resolution methods have been fully successful is a moot point as workers have increasingly resorted to other methods to resolve disputes, including spontaneous strikes, attacking employers, and even on occasions, rather worryingly, to committing suicide (Halegua, 2008).

INTERNAL LABOR DISPUTE RESOLUTION

Most labor disputes in China are settled internally, due partly to the ineffectiveness of the legal and administrative procedures and partly to the Chinese cultural tradition that discourages a judicial approach to resolving disputes (Fox, Donohue, and Wu, 2005).

Yet somewhat paradoxically, dispute resolution institutions or mechanisms in most Chinese workplaces are highly underdeveloped. In recent years the state appears to have accepted the role that workplace dispute resolution institutions can play in preventing and resolving labor disputes as it has sought to strengthen various institutions, including enterprise labor dispute mediation committees (ELDMCs), trade unions, collective consultation, and SWRCs. In addition, an increasing number of employers, either voluntarily or under the pressure of the corporate social responsibility movement, have initiated various employee voice mechanisms to channel workers' grievance (Liu, 2013b).

Consultation and Conciliation

When labor disputes arise, many workers tend not to resort first to the formal labor dispute resolution system or any other workplace dispute resolution mechanisms, but instead seek to negotiate settlements with management either directly or indirectly through their *guanxi* (connections) or social networks (Taylor et al., 2003). This is particularly true in SOEs and COEs where the use of *guanxi* is extensive. Even for migrant workers (rural peasants who work in cities) in private or foreign enterprises, the use of social networks (e.g. relatives, friends, and fellow countrymen) to resolve labor disputes has become popular (Chan, 2010). Workers also have the right to ask enterprise trade unions or other third parties to consult with management on their behalf, and enterprise trade unions may even proactively conciliate labor disputes without requests from workers.

Moreover, to prevent labor unrest, local labor bureaus (recently renamed as bureaus of human resources and social security) and union federations are encouraged to conciliate workplace labor disputes, especially collective disputes. As consultation or conciliation can resolve disputes quickly, cost-effectively, and to everyone's satisfaction, it is often the preferred choice of workers. The ACFTU national survey reveals that 67.3% of respondents chose consultation or conciliation (15.6% for private consultation, 23.7% for asking union's help, and 28% for consultation with top management) as their preferred settlement method (ACFTU, 2010). The 2011 ELDNMR further strengthens consultation and conciliation by stating that parties to a dispute may conclude written agreements, which are subsequently supported by LDACs. However, these agreements cannot be legally enforced and consultation remains largely an informal method of labor dispute resolution.

ELDMCs

Mediation in China has a long history, which can be traced back to the Zhou Dynasty (1066 BC–221 BC) (Liang, 2006); and it has been long promoted by relevant laws and regulations as the preferred method of labor dispute resolution. Therefore, not surprisingly, the first stage of the formal labor dispute resolution system is mediation, which until recently has been mainly conducted within enterprises. Enterprises have been urged to set up ELDMCs to serve as a forum for the airing of grievances and to facilitate negotiations between aggrieved workers and management. Originally, ELDMCs followed the "tripartite" principle, as their membership consisted of representatives of workers, enterprise trade unions, and management. However, this tripartite arrangement was criticized in that it made trade unions a neutral, third party rather than representatives of workers. The 2007 LDMAL and 2011 ELDNMR modified the principle by limiting the composition of ELDMCs to an equal number of two parties: representatives of workers, who are either enterprise union committee members or elected by the workforce, and representatives of enterprises appointed by management. The director of ELDMCs should be an enterprise union committee member or another person agreed by both parties.

In practice, ELDMCs are often under the leadership of SWRCs and positioned, administratively, under enterprise trade unions. The major function of ELDMCs is to mediate labor disputes and to supervise the enforcement of mediation agreements. ELDMCs are also required to educate workers on labor laws, help enterprises prevent labor disputes, ensure worker interests are incorporated into important business plans, and address issues that arise from the enforcement of labor laws at the workplace. In the mediation process, relevant labor laws and regulations are often used as references. However, mediation agreements tend to contain compromises made by both parties, including sometimes significant legal labor rights concessions by workers. If no mediation agreement is reached within fifteen days of initial submission to an ELDMC, either the employer or employee is entitled to refer the case to the next stage. In fact, mediation is optional, as either party may directly file the case to a local LDAC when a labor dispute arises.

Similar to consultation and conciliation, mediation by an ELDMC is not only free but has the potential to reach quick and effective settlements while maintaining harmonious employee–employer relationships. However, it also has three significant drawbacks. First, ELDMCs were not mandatory until 2012 and even then only large and medium-sized enterprises were required to establish them. As a result, ELDMCs have been mainly seen in SOEs and COEs, but are missing from the majority of private and foreign enterprises. As Table 23.2 shows, although the number of ELDMCs has increased in recent years, particularly since the labor law reform in 2007, the percentage of unionized grassroots work units (enterprises or institutions) having ELDMCs declined from 25.96% in 2000 to 12.53% in 2011 (few ELDMCs exist in non-unionized units). Even where ELDMCs exist, many of these do not function properly due to the marginalized position of enterprise trade unions, examined below.

Second, despite the recent change of composition of ELDMCs (i.e. from three to two parties), which emphasizes the role of trade unions as a representative of workers rather than as an independent third party, the neutrality and autonomy of ELDMCs is still in question given the managerial dominance of enterprise unions and workplace governance (Lee, 1999; Gallagher, 2005; Liu, 2010; Liu and Li, 2013). In particular, because members of ELDMCs are employees who are paid and can be fired by employers, and as funding of ELDMCs also comes from employers, mediation by ELDMCs is often heavily influenced by management, which throws into doubt the fairness of the process. Third, the legal enforcement of mediation agreements is still weak, at least in practice. The 2007 LDMAL states that mediation agreements are binding. But it also stipulates that if one party fails to perform its commitment, the other party can bring the case to arbitration for not enforcing the mediation agreement.

The 2011 ELDNMR adds that the two parties can jointly bring the mediation agreement to an LDAC for review within fifteen days from its implementation, and the LDAC can back up the agreement by providing its own certificate, which is likely to make the agreement easier to enforce. Yet obtaining LDAC certification may not be straightforward, as both parties need to agree this procedure and act within a short period of time. The Supreme Court Opinions on Establishing an Institution Linking Litigation with Alternative Dispute Resolution (2009, No.45) regulates that either party can bring the mediation agreement directly to the court to affirm its validity without passing through arbitration procedures. Further, both the 2009 Supreme Court Opinions and the 2007 LDMAL state that where employers fail to enact a mediation agreement on such matters as delayed payment of remuneration and medical expenses for a work-related injury, the employee may apply to the court for a payment order. However, in practice, these measures aimed at strengthening the legal enforcement of mediation agreements are not widely adopted or successfully implemented (Taylor and Li, 2012).

ELDMCs were previously the most important institution used to resolve labor disputes in SOEs and COEs. From 1987 to 1996, ELDMCs handled about twice as many labor dispute cases as LDACs (Ho, 2003). However, the ratio has reversed since the mid-1990s. As Table 23.2 indicates, ELDMCs handled 2.48 times as many cases as LDACs in 1993, but this ratio dropped to 0.25 in 2011. The decline may be for a number of factors. First, as mentioned earlier in this subsection, fewer unionized workplaces have ELDMCs today than in the 1990s. Second, the effectiveness of ELDMCs in settling labor disputes appears to have declined since the mid-1990s. Whereas 81.52% of cases handled by ELDMCs were successfully mediated in 1996, the rate for 2010 was 27.78%. It is interesting to note that the success rate for ELDMC mediations jumped back up to 50.78% in 2011, but to a large extent this may be due to a sharp decline in the number of cases filed with ELDMCs (from 270,000 in 2010 to 193,000 in 2011). Moreover, in 2011, the average number of mediated cases per ELDMC was more or less the same as the previous year (see Table 23.2). Furthermore, the successfully mediated cases in 2011 appeared more prone to breaking down, as a greater share than previously had to file for arbitration at LDACs (Taylor and Li, 2012). Third, workers may have started to view ELDMCs as too prone to taking the side of management and thus not worthy of their trust (Yin, 2011). Interestingly, Table 23.2 shows that although the percentage of unionized workplaces with ELDMCs increased after the LDMAL took effect in 2008, the ratio of labor dispute cases accepted by ELDMCs relative to those filed at LDACs decreased from 0.63 in 2007 to 0.25 in 2011. These trends suggest that efforts by the Chinese government to increase the use of internal mediation to solve workplace disputes may have met with serious challenges.

Table 23.2 Labor Dispute Settlement by ELDMCs

	ELDMCs		Cases Accepted			Cases Mediated		
Year	Total	% of Unionized Grassroots units	Total	% of Cases Filed to LDACs	Ave.	Total	Ave.	% of Accepted Cases
1993	147866	23.60	84824	248.39	0.57	59818	0.40	70.52
1994	123946	21.27	133522	212.11	1.08	91683	0.74	68.67
1995	127669	21.53	93578	87.18	0.73	70713	0.55	75.57
1996	154599	26.35	86045	61.41	0.56	70143	0.45	81.52
1997	127039	24.90	72594	65.69	0.57	47528	0.37	65.47
1998	187102	37.16	152071	108.38	0.81	112659	0.60	74.08
1999			113381	67.21		81234		71.65
2000	222888	25.96	135003	65.03	0.61	80617	0.36	59.71
2001								
2002	164937	9.63	253813	97.08	1.54	57907	0.35	22.81
2003	153113	9.73	192692	67.65	1.26	51781	0.34	26.87
2004	195403	10.10	192119	57.99	0.98	54537	0.28	28.39
2005	230542	9.89	193286	47.45	0.84	42036	0.18	21.75
2006	257544	9.35	340193	76.02	1.32	63020	0.24	18.52
2007	311074	9.74	318609	63.46	1.02	59163	0.19	18.57
2008	388853	10.56	322955	34.70	0.83	66563	0.17	20.61
2009	427000	10.79	276000	31.72	0.65	68000	0.16	24.64
2010	517000	11.97	270000	35.30	0.52	75000	0.15	27.78
2011	660000	12.53	193000	24.63	0.29	98000	0.15	50.78

Sources: *China Statistics Yearbook* (various years); *China Trade Union Statistics Yearbook* (various years).

Enterprise Trade Unions

China has only one trade union, the ACFTU, which is under the tight control of the Communist Party. In line with Leninist trade unionism principles, the ACFTU has the dual-functioning role of representing the interests both of workers and of the state. However, when conflicts emerge between workers and the state, invariably unions side with the interests of the state rather than opting to defend the position of workers (Chen, 2003, 2010). At the workplace, enterprise trade unions traditionally had two major functions: one was to promote production by galvanizing workers to support enterprise plans and the other was to address social welfare issues. To meet the challenge of representing workers in a transitional economy, the 2001 Trade Union Law makes the protection of worker rights and interests the primary role of unions. Resolving labor disputes was also made a major function of enterprise trade unions.

In addition to playing a lead role in ELDMCs, enterprise trade unions engage in the following activities to resolve workplace disputes. First, following a request from aggrieved workers, enterprise trade unions may consult or negotiate on their behalf with management to settle a dispute. When there are spontaneous labor disputes or confrontations on the shop floor, enterprise trade unions may proactively intervene (with or without management involvement) to pacify the parties involved and seek a resolution to the problem. Article 27 of the 2001 Trade Union Law even states that enterprise trade unions, in consultation with management during work stoppages or strikes, should represent the views of workers. Second, enterprise trade unions are entitled to campaign for workplace health and safety. The ACFTU requires that labor protection monitoring and inspection committees (LPMICs) be established by enterprise trade unions to perform this function. On receiving health and safety-related complaints from workers, LPMICs are required to communicate with management on these issues with a view to making improvements. Third, enterprise trade unions also monitor labor law enforcement in the workplace. Labor law monitoring committees (LLMCs) are required to be set up by either enterprise trade unions or SWRCs under the leadership of trade union committee members. Workers may report labor law violations to LLMCs, who then engage with management to correct the problem. Any serious violations of labor law have to be reported to government labor inspection agencies.

Although legally mandated to resolve labor disputes, enterprise trade unions do not perform this role effectively. For a start, although the ACFTU's organizing campaign has significantly increased union density since 2000 (see Table 23.3), a large number of private and foreign enterprises are still union-free. Moreover, due to the bureaucratic, top-down organizing methods of the ACFTU, many newly established enterprise trade unions merely exist on paper and do not carry out any substantive functions (Liu, 2010; Liu and Li, 2013). As can be seen from Table 23.3, only a small percentage of enterprise trade unions had LPMICs and LLMCs and even this tiny number has been in decline since the late 1990s. Compounding the problem is that enterprise trade unions, where they do exist and function, often act in the interest of employers and as a result are considered as largely irrelevant by workers (Liu, 2010; Liu and Li, 2013).

As a mass organization of the Communist Party, the power of the ACFTU comes from the privileged status conferred upon it by the authoritarian regime and not from organic links it has with workers in enterprises. Thus, although some union federations at the national and regional levels, thanks to their special status, may be able to confront employers in certain circumstances, the retreat of the Party-state from workplace management in SOEs and COEs, combined with its relative absence from the ever growing private sector, has rendered most enterprise trade unions either powerless or subordinated to management (Chen, 2009).

What makes the situation worse is that the funding of enterprise trade unions mainly comes from employers, who frequently appoint managers as union leaders, severely compromising the ability of unions to function in the workplace as independent associations. With regard to labor dispute resolution, enterprise trade unions in a few SOEs as well as international joint ventures, usually with the support of the party or government, occasionally may be able to represent the interests of workers in a conciliation process, particularly when the disputes are between workers and low- or middle-level management. But in the vast majority of workplaces, enterprise unions fail to defend the rights of workers, as they operate mostly to bolster the interests of employers (Liu 2009; Liu and Li 2013). As a result, most aggrieved workers do not go to enterprise trade unions for help. Table 23.3 shows that LPMICs and LLMCs, two of the major workplace union dispute resolution institutions, have an extremely limited role in handling workplace disputes. Each LPMIC and LLMC, on average, only accepted 0.70 and 0.19 dispute cases in 2002 respectively, and the figures further decreased to 0.09 and 0.12 in 2011. These figures suggest that these two institutions are largely bypassed by workers. Therefore enterprise trade unions in general are not attractive to workers as a channel or mechanism for resolving their labor disputes.

Collective Consultation

To prevent and resolve collective labor disputes and develop harmonious labor relations, the Chinese version of "collective bargaining," known as the equal consultation and collective contract system, was formally introduced in 1994 and further institutionalized in the 2000s by several major laws and regulations. This system gives the ACFTU, as the representative organ of workers, a formal role to negotiate wages, benefits, and other working conditions. However, it differs from Anglo-Saxon-style adversarial collective bargaining in that it views the consultation process as non-confrontational (Warner and Ng 1999). Collective contracts (including various special agreements such as wage agreements and collective contracts for women workers) are mainly concluded at the enterprise level, though the number of regional and local industry-level collective contracts has been increasing since the mid-2000s (Liu 2013a).

As shown in Table 23.3, the percentage of workers covered by collective contracts has significantly increased in recent years. However, as examined earlier, enterprise trade unions are too weak to take the side of workers. As a result, the process of collective consultation is usually formal, without any meaningful worker involvement, which leads to collective contracts largely reproducing obligations already stipulated in established labor regulations (Warner and Ng 1999; Taylor et al. 2003; Clarke, Lee, and Li 2004; Brown 2006; Liu, Li, and Kim 2011). However, there are a few exceptions. In a few profitable SOEs and international joint ventures, enterprise trade unions, with the support of Party branches or even local governments, may engage in relatively meaningful collective consultations that lead to improved working conditions (usually not that substantively) and to the resolution of collective labor disputes (Liu and Li 2013). In addition, largely due to their relative independence from employers and government, a few innovative industry-level union associations have pursued more aggressive collective

Table 23.3 Labor Dispute Settlement by Enterprise Trade Unions and Related Institutions

Year	Unionized Grassroots Units					Union Density (%)	Collective Contract Coverage (%)	Cases Accepted by LPMICs		Cases Accepted by LLMCs		
	Total (000)	% with SWRCs System	% Convening SWRCs	% with LPMICs	% with LLMCs			Total	Ave. per LPMIC	Total	Ave. per LLMC	Settled (%)
1993	627	57.23	47.85	21.40		37.19						
1994	583	54.60	48.84	18.24		35.62						
1995	593	50.08	43.77	24.50	0.60	34.66				29064	8.14	83.11
1996	587	54.39	47.82	22.45	0.70	32.52	12.09			42326	10.36	86.53
1997	510	56.10	49.71	25.42	15.04	28.42	14.00			32750	0.43	
1998	504	67.92	64.01	30.33	21.98	27.56	20.59			32568	0.29	50.40
1999	509	61.75	58.21		27.58	26.77	14.12					
2000	859	33.53	29.74	22.47	16.29	30.81	17.91			31018	0.22	59.30
2001	1538	18.93				35.78	20.54					
2002	1713	19.33	16.89	7.84	13.07	39.10	17.88	93380	0.70	22585	0.19	62.11
2003	1574	22.29	17.48	9.59	10.31	35.08	18.87	64717	0.43	15100	0.16	58.08
2004	1935	19.05	15.80	9.42	14.65	36.93	18.36	53550	0.29	23482	0.16	44.62
2005	2331	18.52	14.70	9.58	14.48	38.79	25.91	34373	0.15	18391	0.11	66.74
2006	2753	32.71	27.60	9.58	14.71	42.02	27.29	44548	0.17	24532	0.13	66.67
2007	3193	34.02	28.28	10.27	16.77	46.19	29.96	46000	0.14	25000	0.10	68.00
2008	3682	42.58	35.59	11.62	18.60	49.66	34.06	50000	0.12	33000	0.10	69.70
2009	3959	46.45	39.78	12.02	20.16	51.75	37.03	53000	0.11	36000	0.10	75.00
2010	4318	52.11	43.26	12.71	22.37	53.66	41.29	59000	0.11	50000	0.11	76.00
2011	5266	52.81	43.22	12.55	10.10	56.19	48.45	60000	0.09	63000	0.12	55.56

Note: Union densities are calculated as ratios of union members to total non-agriculture employment (total non-agriculture employment is calculated as total employment minus agriculture employment minus self-employed individuals); collective contract coverage is calculated as ratio of workers covered by collective contracts to total non-agriculture employment.

Sources: China Statistics Yearbook (various years); China Trade Union Statistics Yearbook (various years).

consultations with enterprises that have led to higher real wages, improved working conditions, and reduced labor conflicts (Liu, 2010; Pringle, 2011). These exceptional collective consultations may not survive beyond the short term as they require some favorable preconditions, which are by no means assured, such as capable union leaders and strong government support (Liu, 2010).

Staff and Workers Representative Congresses

Another workplace institution intended to prevent and resolve collective labor disputes are SWRCs. First established in 1950, later falling into abeyance in 1957 only to be restored in 1980, SWRCs have legal rights of information, consultation, and codetermination on a wide range of business and employment issues, as well as the right to appraise enterprise directors and managers. While the Regulations on Enterprise Democratic Management (REDM), which took into effect in April 2012, abolished many of the codetermination rights of SWRCs on such matters as wage schemes, rewards and bonus plans, and other important workplace rules, these bodies still possess legal powers. In particular, collective contracts, enterprise restructuring plans, and managerial decisions on the use of workers' welfare funds and the contribution rates to social insurance schemes need to be approved by SWRCs. If properly functioning, SWRCs can provide a powerful platform for workers to collectively voice their concerns and to hold in check managerial prerogative. However, the record suggests that SWRCs usually only "rubber stamp" the decisions of management. Only in crisis situations have a few acted to protect the interests of workers (Zhu and Chan, 2005; Yu, 2011).

Several factors may account for the general failure of SWRCs to resolve or prevent collective labor disputes. First, SWRCs were not mandatory for private and foreign enterprises until the REDM took effect in 2012. As a result, SWRCs have mainly existed in SOEs and COEs. Table 23.3 shows that the percentage of unionized workplaces with SWRCs declined significantly between 1993 and 2005. Although this decline has been subsequently reversed, the majority of SWRCs did not hold conventions (the most important platform for SWRCs to perform its functions) bi-annually as required. Second, although members of SWRCs should be elected by workers, with at least half coming from the shop floor, in practice management often controls SWRCs by designating worker representatives, who are often middle or top level managers (Zhu and Chan, 2005). Finally, enterprise trade unions, the executive body of SWRCs, are usually, as indicated in the subsection of enterprise trade unions under the control or heavy influence of management.

Employer Initiated Workplace Employee Voice Mechanisms

Various employee voice mechanisms such as employee hotlines, suggestion/grievance boxes, manager–employee meetings, and employee committees have recently emerged in many Chinese enterprises, particularly those in export-processing industries. The most important driving force behind this employer initiated development has been the global corporate social responsibility movement that seeks to place pressure on suppliers of multinational corporations in developing countries to improve labor standards and promote employee voice (Yu, 2008, 2009). The Chinese government and ACFTU have also urged enterprises to involve employees in workplace governance as part of a wider effort to develop harmonious labor relations. In addition, a few employers have voluntarily introduced some forms of employee voice with the aim of motivating workers and reducing labor conflicts. For example, it was widely reported in China that Ruide Electronics, a foreign-owned enterprise in the Bao'an District, Shenzhen City, established a system of regular, multilevel manager–employee meetings which helped to reduce labor disputes and stabilize the workforce and production.

According to a 2012 survey of 900 workers in the consumer electronics industry in Guangdong Province, the percentage of workers knowing that their workplaces had suggestion boxes, employee hot lines, dedicated personnel handling grievances, manager–employee meetings, and employee committees were 74.1%, 53.8%, 40.8%, 29.3%, and 21.1% respectively. The percentage of workers having used these employee voice mechanisms (except employee committees), however, were much lower: 41.6%, 26.6%, 20.0%, and 20.6% respectively. Moreover, the results of quantitative analysis show that these employee voice mechanisms have few significant effects on labor standards and working conditions (Liu, 2013b). The shortcomings of employer initiated employee voice mechanisms to prevent and resolve labor disputes are highlighted by the widely publicized labor disputes, riots, and employee suicides at Foxconn, the largest electronics contract manufacturer in the world which has multiple, well-established employee voice mechanisms. The root cause of the problem is that the desire of employers to either control or influence employee voice mechanisms undermines their legitimacy in the eyes of workers, even if these bodies have the trappings of genuine worker involvement, for example direct election to employee committees (Yu, 2008; Chan, 2010).

Workers' Spontaneous Industrial Actions

As mentioned in the section of rising labor disputes, Chinese workers have increasingly resorted to collective industrial actions, including work stoppages, strikes, and protests to resolve disputes and protect employment rights and interests. A large scale survey of migrant workers in South and East China in 2010 found that nearly 3% of respondents had participated in collective industrial action in the previous year, the majority in the form of strikes (Liu, Yong, and Shu, 2011). The major demands of workers in collective actions are payment of wages, wage increases, better working conditions, and more respectful treatment (Cheung, 2012a; Elfstrom and Kuruvilla, 2012). These disputes are often unresolved within enterprises due to the lack of or poor workplace dispute resolution mechanisms examined above. Yet the public or quasi-public labor dispute resolution institutions also find it difficult to settle these disputes given their various limitations (which will be examined in the following subsection). In particular, as both the workplace and public (or quasi-public) dispute resolution mechanisms are mostly geared to solving disputes that relate to alleged violations of employment and labor laws—rights-based disputes—they are unaccustomed to settling interest-based disputes that usually involve matters such as worker demands for wage levels higher than the legal minimum. All in all, however, collective industrial action of some form has become an increasingly popular alternative for workers to resolve their disputes.

Since the right of strike was removed in the 1982 revision of the Constitution, strikes at present are neither legal nor illegal in China. But trade unions are not allowed to lead or organize strikes; and leaders of such collective action run a high risk of being dismissed by employers or arrested by police. These restrictions result in the overwhelming number of labor strikes and protests in China being spontaneous and unpredictable. Invariably, strikes are poorly organized, last for short periods of time, and involve little cross-factory or cross-region coordination (Lee, 2007). Nonetheless, workers are using collective action to prize open the door for collective bargaining, to be conducted either formally or informally with employers (or in some cases government). There is some evidence of this action bringing significant gains. For instance, of the thirty-eight strikes recorded by *China Labor Bulletin* in March 2012, eleven led to collective bargaining with management and in two cases workers achieved their demands (Cheung, 2012b).

Moreover, there are signs that employers are increasingly willing to negotiate with strikers (Cheung, 2012a), which may be attributable to two factors. One is that workers may have gained more market power in particular regions, most notably coastal areas, which have experienced labor shortages; the emerging pattern of strike action also suggests that workers in high-end industries (such as auto and steel) may possess more workplace power than workers in other industries. The greater propensity of workers to exercise industrial muscle may be making employers more prepared to sit at the collective bargaining table. The other factor relates to the increased willingness of government and its affiliates, the ACFTU and the courts, to intervene jointly in worker strikes and protests (Chen, F., 2010; Su and He, 2010; Chen and Xu, 2012). To maintain stability, the government often puts pressure on employers to negotiate with strikers and even to make significant concessions. For example in the highly publicized Honda strike in 2010, Japanese management, under pressure from the Chinese government, agreed to negotiate with the workers and in both 2010 and 2011 made significant concessions on wage levels.

Of course, government intervention can be a double-edged sword as it may also exert pressure on workers to reduce their demands; sometimes government pressure on workers can be more intense than that placed on employers. Overall, spontaneous collective action by workers may not always lead to collective bargaining and even when it does, the collective bargaining process that emerges is usually highly informal, and can be a highly risky method to either resolve labor disputes or to advance the interests of workers. Nevertheless, the recent increase in collective industrial action can be reasonably interpreted as the first green shoots of a genuine labor movement emerging in

China, which will make interest-based labor disputes a more permanent feature of the country's employment system.

External Labor Dispute Resolution

The ineffectiveness of workplace labor dispute resolution institutions or mechanisms has led to the number of labor disputes being filed with external dispute resolution institutions skyrocketing (see Table 23.1 for examples). The hope of the Chinese state is that these labor disputes can be resolved peacefully through institutions either controlled by or under the influence of government, including government agencies, LDACs, the courts, and quasi-government mass organizations such as trade unions and People's Mediation Committees (PMCs). Unsurprisingly, therefore, the establishment or reform of external labor dispute resolution institutions has been the focus of China's recent efforts in settling labor disputes.

Mediation

Although mediation has traditionally been practiced within enterprises by ELDMCs, area and industry-based labor dispute mediation organizations have been emerging since 1993, largely in the wake of regulations issued by the MHRSS or action by ACFTU (for more on the MHRSS regulations, see Yin, 2012). The 2007 LDMAL gave further legitimacy to the role of labor dispute mediation organizations at town/sub-district levels and PMCs in resolving labor disputes. Presently, there are three main types of external labor dispute mediation organizations.

The first is area and industry-based mediation organizations set up by the ACFTU. Since the mid-1990s, a growing number of area and industry-based trade union associations have been established in counties/districts, towns/sub-districts, and villages/communities where there are high concentrations of small and medium-sized private enterprises (see Liu, 2009, 2010, for details). A large number of these union associations have created mediation offices or committees to help resolve labor disputes. Table 23.4 shows that between 2005 and 2011, the number of mediation organizations affiliated to trade unions outside the enterprise has more than doubled. The number of labor dispute cases handled by these mediation organizations increased from about 65,000 to 167,000 in total and about 80% of cases were successfully mediated. Compared with ELDMCs (see Table 23.2), these mediation organizations are more effective in settling labor disputes, which has also been confirmed by a few case studies (Chen, 2004; Halegua, 2008; Liu, 2009; Pringle, 2011).

The second is mediation offices or committees set up by local labor bureaus or government offices at the county/district, town/sub-district, and village/community levels (strictly speaking, village/community level government offices are mass organizations

Table 23.4 Labor Dispute Settlement by External Trade Union Mediation
Organizations

| Year | Mediation Organizations | | Cases Handled | | Cases Mediated | | |
	Total (0000)	% Above-Grassroots Level Trade Unions	Total (0000)	Ave. per Organization	Total (0000)	% of Cases Handled	Ave. per Organization
2005	0.9	15.6	6.5	7.22	5.1	79.2	5.67
2006	1.1	17.5	10.2	9.27	8.3	80.9	7.55
2007	1.1	18.2	8.7	7.91	7.2	82.9	6.55
2008	1.1	17.2	12.3	11.18	10.4	84.2	9.45
2009	1.2	18.2	8.6	7.17	6.9	79.5	5.75
2010	1.5	21.1	12.4	8.27	10.1	81.5	6.73
2011	2.0	26.0	16.7	8.35	13.2	79.1	6.60

Source: Statistical Reports on the Development of Trade Union Organization and Work (2005–11).

with quasi-government status), with either government or quasi-government support. Most of these mediation organizations emerged after 2008 when the Chinese state nationally called on developing a system of "grand mediation"—extensive mediation networks particularly at grassroots administration levels—to resolve various social conflicts. While some of the town/sub-district and village/community level offices set up by local labor bureaus are specifically charged to mediate labor disputes, others are general offices that take on additional functions such as collecting social insurance contributions and inspecting workplaces. Similarly, mediation organizations set up by government offices at the county/district, town/sub-district, and village/community levels are often in charge of mediating both labor disputes and various other social conflicts.

The third is PMCs, mass organizations affiliated to local Justice Bureaus. Originally set up to mediate civil disputes, PMCs have actively expanded their scope to cover labor disputes. According to statistics from the Ministry of Justice, in 2012 there were about 811,000 PMCs covering all towns/sub-districts and villages/communities and these have had a strikingly high successful mediation rate of 96% over the past ten years.

Mediation by these external mediation organizations has some advantages, including providing easy and free access, not being exposed to the same level of employer influence compared to ELDMCs: possessing flexible procedures; being able to conclude quick and simple settlements (thanks mainly to the government or quasi-government authority of these organizations); and reaching settlements that improve relations between the aggrieved parties (Halegua, 2008). Yet, significant limitations also exist on the work of these organizations. First, despite their government or quasi-government status, the authority of these external mediation organizations in settling labor disputes is often questioned by both employees and employers. In particular, legal enforcement of mediation agreements, although significantly strengthened by the 2007 LDMAL and the 2009 Supreme Court Opinions, as mentioned in the subsection of ELDMCs, remains weak in practice (Taylor and Li, 2012). Moreover, either party can still appeal the outcome of mediation in court, which casts uncertainty about the robustness of a mediation agreement. Second, the capacity of these external mediation organizations to settle labor disputes is relatively low as they often lack funding, office space, and full-time, professional staff (Li and Shen, 2011). In addition, the mediators, as government or quasi-government bureaucrats, often lack the necessary knowledge and even at times the motivation to handle complicated or time-consuming cases (Halegua, 2008; Sheng and Jin, 2009; Li and Shen, 2011). Third, in conducting mediation these organizations, rather than using labor laws and regulations as reference guides, tend to prioritize economic growth and stability, which are key government interests. As a result, workers sometimes may be unduly pressurized to accept agreements that are less than desirable (Halegua, 2008). Finally, external mediation organizations have tended not to be very effective at resolving interest-based labor disputes (Taylor and Li, 2012).

Despite these drawbacks, according to MHRSS statistics, the number of labor dispute cases resolved by external mediation organizations has rapidly increased since 2008 and in many areas far exceeded those settled by ELDMCs or arbitration. The rising popularity of external mediation is an outcome of the Chinese government's recent efforts at building an extensive mediation network to resolve social conflicts. In more and more areas, LDACs have started to require labor dispute cases to be handled first by external mediation organizations before they get actively involved in the case, a stipulation that effectively makes mediation mandatory (Halegua, 2008; Sheng and Jin, 2009).

Arbitration and Litigation

Arbitration by LDACs is the second stage of the formal labor dispute resolution process which, unlike mediation, is mandatory. Labor bureaus at the municipal and county/district levels are required to set up LDACs, comprising labor bureau officials and representatives of enterprises and trade unions. LDACs often attempt to conciliate disputes before accepting them. If conciliation fails, LDACs are mandated to attempt mediation; they can even issue mediation agreements before adjudicating a case. If mediation fails, then arbitral awards will be issued. In principle, both arbitration and mediation decisions should be based on or refer to relevant laws or regulations.

As shown in Table 23.5, the number of labor dispute cases filed with LDACs has increased dramatically in the past two decades, especially since 2007 when several new labor laws were introduced, with the effect not only of significantly increasing worker awareness of their labor rights, but also making arbitration more accessible, efficient, and less costly. In particular, the 2007 LDMAL waived arbitration fees and expanded the scope of matters for arbitration to include disputes relating to whether or not an employment relationship exists and to the modification or termination of a labor contract. The new laws also extended the qualifying period for the lodging of an application for arbitration from within 60 days of when the labor dispute arose to one year; shortened the hearing and award-making period from 90 to 60 days; and made arbitral awards on certain disputes final and binding. Together these changes may have encouraged a larger number of aggrieved workers to seek arbitration for their labor disputes. However, the dramatic increase in the caseload since 2008 has imposed a heavy burden on LDACs. Even though arbitrators worked overtime, many hearings were delayed for more than a year, which put off many actual and potential applicants.

Table 23.5 shows that employees are more likely to win cases than are employers. However, there is an increasing tendency not to make awards that favor one side exclusively. Between 2000 and 2011, the percentage of arbitrated cases (completely) won by employees decreased from 53.98% to 33.01%, while the percentage partially won by both parties increased from 28.50% to 54.48%. This trend, which has become more pronounced since 2008, may be due to three factors. First, labor laws and regulations have become increasingly complicated, which may have resulted in aggrieved workers' misunderstanding their legal rights. Second, the expanded scope of arbitrable matters, the extended arbitration application period, and the waiving of arbitration fees since 2008 may not only have widened the range of workers' claims, but also encouraged some workers to try their luck with less legally robust cases. Third, and perhaps most importantly, the faltering of economic growth in the wake of the 2008–9 global financial crisis may have led local governments to impose greater pressures on LDACs to treat employers sympathetically in arbitration (Chen, Y., 2010). In fact, the MHRSS made a national call in 2008 for labor laws to be enforced "softly." Moreover, many local governments gave specific guidelines to LDACs to apply lower labor standards when arbitrating cases. In some areas such as Beijing and Shanghai, previous trends were reversed as after 2009 employers became more likely to win outright labor dispute cases (Taylor and Li, 2012).

Any party dissatisfied with an arbitration decision may embark upon a third stage of litigation by filing the original case with a court. In addition, as a result of a Supreme Court interpretation issued on 24 August 2006 workers with clear evidence of wage arrears may file a case directly with a court. However, for cases involving claims for small amounts or cases arising from the implementation of government labor standards on working hours, leave entitlement, and social insurances, the arbitral awards are final and binding. When hearing a labor case, judges usually first try to mediate a solution. If mediation is unsuccessful, formal judicial proceedings begin. When a verdict is made, any unsatisfied party may appeal to a higher court whose decision will be final. Table 23.6 shows that the number of labor dispute cases filed with courts for first trial more than tripled between 2002 and 2011, which suggests that workers may be electing to bypass the employment dispute resolution machinery and opting to use formal courts to seek vindication of employment rights.

Overall, arbitration and litigation have played a very important role in settling labor disputes in China, largely because workplace dispute resolution mechanisms are pretty ineffective. However, significant drawbacks exist to both of these processes. First, to get access to arbitration or litigation, aggrieved workers have to show evidence of an employment relationship such as a labor contract, payslips, or work identity card. While

Table 23.5 Labor Dispute Settlement by LDACs

Year	All Cases	Cases Conciliated	Cases Accepted							
			Total	Cases Settled	Mediated (%)	Arbitrated (%)	Others (%)	Won by Employers (%)	Won by Employees (%)	Partially Won by both Parties (%)
1994	62949	43851	19098	17962	52.12	19.29	28.59	20.00	47.80	32.21
1995	107333	74303	33030	31415	57.27	23.14	19.60	19.70	51.80	28.50
1996	140122	92001	48121	46543	52.04	27.48	20.48	20.31	50.91	28.78
1997	110505	38981	71524	70792	46.32	21.27	32.40	16.23	56.59	27.18
1998	140307	46838	93469	92288	34.11	27.51	38.09	12.93	52.72	29.65
1999	168696	48505	120191	121289	32.61	28.62	38.77	12.92	51.97	30.88
2000	207605	72399	135206	130688	32.04	41.43	26.55	10.48	53.98	28.50
2001	218560	63939	154621	150279	28.57	48.08	23.35	20.99	47.74	31.27
2002	261458	77342	184116	178744	28.49	43.27	28.24	15.11	47.24	37.65
2003	284842	58451	226391	223503	30.32	42.85	26.82	15.33	49.02	35.56
2004	331311	70840	260471	258678	32.24	42.80	24.95	13.79	47.65	36.35
2005	407334	93561	313773	306027	34.08	43.05	22.87	12.88	47.50	39.63
2006	447483	130321	317162	310780	33.60	45.52	20.88	12.63	46.99	40.38
2007	502084	151902	350182	340030	35.13	43.82	21.05	14.47	46.16	39.37
2008	930748	237283	693465	622719	35.54	44.09	20.39	12.92	44.45	42.63
2009	869977	185598	684379	689714	36.46	42.19	21.35	13.84	44.45	49.17
2010	764862	163997	600865	634041	39.45	42.03	18.52	13.41	36.19	50.40
2011	783582	194338	589244	592823	47.04	41.32	11.64	12.51	33.01	54.48

Source: *China Statistics Yearbook* (various years).

Table 23.6 Labor Dispute Settlement by the First Trial Court

Year	Cases Accepted	Cases Settled	By Manner of Settlement (%)				
			Mediated	Trialed	Rejected	Withdrawn	Others
2002	84693	82886	18.62	59.13	4.78	15.63	1.84
2003	98112	98159	19.31	56.88	5.12	16.51	2.18
2004	109338	108229	21.15	53.33	5.92	17.23	2.37
2005	122480	121516	23.00	51.52	5.86	17.27	2.35
2006	126047	124966	21.63	53.61	4.53	17.93	2.31
2007	150992	147592	25.69	48.08	4.26	19.86	2.11
2008	295531	286221	32.62	43.55	3.73	17.78	2.31
2009	318643	317072	33.33	39.61	3.70	21.08	2.29
2010	321681	327407	42.89	33.68	2.62	18.69	2.14
2011	308622	304228	46.44	30.33	2.36	19.03	1.84

Source: China Statistics Yearbook (various years).

this may seem a reasonable request, it is often extremely difficult for workers, particularly migrant workers, to obtain such evidence (Halegua, 2008; Taylor and Li, 2012). Second, although arbitration has been free since 2008, the cost of going through the lengthy arbitration and litigation process, which often involves hiring an attorney, is still prohibitively high for many workers (Halegua, 2008). Third, it is often difficult to enforce arbitral awards and court verdicts due to lack of legal enforcement power and motivation of LDACs and poor enforcement ability of courts (Halegua, 2008).

Finally, both LDACs and courts are under the control or heavy influence of government. Although LDACs are supposed to be mass organizations that operate on the basis of tripartism, in reality they are under the control of local labor bureaus whose officials serve as directors of LDACs and chief arbitrators (or even single arbitrators for simple cases) of arbitral panels. Because labor bureaus are government agencies whose priority is economic growth, LDACs are often biased in favor of employers. Although courts may take a fairer approach toward workers, they still tend to follow government instructions (Chen, Y., 2010; Su and He, 2010; Chen and Xu, 2012). The possible corruption of labor bureau officials and judges may exacerbate doubts about the fairness of the formal labor dispute resolution system (Halegua, 2008; Liu, 2009). In addition, when dealing with collective labor disputes, both LDACs and courts usually serve the government's interest of maintaining stability. For example, a strategy commonly adopted by both is to "divide and conquer," by disaggregating collective labor dispute cases into individual ones to weaken worker solidarity and to make it easier to obtain settlements (Chen and Xu, 2012).

An interesting trend since 2002 is that the proportion of mediated settlements of total settlements produced by both LDACs and first trial courts has steadily increased: from 28.49% to 47.04% and from 18.62% to 46.44% respectively (see Tables 23.5 and 23.6).

Increases have been particularly pronounced since 2008. Moreover, in 2011, LDACs and courts settled more cases through mediation than through arbitration or judgment. Given the declining mediation rate of LDACs in the late-1990s, these figures suggest that mediation has regained currency in the formal labor dispute resolution system. To a large extent, the upturn in the use of mediation by both LDACs and courts is also due to the Chinese government's strategy of "grand mediation," which as discussed in the subsection of mediation has promoted the development of various external mediation organizations. In many areas, LDACs and courts are firmly instructed by government to first conciliate or mediate labor disputes when handling these. Moreover, mediation rates have become an important criterion in evaluating the performance of arbitrators and judges (Sheng and Jin, 2009; Chen, Y., 2010; Li and Shen, 2011).

Labor Inspection and Petition

Labor inspection agencies, a department of local labor bureaus, are another important institution in settling labor disputes. Because these agencies have the authority to order employers to correct problems and even to fine employers, they may sometimes resolve labor disputes quickly. However, as they are also part of labor bureaus, these agencies tend to suffer from many of the shortcomings bedeviling LDACs, most notably a lack of motivation to enforce agreements and laws thoroughly and a tendency to favor the interests of employers. The work of these agencies is further hampered by workers in SOEs and COEs choosing to use traditional administrative procedures such as petitioning Party organs and other agencies, such as the government's Letters and Visits Offices. These alternative avenues are free and considered simpler than formal labor dispute resolution mechanisms, although they are far from costless as the result may not be a settlement, but may mean petitioning workers being put at risk of detention or a beating (Taylor et al., 2003; Halegua, 2008).

Conclusions

Labor dispute resolution in China has experienced important changes in recent years. First, the labor dispute resolution system has clearly moved away from one characterized by arbitrary administrative discretion in the planned economy toward a regime of legal rules based mostly on individual labor rights. In principle, decisions of all of the three stages of the formal labor dispute resolution system, i.e. mediation, arbitration, and litigation should follow or refer to relevant laws and regulations, although in practice decisions and settlements often fall short of proscribed legal standards. Second, mediation, as the preferred method for settling labor disputes, has regained currency in the formal labor dispute resolution system and has extended from the workplace to industry and regional levels. According to MHRSS statistics, in 2010 and 2011, the number of labor dispute cases handled by mediation organizations outside the enterprise exceeded that of LDACs, and the same is true for the number of cases settled. Third, various workplace dispute resolution mechanisms have been revived or emerged, but remain ineffective due to employer dominance and a lack of genuinely independent worker representation. Finally, spontaneous industrial action by workers leading to some form of formal or informal collective bargaining has emerged as a relatively effective way of resolving labor disputes, especially the rapidly growing number of interest-based collective labor disputes that are difficult to settle through the formal labor dispute resolution system. Thus, despite significant developments in the past two decades, it is clear that more sophisticated institutions and mechanisms of labor dispute resolution are needed to meet the challenges posed by China's further economic and social transition.

Looking ahead, several possible developments are worth noting. First, the Chinese government may further strengthen the strategy of "grand mediation" to resolve the rising incidence of social conflict. Consequently, the number of mediation organizations and the cases handled by them may continue to grow. It is possible that mediation might become a mandatory stage of labor dispute resolution in more areas and may even be written into national regulations or laws. Second, the number of ELDMCs may significantly increase in forthcoming years, as they are now mandatory for medium and large enterprises. The number of enterprise trade unions and some related institutions such as SWRCs and collective contracts may too increase due largely to the continuous organizing campaigns of the ACFTU.

However, a large number of aggrieved workers may continue to bypass ELDMCs and enterprise trade unions, given their subordination to employers. It is possible that the ACFTU may take some steps to reform enterprise trade unions, such as the introduction of direct election to enterprise union committees, which actually has been experimented with in some areas. But without structural changes, it will be very hard for enterprise trade unions to be transformed into bodies that genuinely represent worker interests. Third, as multinational companies and non-governmental organizations are having more and more influence in the Chinese workplace, various employer initiated employee voice mechanisms may continue to grow in popularity. However, their effectiveness in preventing or settling labor disputes may remain limited, at least in the near term. Finally, more and more workers may resort to spontaneous strikes or protests to resolve their disputes. Ever growing worker activism may have the potential to push forward ACFTU reforms and the development of genuine collective bargaining as an effective way of settling labor disputes.

References

ACFTU. 1994–2012. *China Trade Union Statistics Yearbook*. Beijing: China Statistics Press.

ACFTU. 2005–2011. *Statistical Reports on the Development of Trade Union Organization and Work*. Beijing: ACFTU.

ACFTU 2010. *The Sixth Survey of Chinese Workers*. Beijing: China Workers' Press.

Brown, R. 2006. "China's Collective Contract Provisions: Can Collective Negotiations Embody Collective Bargaining?" *Duke Journal of Comparative & International Law*, 16(1): 35–78.

Chan, C. 2010. *The Challenge of Labor in China—Strikes and the Changing Labor Regime in Global Factories*. London: Routledge.

Chen, F. 2003. "Between the State and Labour: The Conflict of Chinese Trade Unions' Double Identity in Market Reform". *The China Quarterly*, 176: 1006–28.

Chen, F. 2004. "Legal Mobilization by Trade Unions: The Case of Shanghai." *The China Journal*, 52(Jul.): 27–45.

Chen, F. 2009. "Union Power in China: Source, Operation, and Constraints." *Modern China*, 35(6): 662–89.

Chen, F. 2010. "Trade Unions and the Quadripartite Interactions in Strike Settlement in China." *The China Quarterly*, 201: 104–24.

Chen, F. and Xu, X. 2012. "'Active Judiciary': Judicial Dismantling of Workers' Collective Action in China." *The China Journal*, 62(1): 87–107.

Chen, Y. 2010. "China's Labor Dispute Settlement: Forced Settlement, Worker Awareness of Rights, and Policy Suggestions." Dissertation, Arizona State University.

Cheung, J. 2012a. "Recent Strikes Show Collective Bargaining is Gaining Traction in China." *Forbes*, 24 Jul.

Cheung, J. 2012b. *China's Workers Emboldened: Strikes Escalate in March*. Hong Kong: China Labor Bulletin.

China Labor Bulletin 2009. *Going it Alone: The Workers' Movement in China 2007–2008*. Hong Kong: China Labor Bulletin.

China Labor Bulletin 2011. *Unity is Strength: The Workers' Movement in China 2009–2011*. Hong Kong: China Labor Bulletin.

China Labor Bulletin 2012. *A Decade of Change: The Workers' Movement in China 2000–2010*. Hong Kong: China Labor Bulletin.

Clarke, S., Lee, C.H., and Li, Q. 2004. "Collective Consultation and Industrial Relations in China." *British Journal of Industrial Relations*, 42(2): 235–54.

Elfstrom, M. and Kuruvilla, S. 2012. "The Changing Nature of Labor Unrest in China." Paper presented at the International Labor and Employment Relations Associations Congress, Philadelphia, PA, Jul.

Fox, J., Donohue, J., and Wu, J. 2005. "The Arbitration of Labor Disputes in China Today: Definition and Implications." *Employee Responsibilities and Rights Journal*, 17(1): 19–29.

Gallagher, M. 2005. *Contagious Capitalism: Globalization and the Politics of Labor in China*. Princeton, NJ, and Oxford: Princeton University Press.

Halegua, A. 2008. "Getting Paid: Processing the Labor Disputes of China's Migrant Workers." *Berkeley Journal of International Law*, 26(1): 254–322.

Ho, V.H. 2003. *Labor Dispute Resolution in China: Implications for Labor Rights and Legal Reform*. Berkeley, CA: University of California Press.

Jiang, S. 2007. "Mass Incidents Caused by Labor Conflicts: A Public Opinion Perspective." *Theory Horizon*, 3: 94–5.

Lee, C.K. 1999. "From Organized Dependence to Disorganized Despotism: Changing Labor Regime in Chinese Factories." *The China Quarterly*, 157: 44–71.

Lee, C.K. 2007. *Against the Law: Labor Protests in China's Rustbelt and Sunbelt*. Berkeley, CA: University of California Press.

Li, X. and Shen, X. 2011. "Legalization Grand Mediation and the Establishment of the Labor and Personnel Dispute Mediation System." *Jianghai Zongheng*, 9: 48–52.

Liang, F. 2006. "China's Ancient Judicial Mediation." *Journal of Henan University (Social Sciences Edition)*, 41(4): 73–7.

Liu, L., Yong, X., and Shu, B. 2011. "Regional Differences in Labor Rights: A Survey of Rural Migrant Workers in the Pearl River Delta and the Yangtze River Delta." *Social Sciences in China*, 2: 107–23.

Liu, M. 2009. "Chinese Employment Relations and Trade Unions in Transition." Dissertation, Cornell University.

Liu, M. 2010. "Union Organizing in China: Still a Monolithic Labor Movement?" *Industrial and Labor Relations Review*, 64(1): 30–52.

Liu, M. 2013a. "China." In C. Frege and J. Kelly (eds), *Comparative Employment Relations in the Global Political Economy*. London: Routledge, 324–47.

Liu, M. 2013b. *Governing Labor Standards in the Chinese Electronic Manufacturing Industry: Labor Market Institutions and Global Value Chain Governance*. Geneva: International Labor Organization.

Liu, M. and Li, C. 2013. "Environment Pressures, Managerial Industrial Relations Ideologies, and Unionization in Chinese Enterprises." *British Journal of Industrial Relations*.

Liu, M., Li, C., and Kim, S. 2011. "Chinese Trade Unions in Transition: A Three Level Analysis." In P. Shelton et al. (eds), *China's Changing Workplace*. London and New York: Routledge, 277–300.

National Bureau of Statistics 1994–2012. *China Statistics Yearbook*. Beijing: China Statistics Press.

Pringle, T. 2011. *Trade Unions in China: The Challenge of Labor Unrest*. Oxford and New York: Routledge.

Sheng, J. and Jin, L. 2009. "Establishing United Guidelines and Jointly Pushing forward Grassroots Mediation." *Labor Security World*, 12: 38–41.

Silver, B. 2003. *Forces of Labor: Workers' Movements and Globalization since 1870*. New York: Cambridge University Press.

Su, Y. and He, X. 2010. "Street as Courtroom: State Accommodation of Labor Protest in South China." *Law & Society Review*, 44(1): 157–84.

Taylor, B. and Li, Q. 2012. "Conflict Resolution in China: The Wrongs of Mediating Rights." Paper presented at the International Labor and Employment Relations Associations Congress, Philadelphia, PA, Jul.

Taylor, B., Chang, K., and Li, Q. 2003. *Industrial Relations in China*. Cheltenham and Northampton: Edward Elgar.

Warner, M. and Ng, S.H. 1999. "Collective Contracts in Chinese Enterprises: A New Brand of Collective Bargaining under 'Market Socialism'?" *British Journal of Industrial Relations*, 37(2): 295–314.

Yin, M. 2011. "Thoughts on China's Enterprise Labor Dispute Mediation Committee System." *Journal of Southwest Petroleum University (Social Sciences Edition)*, 4(1): 39–42.

Yin, M. 2012. "On Regional and Industrial System of Labor Dispute Mediation." *Journal of China Institute of Industrial Relations*, 26(3): 25–30.

Yu, A.L. 2011. "From 'Master' to 'Menial': State-owned Enterprise Workers in Contemporary China." *Working USA*, 14: 453–72.

Yu, X. 2008. "Workplace Democracy in China's Foreign-funded Enterprises: A Multilevel Case Study of Employee Representation." *Economic and Industrial Democracy*, 29: 274–300.

Yu, X. 2009. "From Passive Beneficiary to Active Stakeholders: Workers' Participation in CSR Management against Labor Abuses." *Journal of Business Ethics*, 87: 233–49.

Zhu, X. and Chan, A. 2005. "Staff and Workers' Representative Congress: An Institutionalized Channel for Expression of Employees' interests?" *Chinese Sociology and Anthropology*, 37(4): 6–33.

INDEX